KU-007-432

CRITICAL LEGAL PERSPECTIVES ON GLOBAL GOVERNANCE

This book of essays, written in honour of Professor David Trubek, explores many of the themes which he has himself written about, most notably the emergence of a global critical discourse on law and its application to global governance. As law becomes ever more implicated in global governance and as processes related to and driven by globalisation transform legal systems at all levels, it is important that critical traditions in law adapt to the changing legal order and *problématique*. The book brings together critical scholars from the EU, and North and South America to explore the forms of law that are emerging in the global governance context, the processes and legal roles that have developed, and the critical discourses that have been formed. By looking at critical appraisals of law at the global, regional and national level, the links among them, and the normative implications of critical discourses, the book aims to show the complexity of law in today's world and demonstrate the value of critical legal thought for our understanding of issues of contemporary governance and regulation. Scholars from many countries contribute critical studies of global and regional institutions, explore the governance of labour and development policy in depth, and discuss the changing role of lawyers in global regulatory space.

LIVERPOOL JMU LIBRARY

3 1111 01497 8215

WITHDRAWN

Critical Legal Perspectives on Global Governance

Liber Amicorum David M Trubek

Edited by
Gráinne de Búrca
Claire Kilpatrick
and
Joanne Scott

·HART·
PUBLISHING
OXFORD AND PORTLAND, OREGON
2015

Published in the United Kingdom by Hart Publishing Ltd
16C Worcester Place, Oxford, OX1 2JW
Telephone: +44 (0)1865 517530
Fax: +44 (0)1865 510710
E-mail: mail@hartpub.co.uk
Website: http://www.hartpub.co.uk

Published in North America (US and Canada) by
Hart Publishing
c/o International Specialized Book Services
920 NE 58th Avenue, Suite 300
Portland, OR 97213-3786
USA
Tel: +1 503 287 3093 or toll-free: (1) 800 944 6190
Fax: +1 503 280 8832
E-mail: orders@isbs.com
Website: http://www.isbs.com

© The editors and contributors severally 2015

First published in hardback, 2014

The editors and contributors have asserted their right under the Copyright,
Designs and Patents Act 1988, to be identified as the authors of this work.

Hart Publishing is an Imprint of Bloomsbury Publishing plc

All rights reserved. No part of this publication may be reproduced, stored in a retrieval
system, or transmitted, in any form or by any means, without the prior permission of Hart
Publishing, or as expressly permitted by law or under the terms agreed with the appropriate
reprographic rights organisation. Enquiries concerning reproduction which may not be
covered by the above should be addressed to Hart Publishing Ltd at the address above.

British Library Cataloguing in Publication Data
Data Available

ISBN: 978-1-84946-419-2 (Hardback)
ISBN: 978-1-84946-967-8 (Paperback)

Typeset by Compuscript Ltd, Shannon
Printed and bound in Great Britain by
CPI Group (UK) Ltd, CR0 4YY

Editors' Preface

This volume is a Festschrift in honour of Professor David M Trubek, and the content of the volume reflects this fact. The research questions addressed in the various contributions are those that have animated his wide-ranging, diverse and highly-influential research. The three editors of this volume first came to know and to work with David Trubek in the framework of a series of projects on 'new governance' and labour law governance in the EU. And while his long-standing academic engagement with EU law and policy may seem a long way from his interests in the global legal profession and in law and development issues in Brazil, Duncan Kennedy highlights in his opening chapter how each of these distinct research interests is fundamentally animated by the objective of critically interogating law and institutions with a view to harnessing the transformative potential of law.

David Trubek has been a central figure in critical legal scholarship of the twentieth century and the new millennium. His work has developed an approach that combines critique of conventional legal discourse with a progressive agenda. One of its notable features has been to foster the migration and extension of critical discourse to the new legal spaces emerging and being created by processes of globalisation. The span of his enquiries has been global: from US-focused scholarship, to (what have become known as) the BRICS (Brazil, Russia, India, China and South Africa) and especially Brazil, and beyond the BRICS to the EU as well as to transnational and international institutions, networks and social movements. His perspective has been one of critical engagement: seeking to develop and extend critical inquiry with a view to promoting change and reform. His work has made major contributions to the development of Law and Society scholarship, especially the use of empirical work for progressive legal ends ('critical empiricism'), legal pluralism, the sociology of law and the legal profession; the Critical Legal Studies (CLS) movement; critical perspectives on law and development (most recently, Law and the New Developmental State); and New Governance. Not only has he helped develop these strands and bodies of scholarship, but he has looked for ways of integrating them to form a discourse that would combine critique and reconstruction in the best traditions of Pragmatism and American Legal Realism.

David Trubek's contribution can be seen not only in his writings but also in his significant organisational energy and achievements. Four recent examples illustrate this: the re-issue in 2011 of the edited volume resulting from the German-US critical legal scholars meeting in Germany organised by David with Christian Joerges in 1986; a special session of the Law and Society Association's (LSA) 2010 meeting to discuss his work on critical empiricism, reflecting his long-standing contributions to the LSA; the publication by the *Wisconsin Law Review* in 2010 of a special issue on New Governance and the Transformation of Law, reflecting the central role David and Louise Trubek have played at the University of Wisconsin, Madison, in building New Governance scholarship, especially its EU–US comparative dimension; and the creation of LANDS, the project on Law and the New Developmental State, which has undertaken studies in Brazil, Mexico, Colombia and Venezuela.

This book brings together scholars who have accompanied David on some part of these many academic adventures. A connecting theme of the book is an exploration of the emergence of a global critical discourse on law and its application to processes of global governance. As law becomes increasingly implicated in transnational governance, and as processes related to and driven by globalisation transform legal systems at all levels, critical traditions in law, if they are to remain relevant, need to adapt to the changing legal order and *problématique*. The contributors to this volume include critical scholars from the EU and from North and South America, and they present a variety of critical studies of global and regional institutions and governance practices, including in relation to the 'special case' of the EU. Amongst the themes examined are the transnational governance of labour and development policy, a critical assessment of the meaning and impact of rights discourses, and the changing role of lawyers in the global regulatory space.

There are three main critical approaches visible in David Trubek's work. One is CLS-inspired, one sociologically-inclined and one governance-oriented:

(i)   the CLS-inspired approach seeks to unveil the politics and power implications of traditional legal rules, principles, institutions and thought (such as the rule of law, the ground rules of private and public law, the frameworks and goals of international institutions) in legal education and scholarship;

(ii) the sociological approach seeks amongst other things to examine the shaping of law and institutions through under-examined mechanisms such as social mobilisation, elite network elaboration and litigant analysis; and

(iii) the governance lens examines the limits of conventional legal tools in the face of the complexities of transnationalism and globalisation, and explores new normative mechanisms that seem to expand, adjust or challenge our understandings of law and democracy.

Each of these critical perspectives in Trubek's scholarship entails a rejection of an approach to legal scholarship which rotates 'around the abiding themes that law is vital, legal processes are neutral and rational, legal scholarship authoritative'.[1] Not only do they give different answers to the question 'what is law?' from the answer generally provided by traditional legal scholarship but, as the chapters in this volume demonstrate, they share a stronger interest than traditional legal scholarship in addressing the question: 'what is law for?'

The volume is divided into six main parts. The chapters included in the first section offer an introduction to David Trubek's scholarship and chart its evolution over time. These contributions carry out the work which is usually required of editors in that they tie together and analyse the interactions between different phases of David's academic journey and the different critical-left strands of his scholarship.

I. Critical Pathways in Law

The four chapters in this first part examine different aspects and phases of David Trubek's impressive corpus of academic scholarship, and reflect on their relationship to critique.

---

[1] DM Trubek and J Esser, 'Critical Empiricism and American CLS: Paradox, Program or Pandora's Box?' (2011) 12 *German Law Journal* 116, 119.

Duncan Kennedy's chapter contains a kind of condensed intellectual biography of David Trubek, focusing on his early intellectual influences and the path of his engagement with issues of globalisation from the time he worked for USAID and travelled to Brazil in 1964. Duncan Kennedy presents an engrossing account of the interweaving of the personal, political and intellectual dimensions of David Trubek's journey through the various stages of his academic career. In Duncan Kennedy's words, David has at every stage 'been producing subject-matter specific studies on the way globalisation, legal and economic, generates and perpetuates inequality' and arguing for reform and change to the neo-liberal paradigm of strong property rights for strong parties with no regulatory protection for weak ones.

Bill Simon looks in particular at one of the more recent phases of David's work, namely his engagement with 'new governance' in the EU, and asks whether there are continuities between this less overtly critical project and David's earlier explicitly critical bodies of work within the Law and Development, Law and Society, and Critical Legal Studies movements respectively. Bill Simon identifies and articulates four critical principles deriving from these three bodies of scholarship (anti-foundationalism, anti-determinism, anti-ideology and anti-separation-of-powers), and he then infers four practical criteria or conditions of presumptive political legitimacy (named after four of David's intellectual collaborators or inspirations: Jürgen Habermas, Duncan Kennedy, Roberto Unger and Charles Sabel) which any institution would have to meet to satisfy the four critical principles. He concludes that David Trubek's work on new governance and its potentially progressive role within EU law and politics potentially meets these four prescriptive conditions, and in that is animated by the same kind of integrated normative and critical impulse behind David's earlier work.

Ruth Buchanan's chapter looks at a different part of David's body of work, focusing this time on a particularly influential article he published with Mark Galanter in 1974 in the field of law and development, namely 'Scholars in Self-Estrangement: Some Reflections on the Crisis in Law and Development Studies in the United States'. This essay, which is also discussed in Duncan Kennedy's chapter, had presented a critique of the first wave of law and development scholarship and practice and the liberal-legal assumptions underpinning that project, based in part on the authors' own experiences. Ruth Buchanan's chapter seeks to document the legacy of this important essay in contemporary law and development scholarship, looking not only at its 'afterlife' in the writing of other scholars in the field, but also at its current relevance in alerting scholars to the occupational hazards of critical legal scholarship, including the difficulty of navigating the simultaneous pursuit of reform via fair and effective legal rules even while maintaining the critical stance of social scientists.

In the fourth and final chapter of this first part, Mario Schapiro and Diogo Coutinho, who are currently collaborators with David Trubek on their LANDS project, examine the evolving relationship between political economy and law in Brazil over the last half century. They outline three distinct phases or 'moments' during this time: a phase of development entailing interventionist economic law, a phase of moderate neo-liberalism and economic regulation, and the current phase of the 'new activism' of the state. They identify a number of challenges faced by economic law in this new state activism phase, including what they call the need for selectivity in the use of legal tools, instruments and legal forms, as well as the legitimacy and composition of institutional governance arrangements and particularly the need to develop reforms and new arrangements that are participatory, cost effective and politically responsive.

II. Transformations in Global Governance

In Part II, the chapters contributed by David Kennedy and Peer Zumbansen draw back from these more focused analysis of particular strands of the work and influence of David Trubek, and move instead to look at 'the big picture'.

Peer Zumbansen's chapter aims to connect domestic governance discourses with global governance and global constitutionalism discourses in the context of transnational regulation. He directs our attention to the ways in which information and knowledge (including the ubiquitous 'data-driven' approaches) have become key in development theory and practice today, and to the complexification and intensification of multiple discourses addressing the same set of issues. He points to the range of different new and established fields and sub-disciplinary approaches to the 'intersection between local fragmentation and foreign intervention', including global administrative law, third-world approaches to international law, and transitional justice, and notes how these and other approaches challenge and contest the basis of what counts as the relevant 'knowledge' underpinning policy, and how they carry different assumptions and 'semantic baggage' with them from the domestic to the international arena.

David Kennedy's chapter similarly steps back to survey the larger global landscape, this time with the aim of bringing questions of political economy—and specifically of global political economy—back within academic scrutiny. He identifies the key questions for today not as political questions about governmental or diplomatic action, or economic questions about how markets should operate, but rather questions about the distribution of growth. He argues that the key issue, highlighting the intertwining of political and economic projects, is 'how gains and losses are to be distributed between those who lead and those who lag', and yet notes how little international legal scholarship addresses the global distribution of political authority and economic growth. Internationally-minded lawyers, he suggests, need to reframe and interpret the role of law 'as the cloak hiding asymmetric dynamics of power in political economy of the world' which creates and links centres and peripheries across the global stage. He points out that since law regulates the elements of both political and economic life, the task for critical and reform-minded legal scholars is to imagine the building of a new political economy for a global society.

III. Labour and Globalisation

The five chapters in this part identify different challenges and perspectives on globalisation in relationship to labour standards. All draw on Trubek's scholarship in this area. Perhaps the most prominent preoccupation concerns new spaces and dilemmas for labour standards in a globalised trading system. This includes at least two key issues. One is the effect of global trade on labour standards. If such trade drives down labour standards in advanced economies, as both Compa and Stone assert in their analyses, how can the economic benefits of free trade for developing countries be maintained while combatting this race to the bottom? This dilemma creates tensions between developed and developing economies both globally and within distinctive regimes such as the EU where internal market rules combined with EU enlargement have created east–west dilemmas on labour standards. A second is whether there is an incipient transnational labour regime. Components of such a regime include labour conditionality in trade agreements signed by the US and the EU with third countries, new developments in international labour sources, adaptation of national regimes to meet the challenges of more open regional trading arrangements (such as the EU or NAFTA), and some signs of cross-border worker mobilisation within these new transnational legal spaces.

A second set of pressures on labour regimes and standards, especially their national realisation, comes from the need to adapt to changed social, (macro-)economic and technological as well as political environments. The shift from manufacturing and mass production in labour systems organised around standard employment relationships has, for instance, placed old worker solidarities under very significant pressure, with unions and job security viewed as relics of the past. More sharply, responses to the 2008 financial crisis have highlighted how dismantling labour law can become a default policy response to issues and problems largely unrelated to labour standards. This has led to reflection on how to develop new forms of identity and resistance between those who engage in paid work and other groups and actors, within and beyond the state.

Related to both these profound shifts, and another hallmark of Trubek's scholarly contributions, is attention to how new labour regimes change the nature of law in regulating labour with variants of hard, soft and hybrid legal frameworks becoming more prominent and requiring both careful empirical assessment and critical evaluation.

Harry Arthurs uses the evocative metaphor of 'making bricks without straw' to reflect on the profound difficulties of building a transnational labour regime. He makes the important point that, for reasons linked to both global trade and social-economic-technological shifts, national governments, the linchpin of the post-war welfare consensus, have ceased either to believe in progressive labour policies or to implement them. The crucial missing ingredient in the construction of new labour regimes, nationally and transnationally, is collective worker-identification with that status which has ceased for many to be a central source of common identity. What then of transnational labour regimes 'after labour'? He suggests a reorientation towards all those affected by economic insecurity and subordination to constitute new communities of collective action and resistance to claim standards of decent economic relations.

Lance Compa carefully traces the changing nature and sources used in US labour conditionality in its trade agreements both preceding and post-dating the NAFTA labour side agreement. The rationale is to take labour standards out of competition. He looks at mobilisation within the US political process to obtain such conditionality, the intense battles over the wording concerning labour conditionality, and the law and practice surrounding their compliance mechanisms. In particular, he charts the growing use of the 1998 ILO Declaration on Fundamental Principles and Rights at Work. Despite the problems with these US trade-labour agreements, he suggests that their existence has produced some benefits. It has put the relationship between trade and labour on the global institutional policy agenda, promoted reflective scholarship, and created spaces for transnational mobilisation and collaboration involving lawyers, unions and other activists.

For Katherine Stone the core dilemma is that with global trade, 'labour standards tend to flow to the lowest point'. Because of corporate capacity to deterritorialise, gains from free trade do not necessarily accrue to those living in the territory where the traded goods and services were produced. Under certain conditions, corporate flight to low-labour standard locations as well as regulatory competition by states to attract foreign business, drives down labour standards. Stone identifies and assesses three broad strategies to prevent labour 'drowning in globalisation': using new modes of governance to incite races to the top through processes of peer review; taking advantage of the tendency of some firms to cluster in locations with certain endowments by developing locally-based organising initiatives in those locations; and reconfiguring labour regimes in advanced economies so as to combine firms' needs for flexible innovation-oriented human resources with workers' needs for life security.

Focusing primarily on the post-2008 economic crisis, Kerry Rittich argues for an expanded law of work to take into account a broader set of policy interventions impacting on work as well as a wider range of work relationships, including the borderline between the formal and informal economy. Looking at fiscal and monetary policy, as well as EU bail-out conditionality and crisis deals to save the North American car industry, she illustrates narratives driving the policy response such as the 'belief that labour standards and collective bargaining are per se sub-optimal' which show why critical methods help assess how labour law has come to be central to the resolution of what is essentially a financial and debt crisis.

Concluding this rich section of the volume, Alvaro Santos re-opens three arguments often used to defend the labour law status quo: that it reflects national or regional (EU) identity; that it is inherently progressive; and that the constitutionalisation of social rights enhances their protection. Using the examples of Mexico and recent EU developments, he argues that these assertions are not only unwarranted, they are undesirable. Like Rittich, Santos urges instead analysis of the distributive effects of labour law regimes on wealth and power. Where such analysis reveals undesirable consequences of the status quo in relation to issues such as gender or generational equity, or workers' autonomy and subjectivity, that status quo should be open to progressive critique and re-imaginings. Such distributive analysis also forecloses the view that embedding social rights as fundamental will, in and of itself, prevent regressive social policies.

IV. The European Union

The fourth part in this volume is focused on EU law and governance and explores the potential and possible limitations of a new governance approach. This part opens with a contribution by Kenneth Armstrong, which explores the multiple encounters between (new) governance and law. Like Bill Simon and Duncan Kennedy earlier in the volume, Armstrong argues that new governance has the potential to advance the cause of a progressive law and politics, not least because of the way in which the new governance framing has opened up new areas (including, prominently, anti-poverty policy in Armstrong's own work) for critical engagement in EU law. Contrary to the later chapter by Christian Joerges and Maria Weimer, Armstrong concludes that the current crisis in Europe is as much a crisis *for* law, and a crisis *of* law, as it is a crisis in governance. The economic crisis has created momentum in favour of 'muscular', 'harder rules and sanctions' and has brought in its wake the threat of 'hyper-legalism' rather than a dangerous absence of law. Contrary to received wisdom, Armstrong argues that '[t]he challenge facing Europe is not so much the alleged delegalisation of new governance' but 'a corrosive legal instrumentalism'.

Norbert Reich uses David Trubek's writings on European consumer law, labour law and new governance as an entry point into recent discussion and debate concerning the construction of a European contract law. Reich explores the different phases of European contract law and the different instruments that the EU has deployed. When minimum harmonisation created a new kind of regulatory gap, the EU experimented with different strategies including conflicts-of-law regulation, full harmonisation and a new governance-Open Method of Coordination (OMC) type approach. Reich is critical of the European Commission's current proposal for a regulation on a Common European Sales Law, arguing that it does not satisfy the 'necessity test'. Reich looks to new governance in general, and to David Trubek's contribution to new governance scholarship in particular, for inspiration regarding a possible alternative approach, one which is predicated upon reflexive contract governance with a recommendation rather than a regulation at its core.

Christian Joerges and Maria Weimer offer a less optimistic account of new governance, casting doubt on its accomplishments and suggesting a need for new governance to go back to its critical roots. They argue that the weaknesses of new governance are reflected in current economic governance in the context of the ongoing crisis, and that recourse to 'hybridity' involving both hard and soft law has been not only economically unsuccessful but also socially disastrous. In this setting, new governance is presented as nothing short of a threat to democracy and to the rule of law. Joerges and Weimer begin to set forth an alternative approach which they frame as 'conflicts-law consitutionalism'; an approach that is intended to ensure that 'the idea of law-mediated legitimacy can be preserved, and that the integration project can regain its democratic credentials'. The goal of conflicts-law constitutionalism is to ensure that conflicts between the EU and the Member States are resolved through rules and principles that are acceptable to all, rather than through hierarchy or executive managerialism. The means that conflicts-law constitutionalism deploys is the proceduralisation of EU law.

V. Rights Discourse

Three chapters focus on the deployment of human rights discourse in a range of locations and issues. All set rights, civil and social, in a broader framing so as to provide a rich context for a range of critical approaches.

Henry Steiner's chapter sets the headscarf controversy in France and a number of other European countries in a broader critical and global perspective. Looking at how countries of immigration manage newcomers he contrasts state assimilation policies with policies embracing plural identities. Through careful analysis of relevant French legislation, he makes clear the incoherence of that legislation with its stated goal of protecting *laïcité* (secularity). He also subjects the human rights supervision of the European Court of Human Rights on this issue to searching scrutiny, arguing that, with one recent exception, its jurisprudence is marked by lack of rigour, failure to engage fundamental questions, and leaving too large a margin of appreciation to states such as France, Switzerland and Turkey.

Tamara Hervey's chapter focuses on how to protect social rights before courts in litigation framed by the EU's internal market freedoms. She imagines what EU law could be like if, in its reasoning and its presuppositions, it took social rights seriously by rethinking and rewriting, in an exercise of 're-imagined jurisprudence' a central internal market judgement on health care. In so doing, by foregrounding the collective dimensions of health care, and their allocation on the basis of national or sub-national democratic processes, she makes explicit both the non-inevitability of the Court's current jurisprudence and the opportunity to re-orient it towards greater constitutional symmetry between the supranational and the national, and between market liberalisation and other values worthy of protection.

A different critical approach to social rights and their relationship with the market is provided by Helena Alviar García who asks whether social, economic and cultural rights limit or reinforce the market. Although the Colombian Constitutional Court has been lauded for its emancipatory, market-limiting judgments building on a 1991 Constitution rich in socio-economic provisions, she argues that broader distributive analysis, with greater attention to institutions and policy-shaping, reveals the constitutional rights jurisprudence to largely protect those already in the market for housing and health, hence complementing rather than challenging market-oriented reforms.

VI. The Legal Profession and Globalisation

The sixth and final part of this volume is centred on the study of legal professions and global governance. The first contribution, by Yves Dezalay and Bryant Garth, explores Bourdieu's *Sur l'Etat*, lectures delivered at the College de France in which he returns to ideas first set out in *The Force of Law*. Although rooted in continental European history, Dezalay and Garth argue that these lectures have much to contribute to a law and society understanding of the US Cravath model of lawyering. More generally, they argue that law and society scholarship is set within the paradigm of legal realism and that it tends to be characterised by an almost complete absence of the kind of reflexive sociology that they consider to be indispensable to understanding the constitution of the legal field. While legal scholars purport to increasingly draw upon the writings of Bourdieu, the reflexivity that is central to Bourdieu's research remains neglected all the same. Law and Society scholarship rests upon the 'structural invisibility of hierarchical structures in the field of legal power', with empiricism and cause lawyering both exhibiting the same blindness when it comes to analysing the 'the structures of the field of legal power'.

Mihaela Papa turns her attention to emerging powers, specifically the BRICS, and analyses whether these countries have served, or may be expected to serve, as what she calls agents of social change. Papa offers a conceptualisation of the politics of reforming global governance as involving the interplay between three factors: the existence of a reformist coalition, the context of reform, and the incentive for reform. She then goes on to explore the reformist agenda of the BRICS in the crucial and contested area of investment arbitration, an area in which emerging economies are as concerned to ensure the effective protection of their own investors as they are to promote the fairness of the regime. Papa finds that in the area of investment arbitration, the 'BRICS are unlikely to exert joint leadership as a change-seeking coalition', with the different countries exhibiting different policies and different levels of engagement with global investment governance. Different members of the group are even engaging in investment disputes between themselves. Nonetheless, Papa posits that the relationship between China and Brazil is key in determining how much future cooperation may be achieved.

John Ohnesorge's contribution brings together different themes that have long been present in David Trubek's work, including law and development, the legal profession and global governance. He considers whether it might be appropriate for national governments to offer protection or other kinds of support for business lawyers, treating them as akin to 'infant industries'. Relying principally upon the writings of Jacob Viner, and breaking down the market for corporate legal services into distinct segments, Ohnesorge highlights a number of concerns. While he considers that an infant industry approach facilitates an unusually rigorous analysis of the issues, Ohnesorge reaches the provisional conclusion that it is not at all clear that the provision of infant industry support for local law firms providing internationally-related legal services would constitute 'good public policy', not least because of the consequences of protectionism for the quality and costs of the services concerned. Ohnesorge's analysis is wide-ranging, covering domestic litigation and domestic regulatory work in the protected market, out-going work for business clients from the protected market, and capacity building outside and within government for participation in international governance, including in the settlement of international disputes.

The volume concludes with a chapter by David Wilkins who points to David Trubek's 'uncanny ability to find where the action is'. The main focus of the chapter is on Wilkins' and Trubek's current collaboration on GLEE (Globalization, Lawyers and Emerging Economies). GLEE examines the question of why the legal profession (and specifically the corporate legal sector) is changing so rapidly in countries such as Brazil, India and China and considers what implications this might have for economic development and for the rule of law. This is both a socio-legal and a critical-legal project and in the words of Duncan Kennedy it is one of the projects that currently takes David Trubek 'back to Brazil'.

This has been an especially easy and wonderful project to work on. We have had none of the usual editorial problems of persuading leading scholars to attend the workshop at the European University Institute in Florence in June 2012 or to contribute chapters in a timely fashion to this volume. In fact, such was the general enthusiasm for the project that a number of people who did not write chapters for this volume nonetheless participated in different ways in the Florence event. We would like to thank Dirk Hartog and Catherine Meschievitz for their interventions and insights during the event. We are particuarly grateful to Professor Louise Trubek for her assistance from the beginning to the end of this project. Her support has been invaluable. Thanks are also due to those who contributed financially to the running of the workshop in Florence, namely the Academy of European Law, and the Law Department and the Schuman Centre at the European University Institute (EUI), and New York University Law School.

We owe a very large thank you to Eleonora Masella from the EUI Law Department for making all the arrangements required for the conference held at the EUI in June 2012. Despite the heat and the formidable logistics, she remained calm, competent and good-humoured throughout. Vesselin Paskalev, a PhD researcher at the EUI, has helped enormously in getting the volume ready for publication and we are very grateful for his help.

Finally, we are grateful to David Trubek for his role, together with Louise Trubek, in inspiring each of us in our individual and collective academic projects, in bringing together and prompting new critical and progressive research projects, and in enriching our global, comparative and transatlantic scholarly endeavours with his energy, intellect and friendship.

Contents

List of Contributors

Kenneth A Armstrong is Professor of European law, University of Cambridge.

Harry Arthurs is University Professor Emeritus and President Emeritus, Osgoode Hall Law School, York University, Toronto, Canada.

Ruth Buchanan is Associate Professor and Graduate Program Director, Osgoode Hall Law School, York University, Toronto, Canada.

Gráinne de Búrca is Florence Ellinwood Allen Professor of Law, New York University School of Law, USA.

Lance Compa is Senior Lecturer at the School of Industrial and Labor Relations, Cornell University, USA.

Diogo R Coutinho is Professor at the University of São Paulo Faculty of Law and researcher at CEBRAP (the Brazilian Centre for Analysis and Planning), Brazil.

Yves Dezalay is Directeur de recherches at the CNRS (Centre National de la Recherche Scientifique) at MSN (Maison des Sciences de l'Homme) Paris, France.

Helena Alviar García is Dean of Law at Universidad de Los Andes, Bogota, Colombia.

Bryant G Garth is Dean Emeritus, Professor of Law of Southwestern Law School, Los Angeles, California, USA.

Tamara K Hervey is Jean Monnet Professor of EU Law, University of Sheffield, UK.

Christian Joerges is Professor of German and European Private and Business Law, University of Bremen, Germany.

David Kennedy is Manley O Hudson Professor of Law and Director of the Institute for Global Law and Policy, Harvard Law School, USA.

Duncan Kennedy is Carter Professor of General Jurisprudence at Harvard Law School, USA.

Claire Kilpatrick is Professor of International and European Labour and Social Law at the European University Institute, Florence, Italy.

John KM Ohnesorge is Professor of Law and Director of the East Asian Legal Studies Center, University of Wisconsin Law School, USA.

Mihaela Papa is a Postdoctoral Research Fellow, Globalisation, Lawyers and Emerging Economies Project, Program on the Legal Profession, Harvard Law School, USA.

Norbert Reich is Emeritus Professor, University of Bremen, Germany.

Kerry Rittich is Professor at the Faculty of Law, University of Toronto, Canada.

Alvaro Santos is Associate Professor of Law, Georgetown University Law Center, USA.

Mario G Schapiro is Professor at the São Paulo Law School, Fundação Getulio Vargas (Direito GV), Brazil.

Joanne Scott is Professor of European Law at University College London, UK.

William H Simon is Arthur Levitt Professor of Law, Columbia University, UK.

Henry J Steiner is Emeritus Jeremiah Smith, Jr Professor of Law, Harvard Law School, USA.

Katherine VW Stone is Arjay and Frances Miller Distinguished Professor of Law at UCLA School of Law, USA.

Maria Weimer is a Post-doctoral Researcher in EU and International Law, Maastricht University, the Netherlands.

David Wilkins is Lester Kissel Professor of Law at Harvard Law School, USA.

Peer Zumbansen is Professor at Osgoode Hall Law School, York University, Toronto, Canada.

Part I

Critical Pathways in Law

1

The Globalisation of Critical Discourses on Law: Thoughts on David Trubek's Contribution

DUNCAN KENNEDY

When Gráinne de Búrca asked me whether I would like to participate in a conference to honour David Trubek, I said yes as a matter of course. Some time later, I asked what I should talk about, thinking that I would tell some stories about being his student in first year property at Yale Law School in the spring of 1968, a little anecdotage about Critical Legal Studies (CLS) early days, a bit on his late 80s year at the 'Beirut of legal education', as he called my dear school. The short emailed answer was: 'We'd like you to speak on the globalization of critical discourses on law.' Huh? 'That was what Dave said he wanted.' I said yes as a matter of course, with just a little tremor of angst. Putting it off, putting it off, I finally realised that Dave had bitten off more than I could chew. Then a moment of insight: Dave was asking me to speak not on my topic, but on his!

This will be an attempt to tell the story of one of Dave's most important life projects. First, the critical discourses on law that he has been globalising are not just any and all such discourses, but, I'm thinking, more the discourses loosely joined in critical legal studies, a legal academic movement or school whose origin dates to 1977. Dave was one of the key planners and the site organiser of the first Conference on Critical Legal Studies held in Madison, Wisconsin, where he was teaching law.

The 'critical' in CLS in general, as well as in Dave's particular version, was always ambiguous, in fact doubly so. 'Critical' meant left criticism of the existing legal order on the ground that it was implicitly or explicitly conservative, and should be changed to make it more promotive of egalitarian, communitarian and participatory values. As I will explain, Dave's leftism is not just American liberalism, or even just American left-liberalism, but something more radical, more 'progressive', without being radical in the full-out American New Left sense.

'Critical' also meant a position affirming connection to critical theory, in the European sense. 'Critical theory' was capacious, stretching to include everything from Western Marxism to Max Weber's sociology of law. Marcuse's Freud/Marx/Hegel synthesis, phenomenology, structuralism and existentialism were all important to me as an early participant, though not so much, I think, to Dave. Foucault and Derrida were around the corner but not yet in the room. For Dave, American law and society (that is, the sociology of law) has always been a critical discourse, and he has continually affirmed its at least possible coherence with the more Frankfurt Schoolish varieties of critique.

Dave was one of those who developed from these various strands a number of specific ways to criticise particular legal regimes, and I will be passing these under review in a bit. The second part of the project was to globalise these strands, including both the 'left' part and the 'critical theory' part. This aspect has a very clear origin in Dave's experience in Brazil in the mid 1960s, and went through several quite different phases before gelling in the late 1990s. Again, there is an ambiguity: the globalisation of critique is the critique of globalisation.

Dave has not been mainly interested in finding ways to apply the routines we developed to criticise US legal rules and institutions to the legal rules and institutions of other countries (a first meaning of globalising a critical discourse). Although that is sometimes a part of the analysis, the critique is almost always directed I think, at some aspect or fragment or sector of the global 'system', understood as linking countries all over the world in relationships that have a dimension of power or domination.

Briefly: this is neither classic Marxist analysis of imperialism—the highest stage of capitalism—nor Wallerstein's world system theory, but a much more chastened, small-bore, tentative insistence that we attend to something that should be obvious but is usually ignored. What happens in the global South, as well as in regional peripheries in the North, as well as in the poor parts of large urban areas in the North, is not just a function of what the inhabitants do on their own and for themselves. There are flows of goods and money and equally important flows of ideas, policies and legal norms: in short interdependence, between the weak and the strong. It is not just a question of relative advantage in exchange, but also a matter of relative advantage in the project of structuring exchange over time. This advantage of the strong is crucially important to the outcomes for the weak.

Dave's version of globalising critical discourses includes the diagnosis of the undesirable results (from a left point of view) of the systems that are globalised from the strong to the weak, and he always has proposals for changes that should make the system better (from a left point of view), or an idea of an already ongoing change that could have that effect. It is striking that from early in his career he has been committed, as we will shortly see, to the autonomy as well as to the welfare of the weak.

I. Critical Discourses in Dave's Project: Domestic Origins

During 1961–62, Dave was law clerk to Judge Charles Clark on the US Court of Appeals for the Second Circuit in New York City. Clark had been the Dean of Yale Law School in the 1930s at the height of the legal realist moment in American legal academia. He was not a polemicist in the manner of Thurman Arnold or Jerome Frank. His project was the drafting of the new Federal Rules of Civil Procedure, a monumental attempt to put the ideas of sociological jurisprudence into practical effect, against the pre-existing nineteenth-century procedural regime of classical legal thought. He was a reformer rather than a radical, but one with a very firm commitment to the generational advances of the pre-war period.

While Dave was clerking, Karl Llewellyn published what was supposed to be the crowning work of his career, *The Common Law Tradition: Deciding Appeals*.[1] Clark was an obvious choice to review the book for the *Yale Law Journal* (of which Dave had been an editor), and he delegated the task to his clerk, as was not uncommon in those far-off days. The

---

[1] K Llewellyn *The Common Law Tradition: Deciding Appeals* (Boston-Toronto, Little, Brown, 1960).

review was called 'The Creative Role of the Judge: Restraint and Freedom in the Common Law Tradition'.[2] The review critiqued Llewellyn for ignoring the creative role of the judge, his freedom, in other words, and of thereby backsliding from the realist accomplishment to which Llewellyn himself had been a central contributor. (Twenty-five years later I called an article of mine 'Freedom and Constraint in Adjudication' without conscious adversion to Dave's article which I read and loved as a law student.)

The importance of the article is that it carries forward realist anti-formalism into a period in which Legal Process belief in 'reasoned elaboration' and 'neutral principles' seemed to have won the day. The reader understood that although 'creative' sounded good, and 'freedom' was neutral, both terms opened or re-opened the possibility of analysing the outcome in terms of the judge's politics. 1962 was before the 60s had properly begun and 15 years before the first Crit conference. The article acts as a kind of missing link between pre-World War II legal America and post-Vietnam legal America.

II. Critique as Leftist Legal Discourse

While 'Constraint and Freedom' seems a very good starting point, as soon as we are beyond it things become suddenly and forever-after complicated because Dave always has several projects going, without strong obvious links between them, although they clearly influence one another over time. Here I am just doing what I was told to do, talking about the globalisation of critical discourses, so I will have to slight numerous other dimensions of Dave's work (most notably the civil litigation projects). Sticking to the plan, here is a kind of quick walk-through of Dave's domestic projects that are critical in the sense of leftist, ranging from straightforward American liberalism leftward into the outskirts of radicalism. The topics are familiar, and I will simply list the titles to give a sense of his approach in the 1970s and early 1980s. I should mention at the beginning, his and Louise Trubek's roles as plaintiffs in the federal litigation leading up to *Griswold v Connecticutt*, striking down statutes which criminalised the sale of contraceptives and note in passing that Dave is already a collaborator (very often with Louise).[3]

---

[2] CE Clark and DM Trubek, 'The Creative Role of the Judge: Restraint and Freedom in the Common Law Tradition' (1961) 71 *Yale Law Journal* 255–76.

[3] On exclusionary zoning, see DM Trubek, B Cohen and E Branfman, 'Measuring the Invisible Wall: Land Use Controls and the Residential Patterns of the Poor' (1972) 82 *Yale Law Journal* 483–508; and DM Trubek, 'Law and the Politics of Justice: Rethinking the Open Suburbs Movement' in DH Moskowitz, *Exclusionary Zoning Litigation* (1977). On the environment, see DM Trubek, 'Allocating the Burden of Environmental Uncertainty: the NRC Interprets NEPA's Substantive Mandate' (1977) *Wisconsin Law Review* 747–76; DM Trubek, 'Environmental Defense: Interest Group Advocacy in Complex Disputes' in BA Weisbrod, JF Handler and NK Komesar, *Public Interest Law* (University of California Press, 1978) 151–217. On Consumer protection, see DM Trubek, K McNeil, JR Nevin and RE Miller, 'Market Discrimination Against the Poor and the Impact of Consumer Disclosure Laws: The Used Car Industry' (1979) 13 *Law & Society Review* 695–720; DM Trubek, LG Trubek and JE Zorn, 'Coordinating Consumer Law and Policy in the American Federal System' in T Bourgoignie (ed), *European Consumer Law* 307–59 (1982). On Legal services and public interest law, see DM Trubek, 'Public Advocacy: Administrative Government and the Representation of Diffuse Interests' in M Cappelletti and B Garth (eds), *Emerging Issues & Perspectives in the 'Access to Justice Movement'* 447–94 (1979); DM Trubek, LG Trubek and J Becker, 'Legal Services and the Administrative State: From Public Interest Law to Public Advocacy' in E Blankenburg (ed), *Innovations in the Legal Services* (1980) 131–60.

Exclusionary zoning: 'Measuring the Invisible Wall: Land Use Controls and the Residential Patterns of the Poor.' (1972); 'Law and the Politics of Justice: Rethinking the Open Suburbs Movement' (1977).

The environment: 'Allocating the Burden of Environmental Uncertainty: the NRC Interprets NEPA's Substantive Mandate' (1977); 'Environmental Defense: Interest Group Advocacy in Complex Disputes' (1978).

Consumer protection: 'Market Discrimination Against the Poor and the Impact of Consumer Disclosure Laws: The Used Car Industry' (1979); 'Coordinating Consumer Law and Policy in the American Federal System' (1982).

Legal services and public interest law: 'Public Advocacy: Administrative Government and the Representation of Diffuse Interests' (1979); 'Legal Services and the Administrative State: From Public Interest Law to Public Advocacy' (1980).

III. Critique in the Sense of Critical Theory

Dave's scholarly engagement with critical theory begins, I'd say—but what do I know—in his years as an assistant professor at Yale (friendships with Rick Abel there, and with Unger and Steiner at Harvard were key), specifically in his famous Law and Modernisation seminar, and even more specifically in his passionate engagement with the ideas of Max Weber. To summarise:

1. During the cold war, Weber was mainly known for his views on religion and the rise of capitalism, ingenuously or idiotically or tendentiously interpreted as the anti-Marx manifesto because it supposedly claimed that ideas, particularly religious ones rather than material forces were the main movers of history.

2. At the beginning of the law and modernisation project, Trubek's revisionist story was that Weber was a theorist of how law, rather than religion, played a major role in capitalist economic development. European high formalist legal thought, which protected the autonomy of rational actors from official meddling, guaranteed 'calculability' which encouraged them to grow the economy.

3. In the next stage of the project, there were three big problems:

    (a) the English were the champion developers with a relatively uncertain and unsystematic legal system that Weber regarded as primitive at best;

    (b) we (Dave and his students) thought the legal realist common lawyers had shown that Weber's beloved high formalist system was internally incoherent at the normative level and highly uncertain and biased at the level of legal administration, rather than calculably rational; and

    (c) Weber had nothing but contempt for the post-formalist social law that almost everyone in Europe and America (in 1970) regarded as far superior, both ethically and practically, to its predecessor.[4]

---

[4] See DM Trubek, 'Max Weber on Law and the Rise of Capitalism' (1972) *Wisconsin Law Review* 720; DM Trubek, 'Max Weber's Tragic Modernism and the Study of Law in Society' (1986) 20 *Law and Society Review* 573–98.

'Max Weber on law and the rise of capitalism' (1972);
'Max Weber's tragic modernism and the study of law in society' (1986).

So Weber couldn't be 'the man'; there were just too many problems. The encounter with Weber, however, framed the subsequent encounter with the tradition of Marxist and post-Marxist ideology critique. Ideology critique is the idea that what we loosely call consciousness everywhere mediates between 'facts' and us, structuring perception of the world including our understanding of why bad things are bad and what can and can't be done about them. The critical idea is that elements of consciousness that are false have the effect of restricting people's capacity to act in the interest of their own emancipation. The ideology is 'relatively autonomous' but also serves the interests of those who profit most from the status quo, and is passionately defended, in good faith, by the 'organic intelligentsia' of the privileged strata. All parts of this idea were anathema to American liberal intellectuals in the post-war period, but were revived by the new left in the late 1960s and 1970s.

One of the ways ideology critique came to us early Crits was through the Pashukanis version of the Marxist legal theory of the 'commodity', which was that modern Western capitalist law derived analytically from the capitalist form of property, namely the commodity which has an absolute owner who can do with it whatever he wants and contract about it without any form of regulation. The legal rules were simply the 'reflection' of the supposed underlying truth that in fact, in capitalist society capitalists own the means of production, can do anything they want with them, and compete 'freely' among themselves while contracting 'freely' with propertyless workers. There was a striking structural similarity between Marx and Weber, both of whom accepted that modern law was a coherent working out of a few basic ideas, and that it played the role of facilitating the autonomous dynamic functioning of the economy.

In the very early days of CLS, this Marxist theory had considerable currency among the post-Marxists, who were an important group, allied with but also fighting against the post-liberals, each group having undergone a generationally similar early 1970s disillusionment with what had once seemed their natural reference group. (Due to the descent of Marxists into sectarianism and of liberals into Vietnam and paralysis in the face of racism.)

Dave became a critical theorist in the strong sense when he wrote 'Complexity and Contradiction in the Legal Order: Balbus and the Challenge of Critical Social Thought' (1977).[5] In short, a Marxist social theory of law, like Weber's theory or classical late nineteenth-century legal formalism, that starts from the idea that it has a coherent inner logic and institutions that 'just apply' that logic, ignores everything we've learned from the realist and post-realist critique of law. As a result, the Marxist theory of law as simply the legal reflection of the inner logic of the capitalist commodity, will be weak or simply wrong when it comes to understanding how the social order works through law. Complexity and contradiction, normative and administrative, have to be taken into account, and that will bring the scale of generalisation and dogmatic assertion way down into the lower atmosphere or all the way to the ground. At the same time, complexity and contradiction open law up to emancipatory projects that seem implausible if you think it has an intrinsic oppressive coherence.

---

[5] DM Trubek, 'Complexity and Contradiction in the Legal Order: Balbus and the Challenge of Critical Social Thought About Law' (1977) 11 *Law & Society Review* 529–69.

I would say Dave was looking for a synthesis including legal realism, Marx, Weber, law and society, and the insights of nascent CLS. The Balbus article was the first version of this. He refined and extended it later, in his encounters with Crits who thought the empirical institutionally-oriented side was unlikely to pay off, and with more radical non-lawyer legal sociologists who wanted more evil systematicity.[6]

'Where the Action Is: Critical Legal Studies and Empiricism' (1984);
'Critical Empiricism in American Legal Studies: Paradox, Program or Pandora's Box?' (1989).

IV. The Globalisation of Critique as the Critique of Globalisation

As we turn to Dave as a globaliser of critical discourses about law, the key word is *Brazil*. We began his early story with his year as clerk to Charles Clark, denouncing Llewellyn's sell-out of the realist legacy. Then he went to the United States Agency for International Development (USAID) in Washington, as a desk officer, for two years, then into the field in Brazil. He arrived in Brazil in 1964, at the moment of the Castelo Branco coup of the generals against the left/populist Joao Goulart, whose regime the Brazilian elite and their American private and public backers had come to see as a threat. Dave stayed in Brazil for two years, met Roberto Unger and Henry Steiner, then went off to be an assistant professor at Yale Law School, arriving with a pocket full of money from his former government employer for the study of 'law and modernisation'.

When I first met Dave and Louise in the spring of 1968, they still had a kind of post-Brazil glow about them: bright colours, samba beat, modernist art, feijoada, the sshh sshh sshh'ing of conversation in Portuguese, the aftertaste of splendor and misery as imperial envoys, memories of wild parties and wild politics with violence at right and left extremes, the ferment of native elites eager for collaborators in their struggle for economic development within the fantasy of national greatness.

I imagine that Brazil has stayed so much a part of Dave's life and work because living there combined the thrill of the exotic other with the moral ambiguities of Kennedy-era American liberalism. Liberalism was our dominant national elite ethos, hardly challenged by the Barry Goldwater types. This was not a humanist style. It practised *realpolitik* style covert action against communism and Castro, capitalist economic development through sophisticated New Deal-inspired economic policy without challenging Third World plutocracy (the Alliance for Progress), and the merciless ostracism of liberals who were either too 'soft' for the task or tainted even a little by sympathy for radical leftism. In the period we are discussing, it turned even more brutal, but also simple minded and obtuse, in a way that had been unimaginable in the age of Adlai Stevenson, the losing liberal democratic

---

[6] DM Trubek, 'Where the Action Is: Critical Legal Studies and Empiricism' (1984) 36 *Stanford Law Review* 576; DM Trubek and J Esser, '"Critical Empiricism" in American Legal Studies: Paradox, Program, or Pandora's Box?' (1989) 14 *Law and Society Inquiry* 3.

candidate for president in 1952 and 1956. (But this may be more my own story than it is Dave's.)

V. Critique of Liberal Globalisation

The economists ruled policy in 'underdeveloped countries', and Dave and a few others in the US and in the former British Empire took on the project of working out a legal component of development policy. The inspiration, perhaps, was the central place of lawyers, legal concepts and legal reforms in the New Deal. This model was, of course, intimately connected with the rise of sociological jurisprudence and legal realism, at the Yale Law School in particular.

Applying the model in Brazil involved two odd complexities. First, the economists really and truly thought law was irrelevant, it was not even a shadow within their consciousness: all that counted was a system of modern property rights and markets. Second, the legal order of Brazil, as of most of the global South, was as far as you could possibly imagine from that of the post-New Deal US. First, legal formalism had been challenged in the teens and thirties by social legal thought, but the challenge had largely failed throughout the legal culture, and, second, formal law seemed stunningly irrelevant to what happened in practical life.

Dave's contribution to a liberal project of law and development had two parts, one practical and one theoretical. First, a book in Portuguese called *O Mercado de capitais e os incentivos fiscales* co-authored with Sa and Gouvea Viera and published in Rio in 1971.[7] And second, 'Toward a Social Theory of Law: An Essay on the Study of Law and Development',[8] in the *Yale Law Journal* in 1972.

This was tenure time at Yale for Dave and also for Rick Abel, Robert Hudec and Larry Simon. (John Griffiths had already been fired.) Dave and the others in the 'slaughter of the innocents' were underestimated academically by their senior colleagues (to put it as delicately as possible) and they also came across as unreliable in the generational cultural and political war that the students had initiated at the school beginning in 1968. These were the famous 'dark ages' of Yale, in the words of the 'restore order' dean who took over in 1970. (See Laura Kalman.[9]) Dave was fired, the Law and Modernisation grant from the state department was not renewed, and Dave moved to Wisconsin in 1973.

These intensely painful events were also a liberation (I imagine), and led directly to Dave's justly famous article with Marc Galanter, 'Scholars in Self-Estrangement: Reflections on the Crisis of Law and Development Studies in the United States' (1974).[10] This is a work of critical theory as well as a leftist critique of the liberal internationalist project of

---

[7] English translation, DM Trubek, *Law, Planning and the Development of the Brazilian Capital Market* (New York, NYU Institute of Finance, 1971).

[8] DM Trubek, 'Toward a Social Theory of Law: An Essay on the Study of Law and Development' (1972) 82 *Yale Law Journal* 1–50.

[9] *Yale Law School and the Sixties: Revolt and Reverberations* (University of North Carolina Press, 2005).

[10] DM Trubek and M Galanter, 'Scholars in Self-Estrangement: Some Reflections on the Crisis in Law and Development Studies in the United States' (1974) *Wisconsin Law Review* 1062.

the Kennedy and Johnson years. The liberals had, of course, already suffered their historic defeat of 1968, Nixon had intensified the war in Vietnam, and the US was in full cold war mode. But the critique was not of Nixon but of his predecessors, and of the co-authors themselves, as participants in a project that was bad from the beginning.

To grossly oversimplify (I mean that), bad because it was imperialist and culturally chauvinist and because it chose reactionary allies as its instruments, against the interests of the supposed beneficiaries. What made it a work of critical theory was that this was explained by a world view, a complex set of preconceptions about the Third World, about the political beneficence of the US as an actor, and, crucially, about law and about economics as they would work 'abroad.' Although quite vulgar Marxist analysis of material interests was a common mode of the time, what counted here was something more like 'consciousness'.

It is important to stress, not just for Dave's story as a globaliser of critical discourses about law but for a whole generation of Crits, that the target here was not the right wing, not Nixon; it was the liberal elites described by Halberstam in *The Best and the Brightest*.[11] Their project was discredited at home, for young left liberals, by the Vietnam War and by racial and youth revolt. Its international version was further challenged by the rise of Third World national liberation movements and the theorisation of neo-colonial dependency. Liberal hegemony slowly dissipated, but none of us realised to what an extent 'it was all over' for our frenemy, not because of critique from the left but because of the rise of the right.

Dave, and many others of us, turned away from the international. Between 1974 and the return of law and development around 1993, I count only a couple of forays outward, continuous with the Brazilian moment but no more than that.[12]

'Unequal Protection: Thoughts on Legal Services, Social Welfare and Income Distribution in Latin America' (1978).
'Economic, Social and Cultural Rights in the Third World: Human Rights Law and Human Needs Programs' (1983).
Consultancy: 1982, Guinea-Bissau and Cape Verde (USAID, Portuguese language)

Rather than leading to an alternative international initiative, the deep critique of liberal globalisation of 'Scholars in Self-Estrangement' went to prepare the ground for 'Complexity and Contradiction in the Legal Order' in 1977,[13] which as I tried to explain, was a crucial moment in figuring out the role of law in a critical social theory. Dave turned to major organising roles in CLS and in the law and society movement.

VI. Critique of Neo-liberal Globalisation

Dave's turn to the critique of neo-liberal globalisation was, according to me, the result of a confluence of highly unpredictable events, and full of ironies. In 1986–87, Dave visited

---

[11] D Halberstam, *The Best and the Brightest* (Random House, 1972).
[12] On unequal protection, see DM Trubek, 'Unequal Protection: Thoughts on Legal Services, Social Welfare and Income Distribution in Latin America' (1978) 13 *Texas International Law Review* 243–62; on Human Rights see 'Economic, Social and Cultural Rights in the Third World: Human Rights Law and Human Needs Programs' in T Meron (ed), *International Protection of Human Rights* 206–70 (Oxford University Press, 1984). David Trubek acted as a Consultant to Guinea-Bissau and Cape Verde (USAID, Portuguese language) in 1983.
[13] Trubek, 'Complexity and Contradiction in the Legal Order' (n 5).

at Harvard Law School, in the midst of the controversies we Crits had provoked there. The establishment decided that they had to make some kind of concession to us, since they had recently fired first Daniel Tarullo, currently a Governor of the Federal Reserve Bank, and then Clare Dalton, feminist icon of the time. It seemed a done deal when the faculty voted by more than the required two-thirds majority to hire Dave, but the deal went south when the right protested to Derek Bok, the Prexy of the University, who had a 'crush them before they multiply' attitude toward CLS. He appointed an outside review committee that killed the appointment.

In 1990, Dave accepted the post of Dean of International Studies for the University of Wisconsin, signalling the beginning of his withdrawal from active politics in the law school, and a renewed interest in 'abroad', and he kept at administration of university international matters for the next 15 years. In the meantime, CLS was winding down, through a series of internal conflicts and outward attacks, until by 1993 it was pretty much over. The network of progressive academics remained, although fragmented, and many of them went through a turn toward Europe and or the Third World as the opportunities for fruitful trouble-making in the US more or less disappeared. Paradoxically, as US global military, economic and cultural hegemony surged, and American legal influence along with it, leftists in other parts of the world came looking for possible left legal imports from the US.

At this point there was another surprise. The triumph of the right over the liberals, and particularly over the liberal internationalists of the 1950s and 1960s, had produced from 1980 a dramatic turn in Western development prescriptions for the global South. Since 1945, the dominant Western development prescriptions had been interventionist, albeit staunchly capitalist, and the post-colonial regimes had balanced them against the even more interventionist policies advocated by the Soviet Union. The Washington Consensus (of Reagan, Thatcher and Kohl) required them to dismantle the whole developmental apparatus they had constructed from the end of World War II through the 1970s, to privatise, deregulate and open their markets internationally. A strong background claim was that the globalisation process had reached a historic new stage, presenting developing countries with a clear choice between integration into the world market with the promise of boundless wealth, and 'starving in the dark' of isolation combined with internal economic self-strangulation.

The results of the neo-liberal turn were bad in Latin America, catastrophic in sub-Saharan Africa, and seriously ugly in Russia after 1989 (the 'shock therapy'). In the 1990s, the neo-liberals made an 'institutional turn', and quite suddenly, although consistently with the Hayekian background many of them shared, the Rule of Law became the development panacea.

The 'post-Washington Consensus' version of the rule of law bore some limited similarity to the pre-Washington Consensus version of Dave's youth in Brazil and then at Yale. In each case, there was a critique of the ineffectiveness (and corruption) of legal administration. But the neo-liberal emphasis was on private rather than public law, and therefore on courts rather than administrative law regimes. The neo-liberals were for repealing rather than enforcing the whole developmentalist regulatory apparatus, imagining that the economy would default to the 'free market', organised according to formalised property and contract law administered through adversarial processes. This (fantasy) was a return to the nineteenth-century colonial model, very different from the post-World War II vision of law as an instrument of transformative social and economic policies. When Dave got back into the law and development game, his new critical project was ironically aimed at something a good deal more primitive than what he and Galanter had critiqued in 1974.[14]

Consultant to ARD/Checci-US AID Rule of Law Project in Russia 1993–94
'Law and Development: Then and Now' (1996);
'The Rule of Law in Development Assistance: Past, Present and Future' (2004);
'The New Law and Economic Development: A Critical Appraisal' (co-editor with Alvaro Santos) 2006.

Dave's first re-engagement, 'Global Restructuring and the Law: Studies of the Internationalization of Legal Fields and the Creation of Transnational Arenas' (1994), co-authored with Yves Dezalay, Ruth Buchanan and John Davis,[15] is my favourite of all Dave's articles, a stunning opening shot in the left critical attempt to come to terms with the new global legal order. It describes the emergence of a new legal professional order that is the equivalent and mirror of the new world economic order, presenting it as a function of institutional change that is driven in one sense by the economy but with its own 'relative autonomy'. In the new world order, multinational corporations spawn multinational law firms and overmatched NGOs spawn overmatched public interest law firms, as the organisation of the bar in different countries changes in response to international competitive pressure, but always in strict dependence on local history and local legal culture.

As in every earlier stage of his career, Dave has been producing subject-matter specific studies on the way globalisation, legal and economic, generates and perpetuates inequality, and calls out for institutional responses that reject the basic neo-liberal paradigm of strong property rights for strong parties with no regulatory protection for weak ones.[16]

'Transnationalism in the Regulation of Labor Relations: International Regimes and Transnational Advocacy Networks' (1999);
'The Transatlantic Labor Dialogue: Minimal Action in a Weak Structure' (2001);
'Trade Law, Labor and Global Inequality' (2006).

And again, as in earlier stages of his career, Dave looked for, and found, this time in New Governance, an already existing set of practices (soft law) that had the potential to counter the dominance of the strong, in this case in the European context. He allied himself with the Celtic Fringe (including notably the editors of this volume) in defence of these innovations against conservative legalist critiques, and against left critiques that soft law was doomed to be ineffectual. New Governance in this version is left, at least as I interpret it, because it arises at the moment of disillusion with the European 'hard law' social democratic project, and not just general disillusion. 'Negative harmonisation' in the European Union meant the dismantling of some regulatory regimes of Member States, reconceptualised as being inconsistent with the common market. *Pace* Scharpf, there has

---

[14] See, DM Trubek, 'Law and Development: Then and Now', Proceedings of the 90th Meeting of the American Society of International Law, (1996) 90 ASIL Proceedings; DM Trubek, 'The "Rule of Law" in Development Assistance: Past, Present, and Future' (2004); DM Trubek and A Santos, *The New Law and Economic Development: A Critical Appraisal* (Cambridge, Cambridge University Press, 2006). David Trubek acted as a Consultant to ARD/Checci-USAID Rule of Law Project in Russia in 1993–94.

[15] DM Trubek, Y Dezalay, R Buchanan and J Davis, 'Global Restructuring and the Law: Studies of the Internationalization of Legal Fields and the Creation of Transnational Arenas' (1994) 44 *Case Western Reserve Law Review* 2.

[16] On labour see, 'Transnationalism in the Regulation of Labor Relations: International Regimes and Transnational Advocacy Networks' (1999); 'The Transatlantic Labor Dialogue: Minimal Action in a Weak Structure' (2001); 'Trade Law, Labor and Global Inequality' (2006).

been considerable re-regulation from the centre, but nothing like the rebirth of the social project. Soft law promotes the goals of the social project in a climate of democratic deficit and ideological stalemate.[17]

'Mind the Gap: Law and New Approaches to Governance in Europe' (2002);
'Hard and Soft Law in the Construction of Social Europe' (2005);
'New Governance and Legal Regulation: Complementarity, Rivalry and Transformation' (2007).

The New Governance approach in Europe, if its meaning for Dave was at all what I've just suggested, was not without relevance to the situation of weak parties everywhere in the age of neo-liberal deregulatory globalisation, permitting me to end this introduction to Dave's contributions with another version of the Eternal Return.

VII. Back to Brazil: The New Developmental State

Dave's book on Brazilian capital markets, which seemed to have dropped into the void at the time he wrote it, has been republished in Brazil and hailed as an important contribution to the recasting of the Brazilian economy after the return to civilian rule.[18]

'Direito, planejamento, e desenvolvimento do Mercado de capitais brasileiro 1965–1970' (2011).

It includes a new introduction by a former Minister of Finance who was also chair of Brazil's SEC, but is otherwise exactly the same as the original, as is proper for a book published in the series 'Classics of Brazilian Jurisprudence.'

Dave's re-engagement with Brazil draws together many strands of his career since his first sojourn there from 1964 to 1966. But what is most striking to me is the choice to launch a new project on the developmental state, basing it on the actual practices of the Brazilian government in its latest phase of rapid growth with innovative social transfer programmes that effectively reduce poverty. The developmental state is what the post-war policy-makers wanted, though they didn't want it to be *too* developmental, and it is what the Washington Consensus set out to eliminate, not just practically but theoretically, through neo-liberal critique of state failure and rent-seeking. It is based on developing many existing practices as well as on a commitment to creative new policies. It is rooted today in the notion of agency from the South, rather than the abandonment of policy autonomy to the international financial institutions, or for that matter to well-meaning Northern intellectuals.

I see no reason to think it will be his last project. Without trying for a grand conclusion, I just want to say that it has been one of the great pleasures and great rewards of my academic–political existence to have Dave as a friend and comrade.

---

[17] On new governance see J Scott and DM Trubek, 'Mind the Gap: Law and New Approaches to Governance in the European Union' (2002) 8 *European Law Journal* 1; DM Trubek and LG Trubek, 'Hard and Soft Law in the Construction of Social Europe: the Role of the Open Method of Co-ordination' (2005) 11 *European Law Journal* 343; DM Trubek and LG Trubek, 'New Governance and Legal Regulation: Complementarity, Rivalry and Transformation' (2007) 13 *Columbia Journal of European Law* 539.

[18] D Trubek, JHG Vieira and PF de Sá, *Direito, Planejamento e Desenvolvimento do Mercado de Capitais Brasileiro 1965–1970* (São Paulo, Editora Saraiva, 2011).

2

Critical Theory and Institutional Design: David Trubek's Path to New Governance

WILLIAM H SIMON

David Trubek has played major roles in three important scholarly movements: Law and Development, Law and Society, and Critical Legal Studies (CLS). A major theme of his efforts has been critique. Most often, Trubek has allied with or engaged sympathetically those who have challenged mainstream or established discourse in the name of egalitarian and democratic values.

The relationship of critical analysis to constructive social practice is an issue that has dogged—some might say, embarrassed—scholarship for a long time. Some critical scholars disclaim the responsibility to consider the practical implications of their work. Others have implied by their adoption of conventional left positions that bear no visible influence of their theoretical work that critique functions only defensively, warding off unreflective conservatism to create a space for unreflective progressivism. Trubek, however, has insisted from the beginning of his career that critique could and should inform practice, while conceding that the ways in which it does so were not fully understood or readily generalised.

Now in the latest phase of his career, he has devoted himself to a project the main ambiguity of which concerns, not its practical implications, but the extent to which it involves critique. In a series of collaborations he has provided a sympathetically descriptive account of recent developments in public policy and administration known as 'new governance'. This move makes Trubek a promising case for reconsideration of the question of the relation of critique and prescription. His earlier, largely critical work was exceptionally articulate about the practical implications of critique. And his current work is much more prescriptive than that of most practitioners of critical theory. So it is appropriate to consider how the earlier work relates to the later.

In important respects, new governance, in the form Trubek portrays optimistically, is distinctively responsive to the critical themes in his earlier work. There is a normative criterion of political legitimacy in much critical theory. It is occasionally explicit—notably in Jurgen Habermas' work—but more often implicit. The criterion is this: political institutions acquire presumptive legitimacy to the extent that they anticipate and incorporate the discursive practices exemplified by critical scholarship. Legitimate government institutionalises centrally and continuously in its public decision-making processes the practices of critical reflection and interrogation that critical theory models in scholarship. This general principle leads to some more specific ones. When we measure new governance in the manifestations that Trubek approves we see, at least, important commitments and progress in the direction of these principles.

I first consider what Trubek's earlier work suggests about the practical implications of critique. I then consider how these implications play out in the case of new governance. Throughout the discussion, I refer to CLS practitioners, as well as the self-identified critical practitioners within Law-and-Development and Law-and-Society, collectively as 'Crits'.

I. Critical Principles

I start with what I hope will be an uncontroversial summary of key features of critical theoretical practice in the three legal scholarly movements to which Trubek has contributed, and in particular, in Trubek's own work.

1. *Anti-foundationalism.* The Crits ally themselves with the modernist denial that knowledge can be grounded in some ultimate reality that exists independently of our efforts to understand. The version central to CLS emphasised a particular variation on this claim— the indeterminacy of doctrine. It conceded that there were (or might be) abstract values that were compelling and uncontroversial but denied that there was any neutral method which would generate from these values answers to particular conflicts. The Crits emphasised the ways in which conventional legal analysis tacitly smuggled conclusions into its premises by framing issues to bracket some concerns, by selectively invoking governing values to obscure the extent to which they were in conflict, or by dogmatically asserting non sequiturs.

Law-and-society people tended to treat the indeterminacy claim as too obvious to require demonstration, and they were somewhat surprised and perhaps annoyed that CLS work drew the attention and controversy it did. But Trubek disagreed. Theoretically, doctrinal criticism made an essential, though limited, contribution to explaining the mechanisms by which law legitimated power. Strategically, it seems to have been necessary to engage the legal establishment in the larger critical project. Without it, mainstream legal academics found it too easy to dismiss critique as irrelevant to professional practice.[1]

2. *Anti-determinism.* To begin with, this principle meant a rejection of the Marxist idea that there is a material base independent of an ideological superstructure and that this base determines the superstructure. More broadly, it disputed that there is a limited repertory of tightly structured forms that a modern society can take. There is no reason to believe that contemporary capitalist societies have exhausted the possible range of market-based societies or that the economic productivity of some of these societies necessarily entails their inegalitarian and anti-democratic features.

A lot of critical work has pursued this theme historically, so there has been particular attention to its evolutionary variant—the claim that poor societies must pass through a well-defined path to emerge as prosperous capitalist democracies. Trubek contributed to this critique at both theoretical and practical levels. In his work on Weber, he elaborated what the master himself had recognised as the 'England problem'—a key counter-example to his contention that capitalist development depended on formally rational legal rules

---

[1] DM Trubek, 'Where the Action Is: Critical Legal Studies and Empiricism' (1984) 36 *Stanford Law Review* 576.

(as opposed to the more informal style of common-law judging).[2] In his Brazilian work, Trubek engaged the prescriptive uses of evolutionary determinism. He showed that in the politically and economically oligarchical conditions of Brazil, the prescriptions inferred by the determinists (liberalised capital markets, purposive legal reasoning) turned out not to be conducive to development (much less the democracy for which some had also hoped).[3]

3. *Anti-ideology.* This is best term I can think of to describe opposition to unreflective privileging of the status quo. ('Utopian' would be another, but it has connotations of both intellectual flakiness and programmatic daring, neither of which is deserved by the Crits.) All of the practices to which the Crits object contribute to this privileging, but two are especially important.

The first is the valorisation of the normative commitments proclaimed by established institutions. Doctrinal scholars do this when they assume that the collection of authoritative reference points on particular legal questions reflects some immanent rationality and proceed to construct an account that makes it look harmonious and grounded in basic values. The 'gap' scholarship of interdisciplinary scholars does something similar. It focuses on a particular piece of positive law and proceeds to document the extent to which its presumed prescriptive implications are unfulfilled in practice. It then proceeds in one of two directions. It may suggest that non-enforcement reflects some 'latent function' performed by self-equilibrating social processes. Maybe the law—for example, prohibition of alcohol—was a 'symbolic crusade' designed to ease the pain of status loss for a declining elite rather than to affect mass behaviour. More commonly, the scholar assumes that society would benefit from more enforcement and offers prescriptions as to how to accomplish this. The latter approach is less conservative, but it is still ideological in assuming that there is a social interest in closing the gap simply because the norm satisfies positivist criteria of legality.

The second practice the Crits question is the valorisation of social peace and harmony. The Law-and-Society Crits produced a large body of analysis and research in response to policy discourse of dispute resolution. They showed that it is a mistake to assume, as conventional discourse does, that the emergence of disputes is exogenous to the legal system or that their minimisation is an uncontroversial social good. Legal professionals do not just respond to claims and grievances; they generate and influence them. Their advice can turn disappointment into indignation, whining into claiming. To the extent that professionals facilitate effective collective action, they may increase confidence and solidarity in ways that reinforce and re-shape claims. Conversely, professionals can also 'cool out' clients in ways that reduce expectations and induce resignation. It follows that 'dispute resolution' is not necessarily a good thing. Much social progress has required dispute *generation*. And much of what passes for dispute resolution involves the dampening of potentially progressive political impulses. Of course, the distinction between progressive and regressive change depends on political criteria. The Crits' point is that political criteria are inevitable, and they are best made explicit.

---

[2] DM Trubek, 'Max Weber on Law and the Development of Capitalism' (1972) 3 *Wisconsin Law Review* 720.
[3] DM Trubek, 'Toward a Social Theory of Law: An Essay on the Study of Law and Development' (1972) 82 *Yale Law Journal* 1.

LIVERPOOL JOHN MOORES UNIVERSITY
LEARNING SERVICES

Trubek engaged both gap sociology and the dispute resolution literature in his synthetic essays.[4] With respect to dispute resolution, he also contributed directly to the Law-and-Society critique of the 'litigation explosion' ideology that portrayed litigation as a metastasising social cancer. The research showed that litigation was less prevalent and less expensive than conventional rhetoric claimed.[5]

4. *Anti-separation-of-powers.* Conventional discourse presumes a strong separation between enactment of law and its enforcement. Enactment settles issues of value; enforcement implements the settlement. Enactment occurs through relatively democratic processes; enforcement occurs through relatively technocratic ones. Thus, particular enforcement decisions have democratic legitimacy to the extent that they implement democratic commands. The Weberian view of bureaucracy as a mechanism for automatic implementation of hierarchically-promulgated norms through formal rules fits helpfully into the picture. In the legal academy, the picture is complicated by the acknowledgement that enacted law is characteristically ambiguous and therefore requires the interpretive efforts of lawyers and judges. In both the popular and the professional view, the action is at the top—legislators, judges and elite lawyers make the critical decisions that are then passively implemented by the foot soldiers of the state.

All the Crits insist that the output of top-level legislative and interpretive activity remains too ambiguous to determine street-level decisions (and even if it were determinate, top-level officials lack the practical capacity to enforce compliance by subordinates). The interdisciplinary Crits follow the point up by shifting attention to the street level. In myriad studies, they showed that street-level administration is not a process of passive implementation of centrally-determined commands. It is an unmistakably political process in which unresolved value questions are settled informally in ways usually influenced by social inequality.

The interdisciplinary Crits revised the Weberian picture of bureaucracy but they did not reject it entirely. The difficulties of supervision and the rigidities of rules made bureaucracy a cumbersome tool for most social problems, but a bureaucratic programme that would regulate narrowly and tolerate over-inclusion relative to social need might work. An example would be non-means-tested public assistance that provides benefits to all families with children regardless of income. But to the extent that more precise targeting was needed, bureaucracy would not work. In the tradition of social theory, the prominent alternative was Durkheim's idea of public service professionalism—discretion canalised by socialisation and peer review. Unfortunately, another body of research showed that such street-level public servants often exercised discretion in irresponsible and oppressive ways.

Trubek was not directly involved in the Crit work on street-level administration, but he was strongly associated with it. His Wisconsin colleague, Joel Handler, was a key figure as was Louise Trubek, both as scholar and practitioner.

---

[4] DM Trubek and J Esser 'Critical Empiricism and American Legal Studies: Paradox, Program, or Pandora's Box' (1989) 14 *Law and Social Inquiry* 3.
[5] DM Trubek, A Sarat, WLF Felstiner, HM Kritzer and JB Grossman, 'The Costs of Ordinary Litigation' (1984) 31 *UCLA Law Review* 33.

II. Practical Implications of Critique

The way to infer the practical implications of this critical practice is to ask what kinds of institutions would be immune to it. Not immune in the sense that the institutions had solved all the problems that critique might reveal, but immune in the sense that the institutions had fully internalised the critical practices, or co-opted them in the sense, not of neutralising them, but of incorporating them completely into its standard operating procedures. Taking this approach, we can infer four conditions of presumptive political legitimacy. I have named the four conditions after friends, collaborators and people whom Trubek has acknowledged as influences. The four conditions do not constitute a complete political vision. They presuppose some variation of the conventional elements of liberal democracy such as fair electoral process and civil and welfare rights. But they add an additional set of criteria, which are sometimes overlooked, but that critical theory emphasises and deepens.

1. *The Habermas condition.* Public norms should ideally be based on consensus among affected citizens derived through a process of open, respectful and non-coercive discourse. Crits in the United States legal academy have been ambivalent about Habermas and the discourse principle, but Trubek suggested in 1984 that they might need it.[6] The consensus ideal responds to the practical dilemma that follows the rejection of foundationalism. Consensus is modernity's substitute for traditional and rationalist normative foundations.[7] While the Crit reservations are important (see the next condition), the idea remains useful.

Consensus is not a pre-requisite for collective action. It is impractical for most decisions, and it would be unjust to give those who benefit from the status quo a veto over proposed changes. The consensus condition simply means that we should seek consensus to the extent that is practical and that we should have more confidence in our judgements to the extent that we achieve it. The condition is a useful heuristic even though it is unlikely ever to be fully satisfied for a complex problem. As long as we can measure the proximity of actual circumstances to the consensus ideal, it can serve as a useful measure of legitimacy. Note that this approach differs from claims of legitimacy based on the imagined *possibility* of consent in a hypothetical situation like the Original Position. Here we measure legitimacy by the distance between idealised consent and the quality of consent in the actual decision-making process.

2. *The Kennedy condition.* This condition is the negative implication of the Anti-Determinist position. It requires that public policy and practice be formulated and implemented with maximum possible self-consciousness and transparency. Official decision-makers should forbear from efforts to give their conclusions a veneer of necessity or entailment. There are many Crits whose names we could plausibly attach to this condition, but I have named it after Duncan Kennedy because he has been a major influence on Trubek and because he is probably the legal scholar most closely identified with the position that critique tends to have progressive political effects.[8]

---

[6] Trubek, 'Where the Action Is' (n 1) 597–98.
[7] See M Cooke 'Habermas and Consensus' (1993) 1 *European Journal of Philosophy* 247.
[8] See, eg D Kennedy 'Critical Labor Law Theory: A Comment' (1981) 4 *Industrial Relations Law Journal* 503.

Kennedy's critical practice has been focused on elite judicial and academic discourse. Some Law-and-Society scholars carried on this project at the level of street-level discourse of low-status lawyers and low-level public officials. With their work in mind, we could have called this principle the 'Amherst condition' after the group of scholars centred in Amherst, Massachusetts, whose work Trubek admired (and whose anxious relationship with Kennedy Trubek sought to mediate).[9]

But from either the top or the bottom, the condition is the same. For official decision-makers and their apologists, it requires self-consciousness and candour about the inconclusive and conflicted nature of the authority they invoke, recognition of relevant competing values, and acknowledgement of the political quality of the decision-making process. For advocates and advisers, it means a willingness to acknowledge their own relevant interests and anxieties, to empathetically explore their clients' concerns, and to frame advice in a way that maximises clients' understanding of the range of possibilities and the nature of the constraints that they face.

3. *The Unger condition.* Entrenched social practices and structures should be subject to institutionalised pressures that encourage challenge and induce re-examination. This condition resonates with the rejection of ideology. It is named after Roberto Unger, another Trubek friend whose work exalts the individual and social capacity for self-transcendence.[10]

The Unger condition requires the protection and, indeed, encouragement of diversity in public and private life. In the public sphere, it requires opportunities to challenge concentrated private power through antitrust-type protections and irresponsible public agencies through means such as 'public law litigation'. In social life, it prescribes a kind of education that develops a capacity to thrive in circumstances of diversity and to distance oneself reflectively from convention.

The Unger condition is designed as an antidote to the tendency of consensus and cooperation to congeal into unreflective and dysfunctional conformity. It is, of course, potentially in tension with the Habermas condition, and managing that tension is a critical goal of institutional design.

4. *The Sabel condition.* Institutions and programmes should be designed so that their purposes can be reconsidered and elaborated in the course of implementation. Institutions should facilitate learning, self-assessment and re-orientation. They must combine transparency and provisionality. Institutional goals should be articulated along with performance measures, and both goals and measures should be reconsidered continuously in the light of experience. Practice norms should be fully explicit, but they should not require agents to take actions that contravene the purposes of the programme. When rules conflict with purposes, the response should be neither counter-purposive compliance nor low-visibility adjustment. The agent should disregard the rule and take the action that furthers the programme's purpose, while triggering a process of review that, if her judgement is sustained, leads to the prompt elaboration of the rule to take account of the new contingency. Peer review and the duty to explain take the place of Weberian rules in controlling discretion. The Sabel condition erodes the distinction between free-standing organisations and federations or associations

---

[9] Trubek and Esser, 'Critical Empiricism and American Legal Studies' (n 4).
[10] Eg RM Unger, *False Necessity: Anti-Necessitarian Social Theory in the Service of Radical Democracy* (Cambridge, Cambridge University Press, 1987) 277–312.

of organisations. The techniques of rolling rules and peer review can be applied across organisations as well as within them.

The continuously self-revising organisation (also known as lean production, learning organisation, self-managing organisation, and evidence-based practice) has been shown to be especially effective in the private economy with products and markets that require strong customisation and/or frequent adaptation to new circumstances. Many public problems now seem to call for the same contextualising and adaptive capacities in government organisations. From the point of view of liberal democracy, some variations of these organisations are appealing because the qualities that make them efficient in dealing with some problems also make them conducive to democratic accountability. Such organisations encourage lower-tier administrative creativity and stakeholder participation, and they make practice broadly transparent in ways that facilitate accountability to upper-tier administrators and coordinate political institutions and the public sphere.

The Sabel condition is a negative implication of the rejection of the separation of powers, and, more generally, of the distinction between enactment and enforcement. It is named after Charles Sabel, who has insisted on the pertinence of 'continuous improvement' models of private organisation to the public sphere, and has specifically used such models to develop an account of the European Union.[11]

III. New Governance

The 'new governance' idea arises from convergent efforts to understand the expanding roles of international organisations, the evolution of the EU, and the trend toward decentralising reforms in policy implementation in a variety of countries, especially the US and the UK. These developments have many variations, and there are many interpretations of their general significance. The work on the EU to which Trubek has contributed has been cautiously optimistic, and it thus converges with work on international organisation and domestic policy reform that views at least some manifestations of the new developments as promising. I will not try to assess the plausibility of this cautious optimism about the EU, a task complicated by the current economic crisis. I will limit myself to pointing out those features in Trubek's account of the EU that seem responsive to the institutional implications of critique. (I attribute these ideas only to Trubek, even though he developed them in a series of collaborations, and I will not try to take account of how the ideas overlap and resonate with the new governance literature. Trubek himself might have preferred a less Trubek-centric account, but that is not what the occasion calls for.)

1. *The Habermas condition.* Legally, the EU is an intergovernmental organisation. Traditionally, intergovernmental organisations operate by consensus among member nations, as represented by their diplomats. As the EU has evolved away from this traditional form, the consensus norm has been diluted, but it continues to exert influence.

---

[11] CF Sabel, 'Learning by Monitoring: The Institutions of Economic Development' in N Smelser and R Swedberg (eds), *Handbook of Economic Sociology* (Princeton, Princeton University Press, 1994); CF Sabel and J Cohen 'Sovereignty and Solidarity' in J Zeitlin and DM Trubek (eds), *Governing Work and Welfare in a New Economy: European and American Experiments* (Oxford, Oxford University Press, 2003).

Non-consensus decisions still require a kind of super-majority ('qualified majority'), and they can be made only across a limited range of competences. At the same time, engagement across Member States has increased, including not just senior executives, but a European parliament (though this does not figure in Trubek's picture), and a series of committees and agencies in which mid-level officials, experts and NGO delegates participate. This combination of a diluted consensus norm and a thickened range of cross-national engagement would seem to push the EU along a deliberative path.

Trubek has been especially interested in the phenomenon of 'soft law'. The European Employment Strategy (EES) and the Open Method of Coordination (OMC) create basically procedural duties, and even these are not enforceable in any tangibly coercive way. However, they seem to have motivated substantive change. Trubek has analysed how soft law duties might motivate action. These actions include 'shaming' (fear of peer disdain), 'mimesis' (a desire to justify your conduct as conventional), and 'discursive transformation' which Trubek, following Kirsten Jacobson, describes as 'the construction of "a new perspective from which reality can be descried, phenomena classified, positions taken, and actions justified".[12] Shaming and mimesis sound more like Durkheim than Habermas, and discursive transformation sounds uncomfortably like Foucault. But Trubek also suggests a more Habermasian interpretation in which new governance succeeds 'by bring[ing] people with diverse perspectives together in settings that require sustained deliberation about problem-solving' that leads them to 'collectively redefine objectives and policies'.[13]

2. *The Kennedy condition.* Trubek sees the post-Maastricht EU developments, especially the EES and the OMC, as cracking open conventional legal and political understandings: '[T]raditional principles of legitimacy drawn from state-based models do not work at the European level and may be obsolete at the national level as well.'[14] Notably, there is no visible unitary sovereign to which authority can be attributed. Opponents of the EU attack it for failing to conform to conventional assumptions, and defenders strain to reconfigure or portray it as only a modest departure. But Trubek suggests that practical policy discourse in this terrain has been (or is likely to become) significantly unencumbered by ideological baggage and more open and reflective.

If true, this could be a transitional phenomenon of the sort we expect in moments of dramatic reconstruction but that typically wanes as new institutional forms are consolidated. But some of the aspects of the new arranements that Trubek sees as destabilizing conventional understandingsmight operate in the long term. In particular, there is the commitment to diversity (the Unger condition) and to experimentation (the Sabel condition).

The new governance forms to which Trubek drew attention require policy-makers to both tolerate and take account of diverse perspectives and practices. Decision-makers come from different national cultures. Trubek points out that the problems with which EU social policy has been pre-occupied straddle the boundaries of academic discipline and agency jurisdictions. This straddling contributes another dimension of diversity. The thinner the base of shared assumptions, the greater the pressure to explain, and thus to reflect on,

---

[12] DM Trubek and LG Trubek 'Hard Law and Soft Law in the Construction of Social Europe' (2004) 11 *European Law Journal* 343, 357.

[13] DM Trubek and J Mosher, 'New Governance, EU Social Policy, and the European Social Model' in Zeitlin and Trubek (eds), *Governing Work and Welfare in a New Economy* (n 11) 357.

[14] J Scott and DM Trubek, 'Mind the Gap: Law and New Approaches to Governance in the European Union' (2002) 8 *European Law Journal* 1.

premises that might otherwise be taken for granted. Moreover, the need to take account of the range of viable institutional forms in Member States subverts the tendency to under-estimate the range of viable institutional forms. At the same time, the experimentalist dimension of these reforms requires that deliberators submit their premises to the test of experience. This might subvert tendencies to fundamentalist dogmatism.

3. *The Unger condition*. This condition stipulates that consensus must not come at the expense of the kinds of diversity that stimulate awareness of a broad range of possibilities in culture, politics and the economy. Trubek sees the commitment to diversity as a major strength of the EU. EU consensus is a thin or overlapping consensus that contemplates and indeed protects diversity among and within Member States.

The expansion of the EU has brought increasing diversity among Member States, and association between Member States appears to have some influence on the protection of diversity within Member States. The admission process appears to have had a significant liberalising effect on expansion states. And some of these pressures appear to continue among Member States. Gender equality and social inclusion are among the declared goals of the EES, and there are metrics associated with them.

A pertinent theme in judicial review of administrative action is reduced attention to questions of competence and authority in favour of concern with representation and inclusiveness. For example, Trubek sees the *UEAPME* case as potentially adumbrating a quasi-constitutional principle that would condition recognition of the normative output of stakeholder regimes on adequate representation of affected interests.[15]

4. *The Sabel condition*. Trubek has explicitly interpreted the EES and the OMC as examples of Sabel's idea of experimentalist or directly-deliberative governance.[16] The basic elements are general agreement on goals and measures of progress toward them, followed by Member State plans, self-monitoring and reporting to the EU, followed by peer review, followed by reconsideration and re-elaboration of goals and metrics. These elements are part of a continuous cycle. More recently, Trubek has interpreted develop-ments in international law, particularly around the WTO treaties, in terms of collaborative problem-solving.[17]

As Trubek notes, this approach precludes any strong distinction between rule enactment and rule enforcement. Efforts to implement the norms lead to a greater understanding of them both through local experience and through the pooling of experiences in the peer review process. Political accountability is re-configured. Traditional legal theory empha-sises a backward-looking process in which courts confine administrators to the mandates of generalist legislatures. In the new processes, accountability is more specialised and more prospective. On the one hand, it occurs through the deliberative horizontal engagement of parties with special interests and expertise. On the other, it defers to legislatures by making its activities transparent to oversight by traditional democratic institutions.

---

[15] Ibid.

[16] Trubek and Trubek, 'Hard Law and Soft Law in the Construction of Social Europe' (n 12) 348; Case T-135/96 *UEAPME v Council* [1998] ECR II-373.

[17] P Cottrell and D Trubek, 'Law as Problem Solving: Standards, Networks, and Experimentation in Global Space' (2012) 21 *Wisconsin Journal of Transnational Law and Global Problems* 359.

IV. Conclusion

Readers are struck both by the range of Trubek's scholarship and its continued engagement with new events and ideas. Trubek has never sought the benefits of narrow expertise or yielded to the temptation to rest on early triumphs. However, there is also a notable continuity in his work. Few people have been more ambitious in their efforts to bring critique and prescription together. It remains to be seen whether new governance will prove a durable set of innovations. It does, however, seem deeply responsive to the prescriptive implications of Crit scholarship. No doubt this is not the only programmatic response that could be derived from the critiques. But, thanks in important measure to Trubek, it is the most elaborated one.

3

A Crisis and its Afterlife: Some Reflections on 'Scholars in Self-Estrangement'

RUTH BUCHANAN[*]

> This is a study of the relationship between scholarship and action. It will show how changes in specialised concepts, theories, and modes of scholarly activity affect and are affected by changes in the moral attitude of scholars toward their professional work.[1]

This essay is an extended reflection on the avenues of influence of a single article, one that is arguably the most cited contribution to scholarship on law and development of the last 40 years. In that article, published in the *Wisconsin Law Review* in 1974, David Trubek and Marc Galanter confidently identified and cogently parsed a 'crisis' in law and development studies in the United States.[2] 'Scholars in Self-Estrangement: Some Reflections on the Crisis in Law and Development Studies in the United States' (hereinafter SISE), was undoubtedly a key intervention in the debate over US funding of law reform projects abroad of its time. Yet, as the research conducted for this essay has documented, it continues to be routinely cited by law and development scholars as well as many academics in other fields. In some ways, this tenacity is difficult to fathom—SISE was a piece that was produced at a particular moment of crisis in the field in the US and addresses itself specifically to that moment. It is a piece of writing that is admirably clear about its modest ambitions and the relatively narrow scope of the audience that it explicitly sought to address. The authors note that the paper originated in a report that had been produced for the Research Advisory Committee of the International Legal Centre.[3] Further, they describe the crisis as affecting the 'relatively small group of academics' who are engaged in a 'specialized area of US academic study concerned with the relationship between legal systems and the 'development'—social, economic and political changes—occurring in third world countries'.[4] And yet, the

[*] I wish to thank the participants at the conference on Global Governance: Critical Legal Perspectives *Liber Amicorum* David M Trubek, which took place in June 2012 at the European University Institute in Fiesole, and David Trubek in particular, for their generous response to the paper on that occasion. Marc Galanter also generously read and commented on the draft. Amanda Legeny provided able assistance with the compilation of the bibliographic database and the final editing of the paper.

[1] DM Trubek and M Galanter, 'Scholars in Self-Estrangement: Some Reflections on the Crisis in Law and Development Studies in the United States' (1974) *Wisconsin Law Review* 1062, 1062.

[2] Ibid, 1063.

[3] Ibid, 1062.

[4] It should be noted that at the time, even within the small community of law and development scholars in the US, the paper provoked a considerable amount of comment and controversy. See, for example, the critique offered by Robert Seidman, a prolific law and development scholar and the ensuing exchange. Robert Seidman 'The Lessons of Self Estrangement: On the Methodology of Law and Development' (1978) *Research in Law and*

paper's influence has extended well beyond the circumstances, political era and geographic location in which it was produced.

Part of this continuing resonance might be attributed to its personal tone. There is both an urgency and an immediacy to its critique that emerges from its self-reflective aspect. Both authors were participants in the 'small group of academics' who were seeking to institutionalise a study of law and development in the academy; both had spent a significant amount of time living and working in developing countries, Professor Trubek in Brazil, and Professor Galanter in India.[5] Yet its continuing influence has extended well beyond what might be expected of reflective practitioners, even very insightful ones. Its endurance, in my view, has more to do with the fact that SISE is a pioneering example of critical legal scholarship. Not only does it speak passionately to contemporary readers, it offers many of them insights that resonate with contemporary issues and problems. Most ambitiously, one might propose that revisiting and reflecting upon such a landmark contribution could lead to a renewed and possibly more robust appreciation of the project of critical legal scholarship itself.

The immediate task of this paper is much more modest, however. It undertakes to document the legacy of SISE in contemporary law and development scholarship, through a close reading of the text itself and a review of recent articles in which it has been cited, as well as an analysis of the relevance of its arguments to a body of critical writing in law and development in which it is not usually cited. In considering the ways in which scholars have made reference to SISE over the past decade or so, I observed two distinct approaches. In the first, it stands as a marker for a particular moment in history: the 'crisis' of the 'first wave' of law and development. Law and development scholarship has benefitted from a variety of reconsiderations of that crisis and its aftermath in recent years, as it sought to come to terms with the re-emergence of an interest in law on the part of development institutions and agencies at the end of the twentieth century. In recent times, the historical account continues, the field of law and development has re-emerged, transformed and re-invigorated by processes of globalisation, professionalisation, and a variety of interdisciplinary encounters. A number of these types of accounts have been tremendously influential in framing law and development as a field of study in recent years. I am thinking in particular, of course, of the excellent essays collected by Trubek and Santos in 2006,[6] as well as a number of other recent efforts that might be understood collectively as providing a genealogy of the uses of law in relation to development assistance.[7] Typically, although

---

Sociology 1, 1–29. Trubek and Galanter's response is published as 'Scholars in the Fun House' *Research in Law and Sociology* 1, 31–40; Professor Seidman offers a reply in the same volume at pp 41–44.

[5] Professor Trubek's curriculum vitae indicates that he served between 1962 and 1964 as an Attorney–Advisor at the US Department of State Agency for International Development in Washington DC and between 1964 and 1966 as Legal Advisor and Chief Officer of Housing and Urban Development, USAID Mission to Brazil, in Rio de Janeiro. While Professor Galanter had little direct law and development experience prior to the publication of SISE, he had spent a considerable amount of time in India as a scholar. In the late 1970s, some years after the publication of SISE, he served as an adviser to the Ford Foundation programme on legal services and human rights programme in that country. (Personal communication with Professor Mark Galanter, 9 June 2013).

[6] DM Trubek and A Santos, *The New Law and Economic Development: A Critical Appraisal* (Cambridge, Cambridge University Press, 2006).

[7] T Carothers (ed), *Promoting the Rule of Law Abroad: In Search of Knowledge* (Washington DC, Carnegie Endowment for International Peace, 2006); KE Davis and MJ Trebilcock, 'The Relationship between Law and Development: Optimists versus Skeptics' (2008) 56 *American Journal of Comparative Law* 895; B Tamanaha, 'The Primacy of Society and the Failure of Law and Development' (2011) 44 *Cornell International Law Journal* 209. A voluminous recent overview is contained in J Faundez (ed), *Law and Development* (London, Routledge, 2012).

not invariably, essays in this genre have tended to cite SISE for the purpose of marking a particular point in history, from the perspective of its 'aftermath', or in terms of what came next.

There is also a second, less prominent avenue of engagement with Trubek and Galanter's famous article. In these articles, scholars engage with one or more of the substantive critiques contained in the piece. These engagements tend to emphasise its relevance to present-day dilemmas and highlight continuities in the framing of the role of law in development. Scholarship taking this second approach constitutes, in my analysis, the 'afterlife' of the crisis, that is, the ongoing salience of its critiques to contemporary issues and debates. Later in the article, I will explore a third, more speculative, avenue, through which I conjecture that Trubek and Galanter's 'crisis' continues to exert an influence. In this group, the article itself is not cited, and yet one or more of the critical arguments that it so cogently summarised play a significant role in the argument. These are instances I will describe as 'hauntings'.

Of course, each of these avenues of influence is important and significant in its own way. However, in relation to this famous article, the hunch with which I began this research was that the dominant mode of engagement had been with its place in history; as the crisis of law and development studies, and its aftermath: the demise of that field. And yet it occurred to me that accounts of the crisis and its aftermath that read SISE as part of a 'moment' in a linear history of the field can function to implicitly distance us from its critique by emphasising the gap or discontinuity between that time and our own. In contrast, law and development scholarship can also be understood as a continuous, or at least contiguous, terrain in which certain concepts, tropes or arguments repeat, overlap and fold in on themselves. This is seen more readily through an examination of SISE's other avenues of influence, both in relation to those scholars who engage directly with the contemporary relevance of its critique ('afterlife') as well as the ways in which those critiques continue to haunt contemporary debates.

The analysis in this paper will suggest that these other avenues are both enduring and significant. That is, dozens of scholars writing on a variety of topics across the wide spectrum of issues that might fall within the broad category of 'law and development' have, in returning again and again to the arguments formulated by Trubek and Galanter in 1974, in effect collectively made the argument that while much may have changed in the past four decades, many of the core assumptions that underpin the law and development project have remained the same. Through a closer examination of these other avenues of influence, then, this essay seeks to disinter Trubek and Galanter's remarkably direct and succinct diagnosis of the contradictions of the law and development project from the comfortable historical resting place to which it has been frequently assigned.

Finally, it is worth noting that the intuition that gave rise to this undertaking was formulated in the classroom. Over the past few years, while teaching law and development to students in British Columbia, Toronto and Melbourne, I have found myself annually revisiting Trubek and Galanter's crisis. These engagements have never failed to engender new insights and/or provocations. Indeed, many students respond to this text as if to a whiff of fresh air after a long day in a windowless library carrel. What is it about SISE that draws in readers across several generations, and arrayed across a much broader geographical swath than, its original audience? This essay is, in part, an effort to answer that question.

In what follows, I first revisit the crisis itself, reviewing a number of the key propositions and arguments set out in the article. Secondly, I report on my research into citational history of SISE since its publication in 1974, including tracking citations by year and by type (aftermath/afterlife). In the third section, I analyse the ways in which some key contributions to contemporary critical scholarship on rights and development trace the contours of arguments made by Trubek and Galanter.

I. The Crisis Revisited

For an essay that has attracted so much comment, and which continues to be identified as the 'landmark critique'[8] of the project of law and development some 35 years after its publication, Trubek and Galanter's thesis statement was surprisingly modest:

> The principal thesis of the essay is that intellectual and moral shifts have created a crisis for this small group of academics, a crisis which threatens the future of their efforts to create theories about and to institutionalize the study of law and development.[9]

Trubek and Galanter go on to identify two dimensions of the crisis: first, that individual scholars became increasingly unable to define or to defend the work, and secondly, that there had emerged a lack of consensus around common interests that could be understood as defining a field. Both of these developments were seen as a direct consequence of the loss of faith in the potency of the liberal legalist model of law, both as a model for developing countries to emulate, and as an accurate description of how law actually worked in the US. One of the important critical contributions of the essay is that it breaks down the 'liberal legalist paradigm' into six key propositions.

1. Society is made of individuals and the state; since individuals consent to the state, state control furthers individual welfare.
2. The state exercises control over the individual through law; law is understood as addressed to all individuals similarly situated; the state is constrained by law.
3. Rules are consciously designed to achieve social purposes and formulated through pluralist processes that are fair (that is, not unduly influenced by special characteristics such as wealth or race).
4. Rules are enforced equally for all, in accordance with their purposes.
5. Courts have the principle responsibility for defining and interpreting legal rules; adjudication proceeds on the basis of an autonomous body of learning.
6. The behaviour of social actors tends to conform to the rules.[10]

Trubek and Galanter make three important critiques of the project of law and development in the article, all of which relate to the inadequacy of one or more features of this liberal legalist paradigm. First, they note that the guiding assumption of the law and development movement, that the liberal legalist model could be used as a basis for recommendations regarding legal development in poor countries, had come to seem both ethnocentric and naive to many of those who had been working in the field. That is to say, liberal legalism is not a universal/universalisable model of law in society. As its participants developed a

---

[8]   Davis and Trebilcock, 'The Relationship between Law and Development' (n 6) 915.
[9]   Trubek and Galanter, 'Scholars in Self-Estrangement' (n 1) 1063.
[10]   Ibid, 1071–72.

deeper knowledge of particular legal systems based on fieldwork and exchanges with local lawyers and academics, it became clear that social, cultural, political and legal systems in many countries tended to look very different from the ideal type assumed in each of the above propositions. Moreover, first-wave law and society research (gap studies) was beginning to reveal that many features of the liberal legalist model were not even a particularly accurate description of how law worked in the US. The second critique is directed at the assumption of legal potency itself—Trubek and Galanter suggest that law and development scholars needed to be alive to the possibility that legal change is not instrumentally linked to social change; that is, they must consider the possible irrelevance of law. This critique relates specifically to propositions three, four and six. If changes to specific legal rules cannot be understood instrumentally as relating to or bringing about certain socially desirable outcomes, or even if one imagines that legal reforms might bring about such outcomes but are routinely ignored, then a great deal of the justification for the investment in legally-oriented development assistance disappears. Thirdly, and perhaps most devastatingly, they suggested that legal reforms in developing countries might have a 'negative face'—that is, law reform might in fact do more harm than good judged in terms of such liberal values as promoting greater social equality, political and social empowerment or democracy in a given country. This section is worth quoting directly, as it lays out in some detail the many ways in which well-intentioned legal development assistance can go awry:

> The legalization of areas of social life and the increased formalization of the legal process may increase the costs of protest, deflecting political pressures for social change without any corresponding gains in freedom or equality. Law may be used to justify and legitimate arbitrary actions by government rather than to curb or ban such excesses. The social structure and economic interests of the legal profession may make it a natural ally of conservative groups, and an enemy of groups pushing for fundamental change. Legal changes ostensibly designed to reform major areas of social life and achieve developmental goals may in fact be a form of symbolic politics, the effect of which is not to cause change but to defeat it by containing demands for protest, thereby strengthening, rather than weakening groups committed to the status quo. And increased instrumental rationality in legal processes together with governmental regulation of economic life may contribute to the economic well being of only a small elite, leaving the mass no better, or even worse, off.[11]

The article provides a detailed consideration of both how the crisis emerged and the factors that contributed to the loss of faith in the efficacy of the export of liberal legalism, including the deepening of empirical knowledge of developing states, accelerated in many cases through the contributions of legal scholars from developing countries, the 'turn against law' in the US,[12] doubts about the desirability and universal applicability of the US legal/political system as a model for emulation by developing countries, and finally scepticism about the motives behind government-funded legal assistance. Not all law and development scholars shared all of these concerns, and some continued to adhere to liberal legalism, all of which contributed further to the fracturing of the nascent field.[13] In their concluding section, Trubek and Galanter articulated three possible perspectives on the way forward, that is, justifications on the basis of which scholars might ground their continued

---

[11] Ibid, 1083–84 (footnotes omitted).
[12] See generally M Galanter (2002–03) 'The Turn Against Law: The Recoil Against Expanding Accountability' 81 *Texas Law Review* 285.
[13] Ibid, 1096.

work in the field. They identified them as pragmatic problem-solving, positivist pure science, and eclectic critique.[14]

To the extent that aspects of the 'liberal legalist' paradigm continue to exert a powerful influence over the ways in which many legal development projects are conceived, funded and implemented, the critiques offered in SISE continue to be relevant. Conversely, one might suggest that how much contemporary relevance scholars find in SISE tends to reflect their assessment of how many of the above-noted liberal legalist propositions remain in play. A citational analysis of SISE that reflects not only how many times it has been cited, but also endeavours to capture the ways that it has been used, then, might provide one avenue through which we could ascertain the extent to which contemporary law and development scholars continue to be troubled by the gap between the assumptions of funders and development agencies and what we know about how law works, or doesn't work, as an agent of social change.

II. Noting Up SISE: Two Avenues of Influence

In order to track the influence of SISE, we first compiled a database of citations to this article in English language journals since its publication in 1974.[15] Our searches produced 407 citations in English language journals since that date; 216 of those citations have occurred since 2001.[16] In addition to its citation in a very wide spectrum of US law reviews and social science journals, we found that SISE has been cited in a number of international publications in English, including publications from China, India, Turkey, South Africa, Israel, Australia, the UK, Europe and Canada.[17] Articles citing SISE have been found in

---

[14] Ibid, 1097.

[15] In order to find all of the available English language article citations of SISE online searches were conducted in a variety of databases. We acknowledge that this method is likely to be much more comprehensive with respect to more recent years, as significantly fewer publications would be searchable online prior to the mid-1990s. This search excluded theses and books, as these could not be comprehensively searched by keyword in the same manner. All of this information was saved in a bibliographic database, and put into an Excel spreadsheet for analysis. The searches are recent as at 21 June 2012.

[16] In HeinOnline, ProQuest and Web of Knowledge, the search brought up the original article along with an icon that stated its number of citations and a link to access these. Additionally, in these databases, and in several others (LexisNexis Quicklaw, LexisNexis Academic, Westlaw, LegalTrac, Justis, Ebscohost, Scholars Portal, JSTOR and Springerlink) a search was conducted using the term 'scholars in self-estrangement'. At this point, to verify that the correct article was cited, the search would be narrowed, the citation would be viewed in each article, or both. If the search was narrowed, it was done so by searching the name 'Trubek'. The variants 'Trubeck' and 'Trubec', or the truncated 'Trub', were also searched to account for any misspellings. Additionally, a keyword search was performed through articles that had been found for previous research, on topics of new developmental state and critical empiricism. From here, an article that was not found in the searches mentioned above was discovered, due to a misspelling of the word 'estrangement'. Searches were then conducted in each of the aforementioned databases, with the variant spellings 'enstrangement', 'enstrangment' and 'estrangment'. While a Google Scholar search will produce a higher number of results, closer to 480, our more limited number of citations can be explained by the facts that our search was confined to academic journals published in English, and that the database has been checked for duplications.

[17] See, eg J Goldring, 'Babies and Bathwater: Tradition or Progress in Legal Scholarship and Legal Education' (1987) 17 *University of Western Australia Law Review* 216; D Fitzpatrick, 'Developing a Legal System in East Timor: Some Issues of UN Mandate and Capacity' (2000) 5 *Austrian Review of International and European Law* 5; MM Feeley, 'Three Voices of Socio-Legal Studies' (2001) 35 *Israel Law Review* 175.

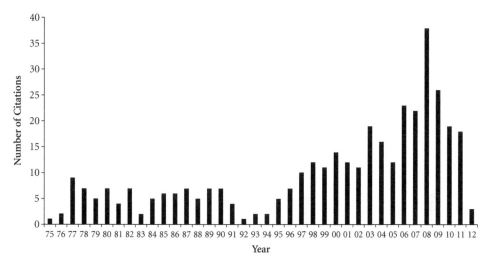

Figure 1: Citations by Year

publications as diverse as the *China Economic Review*, the *Australian Feminist Law Journal*, *IIMB Management Review* (Indian Institute of Management in Bangalore), and *World Development*.[18]

With respect to the frequency of citations, shown in Figure 1, two things are worth noting. First, that there has been no year since its publication that SISE was not cited somewhere, and second, even taking into account the fact that online records are much more comprehensive since the mid 1990s, the number of citations of SISE has increased dramatically over the past decade. While it is only a very rough indication, this increase could be read as a reflection of the growing interest in 'law and development' across a very wide range of disciplines. A review of the titles of some of the articles collected in the database reveals the remarkable diversity of the issues, disciplines, specialisations and regions that are spanned by the descriptor. Without revisiting the fruitless debate over whether law and development is or might be described as a 'field' of scholarly inquiry rather than a 'poorly constructed category that lacks internal coherence',[19] I note that the citations to Trubek and Galanter's article provide, rather than a shared analytic framework or even coherence, a thin thread by which we might trace the outlines of a broad terrain of engagement and contestation that could be identified with the term 'law and development'.[20]

---

[18] See, eg JKM Ohnesorge, 'China's economic transition and the new legal origins literature' (2003) 14 *China Economic Review* 485; E Bertolino, 'The Politics of Subjectivity in the Women, Law and Development Discourse' (2006) 25 *Australian Feminist Law Journal* 119; S Gupta, 'Competition Policy and Law: Academic Perspective' (2007) 19 *IIMB Management Review* (Indian Institute of Management Bangalore) 426.

[19] Brian Tamanaha used this descriptor in a talk published as B Tamanaha, 'The Primacy of Society and the Failure of Law and Development' (2009) *St John's University School of Law Legal Studies Research Paper Series No 09-0172*. In the paper of the same title subsequently published in 2011, he had changed his wording although not his substantive view: 'Conceiving of law and development as a field, I will argue, is a conceptual mistake that perpetuates confusion.' B Tamanaha, 'The Primacy of Society and the Failure of Law and Development' (2011) 44 *Cornell International Law Journal* 209, 220.

[20] See also A Perry-Kessaris, 'Introduction' in A Perry-Kessaris (ed), *Law in the Pursuit of Development: Principles into Practice* (Abingdon, Routledge, 2010).

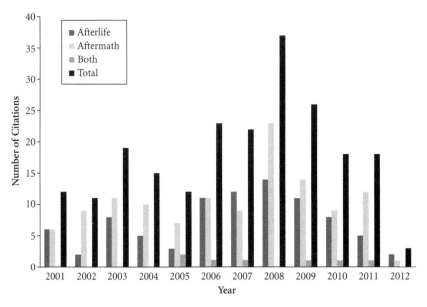

Figure 2: Type of Citation by Year

The second figure reflects our effort to analyse the citations over the last 10 years in terms of the mode or type of engagement, using the distinction between 'aftermath' and 'afterlife' which I drew above.[21] References that emphasised the historical role of SISE, and focused on discontinuities between that era and our own, were coded as 'aftermath'. Citations that focused on the contemporary relevance of the arguments in SISE, identified continuities or sought to apply specific arguments made in SISE to contemporary issues and problems, were coded as 'afterlife'. In a few cases, authors utilised both forms of engagement. What we can see from this figure is that while 'aftermath' references constitute the majority of citations, there were a substantial number of articles in every year that approached SISE from the perspective of its contemporary, rather than historical, relevance. The breakdown of citations since 2001 was 122 'aftermath' references, 88 'afterlife' references and seven that involved both. What can be said on the basis of this analysis is that the substantive critiques of Trubek and Galanter continue to resonate with a significant number of scholars currently publishing in the field of law and development.

---

[21] The criteria that were considered when determining whether each citation was to be coded as afterlife or aftermath were as follows. Generally, qualities of an afterlife citation were having contemporary relevance, emphasising continuity between the time of publication and today, engaging substantively with the arguments of the paper, and including a large number of citations or direct quotations from the text. An example of a citation that was treated as afterlife would be one in which the author noted lessons that could be learned from SISE. Indicators of aftermath treatment were historical relevance, emphasising discontinuity, a short citation without much or any discussion, and fewer citations within the paper. Articles classified as aftermath include those that use SISE to indicate the demise of the law and development movement of the time. When the actual coding was being performed, the continuity or discontinuity, and the contemporary or historical relevance indicated in a paper, tended to be the strongest factors considered.

However, what this coarse-grained overview does not reveal is which of the several strands of critical argument in the Trubek and Galanter paper are the ones most frequently picked up by contemporary scholars, and how they are being used. Anecdotally, I have noted quite a number of references to the critique of 'ethnocentricity' in relation to the export of the American 'liberal legalist' paradigm, especially in the context of the 'legal transplants' debates, and it may well be that this first critique has been the most frequently engaged in the 'afterlife' literature.[22] It has also been suggested that the second and third critiques, that is, the critique of legal potency and the 'negative face' of legal intervention, are less frequently considered in contemporary law and development scholarship.[23] Further content analysis of the 'afterlife' group of articles, along the lines of the discussion in the following section, might help to further advance our understanding of the content of this particular 'critical' or 'sceptical' wing of law and development scholarship.

III. Hauntings: Critical Responses to the Convergence of Development and Human Rights

A familiar strand of debate within contemporary law and development scholarship concerns the emergence of rights-based approaches to development. Usually traced to the influence of Amartya Sen, and linked to creation of the Human Development Reports at the United Nations Development Programme (UNDP), under the leadership of Abub al Haq, the discourse of human rights has made a significant incursion into development debates of the new millenium.[24] It has quickly become a vast terrain of scholarship and practice.[25] Without sidetracking into an exegesis on the Right to Development, the Millenium Development Goals, Rights-based Approaches, or Poverty Reduction Strategy Papers, it can be observed at a general level that efforts at integration between various UN agencies on the one hand and the Bretton Woods institutions on the other, have produced a degree of consensus, at least at the level of discourse, on the need to integrate human rights considerations into the design of development projects, not only in order to ensure that projects do not negatively impact human rights, but because advancing human rights is now understood as both a means to, and an end of development, not unlike the rule of law.

This contemporary narrative of convergence of human rights and development stands in marked contrast to the two solitudes that has characterised these disciplines

---

[22] See, eg S Basheer and S Guha, 'Outsourcing Bayh-Dole to India: Lost in Transplantation?' (2010) 23 *Columbia Journal of Asian Law* 269; M Lawan, 'Liberal Legalism and the Challenge of Development in Nigeria' (2009) 2 *Law, Social Justice & Global Development Journal*; U Mattei, 'A Theory of Imperial Law: A Study on US Hegemony and the Latin Resistance' (2003) 10 *Indiana Journal of Global Legal Studies* 383.

[23] See Trebilcock and Davis, 'Optimists versus Skeptics' (n 6) 45. See also, B Garth, 'Law and Society as Law and Development' (2003) 37 *Law and Society Review* 305.

[24] See, eg the thoughtful account in S Pahuja *Decolonising International Law: Development, Economic Growth and the Politics of Universality* (Cambridge, Cambridge University Press, 2011) 222–28.

[25] See for example, C Rodriguez Garavito, J Keweitel and LT Waisbich, 'Development and Human Rights: Some Ideas on how to Restart the Debate' and the rest of the contributions to the symposium issue on Development and Human Rights in (2012) 9 (17) *Sur International Journal on Human Rights*.

for most of the past 40 years. It fails to fully recognise these discourses as the contested and contingent outcomes of historical struggles, and in so doing, can tend to overlook the importance of contestation in relation to the current situation. These issues have hardly gone unnoticed, however. A number of legal scholars, frequently writing from a perspective located within or sympathetic to developing countries, have offered a variety of critiques of the human rights and development encounter. Without engaging in a full discussion of this significant body of critical scholarship, for present purposes, using a few key illustrations, this section will briefly show the extent to which the legal scholars can be seen to track the three critiques we have identified in SISE. The three critiques again, are:

1.   the critique of universality (ethnocentrism of liberal legalist paradigm);
2.   the critique of (formal) law's potency (significance of informal alternatives); and
3.   the dark face of legal reform (empowering elites, containing protest and so on).

With respect to the first critique, a plethora of examples could be cited; a recent contribution by Issa Shivji to the human rights and development debates is illustrative.[26] Shivji approaches both development and human rights as contentious, fragmented discourses. He identified the UN debates over the right to self-determination in the 1960s and 1970s, during the efforts to promote a New International Economic Order, as pivotal. It was during this era that the developmental and human rights discourses became polarised. From the perspective of newly-independent African states, to the extent that human rights discourses were posited as 'neutral' and 'universal', they were also anti-development, insofar as they could not acknowledge the particular histories, demands and aspirations of peoples in developing countries. Through the era of structural adjustment and since, the growing convergence of development and human rights discourses has led to the narrowing and technocratisation of the former, and the fragmentation and particularisation of the latter. Shivji remains highly sceptical of the emancipatory potential of contemporary reformulations of human rights in the development context. In his analysis the common thread that unites the earlier era with the present has been the marginalisation and containment of developmental concerns and proposals emanating from developing countries. According to Shivji, so long as the dominance of the North over the South in the world system is unacknowledged within human rights discourses, adding a 'developmental' dimension to human rights is unlikely to alter this trajectory.

Shivji's analysis reminds us of the extent to which the first two critiques continue to resonate in the African context. A recent review essay by Sally Falk Moore underscores the ongoing relevance of the second critique, again in the African context.[27] Moore reviews two recent books on law reform efforts in South Africa, in the context of both evolving approaches to legal pluralism in the academy and her decades of fieldwork with the Chagga people of Mount Kilimanjaro, in Tanzania. Her analysis finds more points of continuity than difference between her conclusions regarding the 'potency' of large-scale law reform

---

[26] IG Shivji, 'Human Rights and Development: A Fragmented Discourse' in C Peter and I Juma (eds), *Fundamental Rights and Freedoms in Tanzania* (Dar Es Salaam, Mkuki Na Nyota Publishers, 1999). See also IG Shivji, 'Constructing a New Rights Regime: Promises, Problems and Prospects' (1999) 8 *Social and Legal Studies* 253–76.
[27] SF Moore, 'The Legislative Dismantling of a Colonial and Apartheid State' (2011) *Annual Review of Law and Social Science* 7.

efforts in Tanzania, as they related to the Chagga, and the findings of the more recent ethnographies under review, which concerned the South African Truth and Reconciliation Commission and the land reform efforts in South Africa. In all of these cases, the control of the state, and hence the reach of law, was revealed to be 'necessarily incomplete and uneven'. She further notes that:

> African populations do not passively adapt to legislation but have agendas of their own ... Each case makes plain that control by the state is a partial affair only and that it is deeply affected by the semi-autonomous social fields that exist within the state and their internal and external goings on.[28]

Although legal anthropologists have been teaching us these lessons for quite some time, the persistence of ambitious, formalist and instrumental approaches to law reform in development projects, most recently reframed in the language of rights, suggest that legal scholars and lawyers in development contexts are still loathe to give up on their disciplinary commitments to legal efficacy, even in the face of considerable evidence to the contrary.

This continuing allegiance to formal law as a particularly potent avenue through which to effect large-scale societal transformations that are likely to increase social inclusion, decrease inequalities and improve social justice, especially in the human rights and development context, is even more difficult to sustain, as Trubek and Galanter observed, when one has become aware of the 'negative face' of legal reforms.[29] Yet contemporary scholarly accounts of the dark side of rights talk in the development context are plentiful. A well-known critical formulation of the argument about the implications of the convergence of rights and development is found in work of Upendra Baxi, who claims that the paradigm of universal human rights found in the United Nations Human Development Report (UNHDR) is being supplanted by a new model, which he has described as 'Trade Related Market Friendly' rights.[30] A number of critical scholars have recently both extended and illustrated the argument that in the encounter with development agencies, rights have largely become reformulated as a mode of regulation, in a manner that largely neutralises their potential to be used in contentious politics.[31] For development agencies, the turn to rights is attractive in part because it seems more responsive to the growing demand for accountability, yet as Sally Merry, Kerry Rittich and many others have pointed out, the turn to indicators itself can have insidious effects.[32] For Merry, while rights indicators offer a technology for producing accessible and standardised forms of knowledge, it is important to note the mechanisms by which this technology functions to consolidate power in the hands of experts and obscures the complex political and social choices that are embedded in those measures. According to Merry, indicators 'create a commensurability that is widely

---

[28] Ibid, 14.

[29] Trubek and Galanter, 'Scholars in Self-Estrangement' (n 1) 1083.

[30] U Baxi, *The Future of Human Rights* (New Delhi, Oxford University Press, 2002).

[31] S Pahuja, 'Rights as Regulation' in B Morgan, *The Intersection of Rights and Regulation: New Directions in Sociolegal Scholarship* (Aldershot, Ashgate Publishing, 2007); R Perry, 'Preserving Discursive Spaces to Promote Human Rights: Poverty Reduction Strategy, Human Rights and Development Discourse' (2011) 7 *McGill International Journal of Sustainable Development Law and Policy* 61.

[32] See K Rittich, 'Governing by Measuring: The Millenium Development Goals in Global Governance' in H Ruiz, R Wolfrum and J Gogolin (eds), *Select Proceedings of the European Society of International Law*, vol 2 (Oxford, Hart Publishing, 2010); SE Merry, 'Measuring the World: Indicators, Human Rights, and Global Governance' (2011) 52 (S3) *Current Anthropology* S83. See, generally K Davis, A Fisher, B Kingsbury and SE Merry (eds), *Governance by Indicators: Global Power through Classification and Ranking* (Oxford, Oxford University Press, 2012).

used to compare, to rank, and to make decisions even though the users recognize that these simplified numerical forms are superficial, often misleading, and very possibly wrong'.[33] She argues that the political struggles over what human rights mean and what constitutes compliance are submerged in the turn to indicators by technical questions of measurement, criteria and data accessibility.

What this admittedly very brief and schematic account has tried to suggest is that the contemporary human rights and development encounter is a very contentious and uncertain project. Kerry Rittich sums it up well when she notes that 'in second generation reforms, human rights are better understood not as the answer to the social deficit but as the terrain of struggle'.[34] In this contested terrain, critical scholarship can and should play an important role in questioning assumptions, containing expectations, and challenging the power of entrenched institutions. The three critiques of Trubek and Galanter haunt these debates; in that haunting, perhaps, one might see the potential for another painful, yet ultimately instructive, moment of crisis.

IV. Conclusion

> The crisis itself and the malaise it generates has been of immense value in clarifying major issues in legal theory, social science, and public policy.[35]

SISE is an enduring essay that can be read on many levels. Rereading it today, after so many years, might help us to reflect on the role that we envision for critical scholarship in law generally, and in relation to law and development in particular. As already noted, it is most frequently invoked for its role in articulating, or perhaps even accelerating, the crisis of the 'first moment' of law and development. While it is indeed an article that is deeply embedded in the local scholarly debates of its own time and place, I have argued that it articulates a series of critiques that continue to have relevance in relation to a wide range of contemporary issues, and which are perhaps particularly apt in relation to current rights and development debates. It might also be fruitfully revisited, in the context of the present volume, for what it has to say about the project of critical legal scholarship itself.

To that end, it is useful to recall that SISE was concerned with the loss of institutional support for law and development scholarship in the US; particularly support for a particular kind of interdisciplinary scholarship that enabled the construction of a community of scholars; there is an almost elegiac tone to the conclusion in which the authors note the irony

> in the prospect that the malaise will destroy the field rather than moving it to a higher level of awareness and sensitivity. The malaise resulted from the critical perspective on legal development; this itself was the result of the effort to create interdisciplinary and international centers of social research on law.[36]

---

[33] Merry, 'Measuring the World' (n 30) S85–S86.
[34] K Rittich 'The Future of Law and Development: Second-Generation Reforms and the Incorporation of the Social' in Trubek and Santos, *The New Law and Economic Development* (n 5) 245.
[35] Trubek and Galanter, 'Scholars in Self-Estrangement'(n 1) 1102.
[36] Ibid.

Rereading this passage in 2012 invites consideration of whether contemporary analogies to the lost community of SISE exist, and if so, where they might be found and what their sources of support might be. While a number of exemplary networks have emerged over the years, it would be difficult to assert unequivocally that critical scholarship of the type envisioned by Trubek and Galanter (interdisciplinary, international) has gained a more secure foothold in the academy in recent decades.[37] At this level, SISE is an article that invites critical legal scholars to (once again) reflect on the material conditions of their existence.

SISE is also unapologetically normative. It speaks in the language of morality, which might sound dated to some post-foundational ears.[38] Yet, this tension presents another question for contemporary critical scholars. Where might we find contemporary illustrations of the engaged and committed approach to scholarship embodied by Trubek and Galanter in SISE?

Finally, we might want to consider whether and to what extent the tension identified by Trubek and Galanter between their professional identification as lawyers and their critical stance as social scientists is an enduring feature of critical legal scholarship. As lawyers we are professionally invested in the efficacy of the law, even while we work to reveal its illusions, its injustices, and its incompleteness. Perhaps the most significant contribution of the article has been to alert those of us who came later to the fact that 'self-estrangement' may be an occupational hazard of critical legal scholarship, while at the same time, enlivening us to the possibility that it is an impasse that can nonetheless be productively and successfully navigated.

---

[37] Of course, the Critical Legal Studies movement, which began at a meeting in Madison in 1977, can be understood to have picked up the torch thrown down by Galanter and Trubek in 1974, although CLS remains fairly firmly grounded in the US legal academy. Several more recent networking efforts, such as the International Network on Transformative Employment and Labour Law (INTELL) which began meeting in 1994, and the network of scholars identified with Third World Approaches to International Law, are more international, although effectively unfunded. One might also point to ongoing networks formed as Collaborative Research Networks under the auspices of the Law and Society Association, associated with Harvard's Institute for Global Law and Policy (IGLP), or the Stellenbosch Institute for Advanced Studies in South Africa, as exemplars of vibrant, ongoing international interdisciplinary and critical networks of legal scholars. Whether any of these more recent networks will be able to secure stable long term institutional funding and support is the critical question.

[38] '[L]iberal legalist thought on law and development was always both more and less than science. It was both a form of scholarship that was linked inevitably to action, and a kind of action that used scholarship as its principle tool. Liberal legalism was a fusion of moral aspirations and cognitive assertions. The moral aspects of the current crisis are its most important feature; these can be resolved only by a change in moral views or in the behavior that has created moral doubts.' Trubek and Gallanter, 'Scholars in Self-Estrangement' (n 1) 1101.

4

Political Economy and Economic Law in Brazil: From Import Substitution to the Challenges of the New State Activism

MARIO G SCHAPIRO AND DIOGO R COUTINHO

We cannot interpret laws and regulations without understanding the policies they are designed to 'implement' and the theories which led to these policies. But, on the other hand, there is no way to say what the 'policy' is without studying the law.

David M Trubek[1]

I. Introduction: Economic Law and Political Economy

Political economy and economic law have historically had a unique relationship with each other, yet this relationship has remained relatively unexamined by scholars of economic law. In short, political economy is about the forms of political organisation and how they meet societies' economic needs. In this field, the state figures as the protagonist, in that it establishes connections between political preferences and economic demands.[2] It is economic law, however, that translates economic policy objectives into specific norms.

In other words, while political economy is about the political choices of economic organisation, economic law provides the normative instruments and institutional arrangements by which the objectives of economic policy can be converted into concrete measures and initiatives of public policy. Yet economic law, in a complementary way, can still be observed and described by legal scholars as an angle of analysis or a 'method' by which norms, institutions and legal processes are discussed in terms of application from the point of view of functionality, that is, with regard to the roles they play in the implementation of certain objectives that, ultimately, have been politically defined.

---

[1] DM Trubek, 'Law, Planning and the Development of the Brazilian Capital Market: A Study of Law in Economic Change' (1971) 72–73 *Bulletin Yale Law School Studies in Law and Modernization* 3, 9.

[2] J Caporaso and D Levine, *Theories of Political Economy* (Cambridge, Cambridge University Press, 1992) 1. See G Bercovici, 'Política Econômica e Direito Econômico' (2010) 105 *Revista da Faculdade de Direito da Universidade de São Paulo* 389 for the relationship between economic law and economic policy in the case of Brazil.

Thus, not surprisingly, the movements of political economy can be seen in the structuring of legal instruments and institutional arrangements provided by economic law in different periods. In Brazil, since the second half of the twentieth century, the interaction between political economy and economic law has been quite marked, giving rise to at least three institutional contexts or 'moments': (i) developmentalism and interventionist economic law; (ii) moderate neo-liberalism and economic regulation; and (iii) the new activism of the state and its economic law, which can be characterised as selective and inductive.[3]

This paper aims to describe these 'moments', showing the connections we see between configurations of political economy and elements or functions of economic law. Furthermore, we seek to describe what we believe to be some of the challenges of economic law in the context of the emergence of a new activist state in Brazil, where functions related to selectivity, legitimacy and institutional governance assume a prominent role.

This paper is divided into five sections. Section II retraces the path of economic law and state intervention from the developmentalist period to the economic reforms of the 1990s. Section III describes the most salient features of what we call 'new state activism'. Section IV broadly describes some of the new functions to be accomplished by the economic law in the context of this new state activism. The final section, a conclusion, summarises the central argument and presents some of the challenges we see for economic law as a scholarly field and its relationship to an agenda of applied and empirical research on law and development.

II. Economic Law in the Developmental and the Regulatory State

The transition from the developmental state to economic law in the regulatory state in Brazil is presented briefly in this section.

A. Developmentalism and Interventionist Economic Law

In line with a group of countries with delayed development—which Alice Amsden calls the 'the rest'[4]—Brazil accelerated its development process during the second half of the twentieth century. In that period, there were two visions of political economy being disputed: the industrial transformation strategy versus the belief in comparative agricultural advantages. This contrast, represented by the struggles between the industrialist Roberto Simonsen and the Ricardian Eugenio Gudin in the 1940s, was similar to that experienced by 'the rest' of the countries in the same period. As Amsden reported, throughout the first half of the twentieth century, Latin Americans and Asians found themselves in a dilemma; with their economies losing out to industrialised nations, they were forced to choose

---

[3] For a discussion and periodisation of the history of law and development and its 'moments', see DM Trubek and A Santos, *The New Law and Economic Development: A Critical Appraisal* (Cambridge, Cambridge University Press, 2006).

[4] A Amsden, *The Rise of the Rest: Challenges to the West from Late-Industrializing Economies* (Oxford, Oxford University Press, 2001).

between seeking new forms of competitive advantage or pushing the limits of their existing advantages.[5]

In most of these countries, including Brazil, the path of establishing new competitive advantages prevailed, and countries as distant and diverse as South Korea, Taiwan, Brazil and Mexico implemented similar legal and institutional methods and tools to change the direction of their economies. They replaced 'the market's invisible hand' with the 'the state's visible hand' and industrial policies.[6] The belief was that industry, rather than agriculture, is the dynamic engine of development, broadly understood as the acceleration of technical processes to increase overall productivity and improve the population's general standards of living.[7] In this context, new development theories emerged to explain and support these public actions.

In Brazil, this restructuring began as far back as Getulio Vargas' government, whose policies starting in the 1930s gave rise to a professional bureaucratic apparatus with the creation of DASP (Administrative Department of Public Service), which was necessary to structure bureaucracy and coordinate state actions. Furthermore, this period saw the creation of state-owned enterprises in the industrial and financial sectors, seen as strategic to implement development policies.[8]

This initial push was followed and intensified by the Target Plan (*Plano de Metas*) measures, implemented during the Kubitschek administration (1956–61), when industry became an important part of the economy and the majority of the population lived in urban areas.[9] The end of this prolonged period occurred in 1979, the last year of the Second National Development Plan (PND II). This plan, issued during one of the periods of military rule Brazil experienced in the last century, completed the process of import substitution by providing the national economy with a complete and integrated industrial park.[10] Brazilian development was, in general terms, in line with other successful countries with delayed development, such as South Korea.

One can say that the configuration of this development process was that of a political economy model according to which the state organised economic transformation. This configuration, in turn, was structured by means of a formal institutional arrangement,[11] as well as by tools for state intervention provided by economic law, in order to achieve the goals of the developmental vision—the so-called 'catch up' phase.

Accordingly, law's first role was to establish the normative institutional arrangements of the development model. These arrangements correspond to those which K Pistor and

---

[5] Ibid, 8–13.

[6] Ibid.

[7] As summarised by the Brazilian development economist Celso Furtado: 'development theories are explanatory schemes of social processes in which the assimilation of new techniques and the consequent productivity increase lead to the improved well-being of a population with growing social homogenisation'. See C Furtado, *Brasil: a Construção Interrompida* (São Paulo, Editora Paz e Terra, 1992) 39.

[8] Examples of public-owned enterprises created during that period are Petrobrás (oil and gas), Vale do Rio Doce (iron ore), CSN and Volta Redonda (steel). Examples of public development banks created or reformed during that period are BNDES (the Brazilian National Development Bank) and Caixa Econômica Federal (a Federal Savings Bank).

[9] A Villela and W Suzigan, *Política do Governo e Crescimento da Economia Brasileira* (Rio de Janeiro, Instituto de Pesquisa Econômica Aplicada—Institute of Applied Economic Research (IPEA), 1975).

[10] A Villela and W Suzigan, *Industrial Policy in Brazil* (Campinas, Unicamp, 1997).

[11] It is formal in the sense used by Douglass North to designate institutions shaped according to legal norms or rules, as different from informal institutions, forged by cultural habits and patterns. See D North, *Institutions, Institutional Change and Economic Performance* (Cambridge, Cambridge University Press, 1990).

P Wellons, in their study of law in the development of East Asia, recognise as substantive and procedural roles. For them, the substantive role concerns economic allocation decisions in the sense that it is the legal arrangement that establishes who is responsible for making major economic decisions. These decisions can be attributed to the state, which makes a coordinated decision on the allocation of economic goods. The decisions can also go to private agents, who will make a decentralised decision on the allocation of material goods. The procedural role, in turn, refers to decision-making by the state, which may be more open to discretion or more bound by law.[12]

Consequently, while in liberal market economies such as in the United States[13] the law allocates economic decisions to private decentralised agents and limits state intervention through specific and relatively inflexible laws (or other legal means), in delayed-development models such as in Brazil economic law imbues the state and its bodies with powers to decide the merits of economic actions and also allows a more discretionary public decision-making process. Industrial policies of the developmental period, by ensuring that it is the state that decides what sectors will be considered key, epitomise this kind of arrangement in Brazil.

It is within this framework of institutional design, consisting of a state overseeing economic allocation decisions and possessing discretionary decision-making capacity, that the tools of economic intervention law operate. Such tools, designed to support the developmental state's capacity to intervene, were created to pursue the goals of economic transformation. In the scheme proposed in Brazilian economic law by Eros Grau,[14] there are four types of tools: absorption, participation, leadership and inducement. While absorption and participation represent what Grau defines as intervention *in* the economic domain—a direct intervention— leadership and inducement consist of intervention *on* the economic domain—that is, an indirect action.

Intervention *in* the economic domain brings together the ways in which the developmental state acts as an economic agent, either in the state productive system or in the national financial system through state/public companies and banks. In performing these duties, the state can either monopolise an industry, absorbing it—which occurred in Brazil's oil exploration and production, for example—or can participate in the market, thus competing with other private agents, as seen in the financial system, which includes public and private banks.

The second set of interventions (interventions *on* the economic domain) involves the tools that ensure indirect intervention for the state, whether by imposing behavioural obligations on private players (directing or steering them), or by stipulating rewards that induce these agents to meet certain public interest objectives. These four types of tools can

---

[12] Therefore, typologically, while in the liberal market economies economic decisions are often guided by private cost–benefit analyses, in state-centred models, these decisions are guided by government choices, associated with development policy objectives. *Cf* K Pistor and P Wellons, *The Role of Law and Legal Institutions in Asian Economic Development: 1960–1995*, A Report prepared for the Asian Development Bank (1998) available at www.asianlii.org/asia/other/ADBLPRes/1998/3.pdf, 5.

[13] The notion of a liberal market economy and its association with the US model is put forth by P Hall and D Soskice, who use this typology to describe what they call 'varieties of capitalism'. See D Soskice and P Hall, 'Introduction' in P Hall and D Soskice, *Varieties of Capitalism: The Institutional Foundations of Comparative Advantage* (Oxford, Oxford University Press, 2001).

[14] ER Grau, *A Ordem Econômica na Constituição de 1988*, 4th edn (São Paulo, Editora Malheiros 2000) 158–60.

be understood as situated along a spectrum, whose range covers means which are more interventionist and those which are less so. In this work, we assume that the frequency of use of these tools is consistent with the objectives and the respective tendency of the institutional arrangement adopted, which, in turn, communicates with the configurations of that period's political economy.

In the context of the development strategy, whose objectives are established centrally (top down), and the institutional design attributed to the state, the role of economic law has tipped towards being more interventionist. Specifically, in the context of import-substitution developmentalism, the more evident tools that the state employed to support its development policy were the state-owned enterprises responsible for organising much of the economy. Besides these, there was also the use of planning techniques, price-fixing and control, interest and exchange rates, state monopolies, and, in general, the many and varied means that ultimately restrain the 'economic freedom' of private economic agents.

That does not mean that, in this period, the state did not also make use of direction and inducement. Although the public productive sector and the state financial system assumed most of the investment coordination, the public programming of the economy also made use of indirect intervention through lines of credit and financing, and the non-tax use of the tax law framework.[15] A clear example of this is a study on tax incentives (induction mechanisms) established by Decree 157/1971, which established income tax benefits for businesses that opened their capital to the stock market.[16] This mechanism has been described as the measure of a state responsible for economic planning, which sought, among other objectives, to provide a means of creating a market based on its policies.

The following points summarise this first 'moment' of Brazilian economic law:

— Configuration of political economy: developmentalism
— Interventionist Economic Law:
    — Institutional arrangement: economic allocation via the state;
    — Tools: primacy for 'intervention *in*' the economic domain;
    — Objectives: economic catch-up

B. Moderate Neo-liberalism and Economic Regulation

The political economy configuration that underpinned the development strategy lost steam in the 1980s. This contributed to a new interpretation and new needs on the part of the economic actors. That is, as Roberto Unger suggests, from the 1980s there was a new alignment of ideas and interests, culminating in new policies and, consequently, in a new instrumentality for economic law.

The interpretations that signalled the importance of market failures weighed heavily on the agenda of policy makers and between 1950 and 1980 gave way to analyses that denounced government failures. Authors like Pigou, a pioneer in the identification of the problem of externalities and the need for corrective public intervention and, primarily,

---

[15] See L Coutinho and P Reichstul, 'O Setor Produtivo Estatal e o Ciclo' in CE Martins (ed), *Estado e Capitalismo no Brasil* (São Paulo, Editora Hucitec/CEBRAP, 1977).

[16] *Cf* D Trubek, JHG Vieira and PF de Sá, *Direito, Planejamento e Desenvolvimento do Mercado de Capitais Brasileiro 1965–1970* (São Paulo, Editora Saraiva, 2011).

Keynes, who signalled the limits of laissez-faire economics and highlighted the importance of generating demand through state investment and public planning, were challenged by a new generation of analysts.

The works of Anne Krueger, George Stigler, and James Buchanan, among others, began to point out the defects of government actions in market regulation. From this perspective, bureaucrats, no longer identified with the public interest, came to be seen as individuals maximising their own self-interest (rent seekers); that is, they were not described as agents interested in pursuing the public good. The results of their self-interested actions, combined with the severe information asymmetry between state and market, would be, from this viewpoint, clumsy and costly public interventions that harm rather than help the economy. The diagnosis was, therefore, sceptical with regard to the government: flaws of government are even more severe and difficult to mitigate than market failures.

In particular, in the countries of the 'rest', whose developmental effort had been pursued by state leadership, the new configuration of ideas allows for a re-articulation of interpretations and also of public policy actions and policies. The problems experienced by some of these economies, especially those in Latin America, come to be seen as state problems—a diagnosis consistent with analyses by Krueger, Stigler, Friedman and others. The following passage on the Brazilian case, by Gustavo Franco, President of the Central Bank (BC) in the 1990s, is quite revealing in terms of the new conceptions that prevailed at that period:

> Finally, in conclusion, it remains to be seen that in the new model being drafted, where the mainspring of the process is productivity growth, the government's actions are not in themselves triggers of the development process. The basic dynamics of Brazilian development begins to ignore government actions, especially in relation to major programs and investment projects, although this is not the case with the basic macroeconomic configuration. The government becomes a supporter and the bureaucracies and politicians lose their missionary role taken on over the decades. Progress and growth are obtained increasingly in the private sector, and, in these circumstances, the government must accept displaying an achievement record that is not limited to, nor even prioritizes, the number of projects or programs initiated. Priorities shift from the instruments (programs, expenses) to the ultimate goals (social and economic indicators).[17]

In the actual economic scene in many of these countries, new interests were voiced to foster more economic freedom and less state action. The states' fiscal and financial crisis imposed a comprehensive reform agenda in Latin America, notably in Brazil. Due to this articulation of interests, the meaning and content of this agenda moved towards reducing intervention mechanisms and expanding market spaces—in short, towards deregulation and privatisation. This is a realignment that, similarly to that which occurred in the developmental period, impacted economic law, thereby altering the goals of intervention, the institutional arrangement of economic organisation and the legal means used.

In this scenario, the objectives of economic organisation were no longer catch-up development coordinated by the state and instead became the efficient organisation of the economy, that is, an organisation that valued the allocative capacity of private agents, assuring them economic predictability and calculability through a canonical definition of property rights. Consequently, the earlier legal and institutional arrangement, based on a substantive attribution of economic decisions to the state and prevalence of discretionary spaces, underwent transmutations.

---

[17] G Franco, 'A Inserção Externa e o Desenvolvimento' (1998) 18 *Revista de Economia Política* 71.

Many of the allocative functions formerly carried out by the government were transferred to markets, while discretionary areas were mitigated by the establishment of regulatory constraints that limited the government's ability to make choices. Such choices, in this context, came to be considered illegitimate and often spurious, since they were motivated by goals of a 'political' nature. Finally, the tools used to support economic law had a change in tone: tools of 'intervention *in*' lost centrality and those of 'intervention *on*' gained importance, like a new set of even milder devices, as is the case with self-regulation and the various forms of soft law.

These changes in the substance and direction of economic law were anchored in the economic reforms aimed at changing the pattern of capitalist development in Brazil in the 1990s. These reforms relied on three main sets of measures: (i) economic openness and the drastic reduction in industrial protection measures; (ii) the definition of a macroeconomic policy linked to the maintenance of monetary stability; and (iii) privatisations and partial reform of the state.

Economic liberalisation was implemented in the early 1990s with the reduction of tariff and non-tariff barriers. Between 1990 and 1992, the average decrease in import tariffs was approximately 16 per cent (from 32.2 per cent to 16.5 per cent).[18] Collectively, non-tariff barriers were drastically reduced. This opening process gained new impetus in 1996 when the law on industrial property (Law 9.279/1996) was enacted, incorporating the liberalising provisions of TRIPS (Agreement on Trade-Related Aspects of Intellectual Property Rights) even before the end of the grace period stipulated in the agreement. With this, Brazil came to have patent protection for 20 years (raising the national standard from 15 years) for nationals and foreigners in activities that had not previously been subject to patenting, such as pharmaceutical production.[19] Chart 1 illustrates the Brazilian economy's 'degree of openness' from 1995 to 2010. The vertical axis indicates the percentage of import tariffs.

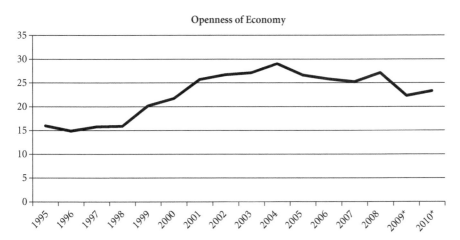

Chart 1. Openness of Economy

Source: IPEA data

---

[18] D Kupfer, *Trajetórias de Reestruturação da Industria Brasileira após a Abertura e a Estabilização*, (PhD thesis, Rio de Janeiro, UFRJ Economics Institute, 1998).

[19] Countries like India, for example, delayed the entry into enforcing the TRIPS guidelines, which experts say would have favoured the protection and development of the Indian drug industry, which today is highly competitive.

In this package of amendments to the institutional framework, monetary stabilisation was another central measure. Since 1994, with the *Real* stabilisation plan,[20] annual inflation has fallen to single digits. The plan was grounded in a combination of monetary policies (including basic interest rates set by the BC) and foreign exchange policies including a floating mode for managing exchange rates (implying a mitigation of discretionary controls on the exchange rate). There are two associated institutional issues underlying the plan: (i) the 'focus' on macroeconomic management; and (ii) changes in monetary and budgetary control.

By electing monetary stability as the central target of macroeconomic policies, the Brazilian federal government prevented these policies from having other goals and outcomes. As Campanário and Silva recall, during developmentalism, industrial policy was part of the macroeconomic policy guidelines, that is, interest rates and exchange controls were also managed according to industrial demands.[21] The change brought about by the introduction of the *Real* currency in 1994 assured, therefore, a macroeconomic management 'focus', guaranteed by a reduction in discretionary spaces—the goals are now linked to inflation control.

Institutionally, this reduction in discretion unfolded as a process beginning in 1986 and completed in 1999. In 1986, the so-called 'transaction account' was closed, in 1988 the Constitution prohibited the development promotion functions of the BC, and in 1999, Decree 3088 established the operational autonomy of the BC.

The 'transaction account' was a Bank of Brazil (BB, a publicly-owned bank) account in the BC, established when the BC was founded in 1964 to ensure the material resources necessary for the BC's operation.[22] Over time, the positions were reversed, and the transaction account became a source of funds for the BB, which could develop its credit activity without a corresponding volume of fund-raising among its account holders. In practice, the transaction account allowed the BB to offer loans by accessing BC funds without these transfers (between the BC and the BB) being publicly controlled, since they were not detailed in the federal government's budget. A second consequence of this adjustment was the existence of a dual monetary authority; as the BB was a source of funds via transaction accounts, its credit capacity was not constrained by monetary policy (interest rates) set by the BC. As noted, in 1986 the National Monetary Council ended the 'transaction account', which ensured greater delineation of functions between the BC, which had strengthened its authority, and the BB, which then began to act only as a state bank. With this leeway, or discretion, BB's economic financing decreased.

Then the 1988 Constitution[23] fixed another problem of public finance. First, it established that issuing money can only be carried out by the BC. Second, it prohibited the CB from lending funds to the National Treasury. Thus, it guaranteed the separation of two important spheres—the monetary sphere, which was left to the BC, and the tax sphere, which came to be administered by the National Treasury Secretariat which had

---

[20] *Real* (R$) is the Brazilian currency.

[21] M Campanário and M Silva, 'Fundamentos de uma nova política industrial' in MT Fleury and A Fleury, *A Política Industrial* (São Paulo, Publifolha, 2004).

[22] F Giambiagi and AC Além, *Finanças Públicas—teoria e prática no Brasil* (Rio de Janeiro, Editora Campus 2008) 89–90.

[23] Brazilian Federal Constitution, Art 164 §1.

been established in 1986.[24] Like the closure of transaction accounts, this was another step towards delineation of functions in budgetary and monetary management, the effect of which was to reduce discretion. Treasury spending came to be publicly recorded in the budget, and no longer had extra-budgetary access to BC resources.

Also, as mentioned above, the final step in this functional separation between monetary management and other government policies occurred in 1999 with the enactment of Decree 3088. From then on, the so-called operational autonomy of the BC was established, and the BC is now formally responsible for pursuing inflation targets set by the National Monetary Council. This activity should be accompanied by periodic accountability and if the annual target is not achieved, the BC president must address an open letter to the Minister of Finance as to the cause of the shortfall.

Economic openness and a macroeconomic 'focus', coupled with the reduction of fiscal–monetary discretion, were accompanied by the third institutional movement of the economic reform period: privatisation. For privitisations, the central development model was altered significantly, that is, the state's allocative power was largely transferred to private agents. In this period important industries including the fertilizer, petrochemical, mining and steel, electrical and telecommunications industries, railways, and state level banking were privatised. Chart 2 shows, for Brazil, the evolution and decrease in the number of state companies between the end of the development period and the neo-liberal period of the 1990s.

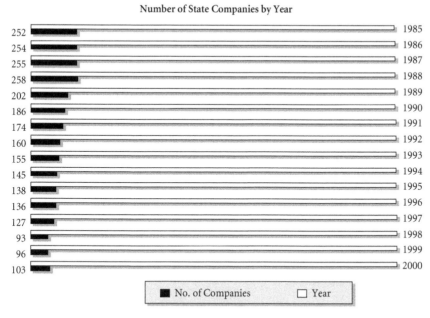

Chart 2. Number of State Companies by Year
Source: Ministry of Planning, Budget and Management

---

[24] Giambiagi and Além, *Finanças Públicas—teoria e prática no Brasil* (n 22) 121.

This was, however, not a complete change. Major state companies, such as the Brazilian National Development Bank (BNDES), Petrobras, BB, Caixa Econômica Federal and the Post Office remained in public ownership. This is why Brazilian reformism was characterised as a moderate form of neo-liberalism (compared, for example, with the experiences of Argentina or Mexico).[25] Even so, the reforms were intense and were supported by a significant change in the regulatory landmark components of the economic order, as noted in Table 1.

In this period, new regulatory agencies were also created, and this strained canons of Brazilian public law by strengthening infra-legal regulation and formally ensuring regulatory stability. A brief explanation of this is called for here. Much of Brazil's public law doctrine is still bound by a formal legalistic understanding which admits only statutory law as a normative mechanism, relegating administrative regulations to the role of merely legal (statutory) concretisation (they are called 'operating regulations'). Evoking Article 5 of the Federal Constitution and Article 25 of the Temporary Constitutional Provisions Act, many jurists contend that legislative delegation does not exist in Brazil thus rendering administrative law regulations unconstitutional. They insist that 'only statutory law innovates in the legal order'.

Contradicting this interpretation, the 'law in action' of regulatory activity has shown the limits of a strict and static understanding of separation of powers since before the reforms of the 1990s: the BC has regulated (and literally legislated on) the banking system through regulations since 1964; like many other sectors it has been regulated for a long time. At the conceptual level, moreover, scholars have revised ideas about legality. They have introduced the notion of 'normative capacity of circumstances' (that is, the ability of the Executive to regulate—practically speaking: legislate—the economic context), which has gained in

Table 1. Regulatory Landmarks

New Regulatory Landmarks of the 1990s	
Constitutional Amendment no. 5	Opening of the gas sector
Constitutional Amendment no. 8	Opening the telecommunications sector
Constitutional Amendment no. 9	Opening of the oil sector
Constitutional Amendment no. 18	The State Administrative Reform
Constitutional Amendment no. 19	The State Administrative Reform
Law 8078/90	Consumer Protection Code
Law 8884/94	Anti-trust Law
Laws 8031/90 and 9491/97	National Privatization Plan
Law 8987/95	Concession Law for Public Service
Law 9427/96	New regulations for the power sector
Law 9472/97	New regulation for the telecommunications industry
Law 9478/97	New regulation for the oil sector

[25] DM Trubek, DR Coutinho and MG Schapiro, 'New State Activism in Brazil and the Challenge for Law' in DM Trubek, HA Garcia, DR Coutinho and A Santos (eds), *Law and the New Developmental State: The Brazilian Experience in Latin American Context* (Cambridge, Cambridge University Press, 2013).

importance.[26] This capacity is exercised through 'authorised regulations', which are regulations derived from abstract and often vague statutory laws aimed at awarding regulatory powers to public administration entities ('legislative authorisations').

With the creation of various American-style regulatory agencies in the 1990s, the regulatory capacity of the Brazilian state acquired more force and they began to exercise a greater degree of autonomy from the government. The institutional design of regulatory agencies stipulated mandates for their directors and financial and operational autonomy, and same-hierarchy appeals are not allowed, so the decisions taken by these entities on the administrative level cannot be subject to appeal to more politicised bodies.[27] This augmented autonomy can also be seen as another measure to restrict the policy discretion of regulatory activity. Table 2 presents the regulatory agencies founded in this period. The following points summarise this second 'moment' of Brazilian economic law:

— configuration of political economy: moderated neo-liberalism;
— regulatory Economic Law:
— institutional arrangement: economic allocation via the market;
— tools: liberalisation followed by economic regulation; and
— objectives: allocative efficiency.

Table 2. Regulatory Agencies

Regulated Sector	Agency	Year	Federal Law
Competition	CADE	1994[*]	8884/94
Electricity	ANEEL	1996	9427/96
Oil	ANP	1997	9478/97
Telecommunications	ANATEL	1997	9472/97
Health Surveillance Agency	ANVISA	1999	9782/99
Bank-monetary	Central Bank (with operational autonomy)	1999	4595/64 and Decree 3088/99
Supplemental Health	ANS	2000	9961/00
Water Resources	ANA	2000	9984/00
Waterway Transport	ANTAQ	2001	10233/01
Land Transport	ANTT	2001	10233/01
Civil Aviation	ANAC	2005	11182/05

Source: Schapiro and Trubek (2012)

[*] CADE was formally created by Decree-Law 7666 of 1945, but it only became effective in 1994 with the enactment of Law 8884/1994, in the scenario of monetary stabilization and partial privatization of the economy.

[26] Grau, *A Ordem Econômica na Constituição de 1988* (n 14) 225–55.
[27] In the case of the BC, its decisions can be appealed in the *Conselhinho* ('small council') of the financial system. See also Opinion 51 of the Office of the General Counsel to the Federal Government of 2006, which discusses the existence of same-hierarchy appeals for agencies and establishes that, if their decisions are contrary to public policy, they can be appealed by a same-hierarchy agency; the opinion was approved by the president of Brazil. The opinion is available in Portuguese at www.agu.gov.br/SISTEMAS/SITE/PaginasInternas/NormasInternas/AtoDetalhado.aspx?idAto=8453&ID_SITE=.

III. New State Activism: Articulation with Market and Social Policies

Recently, the legal scholar David M Trubek proposed a novel research topic in the field of law and development. Trubek considers the possible existence of different and often new roles for law to play in contemporary development strategies and suggests that it is relevant to empirically observe and describe the legal implications of these development trajectories.[28]

Since 2000, and particularly in light of the 2008 financial crisis, a new configuration of political economy has taken shape. In terms of ideas, analyses of government failures, predominant until then, began to give way to new proposals aimed at re-discussing the importance of the state. In terms of interests, the poor results achieved by most developing countries after a decade of neo-liberal economic reforms have stimulated new options in policy making. The result of this reformulation has given rise to a reorientation of state action, which, in another study, we designated 'the new activist state'.[29]

In Latin American countries, Schapiro points out that, in general, greater attention is being given to state solutions.[30] In 2002, Mexico implemented its Economic Policy for Competitiveness, selecting 12 priority sectors and beneficiaries of industry-specific incentive programmes, including textile, leather, footwear, high tech, and motor vehicle industries and manufacturing goods for export. Other countries in the region such as Argentina, Chile, Costa Rica and Uruguay have also returned to the use of industrial policies, but with different strategies, some favouring more horizontal measures and others preferring selective interventions.[31] In the Brazilian case, this redesign was tentatively tried beginning in the late 1990s and pushed with greater force from 2005 onward.

In fact, new ideas had begun to challenge neo-liberal thought in the same way as they had a decade earlier. Academic papers and public policy reports dedicated to interpreting the success of development strategies of Asian countries noted the importance of state economic intervention in the successful cases of Japan, South Korea, Taiwan and other countries. Among the scholarly works, the research of Robert Wade (notably, his *Governing the Market*) was influential. It directly challenged neo-liberal interpretations in vogue and emphasised the importance of industrial policy in the growth of East Asian countries.[32] Wade's work gave similar interpretations and had a similar impact as that of Alice Amsden's book on South Korea,[33] and Peter Evans' book in which he compares the

---

[28] DM Trubek, 'Developmental States and the Legal Order: Towards a New Political Economy of Development and Law' (2008) *University of Wisconsin Legal Studies Research Paper 1075* 2.

[29] Trubek, Coutinho and Schapiro, 'New State Activism in Brazil' (n 25).

[30] MG Schapiro, 'O que a política industrial pode aprender com a política monetária?' (2013) 96 *Revista Novos Estudos*.

[31] W Peres, 'The Slow Comeback of Industrial Policies in Latin America and the Caribbean' (2006) 88 *CEPAL Review* 67.

[32] R Wade, *Governing the Market—Economic Theory and the Role of Government in East Asian Industrialization* (Princeton, Princeton University Press, 1990).

[33] A Amsden, *Asia's Next Giant: South Korea and Late Industrialization* (Oxford, Oxford University Press, 1992).

trajectories of South Korea, Taiwan, Brazil, India and Zaire.[34] In terms of policy analysis, the most important document of the period was the World Bank report of 1993,[35] in which analysts acknowledged for the first time that the mechanisms of state intervention, notably industrial policy, played an important role in the success of that region.

Previously restricted to the Asian panorama, propositions about the indispensable role of state intervention gradually began to make their way into public debates in other developing countries. In Brazil in the late 1990s, the issue of development began to be rescued from ostracism and returned from the exile to which it had been relegated. An example of this was a seminar on economic development organised by José Luis Fiori at the Institute of Economics at the Federal University of Rio de Janeiro in 2000, which had repercussions, as it gathered a group of heterodox intellectuals from different universities to launch the book *Estados e Moedas no Desenvolvimento das Nações* ('States and Currencies in Nations Development').[36] Since then, the theme of development has gradually returned to occupy a prominent role in academic analyses and policy proposals. The authors presented theoretical support that, if did not directly influence the decisions of policy-makers, at least conceptually has helped legitimise the new directions taken by public policies since 2000.[37]

Moreover, in Brazil, this gradual conceptual realignment of the role of the state and development was in accordance with the country's strategic interests. The abrupt opening of the economy and the institutional framework of macroeconomic policy, based on high interest rates and an overvalued exchange rate of the 1990s, had met growing resistance since the end of President Cardoso's second term.[38] In 2002, during the presidential election (won by Lula), industrial interests were rearticulated and began to decisively support an agenda of industrial policy and government stimuli, thus contributing to a redirection of policies adopted since then.[39] As explained by Diniz and Boschi:

> The 2002 electoral setting rekindled the debate over resuming development, in a process in which the convergence of the major corporate entities' proposals was considered the central element. He reiterated the notion that the alternative to the resumption of development would reside in corrections in the process of indiscriminate opening of the economy, initiated during the 1990s. This is how the emphasis of the three proposals that were made public by CNI, FIESP and the IEDI in the first half of 2002 focused on the urgency of adopting a consistent industrial policy of export stimulus and competitive import substitution, to reduce the trade deficit with a series of successive effects, such as the creation of technological capacity, production of goods with high added value, increased productivity and expansion of industrial employment.[40]

---

[34] P Evans, *Embedded Autonomy: States and Industrial Transformation* (Princeton, Princeton University Press, 1995).

[35] World Bank, *The East Asian Miracle: Economic Growth and Public Policy*, World Bank Policy Research Reports (Oxford, Oxford University Press, 1993).

[36] *Cf* JL Fiori, *Estados e Moedas no Desenvolvimento das Nações* (Petrópolis, Editora Vozes, 1999).

[37] See LC Bresser-Pereira, 'From Old to New Developmentalism in Latin America' (2009) 193 *Textos para Discussão—Escola de Economia de São Paulo (FGV-EESP)*; G Arbix and S Martin, Beyond Developmentalism and Market Fundamentalism in Brazil: Inclusionary State Activism without Statism' (Workshop on States, Development, and Global Governance, University of Wisconsin, 12–13 March 2010) and E Diniz and R Boschi, *Empresários, Interesses e Mercado—dilemas do desenvolvimento no Brasil* (Belo Horizonte, Editora UFMG, 2004).

[38] E Diniz and R Boschi, 'Empresariado e Estratégia de Desenvolvimento' (2003) 18 (52) *Revista Brasileira de Ciências Sociais*.

[39] Ibid, 25. '[B]eyond government bureaucracy, in business a significant split was also detected in the whole class' support of liberal policies.' This split became public during the election year of 1998, in an environment marked by the proposed re-election of the president and the debate on the need for a redefinition of directions.

[40] Ibid, 27.

The Lula government responded with a return to more robust policies in (i) industrial, technological and foreign trade, (ii) infrastructure, and (iii) social areas.[41] This new arrangement of features and formats—not yet fully delineated—has combined economic stimulus policies and programmes and a social policy that aims at combining universalism and targeting. As described below, this activist state is some ways both different from and similar to both prior periods, although it has much greater convergence with objectives of the original developmental state.

Like the first period, this third moment pursues an active state role in the economy. However, it is differentiated by state interventions that are less directive and more selective, combining various tools and ways of relating to the market. Moreover, the governance of this new activist state is immersed in a democratic environment, which implies the existence of more complex negotiation processes for public decisions, as they involve multiple actors and are also subject to greater public control.[42]

Regarding the second period, shaped by neoliberal ideology, the differences are greater, since the resumption of state activism in Brazil returned a portion of the power of economic allocation to the state. However, the current legal and institutional framework reflects some of the constraints arising in the period of economic reforms, such as moderation of discretionary decision-making. In addition, other institutional tools and arrangements devised in the neoliberal period that played the role of restricting the space for discretion—such as regulatory agencies, a fiscal austerity law and operational autonomy of the BC—were not abandoned and illustrate the scope of mechanisms available to the state to influence the economy.

Finally, for both periods, there are new factors brought about by the current state activism, notably, social policies and the proposal for a development model that addresses the importance of reducing inequality, given the latest findings concerning the ills economic development engenders, particularly related to poverty. The policies combine universal measures, such as increasing the minimum wage and SUS (the Brazilian universal public health system), with targeted cash transfer programmes for the poor such as *Bolsa Família* (PBF). In summary, the new configuration of state action includes the following elements:

— selective and inductive activism without state dominance;
— moderation of discretion and strengthening of democratic legitimacy; and
— industrial and poverty and inequality reduction policies.

A. Resumption of Industrial Policy and Infrastructure Plans and Actions of Companies and State Banks

Unlike the 1990s, when the country followed the advice that 'the best industrial policy is not having an industrial policy,'[43] three new industrial policies have been implemented since 2004—the Industrial, Technological and Foreign Trade Policy, PITCE (2004–2008), the

---

[41] A de Ávila Gomide and RRC Pires, 'Capacidades Estatais para o Desenvolvimento no Século XXI' (2012) *IPEA, Boletim de Análise Política-Institucional*, 25.

[42] Ibid, 26–27. In the summary of Arbix and Martin, Beyond Developmentalism (n 37) it is an active state, but one that does not dominate the other economic sectors.

[43] This quote is attributed to the former minister of finance under Cardoso's administration, Pedro Malan.

Productive Development Policy, PDP (2008–2010) and, more recently, the Greater Brazil Programme (*Programa Brasil Maior*) PBM (2011–2014). Throughout the decade, the scope of industrial policy also increased. While PITCE prioritised four sectors (pharmaceuticals, capital goods, software and semiconductors), the PDP has brought measures to 24 sectors and the PBM serves approximately 20 sectors.

In the first period alone (2004–2008), four laws specific to industry (Innovation Law 10973/2004, ABDI Law 11080/2004, a Brazilian science and research-oriented federal law *Lei do Bem* 11196/2005 and the Law on Support Foundations, 12.349/2010) were enacted, and a design of governance for industrial policy was established, with the creation of ABDI (Brazilian Agency for Industrial Development) and an agency to promote exports, APEX (under the Ministry of Development, Industry and Trade), which was established through Law 10688/2003.

Currently, the industrial sector has other legal mechanisms, such as the benefits of payroll tax relief (Law 12546/2011), the Automotive System, which provides import tax reduction conditioned on investments in the production of reduced-emissions engines (Law 12546/2011) and mechanisms of preferential margin in public contracts, which benefit products with local content (Law 12349/2010). Between legal and infra-legal measures, the Greater Brazil Programme presented a set of 71 fiscal, pricing, financial (mainly through BNDES) and institutional (such as the assignment of trade defence to the managers) initiatives.

In this resumption of state activism in the industrial area, BNDES, a traditional funder of long-term industrialisation strategies, has once again been elevated to a position of prominence and, since 1999, its disbursements have shown a tendency towards growth (which intensified between 2008 and 2010). In 2010, the bank disbursed R$168 billion into the economy, and in the industrial sector alone the volume exceeded R$78 billion.[44]

In infrastructure, the Plans for Accelerated Growth (PACs) 1 and 2 have been prominent, and have been organised to streamline budget management and to offer qualified monitoring of their implementation. The PACs have been the main mechanism for coordinating government investments in infrastructure and, instead of being executed and monitored in isolation (with each item being executed by the respective ministries), programmes are monitored in a coordinated manner—initially by the Office of the Presidential Chief of Staff and currently by the Ministry of Planning, Budget and Management, which tends to ensure a management with greater technical and administrative capacity. The PACs, in being a broad public investment programme, are instruments of economic inducement, whether by driving the infrastructure work or by supporting industrial segments in supply chain projects. One such PAC programme that illustrates this combination is *Minha Casa, Minha Vida* (My House, My Life), which, in seeking to provide low-income housing, stimulates construction, which is one of the most intense labour-recruiting sectors.

Despite the resumption of state activism, there are important qualitative differences between this type of activism and earlier models, such as the provisions of PND II executed between 1974 and 1979 in the Geisel military administration. Aside from the democratic environment, which involves, among others, negotiated decision-making procedures, a free press and broader powers for the Public Prosecutors Office, the Brazilian market

---

[44] Data available at www.bndes.gov.br/SiteBNDES/bndes/bndes_pt/Institucional/Relacao_Com_Investidores/Desempenho.

environment today has become more complex and diverse. Parallel to the re-positioning of the state as a strategic agent, capital markets also developed between 2000 and 2010.[45] In addition, with greater protection of minority shareholders (Law 10303/2001) and with the stipulation of new corporate governance standards in the São Paulo Stock Exchange (Market Access, Level 1, Level 2 and New Market), the stock market environment is more capitalised and is a reasonable alternative to long-term financing.[46] This partly explains the conclusion that Brazil has an active state role, but one that does not dominate the other economic sectors.[47]

B. Social Policies: Redistributive Initiatives and Reducing Inequality

As is widely known, until the early 1930s, Brazil was an agrarian country. Thereafter, during the process of modernisation and industrialisation, economic growth was probably the main, if not the sole factor responsible for the experiments in poverty reduction, which were few and definitely exceptional. Moreover, Brazilian development was responsible, in the second half of the twentieth century, for a series of socio-economic transformations in the country and the city. These include the disintegration of the social fabric, violence, and marginalisation. These policies led to a 'basic inequality', which was typical of the periphery of capitalism, where the most backward and most modern sectors coexist and create together a tragic complementary relationship.[48]

Inequality in Brazil began to be measured in the 1960s, when there was a remarkable concentration of income.[49] In the 1970s, particularly during the 'economic miracle', when GDP rose significantly, reaching 12 per cent per year, poverty was reduced by 50 per cent.[50] However, in the same period, inequality grew significantly, illustrating a typical Latin American circumstance in which increased wealth clearly favoured elites.

In the same period, the economic performance of some Asian countries was booming compared with growth in Latin American economies, but with much less concentration of income, which ultimately resulted in decreased inequality in some cases. There is evidence that the emphasis on high-quality basic education in these Asian countries, as well as policies directly or indirectly aimed at reducing poverty and inequality, contributed to stimulating economic growth, creating virtuous cycles in which growth and decline in

---

[45] B Stallings and R Studart, *Finance for Development: Latin America in Comparative Perspective* (Washington, Brookings Institution Press, 2006), 248–52.

[46] It is worth mentioning that between BNDES and other public actors, on one hand, and, on the other, the financing alternatives, there is no relation of predation (crowding out), in which the existence of each is only made possible by the exclusion of the other. Differently from this, BNDES, state sources and private mechanisms may pave a path of approximation (crowding in), in which the structuring of operations may have a sharing of sources. Not only can BNDES continue supporting market development by encouraging companies in its portfolio to carry out IPO operations in the stock market, but it can also split the financing of complex projects with private investors, thereby mitigating its costs and risks.

[47] Arbix and Martin, Beyond Developmentalism (n 37).

[48] Cf F de Oliveira, *Crítica à razão dualista/O ornitorrinco* (São Paulo, Editora Boitempo, 2003).

[49] AL Neri, *Miséria e a Nova Classe Média na Década da Desigualdade* (Rio de Janeiro, Centro de Políticas Sociais, Instituto Brasileiro de Economia, Fundação Getulio Vargas, 2008), available at www.fgv.br/cps/desigualdade/.

[50] R Paes de Barros, M Carvalho and S Franco, 'A importância da queda recente da desigualdade na redução da pobreza' (2007) *IPEA Texto para Discussão Número* 1256, 7.

inequality lead to subsequent increases in demand and supply for education, at the same time that lower levels of inequality favourably impacted growth.[51]

In Brazil, there was a further reduction in poverty levels in 1994. With monetary stabilisation, poverty declined by 10 per cent.[52] In the 1990s, the country's growth performance was low; although GDP had grown in the first two years after the introduction of the *Real* currency, the average growth rate between 1994 and 2000 of about 3 per cent was not significant. No decrease in inequality was seen during this period.

In the interval between 2001 and 2005, there was a further reduction in poverty levels in the country. This time, however, the cause was not economic growth, but a small, but significant and unprecedented, decrease in inequality. During this period, the Gini coefficient declined by 4.6 per cent and national income grew only 0.9 per cent per year on average. This means that, considering the modest growth, there was transfer of income in a progressive direction, that is, from the richest to the poorest. In other words, the rich 'lost' and the poor 'gained'. According to data from PNAD 2012 (National Survey through Sampling of Households), the downward trend in income inequality observed from 2001 continues, with the Gini coefficient having reached 0.519 in January 2012.

Chart 3 illustrates the decline in income inequality in the country between 1981 and 2009.

What we note is that since the early 2000s, after remaining almost stagnant for about 30 years, income inequality in Brazil has been gradually decreasing, having reached the lowest levels in recent history in 2012, despite still being very high. Policies such as increasing the minimum wage, rural pensions, inflation control, the Continued Provision (BPC) benefit, among others, have bolstered—in some cases significantly—this reduction, with the PBF as one of the flagship initiatives of this process.

The PBF is a conditional cash transfer (CCT) that benefits poor families with a monthly income per person of between R$70 and R$140. It offers four types of benefits: basic (R$68, paid to families considered extremely poor, with monthly incomes of up to R$70 per person, even if they do not have any children, teenagers or young adults), variable (R$22, paid to poor families with a monthly income of between R$70 and R$140 per person with children

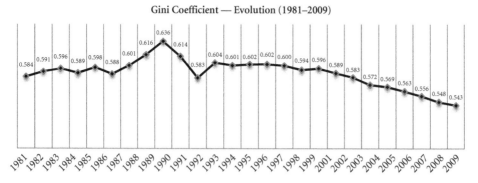

Chart 3. Gini Coefficient—Evolution

Source: IPEA data

[51] N Birdsall, R Sabot and D Ross, 'Inequality and Growth Reconsidered: Lessons from East Asia' (1995) 9 *The World Bank Economic Review* 477.

[52] S Rocha, 'Pobreza e Desigualdade no Brasil: o esgotamento dos efeitos distributivos do Plano Real' (2000) *IPEA Texto para Discussão Número 721*.

up to the age of 15, with each family eligible to receive up to three variable benefits), a variable benefit that depends on the number of teenagers in the household (R$33, paid to all PBF families who have adolescents aged 16 to 17 attending school, with each family eligible to receive up to two variable benefits addressed to the teen) and a variable benefit of extraordinary character, whose value is calculated on a case-by-case basis. To receive cash transfers, beneficiaries must meet some health and education requirements.

In terms of health, the families registered in PBF commit to vaccinating and monitoring the growth of children under seven. Women aged 14 to 44 years must also have medical monitoring, and, if they are pregnant or nursing, they should have prenatal testing and monitoring of their health and that of the child. In the area of education, all children and adolescents aged between six and 15 years must be enrolled in school and must have a minimum monthly attendance rate of 85 per cent. Students aged 16 and 17 years must have an attendance rate of at least 75 per cent.[53]

While CCTs are considered to be a Latin American innovation and have been adopted by various countries on different continents, we can say that PBF has certain characteristics that make it remarkable in the world of CCTs directed to the poorest. These distinctive elements of the PBF include its large scale, its decentralised management mechanism, the use of mechanisms to stimulate administrative performance of the cities that participate in it, its role as an 'integrative social policy'[54] and the fact that it can be described as a 'natural innovation laboratory'.[55]

PBF is believed to have changed the tradition of Brazilian social policies in establishing itself as the leading Brazilian programme for poverty reduction. It differs, therefore, less by being a CCT and more by 'monopolizing policy directed at the poor in a country that has one of the broadest, institutionalized and bureaucratized social welfare policies directed at this population'.[56]

From a legal point of view, *Bolsa Família* is marked by legal and institutional arrangements allowing for the use of incentives for federal-state coordination, the use of behaviour-inducing sanctions, the use of coordination mechanisms based on performance, as well as different types of legal rules whose instrumentation strikes a balance between flexibility (for adjustments, corrections and incorporation of learning arising from the implementation) and stability.[57]

---

[53] In addition, children and adolescents aged up to 15 at risk or taken from child labour should participate in the Services for Strengthening Bonds and Daily Relationships of PETI (Program for the Eradication of Child Labour) and have an attendance rate of at least 85%.

[54] Francesca Bastagli argues that CCTs can be combined with other policies in the field of social assistance for the purposes of transforming fragmented arrangements into inclusive social policy systems. See F Bastagli, 'From Social Safety Net to Social Policy? The Role of Conditional Cash Transfers in Welfare State Development in Latin America' (2009) *International Center for Inclusive Growth (IPC) Working Paper 60*, 2.

[55] K Lindert, A Linder and B de la Briére, 'The Nuts and Bolts of Brazil's Bolsa Família Program: Implementing Conditional Cash Transfers in Decentralized Context' (2007) *Social Protection World Bank Paper 0709*, 2.

[56] SM Draibe, 'Brasil: Bolsa Escola y Bolsa Família' in E Cohen and R Franco (eds), *Tranferencias con corresponsabilidad. Una mirada latinoamericana* (Mexico, Flacso, 2006), 137–78.

[57] *Cf* DR Coutinho, 'O Direito nas Políticas Sociais Brasileiras: um Estudo do Programa Bolsa Família' in DM Trubek and M Schapiro (eds) *Direito e Desenvolvimento: um diálogo entre os BRICS* (São Paulo, Editora Saraiva, 2012).

IV. Functions of Economic Law in the New State Activism: Selective Performance

The earlier sections provided a descriptive analysis of the relations that existed between several different contexts of political economy and the role played by economic law in mediating the relations between the state and the Brazilian market. Therefore, depending on the focal point of the political economy arrangement, the functions exercised by the institutional arrangement and by the legal tools of economic regulation exhibited a set profile. As can be seen, in the context of the policies that were centred on the state, both the arrangements and the tools strengthened economic state allocations and allowed the economy to be directed predominantly by the governmental agencies. In contrast, in the moderate neoliberal period, this standard was different, that is, new arrangements and tools favouring private economic allocations and a market-friendly regulatory intervention gained predominance. This section, in turn, adopts the distinct presupposition of political economy and seeks to construct a normative argument concerning the role of economic law.

With regard to political economy, we understand that no static role has been defined for the state or for the market as vehicles of developmental strategy in this third scenario. Moreover, developmental strategies in Brazil driven by the state began to be drawn up and implemented under the aegis of a democratic political order beginning in 1988. Based on greater hybridisation, we are therefore dealing with an arrangement in which we can observe an uncommon coexistence between the renewed activism of the state, the preservation of private forces as relevant players and the empowerment of civil society and of the democratic spaces of participation and power control. According to this diagnosis, the final part of this text seeks to develop an exploratory argument (to be further tested empirically) that strives to answer the following question: what roles should economic law perform in this peculiar and hybrid arrangement of political economics?

As we have seen, having been summoned to play several key roles in different stages of Brazilian development, economic law suffers pressures and demands in ways we believe to be especially challenging in the context of the new state activism. The performance of the Brazilian state in this context has demanded economic law that selectively takes on varied functions that do not perfectly fit the classic dichotomies of market or state, public or private, nationalisation or privatisation, monopoly or competition. We also argue that, besides being selective, the functions performed by the framework of economic law in this new scenario must, much more than before, ensure the coordination and articulation of public policies and public–private relationships, as well as address the challenge of providing legitimacy to government initiatives, given the plural political context in which these actions occur.[58] In this sense, in our view there are three complex functions to be performed by economic law in the resumption of Brazilian state activism, namely: (i) enable *selectivity*, which reflects potential strategic intervention by the state; (ii) ensure *legitimacy*,

---

[58] We present a separate, but complementary discussion, about the functions of law in the new Brazilian state activism, see Trubek, Coutinho and Schapiro, 'New State Activism in Brazil' (n 25). In this work we use the term functionalities to refer to the following ideas: safeguarding flexibility, stimulating orchestration, framing synergy and ensuring legitimacy.

which is related to the democratic element of this activism; and (iii) forge *institutional governance*, which corresponds to the tasks of planning, administrative coordination and design of public policy actions.

A. Selectivity

The idea of selectivity, which according to our argument should guide the regulatory actions of the state toward developmental policies, presupposes the hybridisation of the political economy aforementioned. Bearing in mind that the dichotomies between the state and the market in contemporary Brazil are no longer enough to guide the vector of economic policy action, the consistency of these policies becomes less dependent on an a priori alignment (favouring the state or the market) and more dependent on a pragmatic definition requiring adjustment and gauging between the type of action needed and the needs and peculiarities of each case. Therefore, given the combined role of the state and the market as relevant agents of development, interventionist policies gain greater vigour the more they draw away from predetermined menus (tool kits) and the more customised their answers are to the specificities of the various economic segments.

Public policy actions and initiatives that characterise the new state activism combine command and control and inducement, planning and free enterprise, discretion and control, punishment, reward, flexibility and stability of rules, public spending, state companies and private investment. Thus, the new patterns of economic law illustrate the Brazilian state's incipient ability to selectively face complex, case-by-case circumstances for which dichotomous explanations based on the pairs listed above are not satisfactory as criteria for analysis and description of the legal reality in the new state activism.

In this scenario, there is an increasing demand for economic law to both create *and* regulate markets, as well as to perform or induce investments in crucial fields such as infrastructure, social welfare and innovation. Accordingly, this requires the simultaneous use of legal tools that are no longer seen as exclusive or incompatible with each other. Thus, the third moment's economic law is largely about selectively designing and managing strategic and systemic planning, regulation, antitrust, privatisation,[59] the various forms of concession and public–private contracts, and as coordination and institutional coordination mechanisms in the management, and governance of public policies.[60]

In short, in the new state activism, it is assumed that the very characteristics of each public policy in its specific sector or segment of the economy at any given time determine which particular legal solutions are to be forged, as opposed to a nationalising/privatising preconception of what the role of the state in the economy should be. As a result, economic law scholarship seems to be more and more challenged to renew itself in its task of

---

[59] It is worth noting that only in exceptional cases (usually the unsuccessful ones) does privatisation make the state 'smaller'. In most successful experiences observed, there is a selective combination, both stable and flexible, of legal and institutional arrangements by which public ownership is replaced and/or combined with the governance of contracts, a robust regulatory apparatus, and the ability to plan and induce investment in important sectors in view of their characteristics and specificities (and not based on abstract formulas). This demands, without paradox, a significant institutional investment in public management expertise, training, an intersectoral approach, coordination, autonomy, participation, accountability and social control of state action.

[60] *Cf* DR Coutinho, 'O Direito nas Políticas Públicas' in E Marques and CAP de Faria, *As Políticas Públicas como Campo Multidisciplinar* (São Paulo, Editora Unesp e Editora Fiocruz, 2013).

providing means for a functional analysis of law, which in turn potentially places it in a privileged position in its complex and multidimensional relationship with the economy.

This is the case of the new industrial policies and those policies designed to combat poverty and inequality. In both cases, what is seen is a selective combination of instruments typical of public law—economic, administrative, tax, financial and environmental—with unusual private tools and rationales in this field. Examples include the use of incentives, conditionalities, inducement-based rewards (in the field of social policies), or the use of mechanisms typical of corporate law, such as venture capital arrangements, to ensure implementation of industrial policies.[61] In this context, the new law on state activism produces innovations within both institutional and normative frameworks to serve more complex political economy goals and, to do so, combines new tools with existing, known legal instruments.

Other examples of this are the challenges that the Brazilian institutional and legal apparatus currently faces regarding promoting immense urgent private infrastructure investments and, at the same time, managing concessions and procurement agreements without losing its ability to ensure systemic planning, integration, universal service and antitrust enforcement, as well as addressing demanding calls to employ legal means to combine the technological upgrading of industrial policies with applicable WTO regulations, or state-owned enterprises with regulatory agencies and modern corporate governance regimes, or conventional administrative law procedures and routines with flexible, revisable and accountable practices.

B. Legitimacy

Describing the challenge of economic law in ensuring the legitimacy of public policies means assuming that, in such programmes, decisions should be made not only on the most sound basis possible, through a coherent and documented argument with open public scrutiny, but also having ensured the participation of stakeholders in the shaping, implementation and evaluation of the policy. In other words, law can provide policies with mechanisms of deliberation, participation, consultation, collaboration and joint decision-making, thereby ensuring that they are permeable to, rather than insulated against, participation.[62] In the same way, law can make agents and processes more discretionary or bound by standards set by law.

Therefore, in a democracy, economic law can be seen as having the central role of ensuring that policies include mechanisms for participation and accountability. That is, legal rules may lead public policies to be more democratic since, through procedural rules that govern public consultations and hearings, and through the publicity of administrative acts, these rules compel public policies to be open to the demands of a plurality of actors, including the least organised and economically powerful. The framework of economic

---

[61] For a description of the legal mechanisms of contracts in industrial policy, see MG Schapiro, 'Rediscovering the Developmental Path: Development Bank, Law, and Innovation Financing in the Brazilian Economy' in Trubek, Garcia, Coutinho and Santos, *Law and the New Developmental State* (n 25). On the roles of law in the *Bolsa Família* Programme, see DR Coutinho, 'Decentralization and Coordination in Social Law and Policy: The *Bolsa Família* Program' in Trubek, Garcia, Coutinho and Santos (n 25).

[62] Coutinho, 'O Direito nas Políticas Públicas' (n 60).

law is also more or less capable of stimulating the mobilisation of actors who would not otherwise engage in monitoring and evaluating public action programmes. Seen in this way, economic law could be comparable to a kind of transmission belt through which society's demands, schedules, ideas and proposals, to a greater or lesser degree, circulate and vie for space in technocratic circles.[63]

In particular, the agenda for policy implementation becomes significant and gains attention: instead of looking for ways to prevent discretion and limit the regulatory capacity, it seeks to understand them as effective tools to increase the intensity of social control and accountability. In this scenario, economic law in the new activist state begins, in short, to aim for the best possible combination of effectiveness and legitimacy—or, to use other terminology,[64] of political and technical-administrative skills.[65] Examples of these challenges are salient in the field of industrial, monetary, fiscal and regulatory polices, as well as in regulatory action. Brazilian institutions such as the BC, BNDES, the Supreme Court, ministries, independent agencies and supervising bodies lack more wide and sophisticated transparency and participatory channels in the country.

C. Institutional Governance

Scholars dedicated to the topic of economic development are prone to say, as a kind of mantra, 'institutions definitely matter'.[66] Consequently, debates and controversies about institutional reform and improvement increasingly focus on the field of means, that is, the study of the forms and mechanisms by which functional institutional arrangements can be produced or reproduced.

In this scenario, the empirical studies conducted, almost always by economists, often seek to describe cases of success and failure and, therefore, to identify and analyse patterns, regularities, innovations and institutional variables. These studies have also strived to create frameworks and analytical methods that can be replicated, within certain limits, in other contexts and circumstances.

But if, undeniably, development depends on good policy decisions, it can be said that it is also, to a large extent, the result of consistent institutional arrangements. Paradoxically, the legal framework, even when identified as a relevant variable in the construction of formal institutions, is rarely scrutinised and studied in Brazil with sufficient in-depth analytical and methodological consistency (nor is this analysis usually performed by researchers from the legal field). As a result, few case studies and little empirical research aim at understanding the means by which the law can (directly and indirectly) both strengthen and catalyse, as well as weaken and paralyse institutions, development processes and policy.

---

[63] On accountability and industrial policies, see Schapiro, 'O que a política industrial pode aprender com a política monetária?' (n 30).

[64] Gomide and Pires, 'Capacidades Estatais para o Desenvolvimento no Século XXI' (n 41).

[65] This agenda is developed, at the time of writing, under the project Strengthening Legal Capacity for National Development, an IPEA initiative, of which we are part. Using case studies, policy and technical-administrative skills in different, concrete public policy initiatives are observed, described and discussed and findings are subsequently published.

[66] This item is in part based on DR Coutinho, 'O Direito no Desenvolvimento Econômico' (2012) 38 *Revista Brasileira de Direito Público* 22.

In the new state activism, understanding economic law as a component of the institutional governance of development policies and actions is to assume that legal rules and institutions structure their operation, regulate their procedures and are responsible for ensuring articulation of the roles of actors directly and indirectly linked to such policies. Attributes of the institutional design of public policies—such as their degree of decentralisation, planning, autonomy and intersectoral coordination and the types of public and public–private relationships they give rise to, as well as their integration with other programmes somehow depend, in summary, on the consistency of the legal framework that holds them together.

V. Conclusion

In this paper we have presented what we consider to be some of the contemporary challenges of economic law in the context of the emergence of a new state activism in Brazil. To do so, we explored different moments of political economy and the main formats of economic law in each of these periods. We described the contours, still relatively tenuous, of the activism and institutional arrangements that the new state activism has demanded and produced. We set forth the argument that economic law is challenged in Brazil to perform functions that were unfamiliar to it both in the period of import substitution and that of the neo-liberal 1990s. In so doing, we adopted a perspective that seeks to consider the role economic law plays in public policy implementation. Thus we explored, in the course of an ongoing research agenda, the dimensions of selectivity, legitimacy and institutional governance as a way to synthesise challenges facing economic law, which is an essential component of national development.

As seen, in the new state activism economic law is strongly linked to the challenging task of promoting the functionality of institutions according to their specific goals.[67] This role has become central in the context of selective state action, in which the governance and effectiveness of public actions are key.[68] This role is also a result of the democratic context in which state activism is established, that is, this context gives rise to the challenge of governing institutional reforms and building arrangements that are cost effective and politically responsive. The task of governance, therefore, involves having the institutional imagination to map problems and normatively formulate new institutional architectures.

Therefore, case studies in which more or less functional legal arrangements are observed may be useful, that is, in cases of success or failure in which the elements of coordination, articulation and definition of institutional roles are analysed from the legal point of view—hence the relevance of more empirical and cross-disciplinary analyses, which are capable of forging skills for this role, allowing lawyers to acquire the ability to capture the real and

---

[67] FK Comparato, 'O Indispensável Direito Econômico' (1965) 353 *Revista dos Tribunais* 26.

[68] As Fábio Nusdeo recalls, to carry out this task well, economic law must encompass politics and economics and, more specifically, of the confluence of the two in forming economic policy. See F Nusdeo, 'O Direito Econômico Centenário' (2012) 1 *Revista Fórum de Direito Financeiro e Econômico* 234. Also on the challenges of contemporary economic law, *cf* HM Huck, 'Discurso de posse como Professor Titular de Direito Econômico-Financeiro da Faculdade de Direito da Universidade de São Paulo' (1998) 93 *Revista da Faculdade de Direito da Universidade de São Paulo* 504.

dynamic functioning of public policy initiatives, as well as to formulate agendas of reform and institutional transformations.[69]

Brazilian scholars (and thus students) nonetheless remain excessively attached to formalistic, doctrinal and static approaches to economic law. As a result, the institutional lenses through which legal arrangements are designed to render polices functional have been neglected, and, practically speaking, this has lead to all sorts of institutional defects: unnecessary rivalries, disputes, gaps, duplications, disharmonies, and resource waste.

Understanding and describing conceptual and research challenges, and, above all, facing them, is a highly complex task that, from the viewpoint of economic law scholars, demands of lawyers interested in economic law a capacity for applied and self-conscious analysis of concrete phenomena.[70] That is, it requires management of empirical methods and analytical approaches aimed at understanding what law 'does' in economic development policies, or, to paraphrase David Trubek, seek to identify 'where the action is'.[71] We very much hope that such an agenda also flourishes in Brazil.

---

[69] Some of these case studies related to legal institutional arrangements are present in Trubek, Coutinho and Schapiro, 'New State Activism in Brazil' (n 25). Other examples are: R Pires, 'Promoting Sustainable Compliance: Styles of Labour Inspection and Compliance Outcomes in Brazil' (2008) 147 *International Labour Review* 1999; AC da Matta Chasin and MM Prado, 'How Innovative was the Poupatempo Experience in Brazil? Institutional Bypass as a New Form of Institutional Change' (2011) 5 *Brazilian Political Science Review* 11; MG Schapiro, 'Development Bank, Law and Innovation Financing in a New Brazilian Economy', submission to *Law and Development Review Manuscript* 1045 (2010) and GC Shaffer, MR Sanchez and B Rosenberg, 'The Trials of Winning at the WTO: What Lies Behind Brazil's Success' (2008) 41 *Cornell International Law Journal* 383.

[70] 'Law and development is an idea that defines a practice and shapes action', explains Trubek. While development goals may be different (eg speed up economic growth, preserve the environment, promote democracy or protect human rights, encourage technical and technological innovation, gains in international trade or reduction of poverty and inequality), '[t]he practice is the *self-conscious* effort to change law and legal institutions to achieve some goal' (emphasis added). DM Trubek, 'The Owl and the Pussy-cat: Is There a Future for Law and Development?' (2007) 25 *Wisconsin International Law Journal* 235, 235.

[71] DM Trubek, 'Where the Action Is: Critical Legal Studies and Empiricism' (1984) 36 *Stanford Law Review* 575.

Part II

Transformations in Global Governance

5

Law and the Political Economy of the World

DAVID KENNEDY*

I. Introduction: Understanding the Big Picture: Global Political Economy

The visible interpenetration of global political and economic life has changed the context for international scholarly inquiry. The central questions today are not political questions—if by that we mean questions to be addressed by governments acting alone or negotiated through conventional diplomatic circuits. They are not economic questions—if by that we mean questions to be answered by the operations of markets, guided by the hand of robust competition in the shadow of regulation. Nor are they questions about the appropriate relationship *between* politics and economics, such as how public power might harness the economy through regulation, or how economic activity might best be supported by and freed from the public hand.

The distribution of growth has displaced ideological hegemony and great power competition as the framework for global political struggle. The global distribution of opportunities to generate and retain rents from economic activity has replaced the question of whether private competition will be liberated from or defeated by the interstate competition in the global economy. How gains and losses will be distributed between those who lead and those who lag and how the struggle between winners and losers will be carried out are questions best addressed by thinking of politics and economics as intertwined projects and close collaborators in the distribution of political authority and economic reward. The answer to these classic questions of political economy will be a function of the interactions among people across the world with diverse powers and vulnerabilities arising from diverse political and economic arrangements. Understanding these dynamics requires analysis of the iterative micro and macro processes through which conflict takes place, whether we think of that conflict initially as 'economic competition' or 'political struggle'.

The intellectual foundations for the return of political economy to academic life have been laid. The demand to understand questions of political economy has challenged the

* This essay summarises and extends a series of studies I have undertaken in the fields of international law, international economic law, comparative law, European law, the law of war and the law of economic development available on my website at www.law.harvard.edu/faculty/dkennedy/publications/. I cite here only works developing examples which I highlight here and which were not cited in those prior studies. Versions of this essay were delivered at the American University of Cairo, 19 February 2012, at King's College, London, 19 April 2012, and at Sciences Po Law School, Paris, 11 May 2012. The article was published in (2013) 26 *Leiden Journal of International Law*.

most robust analytic models in economics and political science to make endogenous social, cultural and institutional factors. Economists are reaching out to understand the institutional, social, psychological and political arrangements which undergird global economic life. Scholars in sociology, political science and international relations have renewed their interest in the impact of international economic arrangements on local, national and global politics. Heterogeneous traditions in social theory, economic and legal scholarship have opened a window on the politics embedded in the basic operations of economic life; the interrelated nature of political and economic life in a world of global markets and local government; the mechanisms by which inequalities between leading and lagging sectors, nations and regions are reproduced; and the modes through which 'governance', whether local, national or global, all too often operates as an unsatisfying cover for economic dominance and political dysfunction. Heterogeneous traditions in law have uncovered the institutional roots of the global economy and polity in local and private rules with transnational effect, in informal networks and professional practice, and in the dispersed regulatory and administrative regimes of many nations and localities. They have identified the glue which binds the global economy together and the institutional forms and practices which fragment, professionalise and disempower our politics.

It is now clear that the elements of economic life—capital, labour, credit, money, liquidity—are creatures of law. The same can be said for the elements of political life—power and right. Law not only *regulates* these things, it creates them. The history of political and economic life is therefore also a history of institutions and laws. Law constitutes the actors, places them in structures, and helps set the terms for their interaction. It often provides the language—and the stakes—for economic and political struggle. As a result, legal arrangements offer a privileged window onto political economic dynamics. Academic inquiry ought to be able to trace the micro- and macro-processes through which people struggle over economic benefits and political authority in their legal entitlements and vulnerabilities. Legal analysis of this type could illuminate the large-scale political economic changes that are upending our world and their roots in the quotidian exercise of entitlements and capabilities in the capillaries of society.

With understanding may come proposals for reform. Economies configured differently will operate differently, just as different allocations of legal capacities and authority will generate divergent polities. By tracing the impact of legal forms on the economic and political actors and activities they constitute, scholars should be able to identify choices among different political and economic trajectories. It should be possible to identify alternative, even equally efficient or democratic, modes of economic and political life with diverging patterns of inequality, alternate distributions of political power and economic benefit and more or less space for experimentation or contestation.

Nevertheless, surprisingly little scholarship in the international legal field aims to illuminate the global distribution of political authority and economic growth. It is hard to say exactly why. Much legal scholarship remains parochial, enthralled by the details of each national legal system's totemic institutions. Taken together, these institutions also structure the world's political economic order, but it is rare to trace their impact on the micro-dynamics of global economic and political interactions, let alone propose their transformation in the name of an alternate global political economic vision. The legitimation of existing institutional arrangements is repeated at the international level, where central banks, the EU, the WTO—even the United Nations—have become objects of a cult-like veneration among the academics who study their operation, no less than the modern corporate form or the various institutions facilitating investment. They simply *must be* honoured, appeased and defended. This academic tendency has parallels in popular wisdom. In the United States, for example, an enormous majority can view the government as a dysfunctional part of the problem without anyone seriously proposing to alter anything about it. The government is crazy—the constitution is sacred.

At the same time, the technical professional conventions governing scholarly production in the legal field discourage pronouncements about the large trends in global political and economic life. The trending legal scholarship is small bore precision analytics, refining and refurbishing the existing lexicons of policy, doctrine and theory. In my view, scholars should not shy away from developing macro-scale pictures of global political economy, if only because thinking about more technical matters often rests on broad convictions about the nature of the world which no longer hold. Take the distinction between 'advanced' and 'developing' economies. Many routine ideas about institutional forms and regulatory arrangements rest on an idea about the 'kind' of society people are talking about—one which is at the cutting edge of history, where economic and political arrangements are 'mature' and most things work, or one which still has 'a long way to go' and is plagued by anomalies. Were this frame to change, much would need to be rethought. And yet it would be more accurate today to start from the premise that all economies, including the world economy, are developing economies.

In this, a fundamental neo-liberal insight was correct: just as the ideological fault line between the first and second world no longer defines global political struggle, the economic fault line between an 'underdeveloped' third world and a 'modern indus-trialised' first world no longer defines global economic relations. Not, however, because liberal democratic politics has become the global default or because the management of routine business cycles in deregulated markets has become the universal national economic challenge—quite the contrary. The diversity of political arrangements has increased. All countries have political characteristics once routinely thought anoma-lous and there is no one 'normal' or mature form for political life. Stable and sig-nificant political regimes come in many varieties—more or less authoritarian, more or less religious, more or less decentralised, more and less technocratic and with different blends of public and private economic power. Few could be said to work well when it comes to addressing large-scale issues of political economy and the dis-tribution of growth. It is not simply that the state has been 'unbundled' or political power 'networked' across boundaries. Politics has everywhere become a diminished shadow of economics as political institutions and elites have been instrumentalised by economic interests. It is not surprising that they find themselves deadlocked—or simply disengaged—when it comes to addressing issues 'in the public interest'.

At the same time, the economic challenges characteristic of the 'developing world' have become common across the industrialised world. All economies face strategic choices between different modes of insertion in the global economy, confront challenges of inequality and structural dualism, find their economies riven with market failures, infor-mation and public goods problems for which they lack instruments to respond, and find themselves talking about new strategies for growth rather than the efficient management of a relatively stable business cycle. In short, the difference between the first and third worlds has eroded because all nations now face political, social and economic challenges once typical of the third world.

A portrait of the political economy of the contemporary world might begin with the observation that across the world, political authority is weaker and more dispersed, and economic flows more varied. The fragmentation and dispersion of political authority has rendered economic life vulnerable to political risks from unanticipated quarters while the forces unleashed by the globalisation of economic life batter political elites from every-where and nowhere at once. This has transformed the arrangement of centres, peripheries and semi-peripheries from the age of colonialism or the cold war. Focus on the 'rise of Asia' or the emergence of a 'multi-polar' world can make it seem that structural inequality has fallen with the demise of a world system of centre and periphery. Nothing could be further from the truth. Economic and political bargaining power remains unevenly distributed—but not along a single axis.

The dispersion of political and economic forces has ignited a rapid global process of factor-price equalisation and technological assimilation among what once seemed the centre and the periphery of the world system. The last two centuries were an aberration as one nation and then a small group of nations rose to unprecedented levels of relative prosperity and political influence in the wake of the industrial revolution. The relative hegemony of a North Atlantic political and economic centre was reinforced for a long time by everything from military power to the structure of the novel, from multinational industrial monopolies to Hollywood movies. This hegemony has been abruptly eroded as the scientific technolo-gies, management institutions and governance arrangements which enabled the dramatic rise of the North Atlantic have become widespread and people everywhere have become able to aspire to a refrigerator, an air conditioner, a car and the government necessary to realise those ambitions.

But economic and political change on this scale is profoundly destructive and rela-tive income equalisation is an extremely uneven business. It certainly does not mean the elimination of income differentials. On the contrary, inequality is everywhere. A global economy is not a uniform economy. Things turn at different speeds. People are left out. People are dragged down. When people turn to their sovereigns for help, the results are terribly uneven. Some are too big to fail—others too small to count. Indeed, the public hand everywhere has become a force multiplier for leading sectors, nations and regions—as it was between nations in the colonial era. As growth here erodes incomes there and consolidates itself as political right, a proliferation of centre-periphery dynam-ics become visible. As a result, the global political economy today rests on an accelerating social and economic dualism between leading and lagging sectors, economies, nations and populations. It is not surprising that we face a revolution of rising frustrations among the hundreds of millions who can see in, but for whom there seems no route through the screen except rebellion and spectacle. Or that we face the restive demoralisation of all those whose incomes, economic opportunities and expectations have fallen—and will probably continue to fall.

The political responses everywhere aim to protect and promote winners, sometimes with a vague promise of transfer payments to compensate losers. But the political challenge is not to find resources to pour on the winners in the hopes they will render our 'nation' competitive. Nations are no longer competing—and winners can usually take care of themselves. In a global economy, it is simply not possible for every nation to be the highest tech, greenest, most innovation-driven knowledge economy, any more than every nation can be the lowest wage manufacturer. These are niche market dreams that function as jus-tifications for mobilising resources behind the successful. They serve to defer rather than underwrite the promise to compensate. The wild horse to be ridden now is the dynamic of dualism between sectors, regions, industries—and nations. The political and economic objective ought to be productively *linking* those who lead with those who lag in reciprocal and virtuous cycles, rather than encouraging growth here to impoverish there in the hopes that one day the losers may be made whole.

In this essay, I encourage legal scholars to improve their ability to speak about the role of law in this kind of large scale re-ordering of political and economic life. I start with the intuition that law has played a central role in two grand, mutually supportive projects which have brought global political economy to this unfortunate point. In the first section, I sketch these two projects. On the one hand, economics has everywhere been disentangled from politics and economic life dis-embedded from political contestation. On the other hand, both economics and politics have been technically consolidated either within or across national boundaries. Both projects have reflected the broad ideological commitments of the policy class and both were carried out as legal and institutional undertakings, supported by the knowledge practices of dedicated professionals. Together they have generated the conditions—the agents and the structures—for a world political economy marked by an accelerating dualism between the regions, sectors and classes to whom much—and little—has been given. My hope is that international legal scholars will develop the intellectual tools to help understand and unravel these dynamics.

As a step in that direction, I propose that legal scholars revitalise two intellectual traditions: the analysis of relations between 'centres' and 'peripheries' in socio-economic systems and analysis of the role of law in the background distribution of bargaining power within such systems. In the second section of this essay, I describe how these intellectual traditions might help clarify the distribution of power and economic opportunity in what might otherwise seem a diffuse jumble of institutional and regulatory structures framing the chaotic operations of political and economic life after globalisation. My claim is that reflection on the role of law in the dynamic relationship between centres and peripheries will focus attention on the crucial questions of global political economy: the dynamics of inequality; the distributions of growth; and the reproduction of hierarchies within and between leading and lagging sectors, regions, nations and cultures. Taken together, strands from these intellectual traditions—heterogenous, institutionalist, realist, critical, sociological, post-modernist, post-Marxist, progressive—offer tools for identifying the political arrangements, discourses, institutions and debates that structure or disrupt those dynamics, and highlighting the role of expertise in rendering them normal, carrying them out—or enabling their contestation and transformation. In the third section, I assess the potential for scholarly work in the field of international law to draw on these traditions to understand and help to remake the political economy of the world.

II. The Grand Political Economic Projects that Brought us Here

A. Insulate Economic Activity from Political Contestation

The first project—the separation of economic activity from political contestation—has its roots in the effort to pursue economics and politics on different scales. The economy has become global while political order remains lashed to local and territorial government structures. The result is a rupture between a local and national politics on the one hand,

and a global economy and society on the other. It is the relative mobility of economics and territorial rigidity of politics that has rendered each unstable. Political and economic leadership have drifted apart. A spiral has begun—as the winners lock in an ever weaker territorial politics and an ever more dominant economic order. Political leadership has everywhere become peripheral to economic management.

The machinery for a territorial politics and a de-territorialised economics is technical and legal. Economic activity can only happen on a global scale if the institutional arrangements are in place to support it, just as political activity can only be concentrated territorially if the institutions responsible for political life have distinct jurisdictions. At a most primitive level, private rights, understood to lie outside or before politics, travel easily—if you own something here, you own it when you get off the plane somewhere else. Public policies, the stuff of politics, do not travel, except as necessary to support the broader market. Political institutions have the legal authority to enforce private agreements and private rights established elsewhere but they cannot regulate beyond their borders. Although your labour law may affect the economy of your neighbour, your writ does not run in your neighbour's jurisdiction. The technical distinction between exercises of public authority which *support* the market and those which regulate or otherwise *distort* the market is crucial—the one travels more easily than the other. As this distinction is interpreted and implemented across dozens of institutional settings, a professional sensibility or common sense emerges about the substantive and territorial limits of public power and about the scale and naturalness of economic flows.

As a political ruler operating in the shadow of this consensus you are a spectator as the waves set in motion by your local actions ripple across the global economy. Your interests, constituencies and authority are defined by a series of distinctions managed and enforced by the ongoing work of various expert votaries who interpret your mandate and explicate the force of legalised economic interests. As a result, the *global* nature of 'problems' and the *local* nature of 'government', whether linked to a city, a state or to the international order itself, is not only a troubling fact to be overcome. It is the product of a very particular political economy written into a historically specific set of legal and institutional arrangements. It generates, in turn, modes of political and economic life which pull away from one another—a self-confident and technical form of global economic management detached from the locations or modes of production, and a media-centred form of political discussion disconnected from the technical management of government, pursued in part as gladiatorial spectacle and in part as an allegorical morality tale. Meanwhile, in the background, government has become technical by division of competences, authorities and mandates, while economics has grown technical by consolidation in ever more rapidly interlinked and speculative markets.

The rift between economics and politics is not simply the result of an ideological commitment to their distinctiveness—a kind of 'neo-liberal' overreach. Popular discourse has been full of voices for and against a laissez-faire separation of politics from economic life for more than a century. Although the professionals who build and manage the political economy of today's world sometimes argue in such hyperbolic terms, when it comes to the details where the rubber meets the road, their differences are minor. At least privately, most easily acknowledge the interpenetration of politics and economics, the unavoidable need for economic regulation and the importance of political leadership for sound economic policy. The roots for the rift between local politics and global economics lie deeper in the dynamic consequences of those everyday details and will require more to reverse than an ideological conversion.

The professional vernaculars through which the political economic order is managed are not based on a sharp conceptual boundary between politics and economics. Economics and politics are not powers absolute within delimited spheres, defined in a kind of global constitutional settlement and managed by the interpretation of formal distinctions and boundaries. Although people sometimes imagine them this way, just as it is common to imagine sharp distinctions between property entitlements—your land/my land—or political jurisdictions and competences, this is not accurate. Individual political and economic 'rights', even to property, rarely work in this kind of on–off way. The relationship between you and me is all about what each of us can do with our land that may affect the other, about the terms of our relationship rather than the demarcation of our difference. When managed by jurists or policy professionals, those terms are detailed matters of more or less, determined by the balancing of competing interests and objectives.

In the professional communities where economics and politics are carried out, this is also widely understood. Just as experts know that private right and public power blend into one another in many ways, they also know that politics can be hard to distinguish from economics in any categorical sense. The practical differences between them are produced almost as a by-product of the routine professional making—and unmaking—of an infinite series of small-scale technical distinctions which can be experienced by the experts who interpret them as matters for subtle balancing rather than sharp line drawing: between public and private, national and international, family and market; between regulations which support the market and those which distort market prices; or between acts of the state which enforce private rights and those which burden them with regulation.

Such distinctions may not, in the end, be logically or philosophically satisfying, but they often work in practice, at least sufficiently so that experts may find professionally satisfactory ways of distinguishing situations that seem to go 'too far' in any one direction. As those who manage the institutions of political economic life repeatedly find ways to draw the line in specific situations, professional traditions emerge devoted to each domain. International private law experts think differently than those focused on transnational regulation. The professions responsible for the management of public and private law, or of market-making and market regulating, have grown apart, coming to occupy different institutional sites and to speak about the world in divergent vernaculars. Over time, the divergent styles of technical interpretation in different disciplines harden the differences between domains that no one thinks distinct.

The same can be said on a larger scale of the difference between economics and politics. In some sense, the relationship between politics and economics is simply a matter of interpretation and perspective. The smallest market transaction—a T-shirt sells in Ghana—can be interpreted to illuminate the politics or the economics of the planet. Yet alternative disciplines and institutional arrangements have sprung up to reflect divergent interpretations of this same transaction. As politics and economics have become increasingly technical, they have come to be served by distinct professions operating on different scales and with different perspectives. Economists and politicians understand the scale and 'logic' of the transaction differently and embed it in a different social, institutional and intellectual context. Their differences emerge as different styles of analysis, different default interpretations and background assumptions. As they pursue their routine work, an intellectually unsatisfying distinction develops into a startling mismatch between institutional, intellectual, social and professional domains. As a consequence, the fault line between politics and economics cannot be undone by legal fiat any more than by ideological reversal. The trick is to understand the rift between politics and economics as a project undertaken everywhere at once by professionals and experts who are simply doing their job, interpreting their competences and pursuing their interests. Only by bending the arc of their routine work will the political economy of the world be transformed.

B. Consolidate both Economics and Politics as Technically Integrated Fields for Professional Management

The second grand project—the technical integration and consolidation of both economics and politics—has also been accomplished through a series of legal, institutional and professional projects. They have been undertaken in the shadow of a loose consensus within the global policy class about the natural teleologies for economic and political life. The economic idea is simple. Although it is common to think of an 'economy' as something nations have—the German economy, the Japanese economy—at least for those who aspire to manage it through policy, to the extent people have also come to think of an economy as a 'market', it is difficult not to also think of an economy as something that can be scaled up or down. And to think that scaling up is generally good. Ever more people, products, resources and ideas ought to be able to find their markets in the shadow of a common price system across ever greater distances. As a result, when putting an economy together, it is a good idea to try to link as many things together as efficiently as possible at the national, regional and global levels. This has always been more idea than reality. Despite the prevalence of local and sectoral specificities, informal networks, oligopolies, barter, intra-enterprise trade, market failures, bottlenecks and other anomalies, it is part of the background consciousness of ruling classes everywhere that fundamentally, the economy is becoming an ever more undifferentiated global market in which 'flows' of goods and services follow prices to more productive uses.

This idea has had dozens of practical and technical corollaries. A system of 'world prices' requires all kinds of institutional arrangements and limitations. Exchange rates must either be stable—effectively a single currency—or so fluid as to ensure they are pushed to parity by market forces. Supply chains, information channels, labour markets and investment patterns ought all to be rendered global through institutional and legal integration. Private actors—investors, employees, managers, corporations—need to understand themselves as capacitated to operate across an ever larger terrain. To do so, they need to be legally disembedded from the kinds of local customary or regulatory arrangements that once made employers feel they must hire from among the members of a particular union, or corporations feel they must respond to the public interest of specific locations or constituencies. Economic entities themselves need to be reconstituted and unbundled, rendered capable of being re-organised, reframed and parcelled out for sale and redeployment. Where regulation or contract impose artificial obstacles to the vertiginous destruction and creative reinvention of economic relations, they need to be unwound. Transnational private legal arrangements and informal standards need to be protected from the regulatory interference of local political and judicial authorities. Territorially enforced public policy which distorts rather than supports market prices needs to be either eliminated or harmonised as part of a stable background for global market transactions. Although there is much media discussion of national economic policy, most of the work of economic management in fact consists of small-scale projects to fine-tune the institutional conditions for market efficiency on a far wider scale. These are carried out by experts working in myriad settings: national and international, public and private. So long as management is carried out in this common spirit, the locus of discussion matters little. Over time, a kind of global common sense has emerged about what governments and private actors *are* and *do* and global economic life on a large scale has been consolidated in ways which set what have come to seem the natural limits of territorial government and public law regulation.

On the political side, the dominant idea is also pretty simple. Politics is all about a 'polity'—usually a community of people associated in some way with a territory. As a result, politics do not scale the same way markets do. Where economies scale horizontally, politics can more easily be deepened and rendered responsive along a vertical axis of representation and accountability. The vertical activity of rulership has become the work of a profession linked to the institutional arrangements we call government. Politics has come to mean the special domain of work performed by government, itself a collection of specialised competences. As politics matures, the work of these people becomes ever more horizontally divided along functional lines. Specialists in transport policy and industrial policy and health policy, as well as political consultants, media commentators, policy advocates and the very specific set of people we call 'politicians'.

Good governance requires that these specialists strengthen the link between policy and the public interest both by strengthening the horizontal specification of mandates or separation of powers and by intensifying the vertical mechanics of rulership through accountability, transparency, citizen empowerment and ruler responsiveness. The perfection of the polity requires and produces a parallel transformation of both rulers and ruled through one or another form of responsive democracy and the 'rule of law'. This is also more idea than reality, but it provides an orienting frame for the work of political specialists. They should aim to perfect their special technical expertise or competence and intensify their representational links to local constituencies through mechanisms of accountability and transparency.

Unsurprisingly, politics built in the shadow of these ideas is characterised by both technical consolidation and division: separating national territories into autonomous states, separating branches of government with different competences and constituencies and separating different levels of government with degrees of relative autonomy. In each setting, political competence is about the management of divided competences, specialised knowledge and local constituencies. At different moments, policy elites seem to become enthusiasts for a similar machinery of 'responsiveness' across the spectrum of special competences, divergent constituencies and levels of accountability: at one moment elections and constituent service, at another, stakeholder engagement and negotiation or transparency. The result is a remarkably homogenous global political order of fragmented government and local politics, operating against the background of an economy organised to link things together by detaching them from the very spatial and communal identifications with which government struggles to intensify its connection.

Most notably, of course, this vision has animated the organisation of the world's political life into the series of ostensibly analogous units called 'nation states'. Again, more idea than reality, yet ruling political classes across the world have become convinced that the world is made up of states and that those who rule have or represent one. The popular media surely encourages the view that the day's 'politics' is focused by whatever the president—or his opponent—did. Although political leaders all speak about the distinctive and exceptional qualities of 'their' state, they also share the view that their *role* as leader of a city, province, ministry or commission is analogous to all the others of its type. This double conviction—analogous roles, distinctive constituencies and specialisations—is the template for their political activity despite the implausibility of both ideas. The 'roles' of heads of state or ministers differ wildly whatever the diplomatic protocol may say, just as those most committed to the distinctiveness of political jurisdictions are often those who represent them, as any trip to the Washington offices of American state representatives will quickly affirm.

Nevertheless, these ideas have spawned a series of technical and institutional projects which have consolidated a government monopoly on political life in one after another location, empowering some and disempowering others while demobilising alternative institutional arrangements and affiliations. At the national level, for example, as the polity came to mean the state, people were reconstituted as individual citizens of specific states—a process requiring a range of technical innovations in identification from passports to voting privileges. A popular and professional vernacular of civil and human 'rights' redefined justice as an appropriate relationship between an individual and a state. The demands of linguistic and other minorities were accommodated either by recognising their demands for political autonomy through secession or, more commonly, assimilating them into a national polity as citizens with enforceable individual and minority rights. Smaller territorial units—cities, neighbourhoods, states—were placed in a hierarchical relationship to larger national units, relations between them managed by professional interpretation of doctrines such as 'subsidiarity', 'states' rights', 'home rule' and the like. Intermediate civic institutions that might once have played a political role—professional guilds, unions, tribes—were either assimilated into national political parties or transformed into cultural and economic rather than political institutions, their members unleashed to engage with the national political world as individuals. At the same time, the emergence of a national media created a national political conversation, reflecting the activity of government back as the privileged site of politics as political parties arose to serve as gatekeepers for the apparatus and personnel of political life. In the end, politics everywhere came to be defined as the activity of specialised people who have, or aspire to have, government power in states.

The fantasy arrangement of the political world into 'states' also equated *world* politics with the diplomatic and military conversations among people linked to governments, re-imagined from this perspective as parallel 'sovereigns'. The development of a horizontal conversation among them, whether carried on by word or deed, led to the emergence of a transnational political class of diplomats and 'non-governmental' representatives of 'civil society' whose members understand their local and global situations to be somehow analogous. Their interaction has encouraged, and has been encouraged by, the emergence of a common global media conversation in which all these people may imagine themselves participating. The emergence of a transnational diplomatic class—including the transnational community of international lawyers—has reinforced a shared vernacular for international political discourse and action, fine-tuning its limits, possibilities and directions. Indeed, the most striking thing about 'world politics' today is the extent to which it is understood to be about the relations among national institutions as they unfold among specialised professionals—diplomats, soldiers and national political leaders. All the other social activity that occurs around the world is something else—commercial activity or cultural activity perhaps, but not 'politics'.

C. The Result: Inequality, Instability and Political Dysfunction

It might seem that a world of national politics and global economics would be ripe for conflict between the two. It is often said that in the first half of the twentieth century the struggle between them was 'won' by national politics, with catastrophic economic consequences, just as it is now sometimes said that the global economy has defeated the potential for meaningful national politics. There is something to both claims, certainly. But more interesting, I believe, are the consequences of their often unequal relationship as it has been sustained over time. If economics means efficient markets and politics means democracy and the rule of law—these all seem like good ideas. It is appealing to think that they go together naturally, or that movement toward one might start a virtuous cycle toward the other. This way of thinking is extremely common among the economic and political professionals who must manage the differences between them. When problems arise, professionals in each area typically respond by calling for more of both—ever more integrated economic markets and ever more responsive and specialised government: more democracy, more efficient markets, both promoted by more rule of law. Where their logics threaten to diverge, the professional challenge is to build intermediate institutions and doctrinal schemes for the technical accommodation of national politics to a global economy and for a satisfying management of the interface between them. The trade regime is the most obvious example—a set of economic and political commitments, doctrines and interpretive institutions designed to encourage national political support for global economic activity and economic accommodation of divergent national political settlements.

Unfortunately, technical management of the tensions between these grand projects has accelerated the distance between politics and the public interest while liberating economic life from the social and political context necessary for its successful stabilisation and management in a kind of perverse feedback loop or vicious spiral, encouraging political impotence and hyperbole alongside economic inequality and instability. Think of Europe. Politics responded to the local demand for growth by ceding ever more territory to a distant economic technocracy which in turn demanded ever further demobilisation of local policy space in the name of the technocratic imperatives of reform and austerity until the local political arrangements began to implode. Across the world, the problems calling out for public policy attention are ever more rooted in global economic movements and ever less amenable to solution on the scale of our political life. Government everywhere is buffeted by economic forces, captured by economic interests, engaged in economic pursuits. The inability of politics to offer public interest solutions to policy challenges has encouraged political cultures ever less interested in doing so. Politics has come to be about other things—symbolic and allegorical displays, on the one hand, and the feathering of nests on the other.

The resulting instability of contemporary political and economic life has manifested itself in a variety of ways since the economic crisis. At the top and bottom of the world economy, people have deracinated themselves, moving increasingly often across greater distances. In relative terms, the middle classes are the ones who have become locked to their territory. For so long the national centre of political gravity, the middle classes of the advanced industrial democracies have become a global periphery, their new political and economic impotence expressing itself in ways which further destabilise political life and economic life. Governments everywhere now operate in the shadow of disenfranchised and disillusioned publics who have lost faith in the public hand—in its commitment to the 'public interest', in its sovereignty, its relevance and its capacity to grasp the levers that affect the conditions of social justice or economic possibility. In the face of integrated supply chains, global markets and financial uncertainty, workers, corporations and banks—all turn to the nation state for redress, bailout and support—only to find there is often little their sovereign will do. Just as the global economy has no 'commanding heights', so the political system has no sovereign centre. The institutional structure for each has been broken up. Political life has drifted into neighborhood and transnational networks, been diffused into the capillaries of professional management, and condensed in the laser beam of media fashion, transformed into a unifying, if impotent, spectacle. From the inside looking out, one finds oneself buffeted by one thing after another—professional common sense chastens the most robust party platform and only the wholesale replacement of politicians by 'technocrats', seems capable of appeasing economic forces. From the outside looking in, however, the centre seems captured, craven and conspiratorial.

Only rarely can a good solution be reverse engineered from critical identification of the problem. Nevertheless, this interpretation of the current political economic dilemma suggests a thought experiment. What would happen were the governance professions suddenly re-oriented to reversing these two large-scale projects? Imagine the daily management of political and economic life aimed in broad terms to reconnect the political and the economic by revising the sinews of legal, institutional and intellectual life through which they have been separated. Imagine the ruling elites also aimed to reverse the technical consolidation of global economic and political life by fragmenting the space of economic activity and multiplying the modes through which politics is undertaken. These broad projects might also be mutually reinforcing. For example, the intermediate institutional forms which could fragment economic space and disrupt the consolidation of national political life may also open spaces for a reconnection of politics with economics.

Such a programme would be familiar to the world's leading risk managers who have seen the dangers of over-integration in economic life. Financial risk management requires the reintroduction of stop-gaps and go-slow provisions against the damage of contagion and the volatility of speculative flows. Supply chain risk management required the reintroduction of inventories to guard against the disruptions of a tsunami here, a nuclear accident there. Imagine continuing on this path, reintroducing institutional forms for economic life linked to territory and to the constituencies the economic and political possibilities of which rise and fall with their location—public unions, publicly-owned enterprises and corporate forms responsive to public policy, as well as shareholder profit, banking and credit reoriented to local economic development. Large-scale regional institutions—central banks, development banks—might be reorganised to be more responsive to diverse local economic and political imperatives, their investments delinked from world market benchmarks. At the same time the experts and professionals who adjust the terms of global political and economic life might aim to strengthen the potential of local politics to pursue their own path. It is not impossible to imagine how this could be done. After all, in the political economy of today's advanced industrial economies a generation or two ago, the intermediary organisations that recently came to look like pure economic irrationality—professional monopolies, corporations linked to local stakeholders, unions forcing negotiations over the forms and costs of public goods—were often also spaces of political engagement. Reinventing such arrangements would require that we re-imagine law less as a common language of economic and political integration than as a shield for alternative paths and powers.

This is simply a thought experiment—a utopian heuristic. People can imagine doing it—indeed, in some areas it is already being done—although it would radically alter the background assumptions which inform the routine professional practices of both economics and politics. Thought experiments like this are important precisely because they focus attention on the large-scale background ideas experts carry around in their heads about what politics or economics are about, where they are heading, and how law fits in. If rulership professionals, including international lawyers, are to develop the analytic habits and perspectives necessary to understand and remap the political economy of the world, they will need to break free of the technical agendas which orient the work of the professions.

It is important to try. When the world's managers focus only on the technical issues of institutional form or regulatory policy which their professional disciplines mark out for attention, they are not simply rearranging the deck chairs on a vulnerable world—they are part of the process by which the world unravels. The legalisation of both politics and economics makes legal institutions and professional practice the glue that constitutes these domains, allocates powers and incapacities between them, and carves the channels through which their separation accelerates. Once this begins, law progressively locks in the gains, for it is the stakes as well as the conduit for interactions between centres and peripheries. How this happens can be traced in the stock of social and legal entitlements each group has been allocated to participate in global economic life. As a result, I am convinced that legal scholars have much to contribute to understanding how the political economy of the world has come undone and what might be done in response. To do so, they will need to rejuvenate two intellectual traditions—the socio-political or socio-economic analysis of centre/periphery dynamics, and the critical analytics first developed by legal realists and socio-legal voices a century ago and developed over the last decades by a variety of critical, progressive and post-modernist voices. I turn now to those heterogeneous inheritances.

III. Centre–Periphery Analytics and Legal Realism: Doorways to Political Economy

The analysis of 'centre–periphery dynamics' has served as the portal to a variety of different political and intellectual projects over the last half century. A brief list would include:

— a project in development economics to foreground the potential for national (or international) economic management to staunch the effects of inter-regional or inter-national dependency and the 'development of underdevelopment' as scholars termed it;
— a project in international politics or international relations to comprehend the dynamics of 'neo-colonial' arrangements limiting the self-determination of newly and nominally 'independent' nations;
— a political project in cultural psychology to understand the dynamics of assimilation, self-marginalisation and rage in the periphery and complacency at the centre of what scholars called the 'world system'; and
— a project of historical recovery to trace the impact of the colonial legacy in liberal internationalism and to de-centre the European and North Atlantic traditions in the discipline of international law.

There were certainly others. 'Centre–periphery dynamics' opens the way for so many critical projects precisely because so many mainstream frameworks edit out both the periphery and the dynamics. Attention to centre–periphery relations opens a window onto the structures of power and hierarchy in a larger system and onto the continuation of war in times of peace through the dynamics of domination and reciprocal influence among unequal actors in such a system.

Before turning to the relationship between political economy and international law, it may be helpful to review in quite general terms what it takes to think about 'centre–periphery dynamics' in a field. Most obviously, you need to identify a 'centre' and a 'periphery'—*of something*. There needs to be a field, a topography, a history, or a system *within which* something is the centre and something else is the periphery. This field provides the coherence; holds the centre and periphery in a relationship. Talking about centre/periphery dynamics forces you to say something about how this larger system functions and coheres. Is it an iron cage? A chaotic accident? Something in between?

For some academic and professional disciplines, it is simply obvious that what they are looking at is a 'system.' In many fields, that idea has entered popular consciousness as well. Economists think of 'economies' as systems whose dynamics can be divined and modelled—by and large, so do lay people. The popularisation of psychological ideas has made it common to think about our internal world as a dynamic economy of desires, reasons, aspirations, pressures, prohibitions and so on. Family therapy models crystallise the idea that families are social systems with dynamics specific to each family and common to families across the culture.

The legacy of academic thinking about international relations and international law is more ambivalent. In some sense, scholars in these fields do encourage the notion that there is an international political system and an international legal system. For almost a century, however, scholarship in both fields has also disputed the idea that these things are 'systems'. Political scientists have stressed the multiplicity and heterogeneity of political life across diverse institutional and cultural forms, and the replacement of a systematic high politics by a communicative process embedded in an unpredictable and chaotic social field. For international lawyers, the point of legalising international relations has always been to replace a political *system* (say, 'balance of power') with a legal *order* among sovereigns. Getting there has required re-imagining both international politics and international law, breaking them down into functional pieces, placing them in an ongoing and diffuse process of argument and collective legitimation, dispersing them across myriad actors, stakeholders, participants in an international legal/political process, embracing a comprehensive legal pluralism. Taken together, focus on legal pluralism, fragmentation and the dispersion of politics throughout social and institutional life has undone the idea that either politics or law coheres as a 'system'. It is as if the political system could be replaced by a legal order only at the expense of both systematicity and orderliness. The result is an open-ended process of competition among all manner of interests which sometimes manage to congeal into what may at best be interpreted as medium-scale 'systems' organising an economic sector, region or domain of activity, prone to overlap, conflict and disintegration as they interact. This legacy makes it difficult to take the first step toward dynamic interpretation of centre–periphery dynamics precisely because doing so requires what seems to be a step back to the more primitive idea that there is, after all, some kind of system.

The erosion of professional attachment to the systematicity of global life was accompanied by the rise of a technocratic and practical sensibility that has transformed rulership.

Ruling is not about grasping the controlling levers of a system or exercising what Weber famously called 'the vocation of politics'.[1] Rulers now occupy functional roles, have delegated competences, and deploy technical tools and instruments to address concrete problems. Rulers have become experts, spoken by their expertise. They operate in a *context*, but they need not attend to any larger *system*. Nor are conflict and distribution central to their work—the point is rather to solve problems, whether in small steps or by bold gestures. Day by day, they inch toward completion of a model city, an international Potemkin village of functional equivalents for ideal–typical national political arrangements. Out there, vaguely surrounding their activity, are various constitutional arrangements, institutional settlements, political expectations, economic forces and cultural fashions—their technocratic world adrift in a haze of system fragments.

Attention to centre–periphery dynamics in this fragmented fog is a way of reawakening the idea of system and focusing on conflict, domination and hierarchy. Indeed, the only systematic element we would need to begin to make sense of global political economy is a kind of permanently floating centre–periphery dynamic which will open the door to a re-imagination of the system *as a system*. Centre/periphery analytics constitute a systemic field by assigning positions to things 'within' it and tracing the interactions, conflicts and hierarchies among them. Seen this way, the 'system' is less a fact in the world, held together by a constitution spelling out actors and structures, than an interpretation. A story about the way things bunch together in uneven patterns and affect one another over time. More conventional narratives are also, of course, stories. But they are stories which occlude attention to the dynamics of power and hierarchy. The point of developing a centre-periphery narrative is to juxtapose an account that foregrounds those elements, challenging the conventional accounts that somehow metabolise them.

As elements in an interpretive story, the metaphor of 'centre' and 'periphery' can refer to just about anything—ideas, regions, nations, groups. The point is the relationship—a relationship that can be spatial, temporal, or just a matter of mental emphasis. The periphery can be 'far away from' the centre, 'more backward than' or 'historically prior to' the centre, or simply less significant, less a matter of focus and attention than the centre. All these are asymmetric relationships or hierarchies.

The centre–periphery metaphor implies a model, an ideal-typical picture, of how centres and peripheries interact. Scholars have generally used the metaphor to assert relationships both of difference and hierarchy. Things that are up-to-date, nearby, are *also* more important or privileged or powerful. Centres have more agency. The structure favours them. Centres exercise powers, get stuff and have status that is not available to peripheries. Perhaps the centre also does bad things to the periphery. Perhaps it keeps the periphery peripheral—or makes it ever *more* peripheral. That is the kind of thing is that centres do.

The danger here is the tendency to exaggerate the clarity and causal determinacy of the model—and the ability to translate generalities about 'centres and peripheries' to whatever is saddled with these labels. Although centres sometimes impoverish or oppress peripheries, sometimes they do not. Sometimes they may lift them up. And sometimes their relative positions are a function of something else entirely—some other system or interest or force

---

[1] M Weber, 'Politics as a Vocation' in HH Garth and CW Mills (eds), *Essays in Sociology* (New York, Macmillian, 1946).

that keeps them in such a relationship. The trick here is to rehabilitate the idea of a system without the baggage of necessity.

Moreover, it is one thing to assert that there is a system and quite another to explain how it works. This requires spelling out with some specificity just what renders the one thing peripheral to the other, how are they differentiated in social, economic and cultural terms, how they then relate to one another, and how various social and material forces generate a dynamic between them. I have long found Gunnar Myrdal's extremely loose analytic framework for thinking about economic and social dynamics useful here.[2] If we start with economic dualism—the city and the countryside, the wealthy North and the poorer South, the inner city and the suburbs, the industrial and agricultural sectors—it is hard to know just what will happen. Certainly good things in one can wreck havoc on the other. A wealthy region can draw investment, people and energy toward it, making it ever more difficult for a poorer region to move ahead. But wealth in one region can also stimulate growth elsewhere. The point is that bad—or good—things in either the centre or the periphery can have a positive or a negative effect on the other. It all depends. Depends on all kinds of things—from attitudes and institutions to politics. Myrdal orients the analysis to identifying the linkages, understanding the dynamics of positive and negative effects, vicious and virtuous cycles, relatively stable equilibria and tipping points through which good or bad things in one have an effect in the other. His method is less an analytic than a list: a list of effects that can arise between a centre and a periphery.

The dynamic dimension is crucial. Statically, it is easy to imagine that things are stable, in equilibrium. Or that the system moves as a whole—growth lifts the rich and the poor, perhaps unequally, but together. It turns out, however, that when you turn on the switch, all kinds of interactions between the centre and the periphery disrupt the equilibrium and threaten the notion of the system moving as one. When things work well, an equilibrium disrupting increase in wealth in one place can stimulate growth elsewhere. When they do not, inequalities and hierarchies may reproduce themselves or become worse. Good intentions have unanticipated bad consequences, surprising feedback loops arise, secondary effects set in, and soon we're in a vicious spiral. Virtues spawn vices. Which way things will go—or whether they will move at all in relationship to one another—depends on the linkages.

This way of thinking blunts the temptation to hunt for large-scale narratives of necessity either for the economy as a whole or for the relationship between its dual elements. The focus is on mid-level social formations. On the macro side, there is dualism—two sub-systems sufficiently differentiated from one another to operate somewhat independently. And there are linkages—sinews of interaction which can strengthen and weaken. These more micro-processes develop dynamics of their own.

This is where law comes in. Legal rules and institutions are sinews of connection and distribution among sub-systems. As a result, attention to law can clarify how centres and peripheries come to be differentiated, as well as the micro-processes that operate to link them. A variety of heterogeneous traditions in legal thought offer tools for identifying these linkages and the channels which structure the dynamic relations among actors in

---

[2] See, eg G Myrdal, 'Appendix 2: The Mechanism of Underdevelopment and Development and a Sketch of an Elementary Theory of Planning for Development' in *An Approach to the Asian Drama: Methodological and Theoretical Selections from Asian Drama: An Inquiry into the Poverty of Nations* (New York, Vintage Books and Random House, 1970).

divergent starting positions. The critical and realist traditions in legal scholarship which stress the role of legal entitlements in constituting actors, allocating rents and establishing patterns of bargaining power offer a powerful lever for grasping the mid-level relationships of differentiation and influence.[3] Socio-legal traditions focus attention on the impact of legal arrangements on human behaviour—and vice versa. The variety of post-modern influences which entered the legal academy over the last decades foreground the communicative, constitutive and performative effects of law in social life. Taken together, these traditions shift analytic focus away from the structure and constitution of 'the legal order' toward the role of law, legal institutions and legal ideas in the hard and soft distribution of entitlements, authority and bargaining vulnerabilities among actors within an economic or political system and to the role of law in the micro-processes of global political and economic struggle.

In this sense, centre–periphery is not a strong model of *power* or *domination* focused on the identification of agency, causation and effect. It is a model of relative *positions* in a field and the dynamics which develop between them over time. The point is not that the centre does this or that *to* the periphery. The actors here are people. The systemic element and the dynamics between centre and periphery arise from what they do. Some system of norms, ideas and expectations, enforced in some way by violence or habit, by shame or charisma, permits actual people situated here to do this and there to do that. The *power* that drives the whole thing, if we can speak of power in that way, runs orthogonal to the field and is exercised as people do things in the shadow of those ideas, expectations and authorities. Power rests with the system of entitlements that links people in relationships of relative privilege and vulnerability, with the habits of society, with the ideas, aims and identities of the participants themselves, and with the objectives and enforcement authority of the state. As people act in the shadow of these authorities and constraints, the complex reciprocal relations between centres and peripheries unfold.

The modest mid-level analytics of Myrdal are useful to develop a checklist of both salutary and perverse links, paradoxical or unexpected effects, vicious and virtuous cycles that can then unfold. A legal focus on the role of background entitlements in the socio-legal dynamics between actors in an economy or a political order is a useful heuristic for identifying the linkages. In a legal system, entitlements to rents are, broadly speaking, the glue that distributes. Finding the entitlement—and the expectations unleashed in the shadow of entitlement—identifies the hand of power. Just as finding the distributive hand of the state in the routine operations of private law adjudication highlights the presence of coercion in what may otherwise seem an equitable process of bargaining and exchange. Doctrinal and institutional arrangements encourage the accumulation of gains, reinforcing the asymmetry. Seen this way, tendentious diagnostics do not require an iron cage. Small rules and good intentions can generate entitlements that reproduce or ameliorate social inequalities as they radiate out through a system structured by centre-periphery asymmetries.

Although Myrdal developed his method to describe linkages among 'economies', it is easy to see that such an approach may also shed light on asymmetric relations in the worlds identified as 'political'. It is common to think of law—public as well as private—as a tool for distributing political authority. Understanding the role of entitlements or legal competences in structuring asymmetric political bargaining and exchange is but a small

---

[3] See Duncan Kennedy, 'The Stakes of Law, or Hale and Foucault!' (1991) XV *Legal Studies Forum* 327.

step. Indeed, such an approach would seem altogether compatible with the disaggregated and distributed understanding of law that has come to dominate the international law field. Myrdal's mid-level analytics embraced the disorderly pluralism and fragmentation of social, economic and political life. That did not eliminate the potential for dualism, for linkages, for spillovers, for the capture of rents and the reinforcement of bargaining power, for vicious—or virtuous—cycles. Far from it. It just makes them harder to find, the mechanics of their operation harder to isolate. The critical and heterogeneous traditions in legal thought give us a place to look for those mechanics.

It is nevertheless surprising how rarely international law scholars focus on the distributive impact of local, national and international legal rules in the global economy, compared to the enormous energy devoted to the quixotic effort to explain how it all may one day add up to a coherent, constituted legal order. The explanation, I am convinced, lies in two unfortunate ideas. First is the idea that international lawyers *should not* focus on issues of political economy. Economics is for someone else, politics precisely what one hopes to beat into the ploughshares of legal order. And second is the idea that questions of political economy can best be answered *either* by large-scale narratives of historical necessity—the nature of capitalism, and so forth—*or* by ethnographies and micro-sociological studies of the impact of 'globalisation' on very particular communities and transactions. The approach I propose differs from both, engaging international lawyers in questions of political economy and focusing on the middle range. The idea is to use the background world of law and legal expertise as a window for interpreting the foreground of world political economy. The hypothesis is that law offers an index of tools and stakes for interaction between centres and peripheries in the world political economic system.

This way of thinking might also illuminate asymmetric relationships among more symbolic 'systems' of ideas, disciplinary sensibilities or national traditions. A focus on the ways in which institutional forms migrate between centres and peripheries could harness comparative legal inquiry to questions of political economy. Comparative law now oscillates between reflection on macro questions of functional equivalence among legal cultures or patterns of influence and transplantation among broad legal traditions or 'families' on the one hand, and micro questions of alternative technical solutions to problems common among modern industrial economies found in different national regimes on the other. The goal of the inquiry is often either to expand the range of plausible national solutions or search for a 'best practice' that might be generalised. In the wake of Myrdal, I would hope comparative legal scholars might rather focus on the asymmetric interactions between the legal ideas and institutions of legal cultures in centres and peripheries, and on the role of legal similarities, differences and influences in reproducing or contesting relations between political and economic centres and peripheries.

To the extent our world is governed by the ideas and practices of experts, it may also be useful to explore the relative authority and reciprocal influences of ideas, disciplines or fields of expertise which are more or less dominant, prestigious or central. In the development field, for example, there is no question that economics has been the dominant discipline for more than 50 years compared to law or other social sciences. The dynamics of the relationship between economics and law in the expertise of development policy makers has some of the characteristics of a centre and a periphery. In repeated waves, an increasingly robust economic model has come to dominate the field, exogenising law, governance and much else, only to find itself chastened by an inability to translate its analytics successfully into policy. At such points, economics has reached out wildly to law, institutions and governance, endogenising one after another aspect of social and political life. In both directions, development economics has overshot the mark—exogenising law and governance in the name of robust analytics to the point of abstract sterility, only to endogenise law and institutions so indiscriminately that a general call for 'good law', 'strong entitlements' and 'human rights' stifles the ability to make choices and establish priorities.

Such patterns of interaction between disciplines are not only the unfolding of a logic and a pendulum between robust exogenising models and context-specific embrace of institutions. Relations between more or less dominant professional disciplines are also matters of reciprocal influence and competition. It would be interesting to know what norms or entitlements structure the relationship between economic common sense (a disciplinary 'centre') and common sense about law, governance and institutions, which has always been more peripheral to development policy. Some of this may be a function of institutional authority, professional resources and prestige and the intellectual path dependence of policy elites. Some may be a matter of ideas. It may be, for example, that a shared commitment to the *instrumental* nature of law might distribute authority asymmetrically between economic ends and legal means. A commitment by both disciplines to avoid seeing legal arrangements as a terrain for political contestation and choice may have kept law peripheral even when economists embrace good governance, formal property entitlements or human rights as the very definition of development. Needless to say, these remain hypotheses. The suggestion is that the diverse knowledge practices of experts may also be understood as centres and peripheries in a field, their relations driven by professional ambitions, desires to affiliate and disaffiliate, dominate and submit, and structured by status hierarchies, institutional arrangements and habits of reciprocal persuasiveness or impenetrability that function in ways analogous to the role of entitlements shaping bargaining powers in political and economic life.

It is not only that symbolic systems have centres and peripheries, the 'centres' and 'peripheries' in economic, political or legal systems may also be symbolic or allegorical. As such, they need to be inhabited or performed, and the effect of such a performance is not certain. Indeed, we might think of domination or hegemony as a performance or assertion of centrality—or an ascription of peripherality—which gives rise, in a significant audience, to the effect of centrality or peripherality. In law, it has become routine to assess assertions of jurisdiction for their effectiveness. The extraterritorial effect of national jurisdiction is a function of the willingness to assert it and the ability to generate cooperation or acquiescence in its exercise. International lawyers are accustomed to speaking about the authority of norms as a matter of their persuasive effect, the legality of political activity as a function of the legitimacy with which it is viewed by the international community, its legitimacy a function, in turn, of its perceived legality. It is odd that this way of imagining legal powers and obligations has so rarely given rise to analyses of the relative persuasiveness or legitimacy of performances from divergent quarters. And yet it seems undeniable that legitimacy and persuasiveness can be both cause and effect of being 'the centre'. When the US makes an assertion to its European allies that the power it wields in one or another disputed context is the exercise of right, what is at stake is not only the one-off legitimacy of the act or persuasiveness of the claim, but also the relative position of European and American authorities in a norm-drenched political system. To say that international law is a 'game of the middle powers' is to say that European nations more readily find themselves occupying the symbolic centre of the global legal order than of the global military or even economic system. Their normative assertions persuade, their action—or inaction—seems legitimate.

Why would this be interesting? For Myrdal the goal was improved policy—what can be done, where are the levers, how can economic analysis be mobilised by planners to encourage upward trends and discourage downward spirals? He imagines a site where these things could be understood and encouraged or contravened—the planning agency, the public hand. And indeed, if you *are* a policy planner, this kind of sceptical, middle-level analytic can be particularly useful: no big story, just an orientation to the kinds of things that might play out among social and economic aggregates and suggestions for dynamics to help or hinder.

At the global level, few scholars today write with this much faith in the availability of a public policy hand. Centre–periphery analytics are deployed more often to criticise than to focus policy proposals. The impetus is less reform than diagnosis, to raise awareness of contestation in the warp and woof of the quotidian. Centre–periphery analytics are useful in critical endeavours precisely because they reframe disciplines grown comfortable with constitutional stability and modest reform to focus on the reproduction of asymmetric power.

Criticism is a rhetorical business. The centre and the periphery are positions that must be claimed, denied, asserted or attributed. It is them and us—and we, we are the periphery! (Or, anyway, it is we who affirm their marginality and represent their interests.) The danger here is the tendency to overstate. Analysis of the relationship between a centre and a periphery seems most effective as criticism when the centre and periphery are hard-wired by history, when the centre has all the stuff, exercises all the power, reproduces the hierarchy. The gold standard for criticism, in this sense, is the iron cage. Where the whole arrangement is loose and unstable, or the results just a lucky—or unlucky—coincidence, the critical sting seems less potent. It might actually be an iron cage, of course. But it may not. Things can go poorly even when the periphery captures the spoils, inheriting the moral pleasures of marginality or relief from the burdens of rulership. Indeed, the most interesting hierarchies, the most obdurate dominations, can arise where power does not simply flow downhill from centre to periphery. Nor is there a persuasive model or compelling analytic reason for thinking that centres will always oppress peripheries. Sometimes there are virtuous cycles and all boats do rise.

Critical claims to peripherality and allegations of centrality must overcome the background complacency which comes from thinking there is no system—or everyone is, in some sense, on the same footing. It no longer seems that the 'system' has a 'logic' any more than that history marches to a dialectic. Much is coincidence. Often there are unanticipated disturbances, external shocks, puzzling reversals and creative re-inventions. To claim that *this* is peripheral to *that* requires a suspension of awareness of life's complexity, irrationality and unpredictability. Even with this suspension, it can be difficult to tell just who is the centre and who is the periphery. There are centres in the periphery; peripheries in the centre. More importantly, perhaps, centres can *feel* peripheral, style themselves marginal and bemoan their distance from power. And in every family we can identify the peripheral drama queens around whose instability and weakness the entire family rotates. In the end, centre–periphery analytics are both interpretations—this is how things are—and, when the interpretation holds, persuades, reconfigures the situation, interventions. To call out the perpetual drama queen victim on his centrality is to name and to shame, whether the ostensible victim is an adolescent or a nation.

Centre–periphery analytics provide a framework for criticising the status quo by asserting the presence of a power and a hierarchy that is otherwise denied. To the extent the political and economic world has come to be managed by experts, the hierarchies and power dynamics of contemporary life are often denied by the routine sensibility, belief system and practices of expert professions. Centre–periphery analytics can also be useful in scrutinising the complacency of an intellectual discipline or professional sensibility, most powerfully by articulating a scandal in a profession's relationship to power, uncovering a profession's implication in producing hierarchies it either denies exist or claims to be subverting.

This can often happen when a field is confident it has inequality under control—either because it is not bothered by the inequality or believes it offers a remedy. For example, it would not have been a particularly trenchant critique of those who built the colonial system to demonstrate that it spawned hierarchies between centres and peripheries—that was the whole point of the operation. Exposure of a dynamic inequality between the imperial centre and the colonial periphery might have scandalised those who believed it was all done from *noblesse oblige* or as the expression of humanitarian and religious motive, but even they probably understood what was going on—that was precisely why their own good ministrations were needed. It would be a scandal, however, if those ministrations were part of the mechanism by which the dynamic inequality between the imperial centre and colonial periphery were heightened or reproduced. Where the presence of humanitarian actors and a religious justification can be shown in fact to have been a link in the socio-economic process by which the centre exploited the periphery, you have a scandal.

For international law, colonialism is not a scandal so long as the discipline can say 'obviously colonialism was terrible, but we got rid of it and are working to undo its legacy'. Nor is it a scandal to demonstrate that international doctrines articulated then or now were unrealistic—the native populations were not really treated as equally 'human' and sovereigns are not really 'equal'. International lawyers, then as now, know this. That's what they are against. That is the reason to separate the good, if imaginary, world of international law from the bad world of international politics, and for redoubling efforts to bring about the progressive civilisation of those politics by law. It is a scandal, however, if it turns out international law doctrines proclaiming the humanity of indigenous peoples or the equality of sovereigns as they are applied are in fact part of the machinery by which the slaughter of indigenous peoples was justified or the inequality of nations has been sustained. Antony Anghie makes just such a claim about international law from the sixteenth to the twentieth century: humanist doctrines, doctrines of positive equality and institutions of affirmative development, have all in fact functioned to sustain and heighten global inequality.[4] To the extent the inequality of centre and periphery in the world system is structural, international law is part of the structure. When international law turns out to be colonialism by another name—the name 'self-determination'—we have scandal, for self-determination is just what the discipline felt it had to offer as a remedy.

Recent work on European law is also harnessing centre/periphery analytics to criticise the dominant professional consciousness of European law professionals. For professional Europeanists, it is not scandalous to hear that despite the 'single market', European national economies and regions remain unequal and distinct. They know that. The whole point of extending the four economic freedoms—and of the 'cohesion' and 'structural' fund transfer payment systems—is to ensure that through integration economic growth is possible

---

[4] A Anghie, *Imperialism, Sovereignty and the Making of International Law* (Cambridge, Cambridge University Press, 2007), also argues that while international law saw itself as preoccupied with extending a universal normative order to ever more sovereign equals, it was actually preoccupied with managing the dynamics between unequal civilisations or cultures.

throughout the Union. The EU project is all about linking centres and peripheries to equalise and grow. As a result, it does pose a critical challenge to the European law field to show that the general legal principles—such as 'free movement' or 'social considerations'—at the core of the endeavour are applied in ways which heighten the inequality between the economies of the European centre and periphery.[5] The devil here is in the details—in the precise ways that universal principles turn out to have diverse meanings and get applied in ways that contribute to dualism. Or in the specific ways a universal programme designed to equalise relations across the EU turns out to accentuate the distance between the centre and periphery. For example, if the structural and cohesion funds effected a net transfer from a periphery to a centre, or if general policies adopted in the name of 'democratisation', 'rule of law' or 'economic development' aiming to bring the periphery into harmony with the centre had the effect, at the periphery, of undermining parliamentary democracy, encouraging de-industrialisation, strengthening the security state, and the like, there would be a scandal.[6] In each of these cases, the villain is not the centre—it is the glue of entitlement that sets up an asymmetric and disempowering dynamic and the cloak of self-narration that covers it up.

IV. International Law and Political Economy

International lawyers and legal scholars have much to contribute to understanding and transforming global political economy. Heterogeneous strands within the discipline have helped prepare the way for a more sustained focus on the role of law in structuring relations among actors in the centre and in the periphery of the world economic and political system. Unfortunately, the mainstream international legal academy has moved ever further from tackling such large scale questions. It is important to understand both how the discipline has insulated itself from political economic engagement and what existing critical traditions could contribute to turning things around.

A. Why is it so Difficult for a Discipline Devoted to the Law of the International System to Address Issues of Global Political Economy?

Since modern 'international law' emerged as a practical and scholarly profession more than a century ago, it has aimed to civilise international politics with the balm of normative regularity and rational dispute resolution rather than diagnose and transform the political

---

[5] Damjan Kukovec's ongoing doctoral work argues precisely this. See, D Kukovec, 'Whose Social Europe?', talk delivered at Harvard Law School (16 April 2010) available at www.harvardiglp.org/new-thinking-new-writing/whose-social-europe-the-lavalviking-judements-and-the-prosperity-gap/; D Kukovec, 'A Critique of the Rhetoric of Common Interest in the EU Legal Discourse', talk delivered at Harvard Law School (13 April 2012), available at www.harvardiglp.org/new-thinking-new-writing/a-critique-of-rhetoric/; and D Kukovec, *A Critique of the Rhetoric of Common Interest in the EU Legal Discourse*, SJD Dissertation (Cambridge MA, Harvard Law School, forthcoming).

[6] Ermal Frasheri makes this point in E Frasheri, 'Transformation and Social Change: Legal Reform in the Modernization Process' *Nellco Legal Scholarship Repository*, 9 May 2008; and in his ongoing doctoral work, E Frasheri, *Of Knights and Squires: European Union and the Modernization of Albania*, SJD Dissertation (Cambridge MA, Harvard Law School, forthcoming).

economy of the world. In moments of crisis—most dramatically in the years after World War I—some in the discipline have offered international law as a terrain for renovating cultural and political life, but such moments are rare. More often, international lawyers have taken the structure of economic life as understood by economists, and the structure of political life is understood by diplomats, at a given moment, for granted. Over the last few decades, the internationalisation of every technical legal field—and the technical specialisation of international legal arrangements—has kept the profession from considering wider questions about the role of law in the world's political and economic organisation.

The theoretical issues that move the field have always been small bore adjustments or reassessments of existing institutional arrangements—and of law's own status in a world of political facts and economic forces one simply had to accept. Just how and why and when do norms bind? Might stable behaviour be reinterpreted as constitutionally compliant? Might existing transnational legislative, administrative and adjudicative processes be adjusted to be more transparent or effective? Nevertheless, a generation ago, the best comparative and public international lawyers were worldly and cosmopolitan, their disinterest in the parochial details of any nations legal arrangements making them lonely figures in law faculties which were everywhere linked to national political institutions and cultural traditions.

In recent years, the relevance of a specifically international legal field has become harder to see as every national regulatory or private law subject matter has been touched by international or foreign developments. Suddenly, everyone in the legal academy is an internationalist—but none have the brief to analyse law's role in the world system. Their remit is focused on transnational dimensions of their own field. In Europe, legal scholars in every field have become Europeanists, while American law professors, from family law to intellectual property, have become expert in the impact of their regime on the world and of the world on their regime. National regulatory subjects which particularly seem to implicate global economic life have blossomed as fields of their own—international banking and finance, international or comparative antitrust, international taxation and the like. Perhaps most strikingly, even American constitutional law, that most isolated of academic cargo cults, has become newly focused on the foreign affairs power, on compliance with international norms, on war powers and the regulation of war, and even on the comparative study of systems thought loosely analogous—Canada, Australia, South Africa, Israel, or the United Kingdom. As a result, the study of international legal phenomena has become linked to the ups and downs of national legal projects of public order, regulation or private law enforcement. The issues are technical, the perspective pragmatic problem solving. International legal study has become a fragmented reflection of national policy concerns, as if becoming an international lawyer meant becoming an internationalised American or European lawyer, rather than someone able to navigate a global legal order infiltrated by the transnational extensions of multiple national legal arrangements but with its own political and economic coherence.

At the same time, the international law field has itself responded to the multiplication and dispersion of legal authorities with global reach by repeatedly splitting into ever more technical subfields, each with its own favourite institutional regime and preferred disciplinary interlocutors. In some sense, modern international law was split at the root. The field came of age in the late nineteenth century by repeated division: 'public international law' from 'private international law', the 'law of war' from the 'law of peace', the 'law in war' from the 'law of war', and so on. Although the distinctions did not remain particularly sharp or formal, the process of division continued throughout the twentieth century. An early and significant disciplinary division—public international law spawning international economic law—bore witness to a moment in which politics and economics were comfortably separate.

In the process, public international law became one specialised field among many, oriented to baseline rules about sources of law, the procedures and institutions of inter-state diplomacy and those substantive matters which had become the topic of multilateral rulemaking—but not to the role of law in the large dramas of global political and economic affairs. Instead, international law was preoccupied with its own status as law in a political world—a concern it translated into endless rumination on its 'binding' quality and the machinery of its 'enforcement'. This theoretical focus translated into a doctrinal obsession with sources of law and the procedures for making claims, settling disputes, enforcing law and holding states 'responsible'. The field's substantive energy focused only on domains which had explicitly been the subject of binding international rules, from the environment and human rights to the use of force and the regulation of armed conflict. Assessing the substantive impact of international law on the world political and economic order meant measuring the impact of these positive norms. International law was implicated in the protection and despoliation of the global environment to the extent the Kyoto Protocol applied and was enforced.

Although the field may at first have seemed foundational—both the base upon which all other international legal fields would be built and the legal foundation for global political activity—public international law soon developed a distinctive perspective and a far more limited domain of interest and engagement. This encouraged the claims by other international legal fields that they were at least as foundational to global legal order, if not more so. In the process any sense of the international system's political specificity was diluted.

In the middle of the last century, it may have seemed the field had discovered a path to renewal. International law's big mid-twentieth-century ideas—transnational law, policy science, functionalism—framed a sociological inquiry into the operations of law in the world and opened the door to a disaggregated and legalised conception of the 'global policy process'. The unfortunate result was a re-interpretation of transnational political and economic activity in legal and increasingly technocratic terms. The functional dispersion of 'regulatory', 'administrative' and 'dispute resolution' capacities spawned a wave of new scholarship seeking the effect of international law wherever two are gathered in its name, dulling the professional experience of a distinctive global framework linked to a global political or economic system. Although ostensibly close to the diplomatic worlds of international organisations and adjudication, its interdisciplinary reference points drawn from political science, international relations and diplomatic history, its mission bringing law to the world of interstate power, the public international law field drifted ever further from focus on the political choices and distributional consequences of legal arrangements. As public international law embraced the fragmentation of the international legal field, law became a way to speak about politics, and politics a way to assert legal entitlements. Along the way, the aspiration to offer a distinctive global perspective on the structure of the world political system withered and the experience of conflict, decision and responsibility were leeched out of our disciplinary images of global order.

At the same time, the field's substantive preoccupations became ever more specific and idiosyncratic. The field promised that law would become the vernacular of legitimacy as legitimacy became the currency of power—and we got a proliferation of international tribunals focused on Africa, an intensification of public naming and shaming rearticulating the division between civilised and barbaric, and a defence of everything from bombing and regime change to life without parole, in the language of human rights. A steady focus on 'crisis' and 'transition' and 'intervention' has made it increasingly difficult to pose questions about law's role in the quotidian structures of conflict and distribution embedded in the economic and cultural global order. Rather than people taking responsibility for decisions, international lawyers imagine a drifting gauze of judicial networks and diffuse stakeholder conversations among a disembodied 'international community' about what it might be legitimate to do about this or that unfolding crisis.

Meanwhile, 'international economic law' and a rejuvenated 'private international law' split off to become fields of their own. Leaving general inquiry into public order behind, international economic law focused on supporting the integration of a global market through the national and international regimes regulating trade. The interdisciplinary reference point shifted from international politics to economics, but not in a way which encouraged focus on law as a link between centre and periphery or as a distributive tool—rather the opposite. A set of ideas about the economics of trade provided an orientation for institutional and doctrinal efforts to harness national regulatory machinery to the expansion of global markets and the erosion of national or local political ambitions to challenge their distributional impact. 'Private international law' focused on the transnational effect of private rights and the procedures of transnational commercial arbitration. Private entitlements are a crucial arena for investigation of the links which bind centres to peripheries and structure global political economy. Unfortunately, the field assiduously avoided such questions, imagining the transnational private legal order as a space outside 'public policy'.

An international law responsive to the political economy of the world will need to escape the grip of these divergent professional styles. International lawyers will need to cross-train, learn about economics and relearn politics as a quotidian matter of hard decisions rather than an intermittent matter of diffuse conversation. The governance challenge is not to bring political actors into law—they are already there. Nor is it to establish—and then work to complete—functional equivalents for familiar national governmental institutions. Projects of functional equivalence—an international criminal law, an international administrative law, an international constitutional law, an international judiciary—are notoriously limited in their ability to grasp the global order as a whole, tending rather toward an infinite ritual of 'progressive development', their completion on an ever receding horizon and their form an abstraction far removed from the national legal and political realities they were established to imitate. Conceived as general global competences, they act in the world as narrow site-specific interventions. None are oriented to the challenge of establishing a public hand capable of taking decisions about the distribution of economic growth. Whether done locally, regionally, nationally or transnationally, this will require new ways of thinking, new modes of professional expertise, and new uses for old institutions.

At the same time, international economic lawyers will need to re-learn the significance of political choice and the dynamic social, political and economic impact of alternative institutional and regulatory arrangements. The economic target is no longer the efficient allocation of existing resources under constraint or the maximisation of comparative advantage. The economic challenge is to understand and make the political, institutional and social choices to place the global economy on one rather than another growth trajectory. An institutional interface to accommodate divergent national conceptions of the regulatory background for 'normal' market activity is not enough. At stake are less the global gains from trade than the distribution of those gains, the bargaining powers through which those distributions occur and the dynamic social and political consequences of the alternative distributions which come with different economic trajectories. In the same spirit, private international law will need to focus on the role of private law forms and relationships as actors in the distribution of economic and political powers.

In short, to analyse and engage with the political economy of the world, international law will need to abandon many of its most significant twentieth-century programmatic preoccupations, methodological accomplishments and disciplinary boundaries. To grasp international law's political economic significance as a constituter of centres and peripheries or a link and channel between them, the debris of the traditional Westphalian narrative and its twentieth-century modernisations will need to be hauled away. Over the last few decades, a variety of critical and alternative strands of scholarship within the international legal field have pushed in these directions.

B. What Heterogenous and Critical Traditions within the Field have already Accomplished to Turn Things Around?

The most important legacy of critical work in the field over the last decades may simply have been the identification of the very limited imagination of the international legal establishment and the tracing of the routines by which it reproduces those limits in the name of transcending them. That work may help open the door to a more broad-ranging engagement with law as a site for ongoing political and economic struggle. To get there, international lawyers will need to set aside the false promises the field makes about its own significance and potential function in international society.

Many look to international law for the expression of universal values, most commonly in the human rights canon. Critical traditions within the field have stressed the narrow specificity of international law's purportedly universal vision in a world where people disagree about the most fundamental things and values are not, in fact, universal. Projects to pursue particular ends in the name of universal values run into characteristic difficulties and generate predictable blind spots among those who pursue them. The support of human rights, a very specific late twentieth-century endeavour, is no exception. Human rights can as often be part of the problem as well as part of the solution. The proliferation of 'rights' is not only a way to speak truth to power. Power also routinely asserts itself as right—perhaps particularly as the expression of human rights.

International law also promises to identify the legitimate actors in the international system and their powers—most formally by enumerating the 'rights and duties of states'. This is partly sociological—simply registering the powerful and their capacities. And, of course, it is also normative—offering a measure of the legitimate uses and misuses of power which may be useful in resolving disputes about who can do what. In fact, the field is neither describing the world as it is nor helping us to imagine and construct a world that could be. Indeed, the field's universalist descriptions of actors and structures more often occlude the way power flows through the capillaries and commanding heights of global society. Nor is the discipline's fantasy-land of institutions and regimes—an international community of stakeholders, a global society of rights-bearing individuals, a universal international criminal law, a transparent international administrative law—a plausible programme of action. These are the programmatic fashions of particular transnational elites, reassuring distractions from understanding how the world is put together and how it might be changed.

Perhaps most importantly, international law promises a catalogue of policy tools and institutional arrangements with which to confront global problems. International lawyers have long said that, like the EU, only with greater strength, the international order governs by a system of law rather than of budgets or a monopoly of force. It is no longer surprising to find in one after another area that international law's most coveted projects and proposals are wildly inadequate to the tasks they purport to address. Their architects are embedded in the machinery of global political and economic power responsible for the difficulties in the first place. That their best efforts in response would be limited by fealty to the limits imposed by that machinery is to be expected. Nevertheless, for whatever reason, the International Criminal Court could triple its budget and jurisdiction, the United Nations could redouble its peacekeeping efforts, the international human rights community could perfect its machinery of reporting and shaming—and it would not prevent the outbreak of genocide or the collapse or abuse of state authority. Every American and European corporation could adopt standards of corporate responsibility, every first world consumer could be on the lookout for products which are fairly traded and sustainably produced, and it would not stop the human and environmental ravages of an unsustainable global economic order. America could sign the Kyoto Protocol, could agree with China and India and the Europeans on various measures left on the table at Copenhagen, and it would not be enough to prevent global warming. The United Nations' Millennium Development Goals could be implemented and it would not heal the rupture between leading and lagging sectors, cultures and classes. The Security Council could be reformed to reflect the great powers of the twenty-first rather than the twentieth century, but it would be scarcely more effective as a guarantor of international peace and security. Global administrative action could be everywhere transparent and accountable without rendering it politically responsible.

Each of these efforts might be salutary. Some may be terribly important. At best, however, the implementation of these schemes would postpone a decision, manage expectations, render the problems to which they are purportedly being addressed sustainable, and thereby reaffirm the current distribution of powers and the centrality of the centre. As a result, completing the programme of international law would not renew the political economy of the world—any more than finally 'completing' the EU would resolve the dynamics of dualism which have rocked the project from Brussels and Frankfurt. The project of continuing the project is one way in which those dynamics are sustained. In Europe, a permanent transition toward an ever-receding goal of a 'political' union sustains the technocratic separation of economic and political imperatives—and reinforces the divide between leading and lagging regions. Globally, the permanent transition toward a universal legal order of equal sovereigns sustains one after another project of hegemony. As a result, rather than a toolkit of policy solutions which might be adopted in the global public interest, it would be more accurate to see international law as a continuation of the politics of war and economic struggle, as a legitimating distraction from the effort to remake those politics or reframe that struggle, and as an effort to institutionalise the ideology of a particular time and place as universal.

Only after pushing past international law's classic self-conception—as the highest expression of universal values, the best map of the world's political actors and their powers, and toolkit of policy solutions—will international lawyers be able to use international legal materials to illuminate the global political and economic process. A crucial first step is to change the profession's default perception of the distance between legal and political arrangements. Although international law has long sought to throw a fragile net of rules across the roiling waves of global politics, its relationship to power is a far more intimate one. Critical traditions focus on law as the language in which governance—even war—is written and performed. But this has not civilised global politics into a legal 'order'. Political struggle continues in and through the regimes and vernaculars of international law. The global political/legal system remains extremely disorderly, plural and uncertain. International legality is less a matter of either normative validity or persuasion than it is a form of effective assertion or performance of authority. When international lawyers say that compliance with international law legitimates, whether on or off the battlefield, they mean that grinding poverty, terrible inequality, environmental destruction, and the premeditated destruction and death caused by war have become acceptable. It would be more accurate to count the vernaculars of legitimacy and the cramped channels of public order entrenched by international law among the root causes for the difficulties facing the world.

This way of thinking opens the door to rethinking international law as a terrain for political engagement rather than as a normative or technical substitute for political choice. In a similar way, it should be possible to shrink the experience of distance between international law and the routine operations of the economy. International law has long been unconcerned with economic affairs. Economics either happens elsewhere on different scale—within the nation—or is the domain of other legal disciplines, most prominently 'international economic law'. I see this routinely among students aspiring to work in the field of human rights, on the one hand, and those aiming to contribute to the management of the global economy or to national economic development, on the other. Too often, the first group is uninterested in economics, except to the extent that social or economic development objectives might be the happy consequence of human rights enforcement. The latter are unconcerned about international public law other than the few institutions marked out as part of the global economic order, the WTO in particular.

Critical strands within the field have aimed to unravel public international law's economic innocence. The structures of authority articulated in public international law— first among them territorial sovereignty—and the institutional separation of public and private powers ratified by the field are crucial in setting the background conditions for both national economies and global economic activity. At the same time, the disciplinary claim by 'international economic law' to be *the* law behind global economic activity is wildly inaccurate. International economic law is a far narrower institutional and normative project focused on the relationship between national regulatory structures affecting trade. The law behind global economic activity is much broader—it is a vast and very uneven field. Private law here, local regulations there, informal industry standards in this sector, public administrative regulation in that sector, habits of jurisdictional assertion and forbearance, internal corporate policies, and the customary norms of illegal and shadow markets are all part of the story.

As the profession's view of the laws structuring global political and economic life expands, it becomes increasingly obvious that global politics and economics are anything but distinct. In the same way it becomes clear that the law of the economy covers an area of political choice and struggle, or that the legislation of political life has structured the distribution of economic opportunity and reward. It is in this sense that critical work has proposed to think of private law and corporate governance as part of the constitutional infrastructure of global governance, and private obligations as background limits on public power. Think of the network of obligations which tied our global financial system in knots—collaterised debt obligations; credit default swaps and securitisation so complex and markets so rapid that no regulatory authority can unravel them; or corporate governance so fluid and inscrutable that one rarely knows who calls the shots. All these stand in a long line of private arrangements—including slavery—made in one place that restrict public policy alternatives elsewhere.

Taken together, these critical efforts aim to reframe international law both to expand the range of normative and institutional material to be considered when contemplating the world's legal regime, and to break the habit of thinking of international law as being distinct from politics and economics. In some sense, of course, this is not new. The world's political and economic elites have long learned to inhabit a fluid policy process in which they as often make, as follow, the law. If international lawyers now draw the consequences of that knowledge as scholars, they will be more likely to remember that things they do not like are also legal institutions and structures of governance: poverty, war, inequality. Only by abandoning the comforting idea that 'international environmental law' concerns only environmental protection and remembering that law also comforts those who would cut down the forest, can the profession come to explore the role of law in the reproduction of poverty or the continuity of war in peacetime.

These critical reinterpretations open the door to treating international law as a political economic space by displacing the field's self-conception and identifying a wider range of materials which might serve as sinews of connection distributing political or economic power among centres and peripheries of the world system. To the extent that critical voices are prone to think the global political order is dominated by statesmen and politicians from an hegemonic centre—or that the economy is directed by 'investors' and 'multinationals' pulling the strings from some Davos-inspired aerie—an expanded conception of the legal terrain across which political and economic forces contend can serve as a useful corrective. The political economy of the world is a more diffuse, dynamic and multi-directional system. The process by which authority, opportunity and reward is distributed among people operating in that system is far more difficult to decipher.

This is particularly the case to the extent the sinews binding the political economic system together are less norms enforced by institutions than ideas diffused across the world about who is entitled to what. Heterogeneous strands in the international law field have also explored international law as a set of ideas, a mental map of the world, a set of beliefs about legitimate and illegitimate action, a form of technical or professional expertise. It is difficult to understand how *knowledge* about the world distributes power between centres and peripheries, how it encourages or enables some actors to extract political and economic rents from others. A first step is simply to understand more fully how a field of knowledge such as international law operates as a pattern of authority.

It is clear that the shared vernaculars of professional experts can influence what individual and institutional actors believe they ought and ought not to be doing. After all, if for a generation everyone thinks an economy is a national input/output system to be managed, and then suddenly they all become convinced that an economy is a global market for the allocation of resources to their most productive use through the efficiency of exchange in the shadow of a price system, lots has changed. That is also governance. Indeed, to the extent that expertise has become the global currency of rulership, understanding the political economy of the policy expertise system has become a crucial part of understanding how we are governed. A better map of the intellectual and institutional system of rulership-by-expertise may open up new opportunities for innovative policy and political contestation.

For example, it is important to recognise that the profession's insistence that international law has domesticated the pre-Westphalian world of empire, religious strife and war by rendering religious confession and ideological conviction matters of domestic concern and harnessing violence to the enforcement of right, while comforting, is not accurate. Global governance remains as much a matter of religion, ideology and war as of persuasive interaction among the elites we call the 'international community' about what is legitimate. In fact, the informal and clandestine, the sacred, the violent and the spectacular are part of how the world is governed. The disciplinary urge to push them off-screen, either back in history or below the waterline of sovereignty, nevertheless has a powerful impact. People who see themselves as religious actors on the global stage have a hard time seeing themselves reflected in the vernaculars of authority through which that stage is built. People who work in institutions which pride themselves on their centrality to global political and economic order have a correspondingly hard time figuring out how to think about religion other than as a matter of personal belief or local culture. It would not be surprising to find that these ideas about religiosity helped distribute the experience of authority to act in the political economy of the world in various ways.

It is difficult to develop a satisfying picture of the ways in which the focal points, blind spots and biases of expertise help to construct relations between centres and peripheries. More often, scholars focus on the authority of agents they can see to act within structures they understand. Legal scholars have paid too little attention to the myriad ways in which power flows through common sense, affiliation, or the experience of victimisation, pride or shame. All these things move like a virus or a fad, but the discipline's epidemiology is weak and the sociology of status, convention and emulation at the global level is rudimentary. Indeed, to trace the contours of global governance is to follow the hand of knowledge in arrangements of power. Doing so would help to reframe international law less as a box of tools, a catalogue of actors or a catalogue of universal values than as the articulation of a shared world.

There is a long way to go to understand how our world is made through articulation and assertion, how the practice of assertion is structured by institutional and professional technologies, and how these, taken together, distribute opportunity and authority. Forty years ago it was common to say that the most significant product of the space race was a distant photo of planet earth—and there was something profound in the observation. Such things constitute a world long before scholars begin to identify actors or structures, assert rulership or solve problems. Of course, such ideas arise from somewhere. Without a space programme, perhaps without a cold war, without *Life* magazine, we might not have had those photos at that moment in that way, and the idea may have arisen differently, at a different moment, or have seemed less compelling. The disciplinary practices of experts are part of the technology through which the world to be governed—a world of centres and peripheries—is assembled.

The role of knowledge in global power is particularly easy to see because global governance is so often an assertion, an argument, a programme of action or a call to resistance. Indeed, when it comes to global governance, saying it is so can make it so. Or, perhaps better, saying it is so is often all there is to it. This is always true of public authority—it comes into being and functions as an assertion. In other contexts we have become used to this. People forget, other than in moments of revolutionary turmoil, that the sovereign is just a person who says he is king. The institutionalisation of public power makes authority seem 'real'; the distinction between 'public' and 'private' natural. In global governance, the saying and performing are right on the surface. Global governance must be *claimed*, through an assertion that this or that military deployment or human rights denunciation is the act of the global public hand—the 'international community' in action. The rhetorical dimension of global power is equally significant for those who would resist. Saying it is *not* so is rarely enough to unravel the world's structure. Nevertheless, identifying the global hand in local unpleasantness is also an assertion—and an allegation of responsibility. Whether one aspires to bring global governance into being or fears its power, one must name it, assert it, and identify it, before it becomes something to build or destroy. Indeed, in a sense, 'global governance' is simply the sum of what those who wish to manage and to resist globally have jointly drawn to our attention as governance.

One way in to this set of issues may be to explore further the way in which international law is performed as an argument about international law itself—its limits and its potential. Modest differences between policy proposals are routinely debated as if the very possibility of legality were at stake. This tendency is common in discussions about global governance. The 'international community' discusses intervention—whether in Libya or Syria or Sudan—in a way which focuses as much on its own credibility and authority as on the local consequences of one or another course of action. At stake in debates about economic stimulus or austerity plans is not only or even primarily who gets what, but rather the credibility and stability of the regime itself—the Euro, the EU, the market. And this kind of association can be self-fulfilling. If everyone thinks the stability of the Euro is at stake—then, the stability of the Euro *is* at stake. In this sense, the constitution of a world is ongoing, a technical and institutional practice as well as a communicative and performative work of the imagination.

C. Implicating International Law in the Relations between Centres and Peripheries

Understanding the world-making effects of the knowledge practices of rulership is an enormous programme for thought. International legal scholars could contribute by situating international law in the larger global political and economic system, interpreting its role as the glue linking leading and lagging ideas, regions, or economic sectors, or as the cloak hiding asymmetric dynamics of power in political economy of the world. Conventionally, the field articulates a universal and homogenous world from which it stands somewhat apart. There are inequalities, of course, but the world it sees—and it would make—is a far more equal one. To reframe the world international law conjures into being as a system of centres and peripheries would already begin to articulate a quite different place into being.

To re-interpret international law as the language constituting centres and peripheries in the world's political and economic system would certainly transform the discipline's self-image. As it sees itself, international law is the handmaiden, the gentle civiliser, the voice crying out in the wilderness, articulating valid norms, naming and shaming from the sidelines. Its kingdom lies in the future and is present now only as a promise. International lawyers can find it absurd to be treated as 'the centre' of anything. Don't we see how hard they are struggling just to stay in the game at all? Why stigmatise *them*, for crying out loud, when there are so many bigger fish to fry?

To critique the rulership of international law, you must *establish* it and implicate this field in this order: constituting actors, channelling interactions, validating or emboldening reciprocal claims; nail down the role of international legal doctrine, legal professionals, legal institutions and structures in governance. Who navigates by their maps? For whom is international law the language of social or political enforcement? What bureaucracies have been spawned in their image? Who is thrust aside, who canonised as the apex of the international community? There has always been something paradoxical here—the discipline also insists (if in a different voice) that its norms are effective, enforced and important. The odd thing is that establishing the rulership of international law can nevertheless be a scandal.

The critical point is that the field governs differently—and for different interests—than it imagines. International law feels it governs from the *periphery*—that states make the norms and enforce them. That power lies with politics. Those working in a more critical vein have proposed something different—first, that international law is a centre which exercises power in the old-fashioned hierarchical sense: human rights as governance, governance feminism, international law forged in and facilitating the colonial encounter. Second, that international law has been the stage on which projects of centrality and marginality have been staged. Arnulf Becker, for example, has traced this theatre in the efforts of intellectuals from the semi-periphery to build international law in the centre as they simultaneously pursued political projects of the periphery in what they took to be the centre of the world's cultural, political and economic order.[7] International law frames a hub and spoke world between the developed North Atlantic industrial democracies and everyone else when it consigns the second to the law of coexistence or the cold winds of free trade, while embracing the former as an advanced space for regional integration and industrial policy, for the law of cooperation and the dense fabric of collaboration characteristic of relations among liberal democracies.[8] In all these ways, international law offers a normative vocabulary of entitlements that constitutes and structures relations among actors, interests and ideas in ways which leave some at the periphery and honours others as central. It is the glue that binds them together.

International law also constructs a world when its votaries imagine international law as an *artificial* construct atop the *real* world of politics among nation-states, or when they imagine that international law exiled religion to the pre-Westphalian past, pushing confession below the waterline of sovereignty, or when they exile women into the private, the local and the cultural, or place private commercial activity outside the domain of international politics and governance. These ideas generate narratives, institutions and expectations which shift the powers and status of people inhabiting these identities to the periphery. And all the while international law speaks the language of universals, embracing and arrogating to itself the universal ethics of human rights, the criminal power to tell right from wrong, the astute political calculation by which necessity and proportionality are measured out in war. In doing so, it has also become the cloak.

International legal scholars could do more to understand how this generates asymmetries—between the religious and secular, or between the reality of politics and the artificialities of

---

[7] See, A Becker, *Mestizo International Law: A Global Intellectual History, 1850–1950,* (Cambridge, Cambridge University Press, forthcoming).
[8] See, eg W Friedmann, *The Changing Structure of International Law* (New York, Columbia University Press, 1964); A-M Slaughter, 'A Liberal Theory of International Law' (2000) 94 *American Society of International Law Proceedings* 240; D Kennedy, 'Turning to Market Democracy: A Tale of Two Architectures' (1992) 32 *Harvard International Law Journal* 373.

law. Does this have some bearing on the way relations between 'real' states like Israel and artificial 'entities' like the Palestinian National Authority become asymmetric? International law is part of the field, the terrain, the language, the structure, through which asymmetries between secular ethics and religious confession, or the diplomatic world of international relations and the economic world of private markets, arise and are reinforced. It provides the normative fabric, the marker of status, the purveyor of *entitlement* through which the routine operations of people pursuing politics and economics, ethics and religion, generate asymmetry and hierarchy. The point is less that international law exercises power as the centre than that it makes itself available as a lexicon of entitlement in a field characterised by dynamic asymmetry.

The potential of centre–periphery analytics for international legal analysis will only be realised if critical scholars can relax the iron-cage top–down pre-Foucauldian model of power so commonly associated with centre–periphery dynamics and learn from international law's own insistence that the world's legal and political order are far more mixed up and fluid than that. Twentieth-century international law was on to something—or created something—when it refigured world order as an open and shifting process whose 'governance' was more a functional reinterpretation of things dispersed across the institutional and political life of the planet than the work of agents empowered by structures. In its own imagination—and in life—international law no longer sits 'on top' governing the relations between states. It prides itself on having become diffused through the global political process as a vernacular of legitimacy, as a horizontal theatre of argument, performance, claims and assertions. Antiformalism, anti-foundationalism, and the embrace of the dispersed theatrics of global power have been hard won in the international legal field. To focus on international law's role in the reproduction of hierarchies of centre and periphery in the world, international lawyers need not turn back from these discoveries. It only remains to develop a centre–periphery analytics every bit as anti-formal, anti-foundational and attuned to the dispersed powers of social performance and expectation.

How, for example, does the commercial arbitration regime reinforce the centrality of the North, the private and the economic vis-a-vis a periphery of the south, the public and the political? It is hard to say. The regime looks evenly balanced. States—like companies—sign up. The regime itself could hardly be more dispersed or ad hoc. The developed world is learning that its own regulatory regimes may yet come to be as vulnerable to attack by trading partners as those of the emerging markets whose policy space was meant to be constrained by the discipline of bilateral investment treaties. And yet, somehow commercial arbitration has metastasised to become an adjudicator of last resort for reviewing the legislative, administrative and even judicial decisions of the developing world. Just how do commercial and financial imbalances translate into political restraint? Could we actually imagine third-world investors using arbitration to contest—and successfully stay—the implementation of a US Supreme Court decision as recently happened to Ecuador in the ongoing *Chevron* case? If not, what are the legal, professional, ideological, commercial or political sinews that reproduce this imbalance? As commercial arbitration, in Garth and Dezalay's compelling phrase, goes about 'dealing in virtue', how are hierarchies left in its wake?[9] The answer will be fine-grain, even if the outcomes are stark.

---

[9] B Garth and Y Dezalay, *Dealing in Virtue: International Commercial Arbitration and the Construction of a Transnational Legal Order* (Chicago, University of Chicago Press, 1996); See also, A Shalakany, 'Arbitration and the Third World: Bias under the Scepter of Neo-Liberalism' (2000) 41 *Harvard International Law Journal* 419.

Centre–periphery analytics might also help us understand the *internal* economy of a profession for which rulership is both a scandal and a dream. There is asymmetry and dualism within the self on the terrain where the field's will to power and to marginality are managed, a centre and a periphery in phases of the international legal professional's sensibility and self-image. This internal ambivalence drives international lawyers working in the humanitarian field, for example, to oscillate between situational pragmatism and a more ethically self-confident universalism. Perhaps they are pragmatic in the field and ethically self-confident in headquarters, savvy over lunch and sanctimonious in their pitch to donors. Both are part of their professional style. Relations between them are fluid and differ over time and in different institutional settings. It is difficult to understand how these postures fit together in a professional style. Often, however, there is asymmetry, pragmatism the central professional sensibility at the International Committee of the Red Cross, ethical self-confidence at the centre for human rights organisations addressing the same battlefield activity. Relations between these institutions, between the doctrines and priorities embedded in each, in part may be a function of the dynamic between these different professional sensibilities. A further avenue for research: in the shadow of what psycho-social or professional rules do these sensibilities relate to one another? Do these asymmetries arise?

In all such matters of interpretation, perspective matters. Talking about centres and peripheries sounds different at the periphery. Stories about difference and domination which make powerful politics in the centre can also offend—identifying the excluded subjects, the unrepresented stakeholders, pinning victims to their subjugation. How does it sound at the periphery to hear it said that sovereignty is just a 'bundle of rights' or, in the words of the 1949 ICJ, 'an institution, an international social function of a psychological character'.[10] Thanks, but we just got here—we'll stick with sovereignty as exclusive political power within a territory. When the EU tells new members how privileged they are to have joined a club of equals, it speaks to their hopes, their dignity. Why should they want to hear that they are still 'the periphery'? A lot depends on how angry the audience is to begin with. Those of us who talked about centre–periphery relations in the Euro-zone seemed like spoilsports as the 1992 'internal market' programme took off; less so now.

I routinely ask my students how they see their generation's project. Is 2012, I ask, like 1648 or 1919 when it seemed everything needed to be rethought? Or is it like 1945, when the international order seemed to need reforming—but not remaking? Tweak the League Covenant and you have the UN. Replace European empire with self-determination under American hegemony and continue. Or is this like 1989, when the demand was not for reform but implementation—with communism defeated the solutions put forward a generation before could finally be implemented?

Unsurprisingly, many go for the middle position: reform, add Brazil to the Security Council, sort out the democracy deficit and currency travails in Europe with another round of treaty-drafting. But an ever increasing number say 2012 is their 1648. As we talk it through, it often seems that the division reflects, as we say, 'where the students are coming from'—not necessarily their nationality—but their sensibility. In this sense, the political appetite for criticism has a centre–periphery dynamic of its own. Those who

---

[10] *The Corfu Channel Case (United Kingdom of Great Britain and Northern Ireland v Albania)* (Merits), Judgment of 9 April 1949, Individual Opinion of Judge Alvarez, 39, 43.

hope to inherit the commanding heights split between 1945 and 1989. Those who feel their interests, politics and national projects, have been stymied by forces beyond their control opt for 1648. The conviction that the preoccupations of the international legal field pale before the injustice of the world is not a recipe for reform or renewal. It is a recipe for disenchantment, for a withdrawal of confidence, affiliation, interest, from the machinery we know as 'governance'.

Indeed, the plausibility of centre–periphery stories depends on where you stand. At the centre, the system seems far too uncertain, malleable and unstable for there to be a centre–periphery dynamic. At the periphery, the dynamic seems far too obvious for the centre to be squishy. Discussion between these positions is unlikely to be productive—indeed, the difference between them is likely to be exacerbated by dialogue, for each is denying what the other finds most true. Moreover, in some sense both sides err. Just because the order is plastic, the centre squishy, doesn't mean there is no centre and no periphery. But just because there is does not mean there's an iron cage—or an iron will. It can be unfair and hierarchical and still not be a conspiracy; diabolically difficult to change and still not be necessity.

For the last few years, I have been participating in discussions at Davos on global policy, risks and governance. Just after the crisis, much seemed up for grabs—the World Economic Forum launched a Global Redesign Initiative to support what they called a 'fundamental reboot' of the 'global architecture'. They were clear, however, that this was not 1945—let alone 1648. No large institutional reorganisation seemed possible—or wise. What was necessary was a new spirit at all levels, and a new willingness to use the tools at hand to respond to urgent issues in new configurations. From this 'centre', global governance was something already constituted global elites could and should undertake—if only they had the will. Will was hard to generate, however, with governance so fragmented, so disparate and so powerless in any particular site.

It looks more like 1648 if you feel the world is *already* governed but you are not part of it. If you can feel that the global economic forces that shake the economy, the society or your own family are facilitated by *some* institutional or legal arrangements. From this perspective, economic instability or poverty are not problems which *escape* governance. They are the by-products—or even the intended consequences—of the current governance arrangements. It is easy to conclude that the people at Davos must want it to turn out this way and have got what they want.

There is little direct dialogue between these positions. At Davos there were demonstrators and lots of barbed wire—one friend came back through security to the conference hall proud to have collected a couple of rubber bullets. But these perspectives do interact. In recent years, a new vernacular has arisen in governance circles to discuss the interaction between these perspectives. To this way of thinking, the relationship between a centre that realises it is too squishy to do more than play for time and a periphery outside demanding more, should be understood as a matter of social-political risk management and 'sustainability', a term detached from its origins in environmental science. The basic question for rulers: how much time do we have? How long can we defer a decision, trying to get things right, before the problem swamps us through the machinery of political or social unrest? Global fiscal imbalances are unsustainable, in this sense, for example, if they will lead to political rupture before we can turn them around. Although most social institutions are all too sustainable—poverty, inequality, ill health—relations between the centre and the periphery often do seem to implicate the system's own sustainability.

This new 'sustainability' analysis is a governance vernacular for managing centre–periphery dynamics. It does not involve demonstrations facing off against bullets, rubber or otherwise. Everyone is also calculating, interpreting, imagining their situation relative to the other and communicating. It is not clear, ultimately, who is 'the centre'. Those on the street can also play the sustainability game—perhaps they will hold on long enough for something to crack. For the rulers, knowing how little can be controlled, it is easy to overestimate the potential for everything to slip out of hand. Moreover, the willingness of the periphery to stand it is itself a moving target, shifting, in part, as belief in the plausibility of the narratives of the centre waxes and wanes.

This kind of symbolic system seems ripe for analysis in Myrdalian terms. There is a loose dualism—those outside, those inside; those near and far from some 'centre'. Their relative positions are themselves part of what is at stake in their interactions, each by turn claiming the modesty of the periphery and authority of the centre. The interaction is structured. The positions are constituted by 'entitlements' which rest in law and social expectation. There are avenues of reciprocal influence, tendencies to spiral, whether viciously or virtuously.

I have looked at a number of international doctrinal worlds over the years—most recently the complex duet between humanitarians and military strategists over the legitimacy of war. They all have something of this structure. A loose vernacular between an 'outside' and 'inside' that seems amenable to interpretation in dualist terms, avenues of interaction, patterns of persuasion, all nested in a set of what we might think of as entitlements. The difficulty is to figure out how it will work when you turn it on. Will human rights and humanitarian law civilise the military or be co-opted by them? Can anything be said about how the relative persuasiveness of their positions will develop over time? Increasingly, I believe the answer is yes.

V. International Lawyers and the Remaking of World Political Economy

Such an analysis may not be politically satisfying. If you are occupying Wall Street or, for that matter, Tahrir Square, the centre–periphery dynamics in international law seem to be an astonishingly elite preoccupation. What about *real politics!* As an Egyptian friend of mine put it: 'excuse me, but we have a revolution going on'. And revolutions call out for bolder centre–periphery narratives, clearly identifying whom to favour and whom to oppose. The difficulty is that even revolutionaries sometimes lack a strong theory—or even a good sociological picture—of how things hold together. It can be tempting to turn back from a twentieth-century embrace of power as performance and argument and identity, to the firmer stuff of interests, structures and classes: real centres and real peripheries. The critical project I propose leans against this kind of political demand. Centre–periphery relations are far less mechanical than that and better thought of as matters of interpretation and assertion, tools for the development of dynamic accounts of mid-level relationships among positions, sectors, regions or ideas, frameworks for uncovering the distributive work of legal arrangements and expert knowledge practices.

At the same time, for international lawyers to take on the challenge of understanding and transforming the political economy of the world, they will need to turn against professional demands for an account of what international law permits and forbids or how the world is legally constituted. The world simply is not constituted in the sense that things fit together in ways articulated in foundational legal documents. Stories about the UN Charter, the WTO and the human rights corpus as world constitutions are fairy tales and international law is far too fluid to serve as a judge of the permitted and prohibited. International law is better understood as part of the glue that holds people, positions and places in dynamic relations with one another, the sinews that link centres and peripheries, and the cloak that obscures the dynamic operations of hierarchy.

Thinking about political economy has become difficult because politics and economics have been structured to operate on different scales, with different players, served by different professions, and interpreted by different academic and expert disciplines. Politics and economics will not be brought together like great powers negotiating a new treaty. Nor will they be brought together by academic theories of their inseparability. They will be reunited by reconfiguring the doctrines, institutions, professional practices and simple common sense through which they have become separate. This is the point of intellectual and professional cross-training: to disestablish the parallel cadres that service the public and the private, the political and the economic. This is the goal of unravelling the distinctions whose expert interpretation and management confirms the separation—between public law and private law, between market supporting and market distorting public policy and so forth.

For the professional political class to remake the world's political economy, they will need to find new institutional channels to integrate transnational interests and new levers to contest faraway decisions which affect their interests. The global political–economic regime will need to make policy space for alternative national and local experiments and strategies designed to manage the internal distribution of growth between leading and lagging sectors or regions and improve the national capacity to capture gains from trade and structure its own insertion into the global economy. Effective governance is no longer a matter of eliminating the corruption or capture of public authorities—difficult as that is. Nor is it a matter of sound corporate governance, corporate social responsibility and effective regulatory supervision—difficult as those are. Effective governance requires that the public and private actors become adept at something which currently none are well organised—or well disposed—to attempt: managing the distribution of growth, linking leading and lagging and managing the political economy of dualism. And they must do this not only in their backyard, in their territory, in their sector, but in a new world of shifting relations and linkages, where small things have large effects, where local rules govern global transactions, and where very little is transparent or predictable. Only by considering economic and political objectives at the same time and on a parallel scale will it be possible to respond to the global challenge of linking experimental, leading-edge economic dynamism wherever it occurs with everyone else—across cities, within and between nations, in regions, across the world.

International lawyers have much to contribute to such a project, particularly if they grasp the depth of injustice in the world today, the urgency of change and the significance of their professional routines in the reproduction of political incapacity. Legal scholars have generated new economic and political ideas before—not all of them sensible. They could do so again. Indeed, the presence of law in the foundations and ongoing practices of both economics and politics makes it surprising that they do not. Nevertheless, a great deal of intellectual work remains to be done.

If we undertake such a critical project, we will want to recall how long it took to disentangle politics and economics; to invent a national politics and organise the world in nation states—and then to build a global economy. For all the agony that has come with success, building a national public politics across the planet had a strong emancipatory dimension—slaves, women, workers, peasants and colonial dominions obtained citizenship in relationship to the new institutional machinery of a national politics. It will not yield easily. It was equally difficult to build a global economy atop that political order. For all the vulnerability, instability and inequality wrought by the effort, the global economy has also lifted hundreds of millions from poverty. It will not be unbuilt in a day. Building a new political economy for a global society will be equally difficult. The promise is equally large. The spirit of new approaches is to begin.

6

Knowledge in Development, Law and Regulation, or How are We to Distinguish Between the Economic and the Non-Economic?

PEER ZUMBANSEN*

I. Introduction

On Sunday, 17 June 2012, while Germany commemorated the 1953 uprising in Berlin of workers and citizens protesting against the East German government, the citizens of Munich were called on to cast their votes in connection with the city and its airport's proposal to build a third runway. With a 33 per cent turnout, 54.3 per cent of Munich's voters rejected the expansion plans for the airport—against an approving 45.7 per cent. In political commentary the following morning, the triumphant voters, rallied around, inter alia, civic initiatives such as 'Plane Stupid Germany'[1] and '*Aufgemuckt*' (which could be translated as 'up in arms'), represented the results as a clear signal that people wanted to 'put an end to the growth mania' and economic exuberance. By contrast, the proponents of the airport extension, a conglomerate of mostly conservative political parties and industry representatives,[2] believed that the decision against the runway communicated a lack of understanding for the importance of the expansion to foster economic growth and prosperity and future-oriented sustainability.[3]

And so, we might say, the story goes. And goes and goes and goes. While the sites and instances might change, the vocabularies remain the same, reflecting perhaps the predictability and polemics of politically opposed views. Seen that way, it would appear as if things have always been relatively simple, refreshingly black or white: Interests, viewpoints and

---

* I am grateful to Marta Jankovic, Hengameh Saberi, Sujith Xavier and to the participants of the conference Critical Legal Perspectives on Global Governance: *Liber Amicorum* David M Trubek, held at the European University Institute, 28–30 June 2012 for helpful feedback.

[1] www.airportwatch.org.uk/?p=2019.

[2] See, eg www.planestupid-germany.de/en/home-en/95-stop-the-third-runway-madness.html; www.ja-zur-3. de/England, and www.munich-business-school.de/nc/en/experience-mbs/news/news-detailview/artikel/munich-business-school-tritt-dem-buendnis-zur-unterstuetzung-des-ausbaus-der-dritten-startbahn-am-flug.html?tx_tt news[backPid]=28&cHash=2629b63e97.

[3] 'Bürgerentscheid in München: Startbahngegner stoppen Flughafenausbau' (*Spiegel Online* German edn, 18 June 2012), available at www.spiegel.de/wirtschaft/soziales/flughafen-muenchen-startbahngegner-stoppen-wohl-ausbau-a-839408.html.

arguments can surely be demarcated along the distinction between economic and non-economic, as if such a distinction were possible.

Yet, how does this observation relate to the discourses that we all find ourselves in these days—sometimes actively as contributors, at other times more passively as listeners, readers or bystanders? Discourses focus on seemingly unruly, boundary-less, problematic concepts; concepts that resist containment and fail to synthesise issues. Consider concepts such as 'global governance', 'regulatory capitalism', 'global legal pluralism', 'global constitutionalism' and 'transitional justice'. Such discourses seem to be, above all, marked by an inquiring, conceptualising impulse, in that they open up vistas and raise questions about connections between different approaches, even as they too often disappoint (possibly for being too modest).[4]

But, still we seem to endorse the intriguing nature of today's deliberations about the functions, the scope and the—fragmented—foundations of global governance instantiations, precisely because we are experiencing the cacophony of descriptive versus prescriptive, sociological versus normative, traditional versus innovative assertions as unavoidable.[5] If we are to crystallise rules for the global governance definition game, then surely there is no way around an earnest engagement with both multi-disciplinarity and inter-disciplinarity views. Increasingly aware of how global governance confronts us with a host of methodological questions, we are finding ourselves engaging with wide-ranging materials from a host of disciplines. Meanwhile, however, the question of method seems to beg another question possibly just as important. What is at stake, really, in this labour-intensive investigation into the different layers of so-called 'global governance'? And, for whom? What lessons, if any, are we able to draw from such efforts—in a more concrete, political way?

Through a dialogue with some of the themes introduced into the scholarship in law and development (L&D) and global governance by David Trubek, this paper hopes to explore ways in which it might be possible and eventually rewarding to pick up on both of these challenges. The chosen approach is a short-circuiting of a number of debates which have been, and continue to be, central elements in fast-evolving global governance discourses. The goal behind this linking exercise is to lay bare continuities and legacies of certain currently fashionable, approaches and concepts in global governance debates in order to show the degree to which we can see that some of them are re-instantiations, reformulations or rediscoveries of concepts and terminologies which were introduced at a much earlier stage and which might seem dated or simply of no use in the context of today's debates. There seems to be little need to justify such an endeavour. Historically and theoretically informed and insatiably curious scholarship bears the inspiring hallmark of both being 'right on the money' and ageing well.[6] The following sections will begin to explore the scope and

---

[4] N Krisch, 'Global Administrative Law and the Constitutional Ambition' in P Dobner and M Loughlin (eds), *The Twilight of Constitutionalism?* (Cambridge, Cambridge University Press, 2010) 245.

[5] G Teubner, 'Fragmented Foundations: Societal Constitutionalism beyond the Nation State' in Dobner and Loughlin (eds), *The Twilight of Constitutionalism?* (n 5) 327, and see now his monographic study, G Teubner, *Verfassungsfragmente. Gesellschaftlicher Konstitutionalismus in der Globalisierung* (Berlin, Suhrkamp, 2012).

[6] See, eg DM Trubek, 'Max Weber on Law and the Rise of Capitalism' (1972) *Wisconsin Law Review* 720; DM Trubek, 'Toward a Social Theory of Law: An Essay on the Study of Law and Development' (1972) 82 *Yale Law Journal* 1; DM Trubek, J Mosher and JS Rothstein, 'Transnationalism and the Regulation of Labor Relations: International Regimes and Transnational Advocacy Networks' (2000) *Law and Social Inquiry* 1187; DM Trubek and LG Trubek, 'Hard and Soft Law in the Construction of Social Europe: The Role of the Open Method of Coordination' (2005) 11 *European Law Journal* 343.

boundaries of L&D in relation to a fast-intensifying discourse on 'transitional justice' (TJ) (Section II) and then contextualise this analysis in a conception of 'spatial' governance (Section III). The concluding sections (Sections IV and V) will investigate the category of 'knowledge' as the crucial variable in the linking of domestic and transnational governance discourses (Section IV).

II. Law and Development and Transitional Justice as Global Governance Discourses

Contributing to a symposium around David Trubek's long-standing work in critical legal scholarship, law and development, new governance and legal theory inevitably prompts reflections on the trajectories, lessons and prospects of such an endeavour. In that respect, the *oeuvre* of such a scholar can fruitfully be seen as a timekeeper, seismographic instrument and yardstick. Inspired by the arc drawn in his work from the critical self-reflection on development law in the 1970s to the scrutiny of different competing models of the state in the present phase of law and development, I hope to offer a supportive and complementary account, which connects domestic governance discourses with global governance and global constitutionalism discourses in the context of the transnational regulatory landscape. By contrasting *domestic* accounts of the state's institutional and normative 'infrastructure' such as the rule of law, due process, rights and constitutional hierarchy with the apparently fragmentary and deficient elements of an evolving *global* legal order, it might be possible to gain insights into the dynamics of 'development law' in the global context today. As domestic regulatory paradigms are being revisited, scrutinised, and tested as to their compatibility with and transferability to the global realm, we now, more than ever, have to recognise the connections and interdependencies between the understandings of 'our' and 'foreign' law, or 'our' and 'foreign' models of the state, of 'our' and 'other' perceptions of law's role in society. In other words, reflecting on a legal theory of law and development and global governance becomes an exercise in epistemology, an ascertaining of how 'we' and 'the other' have learned to conceive of regulatory challenges as legal ones, of competing models of the state, of democratic governance or of economic regulation.

As such, this chapter engages with and comments on David Trubek's innovative scholarship on both law and development L&D[7] and 'new governance'.[8] First, I hope to underline the particular quality and character of an intellectual and political approach to the development of a critical legal research programme that critically illuminates the *context* of legal debates and scrutinises the use of allegedly neutral legal categories (such as the rule

---

[7] See DM Trubek, 'Toward a Social Theory of Law: An Essay on the Study of Law and Development' (1972) 82 *Yale Law Journal* 1; DM Trubek and M Galanter, 'Scholars in Self-Estrangement: Some Reflections on the Crisis in Law and Development Studies in the United States' (1974) *Wisconsin Law Review* 1062; DM Trubek and A Santos, 'Introduction: The Third Moment in Law and Development Theory and the Emergence of a New Critical Practice' in DM Trubek and A Santos (eds), *The New Law and Economic Development* (Cambridge, Cambridge University Press, 2006) 1–18, and DM Trubek, 'Developmental States and the Legal Order: Towards a New Political Economy of Development and Law' (2008) *University of Wisconsin Legal Studies Research Paper No 1075*.

[8] See, eg Trubek and Trubek, 'Hard and Soft Law in the Construction of Social Europe' (n 7).

of law, property, or the state) in a charged discursive universe.[9] Secondly, I hope to be able to highlight the general significance of the field of 'law and development' L&D for a better understanding of the relationship between legal and economic governance discourses, which informs this field perhaps more than any other. Lastly, by focusing on the concept of 'knowledge' as it has been employed by Trubek in his more recent work on the 'new developmental state',[10] I want to draw connections between the assertions of the critical role of knowledge in development contexts, on the one hand, and domestic governance contexts, on the other.

Law and development, one of the fields where David Trubek has made some of his most important scholarly contributions, has always been an area which can neither be neatly and clearly defined nor boxed into clear-cut categories. The field has long been a battlefield for opposing concepts of law, political and economic order and the role of institutional governance,[11] and as such has always been a laboratory for audacious experiments with explosive material. Categories such as 'progress', 'development' or 'order' are invariably contentious, and in the context of L&D are employed as bargaining chips in a high-stakes game over political and economic influence, autonomy and, emancipation.[12] While specific local contexts of L&D became the *loci* of such contestation, often enough under the magnifying glass of international and national development agendas, market integration and state reform, one of the most striking discoveries to be made here relates to the fact that the contentious items in the L&D context are also those which have long informed a critical analysis of law and governance in the context of the nation state.[13] As such, the boundaries between the developing and the developed world, between those countries receiving and those exporting or providing legal (or economic) aid become porous, and a legal theory of L&D can fruitfully build on its older domestic sister.

Among the important scholarly projects pursued by L&D scholars has been the discovery and analysis of the *legal pluralist* nature of the governance orders in the context of development.[14] With a growing awareness of the different, existing ordering structures 'on the ground' in the development context came the realisation that *any* legal order challenges the observer to acknowledge the parallels between and the co-existence of formal and informal, hard and soft law, of legal and non-legal norms.[15] This realisation prompted L&D scholars to acknowledge but also to build on the idea that many of the challenges pertaining to a law/non-law distinction that had been identified as specific to

---

[9] For a powerful illustration of such an approach, see PS Gupta, 'The Peculiar Circumstances of Eminent Domain in India' (2012) 49 *Osgoode Hall Law Journal* 445, 453–56.

[10] See the overview at www.law.wisc.edu/gls/lands.html.

[11] D Kennedy, 'Laws and Development' in J Hatchard and A Perry-Kessaris (eds), *Law and Development: Facing Complexity in the 21st Century—Essays in Honour of Peter Slinn* (London, Cavendish Publishing, 2003) 17.

[12] For a brilliant deconstruction of the post-war conceptual division between political and economic emancipation of former colonial states, see S Pahuja, *Decolonising International Law: Development, Economic Growth and the Politics of Universality* (Cambridge, Cambridge University Press, 2011).

[13] The masterful analysis is still Trubek and Galanter, 'Scholars in Self-Estrangement' (n 8).

[14] K Pistor and D Berkowitz, 'Of Legal Transplants, Legal Irritants, and Economic Development' in P Cornelius and B Kogut (eds), *Corporate Governance and Capital Flows in a Global Economy* (Oxford, Oxford University Press, 2003) 347; K Pistor, 'The Standardization of Law and Its Effect on Developing Economies' (2002) 50 *American Journal of Comparative Law* 97.

[15] HW Arthurs, *Without the Law: Administrative Justice and Legal Pluralism in Nineteenth-Century England* (Toronto, University of Toronto Press, 1988); RA Macdonald and J MacLean, 'No Toilets in Park' (2005) 50 *McGill Law Journal* 721; SF Moore, 'Law and Social Change: The Semi-Autonomous Field as an Appropriate Subject of Study' (1973) 7 *Law & Society Review* 719.

the development context, were in fact detachable from any legal governance framework. Indeed, the inadequacy of existing legal governance thinking pointed to the need for a different theoretical—but also doctrinal—attention.[16]

It is this realisation that allows for a better appreciation of the questionable foundations of a legal order of the embeddedness of legal governance in a particular institutional setting (for example, the state) and at a particular moment in (geo-political) time.[17] To the degree that the struggle over law 'reform' in the context of development is seen as not entirely removed from contestations of legal (political, economic) order in the domestic context, L&D emerges as a field, which is just as much concerned with the relationship of law to its (particular, local) social environment and context as has been the case for any other legal theoretical or legal sociological inquiry.[18] But, accepting this perspective also implies accepting the loss of an outside observer's standpoint. Precisely by acknowledging the inseparability of critical legal analysis in the domestic and the development context, we lose the comfort of being outside of the sphere which we are purporting to study and to examine in a disinterested manner.[19] Instead, the demarcation of the L&D context from that of one's home legal system and jurisdiction becomes questionable in itself, because the assertions of law's precariousness in the development context apply to the domestic home context with equal force. On that basis, the distinction between governance challenges 'there' and 'here' appears artificial. Indeed, the distinction seems designed to insulate the domestic context from critique while depicting the development context as deficient and requiring 'aid' and assistance. The identification of a series of legal governance questions as arising from within the context of a 'developing country' inevitably leads to these questions having to be seen as already pertinent much earlier, that is, already present and evident in the context of domestic legal critique.

A striking feature of this contextualisation of L&D as part of a larger exercise in investigating law's relationship to, and role in society, is the way in which the field opens itself up to an engagement and exchange with complementary discourses about regulatory places and spaces. Both legal scholars[20] and sociologists[21] have been scrutinising the conceptual and constituted nature of such regulatory spaces; spaces which escape a straightforward depiction from a single discipline's vantage point. Just as this critique has become pertinent with regard to the analysis of different, specialised regulatory arenas, ranging from

---

[16] Macdonald and MacLean, ibid. See also C Scott, 'A Core Curriculum for the Transnational Legal Education of JD and LLB Students: Surveying the Approach of the International, Comparative and Transnational Law Program at Osgoode Hall Law School' (2005) 23 *Penn State International Law Review* 757.

[17] Begoña Aretxaga, 'Maddening States' (2003) 32 *Annual Review of Anthropology* 393.

[18] R Cotterrell, 'Why Must Legal Ideas Be Interpreted Sociologically?' (1998) 25 *Journal of Law & Society* 171; R Banakar, 'Law Through Sociology's Looking Glass: Conflict and Competition in Sociological Studies of Law' in A Denis and D Kalekin-Fishman (eds), *The ISA Handbook in Contemporary Sociology* (London, Sage Publications Ltd, 2009); P Zumbansen, 'Law's Effectiveness and Law's Knowledge: Reflections from Legal Sociology and Legal Theory' (2009) 10 *German Law Journal* 417.

[19] Trubek and Galanter (n 8). See also DM Trubek, 'Toward a Social Theory of Law: An Essay on the Study of Law and Development' (1972) 82 *Yale Law Journal* 1.

[20] R Ford, 'Law's Territory (A History of Jurisdiction)' (1999) 97 *Michigan Law Review* 843.

[21] S Sassen, 'The State and Globalization' in JS Nye and JD Donahue (eds), *Governance in a Globalizing World* (Washington, Brookings Institution, 2000) 91; S Sassen, 'The Places and Spaces of the Global: An Expanded Analytic Terrain' in D Held and A McGrew (eds), *Globalization Theory. Approaches and Controversies* (Cambridge, Polity, 2007) 79; D Harvey, 'The Sociological and Geographical Imaginations' (2005) *International Journal of Politics, Culture and Society* 211.

labour[22] to corporate,[23] from environmental[24] to criminal law,[25] altogether suggesting a methodological shift from comparative to transnational law,[26] L&D has become a very active laboratory for a renewed engagement with a critical and contextual analysis of law in a fast-changing and volatile environment.

This aspect has been underlined, perhaps most tellingly, by the recent approximation of L&D with the field of 'transitional justice', which testifies to an increasing awareness among interested experts of the close connections between investigations into the 'legacies' of past injustices with programmes of future-directed legal and economic aid.[27] Closely connected to, and oftentimes overlapping with this very vivid scholarly engagement has, of course, been an equally vibrant 'literary'[28] and cultural engagement with 'transition' periods. After the seminal (inevitably colonial) portrayals by Joseph Conrad in *An Outpost of Progress* (1897) or *Heart of Darkness* (1899), post-colonial novels such as Chinua Achebe's *Things Fall Apart* (1958) and JM Coetzee's *Waiting for the Barbarians* (1980) have again poignantly scrutinised the slippery slope between 'us' and 'them' that inescapably pervades any intervention or development context. How in the context of public international law's attempts to address transnational military and civil conflict, this slope has become painfully obvious again, was powerfully illustrated in Anne Orford's critique of the hidden, hegemonic aspirations of recent instances of humanitarian intervention.[29] Excavating the challenges of concepts such as change, reform and progress, as they have been central to seminal TJ

---

[22] Trubek, Mosher and Rothstein, 'Transnationalism and the Regulation of Labor Relations' (n 7); G Mundlak, 'De-Territorializing Labor Law' (2009) 3 *Law & Ethics of Human Rights* 188; HW Arthurs, 'Extraterritoriality by Other Means: How Labor Law Sneaks across Borders, Conquers Minds, and Controls Workplaces Abroad' (2010) 21 *Stanford Law & Policy Review* 527.

[23] LC Backer, 'Private Actors and Public Governance Beyond the State: The Multinational Corporation, the Financial Stability Board, and the Global Governance Order' (2011) 18 *Indiana Journal of Global Legal Studies* 751; P Zumbansen, 'Neither "Public" nor "Private", "National" nor "International": Transnational Corporate Governance from a Legal Pluralist Perspective' (2011) 38 *Journal of Law & Society* 50.

[24] L Gulbrandsen, S Andresen and JB Skjærseth, 'Non-State Actors and Environmental Governance: Comparing Multinational, Supranational and Transnational Rule Making' in B Reinalda (ed), *The Ashgate Research Companion to Non-State Actors* (Aldershot, Ashgate, 2011) 463; N Craik, 'Deliberation and Legitimacy in Transnational Environmental Governance' (2006) *IILJ Working Paper 2006/10*, New York University, Global Administrative Law Series; C Kamphuis, 'Canadian Mining Companies and Domestic Law Reform: A Critical-Legal Account' (2012) 13 *German Law Journal* 1456; S Seck, 'Home State Regulation of Environmental Human Rights Harms As Transnational Private Regulatory Governance' (2012) 13 *German Law Journal* 1360.

[25] N Boister, 'Transnational Criminal Law?' (2003) 14 *European Journal of International Law* 953; N Boister, *An Introduction to Transnational Criminal Law* (Oxford, Oxford University Press, 2012); RJ Currie, *International and Transnational Criminal Law* (Toronto, Irwin Law, 2010).

[26] CM Scott, '"Transnational Law" as Proto-Concept: Three Conceptions' (2009) 10 *German Law Journal* 859; P Zumbansen, 'Transnational Legal Pluralism' (2010) 1 *Transnational Legal Theory* 141; P Zumbansen, 'Transnational Law, Evolving' in J Smits (ed) *Elgar Encyclopedia of Comparative Law* 2nd edn (Cheltenham, Edward Elgar, 2012), 898–925.

[27] See, eg R Mani, 'Dilemmas of Expanding Transitional Justice, or Forging the Nexus between Transitional Justice and Development' (2008) 2 *International Journal of Transitional Justice* 253, and the contributions to P De Greiff and R Duthie (eds), *Transitional Justice and Development: Making Connections* (New York, Social Science Research Council, 2009).

[28] See the insightful discussion of the prose/poetry debate in India around the work of Rabindranath Tagore, in D Chakrabarty, *Provincializing Europe: Postcolonial Thought and Historical Difference* 2nd edn (Princeton, Princeton University Press, 2007, first published 2000).

[29] A Orford, 'Muscular Humanitarianism: Reading the Narratives of the New Interventionism' (2003) 10 *European Journal of International Law* 679.

debates as those concerning South Africa[30] or Sri Lanka,[31] Achmat Dangor's *Bitter Fruit* (2001) or films such as Vithanage's *Death on a Full Moon Day*, have become inseparably intertwined with the scholarly, 'expert' discourse around these instances of TJ.

III. The Transnational Space of the Contemporary 'Human Condition'

What can this intersection of scholarly, literary and cultural engagement tell us about the methodological challenges arising in the L&D (and TJ) context? To the degree that we can already build on a host of critical work to scrutinise the orientation, method and contentions of L&D and TJ theory, an additional aspect of this enterprise concerns the acknowledgement of and engagement with non-scholarly content. Another question concerns the demarcation of places and spaces in this context. What, we may ask, distinguishes the focus of Achmat Dangor's poignant analysis of family relations in post-apartheid South Africa[32] from the haunting account of Mourid Barghouti's return to Palestine after an involuntary 30-year exile?[33] Emerging from these accounts, is a powerful illustration of what we might call the 'transnational human condition', marked by multilayered and multi-tiered relations of belonging and 'citizenship'. It is this dimension of the 'human condition' that could arguably be seen as the fourth dimension of Hannah Arendt's depiction of labour–work–action,[34] scrutinising the possibilities of political, social belonging in a post-national environment, which is marked by the fragility of political communities and, again, an increased precariousness of political voice.[35]

Chinua Achebe recounts in his 2009 collection of short stories, *The Education of a British-Protected Child*, numerous instances in which he and the audiences he speaks before, are confronted with the porosity of the lines that divide 'home' and 'abroad', the 'here' and the 'there'. In Achebe's rendering, these experiences illustrate the tensions in people's lives when trying to make sense of their deeply-felt attachments to places of origin and places of meaning, when—at the same time—they find themselves on an inchoate and often swirling trajectory, which takes them through different places, communities, spheres of interaction, places of engagement and confrontation—with others, who have come to these places through similar patterns of predictable unpredictability. Achebe's stories recount numerous instances of frustration in the face of alienation, cliché and stereotype that seem to repeat themselves—over and over again. The author presents them in an uncompromisingly and tirelessly analytical manner, the various accounts underlining the importance of

---

[30] H Corder, 'Prisoner, Partisan and Patriarch: Transforming the Law in South Africa 1985–2000' (2002) 118 *The South African Law Journal* 772; A Gross, 'Reconciliation in South Africa' (2004) 40 *Stanford Journal of International Law* 40.

[31] J Derges, *Ritual and Recovery in Post-Conflict Sri Lanka* (London, Routledge, 2012).

[32] A Dangor, *Bitter Fruit* (Cape Town, Kwela Books, 2001).

[33] M Barghouti, *I Saw Ramallah* (London, Bloomsbury, 2004).

[34] H Arendt, *The Human Condition* (Chicago, Chicago University Press, 1958).

[35] See R Cotterrell, 'Spectres of Transnationalism: Changing Terrains of Sociology of Law' (2009) 36 *Journal of Law and Society* 481 and N Fraser, *Scales of Justice: Reimagining Political Space in a Globalizing World* (New York, Columbia University Press, 2009).

difference in that which seems to be the same, the varying conjectures of people's meetings, confrontations and clashes of viewpoints and observations that cannot be simply traced back, as emerges from story to story, to one particular stance, one easily demarcated political viewpoint or a comprehensively-founded moral choice. Instead, Achebe highlights the numerous crossroads in people's perceptions and judgements, the complex overlapping of context and intent that shape the moment when one formulates and utters one's view. He seems to say 'look again', 'think again' and 'look again', and it is this back and forth wandering of our gaze, which may help to grasp the challenges in contemporary L&D and TJ contexts. These contexts are intricately marked by the simultaneous existence of the 'new' and the 'old'. And yet we are asked to reject this (overly neat) juxtaposition for the ways in which it imposes an evolutionary narrative of progress onto a sphere that needs to be studied through its complex relationship between local and global consciousness.[36] Similarly, both L&D and TJ become mere instantiations of a renewed effort to reflect critically on the methodological basis of legal–political governance.

David Trubek's immensely rich body of scholarly work, developed over the span of many years, is a very appropriate platform for the launching of such a renewal. The subject matter of this work has been intricately located in different places and in different spheres of conceptual imagination. As in Achebe's accounts, these spaces are both geographical and intellectual, both real and constructed. And, as is highlighted by the scholarship in the area of L&D that David Trubek has himself significantly shaped, challenged and helped to establish and sustain, the critical engagement with these allegedly *dividing* lines between 'real' and 'constructed', between, say, field work, empirical data, news reports and statistics, on the one hand, and description, critique, deconstruction and argument, on the other, are at the core of what L&D is really all about. To both emphasise and simultaneously question the categories by which we draw lines between 'here' and 'there', 'home' and 'abroad', 'ours' and 'theirs', becomes a lifetime occupation, one that is only inadequately captured by a faculty website indication of 'law and development' as being someone's 'interest' or 'field of research'. Seen, studied, theorised and practised in this critical way, L&D becomes an instantiation of a much more comprehensive engagement with the 'concept of law', with the categories by which in research and curriculum lines are drawn between 'domestic' and 'foreign' laws and legal cultures. Thus, a scholar of L&D of this calibre is inevitably a threat to the standards and routines of scholarship as it is carried out in law reviews and conferences and as it, in myriad ways, influences and shapes law school course design and the programming of legal education. The particular approach to L&D taken here threatens the daily routine of law schools pretending to teach their fee-paying clients to 'learn to think like a lawyer' as it scrutinises this entire routine and suggests that it could all be in fact very different if only we cared to reflect more on the connections between 'here' and 'there'. As is clear from Achebe's stories, to think about these connections is a tiresome business, one that must remain cautious, self-critical and never-satisfied, one that continues to draw on a wide spectrum of information, data and accounts—in other words, on a complex body of 'knowledge', on which one draws and to which one already and constantly contributes.

---

[36] Chakrabarty, *Provincializing Europe* (n 29), ch 5 'Birth of the Subject'.

IV. *Knowledge* in Development

The vibrant and increasingly intersecting intellectual discourses around the conceptual and normative foundations of L&D[37] and TJ[38] are increasingly complemented and contextualised by a critical engagement with legal regulation in the north[39] as well as epistemological interventions in the South.[40] Arising from this attention to L&D and TJ is an intensified interest in the nature of *knowledge* implicated in these different engagements. Knowledge becomes a crucial variable as it applies to a host of divergent conceptual and normative programmes. For example, *knowledge* is at the heart of the expertise and 'know-how' retained by a governing body or drawn upon by governmental actors when crafting regulatory instruments and interventions.[41] At the same time, knowledge as a variable and an unknown enters both sides of regulatory interventions—pertaining to what the regulator knows and what is known within the sphere acted upon. This double contingency of what law should know but can never *know* for certain, has long been a concern of legal regulatory theory, and of legal sociology and criminology in particular.[42] Given the complex interplay of domestic and transnational governance discourses and the centrality of knowledge in both,[43] the intensified interest in scrutinising *what we know* when unleashing programmes of aid, reform as well as 'technical' and legal assistance has to be central to any future engagement with L&D and TJ as part of a larger, interdisciplinary theory of global governance.[44] From the vantage point of a critical engagement with knowledge, such an enterprise must develop a methodology able to open up, rather than eclipse avenues of contestation and mutual learning.[45] A central contention in this paper is that the

---

[37] See the contributions to Trubek and Santos (eds), *The New Economic Law and Development* (n 8).

[38] N Roht-Arriazza, *The Pinochet Effect: Transnational Justice in the Age of Human Rights* (Philadelphia, University of Pennsylvania Press, 2005); N Roht-Arriazza and J Mariezcurrena (eds), *Transitional Justice in the Twenty-First Century: Beyond Truth Versus Justice* (Cambridge, Cambridge University Press, 2006); R Nagy, 'Transitional Justice as Global Project: Critical Reflections' (2008) 29 *Third World Quarterly* 275; S Vieille, 'Transitional Justice: A Colonizing Field?' (2012) 4 *Amsterdam Forum* 58.

[39] This depiction is used to mark economic and ideological characteristics rather than a geographic region.

[40] B de Sousa Santos, 'Beyond Abyssal Thinking: From Global Lines to Ecologies of Knowledge' *Eurozine* (29 June 2007). See also the contributions to B de Sousa Santos (ed), *Another Knowledge is Possible: Beyond Northern Epistemologies* (London, Verso, 2007), and R D'Souza, 'Imperial Agendas, Global Solidarities, and Third World Socio-legal Studies: Methodological Reflections' (2012) 49 *Osgoode Hall Law Journal* 409.

[41] S Jasanoff, *Science at the Bar: Law, Science, and Technology in America* (Cambridge, MA, Harvard University Press, 1997); see also the contributions to G Edmond (ed) *Expertise in Regulation and Law* (Aldershot, Ashgate, 2004).

[42] KN Llewellyn, 'The Normative, the Legal, and the Law-Jobs: The Problem of Juristic Method' (1940) 49 *Yale Law Journal* 1355; N Luhmann, 'Some Problems with Reflexive Law' in G Teubner and A Febbrajo (eds), *State, Law and Economy as Autopoietic Systems* (Milan, Giuffre, 1992) 389; P Zumbansen, 'Law's Effectiveness and Law's Knowledge: Reflections from Legal Sociology and Legal Theory' (2009) 10 *German Law Journal* 417.

[43] KW Abbott and D Snidal, 'Strengthening International Regulation Through Transnational New Governance: Overcoming the Orchestration Deficit' (2009) 42 *Vanderbilt Journal of Transnational Law* 501; P Zumbansen, 'The Ins and Outs of Transnational Private Regulatory Governance: Legitimacy, Accountability, Effectiveness and a New Concept of "Context"' (2012) 13 *German Law Journal* 1269.

[44] D Held, 'Reframing Global Governance: Apocalypse Soon or Reform!' in D Held and A McGrew (eds), *Globalization Theory: Approaches and Controversies* (Cambridge, Polity, 2007) 240; FE Johns, 'Global Governance: An Heretical History Play' (2004) 4 *Global Jurist Advances* Art 3.

[45] See, eg JN Pieterse, 'Globalization North and South: Representations of Uneven Development and the Interaction of Modernities' (2000) 17 *Theory, Culture & Society* 129; M-R Trouillot, *The Anthropology of the State in the Age of Globalization: Close Encounters of the Deceptive Kind* (2001) 42 *Current Anthropology* 125; J Ferguson and A Gupta, *Spatialising States: Toward an Ethnography of Neoliberal Governmentality* (2002) 29 *American Ethnologist* 981.

parallels and shared interests in contemporary L&D and TJ discourses are echoed by the connections between domestic and transnational governance discourses. Where we find that L&D discourses are inseparably intertwined with TJ-related questions regarding the appropriate and non-universalising,[46] legal/non-legal *response* to legacies of suppression, exploitation and domination, we are confronted with the co-evolutionary dynamics of legal/non-legal, hard/soft, formal/informal. In short, attending to *knowledge* points us to the *legal pluralist modes of governance* characteristic in settings which we have hitherto tended to study through conventional notions of jurisdiction, that is, through legal *spatial* lenses.[47] However, these co-evolutionary dynamics between L&D and TJ support the emergence of regulatory regimes which can no longer adequately be captured through categories of state sovereignty or jurisdiction. Instead, the emerging transnational regulatory landscape follows to a large degree the fragmenting dynamics of a functionally differentiated world society, prompting, in turn, an intensified investigation as to the legitimacy, that is, the normative and political implications, of the systems theory's world society model.[48]

These debates provide a formidable background to the continuously evolving debate around L&D in that they complement and expand the highly-charged economic and political stakes in this arena. David Trubek's work is of central significance in this regard. His interest in 'knowledge' occupies a crucial place in a long engagement with bridging both national and development governance discourses. An acute sensitivity to the ambiguous role of knowledge has informed his work over the decades, but in the following, I want to focus particularly on his emphasis on the role of knowledge in development processes as articulated in his recent papers on the 'new developmental state'. Taking a closer look at the role of knowledge in the L&D context promises important insights into the future trajectory of this field in the context of interdisciplinary global governance studies sketched above. What drives and motivates developments such as the World Bank's self-description as a 'Knowledge Bank' becomes a matter of critical concern, and prompts our reflection on the origins as well as the experiences that have already been made with such data-driven governance approaches in other places and times. In other words, David Trubek's interest in the role of knowledge in today's development scholarship—and practice—invites us to take a closer look at the connections and differences between the prominence of knowledge in this context and in domestic contexts in the past. To do so seems especially opportune in light of the crudeness of assertions, distinctions and categories that continue to characterise global governance discourses, particularly in terms of the descriptions and analysis of constellations that really deserve a more comprehensive and sophisticated conceptual treatment.[49] Indeed, the persistence of inadequate analytic categories in the field of global governance is at considerable odds with contemporary analysis of knowledge-driven

---

[46] S Vieille, 'Transitional Justice: A Colonizing Field?' (2012) 4 *Amsterdam Forum* 58.

[47] Ferguson and Gupta, 'Spatialising States' (n 46); A Mbembe, 'At the Edge of the World: Boundaries, Territoriality, and Sovereignty in Africa' (2000) 12 *Public Culture* 259.

[48] This tension characterises the interchange between, say, Gunther Teubner and Emilios Christodoulidis. See G Teubner, 'Fragmented Foundations: Societal Constitutionalism beyond the Nation State' in P Dobner and M Loughlin (eds), *The Twilight of Constitutionalism?* (Cambridge, Cambridge University Press, 2010) and the contributions of Emilios Christodoulidis, Gert Verschraegen, Bart Klink and Wil Martens in (2011) 3 *Netherlands Journal of Legal Philosophy*. For Gunther Teubner's most recent, comprehensive attempt to engage with the challenge of normativity, see his monograph, G Teubner, *Constitutional Fragments* (Oxford, Oxford University Press, 2012).

[49] RA Posner, 'Creating a Legal Framework for Economic Development' (1998) 13 *The World Bank Research Observer* 1.

governance.[50] *Knowledge* as an analytic category, particularly as informed by Trubek's work, offers us a way forward.

A. The Boundaries of 'Law and Development'

While never having gained its secured and unquestioned seat in the core, mainstream North-American law school classroom curriculum, 'Law and Development' has long been one of the most innovative, contested and actively discussed theory/practice laboratories to think about a whole range of dimensions of law reform, aid, development, progress and growth, universality/relativism, imperialism, post-colonialism and models of state and society. Among such laboratory work have always been efforts to question the foundations and in/adequacies of western/northern regulatory concepts for developing countries, fully exposing the deeply problematic and contestable nature of any such progress-associated connotations in the first place. Obvious, then, to participants in such work, was the inseparability of law critique in a foreign, distant place and at home. In both contexts, inevitably, scholars would come to realise the fragile and intricate dynamics of their legal orders' evolution, institutionalisation and function. It is sobering to note as well that in both contexts, scholars would come to realise the illusory nature of the separation of these contexts—foreign and domestic—and how crucial the critical reflection on the boundaries of locality must be.[51]

Despite the death knell that was allegedly struck for 'the law and development movement' by Trubek's and Galanter's impressive self-critique in 1974,[52] the consequences of their writing were, arguably, to enliven and galvanise a field of inquiry. Even if measured only by that inadequate measure—the number of citations—their article has made a most important mark. Its analysis continues to trouble and problematise many different areas of legal discourse—well beyond the field of law and development per se. How can this be explained? As alluded to at the beginning of this paper, there is a particular quality of scholarship which distinguishes itself by making ambitious theoretical, conceptual and political claims based on a careful and comprehensive engagement with a well-considered, complex literature. As such, the value of that scholarship endures beyond the narrow window of a current moment. An engagement with Max Weber, for example, becomes a comprehensive and lasting exploration of the complex relations between legal thought and political governance,[53] a scathing self-critique of the hitherto applied methodologies to comparison and law reform in the context of L&D that unfolds into an inspiring inquiry into the role of law in society.[54]

This elevation of the bar can also be seen in more recent work, be that in the context of the complex regulatory arrangements of the European Union[55] or of the much-debated law

---

[50] K-H Ladeur, 'Constitutionalism and the State of the "Society of Networks": The Design of a New "Control Project" for a Fragmented Legal System' (2011) 2 *Transnational Legal Theory* 463.

[51] Trubek and Galanter, 'Scholars in Self-Estrangement' (n 8).

[52] Pahuja, *Decolonising International Law* (n 14) 204, n 152.

[53] DM Trubek, 'Max Weber's Tragic Modernism and the Study of Law in Society' (1986) 20 *Law & Society Review* 573.

[54] Trubek and Galanter, 'Scholars in Self-Estrangement' (n 8).

[55] Trubek and Trubek, 'Hard and Soft Law in the Construction of Social Europe' (n 7).

reforms that are on the way in different parts of Latin America today.[56] The promises—and rewards—of such work are not only keen and timely observations of present constellations of law and regulatory governance, but a better and more comprehensive understanding of the way in which lawyers must consciously draw on an increasingly differentiated and complex, interdisciplinary analysis of evolving governance structures if they want law to retain a voice in the fast-evolving regulatory theory discourses. At the same time, such scholarship appreciates our 'standing on the shoulders of giants', less in devout reverence, than in critical and alert appreciation of an ongoing conversation.

This research offers comprehensive insights into the complexities of political transformation, law reform and global integration through a reconnection of local knowledge with earlier and larger discursive frameworks. Thus, while focusing on one region of the world and a limited number of countries, it soon becomes obvious how immensely rich the tapped-into repository of information is. Trubek's more recent work on the evolving political economy of the 'new developmental state' forcefully connects a careful consideration of facts 'on the ground' with work on political economy, on state-market relations and on legal and regulatory governance.[57] Against the background of a long-standing scrutiny of the methodological and conceptual challenges facing anyone engaged in law and development work, he seeks to demarcate the contours of a political economy analysis in the development context. Poignantly, he comes to this analysis equipped with a toolbox containing both analytical and conceptual instruments, the adequacy and usefulness of which will have to be assessed in the very concrete applicatory context. In that vein, he observes that the "New Political Economy of Development" (NPED) assumes a central role of uncertainty in setting goals of industrial policy, designing and implementing market regulatory instruments and identifying level of global competitiveness of national economy'. The use of the concept of the 'process of discovery' to explain the regulatory approach in the NPED, owed but not attributed to Hayek,[58] puts the finger on the sensible spot of the—constructed!— boundaries of state–market or public–private. 'If we wanted to sum up the NPED in a few words, it might be in envisioning development as a *process of discovery* in which the state seeks to empower the private sector and state and market function best when they are linked in collaborative structures that foster experimentation and revision.'[59] *Hic sunt leones*! Well aware of the beasts lingering in the shadow of volatile and vulnerable governance structures, coming in the form of institutional economists and social norm theorists, Trubek directs our attention to a body of theoretical work that explicitly aims at bringing together economics, law and politics in order to address real-world problems.

A detailed example of the new kinds of institutions and policies can be found in Hausmann, Rodrik, and Sabel's proposal for industrial policy. This proposal reflects the underlying assumptions of the new development economics and illustrates the kinds of novel institutions it suggests. They note several features of developing country markets that lead to sub-optimal performance and justify state intervention. Such markets may fail to identify new products whose profitability creates positive externalities for the national economy; provide mechanisms to coordinate

---

[56] Trubek, 'Developmental States and the Legal Order (n 8).
[57] Trubek, 'Developmental States and the Legal Order' (n 8).
[58] FA Hayek, 'Competition as a Discovery Procedure' (2002) 5 *Quarterly Journal of Austrian Economics* 9 (first published 1968, MS Snow (trans)); see also F Hayek, 'The Use of Knowledge in Society' (1945) 35 *American Economic Review* 519.
[59] Trubek, 'Developmental States and the Legal Order' (n 8) 10.

interrelated investments; or generate knowledge about the public inputs necessary for the success of an industry. To overcome these failures, they propose new approaches to the organization of an industrial policy.[60]

The responsibility falling on the state here is to 'organise a dialogue among the firms in a sector, region or industry and between the firms and the state; provide incentives for the provision of public inputs identified by this kind of collaboration; encourage continuous improvement; create a system to monitor the projects that emerge from the deliberations; and ensure that the fruits of learning through these processes are shared'.[61]

Refreshingly candid in laying out the motivations of such an engagement, Trubek highlights how 'these institutional innovations have significant implications for the law—and vice versa'. His interest in this work on experimentalist governance and industrial innovation policy[62] is driven by the idea that 'their proposals for public-private deliberation and specialised budgets for government input in selected industries will raise a series of administrative law and constitutional law issues'.[63] Against this background, however, Trubek exposes the ambitious claim of his engagement with these bodies of work:

> I set forth a theory of the relationship between economic ideas and various doctrines in the field of law and development. The history of thought about law and development shows that there is an intimate relationship between prevailing economic ideas and dominant notions of the proper role of law in development. ... This law and development doctrine is more than a simple recipe book of projects and less than an autonomous academic theory. Rather, as Alvaro Santos and I have argued, it is best seen as the product of the interaction of legal theory, economic development theory, and the practices of development agencies.[64]

It is here that we discern most clearly the range of theoretical discourses that, according to Trubek, are quintessential to resuscitating the troubled state of law and development theory in a highly-contested and volatile political and economic global context. However, focusing on a concrete case study presents challenges that loom even larger especially when it comes to developing a sound theoretical framework and drawing on locally gained and compared data:

> [I]f evidence of [New Developmental State] NDS state practice is fragmentary, data on legal practices is almost non-existent and the theory of law in the new developmental state has not yet been created. But we would expect that among other things we will find a great deal of interest in creating the legal framework for various forms of public-private collaboration; emphasis on creating the legal structure for a kind of capital market that can identify and reward entrepreneurship; attention to shifts in corporate governance to encourage investment and promote innovation; recognition of the need for flexibility and for ways to encourage experimentation; and efforts to challenge any aspect of international economic law that might hinder state intervention.[65]

---

[60] Ibid, 12.

[61] Ibid, 13.

[62] See R Hausmann, D Rodrik and CF Sabel, 'Reconfiguring Industrial Policy: A Framework with an Application to South Africa' (2008) *Harvard University Center for International Development CID Working Paper No 168*, available at www.hks.harvard.edu/centers/cid/publications/faculty-working-papers/cid-working-paper-no.-168.

[63] Trubek, 'Developmental States and the Legal Order' (n 8) 13.

[64] Ibid, 16.

[65] Ibid, 18–19.

Arguably, the gist of this effort lies, as noted before, in a building on, and in an approximation of development theory with economic theory, above all institutional economics, with industrial innovation policy theory as well as with 'new governance', among which experimental governance occupies a prominent place. This suggestion prompts a number of comments. First, it should be emphasised that Trubek's purposive engagement with complex theoretical approaches is a powerful illustration of the challenges facing both theory and practice in the presence of complex regulatory arrangements today. However, every toolkit has a history of its own, the way it came to be put together, the order of instruments that are stored and arranged on its inside, and the use that has been made of them over time—their application in practice. While this is an obvious point to make, it deserves mentioning in the L&D context, which prompts a host of questions regarding the origin, adequacy and transferability of regulatory models. As with the seemingly never-ending self-inspection and critique of comparative law,[66] L&D is a field forever belaboured and challenged on a complex methodological basis. The following section raises a number of questions in response to the proposal of importing political economy concepts into the study of developing governance structures, as suggested in David Trubek's recent work.

The previous references underscore the relevance of approaching a study of a local regulatory culture from a more comprehensive perspective that allows for a scrutiny of the *actors, norms and processes*, which shape the development context.[67] But, at the same time, I would like to voice a concern regarding the baggage and background assumptions, accompanying and shaping the political economy ideas transplanted from one context—a post-industrialist and post-welfare constitutional state—into another context with institutional and normative dimensions which we might not be able to map with the cartography we are used to. This seems to be of particular importance with regard to the implicit assumptions informing an endorsement of regulatory models such as decentralisation, innovation and regulatory competition. In political and regulatory theory discourses of the last two or three decades, these terms emerged in an intricate intellectual space between economic and political theories and have by now attained an almost sacrosanct character, be that with regard to federal structures in complex polities[68] or in the context of searching for growth models in path-dependent economies.[69] However, as examples of transatlantic transplants already illustrate, the effects of policies that endorse a fine-tuned subsidiarity–federalist framework and that place hope into the regulated self-regulatory dynamics of actors on different levels[70] greatly depend on the historically and politically evolved context in which

---

[66] See the contributions to M Adams and J Bomhoff (eds), *Practice and Theory in Comparative Law* (Cambridge, Cambridge University Press, 2012).

[67] For more background on the A-N-P approach, see P Zumbansen, '*Lochner* Disembedded: The Anxieties of Law in a Global Context' (2013) 20 *Indiana Journal of Global Legal Studies*, 29–69 (available at ssrn.com/abstract=2174017).

[68] S Rose-Ackerman, 'Risk Taking and Reelection: Does Federalism Promote Innovation?' (1980) 9 *Journal of Legal Studies* 593; GA Bermann, 'Harmonization and Regulatory Federalism' in I Pernice (ed), *Harmonization of Legislation in Federal Systems* (Baden-Baden, Nomos, 1996); R Howse and K Nicolaidis (eds), *The Federal Vision* (Oxford, Oxford University Press, 2001); B Galle and J Leahy, 'Laboratories of Democracy? Policy Innovation in Decentralized Governments' (2009) 58 *Emory Law Journal* 1333.

[69] W Lazonick, 'Varieties of Capitalism and Innovative Enterprise' (2007) 24 *Comparative Social Research* 21; JP Murmann, *Knowledge and Competitive Advantage: The Coevolution of Firms, Technology and National Institutions* (Cambridge, Cambridge University Press, 2003).

[70] CF Sabel and J Zeitlin, 'Learning from Difference: The New Architecture of Experimentalist Governance in the EU' (2008) 14 *European Law Journal* 271; see already MC Dorf and CF Sabel, 'A Constitution of Democratic Experimentalism' (1998) 98 *Columbia Law Review* 267.

they are implemented. What might be in itself a very promising conceptual approach to the study of multi-level and multi-polar regulatory systems—and the EU certainly represents just that[71]—will eventually unfold through highly intricate and unpredictable dynamics in a continuously evolving complex environment.[72]

To be sure, it is no more than a trivial insight that these experiences suggest the need to pay close regard to the locally existing rules and regulatory practices—the challenge consists in determining the form and process of 'context sensitive' regulation. It is with this challenge in mind that we are finding ourselves torn between opening our toolbox of well-worn and tested tools and concepts on the one hand, and starting fresh, with open eyes and without prejudice on the other.[73] What is remarkable in this context is the impossibility of 'breaking free' even from the semantic and symbolic stronghold of certain categories, regardless of the degree to which these have been subjected to critique, deconstruction and demystification. This is as true today[74] as it was in the 1970s:[75] in our search for appropriate regulatory approaches to be taken with regard to development contexts (as well as other, similarly complex regulatory spaces),[76] we strive to critically reflect on the usability of the rule of law, learned lessons with regard to democratic accountability, public deliberation or the separation of powers. Meanwhile, we realise how none of these principles can be lifted out of context without losing some explanatory capacity, leading us back to the motivation of why we intended to draw on a particular regulatory experience in the first place. Again and again, we are confronted with the *particularity* of an evolutionary process in a specific space that seemingly frustrates all attempts at translation or transplantation.[77] And yet, precisely because of this confrontation, we return, again and again, to a critical reflection on the categories through which we seek both to explain and to shape spaces of vulnerability and precariousness. There appears to be a crucial difference, however, between an earlier, progressive, critical exercise of such reflection and the more inchoate, interdisciplinary approach that seems to be forming today out of a combination of legal, political, sociological, economic and anthropological theory on the one hand, and historical and linguistic

[71] See, eg G Majone, 'The European Community Between Social Policy and Social Regulation' (1993) 31 *Journal of Common Market Studies* 153, and KA Armstrong, 'Governance and the Single European Market' in P Craig and G de Búrca (eds), *The Evolution of EU Law* (Oxford, Oxford University Press, 1999).

[72] R Boyer and JR Hollingsworth, 'From National Embeddedness to Spatial and Institutional Nestedness' in JR Hollingsworth and R Boyer (eds), *Contemporary Capitalism: The Embeddedness of Institutions* (Cambridge, Cambridge University Press, 1997); R Dore, W Lazonick and M O'Sullivan, 'Varieties of Capitalism in the Twentieth Century' (1999) 15 *Oxford Review of Economic Policy* 102; G Teubner, 'Legal Irritants: How Unifying Law Ends Up In New Divergences' in PA Hall and D Soskice (eds), *Varieties of Capitalism: The Institutional Foundations of Comparative Advantage* (Oxford, Oxford University Press, 2001); P Zumbansen, '"New Governance" in European Corporate Governance Regulation as Transnational Legal Pluralism' (2009) 15 *European Law Journal* 246.

[73] See, eg K Pistor, 'Of Legal Transplants, Legal Irritants, and Economic Development' in P Cornelius and B Kogut (eds), *Corporate Governance and Capital Flows in a Global Economy* (Oxford, Oxford University Press, 2003).

[74] K Rittich, 'The Future of Law and Development: Second Generation Reforms and the Incorporation of the Social' (2004) 26 *Michigan Journal of International Law* 199.

[75] DM Trubek and M Galanter, 'Scholars in Self-Estrangement' (n 8).

[76] N Krisch, *Beyond Constitutionalism. The Pluralist Structure of Postnational Law* (Oxford, Oxford University Press, 2010) ch 4.

[77] GA Sarfaty, 'Measuring Justice: Internal Conflict over the World Bank's Empirical Approach to Human Rights' in K Clarke and M Goodale (eds), *Mirrors of Justice: Law and Power in the Post-Cold War Era* (Cambridge, Cambridge University Press, 2009).

study on the other.[78] While this difference is still hard to pinpoint or to make fruitful, it becomes ever more evident that in close proximity to the continuing stand-offs between conservative and progressive struggles over development policies, the range of theory, vocabulary, categories, frameworks and imaginations is expanding. In that context, the astutely-recorded accounts by Achebe of his interactions with 'third world experts',[79] the extermination of interview protocols and legislative materials of law-making processes in Singapore's 'authoritarian' Rule of Law[80] or the anthropological scrutiny of the World Bank's human rights programmes[81]—they are all and each one of them crucial elements that help draw a richer and more sophisticated picture of the development context today. In other words, we see a significant analytical expansion and deepening of our 'knowledge' basis vis-à-vis the developmental state and the transnational 'aid and development' apparatus that is staring at it. The challenge remains in understanding and drawing the adequate lessons of such an expanding epistemic framework. The remainder of this contribution shall briefly touch on three categories that play an enormous—both practical and symbolic—role in development discourses today: market, constitution and knowledge.

B. Semantic Tools of Power and Domination: Market, Constitution and Knowledge

Questions related to the order and selection of 'tools' come to the surface not only in the context of the re-introduction of (Hayek's) idea of a discovery process marking the spontaneous self-organising dynamics of markets,[82] but in every assertion of the benefits of regulatory competition in comparison to harmonisation models. Self-regulation, decentralisation and empowerment of actors—as governance subjects—are frameworks which linger alluringly in the background and inform the reference to the promise of discovery as a governance principle. However, by turning one's gaze away from the development context here under scrutiny, and back towards the current applicatory contexts where we find long-standing and recently recurring references to discovery, some of the baggage associated with this idea becomes clearer. Drawing on Hayek, but also on Tiebout,[83] private lawyers, economists and regulatory theorists have been insisting for some time on the supremacy of a regulatory competition approach in contrast to harmonisation or unity-based concepts of market regulation.[84] This deserves mention merely to shed some light on the alluring power

---

[78] J Rajah, *Authoritarian Rule of Law: Legislation, Discourse and Legitimacy in Singapore* (Cambridge, Cambridge University Press, 2012), 37–52, 58–60, 288.

[79] C Achebe, *The Education of a British-Protected Child* (New York, Knopf, 2009).

[80] Rajah, *Authoritarian Rule of Law* (n 79) 181–212.

[81] SE Merry, 'Measuring the World: Indicators, Human Rights, and Global Governance' in P Zumbansen and R Buchanan (eds), *Law in Transition: Rights, Development and Transitional Justice* (Oxford, Hart Publishing, 2013 forthcoming); GA Sarfaty, *Values in Translation: Human Rights and the Culture of the World Bank* (Palo Alto, Stanford University Press, 2012).

[82] For a fuller exposition, see FA Hayek, *The Constitution of Liberty* (London, Routledge, 2006, first published 1960).

[83] CM Tiebout, 'A Pure Theory of Local Expenditures' (1956) 64 *Journal of Political Economy* 416.

[84] See, eg J Macey, 'Regulatory Globalization as a Response to Regulatory Competition' (2003) 52 *Emory Law Journal* 1352, or PB Stephan, 'Regulatory Cooperation and Competition: The Search for Virtue' in GA Bermann, M Herdegen and PL Lindseth (eds), *Transatlantic Regulatory Co-operation* (Oxford, Oxford University Press, 2000), 167–202; for a poignant critique, see S Deakin, 'Reflexive Governance and European Company Law' (2007) *CLPE Research Paper Series and Cambridge Centre for Business Research Working Paper No 346*.

of both discovery process and regulatory competition even in discourses that otherwise would have been believed to be firmly in the hands of legal scholars, particularly constitutional and administrative lawyers. (On a side note, law students interested in studying the concept of constitutional order usually do not notice that they are not reading a legal text when taught the ideas of Tiebout and Hayek. Only after being exposed to a critical legal voice laying bare the implicit assumptions, do students catch their breath).[85]

The challenges of employing the idea of regulatory competition in an economic sense are reiterated in Trubek's observation that: 'The new developmental state seems to need both flexibility *and* stability.' The commitment to experimentation 'creates a need for flexible, specialised, and easily revisable frameworks'.[86] It is now an obvious point to make, and Trubek is among the first to acknowledge the treacherousness of endorsing a regulatory framework per se—rather than placing it in a particular context that gives it meaning and contours. The endorsement of flexibility and adaptable, 'revisable' frameworks follows closely on the regulatory experiences in post-welfare state political economies in the North and the West. These have been marked by a significant shift away from substantive, activist rule-of-law conceptions, in which governments would confidently employ legal regulation to further an abundance of social goals. The fundamental transformation of the welfare state[87] opened up a plethora of options on the right and the left, with *law and economics* eventually coming out as the most successful among the emerging 'law and society' methodologies.[88] The dominance of governance theory that places the market at the centre of its regulatory design has been relatively unabashed over the decades since the 1980s, and even the current financial and economic crisis does not yet seem to have induced its demise. At the same time, we see that engagements with 'market' as governance category are untiring. Apart from the temporarily soothing references to Polanyi[89] we are drawn to explore the intricacies of transnationally-constituted markets through an interplay of economic, sociological and regulatory theory. This interplay draws our attention to the dynamics between market processes and evolving organisational structures,[90] and highlights the need for a better understanding of the interpenetration of economics and finance in the construction of today's markets.[91] That such undertakings are now urgent is only underscored by the fast emergence of 'new' economies and the spatialisation of new,

---

[85] D Charny, 'Illusions of a Spontaneous Order: "Norms" in Contractual Relationships' (1996) 144 *University of Pennsylvania Law Review* 1841.

[86] Trubek, 'Developmental States and the Legal Order' (n 8) 20.

[87] P Pierson, 'The New Politics of the Welfare State' (1996) 48 *World Politics* 143.

[88] K Rittich, 'Functionalism and Formalism: Their latest Incarnations in Contemporary Development and Governance Debates' (2005) 55 *University of Toronto Law Journal* 853, 857: 'We know that functionalist arguments can be flipped, and that both law and economics and critical legal studies are realist progeny.'

[89] See, eg N Fraser, 'The Crisis of Capitalism' Lecture before the Normative Orders Research Cluster, Goethe-University, Frankfurt, 19–20 April 2010, available at www.normativeorders.net/de/veranstaltungen/dokumentation/videothek/415-frankfurt-lecture-ii; for further engagements with Polanyi in a transnational context, see the contributions to C Joerges and J Falke (eds), *Karl Polanyi, Globalisation and the Potential of Law in Transnational Markets* (Oxford, Hart Publishing, 2011).

[90] See, eg D Baecker, *Wirtschaftssoziologie* (Bielefeld, Transcript Verlag, 2006) and S Deakin, 'Corporate Governance and Financial Crisis in the Long Run' in P Zumbansen and CA Williams (eds), *The Embedded Firm: Corporate Governance, Labour and Financial Capitalism* (Cambridge, Cambridge University Press, 2011).

[91] See, eg R Dore, 'Financialization of the Global Economy' (2008) 17 *Industrial and Corporate Change* 1097 and E Engelen, 'The Case for Financialization' (2008) 12 *Competition and Change* 111, as well as S Jacoby, 'Labor and Finance in the United States' in Williams and Zumbansen (eds) (n 90).

transnational markets.[92] In response, we find a feverish search for regulatory frameworks, policies and processes, altogether forming the context and background for an assertion of market governance in developing countries. Those bad old times of a crude depiction of a 'legal framework for economic development' appear to have passed, or have they?[93]

C. The Constitutional Promise

Responding to the seemingly ubiquitous *constitutionalist* discourse, which has been asserting its place within global governance debates, a group of scholars from Colombia, South Africa and India convened in 2011 in New York to explore the options of formulating a concept of constitutionalism 'from the global South'. The edited volume, *Constitutionalism of the Global South*, which grew out of this meeting, published in April 2013, is a most welcome contestation of the predominantly Western discourse on 'global constitutionalism' so far.[94] In his erudite introduction, the conference convenor and editor of the collected essays, Daniel Bonilla Maldonado, highlights the ambiguities that characterise a research project on constitutionalism, which is perceived from a particular geopolitical and historical angle, but which can only be opened up to analysis if a whole other set of factors is taken into consideration. Such factors include the fact that throughout the extensive history of colonisation, a great number of constitutional principles were introduced into the legal orders now under scrutiny. At the same time, through the process of decolonisation and more recent legal transplants, the legal orders have undergone a significant transformation, the result of which is in most cases an intricate combination of 'old' and 'new', 'Northern' and 'Southern' constitutional principles and instruments. Furthermore, the perception of the 'foreign' or 'Southern' legal order is greatly influenced by the constitutional understandings that the observer brings to the task. Not only is this complexity aptly reflected in the introduction but the chapter also introduces the main actors in a North–South dialogue on comparative constitutionalism and constitutional reform. As regards the choice of the three countries under scrutiny in this book—India, South Africa and Colombia—Professor Bonilla and the contributors to the book make the pertinent point that while there is less sense in trying to carve out a comprehensive and distinct framework for a constitutionalist approach of *the* global South, the chosen countries provide for representative case studies to illustrate the major traits of post-colonial constitutionalism. All three experiences are instantiations of a far-reaching and complex history of legal reform, offering rich insights into the negotiation between legislative and adjudicatory approaches to legal regulation in the face of great economic inequality, social and cultural diversity, and violence. Studies such as those collected in the book allow for a more adequate, contextual understanding of the legal, but also political and cultural, issues involved. As such, this scholarship gives unparalleled insights into the local discourses, contestations of and engagements with political and judicial actors, scrutinising the tensions between 'activist' courts and

---

[92] 'BRICs, emerging markets, and the world economy—Not just straw men: The biggest emerging economies are rebounding, even without recovery in the West' (*The Economist*, 18 June 2009).

[93] RA Posner, 'Creating a Legal Framework for Economic Development' (1998) 13 *The World Bank Research Observer* 1.

[94] D Bonilla Maldonado (ed), *Constitutionalism of the Global South* (Cambridge, Cambridge University Press, 2013).

governments, extrapolating the local structures and challenges of gaining 'access to justice' and the obstacles of unfolding an ambitious constitutional agenda in the context of dire economic—and political—inequality and social fragmentation.

This brief allusion to the—as yet unpublished—essays in this volume should only point us in the direction of further differentiation when it comes to references to constitutional reform and the 'migration of constitutional standards',[95] especially in the development context. The value of interventions such as those alluded to here, can hardly be overstated, bringing to light as it were, the significant blind spots in a constitutional discourse that, while aspiring to 'global' relevance, remains too embedded in a particular, Northern/Western reference framework.[96] The consequence of this perspective is a silently yet decisively lingering confidence in the 'embedding', 'containing' and 'empowering' function that constitutional law can assume in a context that is otherwise marked by significant regulatory fragmentation and precariousness. Without taking into account the detail of an evolving constitutional culture in a particular social, historical, political and economic context, we are running the risk of blindly endorsing a specific understanding of rights or of constitutional protection that has little if any relevance to the place it is being brought to. One of the authors in the volume, Professor Manuel Iturralde, cautions against foregone conclusions regarding the formation of a unified, coherent constitutional mindset of the 'global South'. Instead, he stresses some of the changes that have occurred in Colombia, but also in other parts of the world, including in the global South. Among such changes was the rise of progressive constitutional thinking, a growing confidence in a strong judicial branch, 'particularly in constitutional courts, as a valuable tool to attain social change'. Drawing on Diego López Medina's influential work on legal theory in Latin America, the author emphasises the decline in importance of legal formalism in comparison to 'new—progressive—constitutionalism' and judicial activism. Importantly, the author cautions against the view that would perhaps too enthusiastically equate the judicial activism evidenced by the example of the Colombian Constitutional Court with real advance in social change. While acknowledging that court pronouncements by themselves cannot bring about social change (the lessons of *Brown v Board*[97] are deeply internalised), the author posits that judicial activism can and does produce instrumental and symbolic effects. In conclusion, the author finds that the Court's jurisprudence has contributed to an opening up of deliberative and democratic spaces.

Surely, paradigm changes are not induced in a simple manner. As is sourly acknowledged from within the field of comparative law in general,[98] constitutional comparisons are still plagued by a great degree of methodological uncertainty and theoretical indeterminacy. But, while '[c]onstitutionalism is sweeping the world',[99] evidenced, for example, by the

---

[95] S Choudhry (ed), *The Migration of Constitutional Ideas* (Cambridge, Cambridge University Press, 2006).

[96] See, eg the critical remarks by P Capps and D Machin, 'The Problem of Global Law' (2011) 74 *Modern Law Review* 794, reviewing Krisch, *Beyond Constitutionalism* (n 77).

[97] *Brown v Board of Education*, 347 US 483 (1954)

[98] O Kahn-Freund, *Comparative Law as an Academic Subject: Inaugural lecture delivered before the University of Oxford on 12 May 1965* (Oxford, Clarendon Press, 1965); O Kahn-Freund, 'On Use and Misuse of Comparative Law' (1974) 37 *Modern Law Review* 1; P Legrand, *Le droit comparé* (Paris, Presses Universitaires de France, 1999); RA Miller, 'Introduction' in S Reza, MJ Bazyler, RA Miller and P Yu (eds), *Global Legal Traditions: Comparative Law in the Twenty-First Century* (Dayton, LexisNexis, 2013).

[99] SH Williams, 'Introduction: Comparative Constitutional Law, Gender Equality, and Constitutional Design' in SH Williams (ed) *Constituting Equality: Gender Equality and Comparative Constitutional Law* (Cambridge, Cambridge University Press, 2009) 1.

fact that 'at least 110 countries around the world' have engaged in constitution writing or reform since 1990,[100] this evidence is itself extremely varied. Both causes and forms of constitutional change are anything but uniform and thus belie all claims regarding a worldwide and universal trend to a specific set of constitutional values or rights. Rather, the intensity of constitutional creation, reform and discourse around the world is illustrative of the complexity of this process. The search, therefore, for a better understanding of these myriad and continuously evolving constitutionalist cultures must reach deep into the constitutive elements of legal and political cultures, where the places, forms and scopes of democracy continue to be 'unsolved riddles'.[101] As 'law and development' forms and reforms itself into an ever more comprehensive reflective framework to investigate the meaning and role of law in evolving societies, such locally-informed studies of constitutionalism hold significant promise.

V. The Elusive Nature of Knowledge

Finally returning to David Trubek's emphasis on the crucial role of knowledge in the conceptualisation of regulatory policy in the new developmental state, in this section we should touch upon some of the challenges in engaging with knowledge in this context. By way of provocation, I should like to posit that the greatest challenge in determining the role of knowledge in the development context lies in designing a process by which it would become possible to assess the type and quality of knowledge, which is being considered as *relevant* in the conceptualisation of regulatory policy. This 'process', however, is more than a mere procedural framework pertaining to methods of information gathering, consultations, timelines and evaluation. Clearly, we are here confronted with much deeper issues regarding the assessment of the collected and evaluated data, issues that touch directly on the contested relevance of any information[102] and critically highlight the precarious basis on which both domestic[103] and developmental[104] policies are so regularly based. As such, our concern with contested knowledge connects related questions arising in the L&D context with long-standing and still evolving debates in domestic and transnational regulatory spaces. Both are telling and relevant for an assessment of 'knowledge' in development, as Northern/Western regulatory experiences and mindsets routinely become transported into the development context, without the necessary reflection on the different contextual circumstances between the exporting and importing state.[105]

---

[100] Ibid.

[101] S Marks, *The Riddle of All Constitutions: International Law, Democracy, and the Critique of Ideology* (Oxford, Oxford University Press, 2000), 103, 146.

[102] See M Valverde, 'Jurisdiction and Scale: Legal "Technicalities" as Resources for Theory' (2009) 18 *Social & Legal Studies* 139 and M Valverde, *Law's Dream of a Common Knowledge* (Princeton, Princeton University Press, 2003) with a telling differentiation of 'small T' and 'large T' categorisations of *truth*.

[103] K-H Ladeur, 'The Evolution of General Administrative Law and the Emergence of Postmodern Administrative Law' (2011) 6 *Osgoode Hall Law School CLPE Research Paper Series No 16/2011*.

[104] Rittich, 'The Future of Law and Development' (n 75); Merry, 'Measuring the World' (n 82).

[105] See, eg A Santos, 'The World Bank's Uses of the "Rule of Law" Promise in Economic Development' in Trubek and Santos (eds), *The New Law and Economic Development* (n 8) and Trubek and Galanter, 'Scholars in Self-Estrangement' (n 8).

Among the many questions that arise against this background are those that relate to the process by which development agencies draw on, generate and employ the information from which development programmes and policies are conceived and designed. Such perennially pressing and well-known questions now find a potentially fruitful echo in explorations of the way in which global governance institutions can themselves be opened towards a broader basis of public participation, input and, eventually, accountability.[106] Such investigations have been brought under way, more recently,[107] under the umbrella of global administrative law (GAL), and have unsurprisingly prompted a lively mix of endorsement and critical engagement.[108] Whatever the continued debate over the real scope and usefulness of GAL[109] might produce, there is an important 'approximation' of previously too isolated discourses occurring here, which will arguably continue to expose the law of international organisations to contestation but, even more, move parallel critical discourses closer to this field. As such, the Third World Approaches to International Law (TWAIL) scholarship[110] has begun to open important vistas on the historical and semantic trajectories[111] of international law and the order it both depicts and constructs. Similarly, the field of 'transitional justice' has recently begun to assume a more important role in the intellectual space of L&D, given its concerns with evolving state structures and constitutional orders, frequently unfolding at the intersection between local fragmentation and foreign intervention.[112]

What these cursory references may highlight at least, is the complex basis of what might be considered to be 'relevant' knowledge in the context of development policy-making and how such assertions are themselves always highly contested.[113] The proliferation of

---

[106] DM Trubek, 'The Owl and the Pussy-Cat: Is there a Future for "Law and Development"?' (2007) 25 *Wisconsin International Law Journal* 235.

[107] For a compelling account of the struggles in the conceptualisation of the Bretton Woods institutions, see Pahuja, *Decolonising International Law* (n 13) 14–25.

[108] See, eg B Kingsbury, N Krisch and R Stewart, 'The Emergence of Global Administrative Law' (2005) 68 *Law & Contemporary Problems* 15; of the numerous, insightful, critical engagements with this proposal, see, eg C Harlow, 'European Administrative Law and the Global Challenge' in P Craig and G de Búrca (eds), *The Evolution of EU Law* (Oxford, Oxford University Press, 1999) and BS Chimni, 'Co-option and Resistance: Two Faces of Global Administrative Law' (2005) 37 *New York University Journal of International Law & Politics* 799.

[109] My own concerns are expressed in P Zumbansen, 'Transnational Comparisons: Theory and Practice of Comparative Law as a Critique of Global Governance' in J Bomhoff and M Adams (eds), *Theory and Practice of Comparative Law* (Cambridge, Cambridge University Press, 2012) and P Zumbansen, 'Administrative law's global dream' (2013) 11 *International Journal of Constitutional Law* 506.

[110] See the landmark studies by B Rajagopal, *International Law from Below: Development, Social Movements and Third World Resistance* (Cambridge, Cambridge University Press, 2003) and A Anghie, *Imperialism, Sovereignty and the Making of International Law* (Cambridge, Cambridge University Press, 2005). For very insightful engagements with the different approaches and challenges to a TWAIL position, see R Buchanan, 'Writing Resistance Into International Law' (2008) 10 *International Community Law Review* 1 and OC Okafor, 'Critical Third World Approaches to International Law (TWAIL): Theory, Methodology, or Both?' (2008) 10 *International Community Law Review* 371; JT Gathii, 'TWAIL: A Brief History of its Origins, its Decentralized Network, and a Tentative Bibliography' (2011) III:1 *Trade, Law and Development* 26.

[111] See the brilliant studies by Pahuja, *Decolonising International Law* (n 13), and Rajah, *Authoritarian Rule of Law* (n 79), on the ways in which the semantic 'construction' of a field serves to immunise positions of power sustained by a discursive rationality from contestation.

[112] See R Teitel, *Transitional Justice* (Oxford, Oxford University Press, 2000), and R Nagy, 'Transitional Justice as Global Project: Critical Reflections' (2008) 29 *Third World Quarterly* 275.

[113] B de Sousa Santos, *Toward a New Legal Common Sense: Law, Globalization, and Emancipation* (Cambridge, Cambridge University Press, 2002); J Comaroff and JL Comaroff, *Theory from the South: Or, How Euro-America Is Evolving Toward Africa* (Boulder, Paradigm Publishers, 2012); C Rodríguez-Garavito, 'Ethnicity.gov: Global Governance, Indigenous Peoples, and the Right to Prior Consultation in Social Minefields' (2010) 18 *Indiana Journal of Global Legal Studies* 1, esp 13–14 (with reference to J Comaroff and JL Comaroff, *Ethnicity Inc.* (Chicago, University of Chicago Press, 2009).

contending and competing vocabularies to address questions of legal and political reform, institutional development, market-building and security is illustrative of the multiple layers of meaning, historical experiences, associations and connotations, on which each new assertion of political prudence must be seen to rest. Productively inspired by the early frustration vis-à-vis the failed attempts to make available a set of tested legal theories to the legal-political challenges in a development context,[114] the task today seems to be similar, yet amplified. Not only has the design of a regulatory framework that would arguably befit a progressive political agenda become much more elusive, given the troubled and ironic reversal of post-welfare state liberal legal theory into neo-liberal functionalism,[115] but also the reference field for the construction of such a framework has become decisively more differentiated and complex. While it is still true that a concept such as the 'rule of law' can and should, particularly in the context of development, be understood as a platform for contestation and critical engagement with competing viewpoints and interests,[116] it seems that we are today asked to reflect on even more aspects of the Rule of Law (RoL) model than before.[117] Despite the legacy of hundreds of RoL programmes developed and pursued under the auspices of the World Bank, the form and content of the RoL is today more contested than ever.[118] Such contestation is both sobering and significant, especially in a context of intensifying transnational thought exchange regarding the meaning and structure of the RoL.[119]

What seems to emerge from this complexification and intensification of discourses, both of which are driven by a growing interdisciplinary engagement with and contestation of the categories and vocabularies which are being employed, are elements of a transnational discourse that can only inadequately and incompletely be captured under thematic formulas such as 'global governance', 'global constitutionalism' or 'regulatory capitalism'. Indeed, today's investigations into the form(s) and the role of law in development contexts cannot be confined to a space designated as 'law and development'. It is important to highlight the semantic and symbolic baggage that each one is bound to carry from 'domestic' regulatory experiences into the development arena. Neither form of baggage is easily or even adequately captured by a political connotation of 'right' or 'left'. This much the complex regulatory experiences over the last decades have shown.

The question then becomes: where can a political legal theory become attached, if the shift from government to governance, greatly amplified by the emergence of a transnational legal pluralist landscape, confronts us with the unavailability of distinct centres of political decision? Without such centres of decision-making, predictable patterns of norm implementation and adjudication and legitimate processes of political participation, is there a focus for a political legal theory or does the framing of such a question regress us

---

[114] Trubek and Galanter, 'Scholars in Self-Estrangement' (n 8).

[115] P Zumbansen, 'Law After the Welfare State: Formalism, Functionalism and the Ironic Turn of Reflexive Law' (2008) 56 *American Journal of Comparative Law* 769.

[116] D Kennedy, 'Laws and Development' in J Hatchard and A Perry-Kessaris (eds), *Law and Development: Facing Complexity in the 21st Century* (London, Cavendish Publishing, 2003).

[117] For series of insightful engagements, see still AC Hutchinson and P Monahan (eds), *The Rule of Law: Ideal or Ideology* (Toronto, University of Toronto Press, 1987).

[118] *Cf* eg Santos, (n 104) with B Kingsbury, 'The Concept of "Law" in Global Administrative Law' (2009) 20 *European Journal of International Law* 23.

[119] AN Licht, C Goldschmidt and SH Schwartz, 'Culture Rules: The Foundations of the Rule of Law and Other Norms of Governance' (2007) 35 *Journal of Comparative Economics* 659; Rajah, *Authoritarian Rule of Law* (n 79) 37.

to a past of spatial, jurisdictional thinking? Such questions are arguably situated further on the normative scale than on the descriptive, sociological one. To be sure, the descriptive, sociological scale has come to such prominence in the global governance discourses of recent years but the normative scale is increasingly difficult to avoid. In light of ever more differentiated accounts of transnational rule-making and networked interaction,[120] the pressing nature of 'constitutional' questions investigating the seemingly elusive basis of transnational, post-national legitimacy becomes ever more apparent.[121] Exploring further concepts of global pluralism[122] or cosmopolitanism[123] promises to bring important insights into the concrete interaction between different vertical layers of governance and adjudicatory bodies as well as between horizontally interacting organisations on the international level. But, here too, the problem remains of how to convincingly bring together a sociologically informed account of transnational governance with the political philosophical anxieties, which have for so long been inspiring international thinkers.[124] On the other hand, engagements with the problem of legitimacy on the basis of a systems theory model of world society, which is characterised by functional differentiation and a seemingly irresolvable fragmentation of competing rationalities of 'meaning',[125] also illustrate how the quest for the political remains as elusive as it is perceived as urgent.[126] Simple recipes being unavailable, the task appears to be to get back into the midst of it. David Trubek's work is a great motivator in that regard. Never confining himself to an ivory tower, his scholarship always carries the mark of a political thinker, drawing on an impressive range of theoretical work, never for its own sake, but to lay bare the shortcomings of simplifying accounts and of parochial thinking. Just as he would confront the tensions between a self-forgotten development mandate 'out there' and continuing efforts to build an inclusive justice system domestically, he would likely raise his eyebrows at the mind-numbing depiction of the stakes in Munich's recent airport expansion referendum. Can someone really be that naïve, he might ask. With him, we are awaiting an answer.

---

[120] A Héritier and D Lehmkuhl, 'The Shadow of Hierarchy and New Modes of Governance' (2008) 28 *Journal of Public Policy* 1; KW Abbott and D Snidal, 'Strengthening International Regulation Through Transnational New Governance: Overcoming the Orchestration Deficit' (2009) 42 *Vanderbilt Journal of Transnational Law* 501.

[121] A Stone Sweet, 'Constitutionalism, Legal Pluralism, and International Regimes' (2009) 16 *Indiana Journal of Global Legal Studies* 621; N Walker, 'Taking Constitutionalism Beyond the State' (2008) 56 *Political Studies* 519; W Mattli and N Woods, 'In Whose Benefit? Explaining Regulatory Change in Global Politics' in W Mattli and N Woods (eds), *The Politics of Global Regulation* (Cambridge, Cambridge University Press, 2009).

[122] Krisch, *Beyond Constitutionalism* (n 77).

[123] M Kumm, 'The Cosmopolitan Turn in Constitutionalism: On the Relationship between Constitutionalism in and beyond the State' in JL Dunoff and JP Trachtman (eds), *Ruling the World? Constitutionalism, International Law, and Global Governance* (Cambridge, Cambridge University Press, 2009).

[124] I Kant, *To Perpetual Peace: A Philosophical Sketch* (Indianapolis, Hackett, 2003, first published 1795, T Humphrey (trans); see also the opening observations in Capps and Machin, 'The Problem of Global Law' (n 96), with reference to George Scelle.

[125] N Luhmann, 'Globalization or World Society: How to Conceive of Modern Society?' (1997) 7 *International Review of Sociology* 67; A Fischer-Lescano and G Teubner, 'Regime-Collisions: The Vain Search for Legal Unity in the Fragmentation of Global Law' (2004) 25 *Michigan Journal of International Law* 999.

[126] G Teubner, *Verfassungsfragmente: Gesellschaftlicher Konstitutionalismus in der Globalisierung* (Berlin, Suhrkamp, 2012), 49–55, 175–88; for a shorter account of this position, see G Teubner, 'Fragmented Foundations: Societal Constitutionalism beyond the Nation State' in P Dobner and M Loughlin (eds), *The Twilight of Constitutionalism?* (Cambridge, Cambridge University Press, 2010) 327.

Part III

Labour and Globalisation

7

Making Bricks Without Straw: The Creation of a Transnational Labour Regime

HARRY ARTHURS*

I. Introduction

David Trubek, amongst his other improbable endeavours, has shown us how we might construct a regime of transnational labour regulation.[1] This, one might say, is 'like making bricks without straw'. Of course, the analogy is one commonly used to describe any task that is impossibly difficult, but it also happens to be particularly relevant to the themes of this conference. Recall the origins of the phrase. In one of history's earliest recorded labour disputes, the Israelites—a community of undocumented migrant workers—petitioned on religious grounds for a three-day respite from their work at Pharoah's brickworks.[2] Pharaoh took umbrage, and ordered the Israelites to maintain production. Moreover, to discourage future impertinences, he refused to provide them with straw, the binding agent that holds mud bricks together. Instead, he decreed, the Israelites had to provide their own straw, which was very hard to come by locally and had to be sourced through an extended supply chain. Pharaoh's unfair labour practices in turn provoked the world's first general strike, the Exodus.

* I have benefited greatly from the research assistance of Satomi Aki, a JD candidate at Osgoode Hall Law School, York University, and from discussions with participants in the conference Critical Legal Perspectives on Global Governance: *Liber Amicorum* David M Trubek, held at the European University Institute in June 2012.

[1] See 'Is There an Emerging Transnational Regime for Labor Standards?' (1999) 93 *American Society of International Law Proceedings* 380 (Panel Summary of the Proceedings of the 93rd Annual Meeting, Washington DC, 24–27 March 1999, with remarks by DM Trubek, J Rothstein, L Compa, KWV Stone and G Ross, reported by J Rothstein); DM Trubek, J Mosher and J Rothstein, 'Transnationalism in the Regulation of Labor Relations: International Regimes and Transnational Advocacy Networks' (2000) 25 *Law & Social Inquiry* 1187; J Knauss and DM Trubek, 'The Transatlantic Labor Dialogue: Minimal Action in a Weak Structure' in MA Pollack and GC Shaffer (eds), *Transatlantic Governance in a Global Economy* (Lanham, Rowman & Littlefield, 2001); J Zeitlin and DM Trubek, *Governing Work and Welfare in a New Economy: European and American Experiments* (Oxford, Oxford University Press, 2003); D Trubek and L Compa, 'Trade Law, Labor and Global Inequality' (November 2005) *University of Wisconsin Legal Studies Research Paper No 1001*, available at dx.doi.org/10.2139/ssrn.845244.

[2] Exodus 5. Strikes by construction workers were apparently not unknown in ancient Egypt. A somewhat later incident is documented in P Frandsen (trans), 'Editing Reality: The Turin Strike Papyrus' in S Israelit-Groll (ed), *Studies in Egyptology Presented to Miriam Lichtheim*, vol 1 (Jerusalem, Magnes Press, 1990).

The outcome of this dispute is instructive for our purposes: denied their rights under national law, the Israelites managed to persuade a supranational agency—located, like today's International Labour Organization (ILO), on a hilltop—to proclaim the six-day working week as a core labour right. This ought to have been an inspiring, if not controlling, precedent for contemporary efforts to construct a transnational regime of labour regulation. However, the prospects for such a regime are not bright. Most of its constituent elements are degraded or defunct. Pharaoh is long gone: globalisation has radically impaired the willingness and ability of nation states to regulate labour markets. There is, of course, no readily available straw; we have long since ceased to expect that materials will be sourced anywhere near where things are produced or consumed. Moreover, fewer bricks are being made these days, at least in the developed economies where wealth is most often generated not by control over physical processes or corporeal products, but rather by ownership of intellectual property, intangible goodwill, and itinerant capital. And most seriously, there are no more Israelites: no working class, no solidarity, no mass mobilisation, no burning bush of socialism or syndicalism, and no new Jerusalem under construction or on the drawing boards.

The consequences are easily observed. Few stone tablets—few hard laws to protect workers—descend these days from Mount Sinai or Geneva, or indeed from Westminster or Washington: only soft, law-like codes of conduct or international conventions with vague admonitory norms like 'freedom of association' and 'decent work'. Worse yet, where hard labour law still exists, due to the widespread decommissioning or disregard of regimes of labour market regulation, it is often ignored—just like the Fourth Commandment to cease work on the Sabbath.

In the following sections of this essay, I will move first from analogy to critique, and then from critique to prophecy.

II. From Analogy to Critique

A. Pharaoh's Decline and Fall: The Unwillingness and/or Incapacity of Nation States to Regulate

The post-war period—the 'golden age' of labour market regulation in the advanced economies—was an era in which the state ruled in Pharaoh-like fashion. The spread of collective bargaining, the enhancement of labour standards, the expansion of the social safety net, the growth of consultative, corporatist or tripartite institutions: all of these were the work of national governments, usually acting in close collaboration with the social partners. From 1945 to, say, the 1970s, most governments adhered to social democratic or social market policies, either because they believed in them or because it was expedient to act as if they did. Their collaboration with the social partners in protecting the rights and interests of workers was sometimes voluntary, sometimes coerced, but almost always sufficiently sustained and multifaceted to maintain everyone's commitment to what became known as 'the post-war compromise' or 'welfare capitalism'. Of course, labour market regulation was only one part of that compromise, of that form of capitalism. Another key element was the provision of extensive public goods and services. And a third was the development of effective and reciprocating institutions of private and public governance designed to coordinate and reinforce the whole arrangement.[3]

Obviously, welfare capitalism took many forms reflecting the alignment of political forces and the economic profile of different countries. America was not Italy and Italy was not Sweden. Nonetheless, each of these countries—and all the other advanced economies—adopted its own national version of the post-war compromise. In this sense, labour law was indisputably national law. Indeed, it was so 'national' in character that labour law was the case-in-point most often cited to prove that the 'transplantation' of legal systems, even from one advanced economy to another, was doomed to failure.[4]

This is not to deny that ideas about labour market regulation—like goods, capital, technology and people—moved from country to country during the post-war period.[5] But 'globalisation' as we know it was in its early stages of development. That is to say, we had not yet experienced the hegemony of market fundamentalism, the triumph of monetarism, the populist revolt against taxation and government spending, the functional and legal integration of regional economies, the new international division of labour, and the ubiquity of transnational value chains, all of which have combined to radically undermine national systems of labour market regulation. Since the 1970s, however, things have changed considerably. While national governments retain considerable formal power to regulate, and occasionally exercise it, in general they do so reluctantly and at their peril. To provide workers with access to decent pensions, health care or unemployment benefits is to risk the wrath of central bankers and bond-rating agencies. To effectively protect workers' rights to unionise, strike, and exercise collective voice is to remind employers of their right to relocate to some other, less foolhardy jurisdiction. To talk the language of solidarity, inclusion and compassion is to provoke political responses that range alphabetically from amusement to xenophobia—none of them responses governments want to provoke. To reiterate: national governments—the Pharaohs of the post-war era—have either ceased to believe in progressive labour policies or have become afraid to implement them.

Now to translate analogy into critique: national systems of labour regulation may be designed to reinforce (or transform) the larger political economy; they may reflect (or seek to revise) historical and sociological imperatives; they may be shaped by (or constitute a reproach to) constitutional norms and legal cultures. They are therefore deeply embedded in the *congeries* of regulatory systems we usually call 'the state'. In assessing the prospects for a transnational system of labour market regulation, however, we are necessarily imagining what that system would look like 'without the state'.[6]

---

[3] See generally, B Western, *Postwar Unionization in the Capitalist Democracies* (Princeton, Princeton University Press, 1997); M Wachter, 'Labor Unions: A Corporatist Institution in a Competitive World' (2007) 155 *University of Pennsylvania Law Review* 581.

[4] HW Arthurs, 'Compared to What? Reflections on the Future of Comparative Labor Law' (2007) 28 *Comparative Labor Law & Policy Journal* 591.

[5] HW Arthurs, 'Extraterritoriality by Other Means: How Labor Law Sneaks Across Borders, Conquers Minds and Controls Workplaces Abroad' (2010) 21 *Stanford Law & Policy Review* 557.

[6] HW Arthurs, 'Labour Law without the State?' (1995) 46 *University of Toronto Law Journal* 1.

B. Neither Bricks nor Straw: Employment and Employment Regulation under Post-Industrial Capitalism

Systems of labour market regulation are not merely embedded in states: they are lodged in the interstices of technological and social systems. In the first four decades of the twentieth century, 'scientific' innovations in management and manufacturing methods achieved improvements in productivity in countries as diverse as the United States, the Soviet Union and Germany that might even have impressed Pharaoh (some of whose coercive strategies the latter two countries enthusiastically emulated).[7] In the capitalist democracies at least, these achievements laid the groundwork for post-war labour policy, in three respects. First, productivity gains were often achieved via internal labour markets which in turn gave rise to what came to be called the 'standard employment contract'.[8] This 'contract'—as much social practice as legal institution—provided workers with decent wages, benefits, and the prospect (if not necessarily the enforceable promise) of long-term employment. Second, the 'standard employment contract' influenced the design, funding, and delivery of public policies dealing with unemployment benefits, retirement income security, health care, skills training, and industrial relations. And third, relative stability in labour markets based on the standard employment contract allowed workers to unionise, acquire purchasing power, become consumers, and embrace welfare capitalism rather than more radical solutions to the 'social question'.

Moreover, the standard employment contract was particularly well-suited to an era when most advanced economies were engaged in post-war reconstruction, when they were making good long-standing deficits in infrastructure and capital goods, when wartime production methods were being adapted to meet pent-up consumer demand, and when Keynesian policies helped to sustain the momentum of post-war expansion and prosperity. But what technology, consumption, and public policy hath wrought, they could also wreck—and ultimately did. Accelerating technological change allowed employers to replace semi-skilled workers with robots or send work to non-union feeder plants locally or in other countries; hyper-consumption led to excessive personal debt; and three or four decades of welfare capitalism ultimately produced its neo-liberal antithesis in the form of resistance to supposedly undue levels of taxation, state expenditure and market regulation.

Conceding that a broad brush is not ideal for etching in fine details, the point is this: mass production manufacturing was the engine that drove post-war prosperity; it was the home of large numbers of unionised workers and centre-left voters; and it provided the paradigm of the standard employment relationship that informed much post-war labour and social welfare legislation. Consequently, the radical decline of employment in the manufacturing sector over the past 40 years has radically altered the landscape.[9] The loss

---

[7] See, eg J Merkle, *Management and Ideology: The Legacy of the International Scientific Management Movement* (Berkeley, University of California Press, 1980); SJ Link, 'From Taylorism to Human Relations: American, German and Soviet Trajectories in the Interwar Years' (Business History Conference, St Louis MO, March 2011) available at eui.academia.edu/StefanJohannesLink/Papers/583663/From_Taylorism_to_Human_Relations_American_German_and_Soviet_Trajectories.

[8] K Stone, *From Widgets to Digits: Employment Regulations for the Changing Workplace* (Cambridge, Cambridge University Press, 2004) 67.

[9] Between 1970 and 2009, manufacturing in almost all OECD countries shrank as a proportion of total employment by one-half to two-thirds. See Organisation for Economic Co-operation and Development, 'STAN Indicators: Manufacturing Share of Employment 1970–2009' (*OECD Stat Extracts*, 5 April 2011) available at stats.oecd.org/Index.aspx#.

of their core membership of industrial workers had devastating effects on national union movements and weakened centre-left political parties.[10] The decline of manufacturing also to some extent rendered dysfunctional laws and institutions designed to regulate the labour markets of industrial economies. And the loss of well-paying manufacturing jobs undermined the ability of many advanced economies to sustain consumer demand, tax revenues, public expenditure and, therefore, the whole post-war compromise.

What lesson should be learned from the demise of the brickworks of industrialised nations? Without bricks or straw, I contend—without manufacturing or its equivalent—no system of regulation is likely to produce social outcomes comparable to those achieved by the advanced economies during the post-war period.

However, it is unlikely that manufacturing in the industrialised West can be resuscitated, especially in an era of global free trade; and it is improbable that large numbers of displaced skilled or semi-skilled industrial workers will soon find well-paid, secure jobs in some other sector. Or to restate the point in more constructive terms, the success of any transnational system of labour regulation depends on the development of effective transnational strategies to correct the structural weaknesses besetting the advanced economies.

C. The Mysterious Disappearance of Israelites: The Demise of Working Class Consciousness, Identity, Solidarity and Power

The departure of the Israelites from Pharaoh's brickworks was not just a strike to secure improved working conditions. It was ultimately an act of solidarity and resistance by economically subordinate and politically disenfranchised people intended to challenge the values and institutions of the society in which they lived and worked. Strikes have always had this dual character: on the one hand, their immediate aim is to threaten or impose economic harm on particular employers in order to win improved wages and working conditions; on the other, their ultimate effect is sometimes to remind ruling elites of the potential of working-class mobilisation to radically revise the social order itself.

Of course, conventional strikes have become rare in the US, and infrequent in most other countries.[11] Working-class mobilisation, whether at the barricades or the ballot box, is episodic at best. And although unions have helped to organise anti-globalisation, anti-finance capital, and anti-austerity demonstrations in many countries, significant numbers of union members vote for political parties that favour globalisation, finance capital and austerity. It is not just that employers hold the trump cards when unemployment is high and jobs can be exported pretty much at will; it is not just that legal protections for collective labour action have been repealed or fallen into disrepair; and it is not just that employers and right-wing governments have repudiated the post-war social contract. It is

---

[10] J Visser, 'The Rise and Fall of Industrial Unionism' (2012) 18 *Transfer: European Review of Labour and Research* 129.

[11] In 1970 there were 381 'major' work stoppages in the US involving 1,000 or more workers; that number declined to 187 in 1980, 44 in 1990, 39 in 2000 and 11 in 2010. US Department of Labor, Bureau of Labor Statistics, 'Major Work Stoppages in 2011' (*Bureau of Labor Statistics*, 8 February 2012) available at http://www.bls.gov/news.release/wkstp.t01.htm.

that the decline in working class consciousness, identity, solidarity, and power have made these things possible.[12]

That decline represents the most fundamental challenge imaginable to labour law. The very concept of 'labour'—whether as a movement, as a sociological descriptor, as a factor of production, or as a domain of public policy and intellectual inquiry—depends on some commonality amongst all those included in the category. That commonality has long since disappeared. Though much of what they used to do is now done by machines, people still work. But they work differently: work that once required close cooperation amongst proximate operatives is now spread around the world; the ties of similar workplace experiences— once intertwined with ties of gender, race, ethnicity, religion or culture—have been loosened by the increasing heterogeneity of the workforce; and dreams of 'full employment' and 'decent work', once promulgated by post-war governments and sanctified by the ILO, have given way to the reality of a polarised knowledge economy comprising 'good jobs' and 'bad jobs', 'standard' jobs and 'precarious' jobs.

These changes in the nature of work, workplaces, and workers have radically challenged the notion that all workers ultimately have common interests. Indeed, workers are now arguably more likely to identify themselves on the basis of their role as consumers rather than producers. What brand of beer they drink, what football team they support, what religious sect they adhere to, what ethnic or national myth they align themselves with: all of these seem more accurately to express their aspirations and more effectively to mobilise their energies than solidarity with fellow workers determined to vindicate their rights and interests through industrial or political action.[13]

As dramatic as is the decline of labour solidarity at the national level, it is even more so at the global level. Workers scattered along the now-ubiquitous global value chains not only often lack the prerequisites for solidarity—common experiences, values and rights; they can seldom even identify their common corporate adversary. And worse yet, they are effectively in competition with each other for available work. 'Workers of all nations unite' was a stirring call to action when it was first pronounced in 1848; but few answered the call then and fewer still would do so today. Nor are there martyrs to inspire them: no little children dying in dark satanic mills, no heroic workers sabred at Peterloo or shot on the Paris barricades. Nor, most importantly, is there a Manifesto, a blueprint for a better future that might rally workers to seize control of their own fate or, more prosaically, to vote or strike in their own long-term economic interests. This is perhaps the most troubling fact of all. Transnational solidarity will arrive—if it ever does—only when 'hard-working', 'middle-class', 'home-owning' men and women who have lost their jobs and savings, their dignity and hopes, come to perceive that they do indeed share their predicament with people around the world, and that their best prospects lie in seeking solidarity for constructive action at all levels—locally, nationally and across traditional state and class boundaries.

---

[12] Questions have been raised about the actual extent and intensity of working-class consciousness in 19th and early 20th century Europe and America. See S Wilentz, 'Against Exceptionalism: Class Consciousness and the American Labor Movement, 1790–1920' (1984) 26 *International Labor and Working Class History* 1. See also C Fisk, 'Law and the Evolving Shape of Labor: Narratives of Expansion and Retrenchment' (2012) 8 *Law, Culture and the Humanities* 1.

[13] HW Arthurs, 'Labour Law After Labour' in G Davidov and B Langille (eds), *The Idea of Labour Law* (Oxford, Oxford University Press, 2011) 13.

Some of these people have sought solace in the Tea Party or the *Front National*.[14] Some have joined the Indignants in Syntagma Square or the Occupy Wall Street movement in Zuccotti Park.[15] But many—perhaps most—remain too confused or dispirited to manifest solidarity in any form or venue.

To return to my analogy: there are no more Israelites.

D. Soft Law from Sinai: The End of 'Hard' Labour Law?

The Commandments handed down on Mount Sinai were hard law, literally chiselled in stone: immutable, clear, and meant to be enforced by severe sanctions. Those handed down by national and transnational governments are increasingly 'soft'. While the situation varies from country to country, and across the electoral cycle, it is broadly true to say that 'hard' labour law plays a much-reduced role today in the regulation of most labour markets and workplace relations. Take the US: the core provisions of the National Labor Relations Act (NLRA) have not been updated since they were enacted in 1935; the collective bargaining system the NLRA was meant to nurture has virtually ceased to operate; and the National Labor Relations Board that administers the Act almost had to suspend operations earlier this year for want of a quorum.[16] Other hard laws—forbidding workplace discrimination and harassment or guaranteeing minimum standards—have been 'softened' by judicial rulings that allow employee complaints to be diverted from independent courts and tribunals to private arbitrators appointed by employers and/or unions.[17] Recent decisions creating exceptions to the egregious doctrine of at-will employment, are likely to provide 'softer' recourse for impecunious rank-and-file workers, who cannot afford to litigate, than for privileged executives and professionals who can.[18] And 'soft' internal complaints procedures, established by employers as part of their so-called 'total HR management' strategy, are becoming increasingly commonplace.[19]

Admittedly, America is the extreme case amongst the advanced economies. In the UK and Australia, for example, a degree of hard-law protection for workers was restored by Labour governments following the anti-union onslaughts of their Conservative

---

[14] See, eg T Frank, *What's the Matter with Kansas? How Conservatives Won the Heart of America* (New York, Holt, 2004); G Gaillard-Starzmann, 'Regarding the Front National' in A Gingrich and M Banks (eds), *Neo-Nationalism in Europe and Beyond: Perspectives from Social Anthropology* (New York, Berghahn Books, 2006).

[15] For an account of the uneasy relationship between labour and the 'Occupy' movement, see M Trudell, 'The Occupy Movement and Class Politics in the US' (2012) 133 *International Socialism* available at www.isj.org.uk/?id=775.

[16] MD Moderson, 'The National Labor Relations Board after *New Process Steel*: The Case for Amending Quorum Requirements under the National Labor Relations Act' (2011) 80 *University of Missouri-Kansas City Law Review* 463;. G Stohr, 'Obama's Recess Appointments Draw Supreme Court Scrutiny', *Bloomberg News*, 24 June 2013, available athttp://www.bloomberg.com/news/2013-06-24/obama-s-recess-appointments-draw-supreme-court-scrutiny.html.

[17] *Gilmer v Interstate/Johnson Lane Corp* 500 US 20 (1991); *Circuit City Stores, Inc v Adams* 532 US 105 (2001); *14 Penn Plaza LLC v Pyett* 556 US 247 (2009).

[18] KVW Stone, 'Revisiting the At-Will Employment Doctrine: Imposed Terms, Implied Terms, and the Normative World of the Workplace' (2007) 36 *Industrial Law Journal* 84; KR Swift, 'The Public Policy Exception to Employment At-Will: Time to Retire a Noble Warrior?' (2010) 61 *Mercer Law Review* 551.

[19] A Colvin, 'Organizational Primacy after the Demise of the Organizational Career: Employment Conflict in a Post-Standard Contract World' KVW Stone and HW Arthurs (eds), *After the Standard Contract of Employment: Innovations in Regulatory Design* (New York, Russell Sage, 2013).

predecessors.[20] Likewise, in many European countries, the hard law inscribed in post-war constitutions, legislation and jurisprudence survives only in diminished form. And at the community level, European Union Directives, and rulings of the European Court of Justice and the European Court of Human Rights once offered workers effective, if selective, hard-law protections.[21] However, those protections seem increasingly ineffective in sheltering workers from the effects of corporate, national and transnational tendencies towards more flexible employment contracts and less inclusive, generous and costly social security systems.[22]

By contrast, soft labour law has become more commonplace: broad declarations of high principle contained in international treaties, conventions or compacts; codes of practice announced unilaterally by employers or adopted under public pressure or compulsion of law; unenforceable 'endorsements' or 'affirmations' of labour rights pasted like fig leaves over the awkward bits of regional trade or development schemes; and 'enlightened' human resources practices announced by employers to forestall unionisation, escape regulatory scrutiny, improve employee recruitment, enhance productivity, win awards or placate critics.

However, there are good reasons to be wary of soft law. It lacks the democratic legitimacy that comes with legislative enactment; it cannot command the coercive power of the state; it is often couched in general, even anodyne, language that leaves considerable room for 'interpretation' by reluctant employers or timid administrators; and it generally positions workers as passive beneficiaries rather than active architects of workplace normativity.[23] On the other hand, perhaps the shift from hard to soft labour law is part of a general trend away from sclerotic 'command and control' models of regulation to more supple 'decentred' systems.[24] This general trend proceeds from several premises: that the regulatory state promised more than it could deliver; that hard law sometimes produced unintended, even perverse, results; and that soft law, especially in its reflexive variant, has the opportunity to operate more responsively and effectively than hard law.[25] These critiques of hard law are telling but whether soft law will, in fact, provide workers with more protection or less remains an open question.

Or perhaps the displacement of state-promulgated labour law by non-state forms of labour market regulation reflects broader tendencies towards a globalised economy, whose institutions of transnational governance characteristically (some would say intentionally) generate soft rather than hard law.[26] Or perhaps what appears to be a trend towards soft

---

[20] See A Forsyth and A Stewart (eds), *Fair Work: The New Workplace Laws and the Work Choices Legacy* (Annandale NSW, Federation Press, 2009).

[21] See generally, B Bercusson, *European Labour Law*, 2nd edn (Cambridge, Cambridge University Press, 2009); B Hepple and B Veneziani (eds), *The Transformation of Labour Law in Europe: A Comparative Study of 15 Countries 1945–2004* (Oxford, Hart Publishing, 2009).

[22] See, eg J Fudge, 'Constitutionalizing Labour Rights in Europe' in T Campbell, K Ewing and A Tompkins (eds), *The Legal Protection of Human Rights: Sceptical Essays* (Oxford, Oxford University Press, 2011) 244.

[23] HW Arthurs, 'Corporate Self-regulation: Political Economy, State Regulation and Reflexive Labour Law' in C Estlund and B Bercusson (eds), *Regulating Labour in the Wake of Globalisation* (Oxford, Hart Publishing, 2007) 19.

[24] See, eg O Lobel, 'The Renew Deal: The Fall of Regulation and the Rise of Governance in Contemporary Legal Thought' (2004) 89 *Minnesota Law Review* 262; DM Trubek and L Trubek, 'New Governance and Legal Regulation: Complementarity, Rivalry and Transformation' (2007) 13 *Columbia Journal of European Law* 542; C Estlund, *Regoverning the Workplace: From Self-Regulation to Co-Regulation* (New Haven, Yale University Press, 2010).

[25] G Teubner, 'Substantive and Reflexive Elements in Modern Law' (1983) 17 *Law & Society Review* 239.

[26] K Kolben, 'Transnational Labor Regulation and the Limits of Governance' (2011) 12 *Theoretical Inquiries in Law* 403.

law is no more than the current manifestation of labour law's historic oscillation between state and non-state forms of regulation, in the course of which legislation and markets, power and fairness and explicit and implicit normativity reinforce, subvert, and reshape each other.[27] Or perhaps one should simply acknowledge that given the labour movement's current and long-standing weakness, the choice may not be between hard law and soft law modes of regulation, but between soft law and none at all.

Whatever the cause of the decline of hard law and the turn to soft law, the crucial question is surely whether this development has left workers better or worse off. By almost any measure—access to jobs and job tenure; prospects for maintaining or improving wages, benefits and working conditions; income security in the event of redundancy, illness, pregnancy or retirement; voice in corporate decision-making; influence over public policy—one would have to say that the situation of workers in the advanced economies has in many respects deteriorated rather than improved over the past 20 or 30 years. At the same time, and with extensive caveats, it would be fair to say that measured by the same metrics, conditions for workers in a number of developing economies have improved to some extent during the same period, and that the turn to soft law as the characteristic mode of regulation in the global economy may have contributed modestly to that improvement.

III. From Critique to Prophecy: The Prospects for Transnational Labour Regulation 'After Labour'

National regimes of labour law and regulation confront an existential question: what will they become now that their traditional proponents and intended beneficiaries no longer answer to the name of 'labour'? One possible response to that question is to restate labour rights as broad political, social and human rights and to entrench them in national constitutions. However, this is unlikely to do much to protect workers. Constitutions tend to reflect and reinforce values that are already deeply ingrained in a society, to define power relations rather than transform them. A second response might be to entrench labour rights in the supra-national equivalent of national constitutions—in the charters, covenants, and conventions that form part of the universal law of nations or the fundamental law of the United Nations, the EU and similar organisations. For reasons outlined above, I regard this response as equally unpromising.[28] It is not that I attach no value to domestic or transnational entrenchment of labour rights. Rather, I regard these two responses as solutions to the wrong problem. The labour movement and its constituents are in dire straits not primarily because of deficiencies in the provenance, form, content or administration of labour laws,

---

[27] HW Arthurs, 'Labour Law without the State?' (1996) 46 *University of Toronto Law Journal* 1.

[28] Although recent decisions of the Supreme Court of Canada appear to suggest that international human rights doctrines can be invoked to protect workers' rights, many Canadian scholars are sceptical about the efficacy and/or desirability of this approach. See, eg PC Weiler, *Governing the Workplace: The Future of Labor and Employment Law* (Cambridge, MA, Harvard University Press, 1990); L Savage, 'Workers' Rights as Human Rights: Organized Labor and Rights Discourse in Canada' (2009) 34 *Labor Studies Journal* 8; HW Arthurs, 'The Constitutionalization of Employment Relations: Multiple Models, Pernicious Problems' (2010) 19 *Social and Legal Studies* 403; E Tucker, 'Labor's Many Constitutions (And Capital's Too)' (2012) 33 *Comparative Labor Law & Policy Journal* 101; Fudge, 'Constitutionalizing Labour Rights in Europe' (n 22).

but because 'labour' is no longer a social force to be reckoned with or (increasingly) even a concept with a social referent. If this is true, my over-taxed Exodus analogy may point towards a different future for labour law.

According to the plain language or fundamentalist reading of the bargain on Mount Sinai, in exchange for agreeing to observe the Ten Commandments, the Israelites were promised land and all the milk and honey appertaining thereto. This particularist inter-pretation of events on Mount Sinai valorises national or religious 'identity', in much the same way that labour law valorises class membership or the employment relation. But there is another—a prophetic or universalist—interpretation. The Israelite narrative (and the narrative of employment) can be understood as a specific instance of injustice that rein-forces the case for adherence to a general principle: everyone is entitled to freedom, dignity and a decent life; everyone should be treated with fairness and compassion. The ultimate value, in this prophetic interpretation, is social justice, not identity.

In the spirit of this second interpretation of the Exodus, I pose a few simple but funda-mental questions:

— Why should labour lawyers not treat the plight of workers as a special instance of a general problem: the problem of controlling super-ordinate economic power?
— Why should we have one set of legal rules and institutions for workers employed under standard employment contracts, and a plethora of others—often less extensive and efficacious—for contingent or autonomous workers, farmers or tenants, mort-gagors or the operators of small, franchised businesses?
— And why, for that matter, should the law be built around recognition of the specific-ity of categories of subordination—employment, race, gender or disability—rather than around acknowledgement of the reality that economic subordination cuts across all of these categories and causes most of the afflictions suffered by the people who populate them?

These suggestions lead to a proposal that is at least worth considering: if national labour law has, sadly, reached a cul de sac, the best way to extricate it is to enlarge its intellectual ambition and clientele as well as its spatial reach.

A. Enlarging Labour Law's Intellectual Ambition

Intellectual ambition first. Perhaps it is time for labour lawyers to stop tinkering with the machinery of labour market regulation and tweaking the rules of workplace relations. Perhaps they should devote more time and energy to finding ways to locate labour issues within a larger critique of the particular predatory form of capitalism that seems to have gained ascendancy in some advanced economies. Everyone—not just 'labour'—has a stake in labour law's intellectual realignment. Take the issue of deregulation, for example: the deregulation of financial markets has generated as much grief for ordinary citizens—including but not limited to, workers—as the deregulation of labour markets. Take the decline of social security systems in many countries: the loss of access to health care, social housing and decent pensions affects everyone, not just the vestigial remnant of the labour movement. Or take intergenerational equity: the growth of economic inequality and insecurity—both closely linked to the demise of collective bargaining—impairs the life chances of future generations as profoundly as the growth of personal and national indebtedness or, arguably, degradation of the environment. In other words, we might begin to think of labour law as one branch of the 'law of economic subordination and resistance'.[29]

B. Expanding Labour Law's Clientele

Seen in this way, labour law would not only be linked to larger and more lively domains of contention; it would address a new and broader clientele. It would concern itself with fairness not just for workers, but for farmers, borrowers and tenants as well, with potentially positive results. It would place at the disposal of new and needy client populations labour law's vast experience with the mechanics of regulation, the promotion of collective action, and the protection of individual rights. It could help a shrinking labour movement to form new alliances and to promote more widespread sympathy for its values and tactics. And merely reflecting on the idea might at a minimum help to reinvigorate labour law which, in the view of many, has become intellectually ossified if not virtually moribund.[30]

C. Extending Labour Law's Spatial Reach

Finally—most importantly for this occasion—the proposed reinvention of labour law might also extend its spatial reach. I mean this in three senses. First, in many countries the contract of employment is conceptually and/or constitutionally presumed to be a private and local matter.[31] By subsuming employment relations into a more general category of 'relations of economic subordination', the systemic—public, non-contractual—character of such relations becomes more apparent. To the extent that economic systems—markets—have become national rather than local in character, states might be encouraged or emboldened to make them subject to national rather than local regulation if they can do so.[32] However, federal states (and by extension the EU) may encounter practical, political and legal obstacles to making regulatory systems congruent with the markets they are intended to order.[33]

---

[29] I acknowledge the origins of this idea in A Hyde, 'What is Labour Law?' in G Davidov and B Langille (eds), *Boundaries and Frontiers of Labour Law: Goals and Means in the Regulation of Work* (Oxford, Hart Publishing, 2006). This idea's potential is explored in HW Arthurs, 'Labour Law as the Law of Economic Subordination and Resistance: A Thought Experiment' (2013) *34 Comparative Labour Law and Policy Journal* 585.

[30] See, eg C Estlund, 'The Ossification of American Labor Law' (2002) 102 *Columbia Law Review* 1527; P O'Higgins, 'The End of Labour Law as We Have Known It?' in C Barnard, S Deakin and GS Morris (eds), *The Future of Labour Law: Liber Amicorum Sir Bob Hepple QC* (Oxford, Hart Publishing, 2004); M Vranken, *Death of Labour Law: Comparative Perspectives* (Melbourne, Melbourne University Press, 2009); R Mitchell, 'Where are We Going in Labour Law? Some Thoughts on a Field of Scholarship and Policy in Process of Change' (2011) 24 *Australian Journal of Labour Law* 45; G Davidov and B Langille (eds), *The Idea of Labour Law* (Oxford, Oxford University Press, 2011).

[31] HW Arthurs, 'Labour and the "Real" Constitution' (2007) 48 *Les Cahiers de droit* 43.

[32] M Barenberg, 'Labor Federalism in the United States: Lessons for International Labor Rights' (2000) 3 *Journal of International Economic Law* 303; G Patmore, 'The Origins of Federal Industrial Relations Systems: Australia, Canada and the USA' (2009) 51 *Journal of Industrial Relations* 151.

[33] But see S Leibfried and FG Castles, 'Bypasses to a Social Europe? Lessons from Federal Experience' (2005) 12 *Journal of European Public Policy* 545 for an argument that federal or transnational systems constrain the growth of the welfare state.

Second, it is now widely accepted that most markets operate across—rather than within—national borders and require some form of transnational regulation. But while an array of private and public transnational institutions structures business transactions, resolves commercial disputes, protects intellectual property, facilitates capital transfers, and ensures the safe movement of goods, services and people,[34] labour markets are treated somewhat differently. While the ILO plays an important role in setting and disseminating labour standards, their adoption and enforcement is left almost entirely to national or sub-national agencies.[35] Global and regional trade regimes—including the EU—treat labour and employment issues far more diffidently than trade and business issues.[36] And transnational corporations tend to adhere to—even insist upon—the low labour standards that prevail in host countries where they produce or acquire goods, rather than use their leverage to export higher labour standards to those countries.[37] Incorporating labour issues into a broader framework of developmental and trade concerns might gain them the same visibility that attaches to, say, environmental or health issues.

Finally, discursive global communities of professionals, academics, commentators and business leaders help to 'normalise' and even intensify existing relations of subordination by demonstrating that they are not only inevitable but morally defensible. Greek pensioners, for example, deserve to suffer significant reductions in their standard of living because of their willingness to tolerate a political system characterised by corruption, tax evasion and fiscal irresponsibility; small-scale British businesses deserve to disappear because only the 'creative destruction of capitalism' will liberate the economy from the inefficiencies they impose on it; and Canadian workers deserve to see their jobs shipped to Mexico or China because collective bargaining and the tax burdens of the welfare state have led to unsustainably high labour costs in the manufacturing sector. In this way, the discourses of market fundamentalism and global neo-liberalism legitimate a system of transnational governance in which the interests of subaltern groups—both labour and non-labour—receive little attention and less sympathy. Acknowledgement of this 'globalisation of the mind' and its adverse effects on a wide variety of groups and individuals in many countries is a first step towards building an alternative governance model.

Enlarging the spatial dimension of labour law is, of course, a matter not merely of will but of way. In this regard, advances in information and regulatory technology have to some extent altered the terrain. As to the former, workers in different countries can now,

---

[34] See, eg RP Appelbaum, V Gessner and WLF Felstiner (eds), *Rules and Networks: The Legal Culture of Global Business Transactions* (Oxford, Hart Publishing, 2001); JH Dalhuisen, 'Legal Orders and their Manifestation: The Operation of the International Commercial and Financial Legal Order and its Lex Mercatoria' (2006) 24 *Berkeley Journal of International Law* 129.

[35] The ILO does investigate, report on and censure violations of its conventions, but other than expulsion from the organisation, has no sanctions available to compel offending states to comply.

[36] This criticism, commonplace before the Lisbon Treaty of 2009, has persisted and even intensified post-Lisbon: see, eg O Holman, 'Asymmetrical Regulation and Multidimensional Governance in the European Union' (2004) 11 *Review of International Political Economy* 714; L Magnusson, 'After Lisbon—Social Europe at the Crossroads?' (2010) *European Trade Union Working Paper 2010.01* available at www.etui.org/Publications2/Working-Papers/After-Lisbon-Social-Europe-at-the-crossroads. For a critique of the failure of other regional free trade initiatives to protect workers' rights and interests see KE Bravo, 'Regional Trade Agreements and Labor Liberalization: (Lost) Opportunities for Experimentation?' (2008) 29 *Saint Louis University Public Law Review* 71.

[37] The empirical evidence is contradictory: see, eg Xiaomin Yu, 'Impacts of Corporate Code of Conduct on Labor Standards: A Case Study of Reebok's Athletic Footwear Supplier Factory in China' (2008) 81 *Journal of Business Ethics* 513 and to the contrary M Busse, 'Do Transnational Corporations Care about Labor Standards?' (2003) 36 *Journal of Developing Areas* 39.

in principle, make contact and plan concerted action. Transnational social networks have mounted successful online campaigns against the egregious abuse of workers' rights.[38] Discursive communities of experts have been able to project worker-friendly models of labour market regulation across national boundaries and ensure that they receive attention in national policy debates.[39] As to the latter, while Europe in particular has initiated a community regime of labour market regulation and social protection that may one day provide workers with guarantees that match or exceed those they enjoy under national laws, *Viking, Laval, Ruffert,* and *Luxembourg*[40] remind us that transnational regimes have the potential to move labour standards downwards as well as upwards. Developments in the EU during the current economic crisis underline the point.[41] In the developing world, it can fairly be argued, nascent forms of transnational labour regulation have enabled some workers to enjoy more extensive rights and better jobs than they might have secured under local law; but many workers employed by firms associated with global production chains remain dreadfully exploited. On balance, it is not yet clear that the development of new information and regulatory technologies have effectively expanded the spatial reach of labour law to counter the heightened risks to workers' rights and interests associated with globalisation.

IV. To the Promised Land? Prospects for Transnational Labour Regulation

Like many labour lawyers, I believe that prospects for transnational labour regulation are dim, at least until the existential crisis of domestic or national labour law regimes has been resolved. However, unlike many of my colleagues in the field, I am at least prepared to contemplate the end of labour law as a distinct domain of scholarship and practice and to imagine its absorption into the broader legal field that I have called 'the law of economic subordination and resistance'. I have suggested that this would require a shift in the intellectual ambition, clientele and spatial reach of labour law. Now, in conclusion, I suggest that it is just possible that the current global economic situation makes such a shift not only desirable, but somewhat more likely.

---

[38] B de Sousa Santos and C Rodriguez-Garavito (eds), *Law and Globalization from Below: Towards a Cosmopolitan Legality* (Cambridge, Cambridge University Press, 2005).

[39] HW Arthurs, 'Cross-national Legal Learning: The Uses of Comparative Labour Knowledge, Law and Policy' in Stone and Arthurs (eds), *After the Standard Contract of Employment* (n 20).

[40] See Case C-341/05 *Laval un Partneri Ltd v Svenska Byggnadsarbetareforbundet* [2007] ECR I-11767; Case C-438/05 *International Transport Workers' Federation v Viking Line ABP* [2007] ECR I-10779; Case C-346/06 *Ruffert v Land Niedersachsen* [2008] ECR I-1989; Case C-319/06 *Commission of the European Communities v Grand Duchy of Luxemburg* [2008] ECR I-4323; S Sciarra, '*Viking* and *Laval*: Collective Labour Rights and Market Freedoms in the Enlarged EU' in C Barnard (ed), *Cambridge Yearbook of European Legal Studies 2007–2008*, vol 10, (Oxford, Hart Publishing, 2008); ACL Davies, 'One Step Forward, Two Steps Back? The *Viking* and *Laval* Cases in the ECJ' (2008) 37 *Industrial Law Journal* 126; European Parliament's Committee on Employment and Social Affairs, *The Impact of the ECJ Judgments on Viking, Laval, Ruffert, and Luxembourg on the Practice of Collective Bargaining and the Effectiveness of Social Action* Report (PE440.275) May 2010.

[41] R Hyman, 'Trade Unions, Lisbon, and Europe 2020: From Dream to Nightmare' (2012) 28 *International Journal of Comparative Labour Law and Industrial Relations* 5.

The 2008 banking crisis, triggered by the collapse of the market for sub-prime mortgages and other unregulated financial derivatives, demonstrated that national governments, entire economies, and significant labour markets can be destabilised by the machinations of financial institutions or the negligence of regulators in far-off countries. As a result, we are preoccupied with attempts to stave off the insolvency of several Euro-zone countries and many American states and municipalities, and to place virtually all OECD economies on a sounder footing. With this preoccupation, citizens of all countries are increasingly coming to realise that international financial discipline entails unpleasant consequences not only for wayward governments but potentially for everyone in the global economy whose livelihood depends on state contracts, employment subsidy or regulation, or on macro-economic, taxation, industrial and trade policies—which is to say all of us.

We ought therefore to be more alert than we used to be about the trans-systemic and transnational character of economic subordination, its deep, widespread, and long-lasting effects, and the extent to which employment relations are typical of those effects rather than unique. However, we have not yet written our own Exodus, our compelling narrative of making bricks without straw in contemporary capitalism, not yet promulgated the ten commandments of decent economic relations in general and employment relations in particular, and not yet inscribed either of these in a 'great code' that might shape the structures of our thought and the rhythms of our discourse.[42]

David Trubek was not (so far as I know) found in the bulrushes nor has he parted any waters lately or lugged large stone tablets down a mountainside. But from his early work on law and development to his current work on transnational institutions, he has been constructing our narrative, prodding us to do a first draft of our ten commandments, and developing a lexicon which will indeed have a lasting influence on how we all think and talk about regulation in an era of globalisation. If we fail in our efforts to make regulatory bricks without the straw of state power, the fault will not be his.

---

[42] N Frye, *The Great Code: The Bible and Literature* (San Diego, Harcourt Brace Jovanovich, 1982).

8

From Chile to Vietnam: International Labour Law and Workers' Rights in International Trade

LANCE COMPA

I. Introduction

I have had the great pleasure of moving through four decades with David Trubek, first as a student advisee and then as a colleague, collaborator, co-author and friend. This conference gives me an opportunity to discuss how developments in the field of trade and labour standards reflect his critical vision of new forms of global and regional regulatory institutions and how he anticipated the role of lawyers in the field.

A research project under Dave Trubek's supervision as a law student in Chile from 1972 to 1973, triggered my abiding interest in international labour affairs. After a brief summary of that experience, this essay will trace the evolution of trade and labour 'linkage' in US law and policy as contending governments and private actors pushed and pulled new institutional structures. Changing norms, obligations and enforcement mechanisms will be discussed.

I begin with the 1984 labour rights clause in the Generalized System of Preferences (GSP). The GSP labour provision epitomised the 'social clause' long sought by labour advocates but denied by multilateral trade-regulating bodies. It prepared conditions for the beneficial tariff treatment of other nations' exports to the United States in their respect for workers' rights.

From the GSP labour clause, the focus moves to the first international trade agreement with commitments to fair labour standards. Taking effect in 1994, the supplemental labour accord of the North American Free Trade Agreement (NAFTA) and the North American Agreement on Labor Cooperation (NAALC) created reciprocal obligations to apply a broad set of international labour principles in national law systems, especially when non-adherence to the principles affected trade between NAFTA partners.

The essay moves next to the post-NAFTA years when the US moved in a new direction on trade–labour linkage. Starting with Jordan in 2000, the most recent agreement being with Colombia (negotiated in 2007 but finally approved in 2012), new trade agreements made labour chapters integral parts of their texts rather than 'side agreements'. They gradually recalibrated the obligations of pact partners. They began making specific reference to International Labour Organization (ILO) standards, especially the 1998 'core' declaration.

Each new version was subtly different from its predecessor, raising knotty issues for international labour lawyers to sort out.

Negotiations now underway for a Trans-Pacific Partnership (TPP) agreement create the newest opportunity for linking trade and labour standards. A disparate, even motley, group of countries, including Vietnam, is engaged in TPP talks. The shape of the labour chapter is still unknown, but Vietnam has a classic communist trade union system in which the Party-controlled union is the only one allowed. This poses new challenges for linkage invoking ILO core labour standards. The essay ends with a discussion of these challenges and the ways in which Dave Trubek's insights contribute to our understanding of them.

II. Setting the Chile Stage

When David Trubek supervised my Yale Law School 'intensive semester' in Chile in the autumn of 1972, linking international trade and labour rights was an entirely theoretical endeavour. The core concept—taking labour standards out of global competition—inspired the founding of the ILO in 1919. But the ILO system did not contain a mechanism to implement such a linkage. It only required member countries, *if* they ratified ILO conventions (they do not have to ratify them), to adapt their national law to the conventions' terms.

An international trade organisation (ITO) with a strong 'social clause' enabling the conditions for trade benefits in respect of labour rights would have been a third leg of the post-World War II Bretton Woods structure, in addition to the World Bank and the International Monetary Fund. But the US scuttled the ITO. The cold war was underway, and the ITO's commitment to full employment and labour rights was too reminiscent of socialistic interference with the free market.[1] Its successor, the World Trade Organization (WTO), has pointedly resisted taking up labour issues, except for an Article XX clause on prison labour. So in 1972, if I had said that I wanted to practice international labour law, the response would have been, 'there's no such thing'.

My study of labour law reform under Salvador Allende's *Unidad Popular* government was an exercise in comparative labour law, not transnational labour law. Comparative labour law looked at German co-determination, Swedish peak bargaining, French political unionism, Argentine corporativism, Communist transmission-belt unionism, Canadian and Japanese variants of the US Wagner Act model, and other country-by-country labour law systems. Talk of learning from best practices and borrowing positive features remained just that—talk. National labour practices and national labour law systems remained deeply rooted in each country's individual history, traditions, cultures and experiences of class struggle, impervious to foreign influence.

Recently arrived at Yale from his work on development in Latin America, Dave Trubek helped me locate my project in 'law and' development/modernisation/policy/society contexts. He assigned Hirschman, Rostow, Cardoso and other development theorists.

---

[1] D Drache, 'The Short but Significant Life of the International Trade Organization: Lessons for Our Time' (2000) *University of Warwick Centre for the Study of Globalisation and Regionalisation Working Paper No 62/00.*

He assigned Weber, Parsons, and a Brazilian at Harvard, intimidatingly my own age, Roberto Unger.

The Allende government's labour law reform had created an industry-wide collective bargaining system in place of a plant-by-plant system. I studied the textile industry, an important sector of the Chilean economy. I was allowed to observe collective bargaining between the textile workers' union and textile company owners' association. I, interviewed union and management negotiators, and watched negotiations proceed to a successful finish. The textile union made significant contract gains, as did workers and unions in other industries. In the overall labour force, trade union membership and workers' coverage under collective agreements grew significantly under the *Unidad Popular*.[2]

Chile's labour policy measured up to ILO norms on workers' organising and collective bargaining rights. If there had been an effective linkage between workers' rights and international trade at the time, Chile might have gained favourable trade treatment from the US. Instead, US policy was to 'make the economy scream' through trade sanctions against Chile.[3] In September 1973, seven months after I returned to law school, General Augusto Pinochet's *golpe de estado* (*coup d'état*) turned economic screams into human screams of those tortured and killed during the coup and its aftermath.[4]

International labour law had no bearing on events in Chile in the 1970s. Whether or not Allende's reforms complied with ILO standards was not part of the discourse that I encountered. But after the coup, ILO action played a key role in the first application of trade labour linkage under US law.

III. Labour Rights in the Generalized System of Preferences (GSP)

Central obligation: 'taking steps to afford internationally recognized worker rights to workers in the country'[5]

In the early 1980s a coalition of US labour, human rights, religious, development and feminist activists promoted the first concrete linkage of labour rights in trade policy. Mostly 60s-generation activists who went into the labour movement to change the world, trade union participants opposed American Federation of Labor and Congress of Industrial Organizations (AFL-CIO) international policy and unions' one-note 'stop imports' trade policy. Human rights and religious actors sought to counter workers' rights abuses in South

---

[2] L Compa, 'Labor Law and the Legal Way: Collective Bargaining in the Chilean Textile Industry under the Unidad Popular' (1973) *Yale Law School Program in Law and Modernization Working Paper No 23*.

[3] The phrase was Nixon's; the policy was Kissinger's. See, among many, P Kornbluh, *The Pinochet File* (New York, The New Press, 2003); J Dinges, *The Condor Years* (New York, The New Press, 2004).

[4] Among those affected were several trade unionists whom I had met in the course of my research and my housemate Frank Teruggi, one of the two Americans murdered in the Chilean coup (Charles Horman was the other). Frank was doing nothing different than I was—talking to activists, going to meetings and demonstrations, and writing for US outlets. The only difference was that I left and he stayed there when soldiers came to our house, took him away, tortured and killed him.

[5] GSP Renewal Act of 1984, Pub L No. 98–573, 98 Stat 3019 (1984), § 2462(b)(2)(G).

Korea, Indonesia, Malaysia and other Asian countries cultivating export-led development, and in Central and South American military dictatorships, including Chile. Development advocates wanted to keep US markets open to imports from poor countries that honoured workers' rights. Women's rights activists backed measures to help the mostly female labour force in 'global assembly-line' factories.

The coalition and allies in Congress found a legislative opening when Congress had to renew the US GSP. Permitted as an exception to the WTO's 'most favoured nation' principle of treating all trading partners equally, GSP programmes in the US, Europe, Japan, and Canada granted favourable tariff treatment to products from poor countries that qualified for GSP beneficiary status.[6]

Let's make labour standards a criterion for benefits, argued the new coalition. We support trade and poor countries' access to the US market, but on a foundation of respect for labour and human rights. No country and no multinational firm should gain a competitive edge in trade by violating workers' rights. Workers have a right to demand protection for labour standards in the global trading system, and to have laws to accomplish this.

GSP programmes are not negotiated. They are unilateral grants of favourable treatment, and the granting country can set whatever conditions it chooses. The US, for example, had long excluded from GSP eligibility communist countries, OPEC members, countries that fail to take sufficiently vigorous action against drug trafficking, and other categories that moved members of Congress to exclude them from coverage based on GSP 'conditionality', as it is often called. Now respect for workers' rights would come into play.

The coalition won a labour rights clause in the 1984 GSP renewal law. Replete with multiple negatives and other idiosyncratic formulations, the provision's language reflected both the complexity of linking trade and labour policy and the often messy process of legislative drafting and compromise.

The eternal tug-of-war between executive and legislative authority was a starting point. The president wanted to wield power over the granting of GSP benefits, but Congress did not want to give him a free hand. Thus, in amending the GSP law to include a labour provision, Congress conceded that: 'The President is authorised to designate countries as [GSP] beneficiary developing countries' but insisted that: 'The President shall not designate any country [that] has not taken or is not taking steps to afford internationally recognized worker rights to workers in the country.'[7]

Here is where writing stylists tear their hair but lawyers' eyes light up. What does 'not taking steps' mean? Indeed, what does 'taking steps' mean? What does 'afford' mean? What are 'internationally recognized worker rights'?

The statute defined 'internationally recognized worker rights' as follows:

— the right of association;
— the right to organise and bargain collectively;
— a prohibition on the use of any form of forced or compulsory labour;

---

[6] The US Most Favoured Nation (MFN) tariff on a selected product (thousands of products are covered) might be 10 per cent if it came from a European country, but 2 per cent if it came from a GSP beneficiary country, giving the latter a slight advantage on price.

[7] 19 USC §2462.

— a minimum age for the employment of children [and in a 2002 amendment 'and a prohibition on the worst forms of child labour']; and
— acceptable conditions of work with respect to minimum wages, hours of work and occupational safety and health.

This formulation predated the ILO core standards declaration by 14 years. The principle of non-discrimination is notably absent from the definition. The labour rights coalition that promoted the bill and congressional supporters on key committees had non-discrimination in the original draft of the bill. But it was removed when the Reagan administration and senate conservatives insisted on dropping it—otherwise the president would veto the law.

The advocacy coalition lost its feminist wing on this point. Women activists told the rest: 'You are selling out millions of women workers in global supply chain factories around the world so that your male union leaders can have their jobs', or a variant thereof. It was a classic moment of truth in any hard bargaining context: gain a substantial part of one's objective (in this case, arguably, most of it), or stand on principle for all or nothing (in the event nothing, if the Reagan administration had carried through on its threat to veto).

In support of women's rights advocates critical of a legislative compromise, some coalition participants said: 'Let's stand on principle and come back after the 1984 presidential elections, when we can get everything we want in a GSP labour bill with a Democratic president.' Pragmatists in the group said: 'Let's take what we have in hand now, and come back for more later'. The pragmatists prevailed and won the GSP labour clause without non-discrimination, but Ronald Reagan's re-election derailed their plans to come back later for more.

The 1984 GSP law did not incorporate ILO standards. Rights of association, organising and bargaining were not grounded in ILO Conventions 87 and 98, nor was forced labour linked to Conventions 29 and 105. The phrase 'internationally recognized worker rights' (abbreviated to IRWR in US discourse, but nowhere else) meant only what Congress had in mind, and the mind of the American Congress is not a model of transparency and clarity.

'Acceptable' conditions of work as a normative requirement obviously posed the question 'acceptable to whom?' The answer was acceptable to US authorities deciding whether to grant or deny GSP benefits to countries whose status was challenged by labour rights advocates.[8]

The new law created a complaint mechanism which enabled labour lawyers to begin *practising* transnational labour law, not just theorising about it. Procedural rules set out no 'standing' requirement. 'Any person' could file a complaint seeking a labour rights review of a GSP beneficiary country. The Office of the United States Trade Representative (USTR) managed the complaints process, chairing an inter-agency Trade Policy Staff Committee (TPSC) that included other cabinet departments such as State, Labour, Commerce, Agriculture and Defence.

As part of the complaints process, USTR held public hearings in which advocates, foreign government officials, and workers from countries under scrutiny could testify. The hearings were voluntary in nature, not involving compelled testimony or examination, cross-examination or rules of evidence. But foreign countries were effectively in the dock,

---

[8] For sharp criticism on this point, see Philip Alston, 'Labor Rights Provisions in US Trade Law: "Aggressive Unilateralism"?' in LA Compa and SF Diamond (eds), *Human Rights, Labour Rights, and International Trade* (Philadelphia, University of Pennsylvania Press, 1996).

eager to maintain their GSP status and facing a sharp economic sanction if they lost it. Advocates were equally committed to proving violations and stripping the benefit from offending countries. The hearings created an arena of lawyerly combat that involved drafting statements, preparing witnesses, making oral arguments to the TPSC, rebutting the other side with supplemental briefs and so on.

Chile was one of the first countries put to the test.[9] As a developing country, Chile had long benefitted from GSP treatment of exports to the US. Its status had not changed under the now more than 10-years-old Pinochet military dictatorship. In 1986, when the complaints procedure first opened, the AFL-CIO and the independent United Electrical Workers Union (UE) filed petitions to remove Chile from GSP beneficiary status based on labour rights violations.

Despite their absence from the GSP statutory framework, ILO standards became part of the hearing procedure and record. The ILO Committee on Freedom of Association had made repeated findings that the Pinochet government violated workers' rights of association, organising and bargaining. Advocates cited ILO findings in the GSP proceedings to insert authoritative evidence of police harassment, beatings, jailings and military death squad assassinations of trade union leaders and activists. They also pointed to restrictions in the Pinochet labour code that on their face violated workers' rights. For example, workers needed permission from local police officials to hold meetings, and police officers monitored the meetings.

Chilean government officials insisted that workers' rights were respected, and brought a puppet Pinochet unionist to back up their story. The Chilean government engaged a prominent Washington, DC law firm for the GSP proceedings to argue that the passing of a new labour code was 'taking steps' to afford rights to Chilean workers. Facing them were unpaid volunteer lawyers who worked with Chilean democratic unionists risking their lives to testify against the government.

Based on clear evidence of labour rights violations, the US suspended Chile from GSP beneficiary status in February 1988. The GSP cut-off jolted Chilean business and political elites by imposing economic sanctions just when they hoped to expand exports to the US. In strictly economic terms, the GSP move did not affect a major part of exports to the US. Copper, the mainstay of the economy, was not a product that benefitted from GSP tariff preferences. But the sanctions had a strong signalling effect implicating all Chilean business intersections with the American economy. GSP today—what next?

A plebiscite on Pinochet's continued rule was set for October 1988. After the GSP cut-off in February, a significant part of the business community moved to support a 'no' vote—that is, a vote against Pinochet and for a return to democracy. The ruling shook Chilean business interests' confidence in their relationship with the US. Clear-eyed, longer-term-thinking business leaders realised the need for change. The 'no' prevailed in the 1988 referendum, beginning Pinochet's ultimate slide towards arrest and disgrace, not only as a murderous dictator but as a common crook.[10]

It would be too much to attribute cause and effect to the GSP cut-off. Chile's return to democracy was a complex, multi-layered, multi-actor process. But at a key moment, the

---

[9] Others included El Salvador, Guatemala, Indonesia, Malaysia and Romania (which the Ford administration had granted GSP status in the 1970s as part of a presumed 'opening' by the Ceausescu regime).

[10] See E Vergara, 'Pinochet's widow, children arrested in Chile; Many others are also held in a corruption inquiry stemming from a $20-million US fund tied to the ex-dictator' (*Los Angeles Times*, 5 October 2007) A11.

labour rights clause won by advocates for workers' rights in the US legislative process gave important backing to Chile's transition to democracy.

The creative use of the new GSP labour rights clause brought other positive results. The government of Guatemala adopted positive labour law reforms, some important strikes were resolved favourably for workers, and some workers were reinstated to their jobs thanks to pressure from a GSP complaint—one that also used public hearings and public advocacy. Costa Rica ended a system favouring management-dominated *solidarista* associations after Costa Rican unions and US allies filed a GSP complaint. A long-serving ILO official told me: 'For ten years we've been trying to get Costa Rica to fix this problem through decisions of the Committee on Freedom of Association. You did it in six months with your GSP clause.'

I do not want to exaggerate. Other GSP petitions did not fare so well. Advocates did not prevail in complaints against Malaysia and Indonesia in the late 1980s and early 1990s over conditions similar to those in Chile and Guatemala. The lobbying firepower of US multinational companies—electronics firms in Malaysia, mining and energy firms in Indonesia—was too heavy. At bottom, because the GSP labour clause vests discretionary power in the president, geopolitical considerations trump labour rights concerns.[11]

But even in Indonesia, some labour leaders were released from prison to buttress governments' claims of 'taking steps' on workers' rights. In summary, the GSP's new institutional mechanism provided the advocacy community with a chance to apply soft legal formulations like 'taking steps' to win hard results—including laws changed, strikes settled, workers reinstated and union leaders released from jail.

The GSP labour clause also created an opportunity for cross-border collaboration among advocates, particularly, though not solely, among lawyers. US supporters of workers' rights did not operate in a bubble. To craft credible complaints and to exploit the public hearing process, they had to learn from counterparts abroad and jointly develop strategic approaches to the GSP process. In the Guatemalan case, for example, allies from the two countries called publicly for sanctions against Guatemala, but privately told the TPSC that they did not really want the sanctions to be imposed—they just wanted the government of Guatemala to think there *might* be sanctions.

It was the classic sanctions dilemma. Too many Guatemalan workers might lose their jobs under sanctions. The point is that the differing public–private strategy was crafted among Guatemalan labour and human rights advocates after both countries came up with an agreed approach. Lawyers from both countries played a central role in these strategic discussions because the entire GSP regime was rife with legal technicalities, legal issues and legal challenges. A new practice of international labour law was taking shape.[12]

---

[11] Labour advocates filed a lawsuit arguing that the Executive failed to implement the law in the cases of Malaysia and Indonesia. The federal district court dismissed the suit, saying: 'GSP contains no specification as to how the President shall make his determination. There is no definition of what constitutes 'not taking steps' to afford internationally recognised rights. ... [T]here is no statutory direction which provides any basis for the Court to act. The Court cannot interfere with the President's discretionary judgment because there is no law to apply,' *International Labor Rights Education and Research Fund v George Bush et al*, 752 F Supp 495 (1990) (affirmed on other grounds, *International Labor Rights Education and Research Fund v George Bush et al*, 954 F 2d 745, DC Cir, 1992).

[12] Sometimes joint decision-making arrived at an agreement not to act. When US labour advocates asked Brazilian trade unionists and attorneys about filing a GSP petition on labour rights abuses during and after that country's military rule in the 1980s, Brazilian counterparts said: 'Thanks, but no thanks. We'll handle this in-house.'

IV. NAFTA and the NAALC

Central obligations: 'provide for high labour standards ... promote compliance with and effectively enforce its labour law through appropriate government action'[13]

Negotiated in 1993 by Canada, Mexico and the US, NAFTA's supplemental labour pact, the NAALC, sets forth 11 'Labour Principles' that the three signatory countries commit themselves to promote:

1. freedom of association and protection of the right to organise;
2. the right to bargain collectively;
3. the right to strike;
4. forced labour;
5. child labour;
6. minimum wage, hours of work and other labour standards;
7. non-discrimination;
8. equal pay for equal work;
9. occupational safety and health;
10. workers' compensation; and
11. migrant worker protection.

As with the GSP articulation of 'internationally recognized worker rights', the NAALC's labour principles are not based on ILO standards. This time, rather than US Congress declaring international 'rights', the three NAFTA governments declared a set of 'principles' without reference to ILO standards, except for certain phraseological parallels. They pledged to effectively enforce their *national* labour laws in these 11 subject areas.

With this last, the NAALC introduced what has become a constant among labour provisions in trade agreements: the obligation to effectively enforce national labour laws rather than to directly incorporate and apply international norms. Unlike much commercial law, labour law is tightly bound to national traditions and cultures of labour–management relations. Labour law reflects the compromise struck over a long period of class struggles within national boundaries.

Governments are loath to yield sovereignty over labour law in the way they might yield sovereignty over intellectual property or investment law. The early versions of labour clauses in trade agreements could not immediately jump to supranational standards and supranational enforcement. Effective enforcement of national law is a reasonable starting point, especially since much national labour law is favourable to workers and unions.

The NAALC principles ranged well beyond the later ILO 'core labour standards' of 1998. The ILO's 'core' addresses organising and bargaining rights, forced labour, child labour and discrimination. The NAALC included all these, as well as the 'acceptable conditions' in the GSP clause (wages, hours, health and safety), workers' compensation for workplace injury, and illness and migrant workers' rights.

The NAALC's ample subject matter jurisdiction created opportunities for advocacy not offered in other trade–labour systems. As recently as May 2012, a coalition of US and

---

[13] North American Agreement on Labour Cooperation (NAALC), US-Can-Mex, 32 ILM 1499 (1993).

Mexican trade unions and lawyers' groups filed a complaint with the Mexican labour department against anti-immigrant legislation in Alabama and other US states.[14] They argued, in imaginative lawyerly fashion, that these state-level anti-immigrant laws made it impossible for the US to effectively enforce its labour laws in workplaces with migrant workers. No other trade agreement's labour chapter contemplates complaints over migrant workers' rights.

The NAALC's complaint procedures reflect a mostly soft-law system with investigations, public hearings, research and written reports, government-to-government consultations, independent evaluations, non-binding recommendations and similar measures. But a hard-law edge can be applied for three labour principles: those covering minimum wage, child labour and occupational safety and health. An independent arbitral panel is empowered to fine an offending government for a 'persistent pattern of failure to effectively enforce' domestic labour law. If the fine is not paid, the panel can apply trade sanctions on the firm, industry or sector where workers' rights violations occurred.

For advocates willing to put it to the test, the NAALC has emerged as a viable arena for creative transnational action. With its unusual 'cross-border' complaint mechanism, the Agreement provided an opportunity for workers, trade unions and their allies in the US, Mexico and Canada to work together precisely to defend workers' rights against abuses by corporations and governments.

The 40 cases filed since 1994 involved transnational coalitions of unions and allied human rights and community groups who found in the NAALC's mechanisms new opportunities to develop relationships and joint action. Advocates demanded investigations, public hearings and government consultations on workers' rights violations. With the NAALC, they had space to strategise in a sustained fashion, gathering evidence for drafting a complaint, crafting its elements, setting priorities, defining demands, launching media campaigns, meeting with government officials to set the agenda for a hearing and to press them for thorough reviews and follow-up, preparing to testify in public hearings, engaging technical experts to buttress a case with scientific elements (a health and safety case, for example), influencing the composition of independent experts' panels and the terms of reference of their investigation, and other concrete tasks.

To take just one example of many: two US-based human rights groups, Human Rights Watch and the International Labor Rights Forum, along with the Mexican National Association of Democratic Lawyers (ANAD), filed a complaint with the National Administrative Office of the United States (NAO) in May 1997 alleging 'a pattern of widespread, state-tolerated sex discrimination against prospective and actual female workers in the *maquiladora* [supply-chain assembly factories] sector along the Mexico-US border'. The submission alleged a common practice of requiring pregnancy testing of all female job applicants and denying employment to those whose test results are positive. The complaint also said that employers pressure employees who become pregnant to leave their jobs.

The groups submitting the complaint argued that the practice by employers and the failure of the labour authorities to combat it—sometimes by omission, sometimes by overt

---

[14] See S Higgins, 'Union Fights Alabama Law in Mexico, Labor is using trade pact that it has long opposed vs state immigration law' (*Investor's Business Daily*, 1 May 2012) A1. The NAALC sets up a cross-border complaint mechanism: advocates must submit a complaint to the labour department of *another* NAALC partner, not the labour department of the country in which alleged violations occurred—this, to avoid dual and potentially conflicting case handling, since alleged abuses can be the subject of complaints under national labour law systems.

support for the employers' discriminatory policy—violates Mexico's obligations under the NAALC. The US labour department accepted the case and held public hearings in cities along the Mexico–US border. Related campaigns and demonstrations by workers and support groups on both sides of the border created a media firestorm. Several US companies in the *maquiladora* zones announced they would halt pregnancy testing, and the Mexican federal government prohibited pregnancy testing of women applying for employment in federal ministries.

The NAALC case gave new credibility and weight to women's rights advocates in Mexico. In Shareen Hertel's words: 'The creation of the NAFTA side accord presented activists with a new political opportunity ... Submission 9701 put pregnancy testing on the map internationally, and Mexican activists used that international attention to pressure their government for domestic reforms.'[15]

The new instruments and institutions of international labour rights advocacy reflected in the NAALC were flawed. But they created spaces, terrains, platforms and other metaphorical *loci* where advocates could unite across frontiers to promote new norms, mobilise actors, call to account governments and corporations, disseminate research findings, launch media campaigns, educate each other and the public, challenge traditional notions of sovereignty, and give legitimacy to their cause by invoking human rights and labour rights principles. In summary, advocates redefined debates and discourse by breaking up old frameworks and shaping new ones.

As in the GSP process, lawyers played a driving role in NAALC complaints and case processing. Labour and human rights attorneys in the three NAALC partners created an enduring network that meets on a regular basis to review cases and make strategic choices for new ones.

V. Labour Rights in Post-NAALC Trade Agreements: First Generation

Central obligations: 'strive to ensure that [ILO core declaration principles] and [the US definition of] internationally recognized worker rights are recognised and protected by domestic law ... [and] ... not fail to effectively enforce its labour laws ... related to [the US definition of] internationally recognized worker rights'[16]

Trade–labour linkage evolved from the GSP and NAFTA-NAALC foundations as the US continued pursuing bilateral and regional free trade agreements. A 2000 Free Trade Agreement (FTA) with Jordan began to create a new template. In part, it responded to sharp criticisms of the NAALC's status as a 'side agreement' and its failure to refer to international standards.

---

[15] S Hertel, 'Discrimination, the Right to Work, and Reproductive Freedom: The Case of Mexico' in S Hertel, *Unexpected Power: Conflict and Change among Transnational Activists* (Ithaca, Cornell University Press, 2006).

[16] US-Jordan Free Trade Agreement (2000), available at http://www.ustr.gov/trade-agreements/free-trade-agreements (accessed August 30, 2013).

The US–Jordan trade agreement included a labour chapter as an integral part of the agreement. I did not believe that the NAALC's 'side agreement' status was a fatal flaw. An international agreement is an international agreement—front, back or side. What is important is what it says and how it is implemented. But 'side agreement' became a fighting epithet for many labour advocates. (Canadians always said 'side deal' with a sneer for good measure.) Getting rid of side agreements became a point of principle, one that the Clinton administration responded to in the Jordan pact.

One key change in discourse between the 1994 NAALC and the 2000 US–Jordan Agreement was the ILO's adoption in 1998 of its Declaration on Fundamental Principles and Rights at Work. The Declaration set out four 'core' items on: (1) rights of association and collective bargaining; (2) forced labour; (3) child labour; and (4) non-discrimination. These are often called ILO core standards for brevity's sake, and I use that loose term here instead of saying 'fundamental principles and rights' at every turn. Examine the actual text with a lawyer's gimlet eye:

> [A]ll Members, even if they have not ratified the Conventions in question, have an obligation aris-ing from the very fact of membership in the Organization to respect, to promote and to realise, in good faith and in accordance with the Constitution, the principles concerning the fundamental rights which are the subject of those Conventions, namely:
>
> (a)   freedom of association and the effective recognition of the right to collective bargaining;
> (b)   the elimination of all forms of forced or compulsory labour;
> (c)   the effective abolition f child labour; and
> (d)   the elimination of discrimination in respect of employment and occupation.[17]

Every word except 'the' was a subject of debate and contention in shaping the Declaration's language.[18] Why does it cover freedom of association and collective bargaining without mentioning the right to organise? Why 'effective' recognition of collective bargaining and 'effective' abolition of child labour compared with outright 'elimination' of forced labour and discrimination, when 'effective' suggests almost but not entirely? The answer is because organising, collective bargaining and child labour are more contested than freedom of association, forced labour or discrimination.

Now look at the convoluted form of the obligation: 'to promote and to realise … the principles concerning the fundamental rights which are the subject of those Conventions'.[19] 'Those conventions' are two each of the four subjects of the Declaration: Conventions 87 and 98 on freedom of association, the right to organise, and collective bargaining; Conventions 29 and 105 on forced labour, Conventions 138 and 182 on child labour, and Conventions 100 and 11 on discrimination.

---

[17]   ILO, *Declaration on fundamental principles and rights at work* (1998) available at www.ilo.org/public/english/standards/relm/ilc/ilc86/com-dtxt.htm.

[18]   Even 'on' and 'at' in the title resulted from negotiation and compromise. Workers wanted '*of* fundamental principles and rights', and '*of* workers'. Employers said that this would imply some new grant of rights empowering workers when it should be just a restating, in a focused way, of existing principles and rights. Thus, 'on fundamental principles and rights' and '*at* work'.

[19]   Employers wanted to stop at 'promote'; workers insisted on adding 'realise'. One can 'promote' forever without getting anywhere.

A large body of legal analysis and decision-making by ILO oversight bodies, the Committee on Freedom of Association and the Committee of Experts on the Application of Ratified Conventions, provide clear legal standards for what constitutes violations of ILO conventions. But the Declaration does not clearly call for direct adherence to the conventions. It interposes 'principles', 'rights' and 'subjects' before finally referring to the conventions, leaving ambiguous the relationship between the Declaration's obligations and the conventions.

The ILO Declaration leaves ambiguous the extent to which its 'fundamental principles and rights' tend toward hard, binding norms or soft, voluntary guidelines. It is not at either extreme but somewhere on a continuum between the two, creating a legal space for lawyers to forge new legal strategies. Thus, labour advocates make the case that the Declaration creates discernible standards derived from the relevant conventions. That is, 'principles', 'rights', 'subjects' and 'conventions' is an unbroken line, so that the detailed rules elaborated by authoritative ILO oversight committees must be 'realised'.

Employers argue the contrary (stressing promotion, not realisation). They contend that only undefined general 'principles' are implicated by the Declaration, while the rest is just a gloss. Thus, in the words of the US federal district court examining the 'taking steps' standard under GSP, 'there is no law to apply'.

I am in the labour camp here. 'Principles' in the ILO Declaration has no meaning unless the principles are grounded in conventions and related jurisprudence giving them shape and content. I have often seen a cat without a grin, but never, unlike Alice, a grin without a cat. The employer interpretation of the Declaration is a grin without a cat. Once the question 'What do you mean by "principles?"' is posed, the response can only end with the conventions and their detailed treatment by the two oversight committees.[20]

Despite the ambiguity, many labour advocates saw the ILO 'core' formulation as an advance. For many, it was a riposte to the WTO's 1996 refusal to encompass workers' rights in trade rules. It gave sharp focus to central labour demands. It gave the ILO a new, stronger platform to inject labour concerns into global economic debates.

Reflecting the power of the simple concept over complex reality (everyone is proud to be able to recite the four ILO core labour standards; no one can recite the 188 ILO conventions), all sides of international labour affairs communities converged on the ILO core labour standards as the definitive formulation of workers' rights. I never saw it that way. I argued that the rush to four core standards invites a logical response that other labour concerns such as health and safety, migrants' rights, fair pay, social security and other economic and social concerns, are second-class, not worthy of equal standing and advocacy.[21]

I lost. Obeisance to the ILO core labour standards is de rigueur not only in trade agreements, but in every workers' rights formulation—in guidelines from the Organisation of Economic Co-operation and Development (OECD), World Bank performance standards,

---

[20] This is more than a linguistic digression, as we shall see when we come to the May 2007 trade–labour 'template' and 'Footnote 2' in new labour chapters of trade agreements.

[21] L Compa, 'Core labour rights: promise and peril' (2002) 9 *International Union Rights* 20. I am in good company on this point; see P Alston and J Heenan, 'Shrinking the International Labor Code: An Unintended Consequence of the 1998 ILO Declaration on Fundamental Principles and Rights at Work?' (2004) 36 *NYU Journal of International Law & Politics* 101.

corporate codes of conduct, global framework agreements, John Ruggie's protect–respect–remedy approach for the UN, and more.

The US–Jordan FTA was the first to incorporate international norms in the form of ILO core standards, as distinct from the US statutory IRWR formulation. That is, it incorporated the 'labour principles' contained in the 1998 ILO declaration, but with a 'soft' obligation to 'strive to ensure' that such principles are reflected in national law. This is an elastic standard of behaviour, akin to 'taking steps' in the GSP clause. A government could say, for example, that it introduced legislative reforms favourable to workers and unions knowing full well that its parliament would never adopt them, and claim it was 'striving'.

The US–Jordan FTA imposed the same 'strive to ensure' obligation on the fictional 'internationally recognized worker rights' first enunciated in the GSP provision—the US Congress' idiosyncratic definition of international labour standards. However, it only required 'effective enforcement' of laws implementing the US-engendered IRWR standards, not the ILO core standards.

The Jordan model omitted from the 'effective enforcement' rule the core ILO principle of non-discrimination. Neither country had to effectively enforce its anti-discrimination laws. With migrant workers also left out in the cold—migrant rights are not included in the ILO core definition, nor in the US IRWR definition—the US–Jordan trade pact failed to address the rights of two of the largest segments of the labour force in both countries: women workers and migrant workers.

The Clinton administration negotiated the Jordan agreement. It claimed another big step forward, compared with the NAALC, by subjecting labour disputes to the same mechanism as the agreement for commercial disputes. This held out at least a possibility of economic sanctions if a dispute resolution panel of arbitrators found one party in violation of its commitments.

The Bush administration was in power when Congress finally approved the Jordan agreement in 2002. In fact, the administration, business lobbyists and congressional Republicans wanted to weaken the labour clause. But Democrats made its approval the price of re-authorised five-year 'fast-track' negotiating authority for new trade agreements, something the administration badly wanted.

Congress approved the Jordan trade pact and gave Bush his trade promotion authority (TPA).[22] But in what Democrats saw as a betrayal of their deal, Bush's USTR proceeded to sign a side letter with Jordan promising never to seek economic sanctions in a labour dispute. Instead, the parties would rely solely on 'consultation' to resolve the disputes.

In 2006, the Bush administration negotiated a trade agreement with five Central American countries and the Dominican Republic, usually called CAFTA. It maintained the same elaboration of norms and obligations as those of the Jordan agreement. However, rather than applying the same dispute resolution mechanism as that for commercial

---

[22] Anti-free trade activists had always exploited the term 'fast-track' (eg 'they're putting your jobs on a fast track to Mexico'). The phrase had been traditionally used on all sides to describe Congress' grant of trade negotiating authority to the President coupled with a promise that Congress would vote 'yes' or 'no' on a completed agreement with no amendments and within a prescribed period of time—hence 'fast-track'. The Bush administration insisted on the more neutral 'trade promotion authority', and this term has taken hold.

complaints which might result in trade sanction, CAFTA only contemplated fines as a means of enforcement.

Democrats took control of the House of Representatives after the 2006 mid-term elections. The new legislative configuration shifted the balance of power in trade–labour linkage debates. For one thing, it blocked any repeat of the Jordan side letter with CAFTA parties. The Democrats also sought new concessions from the administration as the price of approving CAFTA and renewing TPA authority, up for another vote after five years. President Bush was again seeking TPA negotiating authority to press ahead in the Doha Round negotiations in the WTO. But Democrats also insisted that Bush re-negotiate trade pacts with Peru, Korea and Colombia with new, stronger labour chapters.

The result was a grand bargain. Congress gave Bush TPA and CAFTA. Under CAFTA, trade sanctions were off the table, but there would be no Jordan-style side letter. For Peru, Korea and Colombia, Bush promised the Democrats a new, stronger formulation of labour norms and obligations and trade sanctions as a potential measure against violators.

Like the NAALC, all the post-NAFTA labour chapters in trade agreements provided for myriad forms of government-to-government consultation to avoid the formal dispute resolution process. Indeed, no NAALC case ever reached that stage, although the recent complaint over Alabama's anti-immigrant law holds out such a possibility, since it alleges failure to effectively enforce workplace health and safety and minimum wage and overtime laws, two of the three subject matters (along with child labour) susceptible to sanctions.

But a complaint under the CAFTA labour chapter has reached the stage at which an arbitral panel is to be formed. A coalition of unions and human rights groups in Guatemala and the US filed a complaint alleging the Guatemalan government's failure to effectively enforce its labour laws. According to the complaint, factory owners deny entry to labour inspectors—and nothing happens. Or inspectors enter and find violations—and nothing happens. Or the labour ministry imposes fines—and nothing happens. Or a court orders fines to be paid—and nothing happens. This, in addition to continuing threats, assaults and assassinations of trade union activists.

The US labour department and USTR went through multiple consultation steps with the Guatemalan government without results. Most recently, US officials called for the formation of an arbitral panel that could impose fines against Guatemala.[23] The selection of arbitrators is underway in what could become the first real test of 'hard' labour rights application in contrast to 'soft' application in earlier NAALC cases. The latter often gained positive outcomes, but indirectly, through side-door strategies rather than front-door enforcement.[24]

In March 2012, a labour-human rights coalition filed a CAFTA complaint against the government of Honduras raising issues similar to those of the Guatemala case.[25] The US

---

[23] See US Labor Education in the Americas Project, 'United States Seeks Arbitration with Guatemalan Government over CAFTA Labor Violations', 12 August 2011, available at usleap.org/united-states-seeks-arbitration-guatemalan-government-over-cafta-labor-violations.

[24] For a political scientist's analysis and a sociologist's analysis, respectively, of creative 'side-door' uses of the NAALC, see J Graubart, *Legalizing Transnational Activism: The Struggle to Gain Social Change from NAFTA's Citizen Petitions* (University Park, Pennsylvania State University Press, 2008) and Tamara Kay, *NAFTA and the Politics of Labor Transnationalism* (Cambridge, Cambridge University Press, 2011).

[25] See US Labor Education in the Americas Project, 'Honduran Unions, with AFL-CIO, File CAFTA Labor Complaint with US', 30 March 2012 available at www.usleap.org/honduran-unions-file-cafta-labor-complaint-afl-cio.

quickly decided to accept the complaint for review. The review starts with 'soft' procedures such as exchanges of information, field investigations, reports, hearings, recommendations, action plans, consultations and so on and then, if these yield no result, can move to dispute resolution by an arbitral panel.

As with labour rights petitions under the GSP and the NAALC, the Guatemala and Honduras petitions flow from close consultation, collaboration and strategising among labour and human-rights lawyers in Central America and the US. The nearly 100-page petitions take the form of legal complaints, with a detailed recitation of facts, careful citing of the CAFTA labour chapter's standards and obligations, and closely-reasoned legal arguments tying the facts to CAFTA labour 'law'.

VI. Labour Rights in Post-NAALC Trade Agreements: Second Generation

Central obligations: 'adopt and maintain in its statutes and regulations, and practices thereunder, rights stated in [the ILO core declaration] … [and] not fail to effectively enforce its labour laws related to the ILO core declaration and [the US definition of] internationally recognized worker rights'[26]

In negotiations that resulted in what became known as the May 2007 'template', the House of Democrats and the Bush administration agreed on new trade–labour language in re-negotiated agreements with Peru, Korea and Colombia. In line with the template, the US and each of these bilateral trading partners would:

— adopt and maintain in their laws and practice the labour principles as stated in the ILO Declaration on Fundamental Principles and Rights at Work;
— assume an enforceable obligation to effectively enforce labour laws on the labour principles from the 1998 Declaration, plus acceptable conditions of work [from the US IRWR formulation—wages, hours and health and safety]; and
— subject labour obligations to the same dispute settlement procedures and remedies as commercial obligations, with both fines and trade sanctions as available remedies.

Labour advocates saw these three measures as a signal advance in trade–labour linkage. A move from 'strive to ensure' to 'adopt and maintain' ILO core principles in national law meant that governments had to deliver on promised labour law reforms, not just introduce them. By incorporating ILO core standards into the 'effective enforcement' obligation, the 2007 template for the first time subjected anti-discrimination laws to the same enforcement requirement as that for organising and collective bargaining, forced labour, child labour and 'acceptable conditions'. Finally, the template restored trade sanctions as a potential enforcement mechanism.

---

[26] US-Peru Free Trade Agreement (2007), available at http://www.ustr.gov/trade-agreements/free-trade-agreements (accessed August 30, 2013).

One question, left open in the 'template', brings us back to the debate over the meaning of 'principles' in the ILO Declaration. As a matter of fact, there is not a single text of the 2007 template. It was embodied in competing 10 May press releases from Bush's USTR and from the House Democratic Leadership. Both were rushed, badly-written efforts to put each side's gloss on what the template meant. For example, the Republican USTR stopped at 'adopt and maintain' ILO core principles, while the Democrats' version had 'adopt, maintain and enforce'. The key is how the Peru, Korea and Colombia agreements incorporated the template.

The Bush administration and House Democrats agreed (with slightly differing language in their respective press releases) that the template's 'adopt and maintain' obligation refers 'only to the ILO Declaration on Fundamental Principles and Rights at Work'. The template-driven trade pacts with Peru, Korea and Colombia reflect this point in a footnote (the notorious 'footnote 2' as it is known, at least among trade–labour policy experts) to the 'adopt and maintain' obligations. The footnote states that 'the obligations [to adopt, maintain, and enforce ILO core standards] … refer only to the ILO Declaration'. This takes us full circle to what the Declaration means in the progression from 'principles' through 'rights' and 'subjects' to the 'conventions' and whether they should be merely promoted or fully realised. Ultimately, we will know what this means when an arbitral panel has to rule on a complaint that a country has failed to comply with the obligation.

The governments of Peru, South Korea and Colombia had to come back to the bargaining table to conform their earlier-agreed labour chapter to the requirements of the new template. One presumes reluctantly, but the dynamics of US trade and labour politics made it necessary. Congress quickly endorsed the Peru pact. Unusually, the AFL-CIO did not oppose it, counting the strengthened labour clause as a significant gain for workers. But the agreements with Korea and Colombia languished for four more years before Congress approved them.

The South Korea dispute mainly turned on automobile industry concerns. When the Obama administration felt they had been sufficiently addressed, the president called in the debt of the United Auto Workers (UAW), securing the union's support as payback for the automobile industry bailout in the 2008 financial crisis. Other US unions denounced the deal, but Obama had the labour cover he needed to insist that he was standing up for workers' rights.

The situation with Colombia was more complicated. Trade unions remained united in their opposition to the US–Colombia FTA because of continuing cases of violence against trade union leaders and members. The Obama administration extracted a far-reaching 'Action Plan' from Colombian labour authorities with quantifiable indicators of progress— new labour courts, new labour inspectors, increased labour law budgets, more prosecutions of employers for violations, more criminal prosecutions for violence, and other measures. Congress approved the pact in October 2011, but it did not take effect until President Obama certified in April 2012 (against continued trade union opposition) that Colombia had met the Action Plan goals.

Having lost the battle to stop the US–Colombia FTA in Congress, labour advocates are now preparing a complaint that can put the meaning of 'refers only to the ILO Declaration' to the test before an arbitral panel. As with all the trade–labour complaints, union leaders are involved in decision-making, but union lawyers are crafting the complaint and the legal strategy to carry it forward.

VII. Vietnam and Labour Rights in the Trans-Pacific Partnership (TPP) Negotiations

The newest arena for forging trade–labour linkage is in TPP negotiations among Pacific Rim nations including Australia, Brunei Darussalam, Canada, Chile, Malaysia, Mexico, New Zealand, Peru, Singapore, Vietnam and the US. In Thomas Friedman-esque trade cheerleading style, the USTR is promoting the TPP as an 'ambitious, next-generation, high standard, 21st-century' trade agreement.[27]

The expected coalition of unions, anti-globalisation NGOs, a bloc of congressional Democrats and other free-trade critics are mobilising to defeat the TPP if a completed agreement comes to a vote in Congress.[28] In the same way, they mobilised to defeat NAFTA, CAFTA and FTAs with Korea, Colombia and others—and failed.

The US Congress has always had a sufficient combination of its ideologically pro-free-trade Republicans and enough business-backed Democrats to pass trade agreements. Successive administrations, including those of nominally pro-labour presidents Clinton and Obama, were always eager to show they could accomplish something big. They inevitably responded to corporate importuning and pushed trade agreements through to approval—in Obama's case, directly contrary to promises he made in his 2008 campaign.

The same scenario would likely play itself out with the TPP, if negotiations ever conclude an agreement. However, the TPP labour chapter looms as a potential obstacle to agreement, especially because of Vietnam's participation in TPP negotiations. This is not because Vietnam has a socialist system. Socialist ideals still prevail in public discourse, but they are belied by Vietnam's large and growing private sector and large-scale investments by multinational corporations in apparel, electronics, energy, mining and other sectors.

The central problem is that Vietnam is a one-party communist state with a one-union labour system. The Vietnamese General Confederation of Labour (common usage is VCGL—not VGCL as one might assume) is organically tied to the Communist Party, the only union legally permitted to exist and operate in Vietnam. The head of the VCGL sits on the Party Politburo. The union's role is to transmit Party policy to workers and ensure labour productivity and labour discipline. In many workplaces, human resources managers are the VCGL union leaders. Any workers who try to form a union outside the VCGL are acting unlawfully and are subject to arrest and imprisonment.[29]

All these features run contrary to international human rights standards and ILO standards on freedom of association. If the US insists, as reflected in the evolution of trade–labour linkage in trade agreements up to the present, that Vietnam 'adopt and maintain' labour laws consistent with ILO norms, Vietnam would have to fundamentally change its labour law system to allow non-VCGL unions. Vietnam is not disposed to make such a change. Opening up trade union organising to alternative unions is tantamount to opening up the political system to alternative parties—not an outcome that analysts expect in the near or medium future.

---

[27] See the USTR TPP website at www.ustr.gov/tpp.

[28] See, eg Citizens Trade Campaign, 'Help Prevent a NAFTA of the Pacific', 25 August 2011, available at www.citizenstrade.org/ctc/blog/2011/08/25/help-prevent-a-nafta-of-the-pacific/.

[29] Essentially the same is true of Brunei, but its economy is so tiny that no one is paying attention.

Still, Vietnam badly wants to be part of a TPP trade pact for both the commercial benefits and the status enhancement it would bring. And Vietnam does not have to apologise for much of its labour practices. The biggest labour problem is that of large-scale, spontaneous strikes by thousands of workers at a time seeking wage increases in line with inflation. These strikes take place entirely outside the labour law system and without any involvement of VCGL union officials.

The strikes are spontaneous in the sense that they do not follow from a collective bargaining impasse. They are not unplanned. Indigenous workplace leaders organise and lead strikes, now often with the use of mobile phones and text messages. But instead of sending police and soldiers to break strikes, arrest leaders and force workers back to their jobs, Vietnamese government officials usually pressure business owners to meet workers' demands to end their strikes.

In an effort to address the likely US insistence on ILO standards in a TPP labour agreement, Vietnam's labour ministry proposed a revised law allowing the establishment of a 'representative board of collective labour in non-unionised enterprise', as an English translation by the ILO has it. The clause is not further elaborated and the government has not yet adopted a revised labour law, but an expansive reading might see it as a vehicle for workers to join organisations 'of their own choosing'—the central international norm—as long as they don't call them unions or try to compete with the VCGL. Still, without further explanation, this language is not likely to meet the 'adopt and maintain' standard where the bar is now set for US approval of a trade agreement.

US labour proposals in TPP negotiations are still not public, but many analysts have said that the US is seeking a 'template-plus' agreement which would set the bar even higher. According to the specialised weekly journal *Inside US Trade*, 'the US proposal in TPP goes into greater detail on what countries must do to uphold these rights, and also includes new details on other labour issues, such as how TPP countries should handle complaints about labour rights violations submitted by the public'.[30] The same report notes, 'These aspects of the proposal have raised the ire of congressional Republicans, who argue it goes beyond the May 10 deal' [the 2007 template].

For the labour movement and its allies, the 'plus' in template-plus is the key. The International Trade Union Confederation (ITUC) is urging government negotiators to adopt language it has drafted for a TPP labour chapter that adds migrant workers' rights to covered subjects, bans imports of all products made by child labour, incorporates and makes enforceable the OECD Guidelines for Multinational Enterprises, requires international framework agreements between 'pan-Pacific enterprises' and global union federations, and establishes a TPP Labour Secretariat to research, report, and oversee implementation of the labour chapter.[31]

Even a US negotiating team committed to 'template-plus' in the TPP labour chapter is unlikely to go as far as the ITUC is demanding. The outcome of TPP labour chapter negotiations will signal the course of further evolution of trade–labour linkage—forward toward more 'teeth', standstill with the 2007 template, or backward to something less. Whatever the results, both in language of a TPP labour chapter and later complaints and cases under

---

[30] See, 'TPP Partners Willing To Discuss Scope Of US Labor Text; Enforceability Is Major Hurdle', *Inside US Trade*, 15 May 2012.
[31] See ITUC, 'The Trans-Pacific Partnership Agreement A New Model Labour & Dispute Resolution Chapter for the Asia-Pacific Region', 1 September 2011, available at www.ituc-csi.org/the-trans-pacific-partnership.html.

it, we will learn new lessons about the efficacy and the challenges of this evolving form of contemporary international governance and regulation.

VIII. Conclusion

The argument can certainly be made that the US is bullying its trading partners into acceptance of a trade–labour linkage that is largely driven by domestic US politics and marked by eccentric American notions of international labour standards. And the argument would be largely correct.

US trade unions and NGOs demanding more power in trade–labour linkage and their Democratic allies in Congress, have pushed successive administrations to strengthen labour clauses in trade agreements. Seemingly oblivious to the fact that it has not ratified several of the 'core' ILO conventions, and itself, in many aspects of American labour law and policy, violates international freedom of association standards[32] and other ILO core labour standards,[33] the US blithely imposed a quirky definition of 'internationally recognized worker rights' in all its trade agreements.

In a perfect world, governments would see the logic of trade–labour linkage and arrive smoothly at a consensus for achieving it. But real life is different. Trade–labour linkage is contested terrain. Countries might wait forever for consensus on such a new form of international governance, as the WTO has shown.

It was not elegant and had some bull-in-a-china-shop moments, but the US push for labour rights in trade over the past quarter-century has forced trade–labour linkage to move towards the top on the global governance agenda. US insistence on labour rights in trade agreements unleashed currents with wide spillover effects. It made the ILO more relevant and enhanced the role of national and international labour and human rights civil society groups. It prompted the European Union to inject labour standards into the EU GSP programme and EU trade agreements with various countries. It pressed the OECD, World Bank, IMF and other financial institutions to take labour rights into account in their lending programmes. It drove developments of corporate codes of conduct and corporate social responsibility initiatives. It influenced efforts at the United Nations to develop human rights standards for multinational business, from the early 2000s UN Human Rights Norms for Business to the latest protect-respect–remedy framework of the UN Guiding Principles for Business and Human Rights.

The persistent demand for labour rights in trade has created new forms of global governance—newly-defined international norms, newly-formulated obligations to comply with the norms, and newly-designed supranational mechanisms for measuring compliance and sanctioning violators. These all came in hybrid forms with hard edges, soft edges,

---

[32] See Human Rights Watch, *Unfair Advantage: Workers' Freedom of Association in the United States under International Human Rights Standards* (2000) available at www.hrw.org/reports/2000/uslabor/.

[33] For example, US law does not meet the international non-discrimination standard of equal pay for work of equal value (it provides only equal pay for equal work); it allows young children to labour in agriculture, contrary to child labour standards, and it allows products made by prison labour to enter the stream of commerce in violation of compulsory labour standards.

and somewhere-between-hard-and-soft edges, as Dave Trubek anticipated in his own new governance analyses over the years.

In the same way, the drive for trade–labour linkage created new legal spaces into which labour and human-rights lawyers moved and thrived.[34] In cross-border collaboration, they developed strategies to fit the new trade–labour regimes and married legal and activist campaign tactics to make concrete gains for workers and their trade unions. In this new practice of transnational labour law, legal activists have learned, as Dave Trubek put it, 'to stop thinking about law as command, rule, or doctrine and start thinking about it as system, symbol, and behaviour'.[35]

[34] However, lawyers have not thrived financially, at least on the labour–human rights side. I have served as a volunteer, or at most a modestly-compensated legal adviser, in many complaints and cases under the GSP and trade agreements discussed here, while well-heeled and high-fee-charging corporate law firms advised companies and governments on the other side.

[35] DM Trubek, 'Back to the Future: The Short, Happy Life of the Law and Society Movement' (1990) 18 *Florida State University Law Review* 4.

9

Globalisation and the Middle Class

KATHERINE VW STONE

I. Introduction

In 1992, Ross Perot famously warned that there would be a 'giant sucking sound' as millions of jobs in the United States move to Mexico. His claim, greeted with widespread mockery at the time, may not have been quite as outlandish as it seemed. While there has been no thundering 'shluurrp' or any similar sucking sound, there has been a gradual but steady movement of jobs overseas, first in manufacturing and then in some services over the past twenty-five years. And for those jobs still in the US, wages have stagnated because middle-class workers are being forced to compete, directly or indirectly, with low-wage workers from around the world.

The most important question for social policy today is: can the US participate in global trade while maintaining a robust middle class? Or does expanded global trade necessarily mean doom for the middle class in the US and other advanced industrial nations? This question might have sounded provocative or just plain silly a decade ago, but it can no longer be ignored. In the stream of global commerce, labour standards tend to flow to the lowest point. The price of labour in China now affects what workers in Detroit can bargain for. Safety conditions in Vietnam now affect the availability of jobs in North Carolina. Yet efforts by developed countries to impose their labour standards on developing countries have met with staunch resistance and accusations of protectionism from developing countries.[1] Moreover, under the current rules of global trade, countries cannot unilaterally use trade sanctions to impose their labour standards on countries with lesser standards.

Some have argued that trade does not lower labour standards globally because multinational corporations (MNCs) raise labour standards in the countries where they locate production. However, evidence that this actually happens is sparse at best. For every Banana Republic, there is at least one Nike. And there are only Banana Republics because non-governmental organisations (NGOs) and consumer advocates have shamed a high-profile name-brand producer into adopting a code of conduct and an external monitoring system, and other corporations do not want similar scrutiny. Moreover, not all corporations are vulnerable to consumer pressure, and consumers, as a whole, are fickle and unreliable advocates in any event. It is true that MNCs offer jobs in places where jobs have been intermittent

---

[1] See K Kolbin, 'The WTO Distraction' (2010) 21 *Stanford Law & Policy Review* 461, 468–71. See also, K Banks, 'Trade, Labor and International Governance: An Inquiry into the Potential Effectiveness of the New International Labor Law' (2011) 45 *Berkleley Journal of Employment and Labor Law* 45, 60–61.

or non-existent, and the jobs they provide usually pay more than the local alternatives, but MNCs also relocate repeatedly as soon as workers demand too much. It is quixotic to expect MNCs to provide Western standards of decent work environments.

Moreover, any salutary intentions Western multinational firms might have to offer minimally decent labour standards when they move to poor countries frequently dissipate once they arrive. In China, Vietnam and other Asian countries, US multinationals are powerful actors in the domestic political arena and have used their influence to resist improvements in, and even to reduce, labour standards in their host countries.[2]

Given the trends in global labour standards, what, if anything, can be done to protect labour standards for the middle class in the developed world? Will protection for labour standards in the developed world contribute to the impoverishment of the developing world? Will declining labour standards in the global North lead to a decline everywhere, so that the tide of trade not only does not raise all the boats, but actually sinks them all instead? Or can labour standards be improved universally through some felicitous dynamic that raises all boats?

Five different approaches have been proposed to try to save the middle class in the industrialised world without impoverishing the developing world.

First, some have called for more powerful transnational institutions that have the power and authority to impose hard law solutions. The argument is that the International Labor Organization (ILO), the World Trade Organization (WTO), or some yet-to-be established global labour tribunal with sufficient power and legitimacy should set minimal standards, define fundamental labour rights, and set up an enforcement mechanism akin to the International Criminal Court to adjudicate and remedy allegations of breaches.[3]

Second, there are some who call not for an equalisation or even a harmonisation of labour standards, but rather for a sufficiently ample safety net to ensure that everyone can have a decent standard of living regardless of trends in labour markets. One scheme of this type is the proposal for a basic income (sometimes called a 'citizenship grant') by which a socially-adequate level of support would be provided to every citizen without any work requirement or other strings attached.[4]

A third approach is to advocate policies that encourage a race to the top that can counterbalance a race to the bottom. As discussed below, there have been several different proposals for mechanisms to facilitate a race to the top.[5]

---

[2] D Barboza, 'China Drafts Law to Boost Unions and End Abuse' (*New York Times Business Section*, 13 October 2006). See also, Labor Strategies, *Behind the Great Wall of China: US Corporations Opposing New Rights for Chinese Workers*, available at laborstrategies.blogs.com/global_labor_strategies/files/behind_the_great_wall_of_china.pdf.

[3] See, eg C Barry and SG Reddy, 'Global Justice and International Economic Arrangements: International Trade and Labor Standards: A Proposal for Linkage' (2006) 39 *Cornell International Law Journal* 545; A Hyde, 'The International Labor Organization in the Stag Hunt for Global Labor Rights' (2009) 3 *Law & Ethics of Human Rights* 154; P Macklem, 'Labour Law Beyond Borders' (2002) 5 *Journal of International Economic Law* 605.

[4] See, eg G Standing, *The Precariat: The New Dangerous Class* (London, Bloomsbury Academic, 2010) 171–73; G Standing, *Global Labour Flexibility: Seeking Distributive Justice* (Basingstoke, Macmillan, 1999); J de Wespalaere and L Stirton, 'The Many Faces of Universal Basic Income' (2004) 75 *Political Quarterly* 266. For a general overview of issues and a collection of Working Papers on Basic Income, see The Basic Income Guarantee Network, at www.usbig.net/whatisbig.php.

[5] See Section III A below.

Fourth, some advocate the creation of local and regional agglomeration economies that will act as counterweights to a race to the bottom. Proponents of this approach—including this author—advocate measures to empower local groups so that workers can obtain a share in the surplus that agglomeration provides.[6]

A fifth approach argues that the only way developed countries can protect their labour standards in the era of global trade is to foster firm-level innovation and develop the skills and human capital of the local population.[7]

Of these five approaches, the first two might be attractive, but are highly unlikely to materialise in the foreseeable future. In today's political landscape, it is almost inconceivable that either a transnational labour authority with genuine rule-making and adjudicatory authority will be established in the foreseeable future, or that national states will choose to provide their citizens with an adequate level of basic income. Hence it is more fruitful to consider the other three approaches—encouraging a race to the top, facilitating agglomeration economies, and fostering flexible labour practices. Each of these approaches has not only been theorised and debated in the scholarly literature—each has actually been implemented in some places.

However, each of the latter three approaches has a dark side along with the bright side. Each one offers the possibility of a fairer form of globalisation and a more promising future for the middle class in the developed world, but each also contains serious dangers. Moreover, to get to the bright side of any of these, there are certain regulatory or institutional mechanisms that must be put in place. None will automatically save the middle class. Each requires political mobilisation and enlightened policy design.

In this chapter, I describe the latter three approaches, report on some places where each has been implemented, and elucidate each one's dark and bright side. I then consider whether these approaches can be braided together and used as a lifeline to save the middle class.

First, though, it is necessary to review the conventional debates about labour and trade.

II. Labour Standards and Free Trade—Shotgun Wedding or Harmonious Marriage?

A. Free Trade in Theory: The Ricardian Argument for Free Trade and its Critics

Almost 200 years ago, David Ricardo showed that free trade between two nations was beneficial for both, regardless of each one's wealth, factor endowments or level of productivity. According to his analysis, each nation would export those goods in which it had a 'comparative advantage' and import those goods in which it did not. In Ricardo's

---

[6] See Section III B below.
[7] See Section III C below.

two-country example, if Portugal can produce both textiles and wine more cheaply than England, and if the cost differential between Portugal and England were greater in wine than in textiles, then it would be beneficial for Portugal to export wine to England and import textiles from England. At the same time, it would be to England's advantage to export textiles to Portugal and import wine, again so long as its cost differential is less for textile production than for wine production. This is because while Portugal has an absolute advantage in both commodities, England has a comparative advantage in textiles.

Another example often used to explain the theory of comparative advantage is as follows. Suppose the best lawyer in a town is also the best typist. The lawyer would still be better off hiring a secretary to do his or her own typing.[8] On a moment's reflection, one would agree that this is correct. After all, working as a lawyer is more lucrative than typing, so utilising one's time as a lawyer and paying someone else to type makes sense.

An overwhelming percentage of economists interpret Ricardo's model as presenting a powerful case for the benefits of free trade, even between countries of vastly different wealth, resources, and levels of technological development.[9] In the classic Ricardian model, overall output is increased by trade. Moreover, free trade permits each country to exploit its own comparative advantage, so that with unfettered trade, the gains are potentially shared. However, the model does not prove that both trading partners are automatically, or always, made better off by trade. Whether both nations gain or only one nation gains depends upon many factors, including the institutional arrangements inside each country, the rules governing international trade, the structure of domestic industry, and the specific values of the goods being exchanged.[10] Moreover, the lessons from trades of wine and textiles, or of lawyering for typing, are not easily applied to nations. Nations are made up of numerous distinct groups that do not necessarily have the same interests, nor the same ability to protect those interests, in the face of global trade.

Some economists have raised theoretical and empirical questions about the Ricardian model. Over time, the model predicts that countries will specialise in production areas where they have comparative advantage. But some question whether specialisation will always occur or will always be beneficial to the specialising country. For example, some posit that to benefit from free trade over time, developing countries first need to develop manufacturing industries, and thus they should shield those industries from global competition to give them a chance to develop.[11] Some also question whether market imperfections or path dependency could impair a country's ability to develop the full potential of its productive capacity.[12] Nonetheless, since Ricardo, it has been an article of faith for most economists that free trade benefits all countries that participate in an open trading regime.

---

[8] See, AS Binder, *Free Trade* in DR Henderson, *The Concise Encyclopedia of Economics*, 2nd edn (Indianapolis, Liberty Fund, 2008).

[9] S Deraniyagala and B Fine, 'New Trade Theory Versus Old Trade Policy: A Continuing Enigma' (2001) 25 *Cambridge Journal of Economics* 809, 809 (reporting the finding that in 1996, 97% of US economists support unrestricted free trade).

[10] See AV Deardoff, 'How Robust is Comparative Advantage?' (2005) 13 *Review of International Economics* 1004, 1005–1006; David Kennedy unpublished memo (on file with author).

[11] For a historical review of the 'infant industry' argument for an exception to free trade, see DA Irwin, 'Retrospectives: Challenges to Free Trade' (1991) 5 *Journal of Economic Perspectives* 201–208.

[12] See Deraniyagala and Fine, 'New Trade Theory Versus Old Trade Policy' (n 9), 812–16 (summarising arguments).

Stripped to its essence, Ricardo's theory shows that overall production is greater with free trade. It also shows that in some circumstances, there are mutual benefits of trade for *nations*. However, it does not address the question of which specific groups or individuals within nations will benefit from trade. Rather, despite the analytic power of the theory of comparative advantage, it does not necessarily predict that everyone within a given nation gains as a result of free trade. Ricardo's theory treats each nation as a black box, but within the box, specific groups can win, lose or draw in a free trade game.[13] As Paul Samuelson writes, the theory of comparative advantage makes an important omission by 'treating all people in each region as different *homogeneous* Ricardian laborers'. According to Samuelson, that assumption obscures 'the realistic cases where some Americans (capitalists and skilled computer experts) may be helped by [the decimation of the] wage rates of the semi-skilled or the blue-collar factory workers'.[14]

Ricardo's theory of comparative advantage does not prove that *all* groups within a nation benefit from free trade: It simply does not talk about distribution within, or between, countries. This omission is not a fatal flaw in the eyes of economists. Most economists evaluate free trade, as well as other economic policies, under a Hicks–Caldor model of efficiency.[15] A policy is 'efficient' under a Hicks–Caldor definition of efficiency if everyone could theoretically benefit, not if everyone actually benefits.[16] That is, a policy is efficient if the winners' incomes were sufficiently enhanced that they could compensate the losers and still come out ahead.[17]

Thus under Ricardo's theory, free trade might or might not benefit all groups within a country. The impact on the middle class in an advanced country would be determined by whether there were distributional measures in place to ensure that firms, workers and other social groups all shared in whatever advantages the trading regime produced.

Furthermore, Ricardo's theory is addressed to the effect of trade on 'nations'. It shows that 'nations' can benefit from trade when they specialise and produce goods in which they have comparative advantages. However, it is not clear from the theory what it means for a 'nation' to benefit. In today's world, most economists measure the wealth of nations in several different ways, with the most prominent being gross domestic product (GDP). But GDP is not the same as the wealth of individuals or entities who reside in the nation.

GDP refers to the total value of goods and services produced within a particular country's territorial borders in a particular time frame. Thus it is theoretically possible for GDP to be large even if all the assets within the country are foreign-owned and all the wages

[13] Deraniyagala and Fine note that the theory has 'a particularly underdeveloped notion of what constitutes a nation', ibid, 816.

[14] PA Samuelson, 'Where Ricardo and Mill Rebut and Confirm Arguments of Mainstream Economists Supporting Globalization' (2004) 18 *Journal of Economic Perspectives* 135, 143–44.

[15] See, eg J Coleman, 'The Normative Basis of Economic Analysis: A Critical Review of Richard Posner's The Economics of Justice' (1982) 34 *Stanford Law Journal* 1105 (discussing and criticising Posner's adoption of Hicks–Caldor efficiency criteria).

[16] N Kaldor, 'Welfare Propositions of Economics and Interpersonal Comparisons of Utility' (1939) 49 *Economic Journal* 549–50. In a Hicks–Caldor efficiency model, it is not relevant whether some groups lose, so long as the winners can compensate the losers. Yet in the real world, the issue of compensation, or redistribution, is very important. See, RS Markovits, 'A Constructive Critique of the Traditional Definition and Use of the Concept of "The Effect of a Choice on Allocative (Economic Efficiency)": Why the Kaldor–Hicks Test, The Coase Theorem, and Virtually All Law-and-Economics Welfare Arguments Are Wrong' (1993) *University of Illinois Law Review* 485, 489.

[17] See JE Stiglitz, *The Price of Equality: How Today's Divided Society Endangers Our Future* (New York, WW Norton & Co, 2012).

and salaries of the workforce are paid to foreign workers. That is, a country could have a high GDP even if all the income went to non-nationals and its own citizens were impoverished.[18]

In Ricardo's era, there were no publicly-traded corporations and no international stock exchanges. Large trading companies had charters that permitted them to monopolise trade with particular regions. Those trading companies often had diffuse stock ownership. Entrepreneurial financiers purchased shares and options across borders, but the bulk of ownership was nationally based.[19] In contrast, company ownership today is dispersed globally, just as are company assets, workers, customers and suppliers. Because the owners of MNCs—that is the shareholders—are dispersed around the globe, trade can benefit owners of productive resources without necessarily creating prosperity for their nations of origin.

The more corporations pull away from their national moorings and operate instead in a global market under disparate legal regimes with shareholders and decision-makers from many nations, the less the effect of comparative advantage will redound to the benefit of inhabitants of any particular nation. Trade, under Ricardo's theory, will create more goods overall, but the distribution of those goods and the benefits that accrue from producing them could be located anywhere. That is, when giant multinational firms have interests that are distinct from individuals or other firms in their nation-states, the conclusion that free trade benefits all *nations* does not necessarily hold.[20] Hence trade policies that maximise advantage for firms no longer translate neatly into beneficial effects for particular nations, no less for all social groups within nations.

B. The Distributional Impact of Free Trade

There are two mechanisms propounded to explain why trade may help some groups in rich and poor countries, but not necessarily everyone. Analysts contend that unfettered trade between rich and poor countries can lower labour standards for working people in wealthier countries, either by triggering a *race to the bottom* or by fostering *regulatory competition*, whereby countries loosen regulatory standards to attract producers.

The prediction that firms will move to locations offering the lowest level of labour standards was used to explain firm relocation decisions within the US when firms in the textile industry moved from New England to the South to take advantage of low-wage and non-union environments.[21] In the latter part of the twentieth century, as capital became more mobile internationally and barriers to international trade declined, the concept of a

---

[18] See, eg RA Brecher and JN Bhagwati, 'Foreign Ownership and the Theory of Trade and Welfare' (1981) 89 *Journal of Political Economy* 497–511, concluding that 'welfare aspects of international trade theory need to be reconsidered, when national and aggregate income differ in the presence of foreign ownership'.

[19] FA Gevurtz, 'The Globalization of Corporate Law: The End of History or a Never-Ending Story?' (2011) in 86 *Washington Law Review* 475, 481–83.

[20] S Hymer, 'Efficiency (Contradictions) of Multinational Corporations' (1970) 60 *American Economic Review* 44, 446–48.

[21] B English, *A Common Thread: Labor, Politics, and Capital Mobility in the Textile Industry* (Athens, University of Georgia Press, 2006). The phrase 'race to the bottom' is usually attributed to Justice Brandeis, who used it to decry the trend of states to weaken their incorporation laws in order to attract corporate charters. See *Louis K. Liggett Co v Lee*, 288 US 517, 559–60 (1933) (Brandreis J, dissenting). He wrote, '[t]he race was one not of diligence but of laxity. Incorporation under [competing state] laws was possible; and the great industrial States yielded in order not to lose wholly the prospect of the revenue and the control incident to domestic incorporation', ibid.

'race to the bottom' was transposed to the international arena. The argument is that if capital is unrestrained, firms will move production away from high-wage locations and locate their production facilities where labour costs are lower. This dynamic will depress wages in the original high-cost locations because more and more jobs will be lost. Corporations that do not move their production overseas, will be forced to lower their wage levels to that of the lowest cost producer. Hence critics of unrestricted trade warn that without some enforceable international labour standards or other external constraint on capital mobility, firms will leave high labour standard countries and relocate wherever they can find the cheapest labour.

A somewhat different critique of free trade is the theory of regulatory competition. Regulatory competition occurs when nations compete for business by keeping labour standards low to attract businesses.[22] The argument about regulatory competition is that globalisation induces domestic nations to revise their regulatory regimes so as to downgrade their level of labour protective regulations in order to retain or attract private capital.[23] Many labour advocates predict that regulatory competition will trigger a downward spiral in which nations compete with each other for lower labour standards.[24] They also fear regulatory competition will mean that labour unions will lose their political allies at the domestic level and thus be rendered powerless to resist the subsequent changes.[25]

The dynamics of regulatory competition and races-to-the-bottom are not mutually exclusive. Each posits different effects of trade on labour, effects caused by the actions of different actors. The race-to-the-bottom dynamic addresses choices made by firms, and it presupposes that firms, at least in some instances, will make locational decisions based on the cost of labour. Regulatory competition presupposes that governments make decisions about levels of labour protective regulation based on the threat of jurisdictional competition for jobs. It is reasonable to believe that both dynamics are operative and reinforce each other, so that firms' search for cheaper labour induces countries to lower labour standards.

C. The Problem of Labor and Trade

There is considerable evidence that firms relocate when they can achieve significant labour cost-savings in low-wage countries.[26] In the mid 1980s, diversified multi-national firms

---

[22] See eg J Yardley, 'Export Powerhouse Feels Pangs of Labor Strife' *New York Times* (23 August 2012) discussing the lengths that Bangladesh officials will go to keep its status as 'an export powerhouse, second only to China in global apparel exports, as factories churn out clothing for brands like Tommy Hilfiger, Gap, Calvin Klein and H&M'.

[23] For a schematic analysis of the dynamics of regulatory competition over labour standard regulations, see D Charny, 'Regulatory Competition and the Global Coordination of Labour Standards' in DC Esty and D Geradin (eds), *Regulatory Competition and Economic Integration: Comparative Perspectives* (Oxford, Oxford University Press, 2001) 311, 315–23.

[24] There are other types of regulatory competition as well. For example, Wolf-Georg Ringe, a professor of comparative law at Oxford University, describes regulatory competition in the field of corporate law in Europe after the European Court of Justice ruled that it was permissible for parties to choose where to incorporate. Numerous countries altered their laws once it became permissible for firms to choose to incorporate in the EU country with the least restrictive capital requirements. See W-G Ringe, 'Sparking Regulatory Competition in European Company Law' in R de la Feria and S Vogenauer (eds), *Prohibition of Abuse of Law: A New Principle of EU Law* (Oxford, Hart Publishing, 2009).

[25] See KVW Stone, 'To the Yukon and Beyond: Local Laborers Afoot in the Global Labor Market' (1999) 3 *Journal of Small & Emerging Business* 93. KVW Stone, 'Labor and the Global Economy: Four Approaches to Transnational Labor Regulation' (1995) 16 *Michigan Journal of International Law* 987.

[26] See, eg J Cowie, *Capital Moves* (Ithaca, Cornell University Press, 1999).

began to develop global strategies to move production between locations in order to exploit cost differentials, exchange rate fluctuations, and disparate labour law regimes.[27] And firms often move repeatedly as these factors shift. For example, many firms moved from Brazil to Haiti, and then from Haiti to Bangladesh when they were faced with the prospects of rising labour costs.[28] In 2005, when the WTO lifted textile quotas, industry analysts widely predicted that retailers would abandon their suppliers in low-cost states such as Cambodia, Mexico and Bangladesh, and relocate to the even lower-cost state of China. Indeed, many multinational firms moved production to China in the first decade of the 2000s, but when Chinese wages began to rise, some moved again to Vietnam. Currently, Bangladesh is expected to become the largest garment manufacturing country in the near future.[29]

Despite the anecdotal examples, firms do not inevitably relocate to the lowest labour-cost countries. Rather, evidence suggests that some firms relocate to take advantage of lower labour costs, but the pattern is often more complex than a simple race-to-the-bottom theory would predict.[30] Industries in which labour costs are not a large proportion of total costs are less likely to move than those that are labour intensive. Some industries, such as the hospitality industry, health services, or building services, need to be near their custom-ers. Others benefit by being near their distribution markets, as evidenced by the decision of Japanese car manufacturers to produce cars for the US market in the US. Some producers benefit from being close to natural resources or research facilities that are important to their production processes. Others do not move production to lower labour-cost countries because they benefit from agglomeration economies that result from proximity to other firms in their field.[31] In addition, some firms require their workforce to possess a high level of skills or education and need to locate where workers with those skills are available. And some producers are willing to shoulder higher labour costs because they place a great value on political stability.

Skeptics of the race-to-the-bottom theory further point out that if it were true, then Haiti and Rwanda would be a great location for multinational firms. But law professor Stephen Diamond explains the fallacy of this argument:

> [T]his misstates the problem. The 'race to the bottom' defines a different and new issue: the ability of sophisticated multinational corporate capital to combine high-productivity technology with labor that is paid substantially less than that found in the developed world. Developing this dynamic is not as simple as finding the worst-paid and most-repressed workers in the world. What one finds, in fact, in countries like Haiti or Rwanda are not workers in the classic sense—ready and available to be part of the disciplined structure of a modern capitalist firm. In large part the populations of those countries are at a near-feudal level of development, with the 'workforce' resembling

---

[27] See, eg CK Prahalad and YL Doz, *The Multinational Mission: Balancing Local Demand and Global Vision* 102 (New York, Free Press, 1987).

[28] Stone, 'To the Yukon and Beyond' (n 25) 97–98.

[29] Christina Passariello *Bangladesh Expected to Gain More Garment Work: Retailers Foresee Shifting Some Sourcing From China,* Wall Street Journal, September 16, 2013. See also, EI Rosen, 'The Wal-Mart Effect: The World Trade Organization and the Race to the Bottom' (2005) 8 *Chapman Law Review* 261, 264.

[30] See, eg E Tucker, '"Great Expectations" Defeated?: The Trajectory of Collective Bargaining Regimes in Canada and the United States Post-NAFTA' (2004) 26 *Comparative Labor Law and Policy Journal* 97, finding that NAFTA did not erode collective bargaining laws in the US, but did have a negative effect on the implementation of collective bargaining laws and the outcomes of bargaining in Canada.

[31] See, eg M Drennan, *The Information Economy and American Cities* (Baltimore, Johns Hopkins University Press, 2002); Annalee Saxenian, *Regional Advantage: Culture and Competition in Silicon Valley and Route* (Cambridge, MA, Harvard University Press, 1994) 128.

peasants, not modern workers. The difference in China or Mexico or Indonesia is that decades of rule there by modernizing authoritarian states has produced a new kind of workforce that is akin to that found in Europe or the United States, but at a wage level far below that of the advanced economies and without the independent political power that characterizes countries with strong labor movements.[32]

Thus it might be more accurate to speak not of a race to the bottom, but a race to middle-level countries that have both cheap labour and stable institutions—a combination that often provides the most attractive locations for mobile firms. Thus a revised race-to-the-bottom hypothesis maintains that firms will move jobs not to the most backward regions with the cheapest labour, but to those regions that also have the institutional structure to provide financial and political stability as well as low labour costs.

The race-to-the-bottom theory needs another restatement as well. When firms have a choice about where to produce, they tend to choose locations with lower labour costs and reasonable political stability for the labour intensive aspects of their production. Or, stated differently, when all else is equal, firms tend to prefer locations with low wages, poor safety provisions, weak protections for unions, and other low labour standards. To be sure, the precondition that all else is equal contains many unstated geographic, political, sociological and economic factors, but with these caveats, firms generally prefer to produce in low labour cost environments. Indeed, firms sometimes rearrange their production processes so as to locate those operations that do not require high skills in lower-wage countries, and locate those operations that require a highly-educated labour force in developed areas.

In addition, even when firms stay in place, the mere threat of moving can have a detrimental impact on labour standards in the home countries. In a recent empirical study, economics professor Minsik Choi found that threats of capital mobility have a significant effect on wages and bargaining. As Choi concludes,

> the increased outward investment by US manufacturing industries has been negatively associated with the wage premium that union members shared during the period from 1983 to 1996. ... This study finds that firms' enhanced locational mobility as a result of the globalization process (eg, the recent launches of NAFTA and WTO) is effective in pressuring workers who fear losing their jobs to concede at the bargaining table and accept a lower share of the rent.[33]

III. Is There a Lifeline for the Middle Class? Three Current Approaches

There have been several proposals for counteracting races to the bottom and regulatory competition without abandoning a commitment to expansive global trade. Each one has some risks and potential benefits, as discussed below.

---

[32] SF Diamond, 'The Race to the Bottom Returns: China's Challenge to the International Labor Movement' (2003) 10 *University of California at Davis Journal of International Law and Policy* 39, 41–44.

[33] M Choi, 'Threat Effects of Capital Mobility on Wage Bargaining' in P Bardham, S Bowles and M Wallerstein (eds), *Globalization and Egalitarian Distribution* (Princeton, Princeton University Press, 2006) 78.

A. Transforming Races to the Bottom into Races to the Top

One approach to the problem of labour and trade maintains that labour standards will not necessarily deteriorate as a result of trade, but rather that labour standards can, and under certain conditions will, rise. This approach posits the possibility of a 'race to the top', at least if the necessary institutional framework is in place.

One often cited race-to-the-top view is the 'racheting labour standards' (RLS) approach advocated by Charles Sabel, Archon Fong and Dara O'Rourke. They argue that firms can be induced to emulate the best practices of other firms if there is sufficient information, transparency and accountability. RLS is a proposal for raising international standards based on the assumption that with a properly-structured meta-framework, a race to the top will occur. As the authors describe:

> [L]ike the metaphorical ratchet wrench we invoke, the [RLS] framework attempts to set into motion a process that begins with the dismal labor outcomes often found in the facilities worldwide, and then gradually, but systematically move them upwards. The standards are based initially upon the best that current performance offers, the regulatory frame compels facility-level improvements, and then re-sets standards at that new, elevated level of realized performance. The ratcheting-rule framework recognizes (like voluntary codes) that we have limited knowledge of the diverse needs of workers in developing countries and of feasible social performance, but aims nonetheless (like the ILO proposal) to provide enforceable standards backed by sanctions.[34]

The racheting labour standards concept is a mirror image of the race to the bottom in that it focuses on the behaviour of firms that act in the global labour and product market. Rather than race to the bottom, RLS advocates assert that sufficient transparency and credible monitoring will pressure firms to race to the top.

Sabel, O'Rourke & Fong describe three prerequisites for RLS to be successful—'[p]ublic transparency, comparison and evaluation, and continuous improvement.'[35] Of these, the first two require specific institutional mechanisms to be in place. As the authors explain, 'transparency' involves requiring firms to disclose their treatment of workers and factory conditions. 'Comparison' involves having a public agency that verifies that firms have used appropriate procedures in their disclosures, identifies best and worst practices, and publishes the disclosures so that comparisons can be made. 'Continuous improvement' is up to the firms. The theory assumes that firms will have an incentive to improve their labour standards once their practices are subject to public scrutiny in a systemic and credible way.

According to its proponents, RLS will result in a race to the top only under a particular complex regulatory framework. Hence it is not a theory of 'natural' trends, but rather a method of countering an underlying race to the bottom. For RLS to operate successfully there must be mandatory transparency and monitoring mechanisms, combined with some sort of transnational body to promulgate the mandates and impose sanctions for non-compliance. At the present time, there is no transnational body with the power to require transparency or comparable disclosures by firms. Nor is there any realistic possibility of such a body being created in the near future. Without such an institution, RSL must revert to advocating voluntary reporting and disclosure—mechanisms

---

[34] C Sabel, D O'Rourke and A Fung, 'Racheting Labor Standards: Regulation for Continuous Improvement in the Global Workplace' working paper available at www2.law.columbia.edu/sabel/papers/ratchPO.html.
[35] Ibid.

that are considerably weaker than those currently provided by the ILO. Another race-to-the-top theory posits that developing nations will seek to emulate the high labour standards of developed nations once they have repeated and sustained contact with them. This approach, termed 'constructive engagement', was used to argue that China should be admitted to the WTO because the experience of trading with developed countries would induce it to raise its labour standards and improve its human rights practices.[36]

The constructive engagement theory disputes the existence of a 'natural' race to the bottom, and maintains instead that there is a tendency for countries to emulate more developed ones with which they have contact. However, there is no hard evidence that this tendency exists.[37] Rather, experience demonstrates that countries only raise labour standards when NGOs, consumer boycotts or labour groups are successful in forcing them to do so.

One currently prominent school of thought argues that races to the bottom can be converted into races to the top by means of a style of regulation called 'new governance'. The new governance approach abjures the use of top-down, one-size-fits-all 'command and control' regulation. In its place, proponents of new governance advocate regulatory initiatives that are locally based and tied to local conditions. In addition, new governance advocates support regulatory initiatives that are dialogic and that permit adjustment in goals and techniques based upon experience.[38] Proponents claim that new governance regulatory techniques deliver flexibility and innovation, ultimately making them more effective than the prevailing command and control form of regulation.

The European Union has adopted a new governance framework for social regulation through a method it calls the 'Open Method of Coordination' (OMC). According to the President of the Lisbon European Council, who coined the term, the OMC

> is comprised of four elements: (1) fixed guidelines set for the Union, with short-, medium-, and long-term goals; (2) quantitative and qualitative indicators and benchmarks; (3) European guidelines translated into national and regional policies and targets; and (4) periodic monitoring, evaluation and peer review, organized as a mutual learning process.[39]

The OMC is an elaborate system for articulating goals, guidelines and policy aspirations, coupled with an on-going system for measuring progress and comparing best practices.

Law professors Louise and Dave Trubek have given a detailed account of the potential for a race to the top for labour standards in their writing about the EU's European Employment Strategy (EES) and the OMC. Writing in 2005, they have shown that the OMC framework operates as a governance mechanism that encourages dialogue, spreads best practices and deters races to the bottom within the EU. They described the EU's OMC and explained how it departs from the previous hard law—the so-called Community Method—for making

---

[36] Diamond, 'The "Race to the Bottom" Returns' (n 32).

[37] Stephen Diamond shows that the constructive engagement approach has not improved human rights or labour standards in China, ibid.

[38] MC Dorf and CF Sabel, 'A Constitution of Democratic Experimentalism' (1998) 98 *Columbia Law Review* 267, 267; C Sabel and W Simon, 'Minimalism and Experimentalism in the Administrative State' (2011) 100 *Georgetown Law Journal* 53, 78–82. See also I Ayres and J Braithwaite, *Responsive Regulation: Transcending The Deregulation Debate* (Oxford, Oxford University Press) 4–7.

[39] B Eberlain and D Kerwer, 'New Governance in the European Union: A Theoretical Perspective'(2004) 42 *Journal of Common Market Studies* 121, 123, citing J Mosher, 'Open Method of Coordination: Functional and Political Origins' (2000) 13 *ESCA Review* 6–7.

social policy.[40] They explain that the OMC was devised to transform European labour relations and social policies so as to enable Europe to be internationally competitive while retaining its commitment to a solidaristic welfare state.

In the Trubeks' account, the OMC is a poster child for new governance. The OMC, like other new governance proposals, involves articulating aspirations at an abstract level and at the same time establishing a process by which those aspirations are concretised, implemented, evaluated and modified over time. The Trubeks give some evidence from the early 2000s of instances where the EES raised labour standards in some fields of social policy.[41]

According to the Trubeks, the OMC is a soft form of regulation, but it is not as soft as it sounds. For the OMC to operate successfully, there needs to be mandatory transparency and monitoring mechanisms, combined with some transnational body to promulgate the mandates and some type of sanctions for non-compliance, even if they are informal. Hence, hard laws need to underlie the soft-law processes of consultations, negotiations, persuasion and informal concertation.[42]

The necessary foundation for the OMC to operate exists in the EU, but it is not clear if it exists anywhere else. For example, efforts by the ILO to institute new governance and soft-law mechanisms have not been promising.[43]

In addition, there are as yet many unanswered questions about the effectiveness of the OMC. Despite some successes, many countries in Europe have been dismantling their labour safeguards without providing any mechanism for labour protection. This process began well before the Great Recession and has continued apace since, so that now, in many countries, the economic crisis and the austerity it spawned threatens the European model of labour protection. Much of the dismantlement has not occurred in the context of OMC negotiation, but rather in spite of it. For example, in the early 2000s, Germany reformed its unemployment system in a way that reduced benefits and pressured unemployed workers to accept low-wage work despite adamant opposition from the unions.[44] In that same period, Italy amended its labour laws to relax job security protection, despite opposition in the form of demonstrations and strikes by three million workers.[45] These changes were not negotiated in a harmonious and consensual way. Was this a failure of the OMC, or a sign of not enough new governance? Could more new governance have led to better outcomes?

Moreover, it is unclear whether the OMC and other EU new governance mechanisms of cooperation and coordination have been effective in the face of the Great Recession. Did the OMC mitigate the consequences of the recession, or would more

---

[40] DM Trubek and LG Trubek, 'Hard and Soft Law in the Conception of Social Europe: The Role of the Open Method of Coordination' (2005) 11 *European Law Journal* 343.

[41] Ibid, 351, fn 20.

[42] Ibid.

[43] For a detailed account of the failure of ILO efforts to move to new governance approaches, see L Baccaro and V Mele, 'Pathology of Path Dependency? The ILO and the Challenge of New Governance' (2012) 65 *Industrial & Labor Relations Review* 195.

[44] In the early 2000s, Germany enacted a series of reforms to its unemployment system that reduced the period of unemployment benefits and changed the definition of 'suitable work', such that after one year, an unemployed person was required to accept any job regardless of previous qualifications or wage levels. There were mass protests in opposition to these measures. See, A Kemmerling and O Bruttel, 'New Politics in German Labour Market Policy: The Implications of the Recent Hartz Reforms on the German Welfare State' (2006) 29 *West European Politics* 90, 96–98.

[45] M Henneberger, 'Millions of Italians Take to the Streets in a General Strike' *New York Times* (17 April 2002) A3.

hard-law, centralised regulation of labour market policies have been a better barricade against the ravages of the financial crisis? We do not know whether the OMC spread best practices, or if it simply gave countries a fig leaf to cover their actions of dismantling labour market protections without creating viable alternatives. These are important questions that must be addressed if we want to consider new governance as an antidote to a race to the bottom in global labour standards.

B. Agglomeration and Sticky Industry Strategies for Labour Organising

A second approach to the problem of labour standards and free trade focuses on the locational decisions of firms. While corporations have a tendency to hopscotch across the globe, jumping over any country that imposes burdensome labour regulations, there is also evidence that some corporations have a gravitational pull toward a particular place. Some firms want to be near their customers, raw materials, or suppliers and hence are loathe to locate overseas. Auto repair shops, dry cleaners, restaurants, hospitals, and numerous other businesses that provide immediate services to customers cannot realistically hope to relocate overseas. And, of course, local government jobs, construction and building services are also necessarily place-based activities.

In addition, some types of manufacturing and high-end service industries are tied to a particular place for reasons other than their customer base. Economists have noted that corporations often want to locate near other firms that produce in their field in order to take advantage of agglomeration economies that exist in specific regional locales.[46] They have found that in certain sectors, firms can get extra value from the sheer fact of agglomeration. One well-known example of a successful agglomeration economy is the Silicon Valley computer software industry.[47] Other examples are the clusters of biotechnology firms around Princeton, New Jersey, of banking and financial firms in New York City, and of computer hardware manufacturing firms around Austin, Texas. Firms in these locations are unlikely to move, at least in the short run. Regional economists attribute much of the positive effects of agglomeration economies to the skills and knowledge that is concentrated in, and shared amongst, the locality's workforce.[48] That is, globalisation is not a one-way juggernaut, but rather it is a process that exists in tension with local embeddedness.

The potential of agglomeration economies for union organising has only recent been appreciated. In the face of union decline, many labour leaders and progressive activists have turned away from the traditional paradigm of federally-supervised union organising and embraced instead an alternative model that focuses on 'sticky' industries and emphasising coalition building with other local progressive groups. These campaigns target firms that are unlikely to move overseas, or across the country, to escape rising labour costs—that is

---

[46] For example, Paul Krugman found that 85% of carpets sold in the US were produced within a 65 mile radius of Dalton, Georgia. See P Krugman, *Geography and Trade* (Cambridge, MA, MIT Press, 1993).

[47] See Saxenian, *Regional Advantage* (n 31).

[48] See generally, J McDonald, *Fundamentals of Urban Economics* (Upper Saddle River, NJ, Prentice Hall, 1997).

firms in industries that offer inherently immobile services, have fiscal ties to local governments, or benefit from operating in an agglomeration economy.[49]

In the US, Los Angeles has been at the centre of the development of this local organizing approach.[50] Labour resurgence in LA began in the early 1980s when a coalition of activists, trade unionists and progressive UCLA academics tried to stop General Motors from closing its automobile plant in Van Nuys. The coalition was successful for a few years, but the plant cut back production throughout the decade and eventually closed altogether in 1991.[51] The fate of the Van Nuys anti-plant-closing campaign convinced some activists that to succeed, they needed to target industries that were not likely to leave the city.[52] In 1993, unions and community groups formed the Los Angeles Alliance for the New Economy (LAANE) to develop and implement a sticky industry strategy. They decided to focus initially on tourism.[53]

Over the past two decades, LAANE has worked with other local organisations on a range of local issues. In concert, these groups have achieved many victories, including the enactment of several broad living-wage ordinances,[54] a 'worker retention ordinance' that prevents firms at the airport from firing workers each time a sub-contract changes hands,[55] a 'sweat-free procurement ordinance' that requires the city's contractors to provide decent working conditions and pay a living wage;[56] and a 'Clean Trucks' ordinance that requires trucking firms at the ports to hire drivers rather than utilise independent contractors.[57]

In addition, LAANE has created an innovative instrument, the 'community benefit agreement', in which local unions and community groups bargain with developers of large real estate projects to ensure that the developers utilise local workers, pay living wages, and provide on-the-job training. In exchange, the unions and community groups pledge public support for the development project and refrain from activities that would interfere with the developers' ability to obtain necessary permits and approvals from the public authorities. These types of agreements were pioneered in Los Angeles and are now found in 40 cities.[58]

---

[49] See generally, KVW Stone, 'Flexibilization, Globalization and Privatization: Three Challenges to Labour Rights in Our Time' (2006) 44 *Osgoode Hall Law Journal* 77.

[50] See KVW Stone and S Cummings, 'Labor Activism in Local Politics: From CBAs to "CBAs"' in G Davidov and B Langille (eds), *The Idea of Labour Law* (Oxford, Oxford University Press, 2011).

[51] Ibid.

[52] Ibid.

[53] Ibid.

[54] *Los Angeles Administrative Code*, ss 10.37 *et seq.*

[55] *Los Angeles Administrative Code*, ss 10.36 *et seq*, known as the Los Angeles Service Contractor Worker Retention Ordinance.

[56] Los Angeles Administrative Code, ss 10.43, *et seq*. As explained by the City's Department of General Services, 'The Ordinance requires vendors who provide equipment, goods, materials, and supplies to the City, to comply with the City's Contractor Code of Conduct. In addition, all garment, uniform, foot apparel, and related accessories vendors are also required to provide a Procurement Living Wage and benefits to employees who work directly on fulfilling City contracts.' See gsd.lacity.org/sms/sweat-free_procurment.htm.

[57] City of Los Angeles, Tariff No 4. The LA Clean Trucks Ordinance has been the subject of extensive litigation. The independent contractor provision was held to be valid on the basis of preemption by the Ninth Circuit in 2011. *American Trucking Ass'n v City of Los Angeles* 660 F3d 384 (9th Cir, 2011).

[58] On the origin and operation of community benefit agreements, see V Parks & D Warren, 2009. The Politics and Practice of Economic Justice: Community Benefits Agreements as Tactic of the New Accountable Development Movement', (2009) 17 *Journal of Community Practice* 88–106. See also, Stone and Cummings, 'Labor Activism in Local Politics' (n 52). On the theory of CBAs, see generally J Gross, G LeRoy and M Janis-Aparicio, *Community Benefits Agreements: Making Development Projects Accountable* (2005). On the operation of community benefit agreements, see RC Schragger, 'Mobile Capital, Local Economic Regulation, and the Democratic City' (2009) 123 *Harvard Law Review* 482.

Local activism has been a dynamic factor in labour politics in other countries as well. For example, over the past two decades, in some areas of Italy, Spain, and the United Kingdom, local labour groups, local employers, and local government officials have negotiated social territorial pacts that set local labour market policy on issues such as unemployment insurance arrangements, worker training programmes, and other labour market measures. In some cases, the territorial pacts are negotiated not only between the traditional social partners—employers' associations and trade unions—but also with civic groups and other organised local constituencies.[59] This kind of territorial bargaining has helped foster agglomeration economies. According to University of Catania law professor, Bruno Caruso,

> territorial employment pacts in Italy have fostered territorial bargaining in the so-called economy of 'districts' … which often correspond to sectors traditionally featuring small firms or craftsmen (textiles, furniture, building, tourism) … [Territorial bargaining has supported] the competitiveness of micro firms by injecting a heavy dose of flexibility (as regards working hours, wages, and geographic location) into both the internal and external labour market. These measures are almost always accompanied by others supporting income levels if not permanent employment security.[60]

Local organising efforts that target sticky industries can be an effective means of raising labour standards despite a decline in the effectiveness of unions at the national level. Local campaigns can achieve improvements for workers not only via hard law, such as local ordinances or statutes, but also via soft law, such as through quasi-enforceable multi-party agreements between unions, community groups and employers. And unlike protectionist measures, local pressures to share in profits from sticky industries do not compromise job opportunities for workers in developing countries because these industries were not likely to move abroad in the first place.

To succeed, locally-focused organising efforts require a national legal system that permits localities to legislate autonomously regarding labour conditions. In the US, the doctrine of preemption has operated as a barrier to many local initiatives in the past.[61] Preemption is a function of the Supremacy Clause of the US Constitution, which provides that when state law conflicts with federal law, the federal law takes precedence.[62] Preemption is implicated whenever localities engage in private sector labour regulation, such as by providing organising rights to private sector workers whose rights to unionise are specified in the National

---

[59] See, I Regalia, 'New Forms of Employment and New Problems of Regulation' in I Regalia (ed), 'Regulating New Forms of Employment: Local Experiments and Social Innovation in Europe' (London, Routledge, 2006) 13. See also, I Regalia, 'Regional and Local Level Experiments in Labor Market Policy in Europe' in K Stone and H Arthurs, 'After the Standard Contract of Employment: Innovations in Regulatory Design' (New York, Russell Sage Foundation Press, 2013).

[60] B Caruso, 'Decentralised Social Pacts, Trade Unions and Collective Bargaining: How Labour Law is Changing' in M Biagi (ed), *Towards a European Model of Industrial Relations?* (Klewer Law International, 2001) 193–225, 210.

[61] For example, the issue of preemption was central in the Los Angeles Clean Trucks Ordinance litigation, *American Trucking Ass'n v City of Los Angeles* (n 59).

[62] There are several different types of preemption in the area of labour, of which the most relevant here are *Garmon* and *Machinists* preemption. In *San Diego Building Trades Council v Garmon* 359 US 236 (1959) the Supreme Court held that any activity that is actually or arguably protected by s 7 or actually or arguably prohibited by s 8 of the National Labor Relations Act is preempted. In the *Machinists v Wisconsin Employment Relations Commission* 427 US 132 (1975) the Court held that states cannot regulate in labour relations matters which Congress intended to leave unregulated and subject to the free play of economic forces.

Labor Relations Act.[63] State law is also preempted when it conflicts with other explicit federal statutes. Preemption is a moving target, and local groups have become adept at framing their demands and ordinances to avoid federal or state preemption. But the rules keep changing.[64]

Other countries have their own versions of preemption rules—sometimes treated under the rubric of 'competency' or 'subsidiarity'—which define when localities are allowed exemptions from national legislation in order to make negotiated concessions at the local level. Hence, the architecture of federal, state and local relations is a design feature that determines the success of local worker organizing initiatives.

In addition, local organising strategies require a healthy local economy with viable sticky jobs. Many of the jobs that are targeted by these local initiatives are relatively low-paid service jobs. However, when local labour groups are active in an advanced agglomeration economy, they can mobilise higher paid workers.[65] For example, highly-trained technical workers in Seattle organised the Washington Alliance of Technology Workers (WashTech), initially to improve their working conditions at Microsoft and later to limit the off-shoring of jobs and to preserve overtime pay for contract workers in the state of Washington.[66]

Local and regional organising can also transform casual low-paid jobs into regular, better-paid jobs. For example, in Los Angeles in 1999, the Service Employees International Union (SEIU) transformed jobs in the home health-care industry by organising 74,000 low-wage health-care workers and creating a state agency to serve as the 'employer of record'.[67]

The strategy of local organising that targets sticky jobs would benefit from public policies that help foster agglomeration economies. That is, to fully realise the potential of agglomeration as a source of labour gains, there needs to be industrial policy that supports regional specialisation.[68] Several countries in Europe have pursued such a policy, thereby enabling unions and local organisations to share in the benefits of regional specialisation.[69]

The agglomeration-plus-local-mobilisation approach can enable labour groups to defend labour standards in the developed world without triggering claims of protectionism or inflicting harm on the developing world. If national economic policy were oriented toward fostering agglomeration economies—such as through industrial policies to

---

[63] See, eg *Chamber of Commerce v Brown*, 128 SCt 2408 (2008) (using *Machinists* preemption to nullify a California Law that required certain employers who received certain types of state funds from using those funds to deter union organising).

[64] There have been numerous preemption challenges to local labour ordinances in the past decade, and the courts have been divided. For example, the DC Circuit upheld a District of Columbia ordinance requiring that contractors retain employees of their predecessors for a period of time. *Washington Service Contractors v District of Columbia*, 54 F.3d 811 (1995). On the other hand, the Seventh Circuit recently invalidated a state law that required hotels in Chicago to give their room attendant employees one day of rest in every seven-day period.

[65] See A Dean and D Reynolds, 'A New New Deal: How Regional Activism Will Reshape the American Labor Movement' (Ithaca, Cornell University Press, 2011) describing the author's regional bargaining strategies in Silicon Valley.

[66] See www.washtech.org.

[67] See, E Boris and J Klein, 'Organizing Home Care: Low-Waged Workers in the Welfare State' (2006) 34 *Politics & Society* 81, 91–95; L Delp and K Quan, 'Homecare Worker Organizing in California: An Analysis of a Successful Strategy' (2002) 27 *Labor Studies Journal* 1.

[68] According to social geographer, J Clark: 'Local policy-makers can promote local and regional institutions that facilitate the development of good jobs and sustainable economic growth in the face of these pressures.'

[69] See, eg A Markusen, 'Sticky Places in Slippery Space: A Typology of Industrial Districts' (1996) 72 *Economic Geography* 293, 297–302, describing Italian industrial districts. See also, M Piore and C Sabel, *The New Industrial Divide* (New York, Basic Books, 1984).

promote regional development—then labour groups could capture some of the gains. But until we have a serious, sustained industrial policy in the US, local labour initiatives can raise wages and labour standards at the bottom of the labour market, but they will not have much impact on those at higher levels of the income scale.

C. The Alchemy of Innovation

A third approach to preserving labour standards in advanced countries is to encourage innovation in the workplace. Since the 1980s, several economists and political scientists have argued that the only way that rich or mid-level countries can maintain their standards of living in the face of practically infinite low-cost and poorly educated labour in India and China, is to stay on the cutting edge of innovation.[70] For example, UCLA economist Ed Leamer writes:

> The policy response to the globalization force is pretty straightforward: we need to make the edu-
> cational and infrastructure investments that are needed to keep the high-paying nonconstestable
> creative jobs here at home and let the rest of the world knock themselves silly competing for the
> footloose mundane contestable jobs.[71]

Today most firms recognise that they have to adapt quickly to changes in technology, product market conditions, resource constraints, supplier availability, customer preferences, trading rules, exchange rates, design ideas and other constantly-moving factors. But adaptation is not enough—they must innovate. Management theorists maintain that innovation in product design, production processes, quality control, cost control and information flows are the key to maintaining a competitive edge. In the words of Harvard Business School's Dorothy Leonard: 'Innovate or fall behind: the competitive imperative for virtually all business today is that simple.' Firms require not only innovation, but continuous innovation, simply to survive.

The quest for innovation puts a spotlight on human resource policies, and particularly those policies designed to elicit knowledge. According to management theorist, Debra Amidon, the advent of the innovation imperative is linked to the discovery of the economic value of knowledge. Amidon writes: 'Knowledge—often defined in terms of Intellectual Capital—is clearly the source of new economic wealth. Innovation is the process by which that wealth is converted into action, products, services or initiatives.'[72]

Harvard Business School professors Thomas Davenport and Laurence Prusak explain the innovation imperative in terms of the velocity and intensity of global competition. They warn that any product, no matter how novel, can be reverse-engineered; any new idea can walk out the door when an employee departs; and any new method of production or marketing can be replicated, transmitted, and implemented more cheaply somewhere else. On the other hand, they conclude 'Knowledge, by contrast, can provide a sustainable advantage.' Further, they opine that in today's marketplace, 'pricing pressures leave no

---

[70] G Garrett, 'Globalization's Missing Middle' (2004) 83 *Foreign Affairs* 84; EE Leamer, 'A Flat World, a Level Playing Field, a Small World After All, or None of the Above?' (2007) 45 *Journal of Economic Literature* 83.

[71] Leamer, ibid at 119.

[72] DM Amidon, *The Innovation Super Highway: Harnessing Intellectual Capital for Collaborative Advantage* (Amsterdam, Butterworth-Heinemann, 2002).

room for inefficient production ... Companies now require quality, value, service, innovation and speed to market for business success.'[73]

Firms in older industrialised countries are particularly vulnerable in today's high-velocity global marketplace because they often have higher fixed costs and legacy costs than newer firms. The task for firms in the industrialised world is thus two-fold: they have to lower their fixed costs while at the same time reorganising work to promote innovation.

Firms also need to cut costs in the face of intense global competition. However, the effort to marry cost-cutting with innovation is an uneasy one. Workers are reluctant to propose innovations that will cut costs if doing so will lead to layoffs. Firms can avoid this effect—what some management researchers have called the 'iron law of layoffs'[74]—if they ensure that there will not be any layoffs. However, in today's economic environment, firms are reluctant to make such a commitment, and even if they do, the promises are not credible. Instead, firms are moving in the opposite direction by making everyone dispensable.

Firms are achieving flexibility by adopting measures that turn fixed costs into variable costs. They can turn some fixed costs into variable costs by renting rather than owning plant and equipment and by minimising inventories through just-in-time contracts with suppliers and customers. Similarly, firms can shift fixed labour costs to variable costs by adopting work practices that give them numerical, functional and operational flexibility. Some examples of such cost-shifting practices are:

— expanding the use of temporary work and independent contractors rather than employing full-time workers;
— utilising outsourcing to locate routine work overseas and/or using a supply chain of suppliers and assemblers to perform routine tasks in low-wage areas;
— turning regular workers into optional workers by relaxing legal restrictions on dismissing workers;
— lowering the cost and increasing the returns on labour inputs by more efficient deployment of human resources through measures such as cross-utilisation, and broad-banding;[75]
— using bench-marking to align labour prices with going rates for comparable tasks in other firms; and
— instituting pay-for-performance compensation systems to provide individual incentives for efficient production.

Each of these measures has the potential to to reduce costs in the short run while simultaneously restructuring labour relations to yield flexibility-engendered cost-savings in the long run. Furthermore, several of the measures enumerated above are touted for their impact on innovation. They are advocated as steps that will help convert workplaces into laboratories of innovation. The first three of the listed practices not only trim excess labour costs, but also help transform the culture of long-term attachment. Having temporary and optional

[73] T Davenport and L Prusak, *Working Knowledge: How Organizations Management What they Know* (Boston, Harvard Business School Press, 1998) 17.

[74] See EK Keating, R Oliva, NP Repenning, S Rockart and JD Sterman, 'Overcoming the Improvement Paradox' (1999) 17 *European Management Journal* 120.

[75] 'Broadbanding' is a human resource practice in which firms cluster a number of jobs within a single 'band', and then move employees between those jobs as needed. It is a departure from the strict job definitions of the earlier era. For more detail, see, KVW Stone, *From Widgets to Digits: Employment Regulation for the Changing Workplace* (Cambridge, Cambridge University Press, 2004) 93.

workers working alongside 'regular' workers undermines a previous culture of permanence. Even more importantly, the use of temporary and short-term contract workers enables firms to bring in workers with specific or rare skills that are tailored to new technologies or products. It also enables them to hire workers on a trial basis and assess their potential contribution over time before making a long-term employment commitment.

These new practices, however, are in tension with the labour law regimes that have persisted for the past century in most of the industrialised world. Until the 1980s, most Western countries had labour law systems that provided iron-clad protection against dismissals, and many even prevented employers from transferring employees between jobs or departments. Most countries placed severe restrictions on the ability of employers to utilise temporary workers or bring in workers with specific skills on a short-term basis. In addition, many had powerful unions that imposed centralised wage setting, so that compensation could not be used to award or incentive performance.

Today new labour law regimes are being constructed that attempt to facilitate flexibility and promote innovation. In fact, labour laws have been revised and rewritten throughout the industrialised world over the past 20 years. Almost universally, the new labour laws are designed to provide firms with increased flexibility in order to reduce costs, foster innovation, and enable firms to respond with alacrity to fast-changing product market trends. For example, Australia abandoned its century-old award system of labour regulation in 2005, and is in the process of revising its entire regulatory framework. Japan has enacted so many new labour laws that it is an open question whether its long-standing system of firm-based lifetime employment will survive. Throughout Europe, new labour laws have been enacted that permit temporary employment contracts, relax dismissal protection, enable firms to utilise workers on a project basis, modify unemployment systems so as to put downward pressure on wages and, in other ways, make employment flexible.[76]

Those changes enable firms to deploy workers more flexibly and change the size of their workforce with ease. Proponents justify these changes in the name of promoting innovation and enabling firms to remain competitive.

There is, however, a dark side to these changes to labour law. They shift onto workers risks that were previously borne by the firm. The changes have also undermined unions; engendered pay disparities within firms, and created a generation of young people who despair of ever finding stable employment arrangements. If left unremedied, the emerging regulatory regimes will lead to a deterioration of the standard of living for workers, heightened insecurity and an increase in inequality.[77]

So if innovation is the key to offsetting the downward pressures on wages created by trade, then it is necessary to couple innovative human resource practices with protection for workers' labour standards and security. Flexible work practices not benefit of the middle class unless they are accompanied by a new kind of safety net that can protect workers when their jobs are 'flexibilised'. In today's labour market, where firms are constantly changing their product and resource mix, jobs are continually in a state of flux. In this world, we need to devise social policies that provide not job security, but 'livelihood security'.[78]

---

[76] See generally, KVW Stone and H Arthurs, *Rethinking Workplace Regulation: Beyond the Standard Contract of Employment* (New York, Russell Sage Foundation Press, 2013).

[77] See Stone, *From Widgets to Digits* (n 78); Standing, *The Precariat* (n 4).

[78] KVW Stone, 'Employment Protection for Boundaryless Workers' in Davidov and Langille, *The Idea of Labour Law* (n 52) 17.

Today's workers move frequently between jobs, and into and out of the labour market, throughout their working lives. Workers need to be able to learn new skills, weather periods of unemployment, retool, engage in entrepreneurial activity, and transition from school to work and from work to retirement. Fluidity and transitions into and out of the labour market are a fact of life for workers today, and therefore social policy needs to address the burdens these transitions create. We need to restructure social programmes that currently rely on long-term job attachment, and instead, design those that enable workers to flourish in an open-ended, boundaryless labour market. This means we need policies for workers in transition, such as income maintenance programmes, lifetime learning opportunities, relocation assistance, child-care assistance, portable benefits, and even housing policies that suspend mortgage payments periodically throughout a person's working life. We need a social safety net that does not draw a sharp line between employment and unemployment, but that gives individuals the ability to move between labour market statuses without risking financial ruin. We need policies to assist people with the inevitable transitions that result from today's employment practices.

IV. Braiding the Approaches to Build a Lifeline

Each of the three approaches I have described offers a plausible path to preserving high labour standards in industrialised countries in the face of global trade, but none of them is a magic bullet. And each has been implemented with some success in circumscribed settings.[79]

It is important to note that the three approaches are not mutually exclusive and that there are potential synergies between them. Indeed, some synergies are in place already. For example, the EU is using the OMC's race-to-the-top technique to promote a policy goal called 'flexicurity'. 'Flexicurity' refers to programmes that attempt to reconcile firms' demands for flexibility with workers' needs for security.[80] The EU adopted 'flexicurity' as one of its primary social policy goals in the early 2000s.[81]

'Flexicurity' describes a nexus of measures that attempt to bridge the gap between flexible production for firms and livelihood security for citizens. According to the European Commission's 2007 and 2008 'Employment in Europe' reports:

> 'Flexicurity' aims at ensuring that EU citizens can enjoy a high level of employment security, that is the possibility to easily find a job at every stage of active life and have a good prospect for career development in a quickly changing economic environment.

---

[79] For in-depth discussions about how several countries are approaching this challenge, see essays in Stone and Arthurs (eds), *Rethinking Workplace Regulation* (n 76).

[80] T Wilthagen, FH Tros and H Van Lieshout, 'Towards "Flexicurity"? Balancing Flexibility and Security in EU Member States' (September 2003) available at ssrn.com/abstract=1133940.

[81] See T Wilthagen and F Tros, 'The Concept of "Flexicurity": A New Approach to Regulating Employment and Labour Markets' (2004) 10 *Transfer* 166. See also, AS Tangian, 'Monitoring Flexicurity Policies in the EU with Dedicated Composite Indicators' (2005) *WSI-Diskussionspapiere, No 137*, available at hdl.handle.net/10419/21581, 9–10, discussing spread of flexicurity policies and discussions throughout Europe in early 2000s.

Implicitly adopting a New Governance approach, the Commission acknowledged that there was not one path to flexicurity, but rather that each nation should devise its own balance of flexibility and security consistent with its own history and labour market institutions.[82]

There are also overlaps and synergies between the local organising and flexible work practices approaches to protecting jobs from outsourcing. For example, some local organising campaigns that target sticky industries also address the problems flexible labour markets pose for workers. The organisers sometimes advocate measures such as regional benefit funds and job training programmes to offer lifetime learning so that displaced workers can continually learn new skills. Measures of this sort could allow firms greater flexibility in their labour practices while also establishing institutions to provide workers with greater overall security.

While the three approaches are potentially mutually supportive, they involve different actors. The new governance approach relies on actions of experts to design and evaluate the policies that are implemented by policy-makers. Indeed, this aspect of new governance has opened it up to criticism that, as a method of regulation, it fails to involve local actors or mobilise grass roots support. Moreover, some contend that the OMC's expert orientation has made it vulnerable to political cutbacks because it has not created an informed public that will defend its mission or its measures in the face of conservative turns in politics or austerity measures imposed from afar.[83]

Unlike the top-down bias of new governance, efforts to promote and target sticky industries involve local labour and community activists. Their success depends upon the existence of strong community groups and unions to pressure firms and local governments to provide benefits to the middle class. The kind of dynamic activism found in Los Angeles over the past 20 years may be unique, but many other cities have their own networks of unions and organisations dedicated to aiding the middle class. Also, in an era of internet communication, success breeds success. Living wage campaigns originated in Baltimore and quickly spread to nearly 140 other cities. Community benefit agreements were first devised in Los Angeles, and are now found in more than 30 cities.[84]

The third strategy discussed above is to permit firms to pursue innovation through the implementation of flexible work practices. In the first instance, it involves actions by corporate managers. However, for this approach to offer promise to the middle class, it requires more than simply simple flexible work practices. If firms are to deploy workers on an as-needed basis and churn their workforces without making long-term commitments, then they will need workers who are instantly available and able to perform the tasks they need. But this kind of on-demand work-schedule is burdensome, particularly for anyone with

---

[82] R Muffels, 'Flexibility and Employment Security in Europe: Setting the Scene' in R Muffels (ed), *Flexibility and Employment Security in Europe: Labour Markets in Transition* (Cheltenham, Edward Elgar, 2008) 15. But see A van den Berg, 'Flexicurity: Theory, Practice or Rhetoric?', Conference of the Centre for Labour Market Research (CARMA) at Aalborg University, Aalborg, Denmark (2008), available at www.epa.aau.dk/fileadmin/user_upload/conniek/konferencer/Papers/W-2-Axel-v-d-Berg.pdf (characterising the EU's pathway approach as a retreat from true flexicurity.)

[83] See, eg K Jacobsson and A Vifell, 'Integration by Deliberation: On the Role of Committees in the Open Method of Coordination', Workshop on The Forging of Deliberative Supernationalism in the EU, Florence, 2003, available at www.sv.uio.no/arena/english/research/projects/cidel/old/Workshop_Firenze/contJacobsson.pdf, 21–22.

[84] V Parks and D Warren, 'The Politics and Practice of Economic Justice: Community Benefits Agreements as Tactic of the New Accountable Development Movement (2009) 17 *Journal of Community Practice* 88.

young children or other care-giving responsibilities.[85] It also breeds tremendous insecurity, because workers do not know how long their present job will last or when there will be another one. As flexible work practices become more prevalent, we need a different kind of social safety net than the one that now exists. We need to provide a new form of security that helps bridge transitions. We need to give people skills and the inducement to acquire new skills, as well as livelihood support when they are between jobs. Thus a new regulatory approach is required.

Changes of the magnitude described cannot happen without a grass roots movement animated by a political vision about how the middle class can be saved in the era of flexible production. Yet the three approaches described are strands in a rope that, if woven together, might form a lifeline that could rescue the middle class from drowning in a tidal wave of globalisation.

---

[85] See S Lambert, 'When Flexibility Hurts' *New York Times* (20 September 2012).

10

Fragmented Work and Multi-level Labour Market Governance: Informality, Crisis Policy and an Expanded 'Law of Work'

KERRY RITTICH[*]

I. Introduction: Situating Work

There could not be a better context in which to reflect on the challenges around the regulation of work than a festschrift for Dave Trubek, for there is a great deal of evidence that the project now compels engagement with fields and analytics that have long been central to his own intellectual biography: law and development, transnational labour studies, critical legal analysis, legal sociology and new governance.

This essay is an exercise in charting a possible future for the field of labour law. It is informed by a number of projects and interests, current and long-standing. One is a preoccupation with the distributive dimensions of contemporary governance initiatives, especially those designed to promote development, economic growth and market integration.[1] A second is an effort to account for the myriad regulatory initiatives that now operate outside, alongside, or in tandem with, state or interstate regulation. A third is a study of the legal infrastructure of informal work. Yet a fourth is a collective effort among a number of labour scholars to 'remap' the law of work.

It is easy to feel slightly apocalyptic about the field of labour law. Workers in the global North have experienced flat and falling incomes for a generation; those in the global South have declining access to traditional work yet uncertain access to work opportunities and unstable prospects for income generation in the modern sector. Across both the South and the North, there is intensified competition for jobs, especially those that might in any way be described as 'good'. Market integration has catalysed a precipitous decline in workers' bargaining power and a correlative transfer of risk and costs to workers.[2] And in many

[*] Deep thanks to Amar Bhatia for research assistance and to the Social Sciences and Humanities Research Council of Canada for financial support.

[1] K Rittich, 'The Future of Law and Development: Second Generation Reforms and the Incorporation of the Social' in DM Trubek and A Santos, *The Future of Law and Development: Second-Generation Reforms and the Incorporation of the Social* (Cambridge, Cambridge University Press, 2006); K Rittich, *Recharacterizing Restructuring: Law, Distribution and Gender in Market Reform* (Alphen aan den Rijn, Kluwer Law International, 2002).

[2] For a recent account that puts workers' declining power at the centre of the analysis of distributive questions, see JS Hacker and N Loewentheil, *Prosperity Economics: Building an Economy for All* (Washington, Economic Policy Institute, 2012) available at www.prosperityforamerica.org/wp-content/uploads/2012/09/prosperity-for-all.pdf.

parts of the developed and developing world, expanding economic inequality testifies to workers' diminishing share of the income of productive activity.

The policy context is scarcely more favourable. The conflicts and pressures that have historically given rise to labour standards and workers' rights are as much in evidence now as they have ever been: inequality of bargaining power between workers and those who use their services; disparate opportunities to participate in markets for work; inadequate income to sustain a basic standard of living; pervasive economic insecurity—all abound in contemporary labour markets. However, they are not always recognised as problems; when they are, the form that any response should take is now contested. Regimes that aim to decommodify work and reallocate bargaining power and resources to workers by conventional means—whether by protecting workers' associations and facilitating collective action among workers or establishing baseline labour rights and standards—are increasingly difficult to locate. Robust social programmes from workplace insurance to income transfers and the provision of public goods are equally out of fashion.

One reason is that labour market institutions have sustained a normative and analytic assault from the exponents of greater labour market flexibility from which they have yet to recover. Both states and international actors seem resistant, if not hostile, to greater recognition of workers' rights, to initiatives that might increase wages and improve working conditions, and to solidaristic initiatives and redistribution for egalitarian purposes. Yet at the same time, many have displayed remarkable sympathy for upwardly-redistributive tax policy and, when faced with crises, considerable ease with massive subsidies to stabilise the financial sector.

But workers' troubles are not just a question of bad times or policy-makers who favour labour market rules that are uncongenial to workers' interests. Even under normal conditions, workers find themselves buffeted by a range of forces. Trade-induced competition from workers in other countries; revolutions in technology and the organisation of production; and changing expectations about the roles and relations of the state and the private sector all leave workers exposed to risks, costs and contingencies which they are in no position to control.

The proposal here is that a broad set of factors now impels us towards an expanded conception of the law that regulates work. This is one in which labour and employment laws are understood to be merely a subset of the rules that affect work relationships; nor are they always the most important. In this discussion, I suggest that engagement with work and workers in developing and emerging markets as well as the policies adopted to manage the ongoing financial crises in the industrialised world both highlight the limits of conventional approaches to improving labour standards and the need for more far-reaching and complex analyses of labour market regulation.

II. Reregulating Work

The changed landscape of work, both factual and normative, suggests that understanding how bargaining power is constituted and how risk is structured and allocated through law should now be a central task for labour law scholars. This is a complex task, and one that is made more difficult because two of the foundational premises of the field have been irretrievably shattered.

One is the possibility of imagining a labour law that is organised around a single normative worker or work relationship. The standard employment relationship that served as an important benchmark for the design and construction of labour law, domestic and international, has declined in importance at the level of fact and norm.[3] As serial, contractualised work relationships that permit employers to avoid the constraints of more structured and stable forms of employment have proliferated, its utility and persuasiveness as a regulatory touchstone has receded in equal measure. It is unlikely that any single work model will, or even could, serve as the basis of labour law in the future. At this point we have to imagine a regulatory project that captures both diverse populations of workers and infinitely more varied forms of work.

The second is a singular focus on regulatory initiatives generated and backstopped by the state. Problems of work have classically been addressed through public law interventions that change the conditions of labour contracting, typically in the form of labour codes and employment standards, supplemented where levels of economic development permit by pension and social protection arrangements. Yet however pertinent such mechanisms remain to many workers, they are increasingly inadequate, whether as a response to the current problems of work or as a diagnosis of how the world of work is in fact now regulated. The global organisation of work frequently defeats effective regulation by any single state. Myriad non-state actors, institutions and networks, moreover, are engaged in the generation of norms and policies about work, and thus are in a position to powerfully influence the fate of workers.[4]

It is common ground among labour law scholars that both the reconstruction of the field and the defence of workers' interests involve better calibrating labour law to shifting patterns of investment, exchange and production. It is also relatively uncontentious that the current disjuncture between economic and regulatory space, as well as the fragmentation of any ideal or normative worker, both alters and complicates the calculus about 'good' labour law in a variety of ways. Yet any consideration of the position of workers outside the industrial world makes it clear that the challenges to the field go still farther.

III. Regulating Work: Outside the Centre, Beyond the Twentieth Century

It might once have been plausible to imagine that the fate of workers in what are conventionally styled as transitional, emerging or developing states, was to become more and more like their counterparts in the 'developed' world. The story would go like this. As states in the economic periphery increased their growth rates through modernisation and integration into global markets, their workers too would improve their socio-economic status by

---

[3] LF Vosko, *Managing the Margins: Gender, Citizenship, and the International Regulation of Precarious Employment* (Oxford, Oxford University Press, 2010).

[4] See, eg the UN Global Compact available at www.unglobalcompact.org/AboutTheGC/index.html, and the Equator Principles available at www.equator-principles.com/index.php/about-ep/about-ep). See also, CA Williams and JM Conley, 'Global Banks as Global Sustainability Regulators?: The Equator Principles' (2011) 33 *Law & Policy* 542.

engaging in work that more or less mirrored work in industrialised countries. In tandem with these developments, and after taking into account national legal traditions and a few necessary concessions to local conditions, states would perforce adopt some version of the model labour law that had already been mapped out in the first world. Indeed, this is not just a story. The conventions of the International Labor Organization (ILO) document the extent to which 'international' labour law looks very much like the transposition and diffusion of the labour law of a particular time and place—largely post-war Europe of the twentieth century—to the global plane.

This is simply no longer a reasonable starting point. Workers' rights and labour market standards have yet to touch the vast majority of workers in the global South. But factual and normative changes in the world of work have made the mere extension of existing rules an increasingly implausible account of the future of labour law in any event.

It is well known that transnationally organised forms of production such as global supply chains confound the possibilities of domestic regulation. Jurisdictional limits to the reach of labour law provide a convenient means of separating legal responsibility from effective control, allowing those at the centre to abjure responsibility for the wages and working conditions in the periphery from which they ultimately benefit. Instead of national, or even international, regulation, what seems to be needed in such situations are regimes that makes the supply chain or industry itself the object of regulation.[5]

But the challenges of regulating work in transnational production turn out to be only the tip of the iceberg. Anyone engaged with labour issues beyond the industrialised world, or anyone thinking of labour law through the optic of development, is immediately confronted with a broad array of work situations and regulatory conundrums that bear little if any relation to those in the global North. In addition to those working in service for others, there are petty traders and entrepreneurs, subsistence workers, and workers engaged in household production for both consumption and market purposes—in short, an incredibly varied group of workers involved in an almost limitless number of economic activities.[6]

Most of these workers are informal, meaning that as a matter of law or fact they lie beyond the administrative and regulatory reach of state.[7] Even where their own biographies and itineraries indicate ongoing involvement with the market for labour, some may not be recognisable, at least at first glance, as workers; still others do not even work in the market except on a sporadic basis. Even though most do massive amounts of economically productive work—many are engaged in household and subsistence as well as market work—they are people we only sometimes recognise as workers. What it takes, in law and policy, to better *their* situation almost certainly goes well beyond the regulation of working conditions: access to land, credit and other resources, and assistance with everything from technology to child care, for example, might all be part of the mix. Even diagnosing the forces that are operating on their economic livelihoods is a daunting task.

Informality is a highly-differentiated condition that includes myriad types of workers. Yet if the classic objectives of labour law include limiting the authority of the

---

[5] See, eg M Quinlan and R Sokas, 'Community campaigns, supply chains and protecting the health and wellbeing of workers: Examples from Australia and the USA' (2009) 99 (S3) *American Journal of Public Health* 538.

[6] T Teklè, *Labour Law and Worker Protection in Developing Countries* (Oxford, ILO, 2010).

[7] See ILO 'Resolution Concerning Decent Work and the Informal Economy' (2002) available at www.ilo.org/public/english/standards/relm/ilc/ilc90/pdf/pr-25res.pdf.

economically-powerful party and democratising the process by which working conditions are determined, then informal workers are surely a constituency of interest. Not only are they indisputably engaged in work; many are among the economically dispossessed, those who lose access to resources and traditional markets and modes of survival in the course of market integration and 'liberalisation' drives. Most importantly, they almost invariably exhibit traits that have historically provoked resistance and organisation by workers and the introduction of labour and employment standards and other forms of 'social' law: economically they are often highly insecure; they have deeply-constrained options, and thus impaired bargaining power in the market; and they may be highly dependent on particular individuals or parties for resources and work opportunities. For all of these reasons, their capacity to vary or influence the terms and conditions of their work is virtually non-existent. Where they are a preponderant part of the population, as is the case virtually everywhere outside the industrialised world,[8] their welfare is indistinguishable from the welfare of the society or state as a whole.

The many workers now engaged in informal markets, whether in a transitory or permanent way, not only pose a deep challenge to the dominant idea of a progressive or transformative labour law project; they have put in question, in fundamental ways, what a labour law looks like in the first place. While the diagnosis of labour market informality that now predominates in the policy technocracy is that informality is a product of dysfunctional regulation,[9] this is a transparently-inadequate account of the forces that sustain and organise informal labour markets. Myriad laws and policies structure the bargaining power and the workplace opportunities of those in informal markets: a short, non-exhaustive list of the most obvious would include trade law and investment policy, zoning law, tax law and policy, family law, property and land law, and creditor–debtor law. By definition, a raft of customary, commercial, cultural and social norms invariably operate on the informal sector as well, intersecting with, modifying, and sometimes superseding, the impact of formal norms.[10]

Although attending to workers at the edges or even off the map of market work takes labour scholars well beyond their comfort zone, recognition that informal workers move in and out of markets and take on different economic roles even as they continue to engage in *work* suggests that labour law scholars should follow them as they do so. Tracking the flows of work and resources both in different markets and across the market/household divide, moreover, seems likely to change the overall calculus about the costs, benefits and consequences of a wide range of legal and economic reforms.[11] All of this suggests that, rather than a relentless focus on labour law—whether positive or negative—we need to start trying to figure out how a broader constellation of rules and policies might shift the position and prospects of different populations of workers.

---

[8] Estimates of the informal sector range anywhere from 30 to 90 per cent of the workforce. See, eg International Institute for Labour Studies, 'World of Work Report 2012: Better Jobs for a Better Economy' (Geneva, ILO, 2012), 9, figure 1.5.

[9] See World Bank, *Doing Business* (various years) available at http://www.doingbusiness.org/; GE Perry, WF Maloney, OS Arias, P Fajnzylber, AD Mason and J Saavedra-Chanduvi *Informality: Exit and Exclusion* (Washington DC, World Bank, 2007) available at go.worldbank.org/ERL4C83K00; H de Soto, *The Other Path: The Invisible Revolution in the Third World* (New York, Harper & Row, 1989).

[10] K Rittich, 'Modeling Informal Labour Markets and Development', draft.

[11] Ibid.

IV. Towards a Broader Law of Work

At this point, the case for adopting a broader view of the law of work seems over-determined. Traditional forms of labour law are increasingly weak and ineffectual. When it comes to informal workers, it is unclear that they are the laws that are most of interest in any event. But attention to the position of informal workers points us towards a more general observation. A focus on labour law and social protection is not enough, even if the question is limited to 'what counts' for workers. A wide range of state rules and policies beyond labour law—financial and trade regulation, corporate and private law, fiscal and monetary policy, for example—now organise the shape and presence of work as well as the market returns for workers. The argument is that (a) we should see these rules as part of the effective law of work; and (b) we need to devise better models for explaining their impact on various groups of workers. The ambition is to capture the full range of laws that might be operating on labour markets, in order to identify those that seem most relevant to questions of risk allocation and bargaining power in specific contexts.[12]

Critical methods provide important clues to the ways that benefits, burdens, risks and advantages are both produced and sustained among different classes of market actors. For example, legal rules might be seen as bargaining endowments[13] or authorised forms of coercion[14] that parties can use in the course of structuring their relationships. How they are designed, therefore, may have much to do with the rising and falling fortunes of the parties. For workers, a key insight is that, far from a property of global market integration *simpliciter*, the question of bargaining power is always also a function of regulatory decisions; indeed *all* factor endowments are also legal endowments. For this reason, critical analytics continue to provide an unparalleled set of tools with which to explain the gulf between the promise of welfare enhancement and the actual experience of psycho-social displacement and material insecurity so characteristic of work in the new economy. However, a number of features of the contemporary world of work require their extension, and some raise issues that have been mostly peripheral to labour law scholarship, critical as well as mainstream, so far.

In brief, the argument is that a range of forces and developments in the world of work now compel us to think in terms of a labour law that is: much broader in terms of relevant legal rules and institutions than has been conventionally encompassed within the discipline; transnational rather than merely national and international in focus; deformalised and broadly normative as well as formally legal in character; and multi-leveled in its structure and operation. We need, for example, to consider the impact of private law as much as public law and human rights norms; and we must grapple (again) with countervailing rights claims as they affect the scope and interpretation of workers' rights.[15] We also need

---

[12] For a parallel exercise in family law, see J Halley and K Rittich, 'Critical Directions in Comparative Family Law: Genealogies and Contemporary Studies of Family Law Exceptionalism' (Introduction to Special Issue on Comparative Family Law) (2010) 58 *American Journal of Comparative Law* 753.

[13] RH Mnookin and L Kornhauser, 'Bargaining in the Shadow of the Law: The Case of Divorce' (1979) 88 *Yale Law Journal* 950–97.

[14] R Hale, 'Coercion and Distribution in a Supposedly Non-Coercive State' (1923) 38 *Political Science Quarterly* 470.

[15] See, eg Case C-341/05 *Laval un Partneri Ltd v Svenska Byggnadsarbetareförbundet, Svenska Byggnadsarbetareförbundets avdelning 1, Byggettan und Svenska Elektrikerförbundet* [2007] ECR I-11767; Case C-346/06 *Rechtsanwalt Dr Dirk Rüffert v Land Niedersachsen* [2008] ECR I-01989; Case C-438/05 *International Transport Workers' Federation, Finnish Seamen's Union v Viking Line ABP, OÜ Viking Line Eesti* [2007] ECR I-10779, hereinafter 'Viking'.

to be able to model the interaction of new governance and hybrid public/private initiatives with traditional forms of legal regulation, including those that traverse the borders of states.[16] In addition, we need some frameworks and tools with which to capture the connections among regulatory discourses and institutional change. For it is evident that the production and mobilisation of ideas about governance are themselves profoundly important to workers.

These propositions, I suggest, can be at least partly illuminated by considering the effects on workers of policy change and regulatory reforms adopted in the course of the financial crisis.

V. Beyond Labour Law: Law and Policy Reform in the Financial Crisis

The financial crisis has disclosed, in ways not visible for a long time, the significance of macroeconomic policy to the broader landscape of work. Beyond this, the structure and the consequences of regulatory decisions and policy choices made in the course of managing the financial crisis suggest (at least) two things about the nature of contemporary workplace and labour market governance. The first is that decisions about fiscal and monetary policy should themselves now be seen as important, perhaps key, elements of the contemporary law of work. Not only do they affect overall levels of economic activity and hence the availability of work; they bear directly on workers' bargaining power and indirectly on the extent to which the gains of productive activity accrue to workers. Secondly, financial crisis management has become a major mechanism and locus of labour law reform and policy-making as well as a vehicle for rewriting employment contracts that are collectively bargained in both the public and private sectors.

The centrality of labour law to the structural reforms, I suggest, also confirms the repudiation of the post-war approach to workers' rights and labour market regulation that was already in process before the crisis. In particular, it makes visible the effort to both normalise and generalise the absence of benchmark standards and collectively bargained wages and benefits within labour markets. But it also marks the arrival in the core or centre of crisis management, tools long familiar as part of structural adjustment and debt-servicing arrangements in the global South.

VI. Fiscal Policy beyond the Social

It is hardly revolutionary to point out that fiscal policy is part of the larger context of work, or to notice that it contributes to workers' effective or 'social' wage. Even in normal times, decisions about taxation and state expenditures are directly relevant to workers' employment, income and bargaining position in a variety of ways. Public-sector wage and employment practices are both important in themselves and typically provide important

---

[16] See C Kilpatrick, 'New EU employment governance and constitutionalism' in G de Búrca and J Scott, *Law and New Governance in the EU and the US* (Oxford, Hart Publishing, 2006) 121.

benchmarks for private sector employment as well. The progressivity of the tax rate structure is an important factor in determining how much of the general burden of financing government falls on labour and how much income remains available to individuals and households for 'discretionary' expenses. Public services, income transfers and other social protection programmes 'decommodify' work: depending on their quality, extent and design, they ensure the delivery of some goods and services either for free or at subsidised rates, thus insulating workers from some of the effects of cyclical variations in the labour market. Apart from their immediate and intrinsic value, they have a potentially-significant impact on workers' bargaining power, removing issues from negotiations and enabling bargaining capital to be expended elsewhere. They may even affect workers' reservation wage, generating or closing off exit options either from specific work situations or the labour market as a whole.

In times of crisis, their impact is more clearly in view. During downturns in the business cycle and more pronounced recessions and economic and financial crises, social transfers and programmes such as employment insurance can represent an outsize part of individual or household income. Because they also operate as 'automatic stabilisers' in the economy as a whole, they help sustain job levels in the private sector and, by extension, the bargaining power of those working, or seeking work, in the market as well. But decisions about supplemental projects such as public works programmes and/or extended access to employment insurance can play a significant role, either attenuating or aggravating the extent of the crisis itself, and mitigating or increasing the costs that job losses, layoffs, and shorter work hours would otherwise impose on workers.

The recent crisis has made it clear that an array of fiscal decisions beyond those that directly operate on employment and labour markets are also crucial to the fortunes of workers. Some of these policy and regulatory choices are directly and obviously anti-labour in design and effect. But others have more obscure and ambiguous consequences. For example, it may well be that widespread bank failures would, in fact, have exacted (more) terrible costs on the economy and, by extension, the labour market. Workers have stakes in the recovery of the financial markets through investments in pension and retirement funds in any event. Yet, whatever the general upside of subsidies and bailouts of the financial services sector, it seems clear that how such interventions are designed, how far they go, and what other reforms they are, or are not, attached to are equally, if not more, significant to workers.

Begin with the general approach to the macroeconomic management of the crisis itself. Except for a brief period immediately following the onset of the crisis, fiscal austerity and concerns about sovereign debt have dominated the debate about the financial crisis, evidence of the shift from Keynesian to monetarist macroeconomic policy that predated the crisis itself.[17] The general agreement that stimulus measures should be adopted to address falling growth rates and rising unemployment was soon displaced by concerns about growing debt.[18] These initial measures almost certainly mitigated job losses[19] and lowered

---

[17] For a discussion of this shift, see F Scharpf, 'Monetary Union, Fiscal Crisis and the Preemption of Democracy' (2011) *Max Planck Institute for the Study of Societies Discussion Paper 11/11*, available at www.mpifg.de/pu/dp_abstracts/dp11-11.asp.

[18] See, 'World Leaders Launch Action Plan to Combat Financial Crisis' (15 November 2008) IMF Survey online available at www.imf.org/external/pubs/ft/survey/so/2008/NEW111508A.htm.

[19] One estimate puts that figure at 3 million jobs by 2010 in the US. See CD Romer, 'What Do We Know About the Effects of Fiscal Policy? Separating Evidence from Ideology', Lecture at Hamilton College, 7 November 2011, available at emlab.berkeley.edu/~cromer/Written%20Version%20of%20Effects%20of%20Fiscal%20Policy.pdf, 15.

unemployment[20] even if they did not prevent widespread upheaval in labour markets. But stimulus measures were unevenly and hesitantly adopted in any event. For example, despite its apparent magnitude, the American Recovery and Reinvestment Act[21] was inadequate to replace the collapse in private spending.[22] In Europe, the preference for austerity and price stability enshrined in the Maastricht Treaty through the deficit limits specified in the Stability and Growth Pact constrained the extent to which the states in the Eurozone could adopt counter-cyclical fiscal measures in response to the crisis;[23] indeed, deficit limits were routinely exceeded even by expenditures on 'normal' social protections during economic downturns.[24] The recently concluded agreement has only intensified those constraints, increasing the pressure that may be applied, especially to less powerful states and, of course, their workers.[25]

Yet despite the rejection of Keynesianism in respect of labour market and social policy, austerity has not, in fact, prevailed across the board. Expenditures in some areas have remained essentially untouched, even unexamined; a number of states have assumed unprecedented amounts of new debt at the same time as they have engaged in sharp retrenchment in labour and social costs. Fiscal austerity, then, says both too much and too little about what is going on: the general policy orientation is perhaps better described as uneven or selective austerity.

A threshold issue, of overwhelming significance to workers is simply the decision that debts must be serviced rather than restructured.[26] This is particularly true as even 'private' debts turn out to be public in the end, and labour, as the residual taxpayer in a world in which capital is largely mobile, ultimately pays the bill. Despite the pervasive idea that debts must be paid, it seems important to point out that debt restructuring *is* an alternative. Not only may it be essential to resolving a financial crisis of the magnitude that now grips Europe,[27] debt restructuring as a condition of financial bailout in times of crisis is historically the normal scenario.[28]

The location and structure of any cuts occasioned by fiscal austerity are obviously of interest to workers, as are any new debts assumed or expenditures undertaken in the name of crisis management. Yet even where direct subsidies or new sovereign liabilities are

---

[20] J Stiglitz, *The Price of Inequality* (New York, WW Norton, 2012) suggests that unemployment in the US is at least 2% lower than it would have been without stimulus measures.

[21] American Recovery and Reinvestment Act (ARRA) of 2009, Pub. L. No 111-5, 123 Stat 115, 516 (19 February 2009).

[22] Romer, 'What Do We Know About the Effects of Fiscal Policy?' (n 19).

[23] Scharpf, 'Monetary Union' (n 17); T Niechoj, 'Does supranational coordination erode its national basis? The case of European labour market policy and German industrial relations' (2009) 13 *European Integration online Papers* art 10, available at eiop.or.at/eiop/texte/2009-010a.htm.

[24] Scharpf, 'Monetary Union' (n 17) 13.

[25] See 'The Euro Plus Pact', 11 March 2011available at ec.europa.eu/economy_finance/economic_governance/index_en.htm.

[26] The telling analogy is, of course, the debt restructuring in Latin America and Sub-Saharan Africa during the 1980s and 1990s. See, eg Vijay Prashad, *The Darker Nations: A People's History of the Third World* (New York, The New Press, 2007) 276.

[27] W Buiter, 'Only Big Debt Restructuring Can Save the Euro' *Financial Times* (15 October 2012) available at www.ft.com/cms/s/0/edd92eee-12de-11e2-aa9c-00144feabdc0.html.

[28] LC Buchheit and GM Gulati, 'The Eurozone Debt Crisis—The Options Now' (October 2012), working paper available at papers.ssrn.com/sol3/papers.cfm?abstract_id=2158850, comparing the terms of current and past debt restructurings in the course of financial crises.

absent, there are reasons that reforms generally involve a massive upfront redistribution of public resources in favour of private equity and bond holders.

An independently important element is the priority given to debt servicing and debt reduction in light of competing demands and claims on state resources. As the terms set by the European Commission, the International Monetary Fund (IMF) and the European Central Bank (ECB)—otherwise known as the 'troika'—for the initial and subsequent Greek bailouts,[29] and the now infamous decision of the Irish government to guarantee all of the debts of Allied Irish and other Irish banks both confirm, the norm now is 'absolute priority' for debt servicing. Such a priority may not be in creditors' ultimate interest, even if it comports with their immediate demands, especially where it forecloses infrastructure investments or public works programmes that plausibly contribute to economic expansion and jobs. It is already evident that debts cannot realistically be serviced in the absence of economic growth; debt ratios will inevitably worsen as a consequence of the falling tax receipts that economic contraction and jobs losses provoke.[30] Yet despite both political wrangling and academic dispute over this issue,[31] so far debt servicing has prevailed in the policy calculus.

Yet another is the decision by states to manage fiscal crises by expenditure cuts rather than tax increases. In addition to the inherent difficulties in taxing capital under regimes of capital mobility, the shift from Keynesianism towards monetarism has made cuts the preferred policy option in many countries. Declining tax rates at the upper end of the income bracket[32] and, in some countries, the maintenance of tax credits and loopholes that benefit higher-income earners, along with the neglect of myriad other possible adjustments to the tax code have all increased the cost of the crisis to the average worker. But they have also revealed a more fundamental issue: cuts are rarely if ever evenly or mechanically implemented; they typically entail decisions about what to maintain, or even increase, as well as what to eliminate in the way of expenditures.[33]

Apart from the sheer burden of servicing debts and subsidies, there are as-yet uncalculated opportunity costs—costs that show up both in the form of cuts to existing programmes and services and in new expenditures that can never be contemplated—that arise from decisions to bail out banks and/or nationalise their private debts. Given the magnitude of the sums involved—the cost of the recent bailout has been estimated at one sixth of world GDP[34]—these foregone investments and expenditures must be correlatively enormous. This is without including the host of knock-on effects arising from the assumption of private

[29] See, 'Assurance of Compliance in the 2nd GRC Programme', available at www.ft.com/intl/cms/853efee4-4918-11e1-88f0-00144feabdc0.pdf.

[30] Ireland's ratio of debt to GDP increased from 44.5% in 2008 to 106.4% in 2011. In Greece, the ratio of debt to GDP increased from 112.9% to 170.6% in 2011. See, 'Euro area government debt up to 90.0 per cent of GDP', Eurostat (24 October 2012) available at epp.eurostat.ec.europa.eu/cache/ITY_PUBLIC/2-24102012-AP/EN/2-24102012-AP-EN.PDF. See also, 'Despite Push for Austerity, European Debt Has Soared' The New York Times (22 October 2012) available at www.nytimes.com/2012/10/23/business/global/despite-push-for-austerity-eu-debt-has-soared.html.

[31] For arguments to the effect that contractionary policy is, in fact, contractionary, see P Krugman, End This Depression Now! (New York, WW Norton, 2012). See also, J Quiggin, Zombie Economics: How dead ideas still walk among us (Princeton, Princeton University Press, 2010), chapter 6, 'Expansionary Austerity'; Romer, 'What Do We Know About the Effects of Fiscal Policy?' (n 19).

[32] OECD, Taxing Wages 2011 (Paris : OECD 2012), http://www.oecd.org/ctp/tax-policy/50131824.pdf

[33] See N Brooks and L McQuaig, The Trouble With Billionaires (Toronto, Viking, 2010).

[34] J Heyes, P Lewis and I Clark, 'Varieties of Capitalism, Neoliberalism and the Economic Crisis of 2008–?' (2012) 43 Industrial Relations Journal 222, 229.

debt, as bondholders, doubting (likely correctly) that states can actually service the enormous new sovereign debts with which they are saddled and at the same time stabilise and even expand their economies, demand ever higher interest rates, which then increases the amount of revenue that must go to service the debt, depressing further both economic growth and expenditures on things other than interest payments. Whatever the ultimate effects of these decisions, there is little doubt about where the immediate costs fall.

Finally, it is worth bearing in mind that fiscal policy may take less obvious forms, some of which may generate severe consequences for workers and households. In recent years, especially in the Anglo-American world, austerity in the public sphere has been accompanied by a deliberate policy strategy to support economic demand through easing credit and catalysing a massive increase in the accumulation of private, household debt.[35] Rightly called privatised Keynesianism,[36] these policies appear to provoke asset bubbles that are followed by recessions, and attendant job losses, that are longer and deeper than those that result from cyclical downturns of the 'normal' variety.[37]

VII. Monetary Policy

Decisions about monetary policy are typically seen as far from the concern of labour (and other) lawyers, something properly consigned to economic technocrats and specialists in view of the expertise required in the assessment of macroeconomic issues. The rise of the independent central bank and its installation as a metric of good governance[38] has only enhanced the perception that monetary policy is properly beyond the realm of ordinary politics and policy-making. This remains the case, despite the ongoing debates about the role of monetary policy in both the emergence of and the response to the current financial crisis.[39]

In 'normal' times, this tends to be uncontentious. As Fritz Scharpf has observed, the consequences of monetary policy may not be immediately visible, and even where they are, they often seem attenuated from specific policy choices.[40] Fiscal policy is, in comparison, more obviously relevant to questions of distribution and class politics, and some decisions

---

[35] RH Clarida, 'What Has—and Has Not—Been Learned about Monetary Policy in a Low-Inflation Environment? A Review of the 2000s' (2012) 1 *Journal of Money, Credit and Banking* 123.

[36] C Crouch, 'Privatized Keynesianism: An Unacknowledged Policy Regime?' (2009) 3 *British Journal of Politics and International Relations* 382.

[37] CM Reinhart and KS Rogoff, *This Time Is Different: Eight Centuries of Financial Folly* (Princeton, Princeton University Press, 2009); M Schularick and A Taylor, 'Credit Booms Gone Bust' (2012) 2 *American Economic Review* 1029.

[38] See T Lybek, 'Central Bank Autonomy, Accountability, and Governance: Conceptual Framework' presentation at IMF LEG 2004 Seminar on Current Developments in Monetary and Financial Law, Washington DC, 24 May–4 June 4 2004, available at www.imf.org/external/np/leg/sem/2004/cdmfl/eng/lybek.pdf; F Amtenbrink, 'The Three Pillars of Central Bank Governance—Towards a Model Central Bank Law or a Code of Good Governance?' presentation at IMF LEG 2004 Seminar on Current Developments in Monetary and Financial Law, Washington DC, 24 May–4 June 4 2004, available at www.imf.org/external/np/leg/sem/2004/cdmfl/eng/amtenb.pdf.

[39] See, eg J Frankel, 'The Death of Inflation Targeting' *Project Syndicate* (16 May 2012), available at www.project-syndicate.org/commentary/the-death-of-inflation-targeting); J Stiglitz, 'The Failure of Inflation Targeting' *Project Syndicate* 6 May 2008, available at www.project-syndicate.org/commentary/the-failure-of-inflation-targeting.

[40] Scharpf, 'Monetary Union' (n 17).

about taxation and expenditures are directly connected to work and employment. Yet like other forms of policy, monetary policy is inevitably subject to discretion, the exercise of which can have significant effects on the labour market. Monetary policy plays a key role in growth rates, and hence at least indirectly affects the labour market. Interest rates affect the practical extent of credit available to the private sector, and hence decisions about expansion and hiring, especially within small and medium-sized enterprises. Changes in exchange rates both fuel and depress external demand for products and services and, at the margins, can represent life or death for firms, entire industries and, of course, the workers they employ.[41] Even where jobs are not directly on the line, wages and non-wage benefits are all affected by interest rates and the competitiveness of the exchange rate.

Thus all efforts to insist otherwise, monetary policy is clearly a political, rather than merely technical, issue; that is, monetary policy decisions dispose significant stakes for different social groups. Indeed, its political colour is sometimes evident in the most basic of ways. An analysis of monetary policy trends in the US, for example, indicates significant differential partisan preferences for, and sensitivity to, interest levels, preferences that cash out in visible differences in growth rates, levels of unemployment and income inequality. Democratic administrations appear to be systematically more likely than Republican ones to 'run the risk of higher inflation rates in order to pursue expans[ionary] policies designed to yield lower unemployment and extra growth'.[42] These decisions, moreover, turn out to be extremely important for workers in the bottom quintile of the income distribution; their incomes are highly variable and sensitive to such decisions, while those at the top are far less affected.[43]

A useful place to start unfolding the salience and impact of monetary policy on work and workers is to observe how the balance between inflation and employment concerns has changed. National central banks typically have dual mandates: price stability *and* welfare enhancement through employment creation.[44] This dual mandate historically ensured that labour market consequences were a part of the calculus when it came to monetary policy. It also reflected a broadly shared commitment to the insights of Keynesian macroeconomic theory and their utility in managing the adverse labour market consequences of cyclical downturns in the economy.[45] Even in 'normal' times, employment levels could be managed to some degree, with the perceived trade-off between jobs and inflation calibrated by attention to indicators such as the non-accelerating inflation rate of unemployment or NAIRU.[46]

---

[41] Scharpf, 'Monetary Union' (n 17); LM Bartels, 'Partisan Politics and the US Income Distribution' (2004) *Russel Sage Foundation Working Papers Series* available at www.russellsage.org/sites/all/files/u4/Bartels_Partisan Politics.pdf.

[42] DA Hibbs quoted in Bartels, ibid, 15.

[43] Bartels, 'Partisan Politics' (n 41) 5.

[44] R Schettkat and R Sun, 'Monetary Policy and European Unemployment' (2009) 25 *Oxford Review of Economic Policy* 94.

[45] For example, this dual mandate was identified as one of the purposes of the International Monetary Fund, to contribute to 'the promotion and maintenance of high levels of employment and real income'. See, Articles of Agreement of the International Monetary Fund, art I(ii), 27 December 1945, 60 Stat 1401, 2 UNTS 39 available at www.imf.org/external/pubs/ft/aa/index.htm.

[46] See L Ball and NG Mankiw, 'The NAIRU in Theory and Practice' (2002) *National Bureau of Economic Research Working Paper 8940*, available at www.nber.org/papers/w8940.pdf; Schettkat and Sun, 'Monetary Policy and European Unemployment' (n 44).

A critical issue for workers in both the short and long term is the balance that is struck between price stability and growth or job creation in the setting of short-term interest rates, the key instrument of monetary policy. Despite the dual mandate of most central banks, monetary policy now persistently favours inflation control over economic expansion and employment;[47] in the case of the ECB, the priority of price stability is specified in the Maastricht Treaty.[48]

The US Federal Reserve has employed unconventional forms of monetary policy during the crisis through successive programmes of quantitative easing involving the purchase of an expanded range of financial assets from commercial banks; the ECB, the Bank of Japan, and the Bank of England have all engaged in related operations.[49] These moves reflect the fact that interest rates are currently close to 0 per cent, the 'zero bound', and cannot in practical terms be lowered further. Although primarily designed to increase the money supply and to improve the balance sheets of banks, like fiscal stimulus measures, these programmes almost certainly abated the jobs crisis as well.[50] Nonetheless, inflation remains the overwhelming concern when it comes to monetary policy. Inflation targeting through the setting of short-term interest rates has been identified as '[a] new policy consensus extended to all central banks in the developed world and many in the developing world at the end of the twentieth century'[51] and, because it is also a central means of signalling commitment to orthodox financial and economic policies and thus financial credibility in general,[52] the 'holy grail'.[53]

Although mainstream economic theory holds that monetary policy is a neutral factor vis-a-vis output and employment, at least in the mid- to long-term, there is increasing evidence of, and analytical support for, an employment/inflation trade-off.[54] One of the most critical consequences for workers, then, is simply the abandonment, explicit and implicit, of the commitment to full employment. A function of the displacement of Keynesianism by monetarism in macroeconomic policy, the abandonment of full employment has been linked both to the general weakening of labour's bargaining position and the wage stagnation that has occurred across many industrialised states.[55] In a move to allay any tension with employment creation, inflation control is sometimes justified as laying the foundation for growth *and* employment; the Federal Reserve, for example, now interprets the dual mandate as full employment *through* price stability or 'maximum sustainable employment'.[56] As even this formulation makes clear, however, job creation has been subordinated to price stability.

---

[47] See Scharpf, 'Monetary Union' (n 17).

[48] Ibid, 9.

[49] See, eg debate by the Bank of England in September about further likely extensions in October, P Iman 'Bank of England expected to pump £50bn into economy', *The Guardian* (4 October 2012), available at www.guardian.co.uk/business/2012/oct/04/bank-england-quantitative-easing.

[50] JC Williams, 'The Federal Reserve's Unconventional Policies' *FRBSF Economic Letters* (13 November 2012) available at www.frbsf.org/publications/economics/letter/2012/el2012-34.html.

[51] J Singleton, *Central Banking in the Twentieth Century* (Cambridge, Cambridge University Press, 2011) 258.

[52] Ibid, 242.

[53] Ibid.

[54] Schettkat and Sun, 'Monetary Policy and European Unemployment' (n 44).

[55] Heyes, Lewis and Clark, 'Varieties of Capitalism' (n 34) 226–27.

[56] D Thornton, 'The Dual Mandate—Has the Fed Changed Its Objective?' (2012) 2 *Federal Reserve Bank of St. Louis Review* 117.

In addition, the effects of monetary decisions are typically uneven: unless they occur within an (elusive) optimal currency area, what is good for one region or nation may be bad, or at least worse, for another.[57] As the unresolved crisis in Europe confirms, peripheral states and regions within currency unions may have very different interests in the direction of interest rate changes than those in the centre; they typically have less power to set or influence those changes as well: contrast for example the position of Germany and Spain in respect of the interest rate policy of the ECB. These uneven effects of monetary policy, moreover, are related. Germany's trade surpluses within the union are, by definition, realised by deficits elsewhere.[58] Low interest rates fueled German exports to other states in the region; they also permitted, and arguably encouraged, German banks to lend freely to the states in the South. Thus, monetary policy might be seen as one of the conditions precedent to the boom and the subsequent crash.

To the extent that regional differences map on economic or industrial differences, monetary policy may favour or disfavour particular sectors, firms and workers as well. Construction workers in Spain, for example, may be the beneficiaries of expanding job markets fueled by easy terms of credit in good times, but suffer brutal job losses once the credit and housing bubble bursts. Industrial workers in Germany, meanwhile, may benefit from the healthy export markets that monetary policy decisions help support. However, the *extent* to which workers gain (and lose) is an entirely separate question, as even monetary policy 'success' can come at a cost to labour. For example, Germany's export strategy, both within the Eurozone and externally, has depended on policies of deliberate wage suppression.[59] The flat level of German wage growth, in combination with the wage inflation fueled by easy money flowing from the core to the periphery, has not only made wages in peripheral states progressively less competitive; it has tilted the internal distribution of the gains to Germany against German workers.

At least some of the disadvantage generated by monetary policy can be mitigated by transfer arrangements ensuring that losses do not simply lie where they fall. Where such arrangements are absent, as is currently the case within the Eurozone, the adverse effects of monetary policy may be both acute and essentially beyond the capacity of the affected states or regions to remedy.

To the extent that decisions on monetary policy contribute to bubbles, collapses, and crises, they may be extraordinarily, if complexly, important to the average person in her capacity as worker. Current levels of unemployment in Greece and Spain are unprecedented, reaching levels that can only be described as catastrophic.[60] Recent statistics on US household wealth, for example, disclose a dramatic decline in the fortunes of households in the past decade: median losses of close to 40 per cent followed the financial crisis of 2008, wiping out gains going back to the 1970s.[61] This decline is itself related to job losses, as well as declining household equity. But its impact on levels of economic security is sure

---

[57] R Mundell, 'A Theory of Optimum Currency Areas' (1961) 4 *American Economic Review* 657.

[58] Niechoj, 'Does supranational coordination erode its national basis?' (n 23) 16–17.

[59] Ibid; K Armingen and L Baccaro, 'Political Economy of the Sovereign Debt Crisis: the Limits of Internal Devaluation' (2012) 3 *Industrial Law Journal* 254; Scharpf 'Monetary Union' (n 17).

[60] International Labour Office, 'Global Employment Trends 2012: Preventing a deeper jobs crisis' Report (Geneva, ILO, 2012) available at www.ilo.org/global/research/global-reports/global-employment-trends/WCMS_171571/lang--en/index.htm.

[61] 'Changes in US Family Finances from 2007 to 2010: Evidence from the Survey of Consumer Finances' (2012) 2 *Federal Reserve Bulletin*, available at www.federalreserve.gov/pubs/bulletin/2012/pdf/scf12.pdf.

to generate a host of work-related consequences as well: delayed retirements, returns to the labour market on less advantageous terms, and inability to accept new labour market opportunities because of housing-related constraints on mobility are among the most obvious.

There is a compelling argument that the crisis in Europe is, at base, a balance of payments crisis rather than a fiscal crisis.[62] Under the constraints of the currency union, the preferred, virtually universal, remedy is internal devaluation, that is, downward pressure on wages, in lieu of the external devaluation that continued membership in the Eurozone renders unavailable. It has long been observed, however, that inflation suppression in surplus countries must drive up unemployment in deficit countries within currency unions.[63] The correlative is that achieving full employment in deficit countries will have inflationary effects on surplus countries; solving unemployment in deficit countries therefore depends on a willingness of countries in surplus to tolerate a measure of inflation, or at least inflationary pressure. Thus, debt restructuring aside, an enduring solution to the acute crises in the peripheral states such as Greece and Spain, requires 'reflation' in the core, that is, higher levels of inflation and wage growth in countries such as Germany to permit the economies of the periphery to become relatively more competitive.[64]

While much of the debate is focused on the very real political and legal challenges that this now 'alternative' path would entail,[65] ideological commitments and analytic premises concerning labour market institutions may be doing some independent work, restraining alternatives to the pursuit of internal devaluation in any event. One is the enduring belief that labour market institutions are distortionary, a source of uncompetitive pressure that renders them undesirable per se. It seems plausible that this belief provides underlying support for the view that, rather than revisit wage and inflation policy within the core countries, the 'right' solution to the crisis is to focus on reforms to labour law in the periphery; indeed, the problem in the periphery *must* be labour market rigidity occasioned by inappropriate labour laws.

VIII. Labour Market Flexibility and Crisis Management, or Labour Law Reform through Bailout Conditionality

A. Reforming the Public

There is little if any reason to think that labour market policy and regulation is the proximate cause of the current financial crises, especially given the other candidates close at hand: profligate lending on the part of banks; loose monetary policy that fueled asset price inflation and the growth of bubbles; and so on.[66] Nonetheless, it has become simply

---

[62] P Krugman, 'Euro Update: The Perils of Pointless Pain', (*New York Times* (26 September 2012) available at krugman.blogs.nytimes.com/2012/09/26/euro-update-the-perils-of-pointless-pain.

[63] Mundell, 'A Theory of Optimum Currency Areas' (n 57) 658–69.

[64] Armingen and Baccaro, 'Political Economy of the Sovereign Debt Crisis' (n 59).

[65] See C Joerges and M Weimer, 'A Crisis of Executive Managerialism in the EU: No Alternative' in this volume.

[66] AW Lo, 'Reading About the Financial Crisis: A Twenty-One-Book Review' (2012) 50 *Journal of Economic Literature* 151.

boilerplate that labour market rigidity is a significant cause of economic malfunction and distress and must be remedied, and changes to labour standards, collective bargaining entitlements, and pensions have been at the centre of bailout conditionality whether the debtor is public or private.[67]

The universal remedy of more labour market flexibility, buttressed by the narrative of the 'lazy Greek worker', may have successfully displaced attention from other issues, such as the paradox of austerity for workers in the context of unprecedented state support of financial institutions, and the inherent problems in a monetary union without a banking union or coordinated macroeconomic policy, at least at the initial stages of the crisis. Yet in a context in which numerous forces are already operating to produce declining wages, highly variable and unstable incomes, and uncertain employment prospects, and when stalled consumer and household demand, some of which is a function of wages that have lagged behind inflation and fixed expenses, is limiting the escape from recession, the pursuit of further wage cuts and labour market flexibility looks puzzling if not simply perverse. The strategy only makes sense, I suggest, if we concede independent operative force to the belief that labour standards and collective bargaining are per se sub-optimal or simply 'bad' for the economy. Thus we might think of the ideals about good labour market governance as part of the cognitive apparatus by which flexibility becomes the centre-piece of structural reforms while other, arguably more pertinent, policy and institutional reforms languish or disappear from the crisis response script altogether.

Labour market flexibility norms have been in wide circulation for the better part of two decades, and have long reached the status of elite common sense.[68] The conventional wisdom holding that labour market flexibility is good has not only normalised a high degree of economic insecurity for workers;[69] it has also transformed that insecurity into an engine of productivity and efficiency gains.[70] Even those states and regions such the European Union that remain nominally committed to the social market now give pride of place to flexibilising labour markets, decentralising wage-setting mechanisms, and ensuring that social benefits do not function to impede labour market participation.[71] However, the ongoing financial crises have presented unparalleled occasions to further this vision of optimal labour market regulation, allowing policy-makers to circumnavigate democratic processes and deflect obstacles that have either slowed or prevented the acceptance of reforms during periods of ordinary politics. Indeed, financial crises appear to have emerged as the most important contemporary catalysts towards the adoption (or imposition) of Anglo-American style labour market reforms.

The case of Greece is exemplary of the general approach. As a condition of the release of funds to cover both primary expenditures and the costs of debt servicing, the troika required Greece to cut its minimum wage by 22 per cent, 32 per cent in the case of youth below the age of 25, with an expected reduction in real wages from 22 to 40 per cent;

---

[67] For a review, see C Barnard, 'Financial Crisis and the Euro Plus Pact: A Labour Lawyer's Perspective' (2012) 41 *Industrial Law Journal* 98.

[68] An important early document charting the technocratic position on labour market flexibility is OECD, *OECD Jobs Study: Evidence and Explanations* (1994), 69. See also Stiglitz, *The Price of Inequality* (n 20) 65.

[69] G Standing, *Global Labour Flexibility: Seeking Distributive Justice* (New York, St Martin's Press, 1999).

[70] K Rittich, 'Global Labour Policy as Global Social Policy' (2008) 14 *Canadian Labour and Employment Law Journal* 227.

[71] See, D Ashiagbor, 'Unravelling the Embedded Liberal Bargain: Labour and Social Welfare Law in the Context of EU Market Integration' (2013) 19:3 *European Law Review* 303.

renegotiate existing collective agreements or simply give up contractually-negotiated terms such as wage increases and pension entitlements; and terminate the employment of 150,000 public employees.[72] The bailout did not resolve the crisis, however: growth has plummeted, tax receipts have fallen, and further funds are required for the government to meet its ongoing obligations.[73] At the time of writing, the troika is demanding a still greater, more radical, overhaul of labour law and labour standards as the price for such funds in the form of reductions in the minimum wage and severance pay, the abolition of collective agreements, and extensions to permitted working hours.[74] Similar cuts and conditions have been standard fare elsewhere as well. Ireland was compelled to cut its minimum wage and to roll back collective agreements, including some covering low-wage service sector and other workers, all in the name of remedying labour market rigidities.[75] Portugal suspended the bonuses of public servants and cut social welfare programmes, as well as reducing public sector pay and hiring, freezing pensions, and reforming unemployment benefits.[76]

These programmes have evoked concerns about intrusions into sovereignty and about the preservation of national traditions of labour law.[77] Yet sovereign control and regulatory diversity is under threat in *any* case in which loans are conditioned upon policy responses or regulatory change. The more substantive question is why *labour* law reform has come to be so central to the resolution of what is essentially a financial and debt crisis.

B. Reforming the Private

Although they have received much less in the way of legal analysis, the early bailouts to the private sector, the automotive industry in particular, are instructive here. In North America if not elsewhere, they, too, signal the centrality of labour concessions to current debt reduction strategies, although many of these concessions appear to be no more objectively warranted in private sector debt negotiations than they are in the public. Parallel concessions demanded by firms that did *not* require a bailout during the crisis also indicate the extent to which the crisis has provided a context, catalyst and cover for reforms to labour law and labour relations in general.

In the wake of the crisis in the autumn of 2008, governments everywhere moved to aid their automotive industries, in the belief that because of the immensely important role

---

[72] Aristea Koukiadaki and Lefteris Kretsos, 'Opening Pandora's Box: The Sovereign Debt Crisis and Labour Market Regulation in Greece' (2012) 41 *Industrial Law Journal* 276, 286–301.

[73] The Institute for International Finance reports that cuts have harmed growth much more than predicted, See P Inman, 'Austerity has worsened Greek crisis, says institute' *The Guardian* (4 October 2012) available at www. guardian.co.uk/world/2012/oct/04/austerity-worsened-greek-crisis.

[74] G Wearden, 'Eurozone crisis live: Spain says bailout is not imminent as Greek deadlock continues—as it happened' *The Guardian* (2 October 2012) available at www.guardian.co.uk/business/2012/oct/02/eurozone-crisis-spain-bailout-greek-troika.

[75] See, Memorandum of Understanding of the EU/IMF Programme of Financial Support for Ireland (16 December 2010), 8–10, 17, 20–21, available at www.finance.gov.ie/documents/publications/reports/2011/euimfrevised.pdf; 2011–2014 National Recovery Plan, 36–37, available at budget.gov.ie/RecoveryPlan.aspx.

[76] See the data on 'Portugal' in Z Laven and F Santi, 'EU Austerity and Reform: A Country by Country Table (*The European Institute*, April 2012), available at www.europeaninstitute.org/April-2012/eu-austerity-and-reform-a-country-by-country-table-updated-may-3.html. See also Employment Trends unit, ILO, *Global Employment Trends 2012: Preventing a deeper jobs crisis* Report (Geneva, ILO, 2012) 17–18 available at www.ilo. org/global/research/global-reports/global-employment-trends/WCMS_171571/lang--en/index.htm.

[77] See Barnard, 'Financial Crisis and the Euro Plus Pact' (n 67).

they play in the economy as a whole, allowing these sectors to fail would generate a series of negative spillovers the consequences of which, although they could only imperfectly be estimated, seemed both too large and too far-reaching to contemplate.[78] A wide variety of strategies were employed to forestall such failures; yet how governments chose to aid their industries was both far from uniform and highly instructive.[79]

In North America, the role played by anti-union ideology in structuring the terms and conditions of the bailout is unmistakable. Some of the provisions dealing with so-called 'legacy' costs, that is the enormous financial overhang caused by pension costs and pensioner health-care costs, were probably unavoidable in any event, given the disadvantage that they created vis-à-vis non-union Japanese 'transplant' firms.[80] However, the bailout was used to further far-reaching labour relations change across the industry, change that impaired the bargaining power of workers and the representative role of unions.

In the course of bankruptcy protection proceedings in the US,[81] General Motors and Chrysler[82] received a raft of financial and policy supports from both the US and Canadian governments, from subsidies for new vehicle rebates to debtor-in-possession financing, loan guarantees and equity investments. This support totaled $81 billion in the US; the support was even greater, on a proportionate basis, in Canada.[83] In exchange, the companies were required to engage in massive restructuring, part of which involved the setting up of trust instruments to manage the health insurance benefits of retired workers. The centrepiece, however, was the renegotiation of labour contracts, the aim of which was the reduction of labour costs to match those of the leading, non-union Japanese operations. Additional gains for the companies were achieved by the introduction of a two-tiered labour contract, with wages for newly-hired workers set at 50 per cent of the rate for other workers;[84] dramatic reductions in employment levels, many through the closure and/or relocation of plants to lower-wage jurisdictions such as Mexico; and the inclusion of a no-strike clause in their collective agreement until 2015.

The automotive industry itself has since rebounded, with all of the companies returning to solvency[85] and some reaching levels of profitability never before seen, despite aggregate sales that are weaker.[86] Nonetheless, the internal picture is vastly different. The insistence on cuts to wages as a condition of financing put an enormous thumb on the scale on the side of the employer and, in tandem with the massive job losses—between 2005 and 2009, about 30 percent of jobs within the North American automotive industry were lost[87]—

---

[78] For example, in Canada, it is estimated that each job in the automotive sector drives the creation of 10 jobs in other sectors. See Canadian Auto Workers Union (CAW) *Re-thinking Canada's Auto Industry: A Policy Vision to Escape the Race to the Bottom* (CAW, April 2012) 4, available at www.rethinktheeconomy.ca/resources.

[79] Ibid, 10–11.

[80] Legacy costs added about $1700 to the cost of each vehicle, see, E Siemiatycki, 'Forced to Concede: Permanent Restructuring and Labour's Place in the North American Auto Industry' (2012) 44 *Antipode* 453, 464.

[81] See, eg 11 U.S.Code §§ 301.

[82] The other large North American car company, Ford, had engaged in defensive financial measures earlier and, having accumulated a sizeable reserve in anticipation of restructuring, did not require a bailout during the crisis. Nonetheless, Ford supported the bailout of the other two companies and accessed a number of other subsidies. See J Stanford, 'The geography of auto globalization and the politics of auto bailouts' (2010) 3 *Cambridge Journal of Regions, Economy and Society* 383, 397.

[83] Ibid, 396.

[84] Ibid, 400.

[85] See CAW, *Re-thinking Canada's Auto Industry* (n 78) 8.

[86] Ibid.

[87] Stanford, 'The geography of auto globalization' (n 82) 401; CAW, *Re-thinking Canada's Auto Industry* (n 78) 6.

catalysed a significant redistribution of power and resources as between the companies and their workers.[88] The effort to move to non-union wage levels may produce less in the way of immediate cost-savings than is supposed, at least in Canada where wages are comparable across union and non-union plants.[89] Nonetheless, the changes are crucial to workers' bargaining power and to benchmark norms, wages and benefits across the industry as a whole over the long term. The deliberate humbling of unions, especially in the form of official policy rather than mere private preference, is therefore a landmark moment.[90]

No concept of workers' fundamental or legislated rights, or even acquired contractual rights, restrained these concessions. Indeed, in a highly-illustrative comparison, collective agreements were subject to mandatory renegotiation while the contractually-guaranteed bonuses of bankers were treated as sacrosanct under claims of *pacta sunt servanda*, even a matter of respect for the rule of law.[91] This was so even though the banks received far greater financial support from their respective governments during the crisis,[92] and continue to benefit to the present day from ongoing subsidies through access to the Federal Reserve's discount window.[93]

These differential approaches to employment contracts surely reflect an interweaving of political power and economic interests. However the insistence on non-union wages as the benchmark for workers in the automotive industry, simultaneous with the support for the contracts of bankers, also discloses the underlying ideology and analytic assumptions concerning markets, law, and the relationship between them: undistorted markets are those without collectively negotiated wages and benefits, while contracts concluded under private law rules can only be tampered with at grave peril to the integrity of the legal order itself.

The situation was quite different elsewhere: in no other jurisdiction were contract renegotiations required as a condition of financing,[94] nor did labour cost reductions occupy the central place in crisis management that they did in North America. Instead, overarching considerations included the preservation of automotive jobs, itself linked to the maintenance of industry market share, as well as concerns about overall levels of unemployment. To this end, industry support strategies included job sharing, reduced hours and short-week arrangements, and wage subsidies. In Germany, for example, workers in the automotive industry accepted a temporary reduction in income that was partly offset by government subsidies. This strategy was widely regarded as successful, as it both avoided layoffs and enabled employers to resume full production at an early stage, although temporary, contract and agency workers lost their jobs in large numbers at the same time.

---

[88] See 'Motor vehicles and parts' under 'Manufacturing, Transportation' from 2002–2012 at Bureau of Labour Statistics, available at www.bls.gov/webapps/legacy/cesbtab1.htm. The resulting chart shows a loss of around 450,000 jobs over the displayed period of years.

[89] *A study of the crisis in the automotive sector in Canada: Report of the Standing Committee on Industry, Science and Technology* (Ottawa, Canada Parliament, House of Commons, 2009) available at www.parl.gc.ca/HousePublications/Publication.aspx?Language=E&Mode=1&Parl=40&Ses=2&DocId=3783523&File=0.

[90] Stanford, 'The geography of auto globalization' (n 82) 384.

[91] 'We are a country of law. There are contracts. The government cannot just abrogate contracts', Larry Summers quoted in 'Summers: AIG Bonus Bombshell "Outrageous"' (*ABC News*, 15 March 2009) available at abcnews.go.com/blogs/politics/2009/03/summers-on-aig.

[92] The banks have been bailed out to the tune of roughly $245 billion versus the under $80 billion to auto companies. See ProPublica, *Bailout Tracker*, see projects.propublica.org/bailout/main/summary.

[93] S Johnson and J Kwak, *13 Bankers: The Wall Street Takeover and the Next Financial Meltdown* (New York, Pantheon Books, 2010); Stiglitz, *The Price of Inequality* (n 20) 49.

[94] Stanford, 'The geography of auto globalization' (n 82) 401.

Outside of North America, plant closures were also rare to non-existent, in part because of laws restraining efforts to simply impose the costs of downturns on labour.[95]

Especially in light of the approach undertaken elsewhere, it is difficult to resist the conclusion that the signal example made of workers and unions in the automotive industry in North America during the crisis had a source beyond mere economic calculation. For example, the insistence on the use of non-union plants as the benchmark failed to reflect the fact that unionised plants are, on average, more productive than non-union plants.[96] North American labour costs in the automotive industry are not high in comparison to other highly successful automotive-producing countries such as Germany, Japan and Korea.[97] The high productivity across the sector as a whole is, under neoclassical economic analysis, a *justification* for higher wages in any event. It had been recognised well before the crisis that the North American producers were in trouble due to long-standing design and management problems.[98] Given that wage costs represented only about 3 to 4 per cent of unit vehicle costs, even in the supposed high-wage jurisdiction of Canada, wage levels never could have been the proximate cause of the crisis in the North American automotive industry.[99] Market share, debt servicing and even advertising costs were much more significant to the emergence of financial problems in the industry even before the crisis.[100] A significant percentage of any labour cost differentials appear to simply reflect speculative pressures on currency markets in any event.[101] In short, there are any number of standard economic rationales on which the existing wage structure might have been defended. In the context of widespread industrial subsidies[102] and set against other cost-savings that were not even considered, let alone attempted,[103] the focus on union wages alone, then, appears nakedly ideological.

But the best illustration of the new labour relations norms enabled by the crisis may lie in the tactics adopted by a firm which was completely outside the official restructuring process and the circumstances of which, moreover, were normal rather than critical. Caterpillar, a heavy equipment manufacturer, demanded a 50 per cent pay cut from their workers at their locomotive plant in London, Ontario, in 2011 as the price of renegotiating a collective agreement, locking its workers out and then permanently closing the plant and moving production to the 'right-to-work' state of Indiana when the offer was refused.[104] No pressing economic necessity occasioned the demand; the company was globally successful and highly profitable.[105] Instead, it seems to be only the most extreme manifestation of the perception that collectively bargained demands could, and should, be resisted.

---

[95] CAW, *Re-thinking Canada's Auto Industry* (n 78) 6–7.

[96] Stanford, 'The geography of auto globalization' (n 82).

[97] Ibid, 391–94.

[98] Canadian Parliament, *Report of the Standing Committee* (n 89) 12.

[99] CAW, *Re-thinking Canada's Auto Industry* (n 78) 20; J Stanford, 'Wage-Cutting as Industrial Strategy: Rejoinder to Shiell and Somerville' (2012) *Institute for Research and Public Policy*, available at www.irpp.org/pubs/IRPPstudy/IRPP_Study_no28_commentary.pdf.

[100] J Stanford, 'Auto Labour Costs and Auto Recovery' (8 August 2011) Progressive Economics Forum available at www.progressive- economics.ca/2011/08/12/auto-labour-costs-and-auto-industry-recovery.

[101] Stanford, 'Wage-Cutting as Industrial Strategy' (n 99) 393.

[102] Stanford, 'The geography of auto globalization' (n 82); Canadian Parliament, *Report of the Standing Committee* (n 89).

[103] Stanford, 'Wage Cutting as Industrial Strategy' (n 99).

[104] See, G McDonnell and J Wrinn, 'Lockout Precedes Diesel Plant's Closure' (2012) 72 *Trains* 9.

[105] Ibid.

IX. Towards a Future Law of Work?

At first glance, the crisis-driven reforms to labour law, employment contracts and pensions seem both directly and obviously adverse to workers' interests. Especially when accompanied by cuts to public services, as was typically the case, it is hard to avoid concluding that many workers received a substantial cut to their social wage. Yet the effects of other fiscal and monetary decisions are more complex and ambiguous. Reforms interact, both with each other and with existing or 'baseline' rules and policies. Even a preliminary effort to assess their effects fractures any (remaining) idea that there could be a single worker's interest at stake in any event; in some cases, we can identify winners as well as losers. But whether they are positive or negative, there seems to be no real question of their immense effects, potential and actual, on workers.

There are reasons to think that some of the adverse outcomes for workers flow from the displacement of strategies to politically manage distributive conflict between labour and capital.[106] The commitment to fiscal austerity and labour market flexibility, especially as the labour market picture continues to deteriorate, also suggests a degree of cognitive capture. Should we, in addition, think about all of these practices as legal developments? Here are some suggestions about why we might.

Post-crisis, it is easier to see that the identification of a labour law should be taken as a question rather than a 'fact'. Not only have fiscal and monetary policy emerged as part of the machinery that regulates labour markets. It is (more) clear how specific decisions might have an impact on the bargaining power as well as the jobs of workers; we can see how access to resources, including those that are crucial to labour market participation, might be diminished or closed off; we can observe how workers, as taxpayers, can be assigned residual economic risk; and we can observe that workers might well be worse off even as the economy as a whole stabilises or 'recovers'. In short, the crisis provides an unusually clear window on the material consequences of a wide range of law and policy choices for workers.

The crisis has also illustrated the extent to which economic policy and regulatory decisions made in one jurisdiction may generate spillovers in the labour markets of others. Some of those decisions may be more dispositive of the terms and conditions of work than *any* regulatory or policy decision made in the domestic realm, confirming in yet another way the observation that labour law is, actually, already transnational.

Beyond this are two inter-related observations. First, the restructuring demanded in the course of the crisis, whether directed to public or private sector workers, should themselves be seen as a species of (labour) law. Changes imposed by fiat and mandated by the law governing the terms of financial assistance clearly prevailed over the rules that would otherwise have governed the employment contracts in question. Think of this as labour law reform by extraordinary means, new in form, but recognisably labour law in substance or outcome.

Second, actions taken in times of crisis can be expected to have an ongoing impact on collective bargaining entitlements as well as labour standards in general. How far, and with what effect, is still hard to discern. But the ease with which legal entitlements were

---

[106] W Streeck, 'The crises of democratic capitalism' (2011) 71 *New Left Review* 5.

eliminated, in some cases wiping out gains won through generations of bargaining, may well induce both governments and private firms to redraw contracts in the future under claim of overriding economic pressure. Thus, the decisions made in times of crisis call into question the extent to which ordinary labour standards and collective bargaining rules still represent good *law*. The explicit adoption of a non-union benchmark for automotive wages in North America undercut the premises as well as the results of collective bargaining. But the widespread policy decisions to (attempt to) abate the financial crisis through internal wage and job cuts demonstrates a similar contempt for basic norms and policy objectives of labour and employment law: redressing inequality and imbalances of bargaining power; ensuring that there is a floor under labour contracts; enabling worker voice in the determination of working conditions; and so on. Following the crisis, we might expect more firms to adopt a strategy of 'permanent restructuring', that is, continuous, opportunistic interventions to undercut the role of unions and decrease the returns that go to workers.[107] But reform strategies may also generate recursive effects on labour market institutions themselves, expanding and entrenching norms of labour market flexibility.

If so, one possible future—by no means inevitable—is that more workers in core, industrialised states will find themselves in a position approximating those in informal markets. As labour market institutions recede in importance and it becomes more difficult to legally (if not actually) distinguish workers from other commercial actors, the other rules and policies that operate on labour markets will come more sharply into view. At that point, the broader law of work that has mostly been in the background until recently will be starkly evident.

---

[107] See E Siemiatycki, 'Forced to Concede: Permanent Restructuring and Labour's Place in the North American Auto Industry' (2012) 44 *Antipode* 453.

11

The Trouble with Identity and Progressive Origins in Defending Labour Law

ALVARO SANTOS[*]

> Just like France, after its Revolution, had the great honour of consecrating in the first of its Constitutions the immortal rights of men, so will the Mexican Revolution have the legitimate pride to show the world that it is the first one to consecrate in a Constitution the sacred rights of workers.
>
> Alfonso Cravioto, Address to the 1916–17 Constitutional Assembly [1]

I. Introduction

Debate about labour regulation is not new. What is new is the urgency with which labour law reform is promoted as an important fix to economic woes. In recent years, calls for reform have resounded in poor and rich countries alike. The economic crisis in the United States and in Europe has intensified these debates, making labour regulation a prime target for reform. In several US states public sector unions have been under attack, depicted as a privileged class that drains public funds with high wages, cosy benefits and retirement privileges that no other workers enjoy. Several European countries have introduced austerity measures that target labour regulation and other foundations of the welfare state as sources of economic waste that they can no longer afford. Moreover, it is argued that 'rigid' labour regulation hampers job creation, which can be strengthened through a programme of making labour more flexible.

On the other hand, there is considerable opposition to labour flexibility from labour activists and scholars who seek to defend the current structure. They regard today's job stability and benefits as historical achievements and fundamental rights. Defenders of labour regulation want to preserve workers' protections, which they see as the last line of defence against enormous pressure from global capital, and resist the rhetoric of flexibility, which they see as the handmaiden of capital.

[*] I would like to thank Harry Arthurs, Dennis Davis, Jorge Esquirol, Michael Fischl, Diego López-Medina, Alejandro Lorite, Naomi Mezey, David Kennedy, Duncan Kennedy, Nina Pillard, Kerry Rittich, Chantal Thomas, David Trubek, and Philomila Tsoukala for conversations and helpful comments on this project. Rachel Evans and Carolyn Cadena provided excellent research assistance.

[1] *Diario de los Debates del Congreso Constituyente, 1916–1917* (Mexico, Imprenta de la Secretaria de Gobernación, 1960).

The dire situation of the labour movement worldwide is reflected in the crisis of labour law as an academic field. The field is in a state of soul-searching, with scholars attempting to determine how labour scholarship can grapple with the defeat of the traditional labour movement and with conditions in the global economy that make its recovery seem impossible.[2]

In this article, I examine two prominent arguments which opponents of labour flexibility have used to defend labour regulation: that labour regulation is closely associated with a nation's identity; and that it is inherently progressive. These arguments have been widely used in national debates in countries with strong traditions of social regulation and welfare state institutions. Resonances of these strands of argument can also be seen in regional debates, such as the debate about 'Social Europe' and the future of social regulation in Europe in light of further market economic integration.

This article focuses on the case of Mexico to show both these arguments' appeal and their drawbacks. Mexico proudly considers itself to be the first country to constitutionalise workers' rights and, for much of its modern life, has seen itself as a social state. In the 1980s, however, Mexico introduced an economic liberalisation programme that has had profound effects on its labour market and social security institutions. Liberal reformers characterise labour law as a key, pending, structural reform to help the country get on a path to economic growth. Defenders of labour regulation see it as one of the last bastions against an economic model that has thus far produced meagre growth and has increased social and economic inequality.

Challenging Mexico's historical narrative, I show how social law was, and still is, a truly transnational phenomenon, not necessarily associated with any one nation's identity. In addition, I examine how, even at the moment of its creation, social law was—and still is—politically indeterminate and thus its inherent association with progressive politics is unwarranted. Finally, I argue that the constitutionalisation of social rights does not guarantee progressive results. These critiques are relevant to the current debate about labour regulation in Mexico, where political actors refer to the great achievements of the constitution to defend existing regulation. This defence fails to engage critiques about the effects of social regulation on different groups of workers and on the economy in general. Social law advocates that use these arguments are prone to idealise existing social regulation, making it harder to consider potential alternatives. Ironically, neo-liberal advocates for labour flexibility have begun to use social law to justify their agenda, reinforcing the assertion that social rights are politically indeterminate.

These insights from Mexico may be relevant to contemporary debates about social regulation elsewhere. In particular, I examine the strong parallels between Mexico and the debate about social regulation in Europe. In the European Union (EU), the project of market economic integration is said to have undermined workers' rights and social entitlements at the national level. Those seeking to advance similar social protections at the regional level have done so on identity terms, speaking of 'Social Europe' as reflecting the continent's true self in need of institutionalisation. These advocates have sought to constitutionalise social rights at the European level to ensure those protections. At the same time, those who regard further economic integration as a threat resist it on identity terms at the national level, seeking to preserve the social protections of the welfare state. Both regionally

---

[2] See, eg G Davidov and B Langille (eds), *The Idea of Labour Law* (Oxford, Oxford University Press, 2011).

and nationally, resorting to social law is supposed to advance progressive aspirations and resist the unfettered march of the market. Relying on national—or regional—identity to justify social regulation, however, creates problems similar to those found in Mexico: failing to engage arguments about the effects of social law and preventing the invention of alternatives. At this moment of crisis for the euro zone, when monetary union's viability is being tested, social law discourse has been employed by the EU even as it pursues an austerity agenda; this indicates that the political valence of this discourse is again in flux.

The chapter is divided into three sections. In the first section, I analyse the traditional narrative of labour law in Mexico and challenge its historical claims to national identity and progressive politics. I use the case of Mexico, the country that first enshrined workers' rights in a constitution, as a paradigmatic example of both the appeal and the pitfalls of the social law position. I examine the insights that the critique of the traditional narrative may contribute to the current debate about labour law in Mexico. In the second section, I explore the caveats that the Mexican case may raise for debates about social regulation elsewhere, particularly in Europe. I analyse how identity arguments play an important role in the concept of 'Social Europe' and the regulations or social provisions that are assumed to be inherent to the nature of the EU. I also show how some European countries have used a national identity argument to defend their social regulation against what they perceive to be a threatening pro-market EU integration programme. In the third section, I examine what could be gained by abandoning identity-based arguments and, instead, analysing labour reform as part of a country's overall development strategy.

II. The Case of Mexico and Its Labour Regulation

The reader might not know this, but the idea of social law and the constitutionalisation of workers' rights originated in Mexico. Well, not quite. But that is, in a simplified way, the traditional narrative in Mexico's labour law scholarship. The idea of social law emerged as a critique of classical legal thought in the late nineteenth century and was developed by German and French jurists. These scholars challenged nineteenth-century classical legal liberalism's individualistic assumptions, critiqued its abuse of logical deduction and condemned its social and economic consequences.[3]

Social law jurists argued that individualistic classical liberal law was inadequate to deal with new, interdependent relations brought about by the industrialisation, urbanisation, economic globalisation and deep social changes of the late nineteenth century.[4] These scholars laid the foundations for and helped develop a new legal sphere called social law, doctrinally situated between traditional private law and public law, in which the state was an active participant. This new sphere introduced legal regimes we now associate with the regulatory state, such

---

[3] See D Kennedy, 'Three Globalizations of Law and Legal Thought: 1850–2000' in D Trubek and A Santos (eds), *The New Law and Economic Development: A Critical Appraisal* (Cambridge, Cambridge University Press, 2006) 37–40; G Gurvitch, *Le Temps Présent et L'idée du Droit Social* (Paris, J Vrin, 1932); M Reimann 'Continental Imports—The Influence of European Law and Jurisprudence in the United States' (1996) 64 *Tijdschrift Voor Rechtsgeschiedenis* 391, 398–99.
[4] Kennedy, ibid, 38.

LIVERPOOL JOHN MOORES UNIVERSITY
LEARNING SERVICES

as labour legislation, social security, housing law, sanitary law and financial regulation.[5] After World War I, there was also the rise of a new international law regime to deal with war that created new institutions based on the idea of interdependence.[6]

Social law is paradoxical. Although it spread globally from Germany and France to become a truly international phenomenon, it was understood as having a unique relation to the particular society of each country where it took hold. Social law was often considered to be grounded on some primordial, traditional or religious character of each society that claimed it.[7]

Mexico provides a useful case study of the use of nationalism by social law advocates. Mexico prides itself on its social legal system, which emerged out of the 1910 Revolution, was enshrined in the 1917 Constitution and has a self-image of being very progressive. The national identity justification of social law is not limited to labour regulation but, indeed, exists in other domains. Establishing a communal form of land ownership, in the form of *ejido*, was justified as an explicit opposition to the liberal and individualistic property rights system and a return to pre-liberal and colonial forms of land-tenure.[8] The defence of the legal regime of natural resources, such as oil and water, is also often justified on national identity terms.

When it comes to labour regulation, two main claims permeate the traditional narrative of Mexican labour law textbooks: first, that labour law is of Mexican origin, and second, that labour regulation is inherently progressive and helps all workers. Mexican labour law scholarship has helped shape and sustain the idea that social law stemmed from a unique Mexican reality—triggering the 1910 Mexican Revolution—and that workers' rights were inserted in the 1917 Constitution thanks to the genius of Mexican intellectuals, scholars and politicians.[9] The fact that the 1917 Mexican Constitution was the first in the world to enshrine workers' rights has lent credibility to these claims. Mexican jurists argue that, just as France gave the world the first Declaration of the Rights of Man, Mexico gave the world the first Declaration of Social Rights. The inauguration of this social legal system within the

---

[5] Ibid, 38–39.

[6] The International Labour Organization (ILO) was founded by the Treaty of Versailles in 1919 to deal with the 'labour question', which was of increasing concern among Western powers and a potential source of international conflict. Its constitution stated that 'conditions of labour exist involving such injustice hardship and privation to large numbers of people as to produce unrest so great that the peace and harmony of the world are imperilled.' See Constitution of the ILO from 28 June 1919, 49 Stat 2712, 2713–14, 225 Consol TS 373, Preamble. The legal regime of labour law, which supersedes classical conceptions of property and contract, has conceptual parallels with a new international law regime that supersedes classical concepts of sovereignty. Both fields were influenced by social law ideas. This parallel is exemplified by the work of George Scelle, a French jurist who started out as a labour scholar and later became a renowned international law scholar. See, eg G Scelle, *Le Droit Ouvrier: Tableau de la Législation Française Actuelle* (Paris, Armand Colin, 1932); G Scelle, *Manuel Élémentaire de Droit International Public* (Paris, Domat-Montchrestien, 1943).

[7] Kennedy, 'Three Globalizations of Law and Legal Thought' (n 3) 46–50; see, eg A Shalakany, 'Sanhuri and the Historical Origins of Comparative Law in the Arab World' in A Riles (ed), *Rethinking the Masters of Comparative Law* (Portland, Hart Publishing, 2001), justifying the civil code socialisation by Sanhouri in Egypt as grounded on Islamic tradition. See also S Kan'gara, *Analytical, Prescriptive and Resistant Characterizations of 'African' Conceptions of Property: A Critique of Mainstream Assumptions about African-Western Incompatibility* SJD Dissertation (Cambridge, MA, Harvard Law School, 2003), on how the social function of property in Africa was justified using indigenous ideas.

[8] See A Nuñez Luna, *Water Law and the Making of the Mexican State, 1875–1917* SJD Dissertation, (Cambridge, MA, Harvard Law School, 2011); EN Simpson, *The Ejido: Mexico's Way Out* (Chapel Hill, UNC Press, 1937).

[9] See, eg A Noriega Cantú, *Los Derechos Sociales, Creación de la Revolución de 1910 y de la Constitución de 1917* (Mexico, Universidad Nacional Autónoma de México, 1988).

1917 Constitution has been closely associated with a progressive Mexican state. The native and progressive characteristics of the social state are so central to the state's identity that to challenge them is to question its foundational justifications. It amounts to unveiling the state's main foundational fictions.[10]

One way to think about the traditional labour law narrative is that Mexico has an originalist constitutional tradition that is progressive and associated with the left. Think of the work of Frank Michelman and William Forbath, depicting a social tradition in the US, wherein welfare rights (work, housing, health) can be based on the constitution.[11] Now imagine that this stance represents the mainstream position.

This section analyses mainstream labour law scholarship in Mexico. I focus particularly on the work of Mario de la Cueva, the foremost labour law scholar and one of the main architects in constructing the legal foundation for the social state. He imagined, argued and worked for the reconstruction of the Mexican legal system around social law.[12] I suggest that De la Cueva is to the Mexican twentieth-century legal system what Diego Rivera is to Mexican art—not because of equal fame or notoriety, but because they shared a passion and a vision about the new social order, and created an aesthetic and legal narrative to support it. Rivera heralds the post-Revolution Mexican state as the modern response to colonialism and economic exploitation. Rivera's murals are an elegy to the new man, the worker, emancipated from his past chains. De la Cueva paints the legal regime that would ensure workers' liberation.

Rivera depicts the country in a path of industrialisation, where nineteenth-century bourgeois capitalism, the old economic regime against which the Revolution rebelled, is superseded by a socialist state. The character of that social state is still not fully defined, but it becomes clear early on that it is not a communist state. De la Cueva's murals are his major Mexican labour law textbooks, which create, document and justify this story in legal theory and doctrine. Describing the creation of Mexican labour law, De la Cueva tells us:

> Mexican labour law is a statute imposed by life, a cry by men that only knew of exploitation and ignored the meaning of the term: my rights as a human being. It was born in the first social revolution of the 20th century and found its most beautiful historic crystallisation in the 1917 Constitution. Before those years there were efforts in defence of men, actions were undertaken and ideas presented, but a regime that gave back to work its liberty and dignity had not been achieved; they were lost in the centuries of slavery, of servitude and of the bourgeoisie's private law. The idea that has now reached a universal character had not been declared: labour law constitutes the new rights of the human person, the base without which the old rights of men are not possible.[13]

This section problematises this traditional narrative, most articulately formulated by De la Cueva. I argue first that the critique of nineteenth-century private law and the proposal

---

[10] I borrow the term 'foundational fictions' from Doris Sommer, who argued that the late nineteenth- and early twentieth-century novels in Latin America intended to foster a 'passionate patriotism' in the new nations. See D Sommer, *Foundational Fictions: The National Romances of Latin America* (Berkeley, University of California Press, 1991).

[11] See, eg F Michelman, 'The Supreme Court, 1968 Term—Foreword: On Protecting the Poor through the Fourteenth Amendment' (1969) 83 *Harvard Law Review* 7 (arguing that equality of opportunity is consistent with the Equal Protection Clause of the US Constitution); F Michelman, 'In Pursuit of Constitutional Welfare Rights: One View of Rawls' Theory of Justice' (1973) 121 *University of Pennsylvania Law Review* 962 (discussing John Rawls' theory of inherent welfare rights based on the tradition of 'western individualistic democratic liberalism'); W Forbath, 'The Distributive Constitution and Workers' Rights' (2011) 72 *Ohio State Law Journal* 1115 (depicting the history and significance of labour and workers rights as fundamental rights).

[12] See M De la Cueva, *El Nuevo Derecho del Trabajo*, 13th edn (Mexico, Editorial Porrúa, 1993).

[13] Ibid, vol 1, 38.

for social law as a way to overcome the doctrinal limitations and undesirable economic consequences of legal liberalism was not purely Mexican in origin. Second, I claim that the nature of the political compromise that enabled the constitutionalisation of labour rights and the creation of new social law institutions was less radical at its inception, and less progressive as applied, than is commonly portrayed.

Before subjecting the traditional narrative to scrutiny, however, I describe its relevance in the current labour reform debates. Political parties, activists and scholars refer to the achievements of the constitution and the historically-progressive character of labour legislation to buttress their positions. Exploring the grip this narrative has on the way actors think and talk about labour regulation clarifies the relevance of its critique and the possibilities that may open if we go beyond it.

A. The Debate about Labour Law Reform in Mexico

Labour law reform has been the subject of political debate in Mexico for the last 22 years, since liberalisation reforms were introduced by the Salinas administration between 1988 and 1994. In this protracted debate, the achievements of the Revolution and the historical legacy of the Mexican Constitution play an important, if not always explicit, role. The nationalist discourse that emerged after the Mexican Revolution, created and consolidated during seven decades of a one-state-party system in which the Institutional Revolutionary Party (PRI) ruled, praised constitutionally-protected workers' rights and labour legislation as a historical achievement. This legislation was considered to be a key pillar of the country's modern social, economic and political life. Today, more than two decades after the introduction of economic liberalisation policies, labour law reform is considered to be a 'pending' structural reform and is once again at the centre of political debate. Since 1990, multiple proposals have been introduced, including bills by the three main political parties: the centre-right National Action Party (PAN), which ruled the country in 2000–2012, the leftist Democratic Revolution Party (PRD) and, in 2011, the PRI. After the 2012 presidential elections and with a newly-elected Congress, outgoing President Calderón introduced a labour bill on which Congress will be required to vote.[14]

The Constitution and federal labour law grant substantial protections to workers. They took employment relations out of the civil law domain and created the country's social security system. In 1917, Article 123 enshrined workers' rights in the Mexican Constitution and granted workers considerable protections.[15] Based on these constitutional rights, federal labour law regulates the labour market in great detail, dealing with both individual and collective employment relations. Article 123 seeks to establish an equilibrium between

---

[14] *Proyecto Decreto que Reforma, Adiciona y Deroga Diversas Disposiciones de la Ley Federal del Trabajo*, LXII Legislature (1 September 2012) available at www.stps.gob.mx/bp/secciones/sala_prensa/Ini_Ref_Laboral_2012.pdf.

[15] See Political Constitution of the United Mexican States (hereinafter Mexican Constitution) Art 123 (1917), which includes the following requirements and provisions: eight-hour maximum workday; minimum one day off per week; double payment for overtime work; prohibition on child labour; paid maternity leave; right to equal pay for equal work regardless of gender; establishment of a minimum living wage; wage protection against discounts or reductions for debt obligations; establishment of employers' liability for workplace accidents and illnesses; establishment of workers' right to a share in the firm's profits; employers' compliance with health and safety regulations; housing requirements for certain sectors; recognition of the right to unionise and the right to strike; prevention of employers dismissing workers without cause; and establishment of a tri-partite arbitral and conciliation board to solve disputes between capital and labour, staffed by government representatives, employers and workers.

workers and employers, and to advance social justice.[16] It stipulates that labour is not an article of commerce; it should safeguard workers' freedom and dignity and guarantee a decent standard of living.[17] Importantly, federal labour law's procedural section is guided by a default rule which stipulates that whenever there is doubt in the interpretation of the law, the Conciliation and Arbitral Board will choose the one that favours workers.[18] The Board is also required to supplement the briefs submitted by workers when they do not request benefits they are entitled to.[19]

Despite these generous protections, Mexico's labour market is in dire straits. The working population totals approximately 50 million people.[20] Every year, one million youths become economically active and ready to enter the labour market; the country's economy has been able to create only half the jobs needed.[21] People migrate to the US to find jobs, but many enter the informal economy by working on petty street commerce or enter the ranks of drug cartels or other criminal organisations.[22] Unemployment is approximately 5.4 per cent, but this number does not capture a significant number of workers: the approximately 8.3 per cent who are underemployed.[23] Of the employed, a great number have very precarious jobs, with meagre wages and no benefits. In fact, real minimum wages have declined dramatically in the last four decades.[24] This suggests that even in the formal economy there is a wide de facto flexibility in the labour market due to low wages, informal or illegal part-time contracting by employers, outsourcing and the non-provision of legally-mandated benefits. This further suggests that a considerable part of the productivity gains in recent years have relied on decreased labour costs. Consequently, the share of productivity gains to labour in general terms has decreased.[25]

---

[16] Federal Labour Law of Mexico (*Ley Federal de Trabajo*) Art 2.

[17] Ibid, Art 3.

[18] Ibid, Art 18.

[19] Ibid, Art 685.

[20] Instituto Nacional de Estadística y Geografía (INEGI), *Indicadores Oportunos de Ocupación Y Empleo* ['Job Indicators'] from 2012, available at www.inegi.org.mx/inegi/contenidos/espanol/prensa/comunicados/ocupbol.pdf.

[21] E Zepeda, T Wise and K Gallagher, *Rethinking Trade Policy for Development: Lessons From Mexico Under NAFTA*, (Washington DC, Carnegie Endowment for International Peace, 2009); J Kurtzman, 'Mexico's Job-Creation Problem' *Wall Street Journal* (3 August 2007) available at online.wsj.com/article/SB118610985048187068.html.

[22] From 1990 to 2010, approximately 8.9 million Mexicans migrated to the US. A recent report, however, found that migration has declined significantly in the last five years. See 'The Mexican-American Boom: Births Overtake Immigration' (2011) *Pew Hispanic Center Report*, 3, available at www.pewhispanic.org/files/reports/144.pdf. Possible explanations include: increased unemployment in the US; a increased deportations from the US; a spike of violence in the border area; decreasing birth rates; and broader economic opportunities in Mexico. See also 'Net Migration from Mexico Falls to Zero—and Perhaps Less' (2012) *Pew Hispanic Center Report*, available at www.pewhispanic.org/files/2012/04/Mexican-migrants-report_final.pdf.

[23] Instituto Nacional de Estadística y Geografía (INEGI), *Indicadores Oportunos de Ocupación Y Empleo* [Job Indicators] from 2011, available at www.inegi.org.mx/inegi/contenidos/espanol/prensa/comunicados/ocupbol.asp.

[24] 'The real minimum wages in 2000 represented only a third of those of 1980; national wages in 2000 were equivalent to 50 per cent of those of 1980. By 2000, wages and salaries in large manufacturing plants had dropped to less than 40 per cent of their level in 1990.' C Salas and E Zepeda, 'Empleo y Salarios en el Mexico Contemporáneo' in E de la Garza and C Salas (eds), *La Situacion del Trabajo en Mexico* (México, Instituto de Estudios del Trabajo, 2003), 55; D Fairris, G Popli and E Zepeda, 'Minimum Wages and the Wage Structure in Mexico' (University of California Riverside, July 2005), available at economics.ucr.edu/papers/papers05/05-09.pdf, 4, 23, 28; Zepeda, Wise and Gallagher, *Rethinking Trade Policy* (n 21) 13–14.

[25] EH Laos, *La productividad en Mexico: Origen y Distribución 1960–2002* in C Salas (ed), *La Nueva, Situación del Trabajo en Mexico 2000–2003* (Mexico City, Instituto de Estudio del Trabajo, 2006) 161, 168–69. Although productivity has remained low in Mexico from 1988 to 2002, workers transferred much of their productivity gains to employers. See also S Polanski, *Mexican Employment, Productivity, and Income a Decade After NAFTA*, Brief

Now consider the reform proposals advanced by the main political parties. Over the past 12 years, each of the two government administrations headed by the PAN has introduced a labour law bill. These bills proposed making labour market regulation more flexible by creating new part-time, trial and training employment contracts. They also proposed changes to collective bargaining rules that would make it harder for workers to strike, prohibit closed-shop agreements, and prevent the automatic withholding of union fees by the employer. The PAN also proposes to introduce transparency and union democracy by requiring free and secret elections (for strikes, control over collective agreements and union leadership), imposing the obligation for unions to publish their balance sheets and make them available to members, and requiring the publication of unions' registration, collective agreements and firms' internal workplace regulations.

Opposition to the PAN bills has come from different sectors. These include the left-wing PRD, unions, activists, NGOs and labour law scholars. Many have emphasised the bill's violation of fundamental workers' rights recognised not only in the Mexican Constitution but also in international conventions. In their view, the PAN bills sought to introduce the neo-liberal flexibility agenda, which jeopardised fundamental workers' rights and threatened to impoverish workers and weaken unions. Activists referred to the conquests of the Mexican Revolution and the achievements of the Constitution as a way to resist the neo-liberal programme, often portrayed as an imported economic agenda designed abroad and supported by employers, foreign economic interests and international financial institutions. In addition, a number of independent unions and NGOs brought a complaint before NAFTA's National Administrative Office, claiming the bill violated NAFTA's labour side agreement.[26] Faced with the PAN's bills, many groups on the left have preferred the status quo.

On the left wing, the PRD and the Workers' National Union (UNT), an association of independent unions, have proposed a bill that seeks to: ensure stable and decent jobs in a manner that could be consistent with productivity gains; dismantle corporatist institutions that benefit official unions and stifle union democracy; and reform the dispute settlement system.[27] The PRD–UNT bill accepts some degree of flexibility, introducing, for instance, a limited version of the trial employment contract, but rejects other flexibility modalities, including the formalisation of outsourcing, proposed by the PAN and PRI. The bill emphasises that decisions on how to deploy labour to ensure productivity, including training and promotion, must be taken bilaterally.[28] It also proposes to index wages to

---

Submitted to the Canadian Standing Senate Committee on Foreign Affairs (Carnegie Endowment 2004), available at www.carnegieendowment.org/pdf/files/canadasenatebrief.pdf.

[26] See US NAO Public Submission US2005-01 from the Washington Office on Latin America, to US Department of Labor, Bureau of International Labor Affairs (17 February 2005) available at www.dol.gov/ilab/media/reports/nao/submissions/Sub2005-01.htm (requesting that the US National Administrative Office work with the Mexican government to eliminate alleged NAALC violations in the labour law reform proposal).

[27] *Gaceta Parlamentaria, Cámara de Diputados*, Número 2989-IV (15 April 2010) available at http://rendicion decuentas.org.mx/data/arch_segui/150410-5.doc

[28] Ibid, Art 116 Bis 2. To ensure that goal, it proposes the creation of a firm-level Mixed Commission for Productivity and Training, see Art 116 Bis 4. The bill requires firms to regularly send financial status reports to its workers, see Art 116 Bis 3. It also introduces some flexibility while preventing jobs becoming precarious via low wages, unstable jobs and scarce benefits, see Preamble. The bill recognises the importance of performance-based promotion along with seniority, as well as the importance of training workers for multiple tasks. See Art 159.

inflation to avoid a further decline in real wages.[29] On collective bargaining institutions, the PRD–UNT bill proposes the creation of an autonomous Public Registry, in charge of registering new unions and ownership over collective bargaining agreements, taking that role away from the Ministry of Labour. It keeps current rules that seek to resolve collective action problems. For instance, it partially keeps the closed shop agreement, requiring workers to become union members when they are hired—if the union and the employer have so agreed—but eliminates the closed shop by exclusion, enabling workers to exit the union without being fired. It also keeps rules that require employers to retain union fees. Finally, on administration of justice, the bill would eliminate the long-standing tri-partite Conciliation and Arbitration Boards and replace them with labour courts, staffed by independent judges under the jurisdiction of the judiciary.[30]

The PRI, which had opposed the labour law reform proposals made by this and the previous PAN administrations and the PRD, introduced its own bill in 2011.[31] The PRI's bill introduces significant forms of flexibility, leaves collective bargaining institutions largely untouched, and preserves the current dispute settlement system. First, it proposes a series of changes to the standard employment contract by introducing flexibility in hiring and firing.[32] It also seeks to formalise and regulate outsourcing, an extended employer practice that is currently illegal.[33] The government would remain in control of union registration, certification of elections and ownership of collective agreements.[34] It consolidates the conciliation and arbitration boards but leaves them as tri-partite bodies largely dependent on the executive power. Thus, it seems that the PRI bill seeks to compromise between two of its traditional constituencies. On the one hand, the bill seeks to satisfy employers who demand greater forms of flexibility in hiring and firing, limits to back-wages payments for unfair dismissal and greater control over the allocation of labour to multiple tasks and over promotion. On the other hand, the bill seeks to guarantee that traditional corporatist unions will continue to enjoy a great degree of control over collective bargaining institutions, keeping independent unions at bay. The government would continue to have considerable say in the unions' governance system, keeping decisions of registration, confirmation of leadership and collective agreement control in the Ministry of Labour.

After 12 years as the opposition, the PRI won the 2012 presidential election. As the party that controlled the presidency and pretty much all branches of government for more than seven decades—and as the creator of the national revolutionary discourse—the PRI's bill is indicative of the debate to come and the new government's agenda. In its Preamble, the PRI bill makes several references to the historical achievement of the 1917 Constitution in enshrining workers' rights:

---

[29] It proposes eliminating the current Minimum Wage National Commission, a tri-partite organisation composed of representatives of government, employers and official unions. Instead, the bill creates the National Institute for Wages, Productivity and Profit-Sharing, dependent on Congress and not on the Executive, see Art 90.

[30] PRD proposes to eliminate the distinction between Section A and Section B of Art 123, regulating private and public sector employment in the same way, see Preamble. This would grant public sector workers collective bargaining rights that they currently lack, primarily the right to strike.

[31] Propuesta que reforma, adiciona y deroga diversas disposiciones de la Ley Federal del Trabajo (PRI bill) Gaceta Parlamentaria Número 3218-II (2011).

[32] The bill introduces hourly wages and multiple forms of new contract terms that would enable widespread use of part-time, fixed-term, and trial employment, see ibid, 32, 40.

[33] Ibid, 24.

[34] Ibid, 23.

The 1917 Constitution created Article 123, which for the first time in history elevated labour law to the highest normative level. This was a fundamental decision, bedrock of the modern State that has received utmost recognition in the world.[35]

At every point, the bill declares that the proposed changes are necessary to improve the country's economic condition but are consistent with the historical achievements of the Constitution and respect workers' fundamental rights:

It is necessary to generate confidence in a private and international investment that creates jobs in the formal economy while observing the basic values of Article 123 and the basic rights of workers ... These rights must be well protected, as they have been since our first federal labour legislation from 1931, and as they should be, being an example for all social legislations in the world.[36]

The PRI revives the national revolutionary discourse to reach a compromise between supportive capital and official labour. It is not surprising that the bill preserves the privileges of the big labour unions traditionally affiliated to the PRI. However, the malleability of the social law discourse is significant: the PRI resorts to social law discourse to introduce a labour flexibility agenda, dear to business actors, that is anathema to many of the labour protections associated with the social position. It does so by appealing to national pride and vowing continuity with the very constitutional principles that the bill purports to modify.[37]

The stakes of labour reform are high. At root lie different visions of how to best increase firms' productivity, the relationship between labour and capital, the state's involvement in unions' governance system, collective bargaining and dispute settlement. These different visions have diametrically different implications for the distribution of power and resources between capital and labour, and for democracy in the workplace. Beyond the particular rules supported by the political parties, I am interested in a common theme in these bills that evokes the historical achievement of the Mexican Constitution. This trope is used both by those who want to oppose the neo-liberal flexibility programme and those who want to preserve the corporativist regime currently in place.

Why, then, is social law rhetoric, particularly concerning the constitutionalisation of social rights, so powerful in Mexico? Why does this alleged historical achievement remain so appealing in contemporary debates? It would be useful to investigate why it exerts so much influence: how it is that it still strikes a chord that seems to go to the very sense of selfhood of the nation? Or, conversely, if nobody believes in it any longer, if the once-faithful citizens have lost their faith, why do the dogmas of such national faith need to be invoked in the debate? Is this just a simulation, a currency political actors have to use

---

[35] Ibid, 20.

[36] Ibid, 21.

[37] As soon as Congress began its session in September 2012, outgoing president Calderón proposed a new labour bill that, under a recently-adopted legislative rule, requires Congress to approve the bill (or not) within 60 days. This bill is very similar to previous PAN bills and is an attempt by the government to leave office with a badge of passing a much-touted 'structural' reform. The bill was met with resistance by the left and provoked massive street demonstrations. The PRI, which now controls the House of Representatives, approved flexibility reforms to the employment contract but eliminated all proposals to democratise the union governance system. Thus, the PRI has achieved the same compromise between flexibility and corporatism it was seeking in its own bill. The PAN seemed willing to forego its union democracy proposals to achieve a labour reform and joined forces with PRI. After a heated debate and a few amendments the bill was finally passed, see Senate of Mexico, LXII Legislature, BOLETÍN-0481 'Avala Senado Reforma Laboral y Envía al Ejecutivo los Artículos Aprobados Por Ambas Cámaras', 13 November 2012.

in the public space, a faith they disbelieve in private but nonetheless profess in public? Whether this professed faith is the expression of an honest belief or a cynical position, it seems worth examining what lies behind this historical assumption. Subjecting this claim to critical scrutiny can shed light on what is at stake in the 'practice' of subscribing to it and reinforcing its validity.

In the following section, I examine Mexico's traditional labour law narrative, outlining its main claims and probing why it has such as grip on the way people think about Mexico's history and its future. As I show, legal scholars played a very important role in weaving a discourse about 'social law' that would become closely associated with the nation's character. Legal scholars' reconstruction of the legal system around the idea of social law, crystallised in the 1917 Constitution, would also be the reconstruction of the nation's self for a large part of the twentieth century.

B. Workers' Rights: A National Invention?

Mexican legal scholars emphasise the national invention of social and workers' rights, and consider Mexico's 1917 Constitution to be a significant contribution to the world's juris-prudential history as the first 'Declaration of Social Rights'. I have identified three main claims: (1) social and workers' rights are the result of the 1910 Mexican revolution and, thus, a response to Mexican socio-economic reality; (2) workers' rights are the invention of Mexican actors, be they intellectuals, revolutionary leaders, legal scholars, or politicians; and (3) workers' rights are the product of the 1917 Constitution and resulted from that historical constitutional debate.

These claims are prevalent in the traditional narrative of Mexican labour law scholar-ship. Affirmed by the canonical texts in the field and passed on to every generation of law students, there seems to be a strong interest in reinforcing the Mexican contribution to the origin of workers' rights and, more broadly, social rights. In this section, I explore these claims and, given the difficulty in sustaining this assumption, I begin to explore the possible reasons for maintaining a nationalistic narrative.

i. Workers' Rights as the Result of the 1910 Mexican Revolution

Traditional labour law scholarship considers the creation of workers' rights and of social rights in general to be an achievement of the 1910 Revolution.[38] According to this view, the revolution was a response to the oppressive social and economic conditions under which workers and peasants lived during the long dictatorship of Porfirio Diaz. This socio-economic reality inspired the development of workers' rights and labour law. According to de la Cueva, the 1917 Mexican Constitution is itself the first Declaration of Social Rights.[39] De la Cueva asserts that this Declaration 'stemmed from the tragedy and suffering of the

---

[38] The Mexican Revolution started in 1910 and lasted for a decade. For a comprehensive treatment of the Mexican Revolution see A Knight, *The Mexican Revolution, Vol 1: Porfirians, Liberals, and Peasants* (Lincoln, University of Nebraska Press, 1990) and A Knight, *The Mexican Revolution, Volume 2: Counter-revolution and Reconstruction* (Lincoln, University of Nebraska Press, 1990). See also J Womack, *Zapata and the Mexican Revolution* (New York, Vintage, 1970).

[39] De la Cueva, *Nuevo Derecho* (n 12) 44.

people, and it was a natural, genuine, and authentic creation of the Mexican people, of the men who offered their life in the war of the revolution'.[40]

The connection between the 1910 Mexican Revolution and the enactment of workers' rights is not as straightforward as the traditional narrative assumes. 'Social' legislation existed before the armed movement. De la Cueva himself references labour legislation in Mexico preceding the revolution. For instance, in the last decade of the dictatorial regime of Porfirio Diaz from 1900 to 1910, two Mexican states enacted pro-worker statutes. In 1904, the State of Mexico enacted a workers' compensation law for injuries caused by workplace accidents, making employers liable for health-care costs and full salary for up to three months.[41] In 1906, the state of Nuevo León also enacted a law for workplace accidents.[42]

Furthermore, according to de la Cueva, the interventionist government of Maximiliano of Habsburg—an Austrian prince imposed by the French government at the behest and with the collaboration of conservative groups in Mexico—enacted Mexico's first labour law, the 'Labour Law of the Empire' (1865).[43] As de la Cueva points out, this law contained some of the workers' benefits later enshrined in the 1917 Constitution.[44] It is telling that so many years before the Mexican revolution, Maximiliano, a European prince arguably detached from the reality of Mexican life, had implemented pro-worker legislation.[45] However, de la Cueva does not seem to give much importance to these historical precedents.

Examples in de la Cueva's books suggest that labour laws were enacted before the 1910 Revolution in at least two states. In fact, a foreign ruler had introduced pro-worker legislation as early as the mid-nineteenth century. This evidence weakens the assumption that only the revolution's unique context had influenced the content of the 1917 Constitution. In fact, existing legal doctrines and ideas about social law originating in Europe and circulating around the world also seem to have provided ammunition in the passing of this legislation. As I discuss below, the revolution may have accelerated the enactment of labour laws by different states throughout the country, and it may have given a justification to the members of the Constitutional Assembly for enshrining workers' rights in the Constitution, but the revolution cannot be considered the sole determinant.

ii. Workers' Rights as the Invention of Mexican Intellectuals and Legal Scholars

Another important argument in labour law scholarship posits that the intellectual origin of workers' rights in the country is entirely Mexican. Additionally, scholars argue that the various labour laws enacted in the country after the Revolution were entirely a domestic development and were not influenced by foreign laws. However, at the time, important ideas promoting the need to establish workers' rights were fermenting in the public debate transnationally. As I show, some of the main intellectuals and legislators promoting the recognition of workers' rights were participants in a transnational movement for labour rights and were influenced by social law discussions in other countries.

---

[40] Ibid.
[41] Ibid, 43.
[42] Ibid.
[43] Ibid, 41.
[44] Ibid.
[45] This may be viewed as an early attempt to import into Mexico some of the legal doctrinal developments and legislation in Europe at the time.

Influence of Foreign Ideas

In his book, *Social Rights: A Creation of the 1910 Revolution and of the 1917 Constitution*,[46] Alfonso Noriega Cantú, an influential Mexican legal scholar, attributed the origin of social rights to the Mexican Revolution and the Mexican Constitution. He explicitly addressed the question of whether the 1910 Mexican Revolution was inspired or influenced by Marx's ideas and those of other critics of the capitalist system.[47] Noriega contended that foreign theories had 'no influence whatsoever' on the actors of the Revolution or those who wrote the Constitution, and concluded that the 1910 Revolution 'formed its ideological content inspired in the Mexican historical reality'.[48]

In the course of arguing about the indigeneity of the 1910 Revolution, Noriega identifies several Mexican intellectuals who promoted the creation of social rights in the period before the Revolution.[49] These were the great critics of Porfirio Diaz's dictatorship whose critiques were expressed in the Programme of the Liberal Party of 1906 and Flores Magón's newspaper *Regeneración*, among other sources.[50] These ideas were articulated in the two most influential manifestos of the Revolution, the *Plan de San Luis* and *Plan de Ayala*, issued by revolutionary leaders Ignacio I Madero and Emiliano Zapata, respectively.[51] Unfortunately, Noriega neglected to investigate the intellectual background of the Mexican critics he refers to, especially the most central among them, Ricardo Flores Magón.

Consider Ricardo Flores Magón, whom Noriega and most labour law scholars recognise as an intellectual influence of the Revolution[52] and of labour law legislation.[53] Noriega failed to inquire into Flores Magón's background and did not notice that he was a participant in a transnational intellectual and political movement critiquing economic liberalism and promoting 'social law' ideas. Flores Magón's publications, along with a variety of biographies, highlight the influence of European and US thinkers on his liberal and anarchist political theories.[54] That Flores Magón was influenced by and was himself in conversation with foreign ideas and intellectuals does not diminish his intellectual stature or originality. It does, however, cast doubt on the assertion that social rights ideas, even those promoted by Flores Magón, were homegrown.

The Catholic Social Doctrine was an additional intellectual source in the creation of social law. The influence of social Catholicism in Mexico can be traced to the second half of nineteenth century.[55] Labour scholars have recognised the importance of this doctrine

---

[46] Cantú, *Derechos sociales* (n 9) 83.

[47] Ibid.

[48] Ibid.

[49] Ibid, 83.

[50] Ibid, 83.

[51] Ibid.

[52] De la Cueva also maintains that the 1906 Manifesto of the Liberal Party, over which Flores Magón presided, is 'the most important pre-revolutionary document in favor of the creation of a labour law'. De la Cueva *Nuevo Derecho* (n 12) 42.

[53] N de Buen—perhaps the most prominent labour law scholar in Mexico today—argues that Flores Magón's influence over some leaders eventually translated into specific legislation as the leaders seized power in a variety of states. N de Buen, *Derecho del Trabajo*, 2nd edn, vol 1 (Mexico, Editorial Porrúa, 2010) 334. For example, de Buen notes that General Manuel M Dieguez, one of the leaders of the strike of Cananea (1906) in which Flores Magón was greatly involved, later enacted a labour law for the state of Jalisco (1914); ibid, 330.

[54] See J Crockroft, *Intellecutal Precurosors of the Mexican Revolution 1900–1913* (Austin, University of Texas Press, 1968) 117–33; G García Cantú, *El Socialismo en Mexico. Siglo XIX*, 1st edn (Mexico, ERA, 1969) 120–29.

[55] García Cantú refers to the influence of Christian socialist Plotino C Rhodakanaty and his association called *La Social*. See García Cantú, ibid, 172–79.

in labour law in general, and in the Mexican labour regime in particular.[56] Notably, Pope
Leon XIII's *Rerum Novarum* advocated the reconciliation of social classes, affirming that
'without work there can be no capital, neither can there be work without capital'.[57] Among
its main postulates, the encyclical included respect for private property, conciliation of
classes, mutual cooperation for capitalist production and workers' welfare and unionisation to assure decent living conditions.[58] If these ideas had an impact in the creation of
labour legislation, it would be further evidence of influence of foreign ideas in the Mexican
intellectual and political milieu that resulted in the protection of workers' rights.

Influence of Foreign Laws

Just as there is a tendency to deny the influence of foreign ideas in the creation of workers'
rights in Mexico, there is also a tendency to deny the influence of foreign laws in the local
labour legislations that followed the 1910 Revolution. De la Cueva, for instance, notes
that the 1918 Labour Law of the State of Veracruz—the first State statute enacted after
the promulgation of the Constitution—emphasised the statute's national character in its
preamble:[59]

> [I]t was a permanent criterion to create a law, that was above anything else, Mexican ... that was
> a product of our environment, a legitimate daughter of our Revolution and of our fundamental
> laws, that faithfully responded to our needs. ...We did not want to fill the law with translations
> or copies of foreign laws, even if wise; we did not want to include any precept for the sake of an
> elegant or precise form which was formulated by legislators of other countries; we fundamentally
> wanted to guarantee the application of the law to our environment, to our social and political
> conditions, to our present situation.[60]

For de la Cueva, this was consistent with Mexican labour law's origin, which was 'born
in the fields and from revolutionary men, and which is not and has never been an extra
logical imitation of other peoples' norms'.[61] According to de la Cueva, Veracruz's statute
would greatly influence the first federal labour law (1931). The assertion of national
origin, however, is in tension with a previous acknowledgment. De la Cueva had already
pointed out that the 1904 and 1906 state laws were greatly inspired by the French Law of
1898.[62] In fact, by 1918 Congress considered it preferable to enact specific laws to address
each of the various aspects of labour relations rather than a single code.[63] According to
de la Cueva, this position explains the two draft laws for 'workplace accidents', 'one of
which ... was preceded by an excellent exposition of the theory of professional risk'.[64] The
theory of professional risk, as de la Cueva noted, was a French legal development. The
importation of this theory into this draft project, and finally into the 1931 federal law,
seems clear.

---

[56] See eg de Buen, *Derecho del Trabajo* (n 53) 191–93.
[57] De Buen, *Derecho del Trabajo* (n 53) 192.
[58] De Buen, *Derecho del Trabajo* (n 53) 192–93.
[59] De la Cueva, *Nuevo Derecho* (n 12) 51.
[60] Ibid, 51.
[61] Ibid, 51.
[62] Ibid, 43.
[63] Ibid.
[64] Ibid, 52.

iii. Workers' Rights as a Creation of the 1917 Mexican Constitution

There is no stronger claim about the Mexican provenance of workers' rights than the proposition that Mexico's 1917 Constitution was the first in the world to enshrine such rights. Labour law textbooks commonly cite Mexico as the 'first country to enact social rights in a constitution'.[65]

Based on this temporal advantage, Mexican scholars often argue that the Mexican Constitution created the concept of social rights, and that such rights were Mexicans' direct response to their country's reality.[66] My interest in this section is not to debate the temporal priority of the Mexican Constitution in the inclusion of these rights, which seems clear, but to inquire about the origin of these ideas and how workers' rights made it into the constitutional text.

Mexico's legislative activity after the Revolution shows that the inclusion of worker's rights in the 1917 Constitution did not happen in a vacuum. Rather, it had an immediate precedent in the legislative work of states during the years of the revolution. Between 1914 and 1917—from the overthrowing of General Victoriano Huerta to the victory of Carranza over the other revolutionary factions—a number of Mexican states enacted labour legislation recognising a series of workers' rights.[67] Some of these laws paid explicit attention to labour laws in other countries.[68]

The existence of foreign influence in the Constitution is evident from the comments in the Constitutional Assembly. In a revealing moment, Alfonso Cravioto made a now widely-cited pronouncement that compared the Mexican Revolution and its Constitution to the French Revolution and the subsequent Declaration of the Rights of Man.[69] Yet, in this same speech, Cravioto made an additional important revelation: he rose to defend Carranza and José Natividad Macías, who, in the heated debates, had been branded 'conservatives' by the radicals. He praised Carranza's interest in labour, noting that 'Carranza had commissioned Macías to go to the *United States* and study there, profusely, the future Mexican labour laws.'[70]

Similarly, labour scholar Alberto Trueba-Urbina, a staunch supporter of the originality of the Mexican Constitution, discusses the 1916 to 1917 Constitutional Congress and the process of creation of Article 123.[71] Among the many documents he refers to, however, one can find the very same project of the *Commission for Article 123*, headed by Natividad Macías, establishing the basis for labour legislation. In the Preamble, the influence of foreign ideas is evident:

> [T]he useful *lessons that foreign countries have given us*, concerning the favourable conditions in which their economic prosperity takes place, due to the social reforms implemented

---

[65] De la Cueva, *Nuevo Derecho* (n 12) 52. Nestor de Buen concludes a chapter about the history of social rights stating: 'thus was born the first precept that granted rights to workers at a constitutional level. Mexico entered history as the first country that incorporated social guarantees in a Constitution.' De Buen, *Derecho del Trabajo* (n 53) 343; see also *Diario de los Debates del Congreso Constituyente, 1916–1917* (n 1).

[66] A Trueba-Urbina, *La Primera Constitución Político-Social del Mundo* (Mexico, Editorial Porrúa, 1971).

[67] De Buen, *Derecho del Trabajo* (n 53) 329–34; De la Cueva, *Nuevo Derecho* (n 12) 98–100.

[68] De Buen notes that these state laws that preceded the Constitution ranged from very simple to sophisticated legislation and that some legislation included comparative law references. De Buen, *Derecho del Trabajo* (n 53) 333.

[69] Declaration of the Right of Man and the Citizen, 26 August 1789, available at www.unhcr.org/refworld/docid/3ae6b52410.html.

[70] P Rouaix, *Genesis de los Articulos 27 y 123 de la Constitución Política de 1917* (Colegio de la Frontera, 1959) 89 (emphasis added).

[71] A Trueba-Urbina, *Derecho Social Mexicano* (Mexico, Porrúa, 1978) 151–52.

... suffice to justify this initiative ... so that it can take effect successfully this time *and fill the existing gap of our codes* ... to maintain the desired equilibrium in the legal relationships between workers and employers, subordinated to the moral interests of humanity in general, and of our nationality in particular...[72]

It is clear that Mexican Congressmen were very aware of labour legislation in other parts of the world. There is an important difference between enshrining workers' rights in the Mexican Constitution and claiming that workers' rights, or more broadly social rights, are the creation of the Mexican Constitution. There is no doubt that those participating in the Assembly deemed these rights necessary for the Mexican socio-economic conditions. But the legal, doctrinal and philosophical developments that led to the creation of those rights did not stem organically from the socio-economic conditions that the new constitution sought to remedy.

Some of Article 123's key provisions, including the eight-hour working day, the prohibition of child labour, and employer responsibility for workplace accidents, were the topics of Mexican and other countries' legislation before the Revolution. Consider the French doctrine imposing liability on employers for workplace accidents, moving away from fault or negligence liability and towards strict liability.[73] The legal theory that the State could regulate relations between employers and workers directly by requiring a minima of conditions, rather than leaving those to the parties' free will; the moral idea that the state had an obligation to stop exploitation and improve the conditions under which workers laboured and lived; and the economic idea that this regulation was beneficial to society all existed before the debates in the Constitutional Assembly.

It is possible to believe that the inclusion of worker's rights in the Mexican Constitution corresponded to a political opportunity that was seized by Mexicans influenced by these ideas at the end of the revolution. In this sense, the struggle for workers' rights and the idea of social law were connected to a truly international phenomenon. But to conclude that social rights—and more specifically workers' rights—were the creation of the Revolution, the original creation of Mexican intellectuals and legal scholars or the product of the 1917 Constitution, does not stand in light of serious scrutiny.

C. The Political Character of Labour Law

i. Labour Law as a Radical Political Project

The twin argument of the national origin of social law in Mexico is that it was a politically-radical programme at its inception. The inclusion of workers' rights in Article 123 is portrayed as the result of a winner-take-all victory and the institutionalisation of a radical programme. The most notable labour law scholars in the country have certainly contributed to this idea, weaving a narrative of a legal regime with huge emancipatory potential.

---

[72] Ibid, 153 (emphasis added).
[73] De la Cueva, *Nuevo Derecho* (n 12) 19 (the workers' compensation law—promoted by Minister Waldeck-Rousseau and other members of the socialist party—was among the first French labour laws adopted after the war of 1870).

According to several accounts, Article 123 was the triumph of the radical legislators over the conservatives in Congress.[74] However, the most important triumph for the radicals was not the definition of the rights, which were already envisioned for a subsequent labour statute, but instead their inclusion in the Constitution itself. Although there seemed to be considerable agreement in the Assembly over the need to legislate for workers' rights, their constitutionalisation was perceived as innovative and radical at the time.

There was a heated debate in the Constitutional Assembly about whether workers' rights should be included in the Constitution. Many thought it was enough to grant Congress the constitutional powers to legislate on labour regulation and argued for letting Congress pass a labour statute later.[75] This position represented the view originally supported by Venustiano Carranza, the drafters of the *Project of the Constitution* and the faction of the *renovators*. This coalition was strongly opposed by a handful of radical Congressmen. In one of the most cited passages of the debates, Heriberto Jara argued:

> [T]he jurists, the publicists, the general experts of legislation, will probably find ridiculous this proposition: How would a Constitution include maximum work hours? How would it point out that the individual should not work more than 8 hours a day? That, according to them, is impossible; that, in their opinion, pertains to the regulation of [ordinary] laws. But precisely, what has this theory done? That our Constitution, so liberal, so broad, so good, had resulted in, as the Scientifics call it, '*a suit of lights for the Mexican people*', because that regulation was never passed. … The eight-hour work-day … is to guarantee the freedom of individuals, it is precisely to guarantee their lives, to guarantee their energies, because until now Mexican workers have only been subject to exploitation.[76]

Several representatives delivered passionate speeches supporting this motion.[77] A proposition to include workers' rights in the Constitution, even to create a whole new title in the Constitution on this theme, gathered momentum.[78] When this trend seemed irreversible, Carranza commissioned representative José Natividad Macías to support the creation of a special constitutional section for labour.[79] Macías had previously elaborated a labour code commissioned by Carranza, which was then the basis for what would become Article 123.[80]

The achievement of the radical faction in the Assembly consisted not so much in the content of workers' rights but in their inclusion in the Constitution. The radicals wished to enshrine what they saw as a key promise of the revolution, probably out of distrust that a future labour code would pass. This accomplishment should not be belittled. As can be

---

[74] De Buen, *Derecho del Trabajo* (n 53) 343.

[75] Fernando de Lizardi, UNAM Law School's Dean, initiated the debate by arguing against the inclusion of the new paragraph in the Constitution. He claimed it was unnecessary, as it was a set of 'very good desires that will find an adequate place in Article 73 [stipulating Congress' powers] as a general basis for Congress to later legislate labour matters'. Rouaix, *Genesis* (n 70) 77.

[76] Rouaix, *Genesis* (n 70) 77–78. This passage is cited in every labour law book. See eg de la Cueva, *Nuevo Derecho* (n 12) 49; Nestor de Buen, *Derecho del Trabajo* (n 53) 343–52; Trueba-Urbina, *Derecho Social* (n 71) 47–48.

[77] Including Hector Victoria, the representative of the state of Yucatán, a state that had already enacted labour legislation, who demanded 'maximum daily hours, minimum wages, weekly rest, health in the factories and mines, industrial agreements, creation of tribunals of conciliation and arbitration, prohibition of evening work for women and children, accidents, insurances, compensation, etc'. Rouaix, *Genesis* (n 70) 80.

[78] This position was advanced by Froylán Manjarrez, arguing that he did not 'care whether this Constitution adjusts to the models foreseen by the jurists … what I care about is that we attend the clamour of the men that participated in the armed struggle and deserve that we look for their welfare … Let us not fear that our Constitution be a little bad in its form … let's go to the substance of the question.' Rouaix, *Genesis* (n 70) 81; *Diario de los Debates del Congreso Constituyente, 1916–1917* (n 2) 986.

[79] De la Cueva, *Nuevo Derecho* (n 12) 50.

[80] De Buen, *Derecho del Trabajo* (n 53) 345–46.

gleaned from the constitutional debate, there was considerable opposition by the legal elite amongst the Congressmen. The radical faction succeeded in doing something that seemed unorthodox for the liberal jurists at that time; in defying the liberal constitutional models available, the radical Congressmen prioritised substance over form and succeeded in constitutionalising workers' rights.

Labour scholars have made two common claims about the progressiveness of Mexican labour law that form part of the traditional narrative: first, that labour law had radical objectives and would inaugurate a new social and economic order; and second, that these radical goals reached their apex during the government of President Lázaro Cárdenas (1934–40), believed to be the golden era for the legacy of the 1910 Revolution.[81] After Cárdenas, the story goes, these principles were subverted or betrayed by subsequent administrations and by the leadership of the labour movement.

De la Cueva was one of the most fervent advocates of the progressive character of labour law and its radical goals. He referred to the creation of social law as:

> [T]he revolution of equality as a guarantee of liberty, dignity, and welfare for all human beings, a political and juridical system in which the Aristotelian phrase of justice 'to give to every one his own' is substituted by the Marxist formula 'to give to every one what he needs'.[82]

According to this view, labour law was a major victory for the working class. It was not only a protectionist law, but also created a status-based law of the working class.[83] Article 123 stood for the elimination of the liberal distinction between private and public law, and for the creation of social law, which would give legal force to labour's struggle against exploitation and for social justice.[84]

Labour law scholars share nostalgia for labour law's presumed original radical aims and for their golden era under President Cárdenas's government. Cárdenas' support for the labour movement is praised and widely acknowledged.[85] Scholars point to the end of Cárdenas' government as the turning point in the labour system.[86] After the Cárdenas administration, the government began deradicalising and weakening labour unions, enabling the ratification of national unity agreements and demobilising the transformative character of the labour movement.[87] For instance, the Confederation of Mexican Workers (CTM)—the largest labour organisation in the country to be created with Cárdenas'

---

[81] De la Cueva, *Nuevo Derecho* (n 12); De Buen, *Derecho del Trabajo* (n 53); Trueba-Urbina, *Derecho Social* (n 71).

[82] De la Cueva, *Nuevo Derecho* (n 12) LI.

[83] Ibid.

[84] De la Cueva, *Nuevo Derecho* (n 12) LVIII. Although scholars agreed on the progressiveness of labour law and saw it as a direct challenge to the liberal legal and economic order, they did not advance identical positions about labour law's objectives. Take, for instance, de la Cueva and Trueba-Urbina. While de la Cueva seemed to regard labour law as a powerful instrument to mediate between capital and labour within capitalism, Trueba-Urbina saw in labour law an institution that would set in motion a radical transformation away from capitalism and towards socialism. De la Cueva, *Nuevo Derecho* (n 12) 85; Trueba-Urbina, *Derecho Social* (n 71) 290–91; see also 121–22, 235.

[85] De la Cueva, *Nuevo Derecho* (n 12) lx, De Buen, *Derecho de trabajo* (n 53) 372; Trueba-Urbina, *Derecho Social* (n 71).

[86] De Buen asserts that 'with Cárdenas concludes the process of fundamental social reforms'. After Cárdenas, Mexico 'takes a definite route toward capitalism. It is not a classic liberal capitalism. … It is a capitalism integrated on one hand with private resources and on the other, with an important state intervention … with certain social direction'. De Buen, *Derecho del Trabajo* (n 53) 376. This transition begins in 1940, only nine years after the enactment of the first federal labour law in 1931.

[87] De Buen, *Derecho del Trabajo* (n 53) 381.

support—substituted its radical slogan: 'For a society without classes' with the more moderate 'For the emancipation of Mexico'.[88] Labour scholars are both nostalgic for Cárdenas' golden age and disillusioned by the deradicalisation of organised labour and of the labour regime in general.[89]

ii. Labour Law as a Political Compromise

Analysing the constitutional debates in the 1916–17 Assembly and the developments that led to Article 123, a different story is available: the labour regime did not emerge as a truly radical project that then declined and demobilised, as prominent labour scholars have argued; rather, it was a non-radical compromise from its inception. Pastor Rouaix, who chaired the Commission in charge of writing the workers' rights' special title in the Constitution, provides a detailed account of this compromise.[90] The preparatory work for the article generated heated debates before reaching a final decision.[91] The outcome, according to Rouaix, was a compromise between the opposing factions participating in the Constitutional Assembly: 'the meetings … were the *fraternal amalgam* of Jacobins and moderates, renovators and military men, Carrancists and Obregonists, united by one sole flag: the flag of fatherland'.[92]

Rouaix's book sought to set the historical record straight after the publication of two books written by representatives in the Constitutional Congress.[93] Both books' authors claimed credit for its respective faction for the social reforms implemented in the 1917 Constitution.[94] That these authors could each appropriate the outcome of the Constitution—to some extent true—further confirms that Article 123 was a compromise between competing factions that suited both the 'renovators'—whose leader was the main author of that article—and the 'radicals'.[95]

Additionally, Social Catholicism was an apparent influence in this ultimate compromise. The meetings took place at the chapel in the Bishop of Querétaro's residence, where 'the

---

[88] De Buen, *Derecho del Trabajo* (n 53) 382. The CTM's original manifesto clearly expressed its socialist aims, declaring the abolition of the capitalist system as a mid-term goal. See ibid, 375.

[89] See Trueba-Urbina, *Derecho Social* (n 71) 124, de la Cueva, *Nuevo Derecho* (n 12) 45 (complaining about the betrayal of labour law's goals and wondering if labour law would ever have the courage of its convictions); de Buen, *Derecho del Trabajo* (n 53) 379.

[90] Rouaix, *Genesis* (n 70) 105. Rouaix, a member of Carranza's cabinet, justifies his selection as chair of this commission by the trust he inspired in Congress: '[I]n the radicals because they knew his past performance as eminently liberal and revolutionary; in the military, because as Governor of the state of Durango … he was one of the men who took up arms for the revolution; in the renovators and moderates for his civilian condition and for his adhesion to Mr Carranza.' Ibid.

[91] Some representatives introduced concepts of 'alarming radicalism' but the Committee sought agreement by consensus. Rouaix, *Genesis* (n 70) 106.

[92] Rouaix, *Genesis* (n 70) 240. (emphasis added). Rouaix claims two alliances emerged at the outset in the Constitutional Congress: (1) moderates or 'renovators' who recognised Venustiano Carranza as leader and Commander-in-Chief, represented in the Constitutional Congress by five former Congress representatives under Porfirio Diaz' dictatorship, and (2) radicals, grouped around General Álvaro Obregón, formed by military men who had fought the revolution, surrounded by young representatives. Ibid, 229.

[93] See ibid, 229–40.

[94] Ibid, 229–40. These books are *Chronicle of the Constitutional Congress* by Juan de Dios Bojórquez, a left-wing friend and supporter of Obregón, and *History of the 1917 Constitution* by Felix F Palavicini, a 'reformer' who supported Carranza. See ibid, 231.

[95] Rouaix, *Genesis* (n 70) 237, 239. Rouaix claims that both books distort the participation of the opposite faction to take credit for the final work. In contrast, his book reflects the impartiality of someone who served as a 'loop of union between exalted extremes, which made possible a great creation'. See ibid, 237.

theoretical principles of Christianity, which so many times had been praised in that place, had their practical realisation'.[96] That the Commission's chair saw Article 123 as an application of the principles of Christianity, even in its most progressive articulation at that time, further suggests that the compromise was far from being a radical victory.

Furthermore, even the labour movement's golden era, under Cárdenas, looks less radical than that which many scholars portray.[97] Cárdenas can be read as explicitly forging a compromise position:

> The main action of the Revolution's new phase is Mexico's march toward socialism, movement that equally sidetracks from the anachronistic norms of classic liberalism and from those of communism.
>
> ...
>
> Within this doctrine, the Mexican state is not limited to be a simple guardian of order, with tribunals to adjudicate according to the law of individuals; neither can it become the head of the national economy, rather it tends to turn into the regulator of the great economic phenomena registered in our regime of production and wealth distribution.[98]

What Cárdenas calls socialism is, in his words, right in the middle of the two radical political options: liberal laissez-faire and communism. Cárdenas describes Mexico's revolutionary path as a compromise between these two positions, in which a private property capitalist system is maintained and moderated through government intervention.

Interestingly, the same scholars who assert Article 123 is a victory of a radical political position acknowledge Cardenas' less than radical actions and legacy regarding labour unions. De Buen, for instance, claims that Cardenas' legacy to the labour movement was the creation of a national labour confederation, the CTM, with a socialist orientation. He explains that Cárdenas created the CTM to weaken and replace the then largest labour confederation, the Mexican Regional Confederation of Workers (CROM), which was strongly associated with Cárdenas' predecessor, former President Calles. Thus Cárdenas needed a labour organisation that would support his administration and his policies.[99] De Buen notes that even though CTM originally had a Marxist orientation, it was never, even at its creation, a combative union. Rather, the CTM 'was born demobilized', since it was Cardenas' instrument to fight CROM's political force.[100] De Buen concludes that Cardenas' formidable work is not exempt from errors: '[H]is love for labour unity led him to create an organism that was later to represent the most negative aspect of the labour movement.'[101]

Employers accused Cárdenas of being communist.[102] As a response, in his labour policy agenda, Cárdenas explicitly rejected the influence of any communist groups in his

---

[96] Ibid, 104.

[97] For an analysis of different historical interpretations of Cárdenas' legacy see A Knight, 'Cardenismo: Juggernaut or Jalopy?' (1994) 26 *Journal of Latin American Studies* 73–107 (arguing that Cardenismo had radical objectives but was institutionally weak and was hijacked by more moderate groups and by opponents). 'After 1940, the key institutions of Cardenismo ... hardly fulfilled the radical high hopes of the mid-1930s; nor, to put it another way, did they realise the lively fears of businessmen and conservatives', p107.

[98] A Navarrete, *Alto a la Contrarrevolución (Testimonios de Atlacomulco)* (Mexico, Editorial Libros de Mexico, 1971) 11.

[99] De Buen, *Derecho del Trabajo* (n 53) 372.

[100] Ibid, 375.

[101] Ibid, 376.

[102] Ibid.

administration, argued for the need to create a single worker's organisation to end industrial conflict, reinforced the role of the government as arbitrator of social life, and stressed that workers' demands would always be considered within the margins of firms' economic possibilities.[103]

A final word about the labour movement before Cárdenas' administration is in order. Scholars refer to the syndicalist group 'La Casa del Obrero Mundial' as combative and with revolutionary aspirations until its leaders made an agreement with Venustiano Carranza in 1914 to join the Revolution.[104] De Buen notes that 'in that moment, the demobilized unionism was born'.[105] During the period from Carranza to Cárdenas (1917–34) the co-opting of unions, or their corporatist alliance with the government, and their transformation into political instruments was accomplished.[106]

These accounts provide a picture of a labour movement at odds with the radical character that labour law scholars often project onto the past. While there were clearly radical elements in the labour movement, it seems that immediately after the Revolution, most unions came into the fold and compromised with the state. They forewent their radical aspirations in exchange for government protection and benefits. Cárdenas' golden era seemed to have continued this corporatist logic. Even if he was pro-labour, as Cárdenas undoubtedly was, he successfully created the CTM to consolidate his political power. The CTM stands today as the monument to corporatism and official unionism, far removed from any progressive agenda.

iii. A Typology of the Political Character of Social Law

The compromising character of the 'social' was not limited to the case of Mexico.[107] Moreover, critiques of classical liberalism seeking to reconstruct the legal system around the social were not necessarily associated with the left or the right. The term 'social' could be claimed by anyone not associated with Marxism or liberalism.[108] Indeed, the strength of the social was that it did not associate ideologically with the political divisions of the time.[109] As to the role of the State, the social favoured equally a reconstruction through the State and a reconstruction through civil society. Thus, the social encompasses two divergent positions with regard to the question of labour: one position for social regulation by the State, and another in opposition to State regulation.[110]

The nature of the social compromise in Mexico was a progressive move from the old classical, liberal legal and economic regime, not a conservative one. It was a corporatist

---

[103] Ibid, 373–75.

[104] Ibid.

[105] Ibid, 365.

[106] De Buen classifies unions into moderate and submissive 'yellow-dog' unions and the anarchist 'red' which regarded the state as the handmaiden of the bourgeoisie set out to ensure capitalist exploitation. President Calles would effectively incorporate the 'red' unions into the National Revolutionary Party—later the PRI—in 1929. Ibid.

[107] See D Kennedy and M-C Belleau, 'François Gény aux États-Unis', in C Thomasset et al (eds), *François Gény, Mythe Et Realités* (Yvon Blais, 2000).

[108] Ibid, 300.

[109] Ibid; see also D Kennedy, 'From the Will Theory to the Principle of Private Autonomy: Lon Fuller's "Consideration and Form"' (2000) 100 *Columbia Law Review* 94, 119–20 (arguing that before World War I social reconstruction did not require the adoption of communist or fascist versions of collectivism because neither yet existed as a developed theory or practice of state power).

[110] Kennedy and Belleau, 'François Gény' (n 107) 301; see also Kennedy, 'Will Theory' ibid, 119–20.

project, but it was not fascist. It was decidedly not a radical project; it was far from being a communist programme or even containing the seeds of it. The groups that did not participate in the reconstruction of the legal order through the State were those who represented the old, liberal capitalist system associated with Diaz' regime and those who wanted a communist regime. The reconstruction was also a secular compromise, not a religious one. The groups that desired a reconstruction through civil society and opposed the State remained at the fringe. This includes groups from both the left and the right. On the left, anarchist groups regarded the State as perpetually in alliance with the dominant capitalist class that oppressed workers and peasants. On the right, Catholic groups resented the State for limiting the role of the Church in public and private affairs, and for limiting religious expression while propagating a secular ideology. These groups entered into conflict with the State at different points following the 1917 Constitution, as the new compromise was consolidating.

D. Explaining the Traditional Narrative

If these critiques are plausible, two questions emerge. First, why did these scholars argue so adamantly for the national and radical character of labour law? Second, why does it matter? I see at least three main projects furthered by this narrative.

(1) *The professional project.* These scholars created a new field in legal scholarship—labour law—and at the same time claimed to be renovating the whole legal system around the idea of social law. This project opened up space for progressive scholars and situated them at the vanguard of an otherwise formalistic and doctrinal private law scholarship.[111] These scholars became the standard-bearers of a fully-fledged renovation of the legal system.

This professional project emerged from a theoretical and doctrinal breakthrough adopted, crafted and claimed as theirs in the domestic legal academy. To gauge the impact on these scholars' professional careers consider the case of de la Cueva, who became not only a renowned legal scholar but also a public intellectual and a government adviser. Labour law became a springboard into constitutional law, legal theory and legal philosophy.[112] Founding the field of labour law marked the beginning of a stellar professional career. He became President of the Universidad Nacional Autónoma de Mexico (UNAM) from 1936 to 1942, Dean of the UNAM Law School from 1952 to 1954, and later Emeritus Professor of Law, and Doctor Honoris Causa. De la Cueva received, from the President of Mexico, the 1978 National Prize of Arts and Sciences in History, Social Sciences and Philosophy. He is also revered as a professor and remembered as a mentor by many law students who would later become legal scholars, writers and politicians. Thus, de la Cueva's creation of the labour law field, along with other renowned scholars, can be seen as an effort to forge a

---

[111] Nevertheless, private law was also being socialised. See I Galindo Garfias, *Estudios de Derecho Civil* (México Universidad Nacional Autónoma de Mexico, 1981); N de Buen, *La Decadencia del Contrato* (México Editorial Porrúa, 2000).

[112] De la Cueva was the first scholar in Mexico to publish a book on labour law (1934). Later, he translated Herman Heller's book, *Sovereignty: A Contribution to a Legal Theory of the State and of International Law* (1965), and published *La Idea del Estado* (México, Universidad Autónoma de México, 1975), *Teoría de la Constitución* (México, Porrúa, 1982) and *El Nuevo Derecho Mexicano del Trabajo* (México, Editorial Porrúa, 1972) among a long list of other writings.

professional project, which involved a serious intellectual agenda and a claim to expertise, a career ambition in the legal academy and state institutions, and a desire to influence his peers as well as future generations.

(2) *The political project.* Labour scholars intervened in the national questions about the distribution of wealth and power. Questions such as how to organise relations of production between employers and workers, how to allocate power between capital and labour, what the state's role should be in mediating between employers and workers and through which institutions should the state intervene. De la Cueva, for instance, was a judicial clerk when he wrote the decision of the Supreme Court's Labour Law Chamber that was the basis for the oil companies' expropriation decree by President Lázaro Cárdenas. He was also Chair of the Commission that wrote the second federal labour statute, enacted in 1970, which was an attempt to reinvigorate worker protections and renovate some of the redistributive and transformative aspirations that de la Cueva believed had stagnated.

Notably, the political project can be seen as facilitated by the professional one, with its claim to authoritative knowledge and expertise. The professional project is also a struggle for the prevalence and influence of ideas that are deemed to have better economic and social consequences in society. For de la Cueva, labour law was not only a new discipline but also, and perhaps primarily, a new tool for the social and economic transformation of the country.

(3) *The transnational project.* This is a project that seeks to establish a new relationship of equals between the geopolitical periphery, where Mexico is situated, and the centre. In this case, de la Cueva and other labour scholars attempted to establish this relationship by arguing that Mexico had transcended, or anticipated, Europe.[113] They claimed the genesis of social rights and pointed to the 1917 Constitution as the first 'social' constitution in the world. De la Cueva asserts: 'We can affirm that life anticipated doctrine, because in 1917 … the first Declaration of Social Rights in history was proclaimed in Querétaro [Mexico], and two years later in Weimar.'[114]

This claim lent enormous credibility to the national project of reconstruction. Furthermore, claiming that the project was progressive enabled these legal scholars to advocate progressive politics in Mexico by reference to the Constitution. It was a claim of progressive originalism. When new questions of interpretation arose, they could argue that the Constitution required the progressive one.

This would not be the first time that legal scholars participated in creating a narrative of national pride. For example, in many of the newly-independent states in Latin America in the nineteenth century, legal elites claimed a specific uniqueness or identity for their country

---

[113] For an incisive analysis of the appeal to identity in the project of nation-building, to provide social cohesion, and to justify a domestic political project, see C Geertz, 'The Integrative Revolution: Primordial Sentiments and Politics in the New States' in C Geertz (ed), *Old Societies and New States: The Quest for Modernity in Asia and Africa* (New York, Free Press of Glencoe, 1963) 105–57 '[P]eoples of the new states are simultaneously animated by two powerful … motives … the desire to be recognised as responsible agents whose wishes, acts, hopes, and opinions "matter", and the desire to build an efficient, dynamic modern state. The one aim is to be noticed: it is a search for an identity, and a demand that the identity be publicly acknowledged as having import, a social assertion of the self as "being somebody in the world". The other aim is practical: it is a demand for progress, for a rising standard of living, more effective political order, greater social justice, and beyond that of "playing a part in the larger arena of world politics", of "exercising influence among the nations"'; see also, E Hosbawm and T Ranger, (eds), *The Invention of Tradition* (Cambridge, Cambridge University Press, 1983); M Weber, 'The Nation' in M Weber, HH Gerth and C Wright Mills (eds), *From Max Weber: Essays in Sociology* (Abingdon, Routledge, 1969).

[114] De La Cueva, *Nuevo Derecho* (n 12) 71.

that preceded the Spanish colonialists and differentiated the new nation from Spain. This uniqueness allowed them to claim a place in the concert of nations as an independent and sovereign entity and provided cohesion for the domestic project.[115] Legal scholars in several Latin American countries were actively involved in defending the sovereignty of their countries. They were busy creating new legal doctrines that would allow their countries to be shielded from threats of foreign intervention. These doctrinal innovations were touted as coming out of the new countries, and belonging to the tradition of, while simultaneously renewing, international law.[116] Thus, these scholars would claim that Latin American international law had contributed something original to the discipline, demanding recognition as peers in the international arena. This claim allowed them to legitimate the projects of their national governments at home.

Although these three projects are analytically distinct, they are certainly intermingled. For instance, in de la Cueva's case, the projects reinforce each other in important ways. The transnational project advocating a historic national contribution seems instrumental in enabling his professional and political projects domestically. International recognition gives credence to de la Cueva's professional aspirations and opens the space for political intervention at home.

So why is it important to problematise the traditional narrative and to show its biases, make-beliefs and contradictions? In my view, there are at least two compelling reasons. First, it has the potential to render the three projects—professional, political and transnational—visible and thus open them up for contestation. Challenging the traditional labour law narrative may open the field to new ways of thinking about labour relations. The challenge may also foster legal institutional imagination and policy innovation.

Second, questioning the traditional narrative may enable a clearer analysis of the consequences of the status quo. At one level, the analysis may illuminate who wins and who loses under the current narrative—whose professional and political projects are advanced and whose are hindered. At another level, the challenge may facilitate a more concrete analysis of the consequences of the labour law regime in place by examining how specific rules and institutions affect the distribution of wealth and power in society.

In the past, social law advocates failed to engage with a number of important critiques to social legislation, coming from all sides of the political spectrum. Feminists challenged labour regulation for its gender bias, creating a division of labour that relegated women to the household and left them out of the market. When women did enter the market, they were discriminated against with fewer opportunities and lower wages.[117] A liberal critique challenged the corporatist character of social law, noting that the labour law regime relied on an alliance between the government, employers and official unions that impinged on

---

[115] See A Becker Lorca, 'International Law in Latin America or Latin American International Law? Rise, Fall, and Retrieval of a Tradition of Legal Thinking and Political Imagination' (2006) 47 *Harvard International Law Journal* 283, 301–302; L Obregón, 'The Colluding Worlds of the Lawyer, the Scholar and the Policymaker: A View of International Law from Latin America' (2005) 23 *Wisconsin International Law Journal* 145, 157–58.

[116] See generally, A Alvarez, 'The New International Law' (1929) 15 *Transactions of the Grotius Society* 35.

[117] See, eg M Ariza, 'Mercados de Trabajo Urbanos y Desigualdad de Género en México a Principios del Siglo XXI' in de la Garza and Salas (eds), *La Situacion del Trabajo* (n 24) (noting the wide disparity in economic earning power between men and women); J Williams, *Unbending Gender: Why Family And Work Conflict And What To Do About It* (Oxford, Oxford University Press, 2000) (discussing ways to alleviate the conflict between domestic and workplace responsibilities by altering labour market opportunities); M Fineman, *The Neutered Mother, The Sexual Family And Other Twentieth Century Tragedies* (London, Rutledge, 1995) (arguing for direct public support of care work but not through marriage).

worker liberty, and led union leaders to disregard the interests of the rank and file, focusing instead on obtaining personal and political benefits in exchange for agreements.[118] Social theorists and social movements challenged the social law regime of the welfare state as a statist, bureaucratic system of social control in the service of liberal capitalism. The labour law regime worked to create an obedient working class that was trained to respect authority and accept its limited and subordinated role in decisions of economic production and distribution.[119] Finally, neoclassical economists challenged labour regulation as a barrier to job creation, firms' competitiveness and economic growth.[120]

Some of these critiques are more warranted than others, and their veracity depends on the particular context.[121] They are critiques of social law and of labour regulation by advocates on the left and the right of the political spectrum. What they have in common is that they are consequentialist. They focus on labour regulation's effects on different groups of workers: female workers, youth, non-unionised or informal workers; on workers' subjectivity and their role in society; on workers' ability to be represented; on employers; and on the economy as a whole.

Defending social law—or labour rights—as a national asset and as the achievement of a revolutionary struggle or as a fundamental pillar in the Constitution are ways to justify a social law regime without addressing its effects. In this way, advocates for labour miss an opportunity to evaluate the consequences of the labour regulation they defend and to engage with critics on their own terms. Once the national identity argument is put aside, new opportunities to both defend some aspects of the current regime and to re-imagine it become apparent.

The critiques of the use of national identity and of the assumption that social law in Mexico is progressive may serve as a warning against the romanticisation of social law as a transformative project. Mexico shows that identity-based and deontological arguments can be successful in creating national pride and mobilising support for specific institutions, but they cannot justify a legal regime based on its effects. Moreover, these arguments might end up legitimating a regime that does not advance workers' welfare.

Currently many progressives in Mexico resist the neo-liberal flexibility programme by invoking the achievements of the Revolution and the 1917 Mexican Constitution. They assert that the current legal and constitutional framework has a progressive character that can help resist calls to dismantle current labour market regulation. As I have explained, however, treating social law as having an inherently progressive character is not historically warranted in the case of Mexico. When progressives retrench behind national pride or constitutional rights arguments to resist the neo-liberal flexibility reform they implicitly concede too much. When their main line of defence is that workers' rights cannot be touched, they concede that the economic effects of the current labour law regime might

---

[118] See, eg A Alcalde and B Luján, *Como Viven La Democracia Los De Abajo* (Mexico, Universidad Nacional Autónoma de México, 1997) 91.

[119] See G Bensusán, *El Modelo Mexicano De Regulación Laboral* (Mexico, Plaza y Valdés Editores, 2000) 27–45 (analysing different interpretations of the role of labour law and of the state in liberal capitalism). See also KE Klare, 'Labor Law as Ideology: Toward a New Historiography of Collective Bargaining Law' (1981) 4 *Industrial Relations Law Journal* 450.

[120] See, eg G Velasco, *Labor Legislation From An Economic Point Of View* (Indianapolis, Liberty Fund, 1973); M Friedman and RD Friedman, *Free to Choose* (New York, Harcourt Brace Jovanovich, 1979) 228–47.

[121] A Santos, 'Labor Flexibility, Legal Reform, and Economic Development' (2009) 50 *Virginia Journal of International Law* 43.

be negative but that they do not have an answer to that challenge. Moreover, this line of defence also makes it harder to think of imaginative, progressive alternatives to current market regulation.

On the other hand, those advocating neo-liberal flexibility reform increasingly use the malleable social law discourse to make their case. In Mexico, this is most evident in the PRI bill, which argues that flexibility reforms are necessary to help workers.[122] The bill claims that the historical achievements of the revolution and workers' rights consecrated in the Constitution will remain untouched.[123] It is perhaps fitting for the PRI to advance such reform. After all, it is the party that institutionalised the national Revolution and used that discourse to legitimate its rule. Now, having been out of power for 12 years, the PRI is trying to craft a compromise between employers' associations and unions. Despite its rhetoric, however, this compromise is likely not to benefit most workers.

A striking feature of the PRI bill is that it frames a neo-liberal flexibility programme for market regulation as a social law programme. Thus the PRI bill maintains that greater flexibility in hiring and firing is necessary to help create jobs, particularly for women and youth, and to promote competitiveness, productivity and growth.[124] PRI promotes these reforms while claiming that it is motivated by the historical achievements of enshrining workers' rights in the Constitution, which will continue to guide labour market regulation. At best, this bill is a promise to legalise the status quo.

E. Implications of the Mexican Story for Debates in Other Countries

The Mexican story offers several valuable lessons for labour law debates in other countries. First, Mexico shows that, despite is traditional association with progressive politics, the social is politically indeterminate. As an international phenomenon, social law took different political valences in different countries, from left to right on the political spectrum, and from democratic to authoritarian forms of government.

Second, Mexico shows that arguments based on national identity and constitutional rights face serious problems. These arguments often fail to diagnose the effects of current labour market regulation, offer no response to consequentialist critiques of current regulation, and offer no proposals for re-imagining labour regulation to increase workers' well-being. Consequently, if neo-liberals promote a flexibility reform couched on social law ideals, pro-labour advocates have a hard time offering an alternative programme.

Third, the social was in fact a truly global phenomenon, despite claims that it was unique to and created by each country where it was introduced. This is important to keep in mind, because the arguments of national identity and constitutional rights considerably constrain the analysis to a specific country. Taking seriously the social's transnational character would help to analyse that country's situation in the global economy, thinking of how it is affected by its place in the world market and its relationship with other countries.

In the next section, I explore the relevance of the insights from Mexico for contemporary debates about labour regulation elsewhere, specifically in Europe. The effects of market

---

[122] PRI bill, (n 31) p 20.
[123] Ibid, p 22.
[124] Ibid.

economic integration in the EU and the perceived hampering of social provisions in the Member States have sparked a debate about the need to ensure the preservation of basic social protections as part of the EU. This debate has been framed in terms of identity and the allegedly inherent progressiveness of social law. I examine parallels between the cases of the EU and Mexico, and use the insights gained from the case of Mexico to raise some caveats.

III. National Identity in Current Debates about Social Regulation in Europe

In Europe, the social position has also been articulated in terms of identity at the regional level. Advocates and scholars associate the creation of 'Social Europe' with values that are considered indigenous to the EU and, therefore, must be defended on those terms. This is not limited to social regulation; these arguments are also advanced in private law, as it is visible in the debate about harmonisation and the call for a 'common core' that reflects European social values.[125]

Simultaneously, at the national level, advocates of social regulation resort to a similar identity argument to defend their welfare state worker protections and social insurance programmes against what is perceived as a menacing European economic integration model. In this view, the EU's market-oriented policies threaten the existence of the welfare state, and with it, something fundamental about the nation's identity. This national level pushback against the EU model may be particularly acute in the aftermath of the financial crisis.

This is not to say that all social position arguments are premised upon national or regional identity; however, these arguments remain powerful and thus deserve critical scrutiny. For progressives, the obvious upside of defending social law on the basis of identity is that it provides an easy and energising point of resistance. The problem is that identity conjures up essences and obfuscates trade-offs and distributional consequences. It also portrays the status quo as desirable and makes it harder to articulate alternatives to the existing law that could potentially better meet progressives' underlying interests and goals. Lastly, the emphasis on national identity eschews analysis of social regulation's implication in transnational problems with transnational constituencies.[126]

A. The Use of Identity and the Push to Constitutionalise Social Rights

Since the start of the European integration project after World War II, whether and how to regulate social policy at the supranational level has remained a central question.

---

[125] See, The Study Group on Social Justice in European Private Law, 'Social Justice in European Contract Law: a Manifesto' (2004) 10 *European Law Journal* 653, 655 (private law an 'expression of cultural identity' and not merely technocratic; which should therefore reflect the European social justice agenda). See also, D Kennedy, *Thoughts on Coherence, Social Values and National Tradition in Private Law* in M Hesselink (ed), *The Politics of a European Civil Code* (Alphen aan den Rijn, Kluwer Law International, 2006).

[126] See, eg DM Trubek, J Mosher and JS Rothstein, 'Transnationalism in the Regulation of Labor Relations: International Regimes and Transnational Advocacy Networks' (2000) 25 *Law & Social Inquiry* 1187.

Progressives in Europe have widely used identity arguments to promote a social rights agenda, which is evident in the debates over 'Social Europe'. Take, for instance, the debate over the contents of a potential European Constitution in the early years of the twenty-first century.[127] Similarly to Mexico, identity was a key force mobilising the establishment of social rights. European progressives argued that European identity was closely connected to the 'social' because of the history of welfare protection in Member States and thus constitutionalising this social identity was the way forward for the EU.

Jurgen Habermas famously asked for the constitutionalisation of Europe's social self. He argued that it was these values, in part, that set Europe apart from the rest of the world and which could provide the necessary glue for the further integration that was sorely needed in the face of unfettered globalisation:

> In Western Europe ... the political tradition of the workers' movement, the salience of Christian social doctrines and even a certain normative core of social liberalism still provide a formative background for social solidarity. In their public self-representations, Social and Christian Democratic parties in particular support inclusive systems of social security and a substantive conception of citizenship, which stresses what John Rawls calls 'the fair value' of equally-distributed rights. In terms of a comparative cultural analysis, we might speak of the unique European combination of public collectivisms and private individualism.[128]

Miguel Maduro, who later served as Advocate General in the European Court of Justice (ECJ), called on the EU to initiate an open discussion on its 'social identity' and its 'social self' in the constitutional debates. Maduro noted the 'subsidiary and under-developed nature of Europe's social citizenship when compared with its original market citizenship' and argued that whatever social rights the EU had granted its citizens, it had done so by virtue of the economic value of these citizens rather than out of respect for their basic dignity.[129] His account of why Europe needed to constitutionalise the 'social' explicitly relied on identity:

> Simply stated, Europe must, as Kierkegaard would say, discuss its identity. ... As it now stands, and in Kierkegaard's terms, it faces despair: the despair of wanting to be oneself and the despair of not wanting to be oneself. I do not know the resolution but I believe that future developments of the Union depend on a discussion of this identity or, perhaps better, on a discussion of its underlying social contract. ... To ignore this 'social identity question' in the forthcoming constitutional debates of the EU may well correspond to the dangerous path of which Kierkegaard warned: 'The biggest danger, that of losing oneself, can pass off in the world as quietly as if it were nothing; every other loss, an arm, a leg, five dollars, a wife, etc., is bound to be noticed.'[130]

---

[127] The Constitution was ultimately rejected. See M Qvortrup, 'The Three Referendums on the European Constitution Treaty in 2005' (2006) 77 *The Political Quarterly* 89.

[128] See J Habermas, 'Why Europe Needs a Constitution' (2001) 11 *New Left Review* 5, 10. 'As Göran Therborn remarks: "the European road to and through modernity has also left a certain legacy of social norms, reflecting European experiences of class and gender ... Collective bargaining, trade unions, public social services, the rights of women and children are all held more legitimate in Europe than in the rest of the contemporary world. They are expressed in social documents of the EU and of the Council of Europe"' ibid.

[129] MP Maduro, 'Europe's Social Self: "The Sickness Unto Death"' (2000) 2 *Webpapers on Constitutionalism & Governance beyond the State* 22.

[130] Ibid, 22.

These positions share a reaction to the negative consequences of market integration in Europe and an identity-based project of building 'Social Europe' as way to include social values in a future European Constitution.[131] The aim was that, once constitutionalised, social rights could provide the social insurance and solidarity mechanisms to reshape economic integration. Social rights would thus achieve equal status with the economic freedoms and the efficiency rationale thus far driving the integration process.[132]

B. Identity as Resistance

Just as social progressives in Mexico use the supposedly close connection between national identity and the 'social' to resist neo-liberal reforms, social progressives in individual European states also resisted the process of further Europeanisation through appeal to national identity.

Take, for instance, the French 'no' campaign against the Constitutional Treaty. The campaign referenced the danger that the imagined low-wage immigrant, such as the 'Polish plumber', constituted for the French social model and the danger that expansion to the East would constitute for French identity.[133] A group of entrepreneurs intervening in favour of the 'yes' vote felt compelled to answer the appeal to national identity. They argued that a France weakened by a 'no' vote would have less influence in the deliberation over the European social model and would not be as able to push for the fundamental values of French society at the European level.[134] Economist Frédéric Lordon reproached the 'yes' camp for failing to note that 'the social State and public services [are] ... fundamental elements of political and symbolic French grammar' and thus '[France] can't renounce them under any circumstances'.[135]

National identity defences of the social welfare model have been even stronger in certain Scandinavian countries, where national identity has been constructed in close connection with the welfare state.[136] Writing on the Nordic model, Mary Hilson notes that 'the welfare

---

[131] Habermas was not unaware of the potential conflicts that might arise in interpreting these values, but he saw constitutionalisation as a mode of initiating a so far non-existent pan-European civic public sphere that would allow Europeans to debate the issues. See K Armstrong, *Governing Social Inclusion: Europeanization through Policy Coordination* (Oxford, Oxford University Press, 2010) 234.

[132] For a famously sceptical take on the desirability of constitutionalising Europe's 'social identity,' see JHH Weiler, 'A Constitution for Europe? Some Hard Choices' (2002) 40 *Journal of Common Market Studies* 563, 570. Weiler argued that Europe should not promise a social redistribution it will not be able to deliver, and, more importantly, it should not foreclose discussion on what the socially progressive choices mean by constitutionalising current contested understandings of social rights.

[133] M Arnold, 'Polish Plumber Symbolic of All French Fear About Constitution' *Financial Times* (28 May 2005) available at www.ft.com/intl/cms/s/0/9d5d703a-cf14-11d9-8cb5-00000e2511c8.html#axzz21o3Kr8le.

[134] 'Appel des Entreprises en Faveur du OUI au Référendum Constitutionnel' (Institut de l'Entreprise, 2005) available at www.institut-entreprise.fr/fileadmin/Docs_PDF/Manifestations/dossier_de_presse_180505.pdf, 3.

[135] F Lordon, 'Le Mensonge Social De La Constitution: Le Oui Entre Vaines Promesses et Imprecations' *A l'encontre* (April 2005) 9 available at www.fredericlordon.fr/textes/crise/tce/pdf/Mensonge_social.pdf.

[136] M Hilson, *The Nordic Model: Scandinavia since 1945* (London, Reaktion Books, 2008) 87–88; VA Schmidt, European 'Elites on the European Union: What Vision for the Future?' in A Gamble and D Lane (eds), *European Union and World Politics: Consensus and Division* (London, Palgrave Macmillan, 2009) 6: '[T]he failures of Denmark and Sweden to join the euro ... [were] based on fears about the EU's impact on the highly generous welfare state, along with sovereignty and identity concerns.' See also M Lubbers, 'Regarding the Dutch 'Nee' to the European Constitution. A Test of the Identity, Utilitarian and Political Approach to Vote No' (2008) 9 *EU Politics* 59.

state is still regarded as an integral part of the meaning of Scandinavia'.[137] The difference Scandinavian countries perceive between themselves as an 'egalitarian social democratic community of destiny' and the 'capitalist and Catholic European continent' fuels opposition to European integration.[138] This identity-based defence of the welfare model has also resulted in a xenophobic discourse that specifically singles out foreigners as a potential burden to the generous welfare regimes of the North.[139]

While the project of national resistance may share the objective of social protection with those seeking to Europeanise social rights through treaty incorporation, it does not share their optimism that regionalisation of social policy would be effective or ultimately beneficial. It is not surprising that some of the most vociferous opposition has taken place in countries with robust welfare systems, which fear that these hard-fought protections would be eroded. Remarkably, both groups use identity as a strategy to mobilise their agenda. At the regional level, social advocates mobilise European identity to propose a positive programme of reform in the EU treaty and institutions; other social advocates mobilise national identity to resist the further encroachment of EU law on their national social protections.

C. Identity to What Effect?

Social progressives' call for the Europeanisation of social rights was partly answered by the Constitutional Treaty, which ultimately failed, and the Lisbon Treaty, which largely replicated the Constitutional Treaty's provisions, and was accepted and entered into force. The Lisbon Treaty also incorporated by reference the Charter of Fundamental Rights, which includes a series of social rights, even though it explicitly excludes an interpretation that would widen the scope of the EU's competences.[140] Moreover, on social policy, the EU is said to be a 'social market economy'[141] striving for 'smart, sustainable, and *inclusive* growth,'[142] while the European welfare states are featured in the Commission's reports as a 'productive factor' rather than as an impediment to growth.[143]

What have been the effects of the inclusion of social policy in the EU? I suggest that the relevance of social policy language in EU law has been tested in two crucial ways. The first test has taken the form of a string of highly controversial cases in the ECJ, where national collective bargaining regulations were in tension with EU economic freedom rights. The second test has been provided by the ongoing euro financial crisis and the European response to tackle it. At a moment of crisis, how the rescue programme takes shape would reveal how substantive the commitments to social protection are and whether the social

---

[137] Hilson, *The Nordic Model* (n 136) 88.

[138] Ibid, 25–26.

[139] '[S]ome would see the Nordic welfare states as vulnerable to the related external pressures of European integration and immigration. The debates on Nordic EU membership during the mid-1990s reflected these fears', ibid, 112.

[140] C Barnard, 'EU "Social" Policy: From Employment Law to Labour Market Reform' in P Craig and G de Búrca (eds), *The Evolution of EU Law* (Oxford, Oxford University Press, 2011) 658–60. For a thorough assessment of the changes in social policy brought by the Treaty of Lisbon, see Armstrong, *Governing Social Inclusion* (n 131) 241–55.

[141] Art 3(3) Treaty on European Union [1992] OJ C191/01.

[142] See Commission, 'Europe 2020: A Strategy for Smart, Sustainable and Inclusive Growth' (Communication) COM (2010) 2020 (emphasis added).

[143] Commission, 'Social Policy Agenda' (Communication) COM (2000) 379, 3.

agenda's aspiration to reshape Europe's economic integration has any chance to succeed. So far, the evidence, although not the rhetoric, seems to suggest otherwise.[144]

First, a new phase in the resistance to Europeanisation began after a series of decisions by the ECJ between 2007 and 2008 created intense anxiety about the future of the Nordic model, especially regarding collective bargaining.[145] The *Viking* case, in which a Finnish ship sought to reflag under an Estonian flag in order to lower its labour costs, provoked strong reactions.[146] The ECJ ruled that industrial action aimed at stopping an undertaking from exercising its freedom of establishment was a prima facie violation of the Treaties. Worker protection was a legitimate goal in the industrial action of the union, but it would have to be established by the national courts that specific jobs were in danger, and that there were not in fact less restrictive means of achieving this goal. All of these requirements were novel for the national labour law regimes.

In the *Laval* case, a Latvian construction company undertook work in Sweden for which it posted Latvian workers to Sweden.[147] The local Swedish union began negotiations with Laval in order to set the wage rates for the Latvian workers. The Swedish industrial relations system leaves setting of wage rates to sector-specific negotiations between management and labour. Laval, which had already signed a collective agreement including the setting of wages with a Latvian union, refused to sign into the local collective agreement for the Swedish building sector. The agreement would have forced it to pay the Latvian workers rates much higher than it had planned. The Swedish union then blockaded Laval construction sites, and a secondary, sympathy boycott was undertaken by the local electricians' union. This industrial action, which was legal in Sweden up until that point, was effective, and Laval had to back out of its contracts and declare bankruptcy in Sweden.

The ECJ decided that labour law as such was not outside the scope of Treaty provisions on free movement. Significantly, it recognised collective action as a fundamental right to be exercised in accordance with the fundamental economic freedoms recognised by the Treaties. The court found that collective action limiting free movement of services, such as the one at stake, needed to be exercised for reasons of public interest and needed to be proportional to its legitimate end. Conceding that the protection of workers was a legitimate end, the Court nonetheless found that the specific industrial action had been disproportionate.

These decisions prompted intense reactions from social progressives, particularly in Scandinavia.[148] Even the European Economic and Social Committee urged the EU to

---

[144] Barnard, 'EU "Social" Policy' (n 140).

[145] For analysis of the Laval and Viking decisions, see generally, C Barnard, 'Viking and Laval: a Single Market Perspective' in K Ewing and J Hendy (eds), *The New Spectre Haunting Europe: The ECJ, Trade Union Rights and the British Government* (Liverpool, Institute of Employment Rights, 2009); C Kilpatrick, 'Laval's Regulatory Conundrum: Collective Standard Setting and the Court's New Approach to Posted Workers' (2009) 34 *European Law Review* 844; B Bercusson, 'The Lisbon Treaty and Social Europe' (2009) 10 *ERA-Forum* 87. For an argument that similar cases to *Laval* and *Viking* would have been judged more favourably to collective bargaining rights, see L Steven, 'Laval, Viking, and American Labour Law' (2011) 32 *Comparative Labour Law & Policy Journal* 1079. Two more decisions of the ECJ add to this line of case law, Case C-346/06 *Dirk Rüffert v Land Niedersachsen* [2008] ECR I-01989; Case C-319/06 *Commission of the European Communities v Grand Duchy of Luxembourg* [2008] ECR I-04323.

[146] Case C-438/05 *International Transport Workers' Federation, Finnish Seamen's Union v Viking Line ABP, OÜ Viking Line Eesti* [2008] ECR I-10779.

[147] Case C-341/05 *Laval un Partneri Ltd v Svenska Byggnadsarbetarefoörbundet* [2008] ECR I-11767.

[148] C Woolfson, C Thörnqvist and J Sommers, 'The Swedish Model and the Future of Labour Standards After Laval' (2010) 41 *Industrial Relations Journal* 333.

strengthen its social protections at the constitutional level, advocating a Treaty change to help balance social and economic rights.[149]

Ulrich Muckenberger, who was involved with the 1997 'Manifesto for Social Europe' advocating the constitutionalisation of social values, urged a 'Post-*Laval* Social Manifesto', claiming that the ECJ's balancing of social rights against civil liberties was legally incorrect.[150] According to this account, the inclusion of social rights in EU law has not made much difference because they remain subordinate to market access rights. This typically progressive stance, however, bears some analysis as well. More specifically, it would be important to analyse the consequences of these ECJ judgments beyond the formal, legal prevalence of one right over another.[151] The language of social rights and 'Social Europe' is equated with the well-being of all workers. But the cases show that the interests of Western and Eastern European workers may not be necessarily aligned—in fact, they may be at odds with one another. This does not mean that they cannot be made compatible, for example, by establishing a minimum floor of labour standards throughout Europe and avoiding capital flight to other continents. It would be necessary, however, to show how that would be pursued. Otherwise, it would seem that European workers would be better off had the ECJ decided these cases the opposite way; this glosses over conditions for workers in Eastern Europe and social development prospects for the new EU Members.

Second, the EU has seemingly incorporated social policy in its formal response to the financial crisis.[152] In response to the crisis, the EU implemented financial reform, financial stabilisation, economic governance reforms, and measures to facilitate growth.[153] Although securing a stable economy through economic governance reforms may help growth, this is unlikely to happen under stringent austerity measures. Because Member States do not have autonomy over their monetary policy and cannot devalue their currency, they are experiencing considerable pressure to turn to labour law deregulation and to scale back workers' protections as a strategy to address their fiscal woes.[154] At the same time, the EU's 2020 strategy for growth would require significant government spending, which, given Member States' indebtedness, seems uncertain.

Of the EU responses, the Euro Plus Pact (EPP)[155] and the Memoranda of Understanding (MoU) between the EU/IMF and countries under bailout assistance[156] have had the greatest

---

[149] European Economic and Social Committee, 'The Social Dimension of the Internal Market' (own-initiative Opinion) [2011] C-44/90.

[150] U Muckenberger, 'Towards A Post-*Viking*/*Laval* Manifesto for Social Europe' (2011) *CELLS online paper series 1*, available at www.law.leeds.ac.uk/assets/files/research/cells/mueckenberger.pdf.

[151] Ibid.

[152] For example, the EU Social Protection Committee published a report *The Social Impact of the Economic Crisis and Ongoing Fiscal Consolidation* (Brussels, Directorate-General for Employment, Social Affairs and Inclusion, 2011).

[153] C Barnard, 'The Financial Crisis and the Euro Plus Pact: A Labour Lawyer's Perspective' (2012) 41 *Industrial Law Journal* 98, 99–103.

[154] Ibid, 98, 103.

[155] The EPP, agreed to in March 2011, commits signatories to consider issues of competitiveness, employment, and the sustainability of public finances, among others, under monitoring and surveillance by the European Commission. See Commission, 'Background on the Euro Plus Pact' Information prepared for the European Council (2011), available at ec.europa.eu/europe2020/pdf/euro_plus_pact_background_december_2011_en.pdf. The EPP is not coupled with strong sanctions. Barnard, 'Financial Crisis' (n 153) 108. The so-called 'Six Pack' of EU legislation on stronger fiscal surveillance now includes surveillance of several macro-economic indicators including labour costs.

[156] European Commission, 'The Second Economic Adjustment Programme for Greece' (2012) *European Economy: Occasional Papers*, 94, available at ec.europa.eu/economy_finance/publications/occasional_paper/2012/op94_en.htm.

impact on national labour laws. Both the EPP and the MoU suggested that Member States reform their labour laws to ensure competitiveness and facilitate growth. The MoU, significantly more intrusive than the EPP, conditions the receipt of financial assistance on implementing labour law reforms.[157] These reforms also have a disciplining effect on other countries in crisis, because they send a message that they, too, should deregulate their labour laws.[158] After an analysis of the EU's response to the financial crisis, Barnard concludes that:

> Traditionally, the EU has been seen as something of a bastion against deregulation at national level, and at least this body of directives continues to provide a floor of rights. Yet, now the EU—whether through the Council formations in the context of its recommendations in the integrated guidelines or at least the heads of state or government—has become responsible for the very deregulation it resisted for many years. Longer term, the EU may be responsible for precipitating a race to the bottom.[159]

In the last two years, the Commission has promoted the goal of defending the 'European social model' in its communications regarding the euro crisis.[160] The Economic and Social Committee also considers the European social model to be so unique that it should be promoted in Europe's development assistance programmes to poor countries.[161]

However, the Lisbon Treaty's inclusion of social rights and the enthusiasm about Social Europe may not have made much difference in the EU's response to the euro crisis. On this front, the character of Social Europe must be measured against the effects of the austerity measures in each nation and how their costs and benefits are distributed between societal groups and among the Member States.

As we have seen, the EU uses identity-based social justifications to pursue policies that might not qualify as progressive. Indeed, a number of progressive scholars have expressed their dissatisfaction with the direction of Social Europe in the last decade, especially considering the ECJ's labour rights rulings.[162] Even progressive supporters of the EU level were disillusioned after *Laval*.[163] It is arguable that the EU's seemingly neo-liberal policies are now being pursued under the guise of 'social' discourse.

What have been the limits of using identity arguments to promote a social rights strategy to advance an economic agenda? Progressives in Europe quite successfully enshrined social

---

See also European Commission, 'An Adjustment Programme for Ireland' (2011) *European Economy: Occasional Papers*, 76, available at ec.europa.eu/economy_finance/publications/occasional_paper/2011/pdf/ocp76_en.pdf and European Commission, 'The Economic Adjustment for Portugal' (2011) *European Economy: Occasional Papers*, 79, available at ec.europa.eu/economy_finance/publications/occasional_paper/2011/op79_en.htm.

[157] Barnard, 'Financial Crisis' (n 153) 98.

[158] Ibid, 112.

[159] Ibid, 113.

[160] In fact, the Commission has proposed the safeguarding of the European social model as one of the reasons why all Member States should pursue measures of fiscal consolidation. See Commission, 'Annual Growth Survey 2012' COM (2011) 815, 4.

[161] European Economic and Social Committee, 'The Social Dimension of the Internal Market' (n 149) Art 1.7.

[162] A Supiot, *Conclusion: Europe's Awakening* in M-A Moreau and I Ulasiuk (eds), *Before and After the Economic Crisis: What Implications for the "European Social Model"?* (Cheltenham, Edward Elgar, 2011).

[163] F Scharpf, 'The Asymmetry of European Integration, Or Why The EU Cannot Be a "Social Market Economy"' (2009) 8 *Socio-Economic Review* 211. For example, Alain Supiot, who advocated the constitutionalisation of social values, became disillusioned after *Laval* and its progeny. See B Bercusson, S Deakin, P Koistinen, Y Kravaritou, U Muckeberger, A Supiot and B Veneziani, 'A Manifesto for Social Europe' (1997) 3 *European Law Journal* 189 for the earlier position; and Supiot, *Conclusion* (n 162) for the later position.

rights in European treaty law, and promoted a Social Europe identity. So far, however, the results seem paltry at best. For example, during the recent euro crisis, adopting a Social Europe model does not seem to have made much difference. This opens social rights to the familiar critique of legitimation, claiming that they are enabling economic policies by reference to their compatibility to the social model, which would otherwise look less palatable. The European experience also shows that resorting to identity and social rights may obscure the distributional effects of policies on different kinds of workers; the insistence on preserving a set of social rights might limit the imagination of alternatives that may perhaps offer greater traction.

IV. Labour Reform and Economic Development: Thinking about Potential Alternatives

New possibilities might open up if one thinks about labour regulation beyond its familiar associations, particularly in the case of Mexico. I have argued that the defence of current labour regulation in the name of revolutionary achievement, cultural pride or constitutional rights should no longer be sufficient without evidence of its social and economic benefits. When progressives cling to these arguments, they, perhaps inadvertently, concede too much. They concede that labour regulation is necessarily bad for firms, markets and the country's growth prospects; they pass on an opportunity to challenge the powerful discourse of labour flexibility; and they forego a necessary diagnosis of the current problem. Thus, they surrender an invaluable opportunity to imagine alternatives. Their main strategy is resistance, and their only alternative is the defence of the mostly indefensible status quo.

Proponents of labour flexibility argue that rigid restrictions and compulsory clauses in employment contract make it harder for firms to hire and fire, which in turn translates to fewer jobs being created, lower productivity and depressed economic growth. Progressives should re-appropriate the language and aspirations of labour flexibility. This should not only mean flexibility for employers to hire and fire at will, but also for workers. Progressives could promote an agenda that makes flexibility a means to turn the workplace into a meaningful life experience for millions of workers. Repetitive and deadening activities in factories and shops, with rigid hierarchies and little or no contribution of workers in firms' productive decisions, are routine in many sectors of the Mexican economy.

Too many firms rely on rigid and outdated systems of production and management. Flexibility could be a rallying cry to reform those modes of production. It could foster innovation by prioritising learning and experimentation so that firms resemble schools and workers are encouraged to contribute ideas. Flexibility could change the hierarchical structure of firms from a rigid, vertical structure, to a horizontal one where employees work in teams and are required to participate in projects over which they have ownership and are encouraged to develop critical thinking and collaboration.[164] Flexibility could mean a workplace where competition and cooperation channel work towards a common purpose

---

[164] See eg R Unger, *Democracy Realized: The Progressive Alternative* (London, Verso, 1997).

and give workers an opportunity to realise themselves. That these goals seem impractical or even utopian in Mexico, says more about the rigidity of our firms' management and systems of production than of the desirability or feasibility of these aspirations.

Flexibility should also mean labour mobility. For too long, employers forewent their ability to fire, hire and bargain over working conditions in return for industrial peace. They obtained stability and the return on their human capital investment by ensuring that the workers they had trained remained in the firm for their entire productive lives. Workers sacrificed their aspiration to participation in management and production decisions—or even of ownership—and their ability to withhold their labour and disrupt production. Workers were promised secure, stable jobs that paid family wages and provided benefits. This bargain worked relatively well for many years when internal labour markets where dominant and the domestic economy was substantially shielded from global competition.

No longer. If global economic and regulatory changes have fundamentally altered this bargain, progressives have an opportunity to contest these conditions and reshape the bargain. A cornerstone of the old bargain was permanent employment, sustained by a rule of just-cause dismissal. Given the new conditions of global economic competition, it makes increasingly less sense for progressives to look for security of workers at firm level in all sectors. Progressives could promote security of workers through helping them develop marketable skills—encouraging worker investment not in the firm, but in their own personal capabilities.[165]

In the old bargain, compensation for unjust dismissal provided a cushion for workers to make ends meet while they re-entered the labour market. This compensation worked as the functional equivalent of unemployment insurance. Progressives could promote the establishment of universal unemployment insurance, paid by society as a whole through the tax system. The details of the insurance and policies to encourage labour market re-entry would need to be worked out, but this would protect workers against dismissal while giving firms the flexibility they demand. Workers would be less dependent on one particular firm and instead encouraged to invest in their skills for the market in general.

Benefits, such as health care and pension funds, were a crucial aspect of the permanent employment relationship. This highlights the fact that labour regulation cannot be analysed in a vacuum, but rather must be seen as part of a broader social bargain between capital, labour and the state, institutionalised as social security benefits. It is not surprising that workers would hang on to job security today because without a formal job they would lose accrued benefits and be deprived of social insurance. Furthermore, jobs with benefits, even in the formal economy, are increasingly hard to find. Once social insurance benefits such as health insurance, pensions, childcare, workers' compensation, and affordable housing are universally available to all citizens, job security becomes considerably less important.

Portable skills without jobs are useless. These reforms would need to be paired with a concerted strategy to stimulate the economy and create jobs. Labour flexibility, as it is currently advanced, is no development strategy. Even though it is currently promoted as one of the pending structural reforms and a key that would open the door to firms' competitiveness and job creation, it is hard to see how that would happen. At best, it is a strategy to increase firms' productivity at the margins through reduction in labour costs and making

---

[165] See, eg K Stone, *From Widgets to Digits* (Cambridge, Cambridge University Press, 2004).

jobs more precarious. This is not a sustainable, long-term strategy for job creation, much less a strategy for economic growth.

To see why the proposal of the dominant flexibility agenda is an illusion, one needs to look no further than how the labour market operates in practice—not simply what the law in the books says, but the rules governing everyday action. There is already rampant flexibility in the labour market. Many economic sectors are already quite flexible, where the employment contract restrictions in hiring and firing are honoured in the breach and benefits are not part of the contract. This de facto labour flexibility is sometimes achieved by breach. Sometimes it is by ingeniously bypassing the law, for example, by hiring workers through a third party. Furthermore, by some estimates, half of the labour force works in the informal economy, which is as flexible as it gets. Flexibility in labour costs can also be measured by looking at the dramatic decline in real wages in Mexico. Mexico has some of the lowest real wages in Latin America.[166] Since the 1990s, the productivity gains resulting from declining labour costs have mostly gone to employers.

To better diagnose the labour market, we must recognise that there are several labour law regimes that operate in the economy. Even though the applicable labour law is the same, its real hold varies. The likelihood of effective enforcement increases with the size and market relevance of firms, effective worker representation, probability of inspection visits and expedited remedies by labour tribunals. Consider three different labour law regimes that I call 'employee-friendly', 'employer-friendly' and 'free-for-all.'[167]

In the *employee-friendly* regime, the current labour law is applied at its fullest. Employees work under permanent contracts and enjoy most benefits provided by law. This regime operates in a few economic sectors such as manufacturing, mining and electricity, particularly medium-size and big firms. These are the traditionally unionised sectors, where workers often have effective representation and employers have an interest in preserving their investment in workers' human capital by avoiding employee-turnover. These are also the firms that are most visible and likely to be caught by inspectors or sued by workers if they break the law.

In the *employer-friendly* regime, labour restrictions are loose and benefits scarce or non-existent. Limitations on hiring and firing are bypassed by outsourcing and by employing workers as independent contractors. Labour law is vastly under-enforced or subverted by legal fictions and, given low levels of worker organisation, firms enjoy de facto labour flexibility. This regime is operative in many sectors, including services, tourism and food preparation, and it is most prevalent in micro, small and medium-size firms.

The *free-for-all* regime is the informal economy, where labour law does not reach and where firms mostly operate entirely outside the regulatory framework. This is a highly flexible regime where workers and employers can bargain depending on their actual power, and can expect very little legal enforcement.

Would making labour regulation more flexible achieve what its proponents promise? Hardly, it seems. The only sector where it could have real bite is the employee-friendly regime, because it is not flexible already. However, the potential benefits need to be analysed. The claim that labour flexibility would create jobs and increase output assumes that the demand for labour is quite elastic. These relevant economic sectors are quite capital intensive,

---

[166] World Bank, 'World Development Report 2013: Jobs' Report (2012).
[167] This discussion draws partly from Santos, 'Labor Flexibility' (n 121) 89–97.

however, with labour costs representing a small share of the total cost of production. When the share of labour costs—such as wages and labour protections—in firm's total costs is small, the labour demand tends to be relatively inelastic. Under this scenario a decrease in labour costs, due to more flexible regulation, is unlikely to have a significant impact on job creation.[168]

Even if cheaper labour costs create jobs in these industries, this may result in the significant deterioration of wages and working conditions. Given fixed capital costs and a small share of labour in total costs, lower wages and labour benefits may not guarantee higher overall productivity. Even if we were to see an increase in productivity, past productivity increases due to lowered wages do not confirm a link between higher productivity and job creation.[169] We can only see this by analysing the employee-friendly regime with the specific sectors it regulates and looking at how the law operates in reality, not by treating it in the abstract.

In the current debate, there is surprisingly little diagnosis of how labour regulation actually works and what flexibility reform would mean for different economic sectors as well as for workers and employers in these different labour regimes. Labour regulation does not have to be the same for all sectors. Different economic sectors can have different forms of labour contracts. Labour regulation is not uniform on the books or in practice. Any labour reform should be part of a broader development strategy, taking into account the conditions of different economic sectors and the role they would play in the overall national strategy for competition and job creation.

One final, crucial element of labour flexibility reform concerns unions and unionised workers. Unions must be able to compete with one another, and workers should be empowered to participate in the governance of their unions and to challenge their leadership. For too long, the democratic aspirations of society have been suspended in the workplace. There is no reason why democratic life and the desire to experience meaningful participation and influence in society should stop at the firm's door, where workers spend a significant part of their lives. Such a reform would require the disentanglement of the government from control over union's existence, elections and governance—much as has happened with political parties. Similarly, an independent body could be entrusted to register unions, monitor their internal elections and ensure electoral competition between them to gain majority control over collective agreements.

If union life is to be democratic—and the unions are to be attractive again to society— there should be competition over union leadership. This requires elimination of re-election or term-limits. Furthermore, serious remedies must be available to workers to challenge their leaders when their interests have been affected. This does not mean dismantling all

---

[168] See, eg G Farkas and P England (eds), *Industries, Firms, And Jobs: Sociological And Economic Approaches* (New York, Aldine de Gruyter, 1994) (expounding the Hicks-Marshall laws of elasticity of demand for labour). For empirical evidence that labour regulation's effects may be quite different between capital-intensive and labour-intensive industries, see A Ahsan and C Pages, 'Are All Labour Regulations Equal? Evidence from Indian Manufacturing' (2009) 37 *Journal of Comparative Economics* 62, 71–75.

[169] The physical volume of manufacturing output in Mexico increased considerably in the late twentieth century. However, this productivity increase has not had an impact on employment levels. In the year 2000, employment levels had not recovered from 1993 levels, despite significant growth in the maquiladora industry in the same period. Lower levels of employment can be attributed to an increase in labour productivity, which grew 46.3 per cent from 1993 to 2000, massive layoffs in the non-maquiladora manufacturing sectors due to an increase in competition from imports, and dismemberment of chains of production in the domestic market. See E De la Garza Toledo, 'Estructura Industrial y Condiciones de Trabajo en la Manufactura' (2003) *La Situación Del Trabajo En Mexico* 251, 254–55.

the elements of the collective bargaining system. Some, which enable workers to organise and help avert collective action problems, may be retained. But these rules, like the closed-shop and compulsory union fees, have been subverted for too long against the interest of workers. These mechanisms of collective bargaining would be worth preserving only if corporatist institutions can be reformed to foster independent unions and a vigorous workforce that makes leadership accountable.

V. Conclusion

In the current global economic conditions, labour law advocates find themselves on the defence. There are strong pressures worldwide to dismantle labour regulations and social security institutions. These regulations were introduced in the twentieth century as modern states stepped in to ensure a minimum level of protection for workers and to mediate conflict between labour and capital. Once seen as a sign of a modern and dynamic industrial economy, labour regulation is derided today as a rigid vestige of the past. The rallying cry for reform is 'labour flexibility', which is associated with all things positive in the new economy and proposes to cure the ills of unemployment, lack of competitiveness, and stagnant growth.

Faced with this attack on labour regulation, advocates of social law resort to three powerful defences: identity and national pride; the historically progressive character of labour law; and labour rights as constitutional or human rights. These powerful arguments may be potential antidotes to deregulatory pressures. Proffered strategically to resist labour flexibility reform, when deemed less desirable than the status quo, these arguments may have some instrumental value. I argue in this article, however, that they also have significant drawbacks. These arguments eschew an analysis of the consequences of existing labour regulation, and they fail to answer the flexibility critiques, even if they are unfounded. Additionally, these arguments make it harder to imagine alternative, progressive regulatory mechanisms to address workers' concerns other than hanging on to the status quo.

Analysing Mexican labour law's traditional narrative, I have challenged claims of workers' rights national originality and inherent progressiveness. I show that the emergence of workers' rights and labour legislation in Mexico was the result of a truly international phenomenon, where foreign ideas and laws played an important role. Moreover, the constitutionalisation of workers' rights and subsequent labour legislation was more the result of a political compromise than the historical victory of a radical programme. These challenges call for rethinking labour regulation, even to defend parts of it, by looking at its current effects rather than by invoking national myths that elude these questions, however dear these stories might be.

In the present debate, the PRI has used the social law discourse, resorting to national pride and to labour regulation's assumed progressiveness, to advance a bill that includes the flexibility recipes for employment contracts and preserves the worst aspects of corporatism in collective bargaining favouring old, official unions. This shows how malleable the social position can be and questions its association with a necessarily progressive political position.

The insights from Mexico may be relevant for other countries where social advocates use similar identity-based arguments and equate labour regulation with necessarily progressive results. In Europe, advocates have used identity-based arguments to defend social regulation, including labour law, at the regional and the national levels. Regionally, advocates have attempted to constitutionalise social rights, arguing that they should be recognised as an inherent part of European identity expressed in the notion of 'Social Europe'. Their aim is to reshape European economic integration by introducing regional social values. Nationally, social advocates less keen on the regional project have used identity to defend domestic labour regulation and national welfare institutions against the inroads of unfettered market integration.

To some extent, these projects might be useful in resisting labour market deregulation. But by portraying existing labour regulation as the best alternative, they obscure its negative consequences and make it harder to think of different legal arrangements. At the EU level, the project of consitutionalising social rights has been successful, resulting in new treaty language and increasingly socially-oriented EU Commission discourse. However, several ECJ cases and the EU's response to the financial crisis make clear that social law is very capacious and can be co-opted by both the neo-liberal version of the market-integration project and the labour flexibility programme. The constitutionalisation of social rights, social advocates have painfully found out, does not necessarily lead to the results they foresaw. This highlights the political indeterminacy of social law discourse and the downsides of a strategy predicated on identity and constitutional rights.

Domestically, the retrenchment to the national welfare state as a strategy to resist the EU integration project may also lose sight of problems within the existing social model. Additionally, it narrows the view to the national arena precisely at the time when vital questions of competition and distribution, between capital and labour and between different groups of workers, involve transnational rules and actors. The critique of the supposed national or regional identity arguments in social law seeks to broaden the scope to the transnational arena, thinking about collective solutions for workers in the face of regulatory competition. By doing this comparison, I do not mean to suggest that the situation in Mexico and Europe is the same or that the critiques in the Mexican context are simply transferable. Instead, I seek to illuminate important parallels in the arguments advanced by social advocates. The insights from the Mexican analysis may be suggestive of a broader phenomenon, perhaps one of progressive originalism running up against arguments of economic necessity.

Using the Mexican case, I suggest that there is an opportunity to engage with the deregulatory agenda for labour flexibility in a more productive way. First, we need a more comprehensive diagnosis of how labour regulation takes hold in different economic sectors. I argue that there are at least three different regimes in operation, ranging from formality and effective enforcement, to loose enforcement and informality. By considering the relationship between these labour regimes and economic sectors, we can better imagine what the results of potential labour reform would be.

In my view pro-labour advocates could challenge the assumptions of labour flexibility without needing to hang on to existing labour market regulation. They could appropriate the aspirations of flexibility to benefit workers, demanding more ambitious reforms that address firms' outdated modes of production and management to create a more participatory and meaningful workplace. At the same time, pro-labour advocates can propose ending the dependency on permanent employment for basic entitlements such as health, childcare and retirement funds, moving toward a universal coverage system. This debate could be an opportunity to rethink legal mechanisms that empower workers under conditions of global economic competition, and to do it while being mindful of the effects on the country's development prospects.

Part IV

The European Union

12

New Governance and the European Union: An Empirical and Conceptual Critique

KENNETH A ARMSTRONG

I. Introduction

The European Union is a striking illustration of a phenomenon evident nationally, internationally and transnationally, namely pluralisation and differentiation in the techniques, tools and methods deployed by public and private actors in the search for more legitimate and/or more effective means of securing economic and social governance. As such, the European landscape has proved fertile terrain for the elaboration of a 'new governance' approach to European integration that is keen to illuminate the limits of a 'traditional' approach to European law-making and law-enforcement—typically associated with the 'Community Method'—and to uncover alternative experiments in European governance. David Trubek and his collaborators have been at the forefront of this empirical mapping of the changing governance landscape and its conceptualisation within legal discourse.

In exploring a wide range of developments in EU governance across a variety of policy domains and over many years, this essay pinpoints the contribution which new governance scholarship can make to our understanding of EU governance, while acknowledging the need for analytical refinement and conceptual clarification. In so doing, the analysis engages with three key themes which resonate with enduring preoccupations of David Trubek's scholarship: a *critical* approach to law and governance; a *pluralist* and *sociological* account of law; and legal scholarship as a contribution to *pragmatic* and *progressive* politics.

A new governance approach to the EU can, and ought to be, a critical approach. While the case-study methodology which has animated much of this scholarship has usefully illuminated a rich and diverse governance landscape, nonetheless, it has risked treating 'new governance' as a state of affairs: the evolution from a traditional to a new governance world. Reorienting scholarship to make new governance the analytical and conceptual frame of reference through which to evaluate the phenomenon of pluralisation in governance rather than simply the object of empirical discovery creates a space to reflect more directly and more critically on the capacity of legal discourse and legal concepts to muster responses to changes in governance.

Admittedly, new governance scholarship has sometimes found itself on firmer terrain in elaborating what is changing in governance compared to its conceptualisation of what is happening to law. This weakness has left new governance scholars open to the criticism that they value governance over law; are indifferent to law and legal institutions; or are announcing or awaiting a 'transformative' legal moment. Yet new governance scholarship does have the capacity to highlight the on-going myriad engagements and estrangements between law and governance. However, delivering on this promise requires two things. First, an evaluation of the degree to which changes in governance do, in fact, pose challenges to law, understood as a function of the capacity of law and our concepts of legality to accommodate such changes. Secondly, in looking for available legal responses, scholarship ought to make a more decisive break with the concept of 'soft law': a concept that is both over- and under-inclusive in its capacity to capture changes in law and governance. The plea, therefore, is not only to mainstream the phenomenon of new governance in the EU within a broader horizon of changing patterns of governance nationally, internationally and transnationally, but also to build the legal and conceptual framework within available concepts of constitutional and administrative law as well as a wider sociology of law and legal pluralism.

Contemporary developments in EU governance have proven to be lightning rods for debates about the capacity of new governance to advance the cause of a progressive law and politics. For its critics, new forms of governance are either too ineffective to act as progressive counterweights to market liberalism, or are the very medium through which markets are being decoupled from their social foundations. For proponents, experiments in governance can be attempts to enhance governance capacity in areas where demographic and global pressures create new social and economic risks but where traditional legislative responses lack credibility or legitimacy. The EU's financial, banking and economic crisis and its governance response crystallises this debate. But if it has highlighted shortcomings and weaknesses in new forms of EU governance it has turned out to be both a crisis for law and a potential crisis of law as legal instrumentalism is deployed towards the politics of fiscal discipline and austerity. The experience of the EU is proving to be a particularly potent frame of reference for the contested conceptualisation of what new forms of governance mean for (European) law, while contemporary developments demand on-going critical reflection upon the institutional design of EU governance and the matrix of law and politics which informs that design.

Like other contributors to this volume, the approach taken here uses the work of David Trubek and his collaborators as both the point of reference and point of departure. Two articles are of particular relevance. The first has become a primary point of reference for discussions of new governance in the EU. Written with Joanne Scott, this framing paper introduced a journal special issue on *Law and New Approaches to Governance in the European Union* (LANAGE in Trubek-speak).[1] The second paper written with a more long-term collaborator, Louise Trubek, was published in another journal special issue published in the *Columbia Journal of European Law*.[2] The ideas presented in these papers are also present in David Trubek's other work on new governance in the EU.[3] This essay seeks to

---

[1] J Scott and DM Trubek, 'Mind the Gap: Law and New Approaches to Governance in the European Union' (2002) 8 *European Law Journal* 1.

[2] DM Trubek and L Trubek, 'New Governance and Legal Regulation: Complementarity, Rivalry and Transformation' (2007) 13 *Columbia Journal of European Law* 539.

[3] JS Mosher and DM Trubek, 'Alternative Approaches to Governance in the EU: EU Social Policy and the European Employment Strategy' (2003) 41 *Journal of Common Market Studies* 63; DM Trubek, P Cottrell and M Nance, '"Soft Law", "Hard Law" and EU Integration' in G de Búrca and J Scott (eds), *Law and New Governance in the EU and the US* (Oxford, Hart Publishing, 2006); DM Trubek and L Trubek, 'The Open Method of Co-ordination and the Debate over "Hard" and "Soft" Law' in J Zeitlin and P Pochet (eds), *The Open Method of Co-ordination in Action: The European Employment and Social Inclusion Strategies* (Bruxelles, PIE-Peter Lang, 2005); DM Trubek and L Trubek, 'Hard and Soft Law in the Construction of Social Europe: the Role of the Open Method of Co-ordination' (2005) 11 (3) *European Law Journal* 343.

develop the approach initiated in these articles, while reflecting on the challenges facing EU governance in the period since they were written. It advances both an empirical and a conceptual critique.

II. An Empirical Critique

As Jachtenfuchs highlights, the 'governance turn' in EU scholarship turned academic attention away from the 'ontological' question of the nature of the EU polity and the forces driving polity formation towards issues of the policy-making process and the outcomes of such processes.[4] Rather than being concerned to pin down the 'nature of the beast',[5] political science sought to map and taxonomise the range of modes and instruments of EU governance,[6] while reflecting upon the scope conditions for their emergence and successful operation when applied to a range of policy problems.[7] 'New governance' scholarship opened up the possibility to give a legal dimension to these changes in governance.

At its heart, the literature on new governance has two central preoccupations. The first is an attempt to give a legal response to the proliferation of modes and instruments of governance as public policy-makers—at local, national, international and transnational levels—seek to maintain social and economic order. The second is an explanatory claim that these changes signify the decline of a 'traditional' world of hierarchical governance struggling to impose order through clear and specific rules promulgated through the legislative institutions of representative democracy and implemented and enforced by the executive and judicial branches in conformity with the legislative mandate. In this way, new governance privileges the analysis of forms of governance which are taken to be not merely manifestations of the pluralisation of governance per se, but rather forms that closely align to a conceptualisation of policy-making as responses to new problems and new risks requiring new knowledge resulting in new instruments that demand on-going elaboration and reflection in the practice of governing. Accordingly, if the subsequent conceptual critique of new governance in the EU is to have any relevance, we must first be clear about the phenomenon of new governance from an empirical perspective. More importantly, the extent to which new governance poses a challenge to, or for, law and, therefore, creates a demand for a conceptual and normative response, is correlated with the extent and significance of the empirical phenomenon itself.

In exploring new governance in the EU, the first challenge is to define the terrain of new governance. In so doing, the so-called 'Community Method' typically acts as a benchmark

---

[4] M Jachtenfuchs, 'Theoretical Perspectives on European Governance' (1995) 1 *European Law Journal* 115.

[5] T Risse-Kappen, 'Exploring the Nature of the Beast: International Relations Theory and Comparative Policy Analysis Meet the European Union' (1996) 34 *JCMS: Journal of Common Market Studies* 53.

[6] See, eg H Wallace, 'An Institutional Anatomy and Five Policy Modes' in H Wallace, W Wallace and M Pollack (eds), *Policy-making in the European Union*, 6th edn (Oxford, Oxford University Press, 2010); O Treib, H Bähr and G Falkner, 'Modes of Governance: Towards a Conceptual Clarification' (2007) 14 *Journal of European Public Policy* 1.

[7] M Citi and M Rhodes, 'New Modes of Governance in the European Union: A Critical Survey and Analysis' in KE Jørgensen, M Pollack and B Rosamond (eds), *Handbook of European Union Politics* (London, Sage, 2007); A Héritier and M Rhodes (eds), *New Modes of Governance in Europe: Governing in the Shadow of Hierarchy* (Basingstoke, Palgrave Macmillan, 2010).

against which a range of governance processes can be compared, contrasted and labelled as 'new governance'.[8] A central difficulty with this approach, however, is that the Community Method itself has to be understood and elaborated. Two rather distinct characteristics of the Community Method need to be unpacked. The first is its institutional dimension and the role played by EU legislative, executive and judicial institutions. The second dimension relates to the 'mode' of governance underpinning the outputs of the Community Method: this is typically understood as the production of governance by 'hierarchy'. In this way, new forms of EU governance are depicted as non-hierarchical and operating outside of the traditional institutional structures of the EU. Yet as Scott and Trubek remind us, new forms of governance are not wholly dissociable from the Community Method.[9] Indeed, what may be identified is not necessarily a shift from hierarchy but a relocation of norm production and norm elaboration to a range of institutional locations outside of, but not unconnected to, the inter-institutional decision-making processes associated with the Community Method. It is this differentiation within EU governance rather than a decisive shift from one state of affairs—the Community Method—to another state of affairs—new governance—that needs to be better characterised so that we might then begin to make sense and attach significance to what is changing in governance and what it might mean for law.

Three dimensions of differentiation can be identified. The first dimension concerns the relationship between the emergence of new forms of governance and the continuing role of the EU legislative process. The second development relates to differentiation and rivalry in the institutional model for executive governance within a multi-level polity. The third development shifts attention more decisively towards the Europeanisation of domestic policy through mechanisms of EU policy coordination. As will become apparent, the significance of these three dimensions should not be understood in terms of being stronger or weaker versions of new governance but rather they each have different functional characteristics that illuminate different limits of the Community Method. There is, therefore, functional differentiation across new forms of governance. As a consequence, the implications for law are likely to vary. If attentive to this differentiation, then new governance opens up the EU governance process to critical analysis.

A. The Community Method and the Legislative Process

When thinking about the relationship between the emergence of new forms of governance and the historic role assigned to legislative institutions, it is important to recognise that there is no fixed pool of governance activity from which to evaluate the rise or fall of legislative action compared to any potential alternative. There is no zero-sum game in which the increase or decrease in legislative activity correlates identically with gains or losses in the use of alternative forms of governance. To take a simple example in the EU context, the turn to the Community Method in the form of legislative outputs to strengthen EU economic and fiscal supervision did not result in a turn away from policy coordination as a governance technique: indeed, policy coordination has been intensified through the

---

[8] R Dehousse, 'The "Community Method" at Sixty' in R Dehousse (ed), *The "Community Method": Obstinate or Obsolete?* (Basingstoke, Palgrave Macmillan, 2011); Scott and Trubek, 'Mind the Gap' (n 1).

[9] Scott and Trubek, ibid.

so-called 'European Semester' of economic and fiscal policy coordination. Rather, changes in patterns of governance are about changes in governance capacity, with the emergence of forms of international and transnational governance as attempts to respond to the challenges facing nation states to supply governance solutions to governance problems. Indeed, the interesting question may well be one of how different governance responses co-exist and coordinate with one another in ways which maintain and enhance governance capacities or alternatively create governance deficits (under-regulation) or surpluses (over-regulation).

In considering the role of the EU legislative process, according to Boussaguet, Dehousse and Jacquot, the EU's legislative outputs have remained relatively constant over the last decade despite the emergence of new forms of EU governance.[10] Of course, what this does not tell us is what is produced by such legislative interventions and indeed, new governance may be the product of legislation particularly where legislative acts create framework norms that are developed and elaborated in a post-legislative phase. Yet it would be wrong to imply that this legislative output consists solely or primarily of framework legislation. There is no apparent loss of appetite for the adoption of substantive and detailed legislative acts including the use of directly applicable regulations. Indeed, in its response to the economic crisis buffeting the Eurozone, of the legislative measures adopted in its initial legislative 'six-pack', five of these instruments are regulations and one is a directive. The subsequent 'two-pack' of proposals to enhance surveillance and evaluation of Eurozone states' budgets also envisaged the adoption of regulations. Binding law and hierarchy have not gone away.

The on-going role and significance of public legislative institutions within EU governance also seems to run counter to the intuition within much of the governance and transnational regulation literature of a heightened role for private actors in new forms of governance. Indeed for Börzel, it is public actors that dominate EU governance not just at the legislative level but also in post-legislative EU governance.[11] Yet it is apparent that private actors do play significant roles within EU governance and autonomously within structures of transnational private regulation operating in the European and international environment. Indeed, for Abbott and Snidal, it is transnational private regimes that exemplify new governance's emergence beyond the boundaries of the nation state and which rival 'traditional' forms of international organisation and international norm-making of which the EU is a particularly intense example. In the EU context we find a range of roles played by private actors either as part of public forms of governance or more autonomously.

One obvious area where private governance could rival EU legislative action is in the social sphere where 'social dialogue' between representatives of management and labour can result in the adoption of binding agreements. One way of looking at social dialogue could be to think of it as an example of bargaining in the shadow of hierarchy with the European Commission's consultation of the social partners and the latter's consequential right to bargain among themselves as creating incentives to pre-empt EU legislative action. Yet this tends to overstate both the credibility of the legislative threat—particularly in areas where there is deep disagreement among legislative actors at EU level—and the capacity

---

[10] L Boussaguet, R Dehousse and S Jacquot, 'The "Governance Turn" Revisited' in Dehousse (ed), *The "Community Method"* (n 8).

[11] T Börzel, 'European Governance: Negotiation and Competition in the Shadow of Hierarchy' (2010) 48 *Journal of Common Market Studies* 191.

of social partners to overcome disagreements to conclude negotiations. The revision of the controversial Working Time Directive (WTD) and the Posted Workers Directive (PWD) are cases in point.

While it is clear that some reform of the WTD is believed to be necessary, the political agreement which would form the basis for revision was absent and so the legislative process failed to reach a conclusion. Although the social partners were consulted as part of that legislative process there was also evident disagreement between the partners as to whether the objective of revision was to increase labour market flexibility or to increase worker protection. Nonetheless, with the failure of the legislative process, the social partners did agree to open negotiations with a view to agreeing a revision to the directive. This is bargaining in the wake of legislative failure rather than bargaining in the shadow of hierarchy. Yet the negotiations between the social partners also failed to produce an agreement. The incapacity of social dialogue to reach an agreed outcome on revisions to the PWD has itself resulted in the EU's legislative institutions commencing negotiations where again there is political contestation. In these examples, social dialogue and legislative action are not rivals in situations where both are self-evidently capable of succeeding. Rather each represents a potential alternative to the failure of the other but with the risk that neither succeeds and overall governance capacity is lost.

Even where social dialogue has resulted in binding agreements, the social partners have often looked to the Community Method to institutionalise bargains in legal texts and to harness the enforcement mechanisms of EU law. In this way, while the negotiation of texts is conducted by the social partners, the legislative process encodes these texts in legislative form and so facilitates their monitoring and enforcement. Once again, the resort to alternative arenas for norm production is not necessarily at the expense of the legislative process.

To concentrate on these examples is, however, to ignore the autonomous sectoral social dialogue texts and agreements that are negotiated and implemented by social partners in areas such as workplace stress and harassment at work together with a wide range of codes of conduct and guidelines. These activities point to an active arena of private governance operating within and alongside EU employment law rather than necessarily as rivals to EU legislative action.

Another arena where we find public and private co-regulation or 'associative' regulation[12] is in respect of the elimination of technical barriers to trade. Private European standardisation bodies play a key role in the adoption of harmonised technical standards, compliance with which is voluntary but facilitates market access. This autonomous and voluntary activity supports EU policies in the realm of procurement policy and sectoral market liberalisation in fields such as telecommunications policy. But it is also harnessed more directly as one means of indicating compliance with EU internal market directives which make market access conditional upon meeting framework public interest goals (so-called 'New Approach' directives). While such directives are binding pre-emptory norms, manufacturers can choose to indicate conformity with these legislative acts directly or by complying with harmonised European standards (giving rise to a presumption of conformity with directives). Like the previous example of private governance in the social

---

[12] M Egan, *Constructing a European market: Standards, Regulation, and Governance* (Oxford, Oxford University Press, 2001).

sphere, harmonisation of standards is both autonomous and yet also linked to public legislative action at EU level.

If social dialogue and the New Approach represent self-conscious efforts by EU institutions to harness private governance towards public ends across policy domains, there are transnational private regimes operating in respect of more particular European policy issues. In much the same way that new governance is often dramatically presented in opposition to the Community Method as a mode of public governance, private governance is also all too easily presented as the rival to public governance in the EU. As Cafaggi suggests, the juxtaposition of private and public governance has had the effect of leaving the former out of the integration through law paradigm of European integration: for him, there is at least institutional complementarity between European public and private governance.[13]

These stories of complementarity or indeed 'hybridity' in the combination of governance tools and approaches offer an alternative narrative to depictions of new forms of governance as the necessary rivals to legislative intervention: a point to which Trubek and Trubek have drawn attention and a point to which we shall return later.[14]

B. Executive Governance

Even if the EU legislative process remains of continuing relevance as an expression of the Community Method, it may simply be the beginning rather than the end of the EU policy process. Alternative sites of norm-production prevail in the post-legislative 'executive' phase. Executive governance in the EU is of particular interest when viewed through the lens of new governance inasmuch as it exemplifies differentiation and pluralisation in the institutional design of EU governance, its multi-level nature,[15] and the difficulty in maintaining a clear separation between legislative mandate and executive implementation particularly under conditions of novel risks and uncertainty.

The dominant institutional form of executive governance in the EU has been the post-legislative exercise of executive rule-making and administrative power by the European Commission through 'comitology'. Comitology is the attempt to bring the national administrations into the exercise of the executive responsibilities of the European Commission. A vast literature exists on the phenomenon.[16] Although a departure from the Community Method in one sense—non-legislative norm production and application—it, nonetheless, is its analogue in seeking to reconcile supranational interests—represented by the central position occupied by the European Commission—with the interests of the Member States and the national administrations. It is also not a departure from hierarchy inasmuch as its outputs are binding norms.

---

[13] F Cafaggi, 'Private Law-Making and European Integration: Where Do They Meet, When Do They Conflict?' in D Oliver, T Prosser and R Rawlings (eds), *The Regulatory State Constitutional Implications* (Oxford, Oxford University Press, 2010).

[14] Trubek and Trubek, 'New Governance and Legal Regulation' (n 2).

[15] D Curtin, *Executive Power of the European Union: Law, Practices, and the Living Constitution* (Oxford, Oxford University Press, 2009).

[16] See inter alia, CF Bergström, *Comitology: Delegation of Powers in the European Union and the Committee System* (Oxford, Oxford University Press, 2005); C Joerges and E Vos (eds), *EU Committees: Social Regulation, Law and Politics* (Oxford, Hart Publishing, 1998).

For Joerges and Neyer, the reconciliation of supranational and national interests informed by expertise created an arena of 'deliberative supranationalism' within comitology.[17] For Joerges, the system of comitology is 'the oldest form of "new" governance'.[18] In this volume, Joerges and Weimer highlight the constitutionalisation and proceduralisation of comitology: a process that was incremental with practice gradually being formalised in Council Decisions, supplemented by judicial oversight. Yet this evolutionary procedural 'legalisation'—which Joerges has contrasted with the apparent 'de-legalisation' of newer forms of EU governance—has been interrupted by the 'constitutional' changes made by the Lisbon Treaty. The treaty attempts to impose a more traditional and formal separation of powers model on the exercise of the Commission's executive powers. Indeed, executive rule-making is now to be more clearly delegated to the Commission without the formalities of comitology albeit that expertise is to inform that decision-making.[19] Following a classical approach to the separation of powers, it is the EU's legislative institutions—the European Parliament and the Council—that are to choose which powers to delegate to the European Commission, for how long, and with ultimate power to revoke the delegated authority. In this respect, 'old' new governance is apparently transitioning to new 'old' governance: centralisation of executive responsibility in the hands of the European Commission subject to the supervision and control of the EU legislator. All of which cautions against assumptions that changes in governance are unidirectional: from old to new; from traditional to experimental.

For Sabel and Zeitlin, while the 'Cambrian explosion' of new forms of EU governance find their origins in the system of comitology, the ecosystem of executive governance is characterised by institutional differentiation and experimental governance.[20] These newer institutional expressions of executive governance take the form principally of European agencies and transgovernmental networks. Agencies are engaged to support EU-level executive responsibilities but with more functional expertise channelled through the creation of European-level bodies. Networks seek to Europeanise national executive responsibilities in the development and implementation of EU rules, particularly in areas of regulatory policy. The result is a more plural and differentiated institutional framework for executive governance in the EU.

As Curtin reminds us, executive power in the EU is a 'compound' power,[21] or as Wessels puts it, a multi-level 'fusion' of administrative power.[22] In this way, the familiar problems of how to ensure accountable and effective executive governance—problems

---

[17] C Joerges and J Neyer, 'From Intergovernmental Bargaining to Deliberative Political Processes: The Constitutionalisation of Comitology' (1997) 3 *European Law Journal* 273.

[18] C Joerges, 'Integration through de-legalisation' (2008) 33 *European Law Review* 291.

[19] Under Art 290 TFEU 'delegated' acts are to be adopted by the European Commission without resort to comitology. Under Art 291 TFEU certain 'implementing' acts are adopted by the European Commission subject to a streamlined comitology process now governed by Regulation 182/2011 laying down the rules and general principles concerning mechanisms for control by Member States of the Commission's exercise of implementing powers that came into force on 1 March 2011 [2011] OJ L55/13.

[20] CF Sabel and J Zeitlin, 'Learning from Difference: The New Architecture of Experimentalist Governance in the EU' (2008) 14 *European Law Journal* 271; CF Sabel and J Zeitlin, *Experimentalist Governance in the European Union: Towards a New Architecture* (Oxford, Oxford University Press, 2010); CF Sabel and J Zeitlin, 'Experimentalism in the EU: Common Ground and Persistent Differences' (2012) 6 *Regulation & Governance* 410.

[21] Curtin, *Executive Power of the European Union* (n 15).

[22] W Wessels, 'Comitology: Fusion in Action: Politico-administrative trends in the EU system' (1998) 5 *Journal of European Public Policy* 209.

that have dominated administrative law scholarship for a century—are compounded in EU multi-level governance where authorship and responsibility may be blurred rather than clearly allocated or delegated. As intimated, the reforms made by the Lisbon Treaty attempt to make the European Commission's executive responsibilities clearer and subject to legislative oversight. Yet the European Commission may not be the original author of its delegated rules. For example, in the wake of the financial crisis, new supervisory authorities have emerged including the European Securities and Markets Authority (ESMA). Its powers include drafting regulatory and implementing technical standards which are then formally adopted by the European Commission using its delegated and implementing powers. Although established as 'European' agencies or authorities, these bodies typically draw membership from national regulators and in the case of ESMA has a Stakeholder Group—including academics, financial services participants, users and consumers—that is consulted and facilitates consultation with stakeholders before draft technical standards are adopted. The blurring of authorship which this illustrates, intensifies as transgovernmental networks develop post-legislative codes and guidance that shape decentralised implementation of EU framework norms.[23] Thus, attempts at constitutionalisation through the imposition of a classical constitutional principal–agent model of control and accountability such as that apparently foisted upon the European Commission's delegated rule-making may appear out of place in such an ambiguous administrative environment.

Not surprisingly, then, the terrain of executive governance has proved fertile for proponents of experimentalist governance. The attempt to manage new social and economic risks in an environment of uncertainty creates the scope conditions for the emergence of new architectures for governance in which the blurring of normative authorship is a manifestation of the blurring of boundaries between legislative and executive action.[24] Yet in critiquing classical constitutional principal–agent models of control and accountability, and in emphasising the functional dynamics of new forms of governance,[25] scholarship has opened itself up to the accusation of indifference to issues of legitimacy and rule of law values, or at least, to betray a preference for output legitimacy. Certainly, for proponents of experimentalist governance there is less reliance on legally-mediated procedures when compared to a faith in mechanisms of 'dynamic accountability' that seek to promote accountability through the political process via aspirations of participatory and deliberative democracy and mechanisms of peer review.[26] Yet this should not be understood as an indifference to law but rather as consistent with critical and sceptical traditions that have cautioned against over-reliance on law and legal institutions as a means to control the executive: traditions that have their origins in domestic debates about the implications for law of the growth of the administrative state.[27] Moreover, in the articulation of the so-called 'gap thesis' (discussed further below), new governance scholars have themselves done much to illuminate the risk that new forms of post-legislative governance are not easily captured by courts in the exercise of their judicial review functions. In this way, the contribution of new and experimental

---

[23] J Scott, 'In Legal Limbo: Post-Legislative Guidance as a Challenge for European Administrative Law' (2011) 48 *Common Market Law Review* 329.

[24] Sabel and Zeitlin, 'Experimentalism in the EU' (n 20).

[25] M Wilkinson, 'Three Conceptions of Law: Towards a Jurisprudence of Democratic Experimentalism' (2010) 2 *Wisconsin Law Review* 673.

[26] Sabel and Zeitlin, 'Learning from Difference' (n 20).

[27] Recall, for example, the distinction made between 'red light' and 'green light' approaches to administrative law: C Harlow and R Rawlings, *Law and Administration* (Cambridge, Cambridge University Press, 1997).

governance scholarship has been not just to excavate the contemporary landscape of EU executive governance or to discover new governance lifeforms (depending on one's preference for geological or biological metaphors), but to provide a point of critical reflection from which to think about issues of institutional design and the reconciliation of functional and normative demands. Whatever the shortcomings of that critical reflection in terms of the promotion of workable institutional designs—and here proponents of experimentalist governance would do well to remember the over-inflated optimism with which comitology was embraced as an ideal legal and institutional framework for the exercise of executive power—suggestions that this scholarship is indifferent either to the role of law or the search for legitimacy, are misplaced.

C. The Community Method and the Open Method

The Open Method of Coordination (OMC) has often been presented as the prime example of new governance in the EU. With its origins in the treaty-based processes for economic and employment policy coordination, the advent of the Lisbon strategy to promote competitiveness and social cohesion in the EU launched the OMC as a potentially generalisable technique for the 'Europeanisation' of domestic policies in a wide range of fields (from anti-poverty, pensions, long-term care and education, to knowledge society and information technology policies) but without resort to EU legislative action.[28] Its methodology—a decentralised approach to policy development in line with broad framework objectives and with reporting and monitoring processes—appeared to be an alternative to past strategies of top-down hierarchical Europeanisation through legislative means. With OMC processes developing as a means of pursuing treaty-based objectives but without its processes or methodologies being institutionalised in law, the OMC also appeared to depart from the integration through law paradigm in its processes as well as its output. However, the OMC turns out not to be wholly disassociated from the Community Method in certain respects. At an institutional level, for the Commission, the OMC may be an alternative channel for seeking supranational influence outside of its traditional role in exercising its right of legislative initiative.[29] While it is up to Member States to choose what they wish to learn and from whom, through policy coordination, the steering role of the Commission may play an influential role in that process.[30] For the Member States, it may open up possibilities for a new style of flexible, even 'deliberative' intergovernmentalism.[31] The OMC has also tended to replicate some of the features of comitology in its use of specialised committees of representatives of national administrations mediating between the European Commission and the Council. In other words, if the Community Method is really about an institutional balance between supranationalism and intergovernmentalism, processes like the OMC

---

[28] P Copeland and D Papadimitriou (eds), *The EU's Lisbon Strategy: Evaluating Success, Understanding Failure* (Basingstoke, Palgrave Macmillan, 2012).

[29] L Cram, 'In the Shadow of Hierarchy: Governance as a Tool of Government' in Dehousse (ed), *The "Community Method"* (n 8).

[30] I Deganis, 'The Politics Behind Consensus: Tracing the Role of the Commission within the European Employment Strategy' (2006) 2 *Journal of Contemporary European Research* 21.

[31] U Puetter, 'Europe's Deliberative Intergovernmentalism: The Role of the Council and European Council in EU Economic Governance' (2012) 19 *Journal of European Public Policy* 161.

may, in a different context and towards different ends, reproduce certain features of that method rather than necessarily depart from it.[32]

Much like the Community Method, the open method is not a precise singular phenomenon. It is an assemblage of methods of objective-setting, reporting, reviewing and monitoring with each method present to greater or lesser degrees. Indeed, there is a high degree of differentiation in the use of the technique across policy fields and over time. This diversity is due not least to the very different rationales that underpin the resort to policy coordination: from the desire to manage externalities from other policy fields (for example, managing the consequences of monetary union), through to the aim of applying common approaches to common problems (for example, in making labour markets more 'flexible'), to the more diffuse aim of supporting the search for policy solutions to different policy problems albeit within a common European framework (for example, combating social exclusion).[33] In other words, the institutional design of policy coordination relates to its functional orientation. Yet there is a more profound functional dichotomy that underpins policy coordination and that is between the use of OMC as a technique of *governance* and OMC as a mechanism for *accountability*.[34]

As a technique of governance, policy coordination is not intended to produce direct first order results and so is not directly comparable with other aspects of EU governance and what they may or may not demand by way of legitimation. Rather, it is a second order process intended to stimulate and inform domestic processes and policy-making. Domestic policy-making has always been informed by international policy frames and paradigms and consensuses. And there is nothing new in states borrowing policy ideas from one another. The OMC organises that individual and collective capacity within a European framework. But fundamentally, decision-making rests with Member States: that is the democratic virtue and the effectiveness vice of the OMC.

To be sure, actors within the coordination process will seek to upload policy frames, policy paradigms and policy preferences and encourage others to download them into the national systems. And for proponents of the OMC who saw it not merely as a 'third way' between the Community Method and intergovernmentalism, but also substantively as a means of promoting progressive left-of-centre politics, the lesson to be learned is that the framework can equally be used to disseminate the policies of the Right as well as the Left. Self-evidently, in the realm of economic policy coordination, the coordination process has been harnessed as part of a wider package of responses (including treaty and legislative responses) that are intended to produce real and radical reforms to the conduct of economic and fiscal policies. It is perhaps the irony of policy coordination that, under the Lisbon Strategy—dominated in its early years by social democratic politics—it produced little substantive policy change, yet under the conditions of economic crisis—from which political parties of the Right were at least initially beneficiaries—policy coordination in combination with other governance tools may be facilitating political consensus-building around policies of austerity. That Member States choose to follow particular political paths

---

[32] S Borrás, 'The Politics of the Lisbon Strategy: The Changing Role of the Commission' (2008) 32 *West European Politics* 97.

[33] See generally, KA Armstrong, *Governing Social Inclusion: Europeanization through Policy Coordination* (Oxford, Oxford University Press, 2010); I Begg, 'Is There a Convincing Rationale for the Lisbon Strategy?' (2008) 46 *Journal of Common Market Studies* 427.

[34] Armstrong, ibid.

or adopt particular policies remains their responsibility whether that process is facilitated by European coordination or not.

Indeed, if our starting point is that Member States remain not only legally competent in the policy fields in which the OMC operates but also politically responsible, then a key function of the OMC may be to facilitate the accountability of Member States for their policy choices and policy performances. The mechanisms and processes for reporting and monitoring open out the domestic policy process to external evaluation and comment. While different from the accountability of Member States under judicial processes scrutinising domestic law compliance with EU substantive law, nonetheless, as a political process the OMC is analogous insofar as the domestic policy process is encouraged to be responsive to out-of-state influences with EU-level political institutions drawing conclusions to which Member States are encouraged to respond.

The OMC is both a focal point and a lightning rod for debates about new governance in the EU. It is poster boy and whipping boy. For its proponents, the turn to mechanisms of decentralised policy coordination in areas beyond EU 'regulatory policy' and its associated Community Method, both exemplify the limits of 'integration through law' and the potential for new governance architectures to address pressing social and economic problems by harnessing the individual and collective policy autonomy of Member States within a common European framework. For some of its opponents, OMC is simply a transitory and fashionable distraction from the continuing relevance of EU legislative and judicial governance,[35] while for others, OMC is either too ineffective to secure its aims or the very means by which Europe's economy and social welfare systems are transformed but in ways which do not match the progressive ideals of its proponents. What is so markedly illustrated by this academic debate is that neither proponents nor opponents of the OMC get to 'win' by default. On the one hand, while the OMC may well highlight the limits of effective and legitimate governance through the Community Method, the methods associated with policy coordination may not fare any better or may even intensify problems. On the other hand, the limits of the OMC are not necessarily going to be solved by a triumphant return of the 'Community Method'. An acceptance of the intractability of the governance dilemmas facing the EU may be the common ground for a more balanced reappraisal of the relevance of new governance and the OMC. Like other innovations in EU governance, our capacity to evaluate the OMC's significance and its implications for our conceptualisation of law, rather depend on concrete empirical evidence and nuanced evaluation.

* * * * *

What the empirical evidence demonstrates is an evolving system of EU governance that, as Scott and Trubek reminds us, is not wholly disassociated from the Community Method.[36] It is not an abandonment of hierarchy but in some respects its extension and in others its modulation alongside other techniques of governance. None of which is to suggest that there are not new and interesting things for lawyers to analyse: there are. Rather, the point is that the more that analysis orients its focus on 'new governance' as if it were

---

[35] T Idema and DR Keleman, 'New modes of governance, the Open Method of Co-ordination and Other Fashionable Red Herring' (2006) 7 *Perspectives on European Politics and Society* 108.

[36] Scott and Trubek, 'Mind the Gap' (n 1).

a discrete manifestation of particular forms of governance that decisively departs from the Community Method, the more stylised and stark will be the claims and the more 'exceptional' will be the conceptual contribution. A more mainstreamed, and indeed critical, approach to the EU's governance landscape would seem to be better placed to make a more decisive contribution.

As a prelude to the conceptual critique below, two important conclusions need to be drawn from the empirical critique. There is a risk that the varieties of change in EU governance described above are treated as if they are simply different points on a scale of governance that starts with the Community Method and then leads towards the OMC. It is clear that the differences are not of scale but of type. The examples of co-regulation such as the New Approach and social dialogue are novel insofar as they bring private actors into primary rule-making. Comitology, agencies and networks represent different institutional engagements of public actors—representatives of national executives or regulators—in implementing and developing legislative norms. The OMC is a framework for the creation of second order effects rather than a direct substitute for first order rule-making. These examples of governance are doing different things: they are not different ways of doing the same thing. These differences in function produce institutional variation and institutional experimentation in ways which have different implications for law and legal institutions. Reducing that variety down to a singular phenomenon or label like 'new governance' or 'experimentalist governance' risks blunting the critical capacity of scholarship to reflect on the implications of pluralism and differentiation in governance, while also rendering that scholarship open to accusations and claims that are misdirected.

The second point returns us to the idea that new governance is characterised by its non-hierarchical modes of governance. As will be elaborated more fully below, we are likely to find a range of modes of governance in operation across the range of locations of EU governance. These may even be arranged in 'hybrid' forms that include elements of hierarchy. The main point of departure and difference between scholars is not so much whether the output of governance is a binding norm, but rather whether the processes and sites of norm-production can be accommodated either within classical constitutional and administrative law hierarchies of control, accountability and legitimacy or within prevailing concepts of law and legality. In the EU context, this manifests in a tension between those for whom changes in governance fall within the 'shadow of hierarchy'—the delegation of rule-making by an accountable principal under threat of direct intervention by that principal—and those who see such changes as signalling a more fundamental decline in the capacities of state institutions (including their international and transnational counterparts) to produce legitimate and effective governance in ways which risk the emergence of 'gaps' between law and governance or inspire a 'transformation' in that relationship.[37] It is to these debates that we now turn.

---

[37] TA Börzel, 'Experimentalist Governance in the EU: The Emperor's New Clothes?' (2012) 6 *Regulation & Governance* 378; Sabel and Zeitlin, 'Learning from Difference' (n 20).

III. A Conceptual Critique

In seeking to bring the law back in to the discussion of EU governance, a number of key themes have emerged within the literature. Three themes will be analysed here. The first theme is the manner in which differentiation and pluralisation in governance is accommodated within legal discourse. To the extent that this has been done by an expansion of the category of 'soft law', new governance is conceptually vulnerable in its account of law. The second theme refers to an idea that new forms of governance might coexist and indeed complement more traditional forms of legal intervention. While the literature highlights the potential for 'rivalry' or 'hybridity' it tends to understand this as relationships between 'law' and 'new governance' rather than as two possible relationships between different governance instruments or governance modes whose legal implications themselves need to be evaluated. The third theme addresses the concern that new forms of governance are either estranged from law—the gap thesis—or provoke a reconceptualisation of law—the 'transformation thesis'.[38]

A. Beyond 'Soft' Law

The paradox of new governance scholarship is perhaps that greater attention has been paid to elaborating the features of a changing governance landscape than its legal characteristics.[39] Indeed, while a rather rich picture has emerged of the plurality of forms of governance, as Dawson notes, law has often been characterised in opposition to new governance with the features of the latter defined by their departure from the traditional institutions and processes of public rule-making.[40] As described above, in the EU context, this gives rise to a distancing of new governance both from the Community Method and potentially from law itself. To avoid this estrangement of new governance from legal discourse, scholars have repeatedly described it as a form of 'soft law'.[41] Yet the very softness of this conceptualisation risks mischaracterising the very phenomenon that legal scholars seek to explain.[42]

As developed within international relations and international law scholarship, 'soft law' refers to a range of texts which in some way fall short of archetypal forms of binding international legal instruments. Abbott and Snidal present this shift from 'hard' to 'soft' law on a spectrum of 'legalisation' derived from variation along the dimensions of 'obligation'

---

[38] G de Búrca and J Scott, 'Introduction: New Governance, Law and Constitutionalism' in G de Búrca and J Scott (eds), *Law and New Governance in the EU and the US* (Oxford, Hart Publishing, 2006).

[39] KA Armstrong and C Kilpatrick, 'Law, Governance or New Governance? The Changing Open Method of Coordination' (2007) 13 *Columbia Journal of European Law* 649; KA Armstrong, 'The Character of EU Law and Governance: From "Community Method" to New Modes of Governance' (2011) 63 *Current Legal Problems* 179.

[40] M Dawson, 'Three Waves of New Governance in the European Union' (2011) 36 *European Law Review* 208.

[41] Trubek, Cottrell and Nance, '"Soft Law", "Hard Law" and EU Integration' (n 3); Trubek and Trubek, 'The Open Method of Co-ordination and the Debate over "Hard" and "Soft" Law' (n 3); DM Trubek and L Trubek, 'Hard and Soft Law in the Construction of Social Europe' (n 3). More confusingly, it is sometimes referred to as 'soft governance': S Kroger, *Soft Governance in Hard Politics: European Coordination of Anti-poverty Policies in France and Germany* (Wiesbaden, VS Verl. für Sozialwissenschaften, 2008).

[42] A distinction has occasionally been drawn between 'old' and 'new' forms of governance in which the latter depart from 'traditional' uses of soft law in the EU: S Borrás and K Jacobsson, 'The Open Method of Co-ordination and New Governance Patterns in the EU' (2004) 11 *Journal of European Public Policy* 185.

and 'precision'—referring to the status and form of texts—and 'delegation'—signifying the presence or absence of institutions with enforcement functions.[43] Certainly, there is a phenomenon which is characterised as soft law and it is found in national, international and EU governance.[44] And elements of this type of soft law—typically formally-adopted texts but which do not have the status of binding legal acts—can play a role in new governance. Yet simply accommodating new governance within this capacious category is to ignore the contribution of new governance scholarship in two related ways.

The first is that while a great deal of emphasis is placed on EU scholarship in the emergence of new forms of governance where the EU lacks legislative competence to adopt binding rules, its development in the context of binding framework norms is at least, if not more, noteworthy. As the discussion of executive governance illustrated, the elaboration of binding norms can be accompanied by differentiation within governance. The second issue relates to the first, namely that what seems to matter more to new governance scholars are the mechanisms and processes by which norms—binding or not—are elaborated and their performance reviewed in the context of their application. To put it another way, what seems to count for new governance scholars is not the formal deviation from hard legal instruments as such: if we think about the way in which legal scholars like Scott and Trubek define the attributes of new governance—multilevel, diverse and decentralised, deliberative, flexible and revisable, experimental—they point to the mechanisms by which framework 'first order' norms are implemented and recalibrated as part of an on-going and reflexive process of governance.[45] The difficulty, however, is that it is the governance side that is doing the work here: the characterisation of law and what is happening to law remains to be determined. As a characterisation of new governance, 'soft' law is both under-inclusive in that it detracts attention from the areas in which binding norms—particularly framework norms—are present, and over-inclusive insofar as the presence of new forms of governance may well signify either gaps between law and governance or the presence of alternative and competing claims to legal authorship and normative authority.

B. Beyond 'Law' and 'New Governance': Rivalry and Hybridity

A different manifestation of new governance scholarship's attempt to characterise the legal implications of changes in governance is the proposition that there are dominant relationships between 'law' and 'new governance'. Trubek and Trubek suggest a triptych of candidate relationships between law and new governance: the relationships of 'rivalry'—law and new governance compete to coordinate an activity—of 'complementarity'—the co-existence of law and new governance techniques in the same field—and of 'transformation'—law

---

[43] KW Abbott, RO Keohane, A Moravchik, A-M Slaughter and D Snidal, 'The Concept of Legalization' (2000) 54 *International Organization* 401; KW Abbott and D Snidal, 'Hard and Soft Law in International Governance' (2000) 54 *International Organization* 421.

[44] CM Chinkin, 'The Challenge of Soft Law: Development and Change in International-Law' (1989) 38 *International and Comparative Law Quarterly* 850; M Cini, 'The Soft Law Approach: Commission Rule-making in the EU's State Aid Regime' (2001) 8 *Journal of European Public Policy* 192; A Schäfer, 'Resolving Deadlock: Why International Organisations Introduce Soft Law' (2006) 12 *European Law Journal* 194; F Snyder, 'The Effectiveness of European Community Law: Institutions, Processes, Tools and Techniques' (1993) 56 *Modern Law Review* 19.

[45] Scott and Trubek, 'Mind the Gap' (n 1).

and new governance combine in ways which transform one another.[46] While there is an important intuition underlying this and other attempts to think about what pluralisation and differentiation in governance means for law, further clarification and refinement of our understanding of these relationships is necessary. This entails a two-step process. The first is to view 'rivalry' and 'complementarity' as the possible relationships between different instruments or modes of governance rather than candidate relationships between 'law' and 'new governance'. The second step is to relate more directly the claim of legal 'transformation' to what is sometimes referred to as the 'gap thesis'. It is the first of these steps that is the focus of this section, whereas discussion of the second will be central to the subsequent analysis.

The difficulty starts with the tendency to treat law as a proxy for hierarchy and new governance as a synonym for non-hierarchical modes of governance. What appears to be a concern with the relationship between law and new governance may be better understood as the relationship between different 'modes' of governance—hierarchy, competition, self-regulation[47]—expressed in different instruments or even within the same governance instrument; or the relationship between different sites and different authors of governance. Thus, the idea that law and new governance 'rival' or 'complement' one another as means for societal coordination may mischaracterise what are essentially two plausible interpretations of relationships *within* governance rather than *between* law and governance.

This point has particular salience when it comes to considering a key theme in new governance scholarship namely the potential for 'hybridity'. At its most basic, the idea of hybrid governance is the recognition that many of society's pressing problems are addressed by multiple forms of intervention. At an instrumental level, these interventions may be legislative and non-legislative. Market mechanisms may co-exist with hierarchical rules and processes for self- or co-regulation. As with the idea of 'rivalry', rather than viewing 'hybridity' as the product of candidate relationships between law and new governance, it seems rather more fruitful to think of hybridity as referring to the combinations of modes and instruments of governance which, in turn, give rise to a range of legal encounters. In other words, the differences that are combined in 'hybridity' are differences between modes and instruments and authors of governance rather than differences between law and (new) governance. This not only allows us to analyse more carefully the ways in which different governance techniques combine, it then allows us to think more clearly about their implications for law.

C. Beyond Law?

When new governance scholarship turns its attention more directly towards the implications of changes in governance for law, two dominant characterisations emerge: the 'gap' thesis and the 'transformation' thesis. As de Búrca and Scott have suggested, in its descriptive form, the 'gap thesis' highlights the risk that changes in governance are simply not recognised in law.[48] In a more normative vein, attention is drawn to potential antagonisms where

---

[46] Trubek and Trubek, 'New Governance and Legal Regulation' (n 2).

[47] Treib, Bähr and Falkner, 'Modes of Governance' (n 6); Héritier and Rhodes, '*New Modes of Governance in Europe*' (n 7); C Scott, 'The Governance of the European Union: The Potential for Multi-Level Control' (2002) 8 *European Law Journal* 59.

[48] De Búrca and Scott, 'New Governance, Law and Constitutionalism' (n 38).

either law's attempt to accommodate new forms of governance stifles some of the latter's potential virtues, or new forms of governance displace, or limit the capacities of, law. If the gap thesis warns of a potential estrangement between governance and law, the transformation thesis suggests that such gaps can be bridged by a reconceptualisation of law and its relationship to governance.

i. Mind the Gap

Changes in governance create certain challenges for judicial review. The legislative and executive acts of the EU institutions together with the acts of its bodies and agencies which produce legal effects for third parties are, of course, open to judicial review. In that regard the EU courts have exercised judicial oversight over the use of social dialogue as a means of developing norms which are then institutionalised in legislative form and has placed obligations on EU institutions to consider the 'representativeness' of the parties negotiating such texts.[49]

The reach of judicial review into the realm of technical harmonisation and standardisation raises complex questions of what can be challenged, by whom and upon what grounds.[50] It highlights the potential for gaps in judicial oversight to emerge while also evidencing the capacity for oversight to occur where public and private governance overlap. Although voluntary standardisation has its own internal processes for adopting and contesting draft standards, standardisation is not immune from the reaches of EU law either as regards the formal processes by which such standards are accepted by EU institutions (giving rise to a presumption of conformity with New Approach directives), or in terms of the compliance of such concerted private norm-making with EU anti-trust rules.[51] To be sure, the EU courts have indicated that their review function is limited to the examination of whether there are manifest errors in the judgements made by EU institutional actors and this may place certain evidential hurdles in the way of plaintiffs. Nonetheless, insofar as the private governance of standardisation intersects with the exercise of powers by the European Commission there is the potential for judicial oversight.

The exercise of delegated powers by the European Commission is similarly open to review with changes made by the Lisbon Treaty relaxing somewhat the standing rules for private plaintiffs to challenge non-legislative acts.[52] Yet gaps in judicial review are likely to emerge in the EU's 'compound' and networked administrative landscape. This is something to which new governance scholars have drawn attention rather than ignored or dismissed.[53] Whether or not such gaps can be closed through the development and

---

[49] Case T-135/96, *UEAPME v Council* [1998] ECR II-2335. See N Bernard, 'Legitimising EU Law: Is the Social Dialogue the Way Forward? Some Reflections Around the UEAPME Case' in J Shaw (ed), *Social Law and Policy in an Evolving European Union* (Oxford, Hart Publishing, 2000); S Smismans, 'The European Social Dialogue in the Shadow of Hierarchy' (2008) 28 *Journal of Public Policy* 161.

[50] H Schepel, *The Constitution of Private Governance: Product Standards in the Regulation of Integrating Markets* (Oxford, Hart Publishing, 2005).

[51] Case T-432/05, *EMC Development AB v European Commission* [2010] ECR II-1629.

[52] Prior to the Lisbon Treaty, private plaintiffs had to cross the formidable hurdle of showing 'individual' as well as 'direct' concern which made it very difficult for applicants to challenge both legislative and executive acts of general application. Post-Lisbon, applicants challenging non-legislative 'regulatory' acts that do not entail implementing measures only need to show 'direct' concern. This opens up the possibility for plaintiffs to challenge Commission Regulations adopted in exercise of the European Commission's delegated norm-making powers.

[53] Scott, 'In Legal Limbo' (n 23).

coordination of administrative law at national and EU levels is largely an open question. It is precisely these sorts of questions which proponents of 'global' administrative law seek to address.[54] The point, then, is that the risk of gaps emerging between law and governance is not only a familiar one from the domestic administrative law experience, it is a risk that takes on new forms and dimensions at EU level, but in ways which are at least knowable and comprehended by new governance scholars.

As intimated earlier, it is the OMC which crystallises concerns about gaps between law and governance in the EU. Yet the extent to which it demands or requires a legal response is open to question. That question was posed very directly in the context of the negotiations to adopt the (failed) Constitutional Treaty. For its proponents, institutionalisation of the OMC within the treaties could underpin political commitments to seek solutions to problems through such collaborative endeavours. Nonetheless, to do so would also risk reducing its flexibility and the very diversity in its methodological architecture which gives it a plural rather than singular identity.[55] For its opponents, bringing the OMC within the control of the treaties could serve to contain and constrain this technique in a way which might 'quarantine' it from undesirable spillover effects,[56] but with the risk that it would also legitimate its operation. Attempts to 'constitutionalise' the OMC highlight the potential gap or indeed antagonism between the EU's constitutional and governance trajectories, and provoke us to think carefully about how to reconcile the functional demands of governance with the legitimacy-conferring role of legal institutionalisation.[57]

That said, the demand to put mechanisms of policy coordination on some sort of legal footing is dependent upon how the OMC is understood in functional terms. Scholars of the EU will be familiar with the not-uncontested argument that insofar as the EU's governance output can be characterised as 'regulatory' policy, it requires little by way of democratic legitimation and more by way of credible, non-majoritarian institutions subject to basic administrative law principles.[58]Applying this argument heuristically, as policy coordination moves beyond the boundary of regulatory policy and into core areas of domestic sovereignty such as economic policy and the welfare state, then the greater the apparent demand for structures of governance that supply not merely effective but also legitimate governance. But inasmuch as the Member States remain in charge of policy-making in these spheres—which is the very essence of the OMC—it is *national* institutional structures which are the primary forum for legitimation. Or to put it slightly differently, should the focus of concern lie with the capacity to control and monitor the creation of a policy consensus or a policy paradigm through EU coordination, or with whether or not Member States—who are the central gatekeepers of the domestic policy process—choose to adopt the consensus or paradigm? The answer to that might vary between different OMC processes: the more

---

[54] C Harlow, 'Global Administrative Law: The Quest for Principles and Values' (2006) 17 *European Journal of International Law* 187; B Kingsbury, 'The Concept of "Law" in Global Administrative Law' (2009) 20 *European Journal of International Law* 23; N Krisch, 'The Pluralism of Global Administrative Law' (2006) 17 *European Journal of International Law* 247.

[55] G de Búrca and J Zeitlin, 'Constitutionalising the Open Method of Coordination: What Should the Convention Propose?' (2003) *CEPS Policy Brief No 31*.

[56] Trubek and Trubek, 'The Open Method of Co-ordination and the Debate over "Hard" and "Soft" Law' (n 3).

[57] KA Armstrong, 'Governance and Constitutionalism After Lisbon' (2008) 46 *Journal of Common Market Studies* 415; De Burca and Zeitlin, 'Constitutionalising the Open Method of Coordination' (n 55).

[58] A Moravcsik, 'Reassessing Legitimacy in the European Union' (2002) 40 *Journal of Common Market Studies* 603; A Follesdal and S Hix, 'Why There is a Democratic Deficit in the EU: A Response to Majone and Moravcsik' (2006) 44 *Journal of Common Market Studies* 533.

intense the consensus and the more vulnerable the nation state to its adoption the more we might worry about controlling consensus formation in the first place. Certainly the experience of the EU's economic crisis is one in which European states—to greater or lesser degrees—are vulnerable to international influence and where the consensus on the need for austerity measures is particularly strong. But the coding of that consensus is not merely through the signals and steers of EU policy coordination but rather in the rush to amend treaty texts and adopt muscular legislation and through the contractual obligations which attend the receipt of stabilisation funds. What this so obviously demonstrates is that our anxieties about what new forms of governance mean for law and for mechanisms of legitimation cannot simply be tackled by isolating particular tools and instruments, but requires an assessment of the overarching governance framework—its levels, its institutions, its modes and techniques—and attention towards any resulting gaps between law and governance.

However, we ought not assume that law can or ought to substitute for opportunities for political contestation. Europe's economic and consequential social crisis is not one which fundamentally makes people ponder any putative legal deficit of EU policy coordination. It is not 'delegalisation' that is troubling let alone irritating.[59] It is hyper-legalism that appears dangerous because of its tendency to seek to take matters out of politics and place them under legal control. The Treaty on Stability, Coordination and Governance, the regulations and processes for monitoring national budgets, the Memorandums of Understanding that attach conditionality to the receipt of funds from EU states and the IMF: these are the legal instruments through which European states are seeking to respond to the economic crisis but in ways which limit domestic political autonomy rather than working through, and with, that autonomy. This is not to say that we should ignore the role that policy coordination might play in combination with these reforming moves; rather, it is about resisting an uncritical faith in law's capacity to deliver effective and legitimate European governance.

ii. Transformation

The gap thesis works with our existing concepts and understandings of law as a baseline against which to reflect upon how changes in EU governance might depart from that baseline. Nonetheless, it may be that changes in governance demand changes in our concepts of law and legality. This essay has attempted to demonstrate that for the most part, pluralisation and differentiation in EU governance, while challenging, is at least comprehensible within legal discourse. However heady may be the allure of novelty, the issue of how to conceptualise new forms of governance within law may turn out to be be more about determining which concepts are appropriate and less about developing new concepts of law. Nonetheless, if we are to venture onto the terrain of legal transformation, it helps to be clear about what is at stake.

At an instrumental level, it is evident that EU legislation is not absent and may be the very means by which new forms of governance are constituted or at least form the basis for normative elaboration in the post-legislative phase. Inasmuch as the legislative form is not simply the vehicle for detailed substantive rules to be hierarchically enforced but rather as the framework for normative development then there is something of a 'transformation'

---

[59] Joerges, 'Integration through de-legislation' (n 18).

in the functional properties of legislation. Nonetheless, our concepts of law and legality remain in place. Yet it is at a more systemic level that EU governance is challenging for legal theory and has been from its very beginnings.

From its inception, the experience of the EU has been precisely one of how to fit a novel system of governance into legal categories. Framing the EU as a *sui generis* legal entity proved to be a remarkably disabling legal discourse.[60] The apparent distancing of this 'new legal order' from international law left its legal identity open to an alternative legal conceptualisation in constitutional terms. Whatever the limits of these two different routes to giving EU governance a legal identity they at least had the value of bringing a wealth of legal resources with them.[61] Perhaps because so much of the differentiation in EU governance remains rooted in structures and processes of decision-making by public actors exercising legislative and executive powers the dominant approach within new governance scholarship has been to relate pluralism in governance to constitutionalism and constitutional pluralism.[62] The conjuncture of developments in EU governance with the EU's self-conscious attempt to adopt a 'Constitution' reinforced that relationship. Constitutional pluralism can itself be thought of as an expression of novel and experimental interactions between sites of legal authority that attempt to avoid conflict and rivalry in favour of a certain complementarity.[63]

Yet there is equally a risk that reconstructing novel forms of international and transnational governance within existing legal concepts and categories is itself disabling in their failure to fully grasp the dynamics of post-national governance and the pluralisation not just of governance but also of law. Indeed, the stretching of the language and discourse of 'constitutionalism' is a particular case in point not just in terms of its usage in the post-national context,[64] but also in the national context.[65] Proponents of directly-deliberative polyarchy are perhaps strongest in their articulation of the perceived decline of the capacities of our traditional institutions and structures and their associated legal concepts to inspire the design of legitimate and effective governance. Yet the extent to which frameworks for 'dynamic accountability' can substitute for these institutions and to form the basis for a transformed conceptualisation of law is more troublesome and often has the sense of a theory waiting for events to catch up.[66] It is also open to criticism for relying on a fair amount of liberal

---

[60] N Walker, 'Legal Theory and the European Union: A 25th Anniversary Essay' (2005) 25 *Oxford Journal of Legal Studies* 581.

[61] For example, we can think of the deployment of Hart and Kelsen's concepts of law as a means of making sense of EU law within legal theory: C Richmond, 'Preserving the Identity Crisis: Autonomy, System and Sovereignty in European law' (1997) 16 *Law and Philosophy* 377; N MacCormick, *Questioning Sovereignty: Law, State, and Nation in the European Commonwealth* (Oxford, Oxford University Press 1999).

[62] G de Búrca, 'The Constitutional Challenge of New Governance in the European Union' (2003) 28 *European Law Review* 814; N Walker, 'EU Constitutionalism and New Governance' in G de Búrca and J Scott (eds), *Law and New Governance in the EU and US* (Oxford, Hart Publishing, 2006); N Walker and G de Búrca, 'Reconceiving Law and New Governance' (2007) 13 *Columbia Journal of European Law* 519.

[63] M Kumm, 'Constitutionalism and Experimentalist Governance' (2012) 6 *Regulation & Governance* 401; CF Sabel and O Gerstenberg, 'Constitutionalising an Overlapping Consensus: The ECJ and the Emergence of a Coordinate Constitutional Order' (2010) 16 *European Law Journal* 511.

[64] N Krisch, *Beyond Constitutionalism: The Pluralist Structure of Postnational Law* (Oxford, Oxford University Press, 2010). More generally, see R Cotterrell, 'Transnational Communities and the Concept of Law' (2008) 21 *Ratio Juris* 1.

[65] J Murkens, 'The Quest for Constitutionalism in UK Public Law Discourse' (2009) 29 *Oxford Journal of Legal Studies* 427.

[66] Wilkinson, 'Three Conceptions of Law' (n 25).

constitutionalism even as it attempts to transcend or transform it.[67] To be sure, governance changes over time can result in more radical breaks with the past. Yet these sorts of breaks and ruptures also risk a disabling effect: an incapacity to deal with an untidy political and legal landscape that in part harks back to the past and in part anticipates a future it does not yet, and might never, have.

The issue for new governance scholars is what these processes of gap emergence and gap closing mean for how we think about law and its relationship to underlying structures of control, accountability and legitimation. The contention is that new governance scholarship is at its strongest when it is at its most critical and that critique operates at the level of a constant troubling of our uses of legal concepts and categories to reveal what is masked and hidden by metaphorical sleights of hand that attempt to make gaps disappear. To be sceptical of the reach and role of prevailing concepts of law and to be reflective upon how law and politics are forged into particular matrices is not to show an indifference to law, but rather is to adopt a critical legal perspective. There is also common cause with those who see developments in transnational governance as creating the opportunity to develop a sociological and pluralist approach to law which accommodates not just differentiation in the sites of public governance but also the multiplicity of locations of private governance.[68] These approaches, which have informed much of David Trubek's work in other fields, together with contemporary developments in administrative and transnational law provide new governance scholarship with the tools and resources to elaborate a critical legal perspective on European governance. What new governance scholarship has also brought to the table is a historical dimension: how past attempts to close gaps and reconcile law and governance shape contemporary developments. The manner in which the 'constitutionalisation' of EU law has driven attempts to develop forms of EU intervention that offer greater flexibility and responsiveness beyond its constraint offers a long run perspective on the forces shaping contemporary EU governance. Whatever the limits and problems of new forms of governance, we at least have to recognise why they have emerged and what that tells us about underlying 'constitutional' settlements and their accommodation of law and governance.

IV. Conclusion

'New governance' has provided a useful intellectual hook for legal scholars to think about the changing patterns of governance in the EU from a legal perspective. By way of a conclusion, three aspects of this scholarship are noteworthy. The first is that it permitted a cross-fertilisation of ideas between the EU and the United States with scholars from both sides of the Atlantic identifying an apparently increasing number of fields where new forms of governance have emerged. David Trubek, in collaboration with leading EU scholars such as Gráinne

---

[67] Kumm, 'Constitutionalism and Experimentalist Governance' (n 63).

[68] R Buchannan, 'Legitimating Global Trade Governance: Constitutional and Legal Pluralist Approaches' (2006) 57 *Northern Ireland Law Quarterly* 654; P Zumbansen, 'Neither "Public" nor "Private", "National" nor "International": Transnational Corporate Governance from a Legal Pluralist Perspective' (2011) 38 *Journal of Law and Society* 50.

de Búrca and Joanne Scott, provided the impetus for this activity and dialogue. This essay has sought to revisit some of the assumptions and concepts within that scholarship with a view to sharpening the analytical focus of new governance scholarship at least in the EU context but with the hope that it has broader resonance.

Secondly, certain key themes in new governance scholarship—governing in the face of uncertainty; the slippage between norm-making and norm-implementation; the risk of gaps emerging between law and governance—were of particular interest to EU legal scholars not simply because the EU was apparently a good example of these phenomena but also because the EU's prevailing integration method—the Community Method—appeared ill-equipped to sustain the European integration project. In the face of the EU's continual struggle to attract legitimacy through institutions of representative democracy while continuing to face new risks and challenges which suggested a need for a European response, new governance offered a seemingly attractive alternative mode of Europeanisation. Yet the European experience is also one in which the emergence of new forms of governance has not necessarily been at the expense of its more traditional tools. Indeed—and as illustrated by the EU's response to the economic crisis—the turn back to the Community Method and the turn to further iterations of treaty-making have not produced a corresponding diminution in the use of more novel modes of EU governance. Instead what we have found is an intensification of efforts to maintain and increase governance capacity. Complementarity and hybridity in EU governance is perhaps its most obvious characteristic.

Thirdly, the extension of EU influence into new policy fields through the use of new governance tools has opened up new areas—especially reform of the welfare state and labour markets—to legal analysis and investigation: areas which while often typical of domestic critical scholarship had not attracted quite so much attention in European legal scholarship. Whether as a means of rethinking traditional areas of EU influence or in opening up new areas for scholarship, the preoccupations of new governance scholarship created a space for reflection on contemporary problems of governance in the EU outside of the traditional analysis of judicial governance. To use Mark Tushnet's term, new governance is a 'political location'—albeit one without clear grid references—where scholars with similar intuitions and inclinations could at least find a common language and discourse to discuss the position of law in Europe's changing governance landscape.[69]

Yet it is important to state that new governance scholarship has attracted criticism not only in terms of its empirical significance and conceptual repertoire, but also as the wrong project for progressive politics and progressive legal scholarship. Insofar as the OMC was the apparent target of this criticism, the complaints were often contradictory: on the one hand, new forms of governance were presented as destabilising and de-institutionalising the linkages between society and the market,[70] and yet on the other, they were attacked for being too 'soft' or incapable of penetrating the domestic systems.[71] All of this gave the OMC the ambiguous identity of an alarmingly irrelevant threat. But beyond whether particular governance tools can act as the vehicle for progressive politics, the charge has been that new governance scholars have happily substituted governance for law. As this essay has sought

---

[69] M Tushnet, 'Critical Legal Studies: A Political History' (1990) 100 *Yale Law Journal* 1515.

[70] C Offe, 'The European Model of "Social" Capitalism: Can It Survive European Integration?' (2003) 11 *Journal of Political Philosophy* 437.

[71] M Lodge, 'Comparing Non-Hierarchical Governance in Action: The Open Method of Co-ordination in Pensions and Information Society' (2007) 45 *Journal of Common Market Studies* 343.

to demonstrate, this is a rather surprising accusation as new governance scholarship has done much to bring a legal perspective to the taxonomies and typologies of the 'governance turn' in EU political science scholarship. But if the point is that Europe's current situation is one which demands a critical approach to law and governance then there is no dispute. The EU is facing a crisis. It is a crisis *for* law, not least in the sense that in some quarters, Europe's economic crisis is the basis for efforts towards further integration through law and indeed for future federalisation. But it is also a crisis *of* law in which demands for harder fiscal rules and sanctions, for new treaties, and for domestic constitutional change attempt to take important economic decisions out of politics and place them under the constraints of law. The challenge facing Europe is not so much the alleged delegalisation of new governance: rather, the challenge comes from an intensification and differentiation in the forms and locations of legal instrumentalism. The governance landscape is again in flux and it demands the critical gaze of a progressive legal scholarship: something which has been at the core of David Trubek's teaching and writing on the EU and beyond.

13

'Reflexive Contract Governance in the EU'—David Trubek's Contribution to a More Focused Approach to EU Contract Legislation

NORBERT REICH

> The ungentle laws and customs touched upon in this tale are historical, and the episodes which are used to illustrate them are also historical ... One is quite justified in inferring that whatever one of these laws or customs was lacking in that remote time, its place was completely filled by a worse one.
>
> Mark Twain, Preface, *A Connecticut Yankee in King Arthur's Court* (1889)

I. An Acknowledgement of David Trubek's Socio-legal Thinking

Having been asked to contribute to a collection of essays—a sort of festschrift—in honour of David Trubek I have to start with some personal remarks. I met David and his wife Louise Trubek when they prepared a study on consumer protection for the 'Integration through Law' series edited by Mauro Cappelletti, Monica Seccombe and Joseph Weiler for the European University Institute (EUI). It resulted in a copious book published in 1987.[1] I had just before published or been responsible—with Hans Micklitz—for a series of studies on consumer law in the Member States of the EC,[2] and this resulted in a series of most rewarding exchanges where I was able to profit from David's 'insight from the outside' of United States federalism on the EEC/EC/EU internal market and consumer policies which were emerging. Indeed, the interrelation between open markets and protective policies has been brilliantly developed in his introductory chapter of the 1987 book, in which he clearly foresaw that the 'further effect of consumer protection law on open borders is that of diversity per se. The more variation there is among the laws of Member States in common markets, the more costly it can be for a seller to supply all the national markets that are included'[3]—an argument which the EU Commission recently used in its attempts to create

---

[1] T Bourgoignie and DM Trubek, *Consumer Law, Common Markets and Federalism* (Berlin, de Gruyter, 1987).
[2] N Reich and HW Micklitz, *Consumer Legislation in the EC Countries—A Comparative Analysis* (New York, Van Nostrand Reinhold, 1980); followed by country reports of the then 9 Member States of the EC.
[3] Reich and Micklitz, *Consumer Legislation in the EC Countries* (n 2) 3.

a Common European Sales Law (CESL)[4] to which I will turn later. David Trubek developed a theory of *de jure* and de facto so-called 'regulatory gaps' which justified Community intervention in consumer policy matters under the then still under-developed competence framework of the EEC (he refers to Articles 100 and 235 EEC requiring unanimity). His pleading for a 'modern political economy of consumer protection'[5] criticising and going beyond mere liberal principles of 'achievable transparency and static intervention' is certainly worth a more in-depth analysis under today's conditions which cannot be done here. His insistence on 'responsiveness, diffuse interests, and access' of regulation[6] conceived requirements and conditions which have become important in my own work. At the same time, he criticised the then rather haphazard approach of the EEC to consumer policy as consisting 'of a series of separate and largely uncoordinated actions which have very different implications of consumer law in Europe and reflect the existence of very different views on consumer protection within the Community institutions'.[7] Has this since been changed?

A shift to employment policy issues in his later work[8]—which I could witness personally during my time as Rector of the newly-founded Riga Graduate School of Law from 2000 to 2004 where he taught and undertook research as a very welcome visitor—demonstrated a similar creativity of David Trubek's socio-legal writing and learning, despite—or because of— his position as an 'outsider' to the EC-law governing doctrines such as 'integration through law', 'supremacy and direct effect', and 'Community method of harmonisation'. The debate on the 'Open Method of Coordination' (OMC) launched by a Commission White Paper on Governance of 2001 found his special interest.[9] It defined the OMC's basic principles of good governance as 'openness, participation, accountability, effectiveness, and coherence'. This paper proposed a number of measures in this direction. These included better structured relations to 'civil society' by involving NGOs, although without questioning the 'Community method' of action as a 'top-down' way to achieve integration.[10] It was, however, quite critical of an exclusive reliance on the OMC method of governance: it 'must not dilute the achievement of common objectives in the Treaty or the political responsibility of the Institutions. It should not be used when legislative action under the Community method is possible'.[11]

In a joint paper Joanne Scott and David Trubek go deliberately beyond the rather restricted and to some extent rhetorical approach of the Commission which they criticise insofar as the EU has not really begun to confront the legitimacy challenge it is facing.

---

[4] Commission, 'Proposal for a Regulation on a Common European Sales Law' COM (635) final, 11.10.2011.

[5] Reich and Micklitz, *Consumer Legislation in the EC Countries* (n 2) 7.

[6] Ibid, 10–12.

[7] Ibid, 23.

[8] DM Trubek, 'The European Employment Strategy and the Future of EU Governance' (2003) *Riga Graduate School of Law Working Papers* 10/2003.

[9] Commission, 'European Governance' (White Paper) COM (2001) 428 final, 25 July 2001; for a broader discussion see C Joerges and R Dehousse (eds), *Good Governance in Europe's Integrated Markets* (Oxford, Oxford University Press, 2002); K Armstrong, 'Rediscovering Civil Society: The EU and the White Paper on Governance' (2002) 8 *European Law Journal* 102; E Szyszak, 'Experimental Governance: The Open Method of Coordination' (2006) 12 *European Law Journal* 486; G de Búrca and J Scott (eds), *Law and New Governance in the EU and the US* (Oxford, Hart Publishing, 2006); M Dawson, *New Governance and the Proceduralisation of European Law: The Case of the Open Method of Coordination* (PhD thesis, Florence, EUI, 2009); W van Gerven, 'Private Law in a Federal Perspective' in R Brownsword, H-W Micklitz, L Niglia and S Weatherill (ed), *The Foundations of European Private Law* (Oxford, Hart Publishing, 2011) 343.

[10] Ibid, 8.

[11] Ibid, 22.

European courts, in their opinion, have 'tended to ignore, or distort, new governance, in order that new governance can be accommodated by the premises of a traditional, positivist concept of law'.[12] They see the advantage of this new type of action as allowing involvement of the actors concerned via 'social dialogue'.[13] They define OMC as a characteristic of 'new governance' which does not aim at hard law subject to implementation and supervision by the Court of Justice of the European Union (CJEU), instead acting as a soft-law mechanism allowing the participation of social actors, particularly in areas where the EU had no or only limited regulatory competences such as employment and social policy (now Articles 145, 151 TFEU).[14] They define the following advantages of OMC over harmonisation:

— 'Participation and power-sharing';
— 'Multi-level integration';
— 'Diversity and decentralisation';
— 'Deliberation';
— 'Flexibility and revisability'; and
— 'Experimentation and knowledge creation'.[15]

In a later paper, Trubek, Cottrell and Nance have tried to combine soft- and hard-law methods in European integration.[16] This could be a method for combining soft law, with regard to 'facilitative' contract law, and hard law, in mandatory law matters such as consumer law, non-discrimination and protection of commercial agents in the internal market.

This author's view on the White Paper was less critical than that of the above-mentioned co-authors. I'm probably too much a positivist EU lawyer with a preference for legislation and 'hard law'. In my opinion, governance in the EU would have to use both the traditional 'Community method' and new methods such as OMC. Forms of law-making involving the social actors seem particularly important to me. In this way it will be possible to try out new forms of *co- and self-regulation* with the participation of those involved. An example involves the rules on decision-making in the area of social policy[17] where the social partners (organisations of public and private employers together with trade unions) agree on measures to be taken. These may then be transposed into law by Community institutions.[18]

A more specific example of David Trubek's work where our minds and interests met again has been the so-called *Laval* saga where the CJEU ruled on the incompatibility of social action of Swedish labour unions against a Latvian company intending to post workers in Sweden who were originally to be subject to (allegedly less protective) standards of the home (Latvia) and not the host country (Sweden).[19] The judgment, which condemned the

---

[12] J Scott and DM Trubek, 'Mind the Gap: Law and New Approaches to Governance in the EU' (2002) 8 *European Law Journal* 1, 16.

[13] Ibid, 4.

[14] Ibid, 4–5.

[15] Ibid, 5–6.

[16] See DM Trubek, P Cottrell and M Nance, '"Soft Law," "Hard Law," and European Integration: Toward a Theory of Hybridity' (2005) *University of Wisconsin Law School Legal Studies Research Paper Series* 1002.

[17] Art 139 EC (now Art TFEU 153), excluding, however, measures on pay, right of association, right to strike and to lock-outs; for a discussion see F Möslein and K Riesenhuber, 'Contract Governance—A Research Agenda' (2009) 5 *European Review of Contract Law* 248, 263.

[18] N Reich, *Understanding EU Law*, 2nd edn (Mosselen, Intersentia, 2005) 309.

[19] Case C-341/05 *Laval un Partneri Ltd v Svenska Byggnadsarbetareförbundet et al* [2007] ECR I-11767; see also the parallel case C-438/05 *International Transport Worker's Federation and Finnish Seaman's Union vs Viking Line ABP et al* [2007] ECR I-10779.

action of the Swedish labour unions as incompatible with EU law and made them subject to compensation under Swedish law,[20] aroused strong criticism in academia, including my Bremen colleagues Joerges and Rödl.[21] I had defended the judgment from a perspective of Latvian companies and workers who had been promised free access to the EU labour markets after their accession to the EU in 2004, while restrictions were allowed only under the conditions of the Posted Workers Directive (PWD) 96/71/EEC[22] which, as the CJEU had found, had not been met by Sweden.[23]

A paper of David Trubek advocated a much more subtle and nuanced approach which is concerned with finding a 'Union mechanism to balance the economic and the social' which he calls a 'reflexive balancing'.[24] It combines 'soft' and 'hard' law, which is particularly important in regulating labour relations at an EU level where only limited competences exist.[25] Directive 96/71 is understood as an effort to coordinate the employment law regimes of the home (Latvia) and host state (Sweden), not by prescribing mandatory labour standards, but by authorising the host state to impose specific listed protective standards under certain conditions on companies and workers from the home state by respecting the principles of non-discrimination and transparency (which he calls universality and foreseeability). I could only agree with their conclusion that it would be unacceptable 'to give to unions powers that are denied to the Member States and [thereby] undermine the whole structure of universality and foreseeability that seems to be the core policies behind the PWD'.[26]

II. How to Balance Open Markets and Consumer Protection Standards in the EU?

The reflections of David Trubek on EU integration and law-making in delicate social fields such as consumer protection and labour standards may present an interesting and useful approach as a fresh perspective on the ongoing and controversial discussion about a European (or rather EU) private or more limited contract law.[27] Without overly abusing

---

[20] U Bernitz and N Reich, 'Case No A 268/04, The Labour Court, Sweden (*Arbetsdomstolen*) Judgment No 89/09 of 2 December 2009, 'Laval un Partneri Ltd *v* Svenska Bygggnadsarbetareförbundet et al'' (2011) 48 *Common Market Law Review* 603.

[21] C Joerges and F Rödl, 'Informal Politics, Formalised Law, and the "Social deficit" of European Integration: Reflections after the Judgments of the CJEU in *Viking* and *Laval*' (2009) 15 *European Law Journal* 1.

[22] Directive 96/71/EC of 16 December 1996 concerning the posting of workers in the framework of the provision of services [1997] OJ L18/1.

[23] N Reich, 'Free Movement and Social Rights in an Enlarged Union' (2008) 9 *German Law Journal* 125; N Reich, 'Fundamental freedoms vs. fundamental rights—did *Viking* get it wrong?' (2008) *Europarättslig Tijdskrift* 851 however criticising the (ab)use of the proportionality argument by the Court in *Viking*; see also E Engle, 'A Viking We Will Go: Neo-Corporatism and Social Europe' (2010) 11 *German Law Journal* 635 insisting on the importance of *Viking* and *Laval* for EU labour mobility against neo-corporatist arrangements of the traditional social state such as Sweden and Finland.

[24] DM Trubek and M Nance, 'The Strange Case of the Posted Workers Directive: EU Law as Reflexive Coordination' (Workshop on Laval and Viking at Cambridge University, 19 September 2008).

[25] See DM Trubek and L Trubek, 'Hard and Soft Law in the Construction of the European Social Model: The Role of the Open Method of Coordination' (2005) 11 *European Law Journal* 343, 345.

[26] Trubek and Nance, 'The Strange Case of the Posted Workers Directive' (n 24) 22.

[27] I continue the discussion which started with David Trubek's invitation to give a talk at the Wisconsin Law School and which was published as N Reich, 'A European Contract Law—Ghost or Host for Integration?' (2006) 24 *Wisconsin International Law Journal* 425.

David Trubek's insightful remarks on EEC/EC/EU policy-making and governance by law, he would probably welcome a more coherent approach to consumer policy, including: consumer contract law which has been an issue of EU legislative activity; case law of the CJEU; and conceptual concerns of the EU Commission over the last 20 years and this has been documented elsewhere.[28] But a paradox resulted from this EU encroachment of a new policy field: instead of making marketing and protection conditions within the EU in the interest of both business and consumers more compatible, the original technique of 'minimum harmonisation' resulted in an even greater diversity than before.[29] In order to overcome this new 'regulatory gap', the Commission devised three contradictory strategies, namely:

— the use of conflict-of-laws regulations to coordinate (not regulate!) diversity—similar to Directive 96/71 which had been so ably analysed by David Trubek in his remarks on the *Laval* saga;
— a shift to the so-called 'full harmonisation approach'—which resulted, as will be shown, in a 'half harmonisation';[30]
— the use of OMC methods in the area of out-of-court dispute settlement schemes (alternative dispute resolution (ADR) and online dispute resolution (ODR)) throughout the EU.

The following lines will give a short overview of the existing state of EU 'hard' and 'soft' consumer law, keeping in mind David Trubek's plea for using more flexible regulatory patterns without abandoning the 'Community/Union method' of mandatory legislation where it is still feasible and necessary.

A. Conflict of Law Methods

A conflict of law method of balancing open market and consumer protection imperatives in area of contracting had already been proposed by the Rome Convention of 1980 which, after ratification by the then 12 Member States, became part of their law on 1 April 1991, even though not as an EU instrument but as an international treaty closely linked to internal market policy. The power to decide on referrals of interpretation was given to the CJEU by the Protocol of 1 August 2004.[31] Consumer protection was regulated in Article 5 and served as a model for later initiatives:

— On the one hand, it allowed traders freedom of choice—which usually meant choosing their home law—even in consumer contracts; the 'default' rule of Article 4 referred to the application of the 'home country' of the trader.

---

[28] N Reich, 'Harmonisation of European Contract Law—with special emphasis on Consumer Law' (2011) 1 *China-EU Law Journal* 55.

[29] See the detailed studies in H Schulte-Nölke, C Twigg-Flesner and M Ebers (eds), *EC Consumer Law Compendium: The Consumer Acquis and Its Transposition in the Member States* (Munich, Sellier, 2007).

[30] See N Reich, 'Von der Minimal- zur Voll- zur Halbharmonisierung' (2010) 18 *Zeitschrift für Europäisches Privatrecht* 7.

[31] See H-W Micklitz, N Reich, P Rott and K Tonner, *Understanding EU Consumer Law*, 2nd edn (Antwerp, Intersentia, 2013) para 7.2.

—   On the other hand, in a choice of law-situation it provided for a 'better protection rule' for the so-called 'passive consumer' described in Article 5(2): the consumer must not be deprived of the protection provided by the mandatory provisions of his home country.[32]

In principle, the same approach was taken by the later so-called Rome I Regulation,[33] even though its scope of application was considerably extended, in particular in cases where the professional 'directed its activities' to the consumers' home country.[34] The 'better protection rule' was maintained in Article 6(2) in case of choice of law by the professional under Article 3.[35] I have argued that this provision in most cross-border consumer disputes in the EU allows a fair balancing between the imperatives of an open market on the one hand, and the requirements of consumer protection either by EU or/and Member States law on the other. In order to avoid *de jure* or de facto 'regulatory gaps', for example, by different implementation of consumer directives in the Member States, allowed under the minimum harmonisation principle, professionals and consumer associations should be encouraged to draw up soft-law 'codes of practice' allowing an EU-wide guarantee of 'high standards' which would make reference to divergent national laws unnecessary.[36] So far this initiative has not yet been taken up, even though the EU Commission has supported it in other areas such as unfair commercial practices and service contracts.[37] But this is not an argument against it.

B. From 'Minimum' to 'Full' to 'Half' Harmonisation

A second strategy used by the Commission to close regulatory gaps in the process of making consumer law compatible with the imperatives of an open internal market has been the so-called 'full harmonisation strategy'.[38] Even though the 'minimum harmonisation approach' found support in the case law of the CJEU, most recently in its *Caja de Ahorros* Judgment of 3 June 2010[39]—though exceptionally subject to limitations under the internal market

---

[32]   Ibid, paras 7.8–13.

[33]   Regulation (EC) 593/2008 of 17 June 2008 on the law applicable to contractual obligations [2008] OJ 176/6, hereinafter 'Rome I Regulation'.

[34]   For a clarification see the CJEU judgment of 7 December 2010, Joined Cases C-585/08 and C-144/09 *Peter Pammer et al v Reederei Karl Schlüter et al* [2010] ECR I-12527; it is not necessary that the contract be concluded by means of distant communication, Case C-190/11 *Mühlleitner v AW Yusufi* (CJEU, 6 September 2012).

[35]   For a detailed analysis see N Reich, 'EU Strategies in Finding the Optimal Consumer Law Instrument' (2012) 8 *European Review of Contract Law* 1, paras 18 and 26; a similar view has been developed by S Grundmann, 'Kosten und Nutzen eines Europäischen Optionalen Kaufrechts' (Special meeting of Zivilrechtslehrervereinigung, 20–21 April 2012 in Cologne, *Archiv für die civilistische Praxis* (*AcP*) 2012, 502.

[36]   This approach has been described in some detail in G Howells, H-W Micklitz and N Reich, 'Optional Soft Law Instrument on EU Contract Law for Business and Consumers (Paper prepared for the European Consumer Association BEUC, 2011) available at www.beuc.org/custom/2011-09955-01-E.pdf.

[37]   For details, see G Howells, H-W Micklitz and T Wilhelmsson, *European Fair Trading Law: The Unfair Commercial Practices Directive* (Burlington, VT, Ashgate, 2006) 185; H-W Micklitz, 'The Service Directive: Consumer contract law making via standardisation' in ALBC Ciacchi, C Godt, P Rott and LJ Smith, *Haftungsrecht im dritten Millennium—Liability in the third millennium, Liber Amicorum Gert Brüggemeier* (Baden-Baden, Nomos, 2009) 483.

[38]   For details, see Reich, 'Free Movement and Social Rights in an Enlarged Union' (n 23) 445.

[39]   Case C-484/08 *Caja de Ahorros y Monte de Piedad v Ausbanc* [2010] ECR I-4785.

imperatives[40]—the Commission found that the leeway given to Member States created new impediments to trade in the internal market.[41] They could only be overcome by 'full harmonisation', that is not allowing Member States to introduce 'better consumer protection' provisions within the scope of a directive, for instance on 'Unfair Commercial Practices' under Directive 2005/29/EC and on 'Consumer Credit' under Directive 2008/48/EC.[42] In a series of cases under the so-called 'black list' of Directive 2005/29 the CJEU supported the strict approach by the Commission and did not allow Member States to set up their own black lists of prohibited unfair commercial practices.[43]

When the Commission proposed a 'Consumer Rights Directive' (CRD) on 8 October 2008,[44] it wanted to modify the 'minimum harmonisation approach' of four consumer contract law directives of the so-called *acquis*—Directive 85/577/EEC on Doorstep Selling,[45] Directive 93/13/EEC on Unfair Terms,[46] Directive 97/7/EC on Distance Contracts[47] and Directive 99/44/EC on Sales of Consumer Goods and Associated Guarantees,[48] by the full harmonisation. Its Article 4 provocatively read:

> Member States may not maintain or introduce, in their national law, provisions diverging from those laid down in this Directive, including more or less stringent provisions to ensure a different level of consumer protection.

This aroused a storm of protest both in academia[49] and in the European Parliament (EP).[50] In a sort of compromise, the final version of the CRD'[51] has 'fully' harmonised the provisions on 'off-premises' (formerly doorstep) and distance contracts, while modifying the 'minimum harmonisation approach' of Directive 93/13 and 99/44 to only a very limited extent. The CRD also contains rules on pre-contractual information, including digital

---

[40] Case C-205/07 *Gysbrechts* [2008] ECR I-9947.

[41] See the references in Micklitz, Reich, Rott and Tonner, *Understanding EU Consumer Law* (n 31) paras 1.8, 1.30, 1.48.

[42] For details I have again to refer to Micklitz, Reich, Rott and Tonner *Understanding EU Consumer Law* (n 31) paras 2.19 and 5.10.

[43] Joined Cases C-261 and C-299/07 *VTB-VAB v Total et al* [2009] ECR I-2949 and later cases, C-140/08 *Mediaprint v 'Österreich' Zeitungsverlag* [2010] ECR I-10909.

[44] COM (2008) 614 final.

[45] Directive 85/577/EEC of 20 December 1985 to protect the consumer in respect of contracts negotiated away from business premises [1985] OJ L372/31.

[46] Directive 93/13/EEC of 5 April 1993 on unfair terms in consumer contracts [1993] OJ L95/29.

[47] Directive 97/7/EC of 20 May 1997 on the protection of consumers in respect of distance contracts [1997] OJ L144/19.

[48] Directive 1999/44/EC of 25 May 1999 on certain aspects of the sale of consumer goods and associated guarantees [1999] OJ L171/12.

[49] Without trying to make a full reference to the many contributions to this debate, I refer to the papers in G Howells and R Schulze (eds), *Modernising and Harmonising European Contract Law* (Munich, Sellier, 2011). See also H-W Micklitz and N Reich, 'Crónica de una muerte anunciada: The Commission proposal for a "Directive on consumer rights"' (2009) 46 *CML Rev* 471.

[50] See the overview by A Schwab and A Giesemann, 'Die Verbraucherrechte-Richtlinie: Ein wichtiger Schritt zur Vollharmonisierung im Binnenmarkt' (2012) *Europäische Zeitschrift für Wirtschaftsrecht* 253; A Schwab was reporting member of the European Parliament for the Consumer Rights Directive. For a critical account see S Weatherill, 'The Consumer Rights Directive: How and Why a Quest for "Coherence" Has Largely Failed' (2012) 49 *CML Rev* 1279; for a more positive view, see O Unger, 'Die Richtlinie über Rechte der Verbraucher' (2012) 4 *Zeitschrift für Europäisches Privatrecht* 270; K Tonner and K Fangerow, 'Directive 2011/83 on Consumer Rights—a New Approach to European Consumer Law?' (2012) *Zeitschrift für Europäisches Unternehmens- und Verbraucherrecht (Journal of European Consumer and Market Law)* 67.

[51] Directive 2011/83/EU of 25 October 2011 on consumer rights [2011] OJ L303/64.

content, as well as on fees for the use of means of payment, on additional payments and on passing of risk and delivery. I have called this approach 'half harmonisation'.[52]

It is certainly possible that the next round of reviewing the 'consumer contract law *acquis*' will again bring modifications of its scope of application, perhaps this time by way of a directly applicable regulation as I had proposed in my Wisconsin paper.[53] A recent study by Twigg-Flesner has advocated the elaboration of a Regulation for cross-border consumer transactions only.[54] It would run parallel to existing EU directives and Member State law. This debate shows, on the one hand, the inherent dynamism and on the other, the conflict potential, of consumer law-making and application in the EU. It will certainly not be solved by the time this paper is published.

C. OMC and Dispute Resolution

Since dispute resolution of consumer conflicts with business is a matter left to the national law under the—controversial—principles of 'procedural autonomy'[55] and only subject to special cross-border instruments aiming at a mutual recognition of judicial and similar instruments according to the general competence under Article 81 TFEU,[56] the setting up of 'alternative dispute resolution mechanisms' is left to Member States and to the market partners themselves. The EU only has an indirect competence in that field, namely by including ADR-mechanisms in sectoral directives, as had been done in Article 24 of the Consumer Credit Directive 2008/48; similar provisions exist in other consumer relevant instruments.[57] The principles under which such instruments are supposed to operate have been laid down in two Commission recommendations[58] which were part of the *Alassini* litigation of the CJEU.[59] The CJEU also referred to the principle of effective judicial protection of Article 47 of the EU Charter of Fundamental Rights, thus 'upgrading' 'non-binding' recommendations beyond Article 288(5) TFEU.

The importance of the *Alassini* case lies in providing certain guidelines as to the principles specific to the ODR procedures. It adds other principles to those set forth in the recommendations. It seems that CJEU hints that a procedure by a court of law need not necessarily be the primary entity to decide consumer disputes. The ODR mechanism may be mandatory on two conditions. First, the mandatory nature of the ODR is proportionate

---

[52] Reich (n 30).

[53] Reich, 'Free Movement and Social Rights in an Enlarged Union' (n 23) 458–63.

[54] C Twigg-Flesner, *A Cross-Border Only Regulation for Consumer Transactions in the EU—A Fresh Approach to EU Consumer Law* (New York–Heidelberg, Springer, 2012).

[55] For a critical discussion see the contributions of A Adinolfi and M Bobek in H-W Micklitz and B de Witte (eds), *The European Court of Justice and the Autonomy of Member States* (Cambridge, Intersentia, 2012) 281, 305; D-U Galetta, *Procedural Autonomy of EU Member States: Paradise Lost?* (Berlin, Springer, 2011).

[56] Again I refer to Micklitz, Reich, Rott and Tonner *Understanding EU Consumer Law* (n 31) paras 7.31–7.45.

[57] Details are given by H Micklitz, 'Brauchen Unternehmen und Verbraucher eine neue Architektur des Verbraucherrechts?' (2012) 69 *Deutscher Juristentag* A84.

[58] Commission Recommendation 98/257/EC of 30 March 1998 on the principles applicable to the bodies responsible for out-of-court settlement of consumer disputes [1998] OJ L115/31 and Commission Recommendation 2001/310/EC of 4 April 2001 on the principles for out-of-court bodies involved in the consensual resolution of consumer disputes [2001] OJ L109/56.

[59] Joined Cases C-317/08 and C-320/08 *Rosalba Alassini v Telecom Italia et al* [2010] ECR I-2213.

to aims pursued. Second, the party required to participate in the mandatory ODR must have the right to bring an action in the court if it is not satisfied with the outcome of the ODR. The ODR procedure must not cause substantial delay for the purposes of bringing legal proceedings and must suspend the period for the time-barring of claims (principle of legality).The ODR should not entail any costs or should impose only very low costs for the parties (principle of effectiveness/fairness); the ODR mechanisms established in Member States must pay due account to the above-mentioned recommendations. Soft law becomes 'quasi-hard law' under the scrutiny of the CJEU!

It seems that *Alassini* encouraged the Commission to put forward two proposals concerning ADR/ODR mechanisms in the Union which have now been adopted by the EP and the Council: Directive 2013/11/EU of 21 May 2013 on Consumer ADR and Regulation (EU) No of 21 May 2013 on Consumer ODR.[60] The first will make it an obligation of Member States to provide for ADR mechanisms in certain specially-defined consumer disputes, including those of traders against consumers (which seems rather strange). These mechanisms will have to follow certain principles, such as expertise and impartiality, transparency, effectiveness and fairness. Member States must give information about 'the types of rules the ADR entity may use as a basis for the dispute resolution (for example, rules of law, considerations of equity, codes of conduct)', Article 7(1)(i) of Directive 2013/11. This is an indirect recognition of 'soft law' to be used at least in the preliminary stage of a legal dispute.

The ODR proposal wants to establish an EU-wide electronic platform which can be used by consumers from different EU countries and which will process complaints to the competent national ODR mechanisms. The question of language will be solved by using an EU-wide form which is available in all EU languages.

Again, I will not go into details.[61] What is important is the recognition by EU institutions, in particular the Commission but also the CJEU, to use 'soft law' mechanisms as an instrument to solve consumer disputes 'in the shadow of the law' and of formal court procedures which proved to be ineffective in particular in cross-border settings.[62] Even though the term 'OMC' is nowhere mentioned by the Commission, the proposed policy certainly qualifies for an OMC label. A new architecture of dispute settlement could be the result of these initiatives, leading to a 'delegalisation' of consumer disputes with a stronger emphasis on efficiency and effectiveness in particular in cross-border transactions, and elevating the status of 'soft law' as an equivalent to 'hard law' which will only give a framework of disputes resolution.

---

[60] Regulation 524/2013 [2013] OJ L 165/1, 63.

[61] For a first assessment, see N Reich, *Individueller und kollektiver Rechtsschutz im EU-Verbraucherrecht* (Baden-Baden, Nomos, 2012) 47.

[62] See the seminal paper by V Gessner, 'Europas holprige Rechtswege' in L Krämer, H-W Micklitz and K Tonner (eds), *Law and Diffuse Interests in the European Legal Order: Liber amicorum N Reich* (Baden-Baden, Nomos, 1997) 163.

III. Optional Instruments for an Optimal EU Contract Legislation—'Ghost' or 'Host' for Integration?

A. From the Draft Common Frame of Reference (DCFR) to an 'Optional Instrument' (OI)

As already mentioned, the Commission has presented a proposal for an EU Regulation for a CESL. Its adoption—even though it is not likely to take place in the near future—would transform the 'ghost' of my Wisconsin paper into a '(permanent?) host' of EU law and integration. Is this a welcome host, or will it remain an unwelcome intruder and 'legal irritant'?[63] This question will be debated along after examining the question, however, one should briefly recapitulate the development stages of an EU-specific contract law over the last five years.

When I wrote my Wisconsin paper, the term 'Common Frame of Reference' (CFR) had already been coined, and a large group of European civil law scholars had been assembled under the two headings of 'Study group' and '*Acquis* group'. In 2007 to 2008, a first interim draft CFR[64] was presented to the Commission, which was followed in 2008 to 2009 by a final version,[65] supplemented by six copious volumes of notes and explanations.[66] An intense academic debate followed.[67] It is not necessary to discuss this any further. However, three points should be noted because they are of relevance for the following discussion on a European contract law:

— The principles and provisions contained in the DCFR went far beyond mere contract law; they contained rules on the law of obligations in general (for example, on non-contractual obligations such as tort, unjust enrichment and *negotiorum gestio*); on a number of specific contracts beyond sales law, particularly in the area of services; and on transfer of property and security interests in movables.

— The DCFR wanted to integrate mandatory consumer law provisions, particularly those from the *acquis*, into the general rules of EU private law which—in contracting—contained

---

[63] See the well-known concept of G Teubner, 'Legal Irritants: Good Faith in British Law, or How Unifying Law Ends up in New Divergences' (1998) 61 *Modern Law Review* 11.

[64] C von Bar, E Clive and H Schulte-Nölke (eds), *Principles, Definitions and Model Rules on European Private Law: Draft CFR Interim Outline Edition* (Munich, Sellier, 2008).

[65] C von Bar, E Clive and H Schulte-Nölke (eds), *Principles, Definitions and Model Rules on European Private Law: Draft CFR Outline Edition* (Munich, Sellier, 2009).

[66] C von Bar, E Clive and H Schulte-Nölke (eds), *Principles, Definitions and Model Rules on European Private Law: Draft CFR—Full edition* (Munich, Sellier, 2009).

[67] See H-W Micklitz and F Cafaggi (eds), *European Private Law after the Common Frame of Reference: What Future for European Private Law* (Cheltenham, Edward Elgar, 2010); H Eidenmüller, F Faust, HC Grigoleit, N Jansen, G Wagner and R Zimmermann, 'The CFR for European Private Law—Policy Choices and Codification Problems' (2009) 29 *Oxford Journal of Legal Studies* 659; N Jansen and R Zimmermann, 'A European Civil Code in All but Name' (2010) 69 *Cambridge Law Journal* 98; M Hesselink, 'The CFR as a Source of European Private Law' (2009) 83 *Tulane Law Review* 919; O Cherednychenko, 'Fundamental Rights, Policy Issues and the DCFR' (2010) 6 *European Review of Contract Law* 39; S Vogenauer, 'CFR and UNIDRPOIT-Principles of International Commercial Contract: Coexistence, Competition, or Overkill of Soft Law' (2010) 6 *European Review of Contract Law* 143; P Larouche and F Chirico (eds), *Economic Analysis of the DCFR* (Munich, Sellier, 2011); G Wagner (ed), *The CFR—A View from Law and Economics* (Munich, Sellier, 2009); not to mention the many French, German and Italian contributions.

mostly 'default' rules. Therefore, Article I 1:105(1) of the DCFR provides: 'A "consumer" means any natural person who is acting *primarily* for purposes which are not related to his or her trade, business or profession.' This definition was broader than the traditional one used in the *acquis* to allow the inclusion of so-called 'double purpose contracts' which would not usually come within the scope of the consumer protective provisions of EU law according to the *Gruber* case law of the CJEU.[68]

— The legal character of the DCFR remained unclear. In its early communications, the Commission regarded it as a 'toolbox' for future legislation—a somewhat dismissive term for the enormous scholarly work which went into it. But the Commission certainly did not want to endorse the work formally because of a 'competence gap' in the EU Treaties regarding general contract and even more private law legislation in the EU.[69] This had not been changed by the Lisbon Treaty on European Union, rather the contrary: Article 5 of the Treaty on European Union insisted on a narrow reading of EU competences based on the principle of 'conferral' and limited by the provisions on subsidiarity and proportionality to which I will turn later.

Couldn't the provisions of the DCFR be used—at least partially—for an OI of EU contract law? Indeed, for many supporters of an EU-specific private law the idea of an optional instrument looked like a remedy to solve the 'competence gap' described above, and numerous academic and political contributions discussed matters of competence, scope and relation to national law of an EU OI, filling an entire issue of the *European Review of Contract Law* after a conference in Leuven in 2010.[70] This debate was to some extent started by a Commission Green paper of 1 July 2010[71] which has been reviewed elsewhere.[72] Many questions found controversial answers:

— The competence basis: internal market under Article 114 or 'reserve competence' of Article 352 TFEU, the first being subject to majority voting, the second needing unanimity in the Council and the consent of the EP?
— The personal scope: only B2C (business to consumer) or B2B (business to business) or both?

---

[68] Case C-464/01 *Johann Gruber v Bay Wa AG* [2005] ECR I-439 was decided under the mechanism of the Brussels Convention.

[69] See Reich, Free Movement and Social Rights in an Enlarged Union' (n 23) 437–49.

[70] Contributions by Riesenhuber, Sefton-Green, Gutman, Howells, Augenhofer, Maugeri, Meli, Twigg-Flesner, Mak, Gome and Ganuza, Hesselink, Cristas, Cartwright, Rutgers and Castermans, in the special issue of *European Review of Contract Law* 2011, 115–366.

[71] Commission, 'Green paper on policy options for progress towards a European Contract Law for consumers and Businesses' COM (2010) 348 final.

[72] C Herrestahl, 'Ein europäisches Vertragsrecht als Optionales Instrument' (2011) *Europäische Zeitschrift für Wirtschaftsrecht* 7; K Tonner, 'Das Grünbuch der Kommission zum Europäischen Vertragsrecht für Verbraucher und Unternehmer—Zur Rolle des Verbrauchervertragsrecht im europäischen Vertragsrecht' (2010) *Europäische Zeitschrift für Wirtschaftsrecht* 767; H Rösler, 'Rechtswahl und optionelles Vertragsrecht in der EU' (2011) *Europäische Zeitschrift für Wirtschaftsrecht* 1; M Tamm, 'Die 28 Rechtsordnung der EU: Gedanken zur Einführung eines grenzüberschreitenden B2C Vertragsrecht' (2010) *GPR—Zeitschrift für Gemeinschaftsprivatrecht* 281; J Cartwright, '"Choice is good" Really?' (2011) 7 *European Review of Contract Law* 335. A comprehensive study with detailed recommendations has been prepared by a working group of the Hamburg Max Planck-Institute for Comparative and International Private Law, see Jürgen Basedow et al, 'Policy Options for Progress Towards a European Contract Law' *Max Planck Private Law Research Paper* No 11/2, published in (2011) 75 *Rabel Journal of Comparative and International Private Law* 373, hereinafter *MPI*-study); Reich (n 31), 5–13 with further references on the questions mentioned below. See also European Economic and Social Committee, Opinion on the Green Paper from the Commission on policy options for progress towards a European contract law for consumers and Businesses, [2011] OJ C84/1.

— The territorial scope: only cross-border or internal and cross-border?
— Use of a so-called 'blue button' proposed by Schulte-Nölke to serve the needs of e-commerce?[73]

B. The 'Feasibility Study' of 3 May 2011 and draft CESL of 11 October 2011

The Commission, eager to push for an EU contract law after long years of only symbolic interest, did not even await the outcome of the consultation procedure and set up an 'Expert Group' to study the feasibility of producing an OI on European Contract Law in April 2010.[74] The Expert Group presented its results in record time after one year of work on 3 March 2011.[75] It proposed a draft European Sales Law, including provisions on general contract law, special (mostly mandatory) rules on consumer transactions, and also general rules on the law of obligations such as damages, restitution and prescription. A short consultation period was planned to end on 1 July 2011. The Commission finally published its draft CESL on 11 October 2011—again in record time—which obviously did not allow for any in-depth discussion.

How to approach a long, complex and many-layered document? The Commission has with some modifications—particularly concerning the inclusion of 'digital content' which did not figure in the Feasibility study of 3 May 2011 and only found a definition and some information-specific provisions in Article 2(11), 5(1)(g), (h), 6(1)(r) and (s) of the CRD 2011/83—more or less taken over the content and the concrete proposals of the Expert group. The proposal of an EU OI has a double-headed structure:

— The Regulation (with an explanatory memorandum and recitals, as common in EU legal instruments) will cover 'general EU law matters' (the so-called '*chapeau*'), such as the objectives and legal basis of the instrument, the definitions, the scope of application, the agreement to and enforcement of a fair and transparent 'opt-in' procedure in B2C transactions, obligations and remaining powers of Member States, and miscellaneous technical issues;
— *Annex I* contains the detailed provisions (186 articles) of the CESL; *Annex II* a 'Standard Information Note' explaining an eventual consumers' opt-in. No recitals or explanations are attached to the Annex.

---

[73] Schulte-Nölke, 'EC Law on the Formation of Contract: From the Common Frame of Reference to the Blue Button' (2007) 3 *European Review of Contract Law* 348f: 'The "Blue Button" would be an Optional Instrument enabling businesses to set up a European-wide e-shop which has only to comply with one set of rules. Such an Optional Instrument would solve most of the cases likely to arise in B2C as well as B2B and C2C relations. When buying goods in an e-shop the client could easily choose the application of the OI by clicking on a 'Blue Button' on the screen showing his or her acceptance of the optional European Law ... If the client chooses the 'Blue Button', the optional European Law would derogate the law which otherwise were applicable to the conflict of law rules.' For critique, see Micklitz and Cafaggi, *European Private Law after the Common Frame of Reference* (n 67).

[74] Decision 2010/233/EU setting up the Expert Group on a Common Frame of Reference in the area of European contract [2010] OJ L105/109.

[75] Commission Expert Group on European Contract Law, 'Feasibility Study for a Future Instrument in European Contract Law' available at ec.europa.eu/justice/contract/files/feasibility-study_en.pdf, reprinted in R Schulze and J Stuyck (eds), *Towards a European Contract Law*, (Munich, Sellier, 2011); *cf* the contributions in the same volume.

This paper will give only a short overview of the structure and the basic content both of the *chapeau* and *Annex I*—without even attempting to analyse their central provisions or go deeper into the already very controversial discussion. The main interest of this paper, as indicated in the opening paragraphs referring to the work of David Trubek, will be to look at its potential contribution to solving or at least alleviating the ongoing conflict between integration and protection in the EU, not to add to the many very technical comments.

The main points can be summarised as follows:

— The CESL is supposed to be a measure of the internal market in the sense of Article 114 TFEU and would therefore follow the ordinary legislative procedure by majority voting both in the Council and the EP—a basis certainly to be welcomed by the EP which has always resisted any competence norm where it is not an equal partner as in Article 352 TFU.[76] This is justified because the proposal removes 'obstacles to the exercise of fundamental freedoms which result from differences between national law, in particular from the additional transaction costs and perceived legal complexity experienced by traders when concluding cross-border transactions and the lack of confidence in their rights experienced by consumers when purchasing from another country—all of which have a direct effect on the establishment and functioning of the internal market and limit competition'.[77]

— CESL has a limited personal scope: it is applicable to B2B/SMU contracts where one of the parties is a small or medium-sized (SMU) undertaking as defined in Article 7(2) which can be extended by Member States), or B2C contracts under the narrow definition of the *acquis* whereby '"consumer" means any natural person who is acting for purposes which are outside the person's trade, business, craft, or profession'. This would exclude most dual-purpose contracts, contrary to Recital 17 of the new Consumer Rights Directive 2011/83.[78]

— CESL is supposed to be available to cross-border contracting, with the possibility of Member States also allowing its use for purely internal transactions (Article 13(a)). In B2C situations, however, the cross-border element is defined very broadly in Article 4(3) depending on the address indicated by the consumer (whether or not it is identical with their habitual residence!); the delivery address for goods; or the billing address. It is therefore not restricted, as one could have imagined by the 'blue button' concept, to distance contracts or e-commerce. This means that in a face-to-face situation where a consumer in Germany contracts with a company established in Germany but delivery will be made in France, the CESL could be used by a special opt-in, alongside normally applicable German law.[79] Is that an attractive perspective for business or consumers? Why allow a 'journey to the unknown' when all parties are used to contracting according to their legal traditions and no real link with a cross-border element is established,

---

[76] See Case C-436/03 *European Parliament v Council* [2006] ECR I-3733 paras 43–44 concerning the legal basis of the European Cooperative Society which was based on Art 352 TFEU and challenged by the EP which lost its case!

[77] See Commission, 'Proposal for a Regulation on a Common European Sales Law' (n 4), the Explanatory Memorandum 9.

[78] See the critique by H-W Micklitz and N Reich, 'The Commission Proposal of a Regulation for an Optional 'Common European Sales Law'—Too broad or not broad enough?' (2012) *EUI Working paper LAW 4/2012*, Part I, paras 18–22, at 12.

[79] See the critique by Twigg-Flesner, *A Cross-Border Only Regulation for Consumer Transactions in the EU* (n 54) 76.

except the rather superficial element of a delivery address abroad as part of the performance of a contract which under normal circumstances in conflict-of-law matters does not have any influence on applicable law?

— Its substantive scope is limited to the 'sale of movables', of 'digital content' and of 'service contracts' related to the sale of goods. Certain combined contracts are excluded, for example, those taking a credit element (Article 6(2)). This makes the use of the CESL unattractive or even impossible if the trader offers means of deferred payment or a leasing contract.

— The use of the CESL in B2C transactions depends on rather complex and separate information and notification requirements as set out in Articles 8 and 9 and paralleled by a sort of warning to the consumer, the terms of which are defined in Annex II. In order to avoid cherry-picking, the parties can only choose CESL in its entirety as a complete package (Article 8(3)). Such strict rules discourage rather than encourage consumers to agree to the use of the CESL. Traders will not find them attractive because they are precluded from using standard terms for the opt-in. The contracting will be split into two parts: agreement about the use of the CESL; and agreement on the contract terms within the framework of CESL.[80] Nothing is said about how the opting-in to B2B/SMU transactions will be carried out: will Article 3 of Regulation 593/2008 be applicable here?[81]

— The relation of CESL to the EU *acquis* and to mandatory national law under Article 6(2) of Regulation 593/2008 is by no means clear. The Commission simply writes: 'Since the CESL contains a complete set of fully harmonised mandatory consumer protection rules, there will be no disparities between the law of the Member States in this area, where the parties have chosen to use the CESL. Consequently, Article 6(2) which is predicated on the existence of differing levels of consumer protection in the Member States, has no practical importance for the issues covered by the CESL'. Article 6(2) is, however, concerned with differing Member States rules, not with EU provisions. There is already a debate in legal literature about how this precedence of the CESL over national law under the conditions of Article 6(2) can be assured— otherwise the choice of CESL by the trader would not give him any advantage because, even by choosing it in its B2C transactions, he could not be sure of being confronted with divergent national consumer law resulting from minimum harmonisation which is still possible under Directive 2011/83 for unfair terms and consumer sales.

— The different parts of CESL contain rather detailed rules on B2B/SMU and B2C contracting within the above-mentioned scope of application. Without saying so, CESL contains two completely different sets of rules: mostly default rules in B2B/SMU transactions with some 'micro protection' of SMUs by provisions concerning good faith (Article 2(3) CESL); remedies for fraud, threats and unfair exploitation (Article 56(1)); 'grossly' unfair contract terms (Article 81/86); damages (Article 171); prescription (Article 186); while in B2C contracting mandatory provisions are the standard—for example, the remedies for mistake (Article 56(2)); *contra-preferentem* interpretation (Article 64); terms derived from pre-contractual statements (Article 69);

---

[80] Micklitz and Reich, 'The Commission Proposal' (n 78) 18.

[81] Heated controversies have already been provoked by the unclear status of CESL to Regulation (EC) 593/2008 of 17 June 2008 on the law applicable to contractual obligations (Rome I) [2008] OJ L 176/6 not to be documented here.

contracts of indeterminate duration (Article77(2)); black- and grey-listed terms (Article 84/85); remedies for non-performance (Article 108); interest for delay in payment (Article 167); and restitution (Article 177). This hybrid structure is important for a closer analysis of CESL not so much under competence, but rather under the proportionality criteria of Article 5(4) TEU.

C. CESL as a Hybrid Contract Law—The Challenges of Proportionality as an EU Constitutional Principle under Article 5(4) TEU

The present debate on CESL concentrates on four main controversies:

— the competence basis in EU law: Article 118 or 352 TFEU;
— the methods and technicalities of the 'opt-in' and the effects on national law;
— a detailed analysis of the many rules proposed under coherence and legal certainty aspects, sometimes with express reference to existing national law, including proposals for improvement; and
— the relation between mandatory and default provisions, mostly in B2C transactions, including whether the specific level of protection is 'high' enough (or not) under Article 12/169 TFEU, Article 38 of the Charter of the Fundamental Rights of the European Union ('the Charter').

Quite frankly: this debate is of very limited interest to me (and probably not to David Trubek himself!) because it does not answer the preceding and more important question: do stakeholders (business, SMUs, consumers, other participants in cross-border trade), Member States and the EU itself really *need* such an instrument.[82] The 'necessity test' is not identical with the competence basis but must be met by *all measures* under Article 114 or 352 TFEU—otherwise it would not have found its separate regulation under the proportionality test in Article 5(4) TEU.

In the following I will argue that there is no need for an OI, whether B2B/SMU or B2C, from an EU constitutional, as well as a political viewpoint. Other adequate mechanisms for contracting in the internal market which fulfil the above-mentioned double criteria— avoiding unwarranted trade restrictions *and* guaranteeing a sufficiently high level of protection—already exist or can be envisaged within the existing EU *acquis* which simply render the OI superfluous, even if in the legislative process it will be made 'more consumer or SMU-user friendly', even if some of the technical defects can be overcome, and even if the 'market for legal regulations' the Commission is hoping for will accept and make frequent use of it. When discussing the 'necessity' test, being realistic about contracting is useful: in most cases, the active partner will propose the contract regime. In B2C transactions, this will always be the business part; the consumer is put on a take-it-or-leave basis; the idea that he can use a 'blue button' in his favour seems rather far-fetched. In the area of B2B/SMU-contracting, the stronger party will generally impose the contract terms, rather than the SMU, unless it is in particularly favourable position.[83]

---

[82] For a critique see Grundmann, 'Kosten und Nutzen eines Europäischen Optionalen Kaufrechts' (n 35); Twigg-Flesner, 'Debate on a European Code of Contracts' (2012) 17 *Contratto e Impresa/Europa* 157.
[83] Twigg-Flesner, ibid, 163.

The insistence on the 'necessity' test seems difficult at first glance because the CJEU has so far indirectly monitored the legality of an EU measure on the basis of not meeting the proportionality test in only one case.[84] The standard formula used by the CJEU in a consistent line of cases is as follows. It has recognised that 'the Community legislature must be allowed a broad discretion in areas which involve political, economic and social choices on its part, and in which it is called upon to undertake complex assessments', even though it was bound by the proportionality principle according to the then Article 5(2) EC (now Article 5(4) TEU).[85] 'Consequently, the legality of a measure adopted in that respect can be affected only if the measure is manifestly inappropriate having regard to the objective which the competent institution is seeking to pursue.'[86] But the scope of this case law should not be over-extended: it has never been tested with regard to contract law matters legislated by EU institutions; never has such a complex instrument as the 186 articles of the CESL been put before the CJEU, and never has such a broad mixture of default and mandatory rules been submitted to its scrutiny.

According to Harbo,[87] the Court so far has used a very 'moderate' approach in controlling Community and in the future Union law measures under the proportionality test—an approach characterised by the vice-president of the CJEU K Lenaerts as applying proportionality in a 'procedural fashion',[88] while it uses much more restrictive language with regard to Member State measures allegedly restricting fundamental freedoms.[89]

i. No Necessity for B2B/SMU Cross-border Transactions

However, even under the 'manifestly inappropriate' criteria, it could be argued against the Commission that it has not explained why the CESL should also cover general contract law matters such as the conclusion, defects in consent and interpretation of a contract, which are not specific to sales (and related services) law, and certain areas of the general law of obligations such as damages, restitution, and prescription.[90] Almost all of them must be qualified as default rules in B2B transactions which can be modified by party agreement; very few provisions of the CESL contain mandatory rules which could be invoked

---

[84] Case C-376/98 *Germany v EP and Council* [2000] ECR I-8419 at paras 99–100, indirectly refers to the necessity test which was not relevant for annulment of the tobacco-advertising Directive; A-G Fennelly presented a more elaborate argument in his Opinion of 15 June 2000 at para 149 concerning the infamous and later annulled Directive 98/43/EC on the approximation of the laws, regulations and administrative provisions of the Member States relating to the advertising and sponsorship of tobacco products [1998] OJ L212/9.

[85] Case C-491/01 *The Queen v Secretary of State for Health ex p British American Tobacco (Investments) Ltd. et al* [2002] ECR I-11453; Case C-380/03 *Germany v EP and Council* [2005] ECR I-11573, para 145; Case C-344/04 *IATA and ELFAA v Department for Transport* [2006] ECR I-403, para 80, referring to earlier cases such as Case C-84/94 *United Kingdom v Council* [1996] ECR I-5755, para 58; Case C-233/94 *Germany v Parliament and Council* [1997] ECR I-2405, paras 55 and 56; Case C-157/96 *National Farmers' Union and Others* [1998] ECR I-2211, para 61, recently confirmed in Case C-58/08 *Vodafone* [2010] ECR I-4999 para 69 referring to the objective of directly protecting consumers.

[86] Case C-491/01 (n 85) para 123.

[87] T-I Harbo, 'The Function of the Proportionality Principle in EU Law' (2010) 16 *European Law Journal* 158, 166, 172, 177.

[88] K Lenaerts, 'The European Court of Justice and Process-Oriented Review' (2012) *Yearbook of European Law* 3, 7.

[89] See the critique of N Reich, 'How Proportionate is the Proportionality Principle' in Micklitz and de Witte (eds), *The European Court of Justice* (n 55) 110.

[90] I follow here the argument used in Micklitz and Reich, 'The Commission Proposal' (n 78) Part I, paras 14–16 at 9.

in particular (but not exclusively) by SMUs as mentioned above. These very broad and general rules which differ among Member States have had no proven impact on cross-border transactions so far. The 'impact assessment' of the Commission staff seems to be highly speculative on this point.

In any case, eventual internal market problems can be solved by the B2B/SMU parties' freedom of choice under Article 3 of the Rome I Regulation within the limits of mandatory provisions of paragraphs 3 and 4 of Article 3 which also apply to B2B/SMU transactions. With regard to provisions specific to cross-border commercial sales law, most of them are already covered by the 1980 Convention on the International Sale of Goods (CISG) which will be applicable either under an 'opt-out' mechanism of Article 1(1)(a), or—for traders not established in the CISG Member States, namely in the UK, Ireland, Portugal and Malta, by an 'opt-in' possibility under Article 1(1)(b). It is true that the EU is not party to the CISG, that CISG is not concerned with the specific need for protection of SMUs, and that the CJEU has no explicit power of its interpretation, but may refer to and thereby indirectly interpret it if a link to EU law can be shown to exist.[91] Still the question remains: why put a second level on cross-border contracting in related matters when the parties to a B2B/SMU transaction already have an instrument at their disposal under which considerable legal expertise and experience has already been accumulated, and which may therefore increase the degree of legal certainty which the Commission invokes for B2B/SMU transactions in the internal market?[92] Why artificially separate international and EU cross-border trade, which will make transactions more complex, instead of giving the parties more clarity about their rights and obligations as promised by the Commission? Therefore, it seems highly doubtful whether under the 'necessity' test the EU has jurisdiction to regulate cross-border B2B/SMU sales (and related service) transactions at all by adopting the CESL instrument in its present or even in an improved form. Is this not covered by Article 7(2) CISG which allows the application of special protective provisions under conflict-of-law rules in favour of SMUs?

This critical analysis cannot be refuted by arguing that CESL is 'only' optional in B2B/SMU transactions. Optional instruments have to pass the 'necessity' test as any other EU legislative act. The 'option' is only concerned with its specific application in a contract between B2B/SMU partners, not with competence of the EU at all to take and propose such a measure to the parties.

ii. Is there a Real 'Necessity' for CESL in B2C Transactions?

In B2C transactions matters are more complex because of the mostly mandatory nature of provisions protecting the consumer under EU and national law reiterated in many judgments of the CJEU.[93] In cross-border transactions this problem is referred to in Article 6

---

[91] In Case C-381/08 *Car Trim v Key Safety* [2010] ECR I-1255, para 36 concerning the interpretation of the concept of 'place of performance' in Art 5(1)(b) of the Brussels Regulation 44/2001 the Court referred to Art 3 CISG.

[92] For a discussion on the (rather marginal) divergences between the CISG and the CESL in commercial cross-border sales transactions see the detailed analysis of Magnus in U Magnus (ed), *CISG vs Regional Sales Law Unification* (Munich, Sellier, 2012) 97 with the exception of digital content which did not exist at the time the CISG was negotiated but would allow an application by analogy.

[93] The case law has been well analysed in the Opinion of AG Trstenjak of 29 November 2011 in Case C-453/10 *Jana Perenicova et al v S.O.S. financ* (CJEU, 15 March 2012) paras 42–45. See the comment by H-W Micklitz and N Reich, '"Und es bewegt sich doch"?—Neues zum Unionsrecht der missbräuchlichen Klauseln in Verbraucherverträgen' (2012) *Europäische Zeitschrift für Wirtschaftsrecht* 126.

of the Rome I Regulation, which has been discussed above. The differences between Member State consumer protection laws which remain despite harmonisation at the EU level, may warrant the adoption of a more coherent and uniform EU regulation focusing on establishing uniform standards of cross-border B2C transactions.[94] However, the proposed provisions of the CESL must be 'necessary' with regard to 'content and form'. In my opinion, this necessity test is not fulfilled with regard to those provisions which try to regulate problems specific to B2C transactions and which have already been the object of EU legislation, lately the CRD 2011/83/EU which has fully harmonised the provisions on 'off premises' and distance contracts figuring in Articles 17 to 19, 24 to 27, and 40 to 47 CESL. Is it really necessary to have *two* layers of consumer protection in EU law, one mandatory for both internal and cross-border transactions, the other with only 'optional mandatory provisions' for cross-border contracting which may not always have been coordinated and updated with the existing protective regime of the *acquis*?

In those areas where CESL contains better or different rules, for example, with regard to the professional seller's liability for non-conforming digital content which was only included in Articles 100 to 105 of CESL and not in the CRD, the protection of the consumer/user of digital content should not depend on whether or not he or she has opted in to the CESL. Another example concerns the differences in remedies in the case of a non-conforming good in the CESL and in the CRD: while the CRD limits the first stage remedies of the consumer to replacement or repair without allowing him or her a right to immediate rejection (which can be introduced by Member State law under the minimum harmonisation principle), such a right is foreseen in the CESL because the professional seller does not have a 'right to cure' (Article 114 (2)), provided that the non-conformity is not insignificant, which has to be proven by the seller. If the trader proposes to the consumer to opt-in to CESL and the consumer agrees, the trader would implicitly waive his 'right to cure' and allow the consumer an immediate right of rejection of a non-conforming good as in UK law.[95] Not surprisingly, this increase in consumer protection has been met with strong opposition in business circles and in academia.[96] On the other hand, isn't the possibility of immediate rejection the only realistic remedy in cross-border contracting, while repair or replacement may be more costly to the trader?[97] Finally, why should this remedy depend on the opt-in to a complex instrument such as CESL whose impact on the protective level the 'normal consumer' will usually not be able to assess? Could the trader not offer a right of immediate rejection on his own by a voluntary marketing action, perhaps in a soft-law instrument negotiated between business and consumer associations? Does one need a legislative instrument for that?[98]

On the other hand, there are some provisions in CESL which seem to lower the extent of consumer protection granted under the CRD or the case law of the CJEU. As mentioned

---

[94] This is the main argument by Twigg-Flesner, *A Cross-Border Only Regulation for Consumer Transactions in the EU* (n 54).

[95] Micklitz and Reich, 'The Commission Proposal' (n 78) Part III, paras 16 at 79.

[96] See the critique by Grundmann, 'Kosten und Nutzen eines Europäischen Optionalen Kaufrechts' (n 35); G Wagner, 'Ökonomische Analyse des CESL' (2012) *Zeitschrift für Europäisches Privatrecht* 797.

[97] F Zoll, 'Das Konzept des Verbraucherschutzes in der Machbarkeitsstudie für das Optionale Instrument' (2012) *Zeitschrift für Europäisches Unternehmens- und Verbraucherrecht (Journal of European Consumer and Market Law)* 9, 21.

[98] Proposal in the study by Howells, Micklitz and Reich, 'Optional Consumer Law Standards' (n 36); Reich, 'EU Strategies in Finding the Optimal Consumer Law Instrument' (n 35) 29.

above, the concept of the consumer in CESL is narrower than that described in Recital 17 of the CRD; fewer individuals will therefore come under the consumer protective scope of CESL.

Another possible discrepancy has indirectly been provoked by the express confirmation of the consumer protection objective of the remedies in Directive 99/44/EC by the CJEU in its *Quelle* judgment;[99] the question of whether the costs for de-connecting and re-installing non-conforming goods have to be borne by the seller if this has not been expressly agreed in the contract, was considered by the CJEU in the *Putz/Weber* case.[100] In its judgment of 16 June 2011, the CJEU, against the opinion of AG Mazak, clearly placed those costs on the seller because he delivered a non-conforming good. The seller's responsibility towards the consumer, who installed in good faith the non-conforming goods, is not based on fault, but rather on the simple consequence of the non-fulfilment of the seller's contractual obligations which do not end with the passing of the risk (paragraphs 46 to 47, referring to *Quelle*). The Court also refers to the consumer protection objective of Directive 99/44/EC and to the express statement in Article 3(3), that repair or replacement should be effected 'free of charge' and without 'any significant inconvenience to the consumer'. The seller's strict liability is not excluded even if the costs of replacement are disproportionate, but may however be limited to a 'proportionate amount' (paragraph 76), to be determined by the national court by reference to the purchase price. Within the limits of the proportionality principle the choice of remedies usually depends on the consumer. It is not clear whether this case law will be taken over by the CESL; at least the consumer cannot be sure that by being encouraged or 'persuaded' to opting-in he or she will have the same extent of protection as under the *acquis*. Article 112(1) CESL seems to restrict the consequences of the *Weber/Putz* judgment insofar that the seller only has to take back the replaced items at his expense but does not say that the seller must also cover the (proportionate) costs for re-installing a non-conforming good.[101]

One could argue, therefore, that the obligation of the EU in its internal market measures to guarantee a high level of consumer protection according to Article 114(3) and 169 TFEU cannot be waived by the consumer through an opt-in of the CESL if it contains a lower level of protection than possible under the CRD. The opt-in mechanism of the CESL would create different levels of consumer protection in the EU against the principle of non-discrimination in Article 12 TFEU and Article 21 of the Charter without being justified by imperative requirements of the internal market. Against Recital 58 of the recently adopted CRD, the consumer could be 'deprived of the protection granted by this Directive' under the opt-in mechanism of CESL. Even if the choice of the parties to a B2C contract would make reference also to the 'default' provisions of CESL and to those mandatory provisions in general contract law which are contained in it, there is still no necessity of an OI because under conflict-rules the business party has freedom of choice under Article 3 of Regulation 593/2008, and Article 6(2) with its flexible principle of equivalence can function as a long

---

[99] Case C-404/06 *Quelle AG v Bundesverband der Verbraucherzentralen* [2008] ECR I-2685, confirmed by Art 112(2) CESL.

[100] Joined Cases C-65/09 *Weber* and C-87/09 *Putz* (CJEU, 16 June 2011), against the Opinion of AG Mazak of 18 May 2010; for comments see JA Luzak, 'Who should bear the risk of the removal of the non-conforming goods? Joined Cases C-65/09 and C-87/09 (*Weber* and *Putz*)' (2012) *Zeitschrift für Europäisches Unternehmens- und Verbraucherrecht (Journal of European Consumer and Market Law)* 35 (note). For the German follow up-case see the judgment of 21 December 2012 of the Bundesgerichtshof (BGH) NJW 2012, 1073.

[101] See the comment by Luzak, ibid, 40.

stop to protect the consumer without placing unnecessary burdens on the trader.[102] The trader can always avoid 'being caught' by the consumer protection provisions of the consumers' home country by voluntarily agreeing to a high(er) level of protection. There is no 'regulatory gap' and hence 'no need' which must be closed by allowing the parties to opting into the CESL under EU jurisdiction.

To sum up: it seems arguable that even if the CESL can be based on the existing EU competence provisions, in particular Article 114 TFEU, its two core elements—to regulate cross-border B2B/SMU and B2C transactions in the internal market—*do not comply with the necessity test* under the proportionality criteria of Article 5(4) TEU:

— In B2B/SMU, there is *no need* because of the prevalence of party autonomy and the possibility of choosing the CISG, also available to SMUs.
— In B2C, there is *no need* for an opt-in instrument because this could create an incentive for traders to remove mandatory protective provisions under primary and secondary EU provisions; still existing differences in the level of (non-harmonised) Member State consumer protection measures do not seem to present an appreciable impediment to cross-border marketing and can be levelled out by an internal market-conforming application of conflict provisions of the Rome I Regulation.

IV. A Tentative Conclusion Following the Path Opened by David Trubek: Open Method of Coordination and Convergence in a Reflexive Contract Governance in the EU

The critique of the legislative approach of the CESL as an OI is not meant as a complete rejection of its utility. It is in this area that David Trubek's reflection on OMC, which goes beyond the 'hard' law approach of the Commission, can be useful.[103] This reflection refers to a broader discussion on 'contract governance' in general. In an overview paper based on comparative research in relation to the 'corporate governance' paradigm, Möslein and Riesenhuber distinguish the following four areas of research and practical relevance of contract governance:[104]

1. 'governance of contract law' (institutional framework of contract law-rule making);
2. 'governance of contracts' (contract law as an institutional framework for private transactions);
3. 'governance by means of contracts law' (design of contract law as an instrument of steering behaviour and for achieving regulatory results—regulatory function of contract law); and
4. 'governance through contract' (contracts as an institutional framework and mechanism of self-guidance by private parties).

[102] Reich, 'EU Strategies in Finding the Optimal Consumer Law Instrument' (n 35) 21.
[103] I refer again to Reich, 'Free Movement and Social Rights in an Enlarged Union' (n 23) 468–70.
[104] Möslein and Riesenhuber, 'Contract Governance—A Research Agenda' (n 17) 260.

In the context of the question on the relevance of the insights of David Trubek on EU contract governance, points 1 and 3 are particularly relevant. The CESL is based on prior comparative law work done by academics, in particular the DCFR. This can be used without formal legislation not only as a 'toolbox', but also as a 'soft-law' mechanism to develop timely and legitimate solutions to ongoing contract law problems in the EU. It is not a source of law, but it is a source of *inspiration*. In this spirit, the DCFR has already been used by several Advocates General in cases at the CJEU concerning private law matters as an informal but legally relevant source of solutions to legal problems within the EU. Particularly interesting have been opinions of AG Trestenjak in cases *Martin*,[105] *Friz*,[106] *VB Pénzügyi Leasing*[107] and *Messner*[108] where she expressly cited several provisions of the DCFR concerning the concepts of fairness, abuse and remedies in B2C transactions. In a similar spirit, AG Poiares Maduro referred to the predecessor of the DCFR, the so-called *Acquis principles*[109] in his opinion in *Hamilton*.[110] In its judgments in the cases *Hamilton*,[111] *Messner*[112] and *Friz*[113] the CJEU indirectly followed suit, not by referring expressly to the DCFR, but to 'the (general) principles of civil law', like good faith, unjust enrichment, satisfactory balancing and a fair division of risks among the various interested parties. In her opinion in *Banco Espanol de Credito*,[114] AG Trestenjak mentioned that the recent EU activities concerning CESL would 'have an important influence on the further development in the field of consumer protection law'. Whether or not this is true or not will not be discussed here any further. Even though no political commitment of the Commission has been behind this rather 'incremental development' of general principles of civil law in the EU, without having a formal legislative basis,[115] it comes close to what the former AG van Gerven called the 'open method of convergence'.[116]

Although I have been critical of constitutional basis of CESL in this paper, this does not mean that the project is not useful. David Trubek's plea for more informal measures of standard-setting in areas such as in employment and social policy where there is a competence gap in the EU, and now in the area of contract law, may show the direction that

---

[105] Case C-227/08 *Martin* [2009] ECR I-11939, Opinion of AG Trestenjak from 7 May 2009, para 51.

[106] Case C-215/08 *Fritz* [2010] ECR I-2947, Opinion of AG Trestenjak from 8 September 2009, para 69 at fn 62.

[107] Case C-137/08 *VB Pénzügyi Leasing* [2010] ECR I-10847, Opinion of AG Trestenjak from 6 October 2010, para 96 at fn 54.

[108] Case C-489/07 *Messner* [2009] ECR I-7315, Opinion of AG Trestenjak from 18 February 2009, para 85.

[109] *Acquis* group, *Principles of Existing EC Private Law*, vol I (Munich, Sellier, 2007).

[110] Case C-412/06 *Hamilton* [2008] ECR I-2383, Opinion of AG Maduro from 21 November 2007, para 24.

[111] Ibid, para 24.

[112] Case C-489/07 (n 108) para 26.

[113] Case C-215/08 (n 106) paras 48–49.

[114] Case C-618/10 *Banco Espanol de Credito* (CJEU, 14 June 2012), Opinion AG Trestenjak from 14 February 2012, para 4, fn 10.

[115] For a comprehensive analysis of this development see M Hesselink, 'The General Principles of Civil Law: Their Nature, Role and Legitimacy in D Leczykiewicz and S Weatherill (eds), *The Involvement of EU Law in Private Relationships* (Oxford, Hart Publishing, 2013); S Weatherill, 'The "Principles of Civil Law" as a Basis for Interpreting the Legislative *Acquis*' (2010) 6 *European Review of Contract Law* 74; J Basedow, 'The Court of Justice and Private Law: Vacillations, General Principles, and the Architecture of the European Judiciary' (2010) 18 *European Review of Private Law* 443; M Safjan and P Miklaszewicz, 'Horizontal Effect of the General Principles of EU Law in the Sphere of Private Law' (2010) 18 *European Review of Private Law* 475.

[116] W van Gerven, 'Needed: A Method of Convergence for Private Law' in A Furrer (ed), 'Europäisches Privatrecht im wissenschaftlichen Diskurs' (Bern, Stämpfli, 2006) 437, 456–60; W van Gerven, 'Bringing (Private) Laws Closer to Each Other at the European Level' in F Cafaggi (ed), *The Institutional Framework of European Private Law* (Oxford, Oxford University Press, 2006) 37, 74–77, van Gerven, 'Private Law in a Federal Perspective' (n 5) 344.

should be taken in future work on CESL. In linking parts one and three of the contract governance paradigm, the Commission could issue a *recommendation* as envisaged in option three of its Green Paper of 1 July 2010 and could regularly report on how CESL is accepted or not in the 'market for contracting', on its practical impact, on *lacunae*, on needs for improvement, similar to the proposals of David Trubek concerning the OMC as an alternative to 'hard law' under the Community/Union method of regulation in fields where the EU has no genuine competence to act. CESL could be used as an instrument for better law-making or law application by the EU and Member States, especially their courts of law.[117] It could serve as a source of inspiration for the business and consumer community to negotiate 'better contracting' practices. This approach could be the true value of the DCFR and of instruments which followed, including the CESL as a kind of guideline for 'fair contracting'. It should be remembered that even the CJEU seems to accept the indirect legal value of Commission recommendations in its *Alassini* case law[118] by linking it to general principles of EU law such as effective legal protection.[119]

---

[117] See the discussion by Hesselink, 'A Toolbox for European Judges' in U Neergaard et al (eds), *European Legal Method*, (Denmark, DJOF Publ, 2011) 185, distinguishing European, traditional and political methods; critique because of its immature legal character by H Eidenmüller et al, 'Der Vorschlag für eine Verordnung über ein Gemeinsames Europäisches Kaufrecht' (2012) *Juristenzeitung* 259 at 288.

[118] Joined Cases C-317/08 and C-320/08 (n 55) para 40.

[119] See N Reich, 'The Principle of Effectiveness and EU Private Law', in Bernitz et al, General Principles of EU Law and European Private Law (Alphen ann deen Rhijn, Walters Kluwer, 2013) 301.

14

A Crisis of Executive Managerialism in the EU: No Alternative?

CHRISTIAN JOERGES AND MARIA WEIMER*

I. Introductory Remarks

'Business as usual'—this is the prevailing reaction to the current crisis in legal science and other branches of legal studies. This reaction is neither surprising nor unreasonable. European integration is a project of such dimensions and complexity that it is inconceivable that it could be transformed comprehensively and deeply by some 'big bang', or that those working in one of the fields would know how to re-conceptualise their praxis under the impression of the current events. The seemingly rational, however, is not only insufficient but even irresponsible if we fail to address the challenges of the present state of the European Union. Needless to say, we, as legal scholars, are not able to 'explain' the origins of the crisis or predict the political future. What we are trying to do in this essay is to both *explore* and *re-consider* the role of law in the integration process. What did law accomplish? Where did it fail? What is law going to endure? What kind of future can it envisage?

These are ambitious and demanding objectives which need to be specified and operationalised so as to bring our endeavours into manageable proportions. Here is how we are going to proceed: we start by re-visiting the flagship of European law scholarship, the project of 'Integration through Law' (hereinafter ItL), its promises, accomplishments and shortcomings, thereby laying particular emphasis on the configuration of the law–politics relationship. We believe that this originally very fortunate configuration has become a victim of its own success and an *impasse* which we now have to overcome. Section II addresses the question of this legacy.

The project of European integration was certainly a response to Europe's bellicose past and to the atrocities of the Second World War. But it was deliberately conceptualised and launched as an economic project. In hindsight, however, we know more: it seems to us that the confidence vested in economic integration was flawed for two reasons. The primacy assigned to 'the economic' has neglected the weight of 'the social' in the societies of post-war Europe, a failure which was to become detrimental to the legitimacy of integration. This failure was aggravated by the disregard for what Karl Polanyi and his successors have called the 'social embeddedness' of the economy and of markets. We review these failures in Section III.

* The authors would like to thank Chris Engert for his help in the editing of their contribution.

What we perceive as design failures by no means went unnoticed by policy-makers and students of the integration project, but became the prime concern of political activities and academic debates after the turn of the century. The malfunctioning of ItL was to be cured by novel 'modes of governance', which were supposed to complement, or even replace, the traditional 'community method'. In our discussion of this innovative move in Section IV, we point to the shortcomings of the new governance scholarship, in particular with regard to the methodological problems of its 'definition-by-contrast', which tends to idealise the 'new' at the expense of the 'old'. Moreover, we also cast doubts on its accomplishments with regard to both Europe's 'social deficit' *and* its commitments to democracy. We suggest that new governance scholarship should go back to its critical roots, and renew its constitutional perspective—one that critically reviews the normative qualities of different 'old' and 'new' forms of governance in the EU, and their compatibility with the principles of the rule of law and democracy.

Against this background, we turn, in Section V, to the present crisis and its management. This management has been perceived by some as the endurance of new governance in the EU, while others have characterised it as hyper-legalism and the betrayal of the new governance ideas. In our perception, however, the weakness of the 'definition-by-contrast' of new governance, together with the lack of a critical constitutional discourse on the values of 'old' and 'new' governance and their hybridity, depicted in Section IV, become evident in the Union's new praxis of economic governance: this hybrid arrangement of hard and soft law instruments has, to date, been economically unsuccessful and socially disastrous, especially in the south of Europe. Similarly, and more importantly, the notion of democratic law (either in traditional or experimentalist understandings) has been replaced by an authoritarian managerialism which remains outside any legal discipline.

Is all this, as Germany's chancellor submits time and time again, really '*alternativlos*' (without alternative)? In our concluding section, Section VI, we sketch out an alternative to both the tradition of ItL and the resort to the 'new modes of governance' and the praxis of executive managerialism. We have coined our approach 'conflicts-law-constitutionalism'. We believe that, within this approach, the idea of law-mediated legitimacy can be preserved, and that the integration project can regain its democratic credentials. These are normative claims, however. We know about Hegel's objections to the *Ohnmacht des Sollens* (impotence of the ought), but are not ready to abandon a good normative cause for invalidated functional necessities.

II. The Legacy of Integration through Law

A core characteristic of Europe's integration project has been its concern with, and reliance on, law. ItL, a title with a programmatic message, can safely be called the foundational project of European law scholarship.[1] The many volumes which it has delivered were—as Joseph Weiler, who inspired the project more than anybody else, recently noted—certainly

---

[1] M Cappelletti, M Seccombe and JHH Weiler, 'Integration Through Law: Europe and the American Federal Experience' in M Cappelletti, M Seccombe and JHH Weiler (eds), *Integration through Law*, vol 1 (Berlin, Walter de Gruyter, 1985).

not subjected to some specific conceptual straitjacket. They were innovative in so many issues that they addressed and were dedicated to a search for 'the meaning of law rather than its instrumental legal content'.[2] And yet, the very fact that Europe was explored so comprehensively under legal auspices confirmed the belief in the centrality of law, which Joseph Weiler and Renaud Dehousse famously summarised in their characterisation of law as both 'the object and the agent' of European integration.[3] This conceptualisation proved to be enormously influential. It has been an often explicit and even more often implicit assumption of European law scholarship—until today, as Daniel Augenstein and Mark Dawson have noted in their introduction to an evaluation of the project's *Wirkungsgeschichte* (conceptual history and impact).[4] This success can be attributed to the orientation ItL provided for the practice of legal research, with its assumption of 'mutual conditioning of legal structure and political process'.[5] The lawyers 'doing' European law were assured not only of the centrality of law for integration, but also of the self-sufficiency of their methods and techniques. The contrast of such assumptions with the state of the art in contemporary legal theory, sociology of law (the flourishing and sophisticated strand of 'law and' scholarship) is striking and, by the same token embarrassing. The fictions upon which the project was based fostered its cause: integration is a good in itself which deserves to be promoted; and its promotion 'through law' and legal institutions, in particular by a supranational court, is a reliable assurance of non-partisanship and practical wisdom.

To be sure, such daring premises could not survive forever and the edifice which was built on such shaky ground was bound to tumble down sooner or later. But such theoretical objections and, even more so, any type of prophecy have to remain aware of the background condition of the integration project, to acknowledge its normative dignity, and to appreciate its practical accomplishments. The law was to shoulder enormous burdens in post-war Europe. Its greatest aspiration was that a legal condition (a *Rechtzustand* in the Kantian sense) would replace the state of nature among Europe's nation states. This legal condition enshrined the promise of eternal peace after centuries of militant enmity and the atrocities of Nazi Germany and World War II. Peace was also, and credibly, associated with the prospects for societal progress and economic wealth.

For all these reasons, the genius of the ItL project is undeniable. And yet, there was a two-fold price to be paid for the weakness of its premises. First, post-war Europe was certainly yearning for peace but the signatories of the European Coal and Steel Community of 1951, of the Euratom Treaty of 1954, and of the Treaty of Rome of 1957 represented advanced and ambitious societies. It was inconceivable that their mixed economies and newly-established welfare systems could be integrated 'through law'. The centrality of law was, at the same time, and even more so in the long term, a more obstinate and complex obstacle to a deepening of European integration, because of its failure to provide a viable configuration of the relationship between law and politics. Joseph Weiler, in another foundational essay, addressed

---

[2] JHH Weiler, 'Epilogue' in D Augenstein (ed), *Integration through Law Revisited: The Making of the European Polity* (Farnham, Ashgate Publishing, 2012) 176.
[3] R Dehousse and JHH Weiler, 'The Legal Dimension' in W Wallace (ed), *The Dynamics of European Integration* (London, Pinter, 1990) 243.
[4] D Augenstein and M Dawson, 'What Law for what Polity? "Integration through Law" in the European Union Revisited' in Augenstein (ed), *Integration through Law Revisited* (n 3) 3.
[5] Ibid, 1.

this issue in a ground-breaking way.[6] The committed advocate of legal supranationalism was well aware of the law's limits. In his early conceptualisation of the European constellation, legal supranationalism was complemented and accompanied by political bargaining processes. This legal–political relationship is not carved in constitutional stone, but is, instead, more adequately understood as a precarious equilibrium, or a razor-edged balance, with no in-built invisible hand which would ensure its stability. This construction could take care of eminent political concerns as long as their defence was ensured by the unanimity rule. Its legitimating potential came, as Weiler himself underlined in his seminal 'Transformation of Europe',[7] with the advent of majority-voting in the Single European Act of 1986. To be sure, Europe could still build upon the democratic legitimacy of the 'Masters of the Treaty'. But, in its secondary law, it became increasingly autonomous. The detection of its democracy deficit was to follow immediately, and the quest for its cure was to become irrefutable.

III. The Law of the European Economy

'*Die Wirtschaft ist das Schicksal*' (the economy is our destiny)—this insight of Walter Rathenau, politician and industrialist, of whom much was expected by the young Weimar Republic before he was murdered in 1922—is anything but trivial. Rathenau did not talk about the functional requirements of growth. His economic philosophy was that of an 'organised liberalism' and the famous motto concerned the state of Germany's first republic—and the European context.[8] This is not the kind of perception of the economy which currently prevails in European law scholarship. This scholarship is, of course, concerned with thoroughly documenting, analysing and discussing each and every element of the European legal materials pertaining to the economy. It is nonetheless characterised by a benign neglect of the fundamental importance of the economy and the failure to comprehend its political dimensions and context, of which Rathenau was so well aware. This forgetfulness is all the more remarkable as the foundational steps were not only a noble and civilising response to our bellicose past; they were also, at the same time—or can and should be so understood—a future-oriented rejection of *economic* nationalism and the nation-state's dedication to, and aggressive striving for, economic power and control of the economic instabilities of capitalism and social integration.[9]

A. The Legacy of Integration through Law in the Disregard of the Economy

The expectation that the debates on the constitutionalisation of Europe would consider such aspects is unwarranted. The benign neglect of 'the economic' seems less surprising

---

[6] JHH Weiler, 'The Community System: The Dual Character of Supranationalism' (1981) 1 *Yearbook of European Law* 268.

[7] JHH Weiler, 'The Transformation of Europe' (1991) 100 *Yale Law Journal* 2403, 2453 ff.

[8] See U Mader, '"Die Wirtschaft ist das Schicksal!" Walther Rathenau als Reichsminister 1921 und 1922' (2002) *WRG-Mitteilungen*, available at www.walther-rathenau.de/fileadmin/Material/Mitteilungen/WRG-Mitteilungen-2002.pdf.

[9] See T Judt, *Postwar: A History of Europe since 1945* (New York, Penguin, 2005) 63 ff.

if one takes into account how well it fits into the ItL project. The economy is not exactly absent, but it is understood as some sort of autopoietic machinery which, the more it operates in line with the functional demands of market societies, the better it will deliver its benefits. The exponents of German ordo-liberalism have captured this potential most consistently when they read into the Treaty of Rome a legal ordering of the economy which relied on the economic freedoms of the EEC Treaty and a system of undistorted competition.

In ordo-liberalism, this type of ordering was understood as a *constitutional* project which was to provide valid responses to Europe's legitimacy *problématique*. This ambition, however, was either not taken too seriously, or at times was bluntly rejected, even in Germany, where European law was understood as a subdiscipline of public law.[10] Outside the German realm, in particular in the Anglo-Saxon world of European studies, it is difficult to find references to 'the economic' even after the enormous growth rate of European constitutionalism following the 2003 European Convention. This persistent disregard is less striking and disquieting in view of the very strong interest of European constitutionalism in human and social rights. It also needs to be assessed in the context of the turn to (new modes of) governance, which has fostered intensive research on the ordering of the economy and a European social model. This is examined in detail in the following section. It remains nonetheless both noteworthy and deplorable that the lack of sensitivity on the part of European constitutionalism to the political dimensions of the economy has blocked the advent of pertinent constitutional traditions at the European level.

B. *Sozialer Rechtsstaat* (Social Rule of Law State) and *Soziale Marktwirtschaft* (Social Market Economy)

Two traditions, *sozialer Rrechsstaat* and *soziale Markwirtschaft* both operate in Germany, although different weight is given to each. Article 20(2) of the German Basic Law assures us that 'Germany is a democratic and social federal state', and the eternity clause of Article 79(3) lists Article 20(2) among the provisions which the legislator must not touch. The formula was coined in the Weimar Republic by the constitutional lawyer Hermann Ignaz Heller, Carl Schmitt's most vigorous opponent until his emigration in 1933. The core of his argument is apparently simple, but it builds upon complex normative and sociological premises. In a nutshell: the promise of social justice is inherent in the very idea of democratic rule. Social justice and democratic rule were, to borrow a Habermasian category, co-original concepts, so that 'the social' can be understood as legally-binding commitment.[11] The second tradition was developed programmatically by Alfred Müller-Armack[12] in the early years of the Federal

---

[10] Tellingly, Hans Peter Ipsen, the doyen of German European legal science, is among the very few who have discussed ordo-liberalism critically. See HP Ipsen, *Europäisches Gemeinschaftsrecht* (Tübingen, Mohr/Siebeck, 1972) 995 ff, 1054–55.

[11] See, in more detail with pertinent references, C Joerges, 'The *Rechtsstaat* and Social Europe: How a Classical Tension Resurfaces in the European Integration Process' (2010) 9 *Comparative Sociology* 65.

[12] See in particular, the collection of essays in A Müller-Armack, *Wirtschaftsordnung und Wirtschaftspolitik. Studien und Konzepte zur sozialen Marktwirtschaft und zur europäischen Integration* (Freiburg iBr, Rombach, 1966).

Republic. It built upon ordo-liberal premises and presented itself as a complementary vision, but it was, in fact, much more dedicated to the establishment of a 'social constitution'.[13]

We can refrain from explaining and discussing the differences between these constitutional schools in any detail. The only point which we need to emphasise is a negative communality. An equivalent to Heller's Social Democracy or Müller-Armack's Social Market Economy cannot be established in the EU. The legal obstacles are simple but compelling. Both of these models require legislative competences in the fields of labour law and social policy, which are not available at the European level. Another obstacle is more subtle and more challenging: in view of the distributional implications of labour and social policy, the legitimacy of the EU to rule in these domains is questionable.

The Europeanisation of Heller's Social Democracy or Müller-Armack's Social Market Economy is—in itself—neither good nor bad. During the early years of the European Economic Community (EEC), it seemed plausible to assume that the opening up of national economies was compatible with the establishment of welfare-state systems at national level, and this expectation proved to rest on solid ground for two decades. The delicate issue which then came to the fore is sociological and political: can the welfare-state models, as they have been established at national levels, co-exist with the European integration project in the long run, or will they be eroded by Europeanisation processes, and in particular by the dynamics of economic integration? The latter diagnosis has been put forward by many political economists and political scientists. One famous version is the 'de-coupling' thesis, submitted by Fritz W Scharpf back in 2002,[14] and recently renewed.[15] Once more, the law–politics configuration in the ItL project is of crucial and growing importance. The reach of directly applicable economic freedoms can be continuously expanded by the Court of Justice of the European Union (CJEU), whereas the growing diversity among the Member States of the enlarged EU is rendering agreements on 'positive integration' increasingly difficult. This asymmetry is bound to cause a neo-liberal tilt in the integration project, argues Scharpf, and lawyers observing the developments of European law confirm the validity of his thesis.

C. Polanyian Counter-movements?

However, this tilt is far from being the end of our story. All the preceding analysis informs us about the structural advantages of the protagonists of neo-liberal policies. Such analyses cannot predict what reactions, if any, the promotion of the neo-liberal cause will provoke. It is precisely this kind of extension that was a core concern of the founding father of economic sociology, Karl Polanyi, whose work is increasingly attracting renewed and broad attention.[16] We refer to it briefly here for two inter-related reasons. One is the apparent topicality of his messages. The other is his insistence on the social embeddedness of the

---

[13] See, for a reconstruction, M Glasman, *Unnecessary Suffering: Management, Markets and the Liquidation of Solidarity* (London, Verso, 1996) 59.

[14] FW Scharpf, 'The European Social Model: Coping with the Challenges of Diversity' (2002) 40 *Journal of Common Market Studies* 645.

[15] FW Scharpf, 'The Asymmetry of European Integration, or Why the EU Cannot Be a "Social Market Economy"' (2010) 8 *Socio-Economic Review* 211.

[16] See, eg J Beckert, 'The Social Order of Markets' (2007) *Max-Planck Institute for the Study of Societies MPIfG Discussion Paper* 07/6.

economy, which is an implicit and stringent critique of the tendency of European law scholarship working in the tradition of the ItL project to underestimate, or to disregard completely, the social conditions for the operation of law and legal institutions.

In his reconstruction of the core instability of industrial capitalism, Karl Polanyi lays heavy emphasis on the role played by three 'fictitious commodities' within capitalist society: money, labour and land. These three fictitious commodities denote 'goods' which nonetheless pre-date and transcend 'the market', and whose subsequent 'commodification' not only provokes crises both within and around capitalism, but also proves to be an impetus for the development of counter-movements to the market.[17] All of these three commodities are, at present, under stress. We will postpone the most pressing example and dedicate a separate section to the by now chronic instability within the European monetary and economic union.[18] We have to refrain here from exploring the commodification of 'land'. But we should not leave out 'labour' because Polanyi's analysis illuminates the just-mentioned *problématique* of the de-coupling of the European economic constitution from national labour law and social policy:

> Labour is only another name for a human activity which goes with life itself, which in its turn is not produced for sale, but for entirely different reasons, nor can that activity be detached from the rest of life, be stored or mobilized.[19]

> To allow the market mechanism to be the sole director of the fate of human beings and their natural environment, indeed, even of the amount and use of purchasing power, would result in the demolition of society ... [N]o society could stand the effects of such a system of crude fictions even for the shortest stretch of time unless its human and natural substance as well as its business organization was protected against the ravages of this satanic mill.[20]

In Polanyi's prognosis, unfettered or 'dis-embedded' marketisation would prompt the evolution of 'counter-movements'. He confirmed this hypothesis with reference to nineteenth-century history:

> While the organization of world commodity markets, world capital markets, and world currency markets under the aegis of the gold standard gave an unparalleled momentum to the mechanism of markets, a deep-seated movement sprang into being to resist the pernicious effects of market-controlled economy. Society protected itself against the perils inherent in a self-regulating market system ...[21]

Following the Second World War, he identified counter-movements within the welfare-state programmes, which were concomitantly designed to prevent the return of the recent fascist past.[22] Polanyi's analysis is perfectly compatible with our preceding observations. During a period of 'embedded liberalism', the EEC and the national welfare/social state were, at first, to co-exist peaceably. This situation was not sustainable as the Europe of the 1980s chose to diagnose its economic ills as sclerosis, and institutionalised the programme for the completion of the internal market in such a manner that this programme would

---

[17] K Polanyi, *The Great Transformation: The Political and Economic Origins of our Time* (Boston, Beacon Press, 2001).

[18] See Section V below.

[19] Polanyi, *The Great Transformation* (n 18) 73.

[20] Ibid, 73.

[21] Ibid, 76.

[22] Ibid, 127 ff.

become the binding reference-point for politics. The consequences were, at the time, anything but obvious. The internal-market programme, and above all, its constitution as a 'regulatory state', were not meant to reproduce the battle cry against re-distributive politics that had been sounded at national level; rather, much faith was invested in the French socialist background of the Commission's President Jacques Delors, and the hope that the integration project would develop a stronger 'social' dimension which would lay the foundation for a *European* social model.

The Eastern enlargement process, however, had a fundamental impact upon this constellation, undermining re-socialisation efforts at EU level. Enlargement brought with it intensified socio-economic disparities within Europe. By the same token, political efforts to deepen integration—noticeably by means of the promise of a European constitution—were also forced to renew their commitment to a 'European social model'. At the same time, however, it became readily apparent that Europe's 'social dimension' would not function as an equivalent for any one of the Member State's socialising templates, and much less would it result in the synthesis of national social models. Even following the Maastricht, Amsterdam and Lisbon Treaties, Europe still lacked the necessary social competences, a fact which was less an accident and more the result and expression of the socio-economic disparities and the historical and political divergence between Member States. Massive redistribution as a response to these asymmetries along the lines of the German re-unification model was not an option. The only strategy that was available was a market-oriented one.

This strategy was pursued with vigour by the European Commission, together with interested parties in both the old and the new Europe, and found its most powerful expression within the legal medium. The *Viking*, *Laval* and *Rüffert* judgments[23] are the most characteristic and the most discussed legal elements of this strategy. This jurisprudence is no more or less than the judicial toppling of the post-war *acquis* of the European labour law constitutions.

Why did this happen? The answer is simple: the EU has proved itself incapable of supplementing its market constitution with a labour constitution because its new (Eastern) members view market rights as guaranteeing their own development potential; European law has also swung into action because welfare-state jurisprudence has been eroded in the old (Western) Member States. Law and case law played a decisive part in the ItL project and its constitutionalisation. The acceptance of the project derived from the fact that this newly-made law might be understood as a common European project situated far beyond traditional political schisms. With its recent jurisprudence, however, the CJEU has now prised open national constitutions and alienated the national constitutional jurisdiction, without, however, being able to offer anything in return other than a neo-liberal European perspective. European law has become political. With this, it has undermined the normative integrity of the ItL project itself.[24] What seems wholly unacceptable is the judicial assumption of a power to destroy the welfare state simply because the EU does not have the competence to evolve its own comprehensive 'social model'. As Simon Deakin has noted,

---

[23] Case C-438/05 *International Transport Workers' Federation, Finnish Seamen's Union v Viking Line ABP, OÜ Viking Line Eesti* [2007] ECR I-10779; Case C-341/05 *Laval un Partneri Ltd v Svenska Byggnadsarbetareförbundet, Svenska Byggnadsarbetareförbundets avdelning 1, Byggettan und Svenska Elektrikerförbundet* [2007] ECR I-11767; Case C-346/06 *Rechtsanwalt Dr. Dirk Rüffert v Land Niedersachsen* [2008] ECR I-01989.

[24] M Everson, 'From *Effet Utile* to *Effet Néolibéral*: Why is the ECJ Hazarding the Integrity of European Law?' in C Joerges and T Ralli (eds), *European Constitutionalism without Private Law: Private Law without Democracy* (2011) RECON Report 14/2011 (ARENA) 31–46.

the chain of the above-cited judgments came in the immediate aftermath of the financial crisis. There is, Deakin adds, no direct link discernable either to the financial crisis or to the sovereign debt crisis. What is apparent, however, is that developments in the constitutional architecture of the EU, of which the European Central Bank (ECB) is one of the most prominent examples, have helped to legitimise a specific way of thinking about the relationship between the legal system and the process of economic integration.[25] What also seems very clear is that the Court's jurisprudence is celebrated by the protagonists of a strand of neo-liberalism which qualifies labour law and social protection as inherently restrictive of economic freedoms.

Does all this mean that the kind of counter-movements which Polanyi expected and envisaged had to give way to a second disembedding political wave? Such a conclusion may be premature. We will now turn to the efforts undertaken by the new modes of governance to redesign European welfarism in novel ways.

IV. Questioning the Old/New Governance Divide in European Studies—The Need for Critical Constitutionalism

Ideas about the progressive role of law in the process of European integration, including the balance between the supranational and inter-governmental structures of the EU legal order as elucidated in the ItL project, have come under considerable pressure with the European turn to new governance. For more than a decade now, we have witnessed a massive development of scholarly research on the so-called new modes of governance in the EU.[26] This notion, which to this day remains highly uncertain and contested,[27] has been put forward mainly to indicate an important shift in the way EU regulation was proceeding in order to achieve its integrationist objectives, namely, a shift away from hierarchical regulation associated with the traditional Community Method (including institutional aberrations or innovations such as comitology) towards soft, flexible, decentralised, and experimental regulatory techniques, which were seen as either a variation or a true alternative to the Community Method.[28] The main thrust of the new governance paradigm of European integration was to point to the limits of traditional EU law to achieve common regulatory objectives—in particular, with a view to the challenge of re-regulation at EU

---

[25] S Deakin, 'The Lisbon Treaty, the *Viking* and *Laval* Judgments, and the Financial Crisis: In Search of New Foundations for Europe's "Social Market Economy"' in N Bruun, K Lörcher and I Schömann (eds), *The Lisbon Treaty and Social Europe* (Oxford, Hart Publishing, 2012).

[26] See J Scott and DM Trubek, 'Mind the Gap: Law and New Approaches to Governance in the European Union' (2002) 8 *European Law Journal* 1; G de Búrca and J Scott, *Law and New Governance in the EU and the US* (Oxford, Hart Publishing, 2006); DM Trubek and L Trubek, 'New Governance and Legal Regulation: Complementarity, Rivalry, and Transformation' (2007) 13 *Columbia Journal of European Law* 539; CF Sabel and J Zeitlin (eds), *Experimentalist Governance in the European Union* (Oxford, Oxford University Press, 2010); K Armstrong and C Kilpatrick, 'Law, Governance or New Governance? The Changing Open Method of Coordination' (2007) 13 *Columbia Journal of European Law* 649.

[27] See, for a recent discussion, M Weimer, *Democratic Legitimacy through European Conflicts-Law? The Case of EU Administrative Governance of GMOs* (PhD thesis, European University Institute, 2012).

[28] See the seminal article, Scott and Trubek, 'Mind the Gap' (n 27).

level under Delors' internal market programme as well as the introduction of the euro—while respecting the cultural and constitutional diversity in the Member States. By the same token, it also nurtured new hopes, and raised new promises, with regard to achieving more legitimate, participatory, democratic and effective governance beyond the state. In particular, the coordination of EU employment and social policy via the Open Method of Coordination (OMC) pledged to achieve a more social Europe, and to correct the above-mentioned asymmetry of the EU's economic constitution.[29]

A. Governance, Proceduralisation and Critique—A Transatlantic Multi-disciplinary Research Agenda

It is worth mentioning that neither the EU nor EU legal scholarship is the actual 'birthplace' of new governance ideas.[30] Governance, as a novel analytical research paradigm, first emerged in institutional economics,[31] and social and political sciences,[32] before it also began to be perceived as a fundamental paradigm shift (a 'game-changer') in legal scholarship. In fact, today governance could be seen as a heuristic term,[33] associating a wide multi-disciplinary academic discourse.[34] Despite varying definitions, the common denominator of governance scholars across disciplines is best described as the widening of the research focus on certain aspects of reality, that is, on certain modes of social coordination which were not previously considered as relevant. In institutional economics, governance opened up the perspective on hierarchy, institutions and rules as modes of economic coordination sometimes bearing lower economic transaction costs than the free market.[35] In contrast, in international relations,

---

[29] See, eg DM Trubek and JS Mosher, 'Alternative Approaches to Governance in the EU: EU Social Policy and the European Employment Strategy' (2003) 41 *Journal of Common Market Studies* 63. However, the ability of the OMC to fulfil these promises in practice has been questioned by many commentators. See, eg C Scott, 'Governing without Law or Governing without Government? New-ish Governance and the Legitimacy of the EU' (2009) 15 *European Law Journal* 160; S Smismans, 'New Modes of Governance and the Participatory Myth' (2008) 31 *West European Politics* 874; and specifically with regard to Social Europe, see C Joerges and F Rödl, 'The "Social Market Economy" as Europe's Social Model?' in L Magnusson and B Stråth (eds), *A European Social Citizenship? Preconditions for Future Policies in Historical Light* (Brussels, Lang, 2005) available at papers.ssrn.com/sol3/papers.cfm?abstract_id=635362.

[30] Scott and Trubek acknowledge this, for example, by referring to new ideas about public administration and law at national level, see Scott and Trubek 'Mind the Gap' (n 6). On the influence of other disciplines, A Benz, 'Introduction' in A Benz, S Lütz, U Schimank and G Simonis (eds), *Handbuch Governance: Theoretische Grundlagen und empirische Anwendungsfelder* (Wiesbaden, Verlag für Sozialwissenschaften, 2007).

[31] See the seminal work of Oliver Williamson on new institutional economics, in which Williamson develops governance as a notion encompassing all modes of coordination of economic life in modern societies; OE Williamson, *The Economic Institutions of Capitalism: Firms, Markets, Relational Contracting* (New York, Free Press–Collier Macmillan, 1985); see also, OE Williamson, 'Transaction-Cost Economics: The Governance of Contractual Relations' (1979) 22 *Journal of Law and Economics* 233.

[32] See, for international relations, above all, JN Rosenau and EO Cziempiel (eds), *Governance without Government: Order and Change in World Politics* (Cambridge, Cambridge University Press, 1992); for national public policy, see RAW Rhodes, *Understanding Governance: Policy Networks, Governance, Reflexivity, and Accountability* (Buckingham, Philadelphia, PA, Open University Press, 1997) and J Kooiman (ed), *Modern Governance: New Government-Society Interactions* (London, Sage, 1993).

[33] Or bridge-term, see K van Kersbergen and F van Waarden, '"Governance" as a Bridge Between Disciplines: Cross-disciplinary Inspiration Regarding Shifts in Governance and Problems of Governability, Accountability and Legitimacy' (2004) 43 *European Journal of Political Research* 143.

[34] For an account with references, see Weimer, *Democratic Legitimacy* (n 28) 60.

[35] See references above, Williamson, *The Economic Institutions of Capitalism* (n 1); Williamson. 'Transaction-Cost Economics' (n 31).

governance served to extend the perspective on the role of non-governmental actors and modes of coordination other than formal hierarchy.[36] Similarly, at state level, scholars across Europe and the US elucidated the role of both policy networks and private actors in policy-making, implementation and administrative reform.[37] What connects all these research efforts is the recognition of the conditions of inter-dependence, fragmentation and limited knowledge in modern societies, and of the need for coordination among the various public and private, national and supranational, actors in order to achieve social change.

These fundamental observations on governance as complex social coordination have not gone unnoticed in legal scholarship.[38] In fact, they resonated well with legal theory research on both sides of the Atlantic concerned with the search for a theory of law able to incorporate both a critique of 'legal formalism' and a sensitivity towards the failures of the legal welfare-state interventionism observed in the 1980s,[39] which has led to the present disenchantment with the regulatory state.[40] The ensuing search for a 'post-interventionist' law was, to a large extent, inspired by the work of Jürgen Habermas, which had revealed how the law of the welfare state contributed to a 'colonisation of the lifeworld'.[41] It became increasingly apparent that economic and social processes were embedded in a much more complex way in modern societies than the dichotomies that pitted market and state, economy and intervention, and law and economics in (quasi-) oppositional relations. 'Proceduralisation of the category of law'[42] and 'reflexive law'[43] became the two main reference points in the efforts to reconceptualise the law as a response to this complexity.

The parallels between these legal theoretical endeavours and governance research are manifest. Both have triggered new research dealing with the search for soft-law and regulatory alternatives to command and control regulation. These research efforts followed the realisation that the law of constitutional democracies is, on the one hand, expected to operate effectively and organise economic and social regulation accordingly, while, on the other hand it needs to maintain its responsiveness to wider social legitimacy concerns; and these research efforts engaged in the refashioning of constitutional and administrative legal spheres, and the development of constructive and legitimate synergies between markets and hierarchies.

---

[36] See Rosenau and Cziempiel, *Governance without Government* (n 2).

[37] See Rhodes, *Understanding Governance* (n 2) and Kooiman, *Modern Governance* (n 2); for the US, see O Lobel, 'The Renew Deal: The Fall of Regulation and the Rise of Governance in Contemporary Legal Thought' (2004) 89 *Minnesota Law Review* 7; CF Sabel and WH Simon, 'Minimalism and Experimentalism in the Administrative State' (2011) 100 *Georgetown Law Journal* 53.

[38] Which takes place under the conditions of fragmentation, interdependence and uncertainty, see, eg Kooiman, *Modern Governance* (n 32): 'No single actor, public or private, has all knowledge and information required to solve complex dynamic and diversified problems; no actor has sufficient overview to make the application of needed instruments effective; no single actor has sufficient action potential to dominate unilaterally in a particular governing model.'

[39] See C Joerges, 'Politische Rechtstheorie and Critical Legal Studies: Points of Contacts and Divergences' in C Joerges and DM Trubek (eds), *Critical Legal Thought: An American-German Debate* (Baden-Baden, Nomos, 1989); see also, D Kennedy, *A Critique of Adjudication [fin de siècle]* (Cambridge, MA, Harvard University Press, 1997); J Habermas, *Theorie des kommunikativen Handelns. Band II. Zur Kritik der funktionalistischen Vernunft* (Frankfurt aM, Suhrkamp Verlag, 1981) 522 ff; J Habermas, 'Law as Medium and Law as Institution' in G Teubner (ed), *Dilemmas of Law in the Welfare State* (Berlin, Walter de Gruyter, 1985) 203.

[40] 'We live in a time of increasing disenchantment with the goals, structures, and performance of the regulatory state.' G Teubner, 'Substantive and Reflexive Elements in Modern Law' (1983) 17 *Law and Society Review* 239.

[41] J Habermas, *Between Facts and Norms: Contributions to a Discourse Theory of Law and Democracy* (Cambridge, MA, MIT Press, 1996) 414.

[42] R Wiethölter, 'Proceduralisation of the Category of Law' in Joerges and Trubek (eds), *Critical Legal Thought* (n 40) 501; Habermas, *Between Facts and Norms* (n 42).

[43] Teubner, *Dilemmas of Law* (n 40).

This historical detour helps us to place the new governance discussion in the EU in the broader context of inter-disciplinary research on governance in general and the transformation of the state and of state law in particular. While governance is not an EU phenomenon, EU integration scholarship (both in law and social and political sciences) has become an important forum for discussing and further developing what has been called new or experimental governance in the EU from the late 1990s until the present day. Similarly to the critical legal research endeavours during the 1970s and 1980s, which were characterised by exchange and mutual influence between leading US and European scholars, the EU new governance debate today is being advanced by, and profits from, a common transatlantic research agenda.[44] It is notable that David Trubek, who was one of the founders of the critical legal studies movement in the US,[45] has contributed significantly to the new governance debate in the EU, driving the process of rethinking EU law as a novel category that breaks away from traditional EU legal doctrine. His contribution can, indeed, be seen as a continuation of the critical tradition based upon a critique of legal formalism, albeit along a new institutional path.[46] The post-Maastricht EU with its single market re-regulation programme, the OMC and other institutional innovations, seemed to be a promising ground to test and expand new non-traditional approaches to post-state law and regulation.

B. New versus Old Governance in the EU—Time for a Reorientation

Over the last decade, such academic experimentation with new governance in the EU has produced a wealth of theoretically ambitious scholarly contributions. To a large extent, new governance research has been a mapping exercise based upon case studies, which have aimed to show the emergence of new or experimentalist features in a range of EU policy fields. In this way, it performed a similar perspective-widening function as governance research in other areas, such as institutional economics or policy research at national and international level (see subsection A above). Its biggest achievement to date can be seen in drawing our attention to certain processes and structures of EU integration and policy-making, which run outside the supranational framework established by the Treaties even in areas where traditional EU competences exist.[47] For legal scholars, the attractiveness of this research has always been its potential to stimulate the process of a normative reconstruction of traditional categories not only of EU law, but also of law more generally.[48]

---

[44] See de Búrca and Scott, *Law and New Governance in the EU* (n 27) and the special issue 'Narrowing the Gap? Law and New Approaches to Governance in the European Union' (2007) 13 *Columbia Journal of European Law* 513–732; see also, the highly influential work of the US scholars CF Sabel and J Zeitlin, eg their recent symposium on experimentalist governance in (2012) 6 *Regulation & Governance*, 371–424, in which several EU and US scholars discuss the concept.

[45] DM Trubek, 'Where the Action Is: Critical Legal Studies and Empiricism' (1984) 36 *Stanford Law Review* 575; DM Trubek and M Galanter, 'Scholars in Self-Estrangement: Some Reflections on the Crisis in Law and Development Studies' (1974) *Wisconsin Law Review* 1062.

[46] For an exploration of David Trubek's path from critical theory to the institutional design of new governance, see WH Simon, 'Critical Theory and Institutional Design: David Trubek's Path to New Governance' ch 2 in this volume.

[47] Such as in EU food safety law or GMO regulation. See Weimer, *Democratic Legitimacy* (n 28); E Vos, 'Responding to Catastrophe. Towards a New Architecture of EU Food Safety Regulation?' in Sabel and Zeitlin (eds), *Experimentalist Governance in the European Union* (n 27).

[48] See, for a sensitive attempt to advance this process of rethinking law, G de Búrca and J Scott, 'Narrowing The Gap? (n 44) 513, 514.

In other words, new governance seemed to make it both possible and necessary to rethink our understandings of some fundamental constitutional principles, such as rule-of-law and democracy, thus finally making the leap towards defining a post-state variant of these principles. However, this is precisely the point where we see a challenge, and the need to reorient the EU new governance debate.

Our main plea is that new governance scholarship needs to return to its critical roots, and to renew its constitutional perspective[49] on how governance as social coordination and collective problem-solving, and law as a normative system committed to the principles of rule of law and democracy, can be brought together in the post-national constellation. Such a critical constitutional perspective is needed principally for two reasons.

First, the increased focus on the 'new' in EU governance, together with its promise to achieve more effective and legitimate rule-making, brings with it a propensity towards the idealisation of the new at the expense of the old. This has to do with the 'binary approach' to defining new governance, or its definition-by-contrast to old governance associated with traditional law.[50] Neil Walker has aptly captured this problem in the following way

> the basic analytical frame through which we construct the idea of new governance creates a propensity towards oppositional thinking, and since the adoption of that frame tends in any case to be linked with an interest in and openness towards the affirmative possibilities of the new, this may result in the integrity and virtue of the new relative to the old being exaggerated.[51]

Such affirmation of new governance indeed begs the question as to whether we are ready to sacrifice the virtues of 'old' traditional law based upon ideas of representative democracy,[52] command and control, rights protection and justiciability, and the stabilisation of expectations via formal legal norms. In addition, even if we were ready to declare traditional hierarchical law obsolete or normatively undesirable, we would face the problem of its de facto persistence in much of existing EU law. It should be noted that new governance scholarship is well aware of these problems. Many contributions have produced important insights with regard to the hybridity between new or experimentalist and traditional EU legal approaches.[53] They have stressed the complementarity and potential mutual re-enforcement between both. Following David and Louise Trubek:

> Particular attention needs to be given to developing a theory of hybrids. The discussion of hard/ soft hybrids is just beginning. We are seeing more and more instances of such hybrids, suggesting this constellation represents an adaptation of legal culture to new circumstances and challenges.

---

[49] Our understanding is based on the defence of European constitutionalism as self-government by the European citizens and the legitimacy of governance and government as being mediated by law. We are aware of the need for their reconstruction at post-national level, and will address the challenges which the European constellation poses to our defence of the discourse theory of law and democracy in Section VI. In this sense, our notion of constitutionalism is reflexive. See on reflexive constitutionalism, Walker, 'EU Constitutionalism and New Governance' in de Búrca and Scott, *Law and New Governance in the EU* (n 27) 15.

[50] See 'Introduction' in de Búrca and Scott, *Law and New Governance in the EU* (n 27) 3.

[51] Walker, 'EU Constitutionalism and New Governance' (n 50) 24.

[52] On the tension between experimentalist governance and representative democracy, see JE Fossum, 'Reflections on experimentalist governance' (2012) 6 *Regulation & Governance* 394, and the response by CF Sabel and J Zeitlin, 'Experimentalism in the EU: Common ground and persistent differences' in the same issue, 410.

[53] See 'Introduction' in de Búrca and Scott (n 27); DM Trubek and LG Trubek, 'Hard and Soft Law in the Construction of Social Europe: The Role of the Open Method of Coordination' (2005) 11 *European Law Journal* 343; G de Búrca, 'Beyond the Charter: How Enlargement has Enlarged the Human Rights Policy of the EU' (2003) 27 *Fordham Journal of International Law* 679.

Scholars have yet to develop explanations for this trend, or to craft the robust theories concerning the relative capacities of hard and soft law that is necessary to create a functional theory of hybrids.[54]

While we strongly support this search for new concepts able to account for the interplay and complementarity between traditional law and new governance, we doubt whether a theory of hybrids is significantly able to advance without overcoming the old/new dichotomy.[55] Instead, we plead for a holistic notion of EU governance, which includes different (hierarchical and non-hierarchical) forms of social coordination while accounting for their interdependence, complementarity or, as may occur in some cases, mutual tensions. Perhaps new governance in the EU could learn from governance research in institutional economics and social sciences, in which governance was used as an analytical—rather than normative—paradigm which aimed to explain institutional change.[56] In addition, we need a discourse on EU constitutionalism, which would allow us to assess the normative constitutional quality of hybrid governance arrangements in the EU, thus accounting for the normative virtues of both 'old' and 'new'.[57] This, however, would require distinguishing between the explanatory or analytical dimension of governance, on the one hand, and the normative dimension of constitutionalism, on the other, based upon the recognition that law and governance constitute two distinct 'value spheres'.[58] This also brings us to our second point.

The second reason that supports our plea for a critical constitutional perspective on EU governance is related to the observation that the new governance discussion is biased towards the problem-solving capacity of new governance.[59] From the outset, new governance developed against the background of a critique of the ineffectiveness of traditional EU law to achieve the regulatory objectives of European integration: for example, to achieve the goals of social and environmental protection. Thus new governance and law were both considered as different regulatory instruments for the attainment of the same goals, although new governance was considered to be the more effective instrument. For example, the theory of experimentalist governance in the EU has emphasised the virtues of decentralised, recursive rule-making, which *because* of its ability to foster mutual learning and review between central and local actors is also better equipped to resolve problems of collective social coordination.[60] It is true that experimentalist governance theoretically presents the most sophisticated concept of EU new governance to date, basing itself upon

---

[54] DM Trubek and LG Trubek, 'Hard and Soft Law', ibid, 364.

[55] See Walker, 'EU Constitutionalism and New Governance' (n 50) which states that 'bias towards the new is bound up with the awkwardness of developing hybrid forms of normative as opposed to explanatory theory' 23.

[56] As a consequence, various modes of coping with interdependency, such as hierarchy, networks, market coordination and others, have been treated, at least at the theoretical level, as value-neutral analytical categories. For the discussion of EU new governance in the context of the wider multi-disciplinary research on governance, see Weimer, *Democratic Legitimacy* (n 28).

[57] See Section VI below on conflicts-law constitutionalism. See also, the suggestion for a hybrid concept of EU constitutionalism by PF Kjaer, *Between Governing and Governance. On the Emergence, Function and Form of Europe's Post-national Constellation* (Oxford, Hart Publishing, 2010) 163–65.

[58] See, on law as a functionally distinct space of meaning and reasoning based upon the notion of value spheres by M Weber and A Grimmel, 'Integration in the Context of Law: Why the European Court of Justice is not a Political Actor' (2011) 3 *Les Cahiers Europeens des Sciences Po*, 10.

[59] On the problem-solving bias of governance research in general, see R Mayntz, 'Governance Theory als fortentwickelte Steuerungstheorie?' in GF Schuppert (ed), *Governance Forschung* (Baden-Baden, Nomos, 2005).

[60] See Sabel and Zeitlin, *Experimentalist Governance in the European Union* (n 27).

theories of democratic experimentalism (or 'directly-deliberative polyarchy'[61]) developed in the US.[62] In this sense, it combines the claim of the effectiveness (or output legitimacy) of experimentalist law with the claim of higher democratic virtue (or input legitimacy) along the lines of a combination between participatory and deliberative democracy. Local actors including civil society and their input into the process of the implementation of EU law, peer-review and the revision of EU regulatory programmes all play a key role in supporting this democratic claim. It seems, however, that the democratic aspect of experimentalism is largely apolitical. Local actors and civil society are included, *because* it is presumed that their decentralised coordination and mutual learning are the only way to identify 'good solutions' to regulatory problems. The potential of political conflict and power asymmetries between the different participating actors of experimentalism are not sufficiently accounted for. Moreover, we doubt that the implementation of the experimentalist approach is, in itself, able to create or mobilise a strong 'political public'. In a system of democratic self-government by EU citizens, such a political public would be necessary in order to exercise sufficient pressure to counteract the technocratic trend towards the rule of experts. In other words, 'a democratically dis-embedded technocracy lacks both the power and a motivation to sufficiently consider demands of the electorate to social justice, security, public services, and collective goods in case of conflict between the latter and the systemic imperatives of market competitiveness and economic growth'.[63]

Developing a constitutional perspective based upon an empirically-informed analysis of different forms of EU governance would allow us to keep more critical distance from the actual exercise of political and technocratic power within EU institutional practices. It should be recalled that law exists to supervise and eventually correct as a normative system with its own legal parameters the potential abuse of power by the EU decision-makers. The underlying assumption here is that, while law is dependent on the political and social context in which it operates, its relation to this context is not purely functional in the sense of being a managerial instrument for the realisation of certain regulatory goals. By conceptualising law and new governance as alternative methods of solving problems and affecting behaviour, the current discussion fails to recognise that law and governance are distinct in nature, and not simply surrogates. While it is an important function of law to advance societal problem-solving, the reduction of law to such an instrumental function loses sight of its constitutional function of controlling and limiting the exercise of power. Thus, our plea for a critical constitutional perspective mainly aims to emphasise the need for a reflexive normative discourse about the conditions under which EU governance—both 'old' and 'new'—can be recognised as legitimate; that is, under which they can be recognised as respecting the principles of the rule of law and democracy. The salience of such critical constitutional discourse is particularly evident in view of the current 'transformation' of EU law and governance in the area of economic governance, the Economic and Monetary Union (EMU), and Euro-crisis responses, to which we now turn.

---

[61] See O Gerstenberg and CF Sabel, 'Directly-Deliberative Polyarchy: An Institutional Ideal for Europe?' in C Joerges and R Dehousse (eds), *Good Governance in Europe's Integrated Market* (Oxford, Oxford University Press, 2002).
[62] See M Dorf and CF Sabel, 'A Constitution of Democratic Experimentalism' (1998) 98 *Columbia Law Review* 267.
[63] J Habermas, 'Gesichtspunkte für die demokratische Legitimation einer neuen "institutionellen Architektur" der EWU' (Starnberg, 2012) unpublished paper, on file with the authors.

V. Economic Governance in (the) Crisis

The European turn to new governance, which the previous section has analysed, had a threefold objective. It sought to loosen the orthodox straitjacket, in which the administration of the internal market operated, to fill the lacunae of the integration project, in particular with regard to its social dimension, and last but not least, to enhance Europe's legitimacy. The assessment of its accomplishments is more positive in the spheres of 'the economic' than with regard to 'the social', while the tightrope walk between functional exigencies and normative aspirations has proven to be risky everywhere. There would thus be every reason to continue the debates of Section IV—if the crisis had not affected the context of these debates so profoundly. The crisis originated in the economy, and has triggered an enormous growth of economic governance, which was/has been accompanied by highly-intensive interventions into national welfare-state entitlements while the promises of social Europe were revoked—partly implicitly and partly explicitly. This strengthening of economic governance at EU level, which is so obvious in a descriptive sense, is nonetheless controversial. Its pragmatic merits and potential to accomplish its economic objectives are uncertain and its societal implications, especially in the South, are provoking harsh social unrest. These consequences affect the social legitimacy of the EU as a whole. Our analysis, however, focuses on normative and legal queries over the forms and mechanisms of the new economic governance which have been established in the EU.

A. Background

Any evaluation of the present economic state of the EU has to depart from the 1992 Maastricht Treaty (TEU). This treaty established EMU which at the time was seen as the crowning moment of internal market policy, and, often enough was even conceived as the forerunner for the federal conclusion of the European project. The move towards EMU was certainly political. But the EMU project, which this move launched, was, not least under German influence and with the backing of the German Constitutional Court,[64] conceptualised in legal terms. The establishment of 'an economic and monetary union whose currency is the euro' (Article 2 Treaty on European Union (TEU), now Article 3(4) Treaty of the Functioning of the European Union (TFEU)) was strictly committed to the maintenance of price stability (Article 105 TEC, now Article 127 TFEU) and shielded from the influence of daily politics. The institutional backing of this commitment was the establishment of the ECB as an autonomous body beyond the institutional structure of the EU (Article 108 TEC, now Article 130 TFEU). This 'hard' legal and institutional core with its commitments to monetarist economic philosophy and to price stability was complemented by the Stability Pact[65] and 'soft' mechanisms of economic governance, which concerned, inter alia, the admission into the new currency area, and, in particular, the fiscal policies of the Member States. Admission was a matter of prestige, and also

---

[64] Bundesverfassungsgericht, Judgment of 12 October 1993, 2 BvR 2134/92 and 2 BvR 2159/92, 89 BVerfGE 155 [*Brunner v European Union Treaty*, [1994] 57 *CMLR* 1].
[65] Resolution of the European Council on the Stability and Growth Pact [1997] OJ C236/01; Art 126 TFEU (ex-Art 104 EC Treaty) in conjunction with Protocol No 12.

connected to access to lower interest rates, which was—deliberately—not monitored so strictly. It was also well understood that the monetary policy commitments could be jeopardised by expansive spending. This is why the Stability Pact provided for a disciplining machinery, and this machinery was very soft indeed.[66] Softness, however, was the price to be paid for its adoption.

At the time of its establishment, the institutionally daring, if not revolutionary, dimensions of this revision were rarely noticed[67] and its economic risks were downplayed. By now, after half a decade of an unending crisis, there is nearly a *communis opinio* that the de-coupling of monetary and fiscal policy was a design failure on the part of EMU, which contributed to the present misery.[68] It therefore seems only logical to replace the soft Stability Pact with a much more stringent regime. This is indeed what is happening.[69] But how confident can we be that more discipline in the future will cure the failure of the past?

What we know for sure is that the original confidence in the orderly functioning of EMU was of short duration. Germany, France, the Netherlands and others failed to respect the rules of the Stability Pact. The Commission's much vaunted efforts to take action against deficits dwindled to nothing. Why did this happen? The German case is particularly instructive. The country was in serious economic difficulties after its unification. It simply could not afford to play by the rules of the game and was not willing to comply. How much blame does it deserve? The 'three per cent ceiling' of the Pact, commented the renowned economist Barry Eichengreen, who had studied Monetary Union from its inception, 'is at best silly and at worst perverse'.[70] The German situation was, of course, unique. The one-size-fits-all philosophy of EMU and the Stability Pact was a gross general error because it failed to acknowledge Europe's diversity; it was particularly ill-suited to Germany: one size fits *no one*. This insight is by now uncontroversial in principle. Should one conclude that we need more diversity? This conclusion seems irrefutable in view of the steadily-growing socio-economic diversity in the EU. Under the provisions of EMU as adopted in the Maastricht Treaty and confirmed by the Lisbon Treaty, however, flexibility is very limited. EMU proved to be, notwithstanding the much-noted and criticised *faiblesse* of the Stability Pact, stable in its substantive orientation. It foreclosed, in particular, a return to Keynesian policies. The one country, France, which had tried this out in the 1980s, had already been taught a bitter lesson.[71] The key to the foreclosure of an autonomous economic policy was the euro, which made currency politics, depreciation and appreciation impossible. EMU has indeed dramatically reduced the political autonomy of the Member States in the sphere of economic policy.[72] The only parameter left to strengthen their international competitiveness was the labour market and social policy—means which Germany has so

---

[66] Council Regulation (EC) 1467/97 of 7 July 1997 on speeding up and clarifying the implementation of the excessive deficit procedure [1997] OJ L209/6.

[67] But see F Snyder, 'EMU Revisited: Are we Making a Constitution? What Constitution are we Making?' (1998) *EUI Working Paper LAW* 6/98.

[68] FW Scharpf, 'Monetary Union, Fiscal Crisis and the Pre-emption of Democracy' (2011) 9 *Zeitschrift für Staats- und Europawissenschaften* 163.

[69] See Subsection B below.

[70] Barry Eichengreen, *Die Zeit* (Hamburg, 20 November 2003).

[71] See Scharpf, 'Monetary Union' (n 69) 169.

[72] See C Joerges, 'States without a Market: Comments on the German Constitutional Court's Maastricht-Judgment and a Plea for Interdisciplinary Discourses' *NISER Working Paper* (Utrecht, 1996).

successfully pursued under the Schröder chancellorship. Advocates of the new modes of European governance have tended to neglect this crucial dimension, which restricts the room for manoeuvre in social policy very considerably.

B. Responses

What we currently observe is the development of an enormously prolific legislative and political machinery which is delivering 'ever more Europe'—and is thereby fundamentally transforming Europe's economic constitution.

The ever-increasing output is well documented on the Commission's website.[73] In March and May 2010, respectively, the Commission developed the 'Europe 2020 strategy'[74] and the 'European Semester';[75] followed, in June 2010, by the European Financial Stability Facility (EFSF) Framework Agreement,[76] and in March 2011, by the European Council's 'Euro Plus Pact'.[77] Simultaneously, on the basis of the simplified revision procedures laid down in Article 48(6) TEU, the European Council also decided, on 25 March 2011, to add a new paragraph 3 to Article 136 TFEU, permitting the establishment of a stability mechanism and the granting of financial assistance, effective from 1 January 2013.[78] This was followed, in November 2011, by a bundle of legislative measures aimed at reinforcing budgetary discipline on the part of Member States. The package is supposed to go down in history under the catchy title of the 'Six Pack' and entered into force on 13 December 2011.[79] The high point so far[80] is the Fiscal Compact (Treaty on Stability, Coordination and Governance, (TSCG)), drafted in December 2011, approved at an informal meeting of the European Council on 30 January 2012,[81] and signed on 2 March 2012 by 25 of the 27 Member States. A debt brake along the lines of the German model will be introduced, and it will be subject to judicial review by the CJEU in the form of institutional borrowing, with one Member State bringing action against another. Support from the European Stability Mechanism (ESM), a permanent crisis fund, will be available only to countries in the euro

---

[73] www.consilium.europa.eu/press/press-releases/economic-and-financial-affairs?lang=en&BID=93.

[74] Commission, 'EUROPE 2020: A strategy for smart, sustainable and inclusive growth' (Communication) COM (2010) 2020 final.

[75] Commission, 'Reinforcing economic policy coordination' (Communication) COM (2010) 250 final.

[76] Confirmed in the conclusions of the European Council, Brussels, 17 June 2010, EUCO 13/10, CO EUR 9, CONCL 2. The Framework Agreement was concluded by the Economic and Financial Affairs Council (ECOFIN) and confirmed by the European Council in Brussels on 17 June 2010.

[77] Conclusions of the European Council, Brussels, 24/25 March 2011, EUCO 10/11, CO EUR 6, CONCL 3 (Annex I).

[78] Decision 2011/199/EU amending Art 136 TFEU with regard to a stability mechanism for Member States whose currency is the euro [2011] OJ L91/1.

[79] The five regulations 1173–1177/2011/EU and Directive 2011/85/EU of 8 November 2011, OJ L91/1.

[80] Two additional proposals for Regulations of 23 November 2011—the 'Two-Pack'—are supposed to perfect the surveillance of economic and budgetary planning. One of them plans 'common provisions for monitoring and assessing draft budgetary plans and ensuring the correction of excessive deficit of the Member States in the euro area', see COM (2011) 821 final. The other is 'the strengthening of economic and budgetary surveillance of Member States experiencing or threatened with serious difficulties with respect to their financial stability in the euro area', see COM (2011) 819 final. The results of the consultations on these matters cannot be foreseen at the time of writing (November 2012).

[81] See COM (2011) 821 final as well as the Treaty on Stability, Coordination and Governance in the Economic and Monetary Union in the final version of 20 January 2012, available at european-council.europa.eu/media/639235/st00tscg26_en12.pdf.

area that have signed the Pact. The TSCG has by now been ratified by the required number of 12 states and is to enter into force on 1 January 2013.

On closer inspection, the new regimes deploy a quite coherent pattern. One lesson learned from the shortcomings of EMU and the Stability Pact was to specify the targets that Member States have to meet. The overall objective is a balanced budget with a tolerance of a structural deficit of, in principle, just 0.5 per cent of the gross domestic product (Article 3(1)(b) TSCG). Compliance is ensured at domestic level 'through provisions of binding force and permanent character, preferably constitutional' (Article 3(2)). The request for a balanced budget in the Fiscal Compact has been prepared by the 'Six Pack' with its procedures 'on the prevention and correction of macroeconomic imbalances' in accordance with Regulations 1174/2011 and 1176/2011.[82] But the Fiscal Compact is explicitly reaching into areas beyond the EU's competences under its primary law. This is why the resort to a new treaty seemed inevitable.[83] This is how the old 'Community Method' is complemented and replaced by what Chancellor Merkel has famously called the 'Union Method', a notion which has now been complemented by the revealing term *Ersatzunionsrecht* (substitute EU law), revealing because 'ersatz' law is an oxymoron which indicates that what the Union Method generates is not 'law' as we knew it.[84] The third dimension of the new pattern becomes visible particularly clearly in the above-mentioned 'Six-Pack'. Among its instruments are Regulation 1176/2011 'on the prevention and correction of macro-economic imbalances', and Regulation 1174/2011 'on enforcement measures to correct excessive macro-economic imbalances in the euro area'.[85] Regulation 1176/2011 provides for systematic information of, and in-depth review by, the Commission for each Member State, and an evaluation of whether there are imbalances of an 'excessive' nature. If these are detected, the Commission will develop recommendations about which it will inform the Council, the European Parliament and the Eurogroup. However, all the measures provided for in Regulation 1176/2011 are non-binding. This is where Regulation 1174/2011 takes the next step. It empowers the Council, 'acting on recommendation from the Commission', to impose sanctions such as an 'interest-bearing deposit' or 'an annual fine' on Member States in cases in which recommendations based upon Regulation 1176/2011 have been disregarded. It is remarkable that recommendations from the Commission can be rejected by the Council only by qualified-majority (Regulation 1174/2011, Article 5 providing for 'reversed qualified-majority voting')—this means a very significant strengthening of the Commission's power.

C. Evaluation

There is much more to discuss and to evaluate. We focus here on topics particularly illuminating for the law–politics relationship, the tensions between law and governance, and the new *Gestalt* of Europe's economic constitution as economic governance.

---

[82] [2011] OJ L306/8 and [2011] OJ L306/25, respectively.

[83] Art 2(2) of the TSCG reads: 'This Treaty shall apply in full to the Contracting Parties whose currency is the euro. It shall also apply to the other Contracting Parties to the extent and under the conditions set out in Article 14.' The drafters seem to reckon on conflicts with the EU law as enshrined in the Treaties and assume that, in such conflicts, the Fiscal Compact will prevail.

[84] See the speech of Chancellor Angela Merkel of 2 October 2010, given on the occasion of the opening of the 61st academic year of the College of Europe in Bruges; the term *Ersatzunionsrecht* stems from a German lawyer and has been cited in the recent ESM decision of the German Constitutional Court from 12 September 2012, see BVerfG, 2 BvR1390/12, para 226.

[85] OJ L306/25 and OJ L306/8.

i. Taking the Letter of the Law Lightly

European integration is a moving target. Its ItL project was continuously exposed to tensions between its doctrinal *acquis*, social change, new functional exigencies and normative–political claims. Mere preservation of institutional and substantive accomplishments was never an option. Europe was bound to change—and to defend the integrity of its project through a dynamic 'law of law production', its *Rechtsverfassungs-Recht*.[86] The delicacy and risks of such a constellation are clearly considerable and apparently overwhelming in the present crisis. One cannot be simply complacent with the interpretation of Articles 122 to 126 TFEU. One should not be silent on the illegality of the procedures provided for in Regulations 1174/2011 and 1176/2011 'on the prevention and correction of macroeconomic imbalances'.[87] They simply disrespect Article 121(6) TFEU, which does not permit the issuing of a regulation that provides for mandatory sanctions.[88] We have to criticise the complete disregard of the order of competences and the principle of enumerated powers. We are not so naïve, however, as to assume that either the drafters of these regimes were not aware of such objections or that they were acting in bad faith. We are, instead, sure that they understood the design defects of EMU perfectly well, and that they therefore felt forced, maybe even legitimated, to embark upon an uncharted sea. We can subscribe to the characterisation of this constellation as a state of exception,[89] but this does not imply, however, that we are ready to subscribe to the Schmittian notion of commissarial dictatorship and its implications.[90] Instead, we are trying to understand both the challenges that Europe is facing and its crisis management in a broader theoretical framework.

ii. Managerial Crisis Management

The above-mentioned Regulation 1176/2011 'on the prevention and correction of macroeconomic imbalances',[91] and Regulation 1174/2011 'on enforcement measures to correct excessive macro-economic imbalances in the euro area'[92] are not just legally indefensible. Their deeper *problématique* lies in the type of managerial crisis management that they have established. This managerialism is a delicate development for three inter-dependent reasons. *First*, through the supervision and control of imbalances, it disregards the principle of enumerated powers, and, by the same token, disrespects the democratic legitimacy of national institutions in particular the budgetary powers of parliament; *second*, in its departure from the one-size-fits-all philosophy orienting European integration in general and monetary policy in particular, it does not arrive at a variety which would be based upon democratically legitimated choices; quite to the contrary, the individualised scrutiny of all Member States is

---

[86] On this notion, see M Everson and J Eisner, *The Making of the European Constitution* (London, Routledge-Cavendish, 2007) 22 ff.

[87] [2011] OJ L306/8 and [2011] OJ L306/25, respectively.

[88] M Höpner and F Rödl, 'Illegitim und rechtswidrig: Das neue makroökonomische Regime im Euroraum' (2012) *ZBW—Leibniz-Informationszentrum Wirtschaft* 219.

[89] E-W Böckenförde, 'Kennt die europäische Not kein Gebot? Die Webfehler der EU und die Notwendigkeit einer neuen politischen Entscheidung' *Neue Züricher Zeitung* (Zürich, 21 June 2010).

[90] C Schmitt, *Die Diktatur. Von den Anfängen des modernen Souveränitätsgedankens bis zum proletarischen Klassenkampf*, 5th reprint (Berlin, Dunker & Humblot, 1989, first published 1921); C Schmitt, *Verfassungslehre*, 10th edn (Berlin, Dunker & Humblot, 2010, first published 1928) 107.

[91] OJ L306/25.

[92] OJ L306/8.

geared to the objective of budgetary balances and seeks to impose pertinent discipline. Under the conditions of monetary unity, the Member States can respond to pertinent requests de facto only through austerity measures: reductions of wage levels and of social entitlements; *third*, the machinery of the new regime, with its individualised measures which are oriented only by necessarily indeterminate general clauses, is regulatory in its nature, establishing a 'political administration' outside the realm of democratic politics and the kind of account-ability which the rule of law requires/demands. This implies, as Damian Chalmers has noted, a transfer of the modes of regulatory policy-making into the spheres of redistributive politics.[93] The new 'regulatory state' is by no means to be equated with the one that Giandomenico Majone advocated in his plea for strong regulatory powers, which were to be entrusted to 'non-majoritarian institutions'.[94] It was precisely for this reason that Majone complained that Europe, with its crisis management, was moving 'from the democratic deficit to a democratic default'.[95] To restate this harsh judgment in our own terms, the new economic governance dispenses itself from the legal frameworks of the EU and its Member States. It is not really comforting that some observers of the crisis management underline that, thanks to these practices, the new modes of governance are surviving.[96] In fact, we are not at all sure that the ideals of new or experimentalist governance, namely decentralised governance allowing learning from difference under the input of a broad range of local actors (including civil society), are actually being realised in this new regime. On the other hand, it is not simply a matter of accusing Germany of imposing its own-sided austerity policy on the rest of Europe as this downplays the social rigity which is inherent in the new transnational regimes. Even the most outspoken critics of German ordo-liberalism and its influence on German and European politics[97] has to acknowledge the fundamental differences between the autonomy of the old *Bundesbank* (which could be changed by simple parliamentary majority) and the independence of the ECB and its commitment to price stability, which cannot be changed by anybody. The European dilemma is that the straitjacket of monetary stability was written in legal stone. It is simply inconceivable, under the rule of the common currency and after the disempowerment of constitutional democracies, to opt for alternative policies.

iii. Financial Stability and Social Austerity 'through Law'

To date, the newest modes of economic governance have not been seriously challenged by any judicial intervention.[98] Germany's Constitutional Court, however, is an exception to the

---

[93] D Chalmers, 'The European Redistributive State and the Need for a European Law of Struggle' (2012) 18 *European Law Journal* 667.

[94] See, eg G Majone, *Regulating Europe* (London, Routledge, 1996).

[95] G Majone, 'Rethinking European Integration after the Debt Crisis' (2012) *UCL Working Paper* 3/12, 19 ff.

[96] M Dawson, 'New Modes of Governance' in D Patterson and A Södersten (eds), *A Companion to European Union Law and International Law* (Oxford, Wiley-Blackwell, 2014).

[97] See C Joerges in all his works on Europe since 'The Market without a State? [1992] States without Markets? [1996] Two Essays on the Law of the European Economy' (1996) *EUI Working Paper LAW* 1/96. Today's praxis and, in particular, German politics are certainly framed in ordo-liberal terms. But this is a prac-tice of 'Fassadenordnungspolitik' (would-be ordo-liberalism); it is ordo-liberalism without law—and for this very reason it is heavily criticised by the leading exponent of the ordo-liberal tradition. See E-J Mestmäcker, 'Ordnungspolitische Grundlagen einer politischen Union' (Foundational Principles for the Ordering of a Political Union) *Frankfurter Allgemeine Zeitung* (Frankfurt, 12 November 2012) 12.

[98] The recent *Pringle* case—Irish Supreme Court, Judgment of 31 July 2012, [2012] IESC 47, *Thomas Pringle v The Government of Ireland, and the Attorney General*—does not challenge European law. That view was fully endorsed by the CJEU (Full Court), in its Judgment of 27 November 2012, Case C-270/12, *Thomas Pringle v Republic of Ireland*, not yet reported.

rule—to some degree. This court was at the forefront at various instances in the past and has already been there four times in the current crisis. Its judgments have always attracted much, mainly critical, attention. At the end of the day, however, the Court has never hindered stopped the integration project significantly. Is there, hence, a kernel of truth in JHH Weiler's remark about the dog that barks and never bites?[99] This is, indeed, the prevailing reaction to the judgment of the German Constitutional Court on the ESM Treaty and the Fiscal Compact of 12 September 2012, in which the Court raised no principled objections against these agreements.[100] Many commentators praised the judgment praised as a wise exercise in judicial self-restraint. As the ECB had announced almost simultaneously that it was ready to launch an open-ended and unlimited bond-buying programme to help the indebted Eurozone countries, 'the markets' did, indeed, breathe a sigh of relief.

This alliance between European constitutionalists and de-nationalised markets may not be so fortunate, however. Jürgen Habermas has, at least, raised some doubts. They talk about democracy, he observed, but have Germany in mind.[101] And indeed, on closer inspection, the judgment reveals a number of ambivalences. The most important one is the Court defence of the budgetary power of the German *Bundestag*. This power is a democratic essential, protected by the eternity clause of the Basic Law. Its importance was already underlined in the previous judgment on the rescue package for Greece.[102] Its validity cannot be questioned in principle. In both judgments, the Court has added, the *Bundestag* enjoyed a wide latitude which the judiciary must respect;[103] through this move, the rights of the *Bundestag* were proceduralised: the parliament must be adequately informed and enabled to deliberate, and it must not delegate its power. This reading is in line with what the Court, in its Lisbon judgment, had called 'integration responsibility',[104] a contested notion but one which can and should, in our view, be understood as the search for a response to the tensions between integration and democracy which seeks to defend the normative integrity (democratic quality) of the integration process. Such a benevolent reading, however, is not possible with regard to the judgment of 12 September. The kind of judicial restraint, which the German court exercised when it gave the green light to the extensive indebtedness of the Federal Republic is not so cautious in view of the conditions which the Court has added to its *placet*. The constitutional weight of the budgetary powers of the *Bundestag* requires that the German parliament retains the power to determine the most important conditions for future successful demands for capital disbursements.[105] This is not an innocent statement. In fact, the Court has once again strengthened the link

---

[99] 'The "Lisbon Urteil" and the Fast Food Culture' (2009) 20 *European Journal of International Law*, 505–509, 505, commenting on Bundesverfassungsgericht, Judgment of 30 June 2009, available at www.bundesverfassungsgericht.de; English translation at www.bundesverfassungsgericht.de/entscheidungen/es20090630_2bve000208en.html.

[100] An incomplete English translation is available at www.bundesverfassungsgericht.de/entscheidungen/rs20120912_2bvr139012en.html.

[101] 'Drei Gründe für "Mehr Europa"' (Three reasons for 'more Europe'), *Forum Europa*, *Juristentag* (Munich, 21 September 2012).

[102] Bundesverfassungsgericht, Judgment of 7 September 2011, 2 BvR 987/10 - 2 BvR 1485/10 - 2 BvR 1099/10—aid measures for Greece and against the euro rescue package; available at www.bverfg.de/entscheidungen/rs20110907_2bvr098710en.html.

[103] See ibid, paras 130–32 and Bundesverfassungsgericht, Judgment of 12 September 2012, n 118, para 180.

[104] Bundesverfassungsgericht, Judgment of 30 June 2009, available at www.bundesverfassungsgericht.de; English translation at www.bundesverfassungsgericht.de/entscheidungen/es20090630_2bve000208en.html.

[105] Para 274 (German version).

between *Bundestag's* budgetory responsibility and the German stability philosophy (that is, price stability and the independence of the ECB above all). As a consequence, the nature of EMU as a 'stability community' (*Stabilitätsgemeinschaft*) is even seen as being protected by the 'eternity clause' of Article 79 (3) of the German Basic Law as an unamendable core of Germany's constitutional identity.[106] After this move the stability principles become the core of a refurbished European economic constitution.[107] All this implies that our democratic rights as German citizens are taken care of. However, as citizens of the EU, we are not at all amused. Why is budgetary autonomy not understood as a *common* European constitutional legacy, the respect of which is demanded by Article 4(2) TEU? The one-sidedness of this argument is all the more disappointing as the Court, in an earlier paragraph of its judgment, had opened another and more constructive perspective: departing from its much criticised decontextualised reading of the 'eternity clause' (Article 79 of the Basic Law), the Court now explained that 'Article 79(3) seeks to protect those structures and procedures which keep the democratic process open'.[108] The Court did not indicate that it would be prepared to address the tensions between democratic commitments and the integration process, which would include the concerns of all Member States. Instead, the Court's reasoning leads to a strengthening of the links between economic stability and social austerity. This kind of judicial self-restraint seems even more questionable in the light of—or, rather, in the shadow of—the Maastricht judgment discussed above.[109] In that judgment, the *Bundesverfassungsgericht* had conditioned the participation of Germany in EMU on the European-wide acceptance of Germany's economic and institutional philosophy. This move is now repeated and significantly modified. While the Maastricht judgment assumed that Europe's economic constitution could be an essentially legal project, the new judgment is moving from law to governmental and executive managerialism, with require-ments defined mainly by Germany and its Northern allies. To put it slightly differently, we find it deplorable that the *Bundesverfassungsgericht* acted as (only) the guardian of the German constitution. The one-sidedness of its decision is certainly difficult to overcome. The German Court is not entitled to act as the Guardian of Europe. What we would expect, however, is a readiness to define Germany as a Member of a Union in which the concerns of all the Member States and their democratic rights deserve recognition. This quest leads us to the concluding section.

VI. From Integration through Law to Conflicts-Law-Constitutionalism?

How should one respond to this fundamental transformation of the EU and its core legal principles into a managerial regime of the state of emergency (*Ausnahmezustand*),[110] which not only breaks away from democratic and rule-of-law principles in the traditional sense,

---

[106] Para 220.
[107] See paras 219–20, 232–33, 239–79, and 300–19.
[108] Para 206 in the English extract, para 222 in the German original.
[109] See Subsection A above.
[110] See Böckenförde, 'Kennt die europäische Not kein Gebot?' (n 90).

but is also hardly a realisation of experimentalist democratic ideals? Constructive proposals are challenging indeed, and the capacity of legal scholars to offer practical solutions to the economic, political and social challenges which Europe faces, is, admittedly, limited. Nevertheless, we do not restrict ourselves to telling unpleasant truths about the legal problems of current economic crisis management in the EU, but also feel compelled to sketch out constructive ideas. We agree that:

> Emergency alone cannot justify politics deviating from principles and rules that have emerged as the legal and jurisprudential core of 60 years of European integration … The European Union is a Union based on the rule of law, not of power (claimed by whomsoever), and this must also hold in times of distress.[111]

It now seems more important than ever to engage in a constitutional discourse about the role of EU law in enabling democratic governance, in holding power to account, and about its precarious relationship with democratic politics. To be sure, this immediately raises the question of what we understand as democratic law beyond the state. We will answer this question by reinvoking the concept of conflicts-law-constitutionalism (c-l-c), which we see as a necessary and promising 'third-way' between or beyond the defence of the nation state, on the one hand, and federalist ambitions for the EU, on the other. In other words, while we think that democracy is possible (and necessary!) in the EU, we do not see the constitutional nation state as a prototype for the modelling of (federalist) constitutional concepts in the post-national constellation, nor do we plead for a renationalisation of law and policy in the EU.

C-l-c as a constitutional framework for the EU has been elaborated over the last decade, and presented in detail in a series of academic publications.[112] Here, we will focus on its main ideas and suggestions. The approach was designed as a counter-move to the orthodoxy of European legal doctrines and an alternative to the mainstream of European constitutionalism, on the one hand, and a defence of the integration project against both the gradual destruction of Europe's welfarist legacy and its clandestine de-legalisation, on the other—with the constructive ambition to defend the European commitments to democratic governance and the rule of law.

Having said this, c-l-c is one of the few concepts of EU constitutionalism that recognises the importance of conflicts for legal theorising in EU scholarship.[113] 'Conflicts are both a central dynamic of EU law and a central consequence of its structures. However legal doctrine and much of the academic debate does not address them directly', notes Damian Chalmers.[114] For c-l-c, the merit of EU law—as it has evolved over the last 60 years—is

---

[111] M Ruffert, 'The European Debt Crisis and European Union Law' (2011) 48 *Common Market Law Review* 1777.

[112] See, recently, C Joerges, 'Conflicts-Law-Constitutionalism, Ambitions and Problems' in P Hilpold, N Lavranos, S Schneider, A Ziegler (eds), *Liber Amicorum Ernst-Ulrich Petersmann* (Leiden, Brill, forthcoming); for a brief restatement see the introductory chapter to C Joerges, PF Kjaer, T Ralli (eds), 'Conflicts Law as Constitutional Form in the Postnational Constellation' (2011) 2 *Transnational Legal Theory* (Special Issue) with contributions by AJ Menéndez, F Rödl, M Amstutz, PF Kjaer, M Herberg and M Everson; Weimer *Democratic Legitimacy* (n 28) has discussed the theoretical basis of c-l-c, explored its potential in a highly contested field ('The Case of Administrative Governance of GMOs'), and submitted innovative and critical insights which have inspired our cooperation in this essay.

[113] See, however, recent contribution by Chalmers, 'The European Redistributive State' (n 94).

[114] See D Chalmers, 'Introduction: The Conflicts of EU Law and the Conflicts in EU Law' (2012) 18 *European Law Journal* 607.

its capability to 'live' with the tensions and conflicts arising in the process of European integration while ensuring their civilised settlement through the medium of law. Such a settlement, however, has never been 'the last word', since it has always been accompanied by competing claims of constitutional authority between the EU and the national legal systems. Much of EU academic literature has been dedicated not only to the observation of such legal and constitutional pluralism in the EU, but also to its conceptualisation as a legitimate constitutional framework for the EU.[115] The constitutional balance between centralisation and diffusion in the EU has, lastly, also been endorsed by the Treaty of Lisbon, which has strengthened the principle of subsidiarity and the role of national parliaments and constitutional courts, and provided a better delineation of competences between the EU and the Member States.[116]

C-l-c aims to preserve this balance and the pluralistic structure of EU law. It defends the idea of *horizontal* constitutionalism, implying the equal validity and co-existence of different legal orders within the EU. EU law should not be understood as an ever-growing and ever more comprehensive body of rules and principles of progressively richer normative quality, but must, instead, learn to live with its diversity and to take the fortunate motto of the otherwise ill-fated Draft Constitutional Treaty very seriously, indeed. 'Unity in Diversity' is Europe's true vocation, and one, we suggest, that can be realised through a new type of conflicts law concretised within the EU's constitutional framework. This suggestion has its technical complexities.[117] However, its main message is clear and transparent: different constituencies (that is, the Member States within the EU) need to resolve the problems and conflicts caused by their mutual inter-dependency through rules and principles acceptable to all, rather than through the hierarchical supremacy rule imposed by a central European authority, or an inter-governmental crisis management regime in the case of the EU's new economic governance. Legal conflicts in EU law, and between different legal orders in the EU, are often an expression of underlying political, social and economic conflicts. The socio-economic and cultural diversity[118] in the EU prevents them from being overcome by the superimposition of some kind of unified federalist legal order based on the hierarchy between the EU and national law. We, therefore, plead for a deliberative reinterpretation of the supremacy of EU law.[119] The way to accomplish this is the proceduralisation of EU law for the sake of preserving the deliberative nature of legal rules and principles.

---

[115] MP Maduro, 'Interpreting European Law: Judicial Adjudication in a Context of Constitutional Pluralism' (2007) 1 *European Journal of Legal Studies*, available at www.ejls.eu/2/25UK.pdf; N Walker, 'The Idea of Constitutional Pluralism' (2002) 65 *Modern Law Review* 317; M Kumm, 'The Jurisprudence of Constitutional Conflict: Constitutional Supremacy in Europe before and after the Constitutional Treaty' (2005) 11 *European Law Journal* 262.

[116] See, in more detail, N Scicluna, 'EU Constitutionalism in Flux? Is the Eurozone Crisis Precipitating Centralisation or Diffusion?' (2012) 18 *European Law Journal* 489.

[117] For an elaboration of the three dimensions and some illustration of c-l-c, see C Joerges, 'The Idea of a Three-Dimensional Conflicts Law as Constitutional Form' in C Joerges and E-U Petersmann (eds), *Constitutionalism, Multilevel Trade Governance and International Economic Law*, 2nd edn (Oxford, Hart Publishing, 2011). For a critical review and an exemplary case study, see Weimer, *Democratic Legitimacy* (n 28) 276.

[118] M Höpner and A Schäfer, 'Integration among Unequals: How the Heterogeneity of European Varieties of Capitalism Shapes the Social and Democratic Potential of the EU' (2012) *Max-Planck-Institut für Gesellschaftsforschung Discussion Paper* 12/5.

[119] See C Joerges, 'Rethinking European Law's Supremacy' (2005) *EUI Working Paper LAW* 18/05. In a similar vein, see also, R Howse and K Nicolaïdis, 'Democracy without Sovereignty: The Global Vocation of Political Ethics' in T Broude and Y Shany (eds), *The Shifting Allocation of Authority in International Law: Considering Sovereignty, Supremacy and Subsidiarity* (Oxford, Hart Publishing, 2008) 163.

The constitutional role of EU law in this deliberative reinterpretation is twofold. First, the supranational European conflicts-law requires Member States of the EU to take their neighbours' concerns seriously—in this respect, it aims at compensating the structural democratic deficits of nation-statehood. Here lies the *inherent* democratic quality of EU law, in sharp contrast to one *derived* from the Member States. Europeanisation and globalisation determine that contemporary societies are experiencing an increasing gulf between decision-makers and those who are impacted upon by decision-making. This schism is a normative challenge to democratic orders. Constitutional states can no longer guarantee a voice for all the people impacted upon by their internal decision-making processes. The democratic notion of self-legislation, which postulates that the addressees of a law are also its authors, nonetheless demands 'the inclusion of the other'. Secondly, European conflicts-law should structure cooperative solutions to problems in specific areas—thereby reacting to the inter-dependencies of modern societies. Nation states are no longer able to cope autonomously with the concerns of their citizens, but need to organise cooperative problem-solving at the supranational level. It is important to stress, however, that this cooperation also needs to follow deliberative ideals. Regulatory cooperation at EU level can only be considered as legitimate if it is constitutionalised so as to prevent the establishment of technocratic rule. In other words, the activities of participating EU agencies, comitology committees, and other public and private actors, which arguably defy meaningful substantial control due to the complexity of their tasks and the de facto power of their specialised expertise, need to be framed through procedural law in order to ensure their law-mediated legitimacy and democratic control. The main normative demands of the second dimension with regard to administrative governance have been formulated as the need to find procedural solutions which enable deliberation within transnational decision-making; the need to establish inclusive procedures in which all the concerns at stake would be considered and balanced; and the need for flexible and revisable regulation which, for example, enables national opt-outs for those Member States whose legitimate regulatory concerns demand a deviation from the common European solution.

The crucial role of EU law in holding Member States to account for the external effects of their policies, however, does not, in our view, suggest that the EU should be turned into a federal entity, even in times of crisis.[120] We do not see the conditions for establishing a European democracy as being in place, and think such an endeavour might expose democracy in the EU to risks which are not worth taking. As long as Europe's citizens are not willing to merge their polities into one unitary body, but nevertheless interact intensively, they must accommodate their activities—and accept that they have to live with 'true conflicts', which no supreme authority is entitled to decide.[121] The tensions between the duty to respect foreign concerns and the dignity of democratically-legitimated institutions need to be resolved through procedural norms and principles which are acceptable to all—a task from which European (conflicts-) law derives its legitimacy.

---

[120] In contrast to other suggestions based upon the 'external effects' argument, especially in relation to the external effects of national economic policies on the stability of the euro as evidenced by the euro crisis, see MP Maduro, 'A New Governance for the European Union and the Euro: Democracy and Justice' (2012) *RSCAS Policy Papers* 11/12, Robert Schuman Centre for Advanced Studies, Global Governance Programme, available at network.globalgovernanceprogramme.eu/wp-content/uploads/2012/10/report.pdf.

[121] The, to date, unresolved contest over the use of atomic energy is discussed in C Joerges, 'The Timeliness of Direct Democracy in the EU: The Example of Nuclear Energy in the EU and the Institutionalisation of the European Citizens' Initiative in the Lisbon Treaty' (2012) 2 *Beijing Law Review* 1.

The Euro crisis does not contradict, but instead stresses the urgency of finding pluralistic solutions which tolerate disagreement, rather than centralisation. The crisis has emphasised the very different economic and political philosophies and needs in the Member States. It has revealed the fundamental shortcomings of unitary monetary policy in the EU.[122] It follows that it is by no means clear that 'building the house' of political and economic union under the 'roof' of Monetary Union will correct these shortcomings, and thus be effective in securing economic growth and prosperity for the Eurozone in the future. Instead of learning from these obvious shortcomings, the current crisis management seems to insist that the one-size-fits-all approach to economic governance in the EU enforced by supranational institutions in a commissarial way and against a wave of social unrest in the Member States concerned, is the only way forward. More, not less Europe is presented as a solution, with no alternative. This one-sided view currently expressed (and solemnly repeated) by leading political figures in the EU not only contradicts Europe's constitutional motto of 'unity in diversity' and its long-standing constitutional tradition of securing the precarious balance between centralisation and diffusion.[123] It also continues a dangerous strategy of EU integration as an elitist project—'integrate, democracy will follow'. This strategy is dangerous today, because the 'permissive consensus' allowing for integration to advance in the foundational period of the EU is eroding. In the present economic crisis, and even before it, it has become both obvious and widely realised that a substantial percentage of European citizens do not profit or no longer profit from European integration, but find themselves on the losing side.[124] Now, more than ever, they feel the redistributive consequences of European policies. The restructuring of the EU constitutional order through current crisis management and economic governance, in fact, will thus not be able to rely on the passive supportive consensus of European citizens, but will instead have to deal with open public opposition and social unrest. This prediction of more, not fewer, political and social conflicts in the Union supports a call for a concept of EU constitutionalism, in which EU law is able to deal with these conflicts in a sustainable and democratically legitimate way.

At this point, some self-reflective remarks seem appropriate. The state of the EU as described above in Section V is uncomfortable not only for both the orthodox defenders of the European *acquis* and the progressive proponents of an ever-closer Union, but also for conflicts-law constitutionalism. This reconceptualisation of European law was designed as an exercise in critical theory with normative perspectives which could, in many ways, build upon the evolutionary steps in the integration process, on institutional innovations, on the ingenuity of so many committed actors, and on their readiness and potential to cope with Europe's complex conflict constellations.[125] This reconstructive side of c-l-c has been seriously damaged. This has already become clear in other areas than in the euro

---

[122] See the references to Scharpf, 'Monetary Union' (n 69) and Majone, 'Rethinking European Integration' (n 96).

[123] See, Scicluna, 'EU Constitutionalism in Flux?' (n 117).

[124] See the findings in N Fligstein, *Euro-clash: the EU, European Identity and the Future of Europe* (Oxford, Oxford University Press, 2008).

[125] C Joerges and J Neyer, 'From Intergovernmental Bargaining to Deliberative Political Processes: The Constitutionalisation of Comitology' (1997) 3 *European Law Journal* 273, 293. The argument submitted in that manifesto of deliberative supranationalism has in the past 15 years developed further, not least in a critical response to the institutional transformations of comitology. The development of Jürgen Neyer's views can be studied in his recent monograph, *The Justification of Europe. A Political Theory of Supranational Integration* (Oxford, Oxford University Press, 2012); see in particular, 85–114. For a thorough legal analysis of the transformation of comitology, see A Pilniok and E Westermann, 'Strukturwandel im Verwaltungsverbund? Eine Analyse des neuen Rechtsrahmens der unionalen Komitologieauusschüsse' (2012) 103 *Verwaltungsarchiv* 379–98.

crisis management discussed in this chapter. Worrying tendencies, such as 'delegalisation', 'technicity' and 'depoliticisation', have been part of EU governance for some time now. The implementation of novel, ideal concepts of governance such as deliberative supranationalism or new governance in the European praxis has proven to be problematical. The latter resorts to deformalisation and hierarchic 'soft' governance. We only need to point to two examples here: the Commission-dominated network governance in competition policy after its so-called modernisation,[126] and the implementation of the revised European GMO authorisation regime.[127] In both examples, apparently decentralised and cooperative network governance reverts to the establishment of new legally non-accountable hierarchies. In the current new economic governance, these trends gain a dramatic new dimension. The European interventions are not confined to a compensation of the democracy failure of the European nation-states. The new institutions and management practices have nothing, or very little, in common with the vision of a constitutionalised cooperation. The new hybrid transnational arrangements operate beyond the supervision and control mechanisms on which c-l-c relies.

What, then, is left of c-l-c? C-l-c has become a critical project with a fading backing in the development of the integration project. There is all the more reason to defend c-l-c's normative aspirations, namely the dedication to 'unity in diversity', the rejection of the orthodox 'one-size-fits-all' philosophy, and the quest for a reconfiguration of the politics–law relationship which creates new space for political processes. It seems at least plausible to assume that insights into the increasing socio-economic diversity will promote a readiness to reestablish decentralised sites of autonomous will-formation. Such quests are well discernible in the enlarged EU. These voices can be understood as counter-movements because they seek to preserve, or to re-establish, the social embeddedness of markets. Would such tendencies generate a 'looser' or 'more modest' Union? Simply through its modesty, the retreat from state- and federation-building may gain renewed supportive attention. The 'unity-in-diversity' vision builds upon the strength of genuine European commitments: the readiness to cooperate and to strive for fair transnational compromises, and, last, but not least, a politicisation of the EU which supports and orients such endeavours. European law and its doctrines have been compared with a sleeping dog that, at some unexpected moment, wakes up and bites. What has so often proved to be an adequate description of the operation of legal doctrines might well become true for their critique and reconstruction.

---

[126] See Z Janewski, *Enforcement of the EU Competition Law on National and Supranational Level: Where is the Enforcement of the EU Competition Law Going and What Kind of Results is the New System Introduced with the Regulation 1/2003 Producing?* (PhD thesis, Universität Bremen, 2012).

[127] See the analysis by Weimer in *Democratic Legitimacy* (n 28): 'instead of producing pluralistic solutions, cooperative administrative governance is turned into hierarchical governance characterised by strong scientification and a strong de facto influence of the private applicant', 182.

Part V

Rights Discourse

15

Muslims in Europe: Population Flows, Cultural Clash, Human Rights

HENRY J STEINER*

Why the fuss in Europe about headscarves? Surely they are no stranger to the West. Now in and now out of fashion, headscarves have long served women's diverse purposes. They vary from the commonplace and modest to the chic and striking, as their wearers seek to attract or shun others' attention.

Some of these familiar purposes figure in today's intense political, legal and cultural debates about headscarves. In the European context, other and novel reasons for wearing them have taken centre stage. Those reasons stem from the substantial immigration over several decades of Muslims from a range of countries to a number of West European states—for example, North Africans to France, South Asians to Britain, and Turks to Germany. Many but far from all Muslim women from such countries wear the headscarf. They do so for any of several reasons, principally for the belief that Islamic law requires them to do so when in public. For such believers, the headscarf will cover hair, ears and neck, and will be worn particularly in the presence of unrelated adult men. Varying in design and amount of facial coverage among states or regions and over time, the scarf can be noticeably different in its colour, shape and texture from those to which Westerners are accustomed.[1]

When worn by Muslim women in these European countries, the headscarf assumes unfamiliar properties of a religious and cultural character. It may serve as a powerful signifier of the wearer's belief in Islam as a religion, or simply suggest her attachment to traditions and practices that have distinct meanings. Today, some among the Western public link the wearer to a politicised version of a fundamentalist Islam. Attitudes of both Muslims and others toward the headscarf can and do change significantly over short periods of time.

The Muslim headscarf strikes many Europeans as alien to their religious and cultural traditions, and even as disturbing, whether or not the wearers have become citizens. At the extreme, it generates anxieties and fears among the host countries' populations that have stirred political unrest, legal assaults on the wearing of the headscarf, and even violence.

---

* I have benefitted greatly from the research assistance of and conversations with Idris Fassassi, a French student at Harvard Law School who gained the LLM degree in June 2013, and who is now working in France toward the doctorate degree in law.

[1] *Headscarf*, the familiar term in English, is perhaps most accurately captured in the French word *foulard*. However, with respect to the controversy over the headscarf, *voile* has become as or more used than *foulard*—even though the comparable word *veil* in English suggests some covering perhaps by mesh of the face itself. The Arabic term for headscarf is *hijab*.

Those anxieties have become greater when Muslims wear starker, more arresting and disturbing Islamic dress, particularly the *burqa* or *niquab*.[2] National leaders, legislatures, courts and political parties have entered the fray and addressed the troublesome issues, as have national and international courts. The issues are deep, complex and important. They will not rapidly go away.

These issues have become more acute because they arise at a time when European and global events have been eroding immigrant states' sense of their separateness, independence and sovereignty with respect to being in charge of their own territory and population. International organisations with regulatory powers that reach into states' internal lives, from economic matters to human rights, play a pervasive role both regionally (Europe is a strong illustration) and globally. Revolutionary media and communications technology together with easier travel lower the significance of cultural and physical frontiers. Foreign literature, architectural design, films, theatre, music, dress and fashion and commercial products, as well as international financial services, business investments and licensing, and, of course, widespread use of English as a new lingua franca, permeate Europeans' cultural, socio-economic and political lives. Newly-empowered East and South Asia challenge the traditional assumption of the West's superior civilisation and achievements, of its deserved role as leader and model to be emulated. Schools and universities, the key institutions for transmitting national culture from one generation to the next, adapt to the imperatives of internationalisation. All such considerations help to form the charged background against which European host populations view the new immigrants, at a time when many in the West associate Muslims with an inferior civilisation, a violence-prone religion, and terrorism.

This chapter does not attempt a systematic, inclusive presentation of headscarf issues in Europe. It does not engage in close doctrinal analysis of laws and cases. Rather, it explores some key issues that together involve historical, religious, political, cultural and psychological perspectives on the controversy. It puzzles about some of the asserted reasons for and purposes of headscarf regulation. France receives principal attention, partly because its modern, post-revolution history bears significantly on the current conflict, and partly because its political process has recently yielded laws that regulate the wearing of both the headscarf and *burqa/niquab* in controversial ways. Such laws place France among Europe's most legally-restrictive countries with respect to the dress of Muslim women. (Dress is not the only subject of these recent laws. Switzerland, for example, has banned further construction of minarets.) Even given the serious concerns of Europeans stemming from the rapid increase in the Muslim population, we can still wonder why female dress has borne the brunt of popular debate and legal regulation.

The French headscarf law enacted in 2004, together with similar measures aimed at Muslims and their dress in several other European countries, have been challenged in political and legal fora. Such challenges rest principally on the claim that these measures violate the principle of freedom of religion that lies at the core of international human rights. This chapter does not examine the national administrative and judicial decisions that have generally rejected the challenges to these laws. But after sketching the political and cultural

---

[2] The *burqa* and *niquab* (the Arabic names) are full-body garments from head to toe, loosely-fitting and usually of a dark colour, including (unlike the headscarf) a face covering that leaves a narrow slit over the eyes. In the case of the *burqa*, but not the *niquab*, that slit is covered by a light mesh veil.

background to the current controversy, it does comment on decisions of the European Court of Human Rights (ECtHR) to which these claimants have resorted. That Court has ruled on whether the challenged laws violate the European Convention on Human Rights (ECHR).[3] The Court's decisions and judgments to which the chapter later turns grow out of laws in France and Switzerland as well as in a Muslim country of emigration, Turkey.

I. Immigration

Substantial Muslim immigration began during Europe's recovery from the ravages of World War II. To an important degree, this migration responded to Europe's need for additional workers. The Turkish immigration to (West) Germany offers a classic illustration. Other traditional motives had their roles, from immigrants' search for a higher standard of living to their escape from lives scarred by repression, prejudice and violence. In several countries of major immigration, the incoming workers, and later their families, arrived from former colonies. For example, North Africans settled in France, and South Asians settled in the United Kingdom. These historical links, including the degrading images of the colonised often held by the colonisers, figured in subtle but important ways in shaping attitudes of the host population toward the newcomers. Some may have seen what was happening as a portent of ongoing population flows that could be imagined as a kind of reverse colonisation.

The principal countries of emigration to Europe were Turkey (about four million), Algeria and Morocco (about three million each), and Pakistan (about two million). The current European total stands at approximately 17 million Muslims. Some predictions of Europe's needs over coming decades for an adequate labor force for production and for support of the elderly through a welfare system, suggest a Muslim population of about 30 million by 2030. France's Muslim citizens and resident aliens now total above five million, or eight to ten per cent of the population. These percentages vary significantly from region to region and city to city, and become substantial in cities such as Marseille.

The infusion of millions of Muslims was bound to raise vexing political, social, economic and cultural issues in the most affected countries, just as large inflows of ethnically distinct peoples have bred serious problems in many non-European countries. The new inhabitants modify or even transform the human landscape. For some or many in a host country's population, a former sense of homogeneity—that we were all the same—may be shattered, whatever its historical accuracy. The economic strains or new tasks of government may themselves cause distress, whether traceable to competition for jobs in hard times or to schools' burden of accommodating many poorly-educated immigrants.

Such a shift in European countries' self-understanding may be particularly unsettling when immigrants who will be a conspicuous minority in a European society arrive in large

---

[3] European Convention for the Protection of Human Rights and Fundamental Freedoms, signed 4 November 1950, entered into force 3 September 1953, 213 UNTS 221, ETS 5.

numbers in a relatively short period of time. From the country's point of view, assimilation of the recent arrivals could calm the host population's nerves. The new ethnic-cultural-religious group could slowly become absorbed into the cultural and political mainstream. Differences—stark and alarming at the outset—are likely to fade, partly because they lose the quality of strangeness and surprise, of representing the 'other'.

On the other hand, a willed insularity stemming from a tenacious communal hold on beliefs, traditions, customs and practices could heighten the population's sense of unsettling diversity and even national fragmentation. That tendency to resist assimilation becomes the stronger if complemented or fostered by exclusionary and discriminatory attitudes of the host state's population or policies of the state. In such circumstances, the society may move toward an entrenched multiculturalism that displaces the earlier sense (which may become a matter of historical contrivance) of cultural cohesion and common identity.

This chapter draws on this distinction. It refers to France to illustrate a country favouring the assimilation of immigrants or indeed in some contexts requiring it, and occasionally to the US as an immigrant country accepting or even expecting new ethnic groups to maintain significant aspects of their traditional culture in such a way as to deepen society's multicultural character. The difference can be captured through the image of a hyphen. In the US, it is not unusual for people to identify their ethnicity or their (or their ancestors') nationality before migrating to America through a hyphenated term such as Irish-American, African-American, Asian-American or Hispanic-American. Recent immigrants show no hesitation in publicly displaying dress or other signs of national origin, religion, ethnicity or other personal characteristics. In France, one imagines this to be less frequent. The Muslim immigrants may hold on to ancestry and customary practices in the private realm of their lives but in the public realm of movement, action and interaction, and under the influence of the majority culture, their goal would likely be to become French citizens like the others, almost an indistinguishable part of the whole.

II. Secularism and Schools

Consider two themes of post-revolutionary French political beliefs that bear on France's recent experience with the dress of Muslim women, and on decisions of the ECtHR about French laws that regulate where some types of such dress may not be worn.

We start with the relatively modern concept of *laïcité*, usually translated as 'secularism' in the sense of referring to a secular state not attached to any one church as opposed to a state with a religiously-based system of government and laws. State relationships with the Catholic Church, long a major issue in French history, underwent a massive transformation from the time of the Revolution. Article 10 of the 1789 Declaration of the Rights of Man and of the Citizen provided: 'No one shall be disturbed on account of his opinions, including his religious views, provided their manifestation does not disturb the public order established by law.' About a century later, the famous Act of 9 December 1905 on the separation of church and state, while not referring specifically to *laïcité*, provided in Section 1 that the Republic shall ensure freedom of conscience and 'guarantee free participation in religious worship'. Section 2 covered the separation of church and state.

By the beginning of the last century, state neutrality between religions had become a key component of *laïcité*. Some argued that *laïcité* should be understood to imply religious pluralism and tolerance. A concept so general and basic inevitably remained open over time to diverse definitions and redefinitions.

Article 1 of the French Constitution of 1946 termed France a secular and democratic Republic. The same characterisation appears in Article 1 of the current Constitution of 1958, providing that: 'France shall be an indivisible, secular (*laïque*), democratic and social Republic.' That Article further states that France should ensure equality of all citizens and should respect all beliefs. The Stasi Commission, created in 2003 by the government to study the role and application of *laïcité* in modern French life, gave particular attention in its Report to the President to the place of Islam and Islamic dress in republican society. The Report discussed the current and increasing threat to secularism, and noted that 'many of our fellow citizens demand the restoration of Republican authority and especially in schools ... where the visibility of a religious sign is perceived by many as contrary to the role of schools, and which should remain a neutral forum'.[4] Note the emphasis on the school as an institution of central importance to the concept of *laïcité*. That Report anticipated by one year the enactment of the Act of 2004 on headscarves.[5]

Intricately intertwined with *laïcité* is the concept of the public and private realms of French life, a concept no more precise and commonly-understood than *laïcité* itself. As employed in one or another political or legal context, the public realm may embrace a vast portion of French life, extending to commerce and the market economy, workplaces, streets and stores, parks and public transportation and state schools; indeed to all aspects of life except for those within the so-called 'private' realm. That realm basically includes the home and internal family life, private car and place of worship. The Act of 2010, forbidding dress that covers the face to be worn in public space, offers a recent illustration of how expansive that place can be.[6] However, other policies and laws address only designated parts of the public realm, such as the Act of 2004 prohibiting students from wearing headscarves in public schools.

The prevailing view of the nature and functions of state public schools (that is, pre-university education) brings several of these ideas together. (The policies and laws referred to below do not extend to private schools, whether secular or sectarian.) Such schools constitute the country's vital socialising institution—in this chapter's context, vital for educating immigrants of diverse backgrounds and practices to become *citoyens français*. They must wrest their students out of particularities of their 'private' lives, perhaps a home and environment committed to one or another minority's religious beliefs or cultural habits brought to France by immigrants. The values taught in the schools will be French values, drawn from the country's rich political and cultural history and evolving notions of French civilisation.

---

[4] B Stasi et al, *Rapport de la commission de réflexion sur l'application du principe de laïcité dans la République* (Paris, La Documentation Française, 2003) 7, 57.

[5] Act No 2004-228, regulating, in accordance with the principle of secularism, the wearing of signs or dress manifesting a religious affiliation in State schools, JO, 17 March 2004, hereinafter 'the Act of 2004'.

[6] Act No 2010-1192, prohibiting the concealing of the face in public space, JO, 12 October 2010, hereinafter 'the Act of 2010'.

Such an orientation of public schools is not, of course, distinctive to France. In many countries, state schools engage in a systematic effort to impress on students the fundamentals of the country's history and political system as well as its cultural contributions. But such emphasis does not rule out other companion goals of a public education system.

Consider an immigrant country like the US. Like the French schools, American public schools would to some degree draw students out of the particularities of their family upbringing and private lives with respect to, say, ancestry, ethnicity, race, class, religion, political ideology, and gender roles. They would often do so, however, not to banish such individual histories or identities in order to replace them with a common sense of American history and what it means to be American, but rather to recognise and explore the diversity of American life present in the classroom. In this sense, conspicuous diversity in the classroom need not lead to national fragmentation, but can rather contribute to a richer education that better prepares students for their participation in an ever more diverse America.

III. French Laws and Policy

During the 1960s to 1980s, the increasing immigration of Muslims produced the first headscarf cases. An advisory opinion of the *Conseil d'État* of 27 November 1989[7] underscored that all public services, including public schools, must be 'neutral'. The freedom of religion assured to students included the right to express and manifest religious beliefs, subject to limitation if such manifestation hindered the service of education. Wearing signs in schools that indicated students' religion was not itself incompatible with the principle of *laïcité*. But students went beyond the boundaries of freedom of religion by displaying signs 'which inherently, in the circumstances in which they are worn, ... conspicuously, might constitute a form of pressure, provocation, proselytism or propaganda' on other students, thereby disrupting orderly teaching activities and teachers' educational role, or interfering 'with order in the school'. The opinion noted penalties for violation of this principle, including suspension from school.

A Circular (directive, instructions) by the Minister of Education of 12 December 1989, on *laïcité* and the wearing of religious signs, declared that, in light of the requirement of the respect for pluralism and the principle that the public service should be neutral, the school community should be 'shielded from any ideological or religious pressure'.[8] Hence students should refrain from displaying 'any conspicuous sign ... that promotes a religious belief'. A further Circular of 20 September1994 referred to 'an unacceptable presence, in ever growing numbers, of signs so ostentatious that their signification serves precisely

---

[7] *Conseil d'État*, avis no 346893, 27 November 1989. The excerpts from this document that are quoted in English in the text are taken from the official English version of a decision of the ECHR, *Dogru v France* ECHR 2008 1579, 49 EHRR 8.

[8] Circular of the Minister of Education of 12 December 1989 on Secularism, wearing of religious signs by pupils and compulsory education. The excerpts in English from this Circular that are quoted in the text are taken from the English version of a decision of the ECtHR, *Dogru v France* (n 7) below.

to distance certain pupils from the school's common rules of conduct. Such signs are inherently of proselytising effect.'[9] The principle of co-existence at the school might be undermined. Nonetheless, when drafting rules banning 'conspicuous' signs, schools should remain 'mindful that the presence of more discreet signs that merely denote an attachment to a personal belief cannot be subject to the same restrictions'.

In 2004, Parliament enacted a law on *laïcité* (Act of 2004) applicable to public schools, to the effect that 'the wearing of signs or dress by which pupils overtly manifest a religious affiliation is prohibited'.[10] Later that year, a ministerial circular of 18 May 2004[11] clarified that the Act of 2004 concerns only 'signs ... such as the Islamic headscarf, however named, the *kippa*,[12] or a cross that is manifestly oversized, which make the wearer's religious affiliation immediately identifiable'. The Circular notes that the law does not affect the right of students to wear 'discreet' religious markers—not further defined, but presumably including small crosses attached to a necklace. It has been estimated that between two and three thousand Muslim students wore headscarves to public schools at the time of the 2004 law. The number decreased sharply after the law became effective.

Although this chapter looks primarily at the headscarf, it occasionally refers to a later Act of 2010 that effectively—that is, not by its specific terms—regulates the wearing of the *burqa/niquab*.[13] Enacted by overwhelming votes of Parliament and including criminal sanctions, the Act of 2010 provides that no-one (subject to obvious exceptions as for health or sports) can dress so as to cover (conceal, hide) the face in the public realm—that is, space open to the public or intended for public service. The number of Muslim women in France who wore the *burqa/niquab* at the time of the 2010 law is estimated to have been in the low thousands.

Note several distinctions between the two laws: (1) The Act of 2004, as interpreted by the 2004 Circular, refers specifically to a headscarf and certain other types of dress, whereas the Act of 2010 refers abstractly to any form of dress that covers the face. Nonetheless, that law was popularly and politically understood to ban the *burqa/niquab*. (2) The Act of 2004 refers only to signs or dress through which students manifest a religious affiliation, whereas the Act of 2010 requires no religious or other signification of the dress. (3) The Act of 2004 is effectively limited to girls of school age while they are on the premises of a public school, whereas the Act of 2010 applies to people of any age and either sex when in the public realm.

---

[9] Circular of the Minister of Education of 20 September 1994. The excerpts in English from this Circular that are quoted in the text are taken from the English version of a decision of the ECHR, *Dogru v France* (n 7).

[10] The Act of 2004 (n 6) 5190.

[11] Circular of the Minister of Education of 18 May 2004. The excerpts from this Circular that are quoted in the text (in English translation) are taken from a decision of the ECHR, in the original French, *Aktas v France* Application No 43563/08, Decision of 30 June 2009.

[12] A skullcap associated with Jews and worn particularly by religiously-observant (Orthodox) men. It is usually quite small, sitting on top of the head. The *kippa* is not based on biblical command. Scholars differ about the historical period and place in which it became customary for Jews to wear it. Some believe that the *kippa* by virtue of its continuous use over many centuries has hardened into a fixed custom that forms part of today's *halacha*, the collective body of Jewish law.

[13] The Act of 2010 (n 6).

The preceding advisory opinions, circulars and laws raise some puzzling questions. The 1989 advisory opinion of the *Conseil d'État* refers to 'conspicuous' signs that might constitute a form of pressure or proselytism interfering with order in the classroom. The 1989 Circular repeats this concern and emphasises the need to protect students against ideological or religious pressure. The 1994 Circular declares unacceptable 'ostentatious' signs of religious affiliation that are 'inherently' of proselytising effect. The 2004 Circular following the enactment of the Act of 2004 refers only to such signs as the Islamic headscarf and the *kippa*, as well as a cross that is 'manifestly oversized'. Discreet markers of religious faith are permitted.

The distinctions drawn by these official documents do not seem to fit within the asserted purpose of protecting the principle of *laïcité*. One major goal of the restrictive legislation is to keep conspicuous religious identity out of the classroom, a place of special importance within the principle of *laïcité* in view of the centuries of conflict between the Catholic Church and the state over the direction and function of state schools. Why does the headscarf (and *kippa*) frustrate that goal, while a discreet cross on a necklace does not?

For pedestrians on the street, the distinction makes a certain logical sense; head coverings are far more obvious to a pedestrian than small crosses worn by some passers-by. They are more 'conspicuous'. As for the small cross, people wearing it are first seen from a greater distance and then quickly pass by others. The cross may not be seen. But in the classroom, students and teacher are close to each other throughout the day, often in close conversation. A cross on a necklace will surely be visible, though perhaps it is less likely to be noticed since frequently worn and familiar, whereas headscarf and *kippa* are the dress of minorities, relatively rare and thus more apt to attract attention. Moreover, if the concealment of religious identity is a goal to be served by banning the headscarf, that identity will be revealed in the classroom in countless other ways that are not regulated. Loose fitting clothing, long robes and solemn colours may suggest the modesty that Islam requires of women. Appearance and names of students of North African origin may themselves indicate a high probability that they are Muslim; fasting during Ramadan will be noticed by classmates; the student may wish to mention her religion to friends.

Moreover, in what sense will the wearer of the headscarf (or *kippa*) be likely for that reason alone to be seen as proselytising or 'putting pressure' on others? Consider the similarities and differences among the headscarf, *kippa*, and cross. Inherently, the cross is a more powerful, intense and arresting symbol of religious belief. It signifies a crucifixion that lies at the very core of Christian faith, whereas the head coverings inherently lack religious significance other than that attached by customary practice and history. The upshot for the critical observer is that the headscarf ban can be understood as discriminatory. The principle of *laïcité* which quietly informs these texts seems to be applied less to preserve a vital secular/religious distinction or to preserve the religious neutrality of the state than to impose a discriminatory distinction. As is usually the case, the discrimination is directed against a minority group, a matter of deep concern throughout the field of human rights.

A more searching question asks why and how permitting the headscarf to be worn in public schools threatens the principle of *laïcité*. If all students were even-handedly permitted to wear in school a sign or dress (within appropriate limits such as size) manifesting their religion—that is, if there were no restrictive law—state action would not in any sense be involved when some students choose to do so. Such students (or their parents) are making their own voluntary decisions. The state acts neutrally and establishes no relations with any religious organisation.

IV. What Does the Headscarf Signify to the Wearer or to Others?

Is wearing a headscarf a religious duty of Muslim women? Some scholars and commentators believe there is such a duty and claim that many and perhaps most Muslims so believe. Others disagree and point to non-religious reasons why women might wear headscarves. The writings of clerics, scholars and commentators offer many points of view on this question.[14]

The Koran does not refer to the headscarf as such, but a number of its verses offer a broader view of women's appropriate dress. Koran 24:30 to 31 offers a reasonably clear statement of that view. It provides that 'believing women' should lower their gaze before men and 'guard their modesty', so as not to 'display their beauty', and should draw their clothing 'over their bosoms and not display their beauty' to adult men except for their husband and a described group of close relatives. The cardinal notion developed in other verses as well is that of modesty. Women's dress, including at the extreme the *burqa*, should be loose rather than close-fitting, so as not to reveal the shape of the female body. The headscarf covers hair that often heightens a woman's sexual attractiveness. Such specific or general commands or customs hardening into obligations point to the avoidance by women in public life of sexually attracting others.

Commentators have pointed to the near unanimity of opinion within French political and law-making institutions that a headscarf of Islamic appearance identifies the wearer as a believer in Islam who is responding to a religious duty. In such circumstances, the principle of *laïcité* has at least a threshold relevance to deciding whether the headscarf should be banned in certain locations. But is this opinion necessarily correct? Would every wearer, or an overwhelming majority of wearers, agree about the headscarf's invariable religious significance and message of duty? If not, the debate about a ban—including judicial debate about the legality of the ban under the terms of the ECHR—should be attentive to wearers' different motives or understandings and to their view of what the headscarf signifies.

Inquiry into these questions draws the researcher into a rich literature in the fields of religion, cultural studies and feminism that has explored Muslims' reasons and motives.[15] This literature does not present much statistical information indicating, for example, the percentages of women who wear a headscarf for one or another reason. Rather it reports interviews between authors or researchers with wearers or non-wearers that have a narrative and

---

[14] See L Ahmed, *A Quiet Revolution: The Veil's Resurgence from the Middle East to America* (New Haven, Yale University Press, 2011) 87–89, 119–25, 207–13, 283–84. Many works on this subject can be found by a simple internet search for 'Is wearing a headscarf an Islamic duty?'

[15] The following books offer important views on the headscarf controversy as well as on themes in other parts of this chapter such as conceptions of *laïcité* and the decisions of the ECtHR. Given their different perspectives, methodological orientations and purposes, the readings will profit readers with a serious interest in the field and a desire to explore the issues in more depth. LL Ahmed, *A Quiet Revolution* (n 14); S Benhabib, *Dignity in Adversity: Human Rights in Troubled Times* (Cambridge, UK, Polity Press, 2011); H Elver, *The Headscarf Controversy: Secularism and Freedom of Religion* (New York, Oxford University Press, 2012); C Joppke, *Mirror of Identity* (Cambridge, Polity Press, 2009); M Nussbaum, *The New Religious Intolerance* (Cambridge, MA, Harvard University Press, 2012); O Roy, *Secularism Confronts Islam* (New York, Columbia University Press, 2007); J Scott, *The Politics of the Veil* (Princeton, Princeton University Press, 2007).

qualitative rather than statistical character. What follows is my absorption of information provided by this literature into my own thoughts and framework of inquiry.[16]

Explanations for wearing the headscarf for a reason other than religious belief and duty abound. Wearers may intend to show respect toward their family's or community's traditional practices that may reach generations back. They honour their ancestors, and in so doing may respond to a sense of their own personal and cultural identity. The headscarf is, as it were, a vital part of the wearer's comfortable and honest self-presentation.

The headscarf may link the wearer to other wearers seen casually on the street, and thereby build a sense of community of like-thinking people finding in their common practice a security and companionship that alleviate feelings of separateness and anomie in a still-alien culture.

The wearer may be asserting her independence and decision about how to react to French efforts to assimilate her in vital respects to the general population. In this sense, wearing the headscarf (together with observing other aspects of tradition) may constitute a form of cultural rebellion against pressure to shed her distinctiveness and become a *citoyen français* like all the others.

Women may find that wearing a headscarf offers protection against unwanted interference or harassment by strangers in the public arena. Its message may be understood to indicate that the wearer is not available for casual or sexual encounters.

The headscarf may be seen as liberating from the perspective of a wearer who has won from her family a greater freedom of independent movement than might have been granted if she had gone into public life uncovered. It may, therefore, signify to others responsibility, caution and dutiful behaviour.

To grasp the broad range of beliefs about the meaning of the headscarf, consider a few reasons (other than disbelief in a religious duty) why Muslims might reject it. To many, and to many in the host populations as well, it signifies gender inequality, the systematic subordination and devaluing of women. To reject the headscarf is to reject this cultural and political tradition, indeed to reject interpretations of Islam that foster such beliefs. Moreover, headscarves are frequently imposed on women by extreme family and community pressure, or indeed by psychological or physical coercion—surely less so, however, in a European country of immigration where Muslims are an 8 to 10 per cent minority, than within conservative communities in their dominantly Muslim countries of origin.

Some find justification for the Act of 2004 in these last considerations rather than as a defense of *laïcité*. For such reasons, many French and some Muslim women support the Act as an avenue toward liberation and emancipation, and as a welcome initiative by the state to achieve greater gender equality by protecting students against powerful pressures or indeed threats from their family or community.

This excursion into reasons why Muslim women may decide whether or not to wear the headscarf underscores how complex and multidimensional a signifier the scarf has become. Commentators have noted that the many French proceedings prior to enactment of the Act of 2004—legislative hearings on the proposed legislation, investigative commissions, civil

---

[16] Note an important caution about one characteristic of these inquiries: just as the percentage of Muslim women wearing headscarves varies over time and space, so do their responses to these kinds of inquiries. Responses are often quite specific to time and place—for example, to particular periods of political and cultural change in a particular country such as Egypt, to a few European countries since the larger Muslim immigration began, or to recent trends among Muslim women in the US as affected by the terrorism of 11 September 2001.

society groups that made proposals—rarely if ever invited the schoolgirls themselves to testify about their reasons. It was as if both officials and the public knew the answers beyond the possibility of correction or illumination. The diversity of reasons became public only through independent interviews.

V. The European Court of Human Rights

The applications to and decisions of the ECtHR about headscarves rest on Article 9 of the ECHR. Section (1) Article 9 assures to everyone freedom of religion, including freedom 'either alone or in community with others and in public or private, to manifest his religion or belief in worship, teaching, practice and observance'. Section (2) subjects the freedom to manifest religion to limitations that 'are necessary in a democratic society, in the interests of public safety, for the protection of public order, health or morals, or for the protection of the rights and freedoms of others'. Most decisions of the Court have turned on whether governments satisfied the conditions for limitation in section (2).

Applicants in the cases to be discussed also invoked several other provisions of the Convention: (1) freedom of expression under Article 10, which includes freedom to impart information and ideas, and which is subject to conditions and restrictions that are necessary in a democratic society and that are in the interests of prevention of disorder and protection of the rights of others; (2) assurance under Article 14 against discrimination on grounds such as sex, race, religion, national or social origin, birth or other status; and (3) Article 2 of Protocol No 1 to the Convention, which provides that states shall 'respect the right of parents' to ensure education in conformity with their own religious convictions. Note that such provisions offer the advocate some powerful arguments both in favor of and against legislative prohibition of the headscarf. For example, Article 10 lends itself to the argument that the wearing of the headscarf expresses important beliefs and ideas of the wearer that she thereby seeks to communicate to others. The Court gave brief and secondary consideration to those claims. As noted above, this chapter concentrates on the issue of freedom of religion.

The jurisdiction of the ECtHR includes only alleged violations of the ECHR itself. Applicants from France and Turkey who brought their headscarf-related claims to that Court could have followed an alternative route to international fora: Optional Protocol No 1 to the International Covenant on Civil and Political Rights.[17] The International Covenant covers broadly the same rights as those set forth in the designated articles of the ECHR. Its Article 27, however, bears directly on the headscarf controversy but finds no close equivalent in the ECHR. It provides that in states whose population includes ethnic, religious or linguistic minorities, individual members of those minorities have the right, 'in community with the other members of their group, to enjoy their own culture, to profess and practice their own religion, or to use their own language'. However complex, indeterminate and variously understood by the national courts and international committee that have

---

[17] International Covenant on Civil and Political Rights and Optional Protocol to the International Covenant on Civil and Political Rights, adopted 16 December 1966, entered into force 23 March 1976, 999 UNTS 171.

applied it, this Article points toward a broad right to cultural survival and thus to one of several ways of characterising the headscarf controversy.

* * * * *

We turn to decisions of the ECtHR that have wrestled with controversies over the headscarf and related clothing that originated in France, Switzerland and Turkey, each of which had restrictive laws or institutional rules that denied the right to one or several people to wear the headscarf (in one case, applicants were men wearing different religion-related garments). As the Convention requires, the applicants had first exhausted administrative and judicial remedies in the states involved. After being denied relief, they brought their claims to the ECtHR, asserting in each case that the dress at issue was worn out of a sense of religious obligation. They thereby brought Article 9 into play.

In these decisions, the ECtHR frequently refers to the established principle of the margin of appreciation (MA)—a principle developed over several decades by the ECtHR without any mention of it in the Convention itself.[18] The principle basically suggests some degree of deference to the decision-making of the State Party to the ECHR that was brought before it. The opinions of the ECtHR over the decades offer sharply different understandings of the MA—what the concept means, how it should be applied. Rather than develop one coherent theory, the Court has put the concept to diverse and inconsistent uses. Nonetheless, invoking the MA can play an important and sometimes decisive role in leading the Court to its decision.

To an important degree, the MA expresses the idea of subsidiarity. Some questions and issues are best resolved by local authorities at the local level where a controversy arose rather than at a distant international court—for example, local authorities justifying a curfew or detentions because of an emergency stemming from violence or a natural disaster. The degree of deference shown to the state may be narrow or broad. By its terms, the principle requires that such deference, however measured or generous, 'goes hand in hand with a European supervision'. In different cases and contexts, that supervision has ranged from rigorous to negligible.

More broadly, the Court and its observers may understand the MA to provide some defence of the sovereignty of States Parties to the Convention, states that have, of course, agreed to the Court's jurisdiction to determine whether their judicial, executive, administrative or legislative measures violated the ECHR. The MA's requirement of some degree of deference may then serve as a protection of states—particularly democratic states—and their sovereignty against what could be thought of as excessive interference in their internal democratic orders by the ECtHR, whose judgments are binding.

Another understanding of the MA emphasises its role in enabling the Court to avoid difficult decisions about rights that might prematurely impose a uniform rule on all Member States. By granting a state a broad margin of appreciation, the Court may be able to postpone a judgment squarely on the merits until a more suitable time arrives for imposing such a rule, perhaps a time when states have come to some consensus or some clear trend that can guide the Court. Naturally, the Court is in a more comfortable position

---

[18] The Brighton Declaration issued at the High Level Conference on the Future of the European Court of Human Rights in Brighton, UK on 19 and 20 April 2012 stated that the ECHR should include the margin of appreciation in its preamble by the end of 2013. Text of Declaration available at hub.coe.int/en/20120419-brighton-declaration/ and (2012) 30 *Netherlands Quarterly of Human Rights* 349.

when it is able to follow the lead of States Parties, to ratify what their internal orders have yielded, rather than impose a rule to which many states are opposed. Its legitimacy is less likely to be questioned.

Of course, too generous a view of the MA may effectively eliminate the role of the Court in protecting human rights within its States Parties, and leave state sovereignty with respect to human rights about where the Court initially found it. Such cannot have been the purpose of the ECHR. Indeed, the headscarf cases highlight the importance of a genuine 'European supervision', for they engage two of the human rights movement's fundamental concerns: freedom of religion, and protection of minorities.

The resort to the MA in the following decisions illustrates a number of these understandings, as well as the degree to which it can shape the Court's decision.

Dahlab v Switzerland (2001).[19] A primary school teacher in the canton of Geneva, who had recently converted to Islam, started to wear a headscarf regularly, including while teaching her class, 'her intention being to observe a precept laid down in the Koran ...'. She was advised by the school authority that this practice violated the Federal Constitution and cantonal laws requiring that public schools observe denominational neutrality and separation of Church and State. The headscarf, to the contrary, constituted 'an obvious means of identification' of a Muslim teacher within a secular educational system. Unless she abandoned it, the teacher would lose her employment.

A Swiss Federal Court upheld this decision. It emphasised that the cantonal legal requirement could be applied to ban the headscarf, a 'powerful' and readily-visible religious symbol. This requirement affected only the teacher, a civil servant subordinate to higher authorities. Moreover, the principle that a teacher should not self-identify as adhering to a particular faith applied only during periods of class instruction. Simply by wearing the headscarf without making others aware of her Islamic faith in any other way, she may have interfered with religious beliefs of a pupil. Such considerations were more serious in view of the pupils' 'tender age' of four to eight, and of the hierarchical relationship between them and the teacher. As a representative of the state exercising authority within the classroom, a teacher could serve as a role model.

The Swiss court noted that if it were to approve the headscarf, the state would also have to accept the wearing by a teacher of a *soutane* (a cassock associated with clerics of the Catholic Church and other Christian churches) or a *kippa*, which were 'powerful symbols of other faiths'. Schools would be in danger of becoming 'places of religious conflict'. Nonetheless, the court observed, the principle of proportionality led cantonal governments to allow teachers to wear 'discreet religious symbols' at school, such as pieces of jewellery—presumably a reference to the common practice of wearing a cross attached to a necklace.

The teacher applied to the ECtHR to determine whether the Swiss decisions violated her right to manifest her religion. Drawing extensively on the Federal Court's opinion, the ECtHR found the application to be 'manifestly ill founded', and hence inadmissible. In its argument, the government stressed that the Federal Court had drawn a 'fundamental distinction' between a headscarf worn by a teacher and by a pupil. Through the ban, the school authorities sought religious harmony. The ECtHR itself was attentive to the age of the students, and concluded that the conditions of Article 9(2) were met.

---

[19] *Dahlab v Switzerland* ECHR 2001–V 449.

The Court concluded that the required finding under Article 9(2)—the restriction was 'necessary in a democratic society'—was adequately supported, and that the restriction was 'proportionate' to the end to be achieved. It relied importantly on the margin of appreciation, giving it a broad scope. Nonetheless, its argument provided a substantial foundation for its decision. The end to be achieved under Article 9(2) was the protection of the rights of others. Accepting that it was difficult to assess the effect of the headscarf on young pupils' freedom of conscience and religion, the Court stated that, nonetheless, 'it cannot be denied outright' that a teacher wearing it 'might have some kind of proselytizing effect', particularly since the headscarf appears to have been imposed by a precept of the Koran. The Swiss authorities had not exceeded their margin of appreciation.

Some features of this case became significant for later decisions. The Swiss and ECtHR opinions stressed two facts. The applicant was a teacher, not a student (students were not restricted in their dress by this decision). Moreover, the students were very young. Many states wrestle with the issue of whether employees (civil servants) of the state of a certain authority and status should be permitted to overtly identify their religion while performing their duties. It might be difficult to decide where to draw the line between state employees who were subject to the restriction and those who were not. Some lines would be evident enough, such as distinguishing between the school's administrative head and lunchroom employees. A state seeking denominational neutrality might well conclude that teachers who are granted academic authority over students, and who are key actors in the performance of the vital state function of education, should appear before students simply as a teacher, without any complication which could lead a student to believe that state and religion were linked. The subject matter being taught—mathematics or European history, grammar or moral thought—or the age of the students could be relevant to such a decision. States may reason in similar ways about forbidding the wearing of overt religious signs or dress by police or judges performing their duties as state employees and representatives, or by other officials with authority and power over us, even though we understand that the self-identification was a voluntary choice on the part of the official and was evenhandedly permitted by the State for members of all religions.

Leyla Şahin v Turkey (2007).[20] The applicant considered it her religious duty to wear a headscarf, including during classes she attended as a student at her state medical school. Consistently with university rules based on Turkish legislation, that school banned wearing headscarves at classes. The applicant left this school and continued her education in Vienna. After exhausting local remedies, she brought an action before the ECtHR on claims that included Turkey's violation of her freedom of religion under Convention Article 9. The Court's Chamber found in favour of the government. The Grand Chamber agreed to hear the case. Its judgment found no violation of the ECHR in an opinion that drew on some of the Chamber's views.

The Turkish Constitution requires the state to be democratic and secular. The Court commented on Turkey's many decades of political drama and secular–religious conflicts since the new Turkish Republic separated religion and the public sphere in 1923. It described the 'defining feature' of the Republican ideal to be women's presence in public life and participation in society; hence they should be 'freed from religious constraints'. Some

---

[20] *Leyla Şahin v Turkey* ECHR 2005-XI 175, 44 EHRR 5 and *Leyla Şahin v Turkey* (Grand Chamber) ECHR 2007-XI 175, 41 EHRR 8.

people, noted the opinion, see the headscarf as a religious duty 'or a form of expression linked to religious identity', while 'supporters of secularism ... see the Islamic headscarf as a symbol of a political Islam'.

While professing to follow a secular way of life, the majority of the population adhered to the Islamic faith. Hence, the Court argued, regulating use of the headscarf consistently with Article 9(2) for the protection of rights of others (in this case, presumably other Muslim students not wearing headscarves but perhaps feeling pressure from the applicant to do so) and for maintenance of public order may be understood as meeting 'a pressing social need', a need all the more apparent since the headscarf recently took on political significance. The Court quoted the observation in the earlier judgment of the Chamber that it would keep in mind the presence of 'extreme political movements' in Turkey seeking to impose on society religious symbols together with a conception of a society founded on religious precepts. It also quoted the Chamber's comment that, consistently with the ECHR, 'states parties can take a stance against such political movements', based on their historical experience.

It was in this context, the Court said, that the university regulations at issue had to be understood, intended as they were to preserve pluralism in the university. Certainly, within the constraints imposed by their educational organisations, Muslims in Turkish universities were free to manifest their religion in habitual ways. The test of proportionality should be applied to the measure taken (the ban on the headscarf) in relation to the objectives noted. The Court, however, then observed that university authorities on the ground were in principle better situated than an international court to evaluate the local needs and conditions. 'Having regard to the Contracting States' margin of appreciation in this sphere', the interference was justified and was proportionate to the aim pursued. A salient dissent by Judge Francoise Tulkens underscored major problems in the Court's opinion.

Several aspects of the opinion invite comment. Its broad references to the *Dahlab* decision are puzzling. The Court makes no effort to explain why an opinion pointedly involving state-employed teachers in a state public school teaching young children lends support to a decision involving not a teacher, and not children, and not a public school, but an adult student at a professional university. Unlike a teacher, the student is neither a state employee, nor a civil servant or state representative. The student made a voluntary personal choice about wearing the headscarf that was neither required nor encouraged by the state. Without comment on these substantial differences between the two situations, the Court expanded the public space and institutions in which certain religious dress is banned, and expanded the category of persons under dress restrictions.

Nor was there serious argument, but rather assertion by the Court, about how the conditions of Article 9(2) were met. After all, these are not light matters; the conditions are strongly stated such that the limitation of a right to manifest religion must be 'necessary'. The opinion tersely notes a 'pressing social need' to protect rights of others or maintain public order, without evidence or argument supporting its conclusion that such rights or public order were here threatened. What in these circumstances would cause other students, including uncovered Muslim students, to feel such a threat? In what way did the headscarf serve to proselytise? How would public order be disrupted? How would the principle of *laïcité* have been eroded? Discussion might have engaged these questions and shed some light on the judgment. For example, if the vast majority of female students in the medical school wore headscarves, those uncovered might feel some pressure to join the majority, a characteristic majority–minority phenomenon in many contexts unrelated to religion. Was this the Court's concern?

As in *Dahlab*, but more generously, the Court invokes the MA to fortify its conclusions. But the 'European supervision' required by this principle was hardly noticeable. Rather, the Court explained that when a sensitive concern such as the relationship between state and religion is at issue, a concern about which opinions in a democracy may differ, the 'role of the national decision-making body must be given special importance, particularly with respect to regulating the wearing of headscarves in educational institutions'. But why do headscarves have this 'special' importance?

The Court notes that the spacious MA that it grants Turkey is particularly justified in view of the diverse approaches of European countries to the headscarf issue, so that: 'It is not possible to discern throughout Europe a uniform conception of the significance of religion in society.' Here, of course, the Court is correct. Populations of some countries have stronger religious traditions and practices. States show considerable variation with respect to church–state relationship. Nonetheless, the Turkish restrictive measures on headscarves do stand out among the States Parties to the Convention, for no other state (at least at the time of this judgment) had extended bans to students at universities.

As here applied, MA appears to grant the state carte blanche to determine whether the conditions in Article 9(2) such as 'necessity', or the test of proportionality, have been satisfied. To be sure, application of the MA in other cases has been far more guarded and accompanied by the Court's close 'supervision'. To be sure, in many cases in which the MA has been invoked, the Court's judgment found a violation of the Convention. But if used primarily as it has been in several cases concerning headscarves, that principle could become a formula for avoiding independent examination of an issue.

Finally, consider the Court's attention to Turkey's turbulent politics over a number of decades, involving secular–religious conflicts and military interventions, as well as its attention to the politicisation of Islam and to 'extreme' political movements against which a government has the right to 'take a stance'. Surely this context is relevant to the Court's judgment and to the application of the MA. Perhaps it holds the key to a better understanding of the judgment. Though not expressed as such in the opinion, the Court may have viewed Turkey as a special case among the States Parties, under ongoing threat that could justify both special measures and special deference.

Dogru v France (2008).[21] The applicant, a student in a public school, wore her headscarf for religious reasons both in academic classes and for sports activities requiring dress that met safety criteria. Consistently with its internal rules, the school forbad her attendance at school unless she removed the headscarf during physical activities.[22] The student refused and was expelled. The Court's judgment concluded that the expulsion was justified under Article 9(2) in the light of the 1989 advisory opinion of the *Conseil d'État* and related ministerial circulars described in Section III above. The sanction of expulsion was 'necessary' and 'proportionate' to the school's objective of health and safety.

The Court drew upon its earlier opinions in *Dahlab* and *Şahin* to highlight certain observations in those cases. It noted that the wearing of religious signs was not 'inherently incompatible' with the governing principle of secularism in schools. In this case, however,

---

[21] *Dogru v France* (n 7).

[22] The relevant events took place before the Act of 2004 had become effective. For that reason, the opinion refers to this law but does not apply it. Hence the school's insistence that the headscarf be removed covered only sports activities rather than the student's whole day at the school, as would have been required under the Act of 2004.

the circumstances in which the headscarf was worn led to a different conclusion. Students had to comply with the school's health and safety rules. In her demand for religious freedom, the applicant had overstepped her right to manifest her religion. The authorities could assure that such manifestation 'did not take on the nature of an ostentatious act that would constitute a source of pressure and exclusion'. The decision by school authorities that the headscarf was incompatible with sports classes for health and safety reasons was not unreasonable.

This judgment was ultimately based on concerns of health and safety, a less contentious, more limited and more contextual basis than *Şahin*. Nonetheless, *Dogru* vividly illustrates the rapid development over these three cases of a jurisprudence on headscarves that is neither based on rigorous argument, nor responsive to basic questions, and that seems ever more expansive in its willingness to view the state measures as consistent with the Convention. The opinion relies on broad observations made in *Şahin* without considering that *Şahin* involved a radically different country. The characterisation of Turkey's political situation in the *Şahin* opinion hardly described French conditions of the day.

Aktas v France (2009).[23] The applicant, a Muslim girl, wore a headscarf to her public school, after the Act of 2004 and related rules including a ministerial circular of 2004, described in Section III above, had become effective. She refused to remove it and was ultimately expelled. After being denied relief in France, she applied to the ECtHR. In this decision, the ECtHR considered only the claim of freedom to manifest one's religion. The Court concluded that the application was not well founded and was therefore inadmissible.

Relying on and quoting from *Şahin*, the Court emphasised that its prior jurisprudence had made clear that wearing a headscarf could be considered 'an act motivated or inspired by a religion'. Since deep differences in opinion about state–religion relationships exist in many states, there was reason to accord particular importance to the role of the national decision-maker, particularly where religious symbols in educational institutions were at issue. Restrictions of such symbols, signs and dress were in the service of protecting the constitutional principle of *laïcité*.

In a democratic society, the Court stated, some limitations on freedoms of religion were inevitable where several religions co-existed in order to reconcile the interests of diverse groups and assure respect for all. In so doing, the state played a neutral and impartial role. Bearing in mind the margin of appreciation which it was appropriate to grant the state in these circumstances, the Court found the application to lack adequate foundation and hence to be inadmissible.

Arslan v Turkey (2010).[24] In 1986 a religious group known as *Aczimendi tarikan* was formed in Turkey. It followed the precepts of its leader. Its distinctive male dress, recalling the dress of its principal prophets, including Mohammed, featured a black turban and tunic. While on public streets en route to a mosque before which a religious ceremony was to be held, 127 group members were arrested. They were later convicted under penal laws whose purpose was to safeguard Turkey's secular government. Those laws included a prohibition on publicly manifesting religious beliefs through clothing. The government claimed that it acted because this group sought to replace Turkey's democratic government with a system based on *sharia*. The group members claimed that their conviction stemmed from

---

[23] *Aktas v France* (n 11).
[24] *Ahmet Arslan v Turkey* (Application No 41135/98, Decision of 23 February 2010).

wearing their turbans in a public place (a street) open to all, and applied to the ECtHR for relief. The Court's judgment concluded that Turkey had violated Article 9.

The opinion stressed that the applicants were 'simple citizens', not representatives of the state, not performing any public function and not exercising any authority of the state. Hence the state could not regulate the public expression of their religious convictions. The state laws applicable to state personnel performing their jobs, and in particular to teachers, were inapplicable. For such reasons, the *Dahlab* decision was not germane. The dress involved in this case, which had a religious significance for the applicants, was worn in the street and not in public places—such as schools or government institutions—in which the state's duty of neutrality would trump individuals' freedom to manifest religion. Hence prior decisions (citing *Şahin*) barring religious symbols in public teaching institutions were not in point. No evidence or allegations supported the view that applicants constituted a danger to public order or applied pressure against or sought to proselytise others on the public street. The necessity for the government to insist on compliance with dress restrictions in this context was not convincingly shown, and the requirement in Article 9(2) of meeting the stated conditions for limiting the freedom to manifest one's religion was not satisfied.

A concurring opinion stated, with respect to Turkey's secular constitutional system, that the Court's judgment was perfectly compatible with the principle of *laïcité*, and also respected Turkey's margin of appreciation.

Compared with the preceding cases, the Court here concentrates on the precise context and factors that are germane to its judgment. The opinion carefully and closely explains the distinctions and devotes less attention to stating broad principles whose relevance may not be made clear. It concentrates on the precise factors that argue against upholding the state's conduct. Carefully and closely argued, the opinion explains the distinctions it makes between this case and the predecessors which it cites. It notes the lack of evidence that would be necessary to support a conclusion such as danger to public order or threat of proselytising. In brief, the Court does more than declare and defer and decide; it informs and advances understanding of the field. Through its critical inquiry, the Court indeed exercises the 'European supervision' on which the classic formulation of the margin of appreciation insists.

VI. Concluding Observations

First, a word should be said about the questions and criticism that this chapter directs to the laws, advisory opinions, circulars and judicial opinions involved in this ongoing controversy. Very probably some of that criticism would not figure in writings of persons closer to and more familiar with the relevant political, legislative and judicial institutions; with their styles, concerns and pressures; and with ideological elements of the controversy. My own perspective as a non-European, educated in a different legal and political system, doubtless becomes manifest at times.

Secondly, this chapter gives scant attention to the Act of 2010 affecting the *burqa/niquab*. That dress associated with Muslim women and Islam presents some of the same issues as the headscarf, but also raises fresh troublesome concerns. The least troublesome of those concerns addresses the ways in which wearing the *burqa/niquab* must be regulated in the interest of safety, national security, identity pictures, checkpoints and other such matters. The serious concerns stem from the far greater reach of the Act of 2010, both as to persons covered and the spaces where the ban applies. Its foundation in basic French political principles as well as in the ECHR seems more fragile. Many people concerned with these issues await with keen interest the day when the Act of 2010 comes before the ECtHR.

Thirdly, in its discussion of the ECtHR cases, this chapter takes into account the margin of appreciation. In several of the headscarf cases, it criticises the summary character and breadth of the Court's deference to states. Perhaps the larger context in which the Court functioned during these years offers at least a partial explanation of its use of the MA. Naturally, the ECtHR has had concerns about maintaining its legitimacy among the States Parties to the ECHR, particularly given that a large number of those states are among the world's oldest and most reliable democracies and rank highly in terms of observance of human rights. Several states, such as the UK, have expressed their concern that the Court may be overreaching in some of its judgments, particularly when fair and democratic processes functioned as they were intended to function with respect to enacting the laws or taking the measures that were challenged before the Court. Such concerns led to the recent Brighton Conference and Declaration.[25]

Moreover, the headscarf regulation enjoyed broad political support as part of the governmental and public reaction to substantial immigration of Muslims. Its popularity does not simplify the ECtHR's task. In these circumstances, the MA may have been favoured by the Court as a cautious and politically-sensible method for deciding these cases, at least until a clear consensus about legal regulation develops among a larger number of States Parties. In the meantime, the Court can in this way affirm the legality under the Convention of what the states have done, without developing a full explanation and argument of its own involving such basic concerns as freedom of religion and protection of minorities.

---

[25] The Declaration sets forth various proposals that would change and in a few respects limit the work of the Court, while reinforcing the role of the States Parties in the protection and implementation of human rights (n 18).

16

Re-judging Social Rights in the European Union

TAMARA K HERVEY[*]

I. Introduction

If legal scholars seek to pursue socially progressive political agendas, what approaches, tools or practices can they deploy?[1] One such approach involves an exploration of how 'social rights' could be enforced through litigation strategies.[2] But how does a social rights agenda fare in the context of increasingly liberalised global markets, where free trade is the central value, and social rights, and other 'local' preferences are constructed as protectionist exceptions to the rules on free movement of commodities and services and fair competition? We see this phenomenon, for instance, in the law of the World Trade Organization, and also in the law of the European Union, which is the subject of this chapter.

A dominant conceptualisation of social rights in the EU, which owes much to Fritz Scharpf, is that the EU suffers from a 'constitutional asymmetry' in matters pertaining to social rights.[3] The application of EU treaty law on free movement or competition leaves a regulatory vacuum, which undermines national social rights provisions. The lack of competence at EU level in social spheres means that the regulatory vacuum cannot be filled by EU social rights law, and neither, according to Scharpf at least, can 'governance'

[*] I am grateful to Kenneth Armstrong, Gráinne de Búrca, Claire Kilpatrick, and Joanne Scott; to my colleagues in the Jurisprudence Reading Group at the School of Law, University of Sheffield, especially Richard Collins and Dimitrios Kyritsis; and to the participants at the SLSA workshop *Exploring the Legal in Socio-legal Studies*, 21 September 2012, especially Rosemary Hunter and Stewart Motha, for helping me to sharpen the ideas in this chapter. All remaining deficiencies are, of course, my responsibility.

[1] See, eg David Trubek's account of how the 'law and society' movement was linked to progressive political movements in DM Trubek, 'Back to the Future: The Short, Happy Life of the Law and Society Movement' (1990) 18 *Florida State University Law Review* 1, at 6–10, 52–55.

[2] See, eg, P O'Connell, *Vindicating Socio-Economic Rights: International Standards and Comparative Experiences* (London, Routledge, 2012).

[3] See eg FW Scharpf, 'The Asymmetry of European Integration, or Why the EU Cannot be a "Social Market Economy"' (2010) 8 *Socio-Economic Review* 211; FW Scharpf, 'The European Social Model: Coping with the Challenges of Diversity' (2002) 40 *Journal of Common Market Studies* 645; see also L Moreno and B Palier, 'The Europeanization of Welfare: Paradigm Shifts and Social Policy Reforms' in P Taylor-Gooby (ed), *Ideas and Welfare State Reform in Western Europe* (Basingstoke, Palgrave Macmillan, 2005); V Hatzopoulos, 'Why the Open Method of Coordination is Bad For You: A Letter to the EU' (2007) 13 *European Law Review* 309; C Offe, 'The European Model of "Social" Capitalism: Can It Survive European Integration?' (2003) 11 *Journal of Political Philosophy* 437.

assist. This means that Member States which tend towards a liberal market economy[4] are less affected by EU free movement law than those that tend towards a social market economy.[5]

This conceptualisation of the place of social rights in EU law begins from the premise that the 'telos' of EU law is to create a liberal market and that the Court of Justice of the European Union (CJEU), which is a key driver and actor in the account, has signed up to the notion that the (or at least a) telos of the EU is such an economy. This notion, according to the 'constitutional asymmetry' position, is what drives the CJEU's interpretation and application of the key rules of internal market law, which leads to the regulatory vacuum that is central to the argument. The underlying assumption is that the 'DOS' or 'Windows'[6] of EU law is based on the view that varieties of capitalism other than liberalism obscure, or even embed, national protectionism, which is undesirable for Europe as a whole. In agreeing to join the EU, Member States agree to comply with internal market law to remove such unproductive protectionism.

The conceptualisation also begins from the premise that the EU was not and still is not a human rights organisation. Human rights, including social rights, thus occupy a 'secondary' position within EU law. As underlying 'general principles' of law (now codified in the EU's Charter of Fundamental Rights), human rights may be invoked to hold the EU's political and administrative institutions to account. But, in terms of their effect on national laws and policies, the relationship between human rights and internal market law is such that the liberalism-based rules of free movement and fair competition are the rule. Human rights (including social rights) are constructed as exceptions to that rule.

But what if we reject those premises? Using a new form of critical legal scholarship, that of 'imaginative jurisprudence', this chapter seeks to explore how the law on social rights in the EU could have been. 'Imaginative jurisprudence' involves a literal rewriting of seminal cases through a critical lens.[7] The method deploys the author's imagination alongside traditional academic skills.[8] Beginning from the premise of an EU with a 'social self';[9] and one which respects, protects and fulfils/remedies[10] social rights, this chapter explores what it might mean to rewrite the seminal judgments of the CJEU that are often cited as

---

[4] PA Hall and DW Soskice, *Varieties of Capitalism: The Institutional Foundations of Comparative Advantage* (Oxford, Oxford University Press, 2001).

[5] But see, J Snell, 'Varieties of Capitalism and the Limits of Economic Integration' (2012) 13 *Cambridge Yearbook of European Legal Studies* 415.

[6] JHH Weiler, 'Introduction: The Reformation of European Constitutionalism' in JHH Weiler (ed), *The Constitution of Europe* (Cambridge, Cambridge University Press, 1999).

[7] See the discussion in R Hunter, 'The Power of Feminist Judgments?' (2012) 20 *Feminist Legal Studies* 135. For examples of 'feminist jurisprudence' in this vein, including the Feminist Judgments Project in England, see R Hunter, C McGlynn and E Rackley, *Feminist Judgments: From Theory to Practice* (Oxford, Hart Publishing, 2010) and the Women's Court of Canada, available at womenscourt.ca/home/. For a different example of something similar to 'imaginative jurisprudence' (though not under that name), defending the thesis that the 'right thinking person' in the law of defamation should be conceptualised as a person who holds liberal values, see L McNamara, *Reputation and Defamation* (Oxford, Oxford University Press, 2007), 218–26.

[8] At the risk, I admit, of falling foul of the negative aspects of the 'New Scholarship', see R Baldwin, 'The New Scholarship: Celebrating the "I" in Ideas' in *LSE Law, Society and Economy Working Papers 5/2012*.

[9] MP Maduro, 'Europe's Social Self: "The Sickness Unto Death"' in J Shaw (ed), *Social Law and Policy in an Evolving European Union* (Oxford, Hart Publishing, 2000).

[10] H Shue, 'The Interdependence of Duties' in P Alston and K Tomasevski (eds), *The Right to Food* (Utrecht, Stichting Studie en Infomatiecentrum Mensenrechten, 1984); J Ruggie, *Protect, Respect and Remedy: A Framework for Business and Human Rights* (UN Doc A/HRC/8/5, 7 April 2008); Sandra Fredman, *Human Rights Transformed: Positive Rights and Positive Duties* (Oxford, Oxford University Press, 2008).

examples of the constitutional asymmetry argument. It does so through focusing on one judgment, that of the *Kohll* case on free movement of cross-border patients in the EU.[11]

The *Kohll* case is selected as the example for this paper, as it encapsulates many of the key features of the 'constitutional asymmetry' debate, in particular in the context of *social* rights (as opposed to labour law, which is where much of the debate has focused). By social rights, I mean rights that are concerned with the material well-being of individuals and communities,[12] usually instrumentalised through the 'big five' areas of social citizenship: social security, welfare, health care, housing and education.[13] These rights are protected in the written constitutions of many of the Member States of the EU, and indeed national constitutions across the globe, and are enshrined in the EU's Charter of Fundamental Rights and other international legal instruments. The particular social right at issue in the *Kohll* case is the 'right to health care'.[14] These social rights are under increased pressure in the context of the EU of the 2010s, given the economic crisis, the responses to that crisis based on reducing government deficits through cutting public spending,[15] and the consequent pressures on national health-care systems.[16]

II. *Kohll*: the Traditional Account

In 1993, Mr Kohll, a Luxembourg national, took his daughter to the doctor for dental treatment. The doctor, probably looking at the waiting times in Luxembourg, recommended treatment from an orthodontist established just over the border, in Trier, Germany. Mr Kohll requested authorisation from the national health insurance body, but the request was refused, on the grounds that the treatment was not urgent and could be provided in Luxembourg. Mr Kohll challenged that decision, and the case was referred to the CJEU, on the question of whether the provisions of the Treaty on free movement of services applied, and therefore such a refusal was unlawful in EU law.

From the point of view of EU law, *Kohll* was utterly unremarkable. All the key elements of doctrine necessary to decide the case were well established in earlier CJEU jurisprudence. That health-care services fall within the scope of EU internal market law had been decided in 1984.[17] That services within EU internal market law need not be paid for by the recipient was decided in 1988.[18] The notion that a 'restriction' on free movement of services was broadly defined, to include anything making cross-border receipt or provision of services more difficult than equivalent service receipt or provision within one Member State, was

---

[11] Case C-158/96 *Kohll* [1998] ECR I-1931.

[12] O'Connell, *Vindicating Socio-Economic Rights* (n 2).

[13] TH Marshall, *Social Policy* (London, Hutchinson, 1975).

[14] The right to health or the right to health care is found, for instance, in national constitutions of Belgium, Finland, Hungary, Italy, Luxembourg, the Netherlands, Portugal and Spain.

[15] Contrast Angela Merkel's approach (and indeed that of Christine Lagarde of the International Monetary Fund) with Francois Hollande's proposed Growth Pact (or indeed Barack Obama's approach).

[16] N Fahy, 'Who is Shaping the Future of European Health Systems?' (2012) 344 *British Medical Journal*, e1712.

[17] Joined Cases 286/82 and 26/83 *Luisi and Carbone* [1984] ECR 377.

[18] Case 352/85 *Bond van Adverteers* [1988] ECR 2085.

in place.[19] That mere economic reasons could not justify a restriction on free movement of services had also recently been established.[20] The CJEU duly decided in *Kohll* that the authorisation rules 'deter insured persons from approaching providers of medical services established in another Member State, and constitute ... a barrier to freedom to provide services.' The rules were not justified on grounds of public health, as the qualifications of orthodontists practising in Germany are recognised by Luxembourg under EU law,[21] and no evidence had been adduced to the effect that the rules were 'necessary to provide a balanced medical and hospital service accessible to all' or 'indispensable for the maintenance of an essential treatment facility or medical service on national territory'.[22]

Yet it is not an exaggeration to say that the health policy communities in the Member States of the EU received *Kohll* with incredulity.[23] Several national governments took the view that the decision could not possibly apply in the context of their health-care system:[24] they were proved wrong.[25] It was feared that the case would lead to critical instability in national health (insurance) systems and threaten the viability of their social goals. Unpredictable influxes and effluxes of patients would make it impossible for governments to plan health services effectively. Human capacity planning was a particular focus: particularly in the hospital sector, national populations are the relevant reference point, and if this were changed, then the consequent pressures on some hospitals (and under-use of others) would jeopardise equality and social equity—fundamental principles of national health (insurance) systems in the European context. The ability of patients to access new and 'unproven' treatments in other Member States would affect national control over health technology assessment and decisions about the scope of the 'basket of care' available through the national health (insurance) system in a particular Member State. In the context of budgetary prudence, the temptation to lower standards in order to cope would lead to a 'race to the bottom', with worsening health service entitlements across the EU. In the context of significant disparities in spending and health outcomes across the EU,[26] the ability of certain mobile patients to access (expensive) health care in the West and North was seen as particularly threatening to health systems in the East and South of the EU. In general, it was feared that the individualisation implicit in litigation based on EU law would undermine collective provision of health-care rights within Europe's national health-care

---

[19] See Case 186/87 *Cowan* [1989] ECR 195; Case C-76/90 *Säger v Dennemeyer* [1991] ECR I-4221; Case C-43/93 *Vander Elst* [1994] ECR I-3803; Case C-272/94 *Guiot v Climatec* [1996] ECR I-1905.

[20] Case C-398/95 *SETTG v Ypourgos Ergasias* [1997] ECR I-3091, para 23.

[21] Paras 43, 47–48.

[22] Para 52.

[23] There have been similar responses from similar communities to other 'constitutional asymmetry' cases, for instance, the Trades Union movement's response to Case C-341/05 *Laval* [2007] ECR I-11767 and Case C-438/05 *Viking Line* [2007] ECR I-10779.

[24] DS Martinsen, 'The Europeanization of Welfare: The Domestic Impact of Intra-European Social Security' (2005) 43 *Journal of Common Market Studies* 1027, 1045.

[25] Case C-368/98 *Vanbraekel* [2001] ECR I-5363; Case C-157/99 *Geraets-Smits* [2001] ECR I-5473; Case C-8/02 *Leichtle* [2004] ECR I-2641; Case C-372/04, *Watts* [2006] ECR I-4325; Case C-444/05 *Stamatelaki* [2007] ECR I-3185; Case C-173/09 *Elchinov* [2010] ECR I-8889, para 49; Case C-512/08 *Commission v France* [2010] ECR I-8833; Case C-211/08 *Commission v Spain* [2010] ECR I-5267.

[26] For instance, in terms of per capita spending on health, Romania and Bulgaria spend, respectively, US$500 and US$522, whereas Denmark spends US$6,648, the Netherlands US$5,995, and Luxembourg a generous US$8,798. According to these figures, average life expectancy at birth varies by seven years, and infant mortality ranges from 11 per 1,000 (Romania), to only 2 per 1,000 (Finland). See World Development Indicators 2011, available at data.worldbank.org/data-catalog/world-development-indicators; European Commission, 'Solidarity in Health: Reducing Health Inequalities in the EU' (Communication) COM (2009) 567.

systems, based on solidarity and equality of access to health care according to need. All of these points are consistent with the 'constitutional asymmetry' argument.

Such fears of a major disruption to the organisation of national health (insurance) systems, following copycat litigation, eventually led the Member States to adopt new EU legislation.[27] Although this goes some way to addressing some of the 'constitutional asymmetry' points (and, incidentally, shows that the EU legislature can, where politically expedient, respond to such litigation), the Treaty provisions on which the *Kohll* reasoning is based obviously remain in place. The existence of relevant EU legislation dating from the 1970s[28] did not prevent the CJEU from using the Treaty provisions to, in effect, undermine that legislation in order to promote the internal market. In other contexts, notably that of workers 'posted' from Central or Eastern European Member States to Northern or Western Member States,[29] the existence of EU legislation purportedly covering the issue did not deter the CJEU from finding that the Treaty provisions on free movement of services and freedom of establishment were applicable.[30]

III. *Kohll*: Re-imagined

But what if the CJEU had approached the *Kohll* case from a different foundation—one where the relationship between social rights and internal market law is differently constituted? How might the CJEU have reasoned and decided the case under those circumstances? Below are excerpts from the *Kohll* judgment, re-imagined in that vein. Alterations to the original text are indicated by underlined (added) and strikeout (removed) text.[31] The method of showing the changes that would be made to the real judgment, is, as far as I am aware, unique.[32] It is used here primarily to demonstrate graphically the extent of the similarities (and the nature of the differences) between the real and the re-imagined *Kohll*.[33] It also reflects the form that CJEU judgments habitually take, and the fact that they often repeat entire phrases verbatim from earlier jurisprudence.

> 1 … the Luxembourg Cour de Cassation referred to the Court for a preliminary ruling under Article 177 of the EC Treaty two questions on the interpretation of Articles 59 and 60 of that Treaty.

---

[27] Directive 2011/24/EU of the European Parliament and of the Council of 9 March 2011 on the application of patients' rights in cross-border health care [2011] OJ L88/45.

[28] Council Regulation (EEC) 1408/1971 on the application of social security schemes to employed persons, to self-employed persons and to members of their families moving within the Community [1971] OJ Sp Ed II/416.

[29] Directive 96/71/EC of the European Parliament and of the Council of 16 December 1996 concerning the posting of workers in the framework of the provision of services [1996] OJ L18/1.

[30] See Case C-341/05 *Laval* [2007] ECR I-11767, Case C-438/05 *Viking Line* [2007] ECR I-10779, Case C-346/06 *Rüffert* [2008] ECR I-1989; Case C-219/08 *Commission v Belgium* [2009] ECR I-9213.

[31] It seems that the real judicial drafting process may, in a similar way, at least sometimes involve keeping various possible versions in play until the final version is reached. Thanks are due to Stewart Motha for sharing his experiences as a judge's associate in Australia on this point.

[32] It differs from that used, for instance, in the feminist judgments projects mentioned above, as they write entirely fresh judgments.

[33] One of the main changes is the reordering of the paragraphs on the justification point, see further below.

15 …, the questions to be considered concern first the application of the principle of freedom of movement in the field of social security, … and … the application of the provisions on freedom to provide services. These questions must be considered in the context of the fundamental human right to health care, a general principle of EU law, respect for which is guaranteed within internal market law.[34]

Application of the fundamental principle of freedom of movement in the field of social security

…

17 It must be observed, first of all, that, according to settled case-law, Community law does not detract from the powers of the Member States to organise their social security systems in order to protect social rights.[35]

18 In the absence of harmonisation at Community level, it is therefore for the legislation of each Member State to determine, first, the conditions concerning the right or duty to be insured with a social security scheme.[36]

19 … the Member States must nevertheless comply with Community law, which requires respect for fundamental social rights, when exercising those powers.

20 The Court has held that the special nature of certain services does not remove them from the ambit of the fundamental principle of freedom of movement.[37]

21 Consequently, the fact that the national rules at issue in the main proceedings fall within the sphere of social security cannot exclude the application of Articles 59 and 60 of the Treaty.

…

Application of the provisions on freedom to provide services

29 The dispute before the national court concerns treatment provided by an orthodontist established in another Member State, outside any hospital infrastructure. That service, provided for remuneration, must be regarded as a service within the meaning of Article 60 of the Treaty, which expressly refers to activities of the professions. It is, however, at the same time, a service of general interest, through which Member States respect, protect and fulfil social rights, and thus Articles 59 and 60 of the Treaty must be interpreted accordingly.

30 It must therefore be examined whether rules such as those at issue in the main proceedings constitute a restriction on freedom to provide services, and if so, whether they may be objectively justified.

Restrictive effects of the rules at issue

…

33 It should be noted that, according to the Court's case-law, Article 59 of the Treaty precludes the application of any national rules which have the effect of making the provision of services between Member States more difficult than the provision of services purely within one Member State.[38]

---

[34] See, eg Case C-5/88 *Wachauf v Federal Republic of Germany* [1989] ECR 2609; Case C-260/89 *ERT* [1991] ECR I-2925; Case C-168/91 *Konstantinidis* 1993 ECR I-1191.
[35] Case 238/82 *Duphar and Others v Netherlands* [1984] ECR 523, para 16, and Case C-70/95 *Sodemare and Others v Regione Lombardia* [1997] ECR I-3395, para 27.
[36] Case 110/79 *Coonan v Insurance Officer* [1980] ECR 1445, para 12, and Case C-349/87 *Paraschi v Landesversicherungsanstalt Württemberg* [1991] ECR I-4501, para 15. In addition for the conditions for entitlement to benefits, see Joined Cases C-4/95 and C-5/95 *Stöber* [1997] ECR I-511, para 36.
[37] Case 279/80 *Webb* [1981] ECR 3305, para 10.
[38] Case C-381/93 *Commission v France* [1994] ECR I-5145, para 17.

34 While the national rules at issue in the main proceedings do not deprive insured persons of the possibility of approaching a provider of services established in another Member State, they do nevertheless make reimbursement of the costs incurred in that Member State subject to prior authorisation, and deny such reimbursement to insured persons who have not obtained that authorisation. Costs incurred in the State of insurance are not, however, subject to that authorisation.

35 Consequently, such rules deter insured persons from approaching providers of medical services established in another Member State and constitute, for them and their patients, a barrier to freedom to provide services.[39]

36 The Court must therefore examine whether a measure of the kind at issue in this case may be objectively justified.

Justification of the rules at issue

43 The Luxembourg Government ~~also relies on grounds based on~~ submits that the protection of public health justifies the rules at issue, arguing, first, that the rules ~~at issue~~ are necessary to guarantee the quality of medical services, which in the case of persons going to another Member State can be ascertained only at the time of the request for authorisation, and, second, that the Luxembourg sickness insurance system aims to provide a balanced medical and hospital service open to all insured persons.

44 Mr Kohll submits, on the other hand, that there is no scientific reason to conclude that treatment provided in Luxembourg is more effective, now that the pursuit of the medical professions is the subject of mutual recognition between Member States. He further submits that the reference to a balanced medical and hospital sector open to all must above all be categorised as an economic aim intended to protect UCM's [the national health insurance institution] financial resources.

45 It should be noted, first of all, that under Articles 56 and 66 of the EC Treaty Member States may limit freedom to provide services on grounds of public health.

46 However, that does not permit them to exclude the public health sector, as a sector of economic activity and from the point of view of freedom to provide services, from the application of the fundamental principle of freedom of movement.[40] Nevertheless, the status in EU law of health services as social services of general interest must also be taken into account in interpreting that principle.

47 The conditions for taking up and pursuing the profession of doctor and dentist have been the subject of several coordinating or harmonising directives.[41]

48 It follows that doctors and dentists established in other Member States must be afforded all guarantees equivalent to those accorded to doctors and dentists established on national territory, for the purposes of freedom to provide services, subject to the interest of the Member States to protect the health of those insured within their national health system.

49 Consequently, rules such as those applicable in the main proceedings cannot be justified on grounds of public health in order to protect the quality of medical services provided in other

---

[39] See Joined Cases 286/82 and 26/83 *Luisi and Carbone v Ministero del Tesoro* [1984] ECR 377, para 16, and Case C-204/90 *Bachmann v Belgium* [1992] ECR I-249, para 31.

[40] See Case 131/85 *Gül v Regierungspräsident Düsseldorf* [1986] ECR 1573, para 17.

[41] See Council Directive 78/686/EEC of 25 July 1978 concerning the mutual recognition of diplomas, certificates and other evidence of the formal qualifications of practitioners of dentistry, including measures to facilitate the effective exercise of the right of establishment and freedom to provide services [1978] OJ L233/1; Council Directive 78/687/EEC of 25 July 1978 concerning the coordination of provisions laid down by law, regulation or administrative action in respect of the activities of dental practitioners [1978] OJ L233/10; and Council Directive 93/16/EEC of 5 April 1993 to facilitate the free movement of doctors and the mutual recognition of their diplomas, certificates and other evidence of formal qualifications [1993] OJ L165/1.

Member States <u>only where there is a serious concern about the quality of the medical services at</u> <u>issue, or an objectively demonstrable risk to the patient or population.</u>

50 As to the objective of maintaining a balanced medical and hospital service open to all, that objective, although intrinsically linked to the method of financing the social security system, may also fall within the derogations on grounds of public health under Article 56 of the Treaty, in so far as it contributes to the attainment of a high level of health protection <u>and consequently the</u> <u>protection of fundamental social rights.</u>

51 Article 56 of the Treaty permits Member States to restrict the freedom to provide medical and hospital services in so far as the maintenance of a treatment facility or medical service on national territory is essential for the public health and even the survival of the population.[42]

52 However, neither UCM nor the Governments of the Member States which have submitted observations have shown that the rules at issue were necessary <u>to prevent a serious concern about the qual-</u> <u>ity of the medical services at issue, or an objectively demonstrable risk to the patient or population,</u> <u>or</u> to provide a balanced medical and hospital service accessible to all. None of those who have submitted observations has argued that the rules were ~~indispensable for the maintenance of~~ <u>a reasonable</u> <u>measure to maintain</u> an essential treatment facility or medical service on national territory.

53 The conclusion must therefore be drawn that the rules at issue in the main proceedings are not justified on grounds of public health.

37 UCM and the Governments of the Member States which have submitted observations <u>also</u> submit that freedom to provide services is not absolute and that<u>, given that health care is a social</u> <u>service of general interest, and that the Luxembourg rules give effect to the right to health care for</u> <u>insured persons,</u> reasons connected with the control of health expenditure must be taken into consideration. <u>The right to health care is not an absolute right, but must be realised in accordance with</u> <u>the economic capacity of the Member State concerned. Unreasonable restrictions on such social</u> <u>rights are prohibited by law.</u> The requirement of prior authorisation constitutes ~~the only~~ <u>an</u> effective <u>and reasonable</u> ~~and least restrictive~~ means of controlling expenditure on health and balancing the budget of the social security system, <u>while providing a social service of general interest and</u> <u>protecting the right to health of persons insured within the Luxembourg social security system.</u>

38 According to UCM, the Luxembourg Government and the Commission, the risk of upsetting the financial balance of the social security scheme, which aims to ensure a balanced medical and hospital service available to all its insured, constitutes an overriding reason ~~in the general interest~~ capable of justifying restrictions on freedom to provide <u>social</u> services of <u>general interest. Where</u> <u>such overriding reasons are the protection of fundamental human rights, Community law respects</u> <u>those rights, in the context of creation of the internal market.</u>[43]

39 The Commission adds that the refusal of the national authorities to grant prior authorisation must be justified by a genuine and actual risk of upsetting the financial balance of the social security scheme.

40 On the latter point, Mr Kohll submits that the financial burden on the budget of the Luxembourg social security institution is the same whether he approaches a Luxembourg orthodontist or one established in another Member State, since he asked for medical expenses to be reimbursed at the rate applied in Luxembourg. The rules at issue therefore cannot be justified by the need to control health expenditure.

---

[42] See, with respect to public security within the meaning of Article 36 of the Treaty, Case 72/83 *Campus Oil v Minister for Industry and Energy* [1984] ECR 2727, paras 33 to 36.
[43] <u>See Case C-260/89 *ERT* [1991] ECR I-2925; Case C-112/00 *Schmidberger* [2003] ECR I-5659; Case C-36/02 *Omega Spielhallen* [2004] ECR I-9609.</u>

41 It must be recalled that aims of a purely economic nature cannot justify a barrier to the funda-mental principle of freedom to provide services.[44] However, it cannot be excluded that the risk of seriously undermining the financial balance of the social security system, <u>through which Member States secure a social service of general interest, and respect, protect and fulfil social rights,</u> may constitute an overriding reason in the general interest capable of justifying a barrier of that kind.

42 ~~But, contrary to the submissions of UCM and the Luxembourg Government, it is clear that reimbursement of the costs of dental treatment provided in other Member States in accordance with the tariff of the State of insurance has no significant effect on the financing of the social security system.~~ <u>It is clear that reimbursement of the costs of dental treatment for a single patient, such as Mr Kohll's daughter, provided in another Member State, in accordance with the tariff of the State of insurance, has only a marginal effect on the financing of Luxembourg's social security system. However, in the context of the obligation of Luxembourg to respect, protect and fulfil the right to health of all persons insured within the Luxembourg system, the effect on Luxembourg's social security system—and indeed those of other Member States—of unlimited movement of patients insured within that system must also be considered.</u>

42a <u>In the absence of harmonisation of social security systems at Community level, respect for the right to health care, a fundamental right recognised in Community law, and health care as a social service of general interest, is given effect through national social security systems. If unlimited movement of patients were required by Community law, the effect would be to make it impos-sible for Member States to respect, protect and fulfil the right to health, according to nationally-determined democratic decision-making procedures, which legitimate decisions concerning access to health care within the limited economic resources available. In that context, national rules restricting reimbursement for health care undertaken outside the national social security system constitute a reasonable restriction on free movement of social services of general interest in the internal market.</u>

54 In those circumstances, the answer must be that Articles 59 and 60 of the Treaty <u>do not</u> preclude national rules under which reimbursement, in accordance with the scale of the State of insurance, of the cost of dental treatment provided by an orthodontist established in another Member State is subject to authorisation by the insured person's social security institution.

IV. Discussion

What can we learn from this exercise in 'imaginative jurisprudence'? I consider three elements here: the types of change made to the real judgment to reach the re-imagined judgment; what the exercise reveals about the nature of the 'constitutional asymmetry' position; and what it reveals about social rights in EU law. The chapter concludes with some observations about the limitations and the promise of the method itself.

A. The Changes Made

The re-imagined judgment begins from a different relationship between the 'fundamental freedoms' of internal market law and 'fundamental (human) rights' including the right to

---

[44] See, to that effect, Case C-398/95 *SETTG v Ypourgos Ergasias* [1997] ECR I-3091, para 23.

health care. It imagines earlier jurisprudence where this relationship is articulated not in terms of the rule/exception approach, but where respect for human rights is embedded in the Treaty rules on freedom of movement.[45] It follows that internal market law *itself* requires respect for human rights, and internal market litigation becomes a site for determining the scope, contours, detailed meaning of and exceptions to human rights, including social rights such as the right to health,[46] rather than a place where human rights are exceptions to the rule of free movement. The re-imagined judgment also makes explicit the relationship between social services of general interest, social security/welfare systems (here, health care systems) and social rights (here, the right to health care).[47] Combining these two ideas, internal market law must be interpreted so as to respect, protect and fulfil social rights. Social services of general interest, delivered within domestic welfare systems are important mechanisms for so doing.

In itself, this alternative approach is not imagined to affect the *scope* of EU law—in principle health care systems still fall to be scrutinised under the free movement provisions, and rules concerning what counts as a 'restriction' on free movement remain unchanged.[48] What is different is the justification stage of the CJEU's re-imagined reasoning. The justification points are re-ordered in the re-imagined judgment, so as to deal first with the justification which fails, and then with that which succeeds. Dealing first with the public health justification, in this case, it is not made out by the Luxembourg government.[49] However, possible future reliance on public health to justify such restrictive rules is set up by recognising that the status of health care services and social services of general interest must be taken into account,[50] and by elaborating what a public health concern would look like, for instance demonstrable concern over quality of medical services; or risk to the patient or the population,[51] and a 'reasonableness' test[52] for assessing this (rather than the current very strict proportionality test). As for the justification concerning protection of the viability of the health-care system, especially the hospital sector, the link between this, social services of general interest, and human rights protection is made explicit,[53] and the nature of the right to health care (not absolute, must be realised within economic constraints of a particular state, subject to a reasonableness test[54]) is discussed. This means that the standard of justification is what is reasonable *in the particular national (here, Luxembourg) context*, a crucial reference point in the context of an EU with very different levels of investment in health-care systems. With all of this set up, at the justification stage, the imaginary CJEU considers not only the rights in internal market law of an individual litigant (Mr Kohll's daughter), but also systemic issues—here the collective provision of the right to health care. There is no EU-level harmonisation of social security. Democratically legitimated decisions about resource allocation take place at national level, on the basis of

---

[45] The reasons for this re-imagined earlier jurisprudence are outlined below; essentially they go to the need to provide a credible re-imagined *Kohll* that does not depart from the previous jurisprudence too significantly, given the CJEU's usual practice of incremental change, and deep respect for its own earlier decisions.

[46] Re-imagined judgment, paras 15, 19 and 38.

[47] Re-imagined judgment, para 17.

[48] Re-imagined judgment, paras 33–36.

[49] Re-imagined judgment, paras 52–53.

[50] Re-imagined judgment, para 46.

[51] Re-imagined judgment, para 49.

[52] Re-imagined judgment, para 52.

[53] Re-imagined judgment, paras 50 and 37.

[54] Re-imagined judgment, para 37.

territorially closed health-care systems,[55] not at EU level. Therefore, the right to health care is given effect through national health-care systems, and that right must be recognised in and respected by EU law. Implicitly, the free movement rules of internal market law cannot lightly interfere with such decisions—hence the reasonableness test and the collective, rather than individual, reference point. It follows that the Luxembourg prior authorisation rules *are* justified.

B. The Nature of the Constitutional Asymmetry Position

As Burley and Mattli[56] and Maduro[57] have observed, the CJEU adheres to a style of formal reasoning that emphasises logical deduction from legal principles, in preference to analysis of substantive economic or social problems or policy goals that contextualise national policies that are consequently judged to be in conflict with internal market law.[58] This is the case even though the legal principles themselves are self-proclaimed, and there is an element of 'boot-strapping' involved in what is presented as logically-coherent juristic reasoning.[59] The formal reasoning that supports the constitutional asymmetry argument includes at least three stages: scope (including cross-border effect), rule, and exception. Examining each of these illustrates how the constitutional asymmetry position relies on the idea that the CJEU accepts a particular version of legal formalism as a given constraint on its decisions.

The first stage involves the scope or reach of EU law. The original assumption of the governments of the Member States was that social services of general interest, such as education, health care and so on, would fall outside the scope of EU law on free movement of services. Beginning with (tertiary) education,[60] the CJEU has subverted this position, by commodifying such services.[61] Equally, the original idea of the scope of EU internal market law was that its aim was to tackle cross-border restrictions, and it would not apply in 'purely internal situations'. Again, the CJEU has, following a self-proclaimed formal rule concerning the *effects*—including *potential* effects—of national policies, enabled litigation challenging national rules that do not obviously involve border-crossing transactions.[62] Where that is so, given the legal principle of equality of treatment of similar situations, the

---

[55] M Ferrera, *The Boundaries of Welfare: European Integration and the New Spatial Politics of Social Protection* (Oxford, Oxford University Press, 2005). But see S Leibfried and P Pierson, *European Social Policy: Between Fragmentation and Integration* (Washington DC, Brookings, 1995).

[56] A-M Burley and W Mattli, 'Europe Before the Court: A Political Theory of Legal Integration' (1993) 47 *International Organization* 41, 44.

[57] MP Maduro, *We, the Court: The European Court of Justice and the European Economic Constitution* (Oxford, Hart Publishing, 1998), 11, 16–25.

[58] Scharpf, 'The Asymmetry of European Integration' (n 3), 216.

[59] J Derrida, 'Force of Law: The "Mystical Foundation of Authority"' (*Deconstruction and the Possibility of Justice* colloquium, October 1989), available at pdflibrary.files.wordpress.com/2008/01/derrida_force-of-law.pdf, 945.

[60] See the case law discussed in B de Witte, *European Community Law of Education* (Baden-Baden, Nomos, 1989) and J Shaw, 'From the Margins to the Centre: Education and Training Law and Policy' in P Craig and G de Búrca (eds), *The Evolution of EU Law* (Oxford, Oxford University Press, 1999).

[61] Other such services include, for instance, long term residential care, see eg Case 70/95 *Sodemare* [1997] ECR 3395.

[62] See, eg Joined cases C-570/07 and C-571/07 *Pérez and Gómez* [2010] ECR I-4629. For further discussion see C Barnard and O Odudu (eds), *The Outer Limits of EU Law* (Oxford, Hart Publishing, 2009).

practical effect of the CJEU's judgments is to challenge domestic situations as well.[63] There is also a major political effect on the practical ability of Member States to determine their internal policies, if they are debarred from particular policy choices with respect to external transactions. This means that integration through internal market litigation directly or indirectly 'undermine[s] the capacity of member states to shape the conditions of production and consumption in their own markets according to national political preferences'.[64] The re-imagined judgment in this paper does not re-imagine either of these aspects of the CJEU's jurisprudence, although recognising the contingent nature of the scope rules as developed by the CJEU shows that they could be so.

The second stage in the reasoning is the rule/exception approach. This embeds 'a procedural asymmetry between rule and exception: if an impediment to the exercise of European liberties is alleged, the Court takes judicial notice of its potential effect—which then establishes the rebuttable presumption of a Treaty violation'.[65] In effect, legal formalism leads to procedural and evidential consequences for how Member States defend their national social policies in the context of internal market law. Once such social policies are constructed as exceptions to the general rule of free trade, it follows according to the standard legal formalist relationships between rule and exception that policies that support or promote social rights must be narrowly interpreted, against a reference point of free trade as being the desired aim.

At the third stage, the exception is scrutinised. As the CJEU has understood the nature of the rule and exception here, national policies must satisfy the proportionality test (which in free movement law at least has its strictest possible version). The burden of proof lies on the Member State to justify its 'restrictive' policy, in accordance with strict proportionality, rather than in the ordinary place, on the litigant seeking to show that their rights have been breached.[66]

In the re-imagined judgment, the CJEU operates more like a 'standard' constitutional court, mediating between different levels in a federation. It becomes one of the places where the relative importance of national/state/provincial/regional/local concerns and federal/EU concerns are discussed.[67] Constitutional courts in established federal states make such judgments on the basis of maintaining a 'stable balance between the mandates, legitimacy bases and functional requirements of both levels of government'.[68] Under the constitutional asymmetry position, the CJEU does not operate on this basis because of the CJEU's internally-constructed role for itself. According to this construction, the CJEU is (only) 'an instrument for promoting a dynamic process of ever increasing European integration'.[69] In order to reach a re-imagined self-appointed role for the CJEU, we have to re-imagine the CJEU's own idea of European integration and what it is *for*. And here we need to look at the history. Accounts of the setting up of what is now the EU focus strongly

---

[63] Scharpf, 'The Asymmetry of European Integration' (n 3), 224.

[64] Ibid, 224.

[65] Ibid, 219.

[66] 'The increasing liberalisation of transnational access to national health care has largely been achieved by tightening the evidentiary standards for proving the proportionality of restrictive rules', ibid, 219, fn 13.

[67] Ibid, 229–30.

[68] Ibid, 228.

[69] G de Búrca, 'The Road Not Taken: The European Union as a Global Human Rights Actor' (2011) 105 *American Journal of International Law* 649; Scharpf, 'The Asymmetry of European Integration' (n 3), 228.

on the EU as a body for promoting peace and development.[70] Economic rights (to move freely within the internal market) are implicitly construed by the CJEU as the basic pre-condition for *all* fundamental (civil, political, social) rights[71]—in other words, peace and material prosperity are contingent on economic freedoms. But again there is nothing that *mandates* such a construction by the CJEU. There is no particular reason why the EU could not have been (cannot be) understood as an institutional arrangement that, in pursuit of peace and development, serves human beings *qua* rights-holders with dignity directly, and not only indirectly through the interest of capital or commodities. Moreover, given that we now understand social equality as crucial to development,[72] we can quite legitimately imagine a CJEU that constructs the idea of European integration as being for more than free movement of capital and commodities, but for creating a developed Europe that shares its wealth with the more vulnerable in society through social welfare mechanisms that are democratically legitimated at (sub)national level, and not undermined by EU level institutions. We might also consider the idea that the CJEU came to understand the EU as having a role in supporting human rights through its internal market law, drawing on de Búrca's work that shows that the EU omitted human rights from its Treaties in 1957 as a 'pragmatic and strategic *interim* step' (italics added), not a deliberate decision to leave for ever clear blue water between the idea of European integration as supported by the EU and that supported by the Council of Europe.[73]

There are aspects of the CJEU's jurisprudence, particularly that of its Advocates General, that show glimmers of how the CJEU might, through considering the place of vulnerable individuals within Europe (and the collectively-organised institutions that support them)[74], have developed an alternative idea of what the EU is for. Advocate General Jacobs' stand-out 1993 Opinion in *Konstantinidis*,[75] drawing on Roman Law notions of citizenship, combined with the freedoms implied in an internal market (and indeed the Roman Empire[76]), is one such example; as is Advocate General Sharpston's much more recent Opinion in *Zambrano*,[77] which goes further in that it extends the application of fundamental rights in EU law to acts

---

[70] See, eg the magisterial T Judt, *Postwar: A History of Europe since 1945* (New York, Vintage Books, 2010); see also AS Milward, *The Reconstruction of Western Europe, 1945–1951* (London, Methuen & Co, 1984); W Wallace, 'Rescue or Retreat? The Nation State in Western Europe, 1945–93' (1994) 42 *Political Studies* 52.

[71] AJ Menéndez, 'The European Democratic Challenge' (2007), *RECON Working Papers*, available at www.reconproject.eu/projectweb/portalproject/RECONWorkingPapers.html, 23.

[72] See, eg RG Wilkinson and K Pickett, *The Spirit Level: Why Equality is Better for Everyone* (London, Bloomsbury Press, 2009); Daniel Dorling, *Injustice: Why Social Inequalities Persist* (Bristol, Policy Press, 2010). On law, equality and development, see, eg DM Trubek and A Santos (eds), *The New Law and Economic Development: A Critical Appraisal* (Cambridge, Cambridge University Press, 2006).

[73] De Búrca, 'The Road Not Taken' (n 69) at 4, 17–18, 50.

[74] Such as welfare systems or health care systems (or indeed trade unions).

[75] Case C-168/91 *Konstantinidis* [1993] ECR I-1191.

[76] Para 46 'In my opinion, a Community national who goes to another Member State as a worker or self-employed person under Articles 48, 52 or 59 of the Treaty is entitled not just to pursue his trade or profession and to enjoy the same living and working conditions as nationals of the host State; he is in addition entitled to assume that, wherever he goes to earn his living in the European Community, he will be treated in accordance with a common code of fundamental values, in particular those laid down in the European Convention on Human Rights. In other words, he is entitled to say "civis europeus sum" and to invoke that status in order to oppose any violation of his fundamental rights.

[77] Case C-34/09 *Zambrano* [2011] ECR I-1177.

of the Member States even where no free movement has taken place.[78] In these examples, human rights are not seen as exceptions to a prior (and implicitly more worthy of protection) rule of free movement—rather the very ideas behind the internal market are imbued with human rights protection, and the link between EU human rights protection and free movement is decoupled.[79] Perhaps more crucially, the commodification of human beings, even as (economic) citizens of the EU, is reversed.[80]

It is these aspects of the *Kohll* judgment—reconceptualising the relationship between free movement and fundamental (social) rights—that are most affected in the re-imagined version. Rather than a rule/exception construction, respect for social rights is deemed to be embedded within internal market law. This reconceptualised relationship entirely disrupts the rule/exception formula, and all that flows from it, including the assumption that free trade is a prior aim (of the EU) to that of social welfare, and hence the application of the strict proportionality test at justification stage. These aspects of the re-imagined judgment reveal that the constitutional asymmetry position is based on the formal legal consequences that are presented as flowing 'naturally' (in the course of 'standard' legal reasoning) from the rule/exception formula. Whereas, actually, there is nothing inevitable about the rule/exception formula, on which the constitutional asymmetry position relies so strongly. Equally, the constitutional asymmetry position relies on the assumption that internal market law requires the commodification of human beings in order to bring them within its scope—which then has consequences for how those human beings, and their human (social) rights are conceptualised. Again, there is nothing *inevitable* about internal market law, or about formal legal reasoning, that requires such conceptualisation.

Moreover, we can see that there is a certain logical incoherence in the constitutional asymmetry position. That position relies on an assumption that the CJEU is committed to a version of legal formalism that stresses constraints on judicial decision-making through formal logics. Accordingly, the constitutional asymmetry position is presented as the legally logical position that inevitably follows, and hence is justified by, the CJEU's legal reasoning, or simply as an unintentional effect of the CJEU's reasoning. Yet at the same time, those who describe the CJEU's role in perpetuating the position of constitutional asymmetry imply that the CJEU is driven by a political motive, of its *certain idée de l'Europe*, and that the CJEU has sufficient judicial discretion to pursue that idea. Here, the CJEU is presented as acting instrumentally, using legal formalism to operationalise, and perhaps even at the same time to conceal, its political preferences. Constitutional asymmetry's version of judicial activism is incompatible with its notion of legal formalism.

---

[78] Para 163; 165–70. The Advocate General accepts that this would be a new role for human rights in the EU, see para 173.

[79] D Anderson and C Murphy, 'The Charter of Fundamental Rights' in A Biondi, P Eeckhout and S Ripley (eds), *EU Law after Lisbon* (Oxford, Oxford University Press, 2011).

[80] AG Sharpston, in Case C-34/09 *Zambrano* [2011] ECR not yet reported, para 84 'It would be paradoxical (to say the least) if a citizen of the Union could rely on fundamental rights under EU law when exercising an economic right to free movement as a worker, or when national law comes within the scope of the Treaty (for example, the provisions on equal pay) or when invoking EU secondary legislation (such as the services directive), but could not do so when merely 'residing' in that Member State.'

C. The Debate over the Nature of Social Rights in the EU

The constitutional asymmetry position is more nuanced than a claim that the CJEU always takes a 'market-liberal' or 'neo-liberal' approach in its judgments. There is, of course, CJEU case law supporting social rights of migrant workers,[81] equal pay and treatment for women,[82] older people,[83] and people with disabilities,[84] access to universities for students studying in another country,[85] and access to welfare systems.[86] EU jurisprudence has evolved into areas where the interests that are being supported by the CJEU are not (or not primarily) those of capital or large firms. 'Liberalisation' in the sense of the constitutional asymmetry account has a different meaning—one focused on enhancement of individual liberty and mobility. The notion of European citizenship developed by the CJEU stresses individual entitlements and rights to exit from, or enter into, national welfare systems which are determined (and financed) collectively.[87] The *Kohll* case is a prime illustration.

In the absence of EU-level mechanisms of social solidarity, Scharpf argues that the CJEU's jurisprudence undermines national systems of solidarity, which are collectively determined, through nationally-based legitimating democratic processes. 'For the new social liberties as for economic liberties, therefore, integration through law maximises negative integration at the expense of democratic self-determination in the national polity.'[88] Hence Scharpf's strong normative, and practical, arguments for the CJEU respecting national preferences for systems and institutions that protect social rights.[89]

Re-writing the judgment in *Kohll* reveals that this critique is a variant of the debate on the justiciability of social rights. A strong criticism of social rights is that pursuing such rights, for instance, the 'right to health', through litigation, has the effect of substituting judicial decisions for political decisions. The proper allocation of the resources of a state should be a matter for appropriately legitimated political processes, not the decisions of courts in those (few) cases that are able to be litigated. Who brings litigation? Actors with a sufficient economic or personal stake in challenging the status quo, and who have, or can access, sufficient resources. Courts (here the CJEU) therefore see only cases involving those who are sufficiently well-resourced to bring litigation, and in the context of EU law, to be mobile.[90] Courts do not see cases promoting the interests of the less affluent, less mobile majority, or those whose interests are served by the status quo.[91] Where courts become

---

[81] Case 32/75 *Christini v SNCF* [1975] ECR 1085; Case 65/81 *Reina* [1982] ECR 33; Case 207/78 *Even* [1979] ECR 2019.

[82] Case 43/75 *Defrenne* [1976] ECR 455; Case 152/84 *Marshall* [1986] ECR 723; Case C-177/88 *Dekker* [1990] ECR I-3941.

[83] Case C-411/05 *Palacios de la Villa* [2007] ECR I-8531.

[84] Case C-303/06 *Coleman* [2008] ECR I-5605; Case C-13/05 *Chacón Navas* [2006] ECR I-6467.

[85] Case 293/83 *Gravier* [1986] ECR 593; Case 39/86 *Lair* [1988] ECR 3161; Case 24/86 *Blaizot* [1988] ECR 379.

[86] Case C-184/99 *Grzelczyk* [2001] ECR I-6193; Case C-224/98 *d'Hoop* [2002] ECR I-6191; Case C-258/04 *Ioannidis* [2005] ECR I-8275.

[87] A Somek, *Individualism: An Essay on the Authority of the European Union* (Oxford, Oxford University Press, 2008).

[88] Scharpf, 'The Asymmetry of European Integration' (n 3), 222–23.

[89] Ibid, 227.

[90] RD Kelemen, *Eurolegalism: the Transformation of Law and Regulation in the European Union* (Cambridge, Harvard University Press, 2011).

[91] N Fligstein, *Euroclash: The EU, European Identity, and the Future of Europe* (Oxford, Oxford University Press, 2008).

involved in adjudicating on social rights, this has the effect in practice of substituting protection of individual rights, for the pursuit of collective entitlements. Thus, for instance, the right to health privileges those who are able to bring litigation, who, by definition, are not the poorest and most vulnerable members of a society, whose health is most in need of protection.[92]

The debate is not identical in the EU context. The political arrangements in the EU, in particular the relationships between the legislature and the courts, are different to those in (federal) states. The EU legislature is probably more constrained by blocking vetoes than national legislatures.[93] What is litigated in cases such as *Kohll* is freedom to move, not social rights per se. But the context is not so different. This is not a new debate—it has been discussed by (constitutional) courts in the context of litigating social rights the world over. Just as those (constitutional) courts take into account the different constitutional contexts when they adjudicate on social rights, and consider the collective solidarity-based arrangements that would be disrupted if they were to undermine national social welfare systems by holding an aspect of them unconstitutional,[94] so can the CJEU—as the re-imagined judgment illustrates.

Again, imagining a different jurisprudence requires imagining that the CJEU is not entirely constrained by legal formalism.[95] The re-imagined judgment includes attention to and explicit analysis of the substantive economic or social problems, the national situation and the rationales for the policy responses that are under challenge by the litigation.[96] The judicial account of the facts is redrawn, so as to pay attention to those broader policy implications of the litigation at hand. It involves a discussion of the implications of a decision in favour of *this* particular litigant in the context of its *collective* effects on national policy (in law and in practice). While there are certainly examples of constitutional courts tackling

---

[92] The counter-argument to this claim points out that well-chosen 'test cases' can have the effect of forcing policy change that improves the position of everyone, including the least well off. The Treatment Action Campaign case in South Africa, for instance, was very carefully chosen, and was not an isolated piece of litigation, but part of a carefully orchestrated political and educational campaign. See A Belani, 'The South African Constitutional Court's Decision in TAC: A "Reasonable" Choice?' (2007) *Center for Human Rights and Global Justice Working Paper: Economic, Social and Cultural Rights Series no 7*; CR Sunstein, 'Social and Economic Rights-Lessons from South Africa' (2000), 11 *Constitutional Forum* 123; KG Young, 'Minimum Core of Economic and Social Rights: A Concept in Search of Content' (2008) 33 *Yale Journal of International Law* 113.

[93] On EU legislative (and other) decision-making see J Peterson and E Bomberg, 'Decision-Making in the European Union' (Basingstoke, Macmillan, 1999).

[94] See, eg the judgments in the Women's Court of Canada project (n 7).

[95] For a discussion of the multiple meanings of legal formalism, especially in European contexts, see J d'Aspremont, *Formalism and the Sources of International Law* (Oxford, Oxford University Press, 2011) 12–29; for the US context, see, eg the review of the history of legal realism at Yale, L Kalman *Legal Realism at Yale: 1927–1960* (Chapel Hill, University of North Carolina Press, 1986) reviewed in J Singer, 'Review Essay: Legal Realism Now' (1988) 76 *California Law Review* 465; CE Clark and DM Trubek, 'The Creative Role of the Judge: Restraint and Freedom in the Common Law Tradition' (1961) 71 *Yale Law Journal* 255; review essay on BN Cardozo *The Nature of the Legal Process* (New Haven, Yale University Press, 1921) and K Llewellyn, *The Common Law Tradition: Deciding Appeals* (Boston, Little, Brown, 1960); more recently see, eg BZ Tamanaha, *A General Jurisprudence of Law and Society* (Oxford, Oxford University Press, 2001); BZ Tamanaha, *Beyond the Formalist-Realist Divide: The Role of Politics in Judging* (Princeton, Princeton University Press, 2009); B Leiter, 'Legal Realism and Legal Positivism Reconsidered' (2001) 111 *Ethics* 278.

[96] The importance of such contextual information is particularly highlighted by the feminist judgments projects, see R Hunter, 'Can *Feminist* Judges Make a Difference?' (2008) 15 *International Journal of the Legal Profession* 7, 12; R Hunter, 'An Account of Feminist Judging' in Hunter, McGlynn and Rackley (eds), *Feminist Judgments* (n 7), 37–40.

social rights litigation using individual-focused approaches,[97] there are also examples of judicial contextual reasoning which considers the institutional, collective or policy implications of a particular decision, on which to draw in the imagining.[98]

And just as other courts use (legal) concepts such as social solidarity; social services of general interest; and proportionality, reasonableness or margin of appreciation to resolve such disputes, so could the CJEU as the re-imagined judgment illustrates. Re-imagining includes re-imagining the CJEU's decision that it is up to the CJEU to decide which mandatory requirements/objective public interests are acceptable, through its application of the (de facto flexible, though currently inflexibly interpreted) proportionality principle. One possibility for the CJEU would be to 'recognise a sphere of national autonomy in which purposes of public policy and the measures through which these are to be realised should be chosen by democratically legitimated political processes',[99] perhaps drawing on the doctrine of 'margin of appreciation' found in the jurisprudence of the European Court of Human Rights.

The aspects of the re-imagined judgment concerning social rights, social services of general interest and solidarity, reveal the fallacy of EU exceptionalism implicit in the constitutional asymmetry position. Certainly, the EU is not *identical* to other legal orders. But it is not so different as to be *incomparable*. And the ability to compare means that we can learn from other (constitutional and international) courts.

---

[97] See, eg the Canadian Supreme Court in *Chaoulli v Quebec (Attorney General)*, [2005] 1 SCR 791, 2005 SCC 35.

[98] In the context of the 'right to health', see, eg AE Yamin and O Parra-Vera, 'How Do Courts Set Health Policy? The Case of the Colombian Constitutional Court' (2009) 6 *PLoS Medicine* e1000032; AE Yamin and O Parra-Vera, 'Judicial Protection of the Right to Health in Colombia: From Social Demands to Individual Claims to Public Debates' (2009) 33 *Hastings International and Comparative Law Review* 431; *Paschim Banga Khet Mazdoor Samity v State of West Bengal* [1996] INSC 659 (6 May 1996); *Rakesh Chandra Narayan v State of Bihar*, AIR 1989 SC 348; *Bandhua Mukti Morcha*, AIR 1984 SC 811; *Common Cause v Union of India*, AIR 1996 SC 929, 929; *Sheeraz Latif Ahmad Khan, Right to Health*, 2 SCJ 29, 30 (1995) (quoting AIR 1995 SC 636); *Mahendra Pratap Singh v State of Orissa*, AIR 1997 Ori 37, 37; cited in SB Shah, 'Illuminating the Possible in the Developing World: Guaranteeing the Human Right to Health in India' (1999) 32 *Vanderbilt Journal of Transnational Law* 435; *Government of the Republic of South Africa v Grootboom* 2000 11 BCLR 1169 (CC); *Minister of Health v Treatment Action Campaign (TAC)* 2002 (10) BCLR 1075 (CC), see EB Kramer, '"No One May Be Refused Emergency Medical Treatment"—Ethical Dilemmas in South African Emergency Medicine' (2008) 1 *South African Journal of Bioethics and Law* 53; CR Sunstein 'Social and Economic Rights? Lessons from South Africa' (2001) *University of Chicago, Public Law Working Paper No 12; University of Chicago Law & Economics, Olin Working Paper No 124*; O'Connell, Vindicating Socio-Economic Rights (n 2); EC Christiansen, 'Adjudicating Non-Justiciable Rights: Socio-Economic Rights and the South African Constitutional Court' 38 *Columbia Human Rights Law Review* 321; J Dugard, 'Court of First Instance? Towards a Pro-poor Jurisdiction for the South African Constitutional Court' (2006) 22 *South African Journal on Human Rights* 261; L Forman, 'Ensuring Reasonable Health: Health Rights, the Judiciary, and South African HIV/AIDS Policy' 33 *The Journal of Law, Medicine & Ethics* 711; MS Kende, 'The South African Constitutional Court's Embrace of Socio-Economic Rights: A Comparative Perspective' (2003) 6 *Chapman Law Review* 137; M Khan, 'Role of Courts in Protecting Socio-Economic Rights' (2008) *SSRN Papers*, available at ssrn.com/abstract=1903648; M Khosla, 'Making Social Rights Conditional: Lessons from India' (2010) 8 *International Journal of Constitutional Law* 739; T Roux, 'Principle and Pragmatism on the Constitutional Court of South Africa' (2009) 7 *International Journal of Constitutional Law* 106; M Tushnet, 'Social Welfare Rights and the Forms of Judicial Review' (2004) 82 *Texas Law Review* 1895.

[99] Scharpf, 'The Asymmetry of European Integration' (n 3), 231.

V. Conclusion: The Limitations and Promise
of 'Imaginative Jurisprudence'

In conclusion, I offer some brief reflections on the process of re-writing the *Kohll* judgment, and on what this kind of critical legal scholarship can add to the academy.

It was *difficult* to write the re-imagined judgment! In part, as the editors of the English Feminist Judgments projects also report,[100] this is because, as I experienced it in the process of preparing this chapter, judicial writing is different from normal academic writing. In normal academic writing, it is quite usual to be explicit about the contingency of claims about truth that one makes, to be tentative about claims to truth, or explore different ways of looking at a contentious issue without reaching a conclusion as to how it should be resolved. Academics can offer a critique (either internal/immanent or external/normative) without coming up with a positive alternative. I am as guilty of this (if 'guilty' is the right word) as others. Judicial writing is experienced as different, and distinctive in nature.[101] Judges must decide. To do so, they must assert facts as truths.[102] They must apply law to facts, and that involves presenting their claims about truth (how the law applies to the facts) as actual truths, not as truths contingent upon the selection of facts and the interpretation of the law.[103] The need to decide is particularly challenging.[104] Cases such as those taken as exemplars of constitutional asymmetry *are* difficult to decide—by definition. They involve finely-balanced arguments on both sides, and it is not possible to have all the information that one might want in order to reach a decision. What is the appropriate pay-off between what is right for an individual patient, and how this might affect all patients? Is it better to allow free movement of services law to challenge practices in national health-care systems that might well be inefficient, or unnecessarily conservative, as well as overtly protectionist? Or is it better to protect national systems as they currently are from disruption *through litigation*—and perhaps to hope that other processes (such as new governance processes[105]) will bring about desirable changes through policy emulation, perhaps over a longer period of time? Are some kinds of health care (such as hospital care or care involving 'heavy medical infrastructure') more vulnerable than others to the vicissitudes of EU internal market law? What difference do—and should—variations in economic development, types of health care system or health outcomes, make in the relevant Member States at issue in a

---

[100] R Hunter, C McGlynn and E Rackley, 'Feminist Judgments: An Introduction' in Hunter, McGlynn and Rackley (eds), *Feminist Judgments* (n 7), 15 hereinafter Hunter et al, 'Introduction'.

[101] E Rackley, 'The Art and Craft of Writing Judgments: Notes on the Feminist Judgments Project' in Hunter, McGlynn and Rackley (eds), *Feminist Judgments* (n 7), 44; Hunter et al, 'Introduction' (n 100), 17.

[102] Because what I am talking about here is appellate court decision-making, the recounting of facts is separate from fact *finding*, which happens at first instance, see ibid, 15.

[103] See Hunter et al, 'Introduction' (n 100) 15. For more on the legal indeterminacy implicit, see the sources in (n 124) below.

[104] Hunter et al, 'Introduction' (n 100) 17.

[105] On 'new governance' in the EU and other contexts, see M Dawson, *New Governance and the Transformation of European Law* (Cambridge, Cambridge University Press, 2011); G de Búrca and J Scott (eds), *Law and New Governance in the EU and the US* (Oxford, Hart Publishing, 2006); J Scott and DM Trubek, 'Mind the Gap: Law and New Approaches to Governance in the European Union' (2002) 8 *European Law Journal* 1; DM Trubek and LG Trubek, 'Hard and Soft Law in the Construction of Social Europe: the Role of the Open Method of Co-ordination' (2005) 11 *European Law Journal* 343.

particular case? 'Imaginative jurisprudence' must go further than asking these questions: for better or worse, it must propose a positive decision, and justify it.

And yet judicial and academic writing are not so different. Both judicial and academic writing involve creativity—they are an 'art', not a science.[106] The actual decision in a judgment is not the whole of the judgment; otherwise judgments would be just one or two lines long. Crafting a judgment is in some senses like any piece of creative writing; it seeks to convey meaning, or a 'message', using text to do so.[107] Thus 'imaginative jurisprudence' seeks to employ text in order to evoke a response, to persuade, a reader or readers. Part of the task involves using words to involve the reader in a process of moving from facts to law to a decision.[108] A key device here is the narrative—the recounting of the story (the 'facts') in a particular way.[109] The author guides the reader along, following the conventions of judicial writing, so that ultimately the reader is convinced of the 'rightness', the 'legality' of the decision reached.

In reaching a decision in a specific case, a re-imagined judgment must therefore be credible to its readers. I found three main challenges in this respect: consistency with legislative texts; consistency with previous jurisprudence; and developing a persuasive style of reasoning. In democratic organisations, courts cannot radically depart from the law as developed by the legislature. This is also true of the CJEU, although the texts of the EU's treaties and secondary legislation are often extremely general in their formulation, and this is the case with the Treaty provisions at issue in *Kohll*. In this respect, credibility was not too much of a challenge: the re-imagined *Kohll* judgment is consistent with the text of the Treaties.[110]

Although the CJEU is not formally bound by its previous rulings, its normal practice (in common with all courts) is to follow them.[111] Of course, legal precedents are flexible—they can be read broadly (establishing a general rule applying to many situations) or narrowly (applicable only to specific facts). Certainly where courts use a common law method, the scope of legal rules or principles is thus developed and refined over time. Even so, in order to be credible in this respect, the re-imagined *Kohll* judgment relies on other, earlier re-imagined judgments, in particular a re-imagined *ERT* that lays the basis for the idea of fundamental (social) rights as embedded in internal market law, which replaces the rule/ exception construction. Part of the reason for this element of the re-imagined judgment was the need to determine which norms were applicable as 'the binding law'. The decision relies on the notion that social rights are binding law in cases such as the re-imagined *Kohll*. It was not, in my view, possible to reach this position credibly in *Kohll* without relying

---

[106] On the 'art' of legal writing, and its relationships to non-legal writing, see, eg JB White, *The Legal Imagination (abridged version)* (Chicago, University of Chicago Press, 1985) especially 207–42.

[107] 'The message of poem ... is not its meaning; likewise, the message (or rule) of the judicial opinion is not its meaning ... The meaning of a poem is not its paraphrase, but the experience of reading it', ibid, 214–15. See also, JB White, *Justice as Translation: An Essay in Cultural and Legal Criticism* (Chicago, University of Chicago Press, 1990) xi–xii.

[108] White, *The Legal Imagination* (106), 224–27.

[109] See further below.

[110] Although it imagines earlier cases that interpret them in different ways than they have been interpreted to date.

[111] Examples where the CJEU has not done so illustrate this point in their very infamy: eg see the development from Case 1/58 *Stork* ECR English special edition, p 17 to Case 29/69 *Stauder* [1969] ECR 419; Case 120/79 *Cassis de Dijon* [1979] ECR 649 to Joined Cases C-267/91 and C-268/91 *Keck and Mithouard* [1993] ECR I-6097.

on re-imagined earlier precedents.[112] The precedents established in cases such as *Cassis* are read in the re-imagined *ERT* as not so broad that they require a strict proportionality assessment of whether rules whose underlying policy is to protect human rights constitute unjustifiable restrictions on free movement of services. The legal device of distinguishing is used to develop a different line of re-imagined jurisprudence for human rights-based policies that restrict free movement. This allows, in the re-imagined *Kohll*, a credible distinguishing of social services of general interest, which protect such social rights, from those ordinary private services at issue in the foundational precedents of the CJEU.[113] The device of earlier, re-imagined judgments was necessary to reach the conclusion in the re-imagined *Kohll*. Without the re-imagined *ERT*, the re-imagined *Kohll* would have departed too far from the CJEU's jurisprudence, and lost credibility for that reason.

Equally, the challenge of writing a persuasively-reasoned judgment was significant. In the re-imagined *Kohll*, the CJEU relies not (only) on formalistic deduction of consequences from abstract rules (whether those rules are determined positivistically, and followed deductively through syllogism (the 'civil law' method); or determined through *stare decisis* and applied by analogy (the 'common law method')). The CJEU also deals explicitly with policy, moral and institutional analysis—it understands the application of abstract rules ('restrictions on freedom of movement of services within the EU are prohibited, unless justified') in the context of what institutional arrangements are made for the provision of the specific service at issue; what type of service it is (a social service of general interest); what policy aims the service provision seeks to achieve (inter alia respect for and protection of the right to health care); whom the service seeks to protect; the models of solidarity upon which European health systems are built; and the broader collective consequences following from a decision that is taken one way or another. Constitutional courts regularly deal explicitly with these types of questions—and do so without departing from defensible judicial practice. Hence, the re-imagined *Kohll* that has the CJEU doing so is credible[114]—it imagines that the CJEU remains constrained by the requirements of judicial reasoning that lend such credibility, but it departs from the particular version of legal formalism upon which the constitutional asymmetry position is founded.

The method of 'imaginative jurisprudence', as I have used it here, is grounded in comparative legal methodologies.[115] Key sources for the re-imagined *Kohll* are both the rulings and (more importantly) the *rationes* of other (constitutional) courts on the right to health care (and other social rights) from across the world. Although I was limited by my linguistic inadequacies to texts available in the English language, I did not confine myself to European sources here, but drew on jurisdictions including Canada, Columbia, India and South Africa. In terms of re-imagining the more fundamental aspects of the CJEU's jurisprudence (in particular, what it considers the EU's purpose, and the integration process, as *for*), as

---

[112] Others may disagree—sometimes courts, including the CJEU, do depart significantly from earlier rulings without distinguishing them on the facts.

[113] See, eg Case 33/74 *Van Binsbergen* [1974] ECR 1299; Case C-55/94 *Gebhard* [1995] ECR I-4165.

[114] If pushed, I admit that the re-imagined judgment reads much more like an Opinion of one of the CJEU's Advocates General than of the CJEU itself.

[115] On comparative constitutional law, see M Tushnet, 'The Inevitable Globalisation of Constitutional Law' (2009) 49 *Vanderbilt Journal of Transnational Law* 985; R Hirschl, 'Comparative Law: The Continued Renaissance of Comparative Constitutional Law' (2010) 45 *Tulsa Law Review* 771. Of course, the method need not be so rooted: as the feminist judgments projects demonstrate, the sources for imaginative judgments could equally include, for instance, political or social theory.

well as national constitutional courts' ideas,[116] I drew on other institutional organisations within Europe that also support the aims of peace and development (particularly the Council of Europe, but also the OECD, WHO (Europe), and even the World Bank and the IMF). The method thus also involves comparative international law.

Credible 'imaginative jurisprudence' may not invent facts. Like the real thing, it must draw on whatever facts are available, although there is space for exercising imagination, or stressing possible interpretations of facts as if they were *the facts*,[117] especially where facts are missing. Judicial story-telling (recounting of facts, selecting which facts to stress and which to exclude), though presented as neutral and excluding irrelevant facts,[118] plays a crucial role in constructing legal arguments—the description of the facts determines as well as describes. Recounting the facts, which lead to the apparently incontrovertible legal conclusion, goes fundamentally to the cogency of a judgment. But it also gives judges a significant discretion in applying law to facts, as well as determining the boundaries between 'law' and 'facts'. And this is not just *which* facts are told; it is also *how* they are told.[119] In the real *Kohll*, the story is told focused around only a single patient: Mr Kohll's daughter. The re-imagined *Kohll* casts its net wider, and brings into the story 'a million Mr Kohlls' daughters':

> It is clear that reimbursement of the costs of dental treatment for a single patient, such as Mr Kohll's daughter, provided in another Member State, in accordance with the tariff of the State of insurance, has only a marginal effect on the financing of Luxembourg's social security system. However, in the context of the obligation of Luxembourg to respect, protect and fulfil the right to health of all persons insured within the Luxembourg system, the effect on Luxembourg's social security system—and indeed those of other Member States—of unlimited movement of patients insured within that system must also be considered.

The conclusion that reasonable restrictions on free movement of health care services are permissible in this context is supported by this version of the facts. A different telling of the story, in a way that radically reframes the issues, allows for a credible reframing (even, potentially, a radical reframing) of the legal response.[120] Opening up to question the 'accepted' notions of the facts is fundamental to critical legal scholarship, and this is something that 'imaginative jurisprudence' can demonstrate particularly effectively.

Taking this point further, if we were to rewrite cases such as *Viking* or *Laval* or *Rüffert*, we might begin from the position that the effect on Western/Northern EU Member States of the presence of Eastern or Central European workers or service providers is very much a matter of opinion, and clear incontrovertible facts are not available. Likewise, if we were to rewrite cases such as *Commission v Austria*, the effects on education systems of free moving

---

[116] See, eg the German Constitutional Court's decisions, such as 2 BvrfG 2/08 *Gauweiler v Treaty of Lisbon* 30 June 2009; *Wünsche Handelsgesellschaft* [1987] 3 CMLR 225; *Internationale Handelsgesellschaft* [1974] 2 CMLR 540; or the Polish Constitutional Court in K 18/04 *Polish Membership of the European Union (Accession Treaty)* 11 May 2005.

[117] The concept of 'judicial notice' is deployed in this respect, certainly in the English context, see Hunter et al, 'Introduction' (n 100).

[118] Rackley, 'The Art and Craft of Writing Judgments' (n 101), 45, citing Lord Neuberger 'First Instance Judgments: Some suggestions' unpublished paper 2009.

[119] Ibid, 46, citing R Posner, 'Judges' Writing Styles (And Do They Matter?)' (1995) 62 *University of Chicago Law Review* 1421; R Hunter, 'An Account of Feminist Judging' (n 96), 37–40.

[120] On the relationships between story-telling and judicial writing (and indeed social change), see Rackley (n 101), 45–48; White, *The Legal Imagination* (n 106) and White, *Justice as Translation* (n 107).

students are unclear. Even more fundamentally, what the EU is, or is for, is not a factual matter—a retelling of that 'fact' makes a crucial difference to the legal consequences that follow. We could imagine a credible rewriting of such seminal cases in EU law as *Van Gend en Loos*,[121] or *Internationale Handsegesellschaft*[122] that takes EU law in a quite different direction to that in which it actually developed.

It should be clear by now that the point here is not that the CJEU can decide cases according to whim. Rather, the point is that it is credible to reason and decide complex constitutional cases, such as *Kohll*, in different ways.[123] As well as doing so by relying on different accounts of the facts, to some extent, the law is also indeterminate.[124] Legal rules alone do not determine judicial decisions. They are too vague to do so, and it is perfectly legitimate for courts to interpret legal concepts (such as 'proportionality', 'reasonableness' or 'discretion') in different ways. Thus it is open to courts (here the CJEU) to choose between different interpretations of the law, and different possible applications of law to facts in the cases before them.

Which brings me to my final point. What 'imaginative jurisprudence' demonstrates—powerfully—is that (EU) law is not necessarily reified in the way that it we currently understand it to be. The version of legal formalism that underpins the constitutional asymmetry position is *not* the only credible basis upon which the CJEU may develop its jurisprudence. It can be reread, and rewritten, in many different ways. Each decision applying a rule is a 'performative act', a (re-)creation of the law anew,[125] an exercise of legal imagination. In exploring how the CJEU's jurisprudence could have been, 'imaginative jurisprudence' implicitly explores how it could be in the future.[126] This is not to say that 'imaginative jurisprudence' *automatically* supports the type of socially progressive agenda for EU law that I pursue in this chapter. It is perfectly feasible to imagine, for instance, CJEU jurisprudence that retains the notion that the EU does not aim to protect social rights, yet respects the autonomy of the Member States to protect and fulfil such social rights, and will not interfere with genuine attempts to do so. That is a summary of the normative position adopted by Scharpf and others. Equally, it is perfectly feasible to imagine a CJEU jurisprudence that is even more supportive of free trade and open competition than the status quo, and which therefore undermines national social welfare systems, and the social services of general interest on which they are based, even further. Indeed, legal formalism may be a (partial) protection against the politicisation of courts in such a way.[127]

---

[121] Case 26/62 *Van Gend en Loos* [1963] ECR 1. See P Pescatore, 'The Doctrine of Direct Effect: An "Infant Disease" of Community law' (1993) 8 *European Law Review* 155.

[122] Case 11/70 *Internationale Handsegesellschaft* [1970] ECR 1125.

[123] Hunter et al, 'Introduction' (n 100), 3; Hunter, 'The Power of Feminist Judgments?' (n 7), 137.

[124] A position that David Trubek has recognised in much of his writing, see, eg DM Trubek, 'Where the Action Is: Critical Legal Studies and Empiricism' (1984) 36 *Stanford Law Review* 575, 577–79, citing eg S Macaulay, 'Non-Contractual Relations in Business: A Preliminary Study' (1963) 28 *American Sociological Review* 55; S Macaulay, 'Private Legislation and the Duty to Read' (1966) 19 *Vanderbilt Law Review* 1051; D Kennedy, 'Form and Substance in Private Law Adjudication' (1976) 89 *Harvard Law Review* 1685; D Kennedy, 'Legal Formality' (1973) 2 *Journal of Legal Studies* 351. Like Dave, I find the 'critique of legal order' 'exhilarating', rather than 'paralysing' (Trubek, 'Where the Action Is' 579).

[125] Derrida, 'Force of Law' (n 59), 961.

[126] Even where a line of legal authority has been apparently incontrovertibly established, it is possible to distinguish, or even to change tack entirely; see, eg the examples cited in n 111 above.

[127] See M Koskenniemi, 'What is International Law For?' in MD Evans (ed), *International Law* (Oxford, Oxford University Press, 2010) 53. Thanks to Richard Collins for directing me to this point.

The formality of judicial reasoning is not as constraining as the 'constitutional asymmetry' version of legal formalism implies. 'Imaginative jurisprudence' thus reveals the underlying assumptions upon which the CJEU has developed its reasoning. The process of re-imagining CJEU jurisprudence not only shows that the CJEU's approach is but one of a number of plausible alternatives, but also implies that the CJEU's approach is insufficiently justified and defended against those alternatives. The assumptions upon which the CJEU relies are not incontrovertible, but must be defended and justified, just as the proponents of a 'social rights' agenda must defend and justify their underlying assumptions. Constitutional asymmetry is thus 'rebalanced': the assumptions on which is it based are just as much up for discussion as those of the social rights agenda, rather than occupying a position of incontrovertible acceptance and indeed invisibility.[128] If we value transparency in judicial reasoning, as an essential component in its credibility, and the underlying notion of the rule of law, then 'imaginative jurisprudence' points the way to a broader, hence richer, debate on the key issues at stake in such constitutional decision-making: what the relationships between liberalism and social rights should be; who should decide, and according to what procedures and principles, in a multi-level context such as that of the EU? Thus the most powerful contribution of 'imaginative jurisprudence' is to bring to light the imbalances of power that are embedded in the unequal requirements to account for, for instance, liberal market and social market preferences in terms of a discussion of what, and whom, the EU (or any constitutionalised or multilevel legal system) is *for*.

Of course, I acknowledge that rewriting judgments is limited as a method of political activism or a way of seeking broader social change or otherwise challenging the status quo. Judgments are a 'constrained and bounded genre'.[129] 'Imaginative jurisprudence' is also limited as an agent of social change in the sense that it accepts the bases of law and its authority.[130] In adopting that view, I implicitly accept 'law's image of itself as a force for good'.[131] So—in the context of EU law—this means accepting EU law's claims to power, and to articulate truths. Equally, I am not arguing for a departure from all constraints of legal formalism: 'imaginative jurisprudence' (as in the feminist judgments projects[132]) requires that the standard values inherent in the idea of the rule of law (consistency with legislative texts, consistency with previous jurisprudence, persuasive reasoning) be followed. After all, as noted above, legal formalism may provide (some limited) protection from unconstrained judicial politics; and there is nothing to guarantee a CJEU that is sensitive to social justice, were we to remove all constraints on its decision-making. However, as I have deployed it here, 'imaginative jurisprudence' does attempt to tackle 'power and authority

---

[128] Thanks to Dimitrios Kyritisis for directing me to these points.

[129] Hunter et al, 'Introduction' (n 100) 5. See also White, *Justice as Translation* (n 107), 89ff.

[130] It is not a Critical method in that sense. This is also recognised in Hunter et al, 'Introduction' (n 100), and Hunter, 'The Power of Feminist Judgments' (n 7). On the different types of Critical and critical legal scholarship, see R Cryer, T Hervey, B Sokhi-Bulley and A Bohm, *Research Methodologies in EU and International Law* (Oxford, Hart Publishing, 2011). The promise, and limitations, of other forms of critical method, including the use of fiction, have been explored by other scholars, see, eg S Motha, 'As If: Constitutional Narratives and "Forms of Life"', forthcoming in Karin Van Marle and Stewart Motha (eds), *Genres of Critique: Law, Liminality, and Literature in South Africa* (Stellenbosch University Press, forthcoming).

[131] Hunter et al, 'Introduction' (n 100), citing C Smart *Feminism and the Power of Law* (London, Routledge, 1989).

[132] See Hunter, 'Can *Feminist* Judges Make a Difference?' (n 96) 15ff, and Hunter, 'An Account of Feminist Judging' (n 96), 30-35.

not from the distance of critique but on [law's] own ground'.[133] It seeks to uncover, and thus disturb, the power relations embedded in the current situation,[134] and it seeks to harness law—classically very much a servant of those already empowered—to do so. In this respect, 'imaginative jurisprudence' is ultimately a subversive activity.[135] But it is not subversion for its own sake—it has an aim, which is law reform.[136] 'Imaginative jurisprudence' harnesses law's power as an important social discourse which creates and reinforces social constructs and communities.[137] Re-imagining judgments involves retelling those narratives, and thus disrupting the 'received wisdom'—a version of truth that invariably privileges certain (human or legal) persons or commodities over others.[138] In this context, ultimately it involves reimagining what, and whom, EU law is for, and fundamentally what the EU is.

---

[133] See Hunter et al, 'Introduction' (n 100) 8.

[134] See Hunter 'The Power of Feminist Judgments' (n 7).

[135] Hunter et al, 'Introduction' (n 100) 8 draws an analogy with the parodic activity of drag artists, which subverts and undermines gender norms.

[136] See, eg Hunter et al,Introduction' (n 100); Hunter, 'The Power of Feminist Judgments' (n 7), 137, 146; McNamara, *Reputation and Defamation* (n 7), 229–32.

[137] White, *Justice as Translation* (n 107), 101–102.

[138] Trubek, 'Where the Action Is' (n 124), 591–95.

17

Social, Economic and Cultural Rights and Economic Development: Limiting or Reinforcing the Market?

HELENA ALVIAR GARCÍA

In 2004 two influential legal academics, Uprimny and García, published an article celebrating the potential for 'emancipation' of Constitutional Court rulings in Colombia. The authors defined emancipation as an impulse against hegemonic capitalism. In the introduction, they described Constitutional Judges' interventions in the following terms: 'The work of the Constitutional Court has been enormous, not only in terms of the number and variety of rulings but because it has surprised Colombian society with a range of progressive rulings.'[1]

On the opposite side of the spectrum, neoclassical economists violently attacked the Court's adjudication on social and economic rights (the same rights that were being celebrated by Uprimny and García) because they interfered with the market and signalled a violation of the separation of powers, and because decisions were taken by individuals with no knowledge of economics.[2]

The objective of this chapter is to provide a different view on this debate. In my opinion, even though it is true that many Court rulings have been able to limit market-oriented reforms, they have not significantly transformed the distribution of resources within Colombian society. Instead, they have privileged the existing status quo, protecting the middle classes who have access to the legal system, and strengthening the individualistic rights-based approach to social policy.

This goal is closely linked to my work over the last few years aimed at understanding why—notwithstanding what some have described as progressive constitutional provisions and legal reforms—Colombia continues to be characterised by high levels of inequalities in wealth among class, gender and race. My aim is to understand the role played by laws, administrative regimes and legal institutions to structurally limiting the progressive impulse of constitutional provision or legal reform.

---

[1] R Uprimny and M García Villegas, 'The Constitutional Court and the Social Emancipation in Colombia' in B de Sousa Santos (ed), *Democratizing Democracy: Beyond the Liberal Democratic Canon* (London, Verso, 2005).

[2] For more on these critiques see H Alviar, '¿Quién Paga o Debe Pagar por el Estado Social de Derecho?' (2009) 22 *Revista de Derecho Público* 1, available at derechopublico.uniandes.edu.co/components/com_revista/archivos/derechopub/pub99.pdf.

LIVERPOOL JOHN MOORES UNIVERSITY
LEARNING SERVICES

In order to do this, this chapter is divided into four parts. In the first section I position this debate within the broader framework of law and development literature. I then describe the historical/legal background that preceded the 1991 Colombian Constitution which included an extensive bill of rights. Finally, I give two examples of how Social and Economic Rights (SER) have interacted with market-oriented economic development plans.

I. The Place of Social and Economic Rights in Law and Development

There are three basic approaches within the literature on the relationship between law and ideas about economic development. The first approach, which I will call classic, is a purely instrumentalist perspective which assumes that economic policies can be easily translated into legal tools and institutions.[3] The use of the word 'translation' comes from David Kennedy, who wrote:

> I use the word 'translation' to highlight the gaps which must be overcome to apply legal or economic ideas. The word apply evokes sense in which the application of such ideas is a matter of argument and persuasion, making an analogy between the context to be addressed and the theoretical framework within which the ideas were developed and refined.[4]

This approach has been the most prevalent among technocrats and policy-makers in developing countries.

Then, there is the instrumentalist law-centred approach, which has a 1960s and a 1990s version. According to the 1960s version, a change in the legal system is a prerequisite to achieve the correct framework to promote economic development. This transformation should establish a liberal legalist paradigm in order to serve as a tool for development. As Trubek and Galanter have explained, this paradigm is a general model that explains

---

[3] This classic instrumentalist approach can be found at different historic moments. When describing a major administrative law reform, one of the most prominent administrative law scholars, Jaime Vidal Perdomo, wrote: 'Reform, then, as we have had the opportunity to show it, is not ideological but instrumental and its centre of gravity is the composition of the branches of government, except for the judicial power, their roles and the relationships between them. The first idea does not mean it does not respond to a conception of the State, since it reflects the inspiration to modernise the instruments of power to suit the requirements of economic and social development and to return to the traditional rules of the partial democratic game transiently altered by the 1957 Plebiscite.' JV Perdomo, *Historia de la reforma constitucional de 1968 y sus alcances jurídicos* (Bogota, Publicaciones de la Universidad Externado de Colombia, 1970) 154. There are many contemporary examples of this classic view. One example in a national planning document (CONPES) of 2005 directed toward the regulation of the financial market, established: 'The contemporary model of state intervention in the economy, which provides that the intervention to regulate economic freedoms will be the exception rather than the rule and will be made only when there are strong justifications.' *Program for the renewal of Public Administration: Institutions reform for the regulation and supervision of the financial market* (2005) (Deparamento Nacional de Planeación (National Planning Department) CONPES 3399) available at www.dnp.gov.co/Portals/0/archivos/documentos/Subdireccion/Conpes/3399.pdf.

[4] D Kennedy, 'Law and Development Economics: Toward a New Alliance' in D Kennedy and JE Stiglitz, *Law and Economics with Chinese Characteristics: Institutions for Promoting Development in the Twenty-first Century* (Oxford, Oxford University Press, 2013).

the relationship between law and society and specifically explains how legal systems and development relate.[5] It contains six basic characteristics:

1. Society consists of individuals, intermediates and the State. The State has the power to coerce individuals and works through individuals. Both the State and intermediates are instruments used by individuals who pursue their own welfare.
2. The State controls individuals through law. It does so according to rules through which the State itself is coerced.
3. Rules are designed to achieve social purposes or attain social principles in a conscious way. The rule-making process is pluralist and there is no systematic advantage of some population over another. Intermediates are the principal actors in the rule-making process because they aggregate individual interests.
4. Rules are enforced equally for all citizens.
5. The legal order applies, interprets and changes universalistic rules. The central institutions of the legal order are the Courts, which have the final say in defining the social significance of law. The typical decisive mode of legal action is adjudication, which follows authoritative rules and doctrine to reach its outcome.
6. The behaviour of social actors tends to follow the rules. When the population does not comply with the rules, officials will enforce them.[6]

On the other hand, in the 1990s the centrality of law was exemplified by the Rule of Law Project promoted by the World Bank.[7]

For the two last approaches law is understood as both a framework and an instrument. In the 1960s it acted as a framework to set in place the liberal legalist model and as an instrument to promote Import Substitution Industrialisation. In the 1990s it acted as a framework to secure market transactions and as an instrument to promote the principles of the Washington Consensus. In summary, both the classical and the law-centred instrumentalist approaches share the same interpretation of the relationship between law and development.

There is a third perspective, the objective of which is to understand the basic assumptions about law held by both lawyers and economists, and how these assumptions create biases and distribute resources. David Trubek and Marc Galanter were among the first academics to study these assumptions and their effects. They describe this analytical impulse in the following terms:

> In the early years of the law and development movement many scholars and assistance officials shared a tacit set of assumptions about the relationship between law and development. In this section we shall set out the basic presuppositions of this paradigm—which we shall call 'liberal legalism'—in the form of a series of propositions about the role of law in society and the relationship between legal systems and development. Only by making the tacit assumptions explicit can we understand and examine the ideas that shaped the early law and development efforts. The task of turning presuppositions into propositions, however, is a difficult one. Although the basic elements

---

[5] DM Trubek and M Galanter, 'Scholars in Self-Estrangement: Some Reflections on the Crisis in Law and Development Studies in the United States' (1974) *Wisconsin Law Review* 1062, 1070–72.

[6] Ibid, 1070–1972.

[7] A Santos, 'The World Bank's Uses of the "Rule of Law" Promise in Economic Development' in DM Trubek and A Santos (eds), *The New Law and Economic Development: A Critical Appraisal* (Cambridge, Cambridge University Press, 2006).

we seek are fundamental, they are also hard to uncover. The analyst must strive to make them clear and explicit, without at the same time distorting or caricaturing them.[8]

This perspective also assumes that there is a dynamic relationship between economic development ideas and law. This dynamic relationship is not only constantly changing according to transformations in laws and institutions as well as changes in styles of legal reasoning, but also allocates resources and gives content to market-oriented ideas of development or State-led distribution. This ever-shifting relationship requires the detailed unpacking of the set of ideas that underlie the role of law.[9] In addition, it entails understanding the multiple ways in which legal transformations as well as theories about law have shifted historically, the way in which law structures the market, the interaction among the different branches of government when targeting a development policy,[10] the choices that policymakers, legislators and judges make about the best way to reach a development goal[11] and the clash between policy design and social and economic rights.

II. Background that Preceded the 1991 Colombian Constitution

This chapter assumes that there is an intimate relationship between economic development ideas, social policies and the role of the State. During the period from the late 1960s to the late 1980s, industrialisation, coupled with policies aimed at increasing saving and attracting foreign direct investment, were the main economic development ideas. Social policy was incorporated to support the aim of achieving full employment. The achievement of full employment required a more active State, with the understanding that only through creating the conditions of formal, well-paid jobs would a virtuous cycle occur that would increase consumption and demand. Social policies aimed at poverty alleviation were focused on removing structural barriers to full participation in the market.

One example of this is the Colombian National Development Plan of 1970 to 1973, which states that: 'There is a need to consider employment as a fundamental objective of the economic development process, and not as a sub-product of the interaction of other variables.'[12] This assumes that employment is a fundamental objective of the economic development

---

[8] Trubek and Galanter, 'Scholars in Self-Estrangement' (n 5) 1070.

[9] This discussion about the role of law is greatly influenced by Duncan Kennedy's work. See D Kennedy, 'Three Globalizations of Law and Legal Thought: 1850–2000' in Trubek and Santos (eds), *The New Law and Economic Development* (n 7); D Kennedy, 'The Stakes of Law, or Hale and Foucault!' in D Kennedy, *Sexy Dressing etc: Essays on the Power and Politics of Cultural Identity* (Cambridge, Cambridge University Press, 1993) and David Kennedy's work on law and development, specifically, Kennedy, 'Law and Development Economics' (n 3) and D Kennedy, 'The "Rule of Law" Political Choices, and Development Common Sense' in D Trubek and A Santos (eds), *The New Law and Economic Development* (n 7).

[10] As I will describe later in this article, the executive branch has had an enormous amount of power in deciding the form and content of social policies in the Colombian context. However, over time this power has been restrained in different ways by both the judiciary and the legislature.

[11] It is not obvious that a development policy should automatically be supported by public law or that criminal law is the only way to prevent undesired behaviour.

[12] Departamento Nacional de Planeación, *Plan Nacional de Desarrollo (Colombian National Development Plan)* 1969–1972; Departamento Nacional de Planeación, *Plan Nacional de Desarrollo (National Development Plan)* 1970–73, available at www.dnp.gov.co/LinkClick.aspx?fileticket=tVPsLE8wyk8%3d&tabid=66.

process, and not a by-product of the interaction of other variables. In addition, the social security system was reorganised and strengthened during this period. As a consequence, support for was extended from working-class benefits to benefits for families, pensions for widows and unemployment insurance. Rural workers also enjoyed these benefits.

Thus, from the late 1960s to the late 1980s, there was a major change in the institutional setting and the legal framework of the field. In 1968, there was a fundamental constitutional amendment which significantly increased the power of the president. This reform was characterised by a strong emphasis on economic issues which gave the State a number of tools to enable it to fully carry out its intervention function. This constitutional transformation was based on the idea that in order to reach the objectives of development (industrialisation with some degree of distribution which would increase the demand for goods and services) Colombia needed to completely change the organisation of the State. In order to do this it had to restructure public institutions into a wide range of public and semi-public enterprises: Mixed Public and Private Partneships, Industrial and Commercial Companies of the State and Public Establishments (*Sociedades de Economía Mixta, Empresas Industriales y Comerciales del Estado, Establecimientos Públicos*) that shared some characteristics of private sector enterprises but were run by central government technocrats.[13]

As a result of this change, during this period a whole system of government was put in place through administrative acts (presidential decrees)[14] with little or no participation from Congress and little individual right litigation. Judges were largely absent from this framework, except for a series of cases brought to court over individual pension agreements.[15]

From the late 1980s to the late 1990s the Colombian development strategy shifted from promoting industrialisation and full employment to strengthening the competitive mechanisms of the market as the only suitable way to achieve economic growth. Import Substitution Industrialisation (ISI) policies were gradually abandoned in favour of free trade[16] and strong market institutions.

The abandonment of full employment as a primary objective of development policy had a tremendous impact both on social policies and their interaction with the legal framework. Workers' benefits were eliminated and direct State investment in health and education was reduced. Rural poverty alleviation programmes were greatly weakened due

---

[13] According to academics writing during this period, the administrative reform of 1968 tried to promote a more centralised, apolitical, technocratic, institutional setting through the creation of a range of state enterprises and the strengthening of the government to handle economic matters. For more information, see V Perdomo, *Historia de la reforma constitucional de 1968 y sus alcances jurídicos* (n 3), 213.

[14] For an in-depth analysis of this reform see C Caballero, 'La impronta de Carlos Lleras Restrepo en la economía colombiana de los años sesenta del siglo XX' (2009) *Revista Estudios socioculturales no 33*, available at www.scielo.org.co/scielo.php?script=sci_arttext&pid=S0123-885X2009000200009; JC Esguerra, 'Carlos Lleras Restrepo y la Reforma Constitucional de 1968' in CL Restrepo, OM Benítez, FV García, JV Perdomo, JC Esguerra, BC Varela and JF Chalela, *Perfil de un Estadista* (Santa Fé de Bogota DC, Ediciones Academia Colombiana de Jurisprudencia, 2000).

[15] Gerardo Arenas describes the period 1977–90: 'At this stage there is a marked influence of the jurisprudence in the development of a social security pension system, as the first justice conflicts over their implementation begin to reach the courthouses. Here the jurisprudence defines important aspects such as the scope of the 'pension-sanction', the definition of when the pensions correspond to the employer, when to the insurance and the decision on the constitutionality of the transit into the Social Insurance.' See GA Monsalve *El derecho colombiano de la seguridad social* 3rd edn (Bogota, Legis, 2011), 89.

[16] The National Development Plan of 1990 establishes two principles in terms of macroeconomic policies. First, free trade and an open economy are basic for development. Second, state 'intervention must not replace the market; it must correct its distortions'. Departamento Nacional de Planeación (National Planning Department), *La Revolución Pacífica*, available at www.dnp.gov.co/PortalWeb/PND/PlanesdeDesarrolloanteriores/tabid/66/Default.aspx.

to a lack of resources. These reforms were accompanied by privatisation of the organisation that provided social benefits. Privatisation was part of the free market import substitution agenda, but it was also an essential part of the critique of neoclassical interventionist policies. Throughout the 1990s a very significant percentage of State-owned enterprises were privatised. As a result, nearly 30,000 employees, according to the government's statistics, and more than 77,000 employees, according to the main Colombian trade union (*Central Unitaria de Trabajadores*), lost their jobs.[17]

Poverty alleviation policies changed their macroeconomic status and became more centered and defined by microeconomics. Social policy shifted from instruments related to promoting formal and total employment, aiding the rural population and at the same time increasing measures to respond to structural violence and poverty,[18] to setting in place cash transfers originally designed to help out households in times of structural adjustment. During the 1990s the *Fondo de Solidaridad y Emergencia Social* was established to provide financial aid for education, health care, sanitation and to improve and strengthen government institutions, and special protection for women, youth and the elderly, as well as emergency employment programmes in the cities and the countryside.[19]

The following table summarises the relationship between economic development, social policies and the role of the State.

Table 1: Economic Development and Social Policy

	Definition of Development	Social Policy	Role of the State
ISI	Industrialisation, urbanisation	Full employment	Central to the design, financing and channelling of services through macroeconomic policy
Neo-liberalism	Export led growth— Free market	Individual, targetted, conditional provisions	When markets fail there is a marginal role for the State to play—microeconomic analysis is prevalent
Post-neo-liberalism	Export led growth— free market with increasing State intervention	Individual, conditional provisions combined with social and economic rights adjudication	The State plays an important role in creating incentives for research and innovation as well sectors to be promoted or protected

---

[17] H Alviar, 'The Classroom and the Clinic: The Relationship Between Clinical Legal Education, Economic Development and Social Transformation' (2008) 13 *UCLA Journal of International Law & Foreign Affairs* 197.

[18] For examples of these policies, see H Alviar, 'Social Policy and the New Development State: The Case of Colombia', Presentation at the LANDS Latin American project workshop, 12–13 May at Cebrap, São Paulo, available at www.law.wisc.edu/gls/documents/helena_alviar_paper.pdf.

[19] J Núñez and L Cuesta, 'Evolución de Las Políticas Contra la Pobreza: de la Previsión Social a las Transferencias Condicionadas' (2006) *Documento CEDE 6-31, Universidad de los Andes* 12.

In summary, from the late 1980s to the late 1990s many workers' benefits were eliminated and direct State investment in health and education was reduced. Nevertheless, there was a significant restriction on the removal of welfare policies. On the one hand, the laws and regulations set in place to minimise the role of the State had to deal with pressing social and economic inequality. On the other hand, privatisation and the elimination of subsidies were restricted by a Constitution that included a generous bill of social and economic rights as well as social corporate responsibility codes aimed at protecting the family unit.[20] Therefore, social and economic rights, including special provisions that demand a guarantee from the State of the protection of human dignity and the provision of education and health to the whole population, provide a background against which any social policy must interact. Therefore, the constitution had a very determinant effect over the content of the norms, the type of regulation established, and the role of judges.

As stated in the introduction, the fact that the Colombian Constitution has an extensive bill of rights and the Constitutional Court has made progressive rulings in terms of SER, does not mean that the distribution of resources and power within Colombian society has been transformed. It has meant, however, that the rights of formal workers have been effectively protected in comparison with the situation before 1991. During this period of time, these rights were covered only by the law but, because of a range of problems including lack of access to justice, they were not effectively protected.[21] In other words, SER have strengthened the liberal welfare State because they have been used to effectively enforce workers' rights. According to the research of Rodrigo Uprimny, Mauricio García and César Rodríguez, roughly 49 per cent of the rulings of the Court have referred to workers' and related rights: the right to health (28.76 per cent) and right to social security (20.59 per cent).[22] More recent data show a similar trend. In this sense and according to the Ombudsman (*Defensoría del Pueblo*), during the period 2009 to 2010 the right to health and social and economic rights represented 52 per cent of all cases brought forward.[23]

Having said this, the 1991 Constitution has provided a limit both for executive branch technocrats and legislators in terms of targeting social policies, putting in place universal coverage in health[24] and education[25] and guaranteeing a minimum wage.[26]

---

[20] The private sector has influenced the configuration of social policy in at least three ways: cooperating with the State on social investment programmes that have subsequently become law; through the creation of independent institutions in charge of social programmes; and more recently, through the establishment of social responsibility codes. Therefore, the dismantling of social policies had to deal with an existing welfare structure promoted by conservative industrialists who were influenced by Catholic ideas of solidarity.

[21] Statistics from the *Departamento Administrativo Nacional de Estadística* (DANE)—National Administrative Statistics Department show that before 1991, more than 50% of labour trials lasted over a year, and more than 30% lasted over two years. See *Departamento Administrativo Nacional de Estadística, La justicia Colombiana en cifras 1937–1994* (Santafé de Bogotaa, DC, Jorge Gómez Vallejo ed, 1996) 226.

[22] M García Villegas, CR Garavito, R Uprimny, *¿Justicia Para todos?: Sistema judicial, derechos sociales y democracia en Colombia* (Bogota, Grupo Editorial Norma, 2009) 359.

[23] Defensoría del Pueblo, *La tutela y el derecho a la salud 2010* (Imprenta Nacional de Colombia, 2011) available at www.acmfr.com/documentos/INFORMEDEFENSORIADELPUEBLO2010.pdf.

[24] For further information on the right to health as a fundamental right see Case T-760 of 2008.

[25] There are many decisions by the Constitutional Court about this subject, among them the most useful Rulings are: T-236 of 2001; T-943 of 2004; C-1109 of 2001; C-673 of 2001; C-925 of 2000.

[26] For example, in 2003 the Constitutional Court declared an increase of 2% in VAT on products considered essential for family subsistence (*canasta familiar*) to be unconstitutional. The Court said that this increase went against the principles of progressivness and equity and would disproportionately affect the poorest in society since most of their income is spent on these goods, Corte Constitucional (Constitutional Court), Sentencia (Ruling) C-776 of 2003, MP (Judge) Manuel Jose Cepeda Espinosa. Along the same lines, in 2001, in a highly

III. SER and Economic Development: Conflict or Complement?

In this section I describe two cases in which market-oriented development policies clashed with rulings of the Constitutional Court. These demonstrate how the interaction between different legal regimes and forms of legal reasoning frame policy-making. After this analysis, I set forth some thoughts about the distributional consequences of this interaction.

A. Right to Housing

In order to understand the background in which market-oriented reforms were set in place, this subsection starts with a brief history of public policy on housing and the legal developments surrounding it. Housing is a very interesting case to illustrate my argument because housing has been understood as both an economic development policy and as a right. I describe two Constitutional Court rulings that brought housing to the table as an SER, and continue with a description of some reactions to the rulings.

i. Historical and Legal Background

Colombia has had a history of State intervention in the housing market since the beginning of the twentieth century up to the new Constitution of 1991.[27] In fact, since the early 1930s the State has created a scheme of financial aid allowing people to have finance available in order to buy their homes.. From this time, access to long-term credit for housing to different groups of the population has been promoted by the creation of various institutions. In the 1930s and 1940s, the main sources of mortgage loans were the Central Mortgage Bank (*Banco Central Hipotecario*—BCH), created in 1932, and the National Loans Institute (*Instituto de Crédito Territorial*—ICT), created in the 1940s. These institutions werein charge of both building for and providing credit to low-income families. Indeed, the State constructed around 20 per cent of low-income housing in cities during this period.

Market-oriented reforms set in place in 1991 were intended to remove the State from financing and building housing solutions.[28] It was copied from the Chilean model, with the characteristic of limiting the State's role to providing a subsidy for housing demand, and leaving the rest to private companies.[29]

---

controversial decision, the Court decided that the salary of low-wage public workers could not be increased below the inflation rate, Corte Constitucional (Constitutional Court), Sentencia (Ruling) C-1064 de 2001, MP (Judge) Jaime Córdoba Triviño.

[27] Colombia lived more than a century under the 1886 Constitution.

[28] According to Art 6 of Law 3 of 1991 which created the *Sistema Nacional de Vivienda de Interés Social*, established the family housing subsidies, and reformed the *Instituto de Crédito Territorial, ICT,* and established that, 'the housing family subsidy is a State compensation in money or goods given for only one time to the beneficiary, with the purpose of providing a housing solutions, without the need for compensation, as long as the beneficiary complies with the conditions established by law'. This subsidy implies that there is no State involvement in the construction or provision of housing.

[29] Following the Chilean model in Colombia the direct participation of the State was abandoned and the only public policy was a direct subsidy to demand, see Adriana Parias Duran in Samuel Jaramillo, *Bogotá En El Cambio De Siglo: Promesas Y Realidades* (Quito, Organización Latinoamericana y del Caribe de Centros Históricos, 2010).

During this period National Development Plans (NDPs)[30] reflect the two main transformations in public policy on housing in Colombia—from a strong State intervention to a privately-financed and operated system.

ii. The Right to Housing: An Effective Limit to the Market?

A fundamental characteristic of housing policy since the 1990s has been its intimate relationship with the availability of credit. Indeed, the fact that the State stopped building houses or directly assigning subsidies, meant that access to housing (in general and for low-income housing in particular) was linked to the financial market. Until 1999, there was a housing finance scheme aimed at both promoting access to credit for the general population and at the same time make it attractive for construction companies and banks to engage in large-scale urban projects. For almost 20 years, the interest rate for a special financial instrument, *Unidad de Poder Adquisitivo Constante* (UPAC, constant purchasing power unit)[31] was pegged to the national inflation rate. In September 1995 the interest rate was linked not to inflation but to the regular interest rate charged by banks, because UPAC was seen as distorting the credit market. This change produced a considerable increase in the amount that debtors were paying for their mortgage loan. As a result, many families saw how their debts increased above the value of their property. Thus, in a relatively short time, these families typically found themselves owing a sum that was several times the amount of the original loan in cash, and more than the current value of the house for which they had contracted the debt.[32] Debtors stopped paying, either because they could not afford it, or because they considered the situation to be unfair. Many families' homes were repossessed by the bank.

In this context, Ruling C-700 of 1999 was issued by the Constitutional Court. The suit was directed at the UPAC finance housing system. The Court argued that the financial system could not be controlled by the market when the right to housing was involved:

> Under Article 51 of the Constitution the norms that Congress issues related to financing of housing in the long term, cannot be uniformly applied to the financial, exchange and insurance systems … but must be linked to the conditions that allow Colombians to own decent housing and to promote social interest housing programs, 'adequate long term financing systems'.[33]

To sum up, the response of the Constitutional Court in this ruling was to declare the UPAC system unconstitutional, based on the above reasons. However, the Court stated that Congress should be in control of designing a new system that complies with Article 51 of the Constitution.

---

[30] As the National Department of Planning says 'the NDP is a formal and legal instrument by which the objectives of a government are established thus allowing the evaluation of its working … according to the Constitution it has a general part and a specific investment plan for national entities'. Departamento Nacional de Planeación, *Qué es el Plan Nacional de desarrollo?* available at www.dnp.gov.co/PND.aspx.

[31] According to Francisco Barreto, this system was created 'as the unit of account of a credit that sought to promote the construction of urban housing on the basis of maintaining the real value of the resources involved'. See F Barreto, *La crisis del sistema UPAC, o el significado de los Derechos Sociales en contextos de cambio en las reglas del juego económico* (on file with the author).

[32] Ibid.

[33] Corte Constitucional (Constitutional Court), Sentencia (Ruling) C-700 of 1999, MP (Judge) José Gregorio Hernández, available at www.corteconstitucional.gov.co/relatoria/1999/C-700-99.

In a ruling the following year[34] the Court reiterated this limit on the market by saying that mortgage interest rates, being crucial to the guarantee of the right to housing, particularly low-income housing, could not be left to the market.[35] In this case the Court demanded State regulation in order to guarantee an interest rate that could protect all housing credit takers. This meant that financing possibilities, in particular when dealing with the exercise of the constitutional right to the acquisition of adequate housing (Articles 51 and 335 of the Colombian Constitution), should be available to everyone, even those on lower incomes. Moreover, the Court emphasised that the right to housing requires the availability of loans to everyone, including those on low incomes.[36]

iii. What Were the Reactions to the Court's Intervention? Who Benefitted from It?

Critics of Constitutional Court's rulings were neoclassical economists and traditional civil court judges. On one hand, neoclassical economists understood the intervention of the Court as unduly interfering in the functioning of both the regulation of financial institutions that should be carried out by the legislature, and the Central Bank. On the other hand, traditional judges saw the ruling as contrary to civil procedure principles and erratic in terms of how foreclosures should end.

In fact, soon after these rulings, Salomón Kalmanovitz, Co-director of the Central Bank at the time, said that 'we, the economists, see with great concern how the Court is making decisions without having adequate knowledge of the field it is referring to and with no consideration of the creation of incentives for citizens not to pay their loans'.[37] He also argued that the Court 'entered constitutionally-defined territories of the Central Bank, the only monetary authority, and predetermined future decisions that Congress should make'.[38]

Civil law judges resisted the ruling for other reasons. The Constitutional Court had ordered all foreclosure procedures begun before 1999 to be immediately suspended in order to protect homeowners who had been affected by the change in the interest rate. Notwithstanding what was said by the Court, civil judges did not stop foreclosures if there was an outstanding debt. These judges argued that the Constitutional Court was not authorised to interpret civil procedure, as the only legitimate interpreter was the Supreme Court; that the Constitutional Court jurisprudence was erratic and contradictory; and that the intervention of the Court on economic matters was inappropriate because this was an issue that should only concern the executive or legislative branch and the Central Bank.[39]

---

[34] Corte Constitucional (Constitutional Court), Sentencia (Ruling) C-955 of 2000, MP (Judge) José Gregorio Hernández, available at www.corteconstitucional.gov.co/relatoria/2000/C-955-00.htm.

[35] Ibid.

[36] Ibid, 'In the mentioned loans, there should be a guaranteed democratization of credit, which means that funding opportunities, particularly when it comes to the constitutional right to acquire decent housing, should be affordable for everyone, even the poor people. Therefore, conditions for too onerous loans, financing systems that make unaffordable loans, high fees, charging uncontrolled high interest rates ... are in violation of the Constitution and must be rejected.'

[37] Salomón Kalmanovitz, 'La Corte Constitucional y la capitalización de intereses', presentation at the conference 'Fallos de la Corte Constitucional en materia económica: ¿Debe el alto tribunal tener en cuenta sólo el derecho? organised by Universidad de los Andes, BID y El Espectador on 23 March 2000, Bogota.

[38] Ibid.

[39] For an analysis of the resistance of civil judges, see MV Alfaro, *Sentencias del Upac, un caso de Resistencia judicial* (forthcoming, on file with the author).

In my opinion, the Court ruling was not as transformative as many had expected. Until 2010 it was estimated that 36 per cent of the Colombian population had no access to adequate housing.[40] This situation was not transformed by the Court's rulings, or by the legislation developed by Congress in response to the Court orders regarding the fulfilment of the right to decent housing. Those who had benefitted (some of them because many civil court judges did not prevent foreclosures) were middle-class property-owners who had mortgages. As a consequence, the rulings did not limit market-oriented reforms; instead they created a series of mechanisms enabling those in the middle classes who had been left outside the market to gain access to it. The Court orders did nothing to transform the understanding of rights as individually-basedand intimately linked to issues of access to the legal system.

B. Right to Health

As with the right to housing, the following section provides the background to the market-oriented reforms that were set in place. I then describe ruling T-760 of 2008 which established that the right to health is a fundamental right. In the final section, I explain who defended and who attacked the ruling as well as who eventually benefitted from it.

i. Historical and Legal Background

The health reform of 1993 is another example of the wave of liberal reforms set in place during the first part of the 1990s. The reform signalled a partial privatisation of the system in order to promote competition between agencies providing health care aimed at increasing the health coverage of the population and reducing state spending. The law created two different affiliation regimes: the contributory and the subsidised. Individuals who are either formally employed, or independent workers capable of paying the insurance fee, are part of the contributory regime. The rest are part of the subsidised regime.[41]

Despite the fact that the system was based on the free market there was significant State regulation. There was, in effect, a hybrid regulatory system, where private institutions would provide health services but public institutions defined the conditions of those insured as well as the services that were to be provided and their costs. The reforms implemented through Law 100 in 1993 were premised on the superiority of market-based allocation of health care. However, what Law 100 envisioned was far from an unregulated market. Unlike a normal private insurance scheme, Law 100 set up a hybrid scheme whereby private insurance companies did not set the capitation rates, did not define deductibles or premiums, did not set the content of benefits packages, and did not decide whom to insure. Furthermore, given

---

[40] For an analysis of the housing deficit in Colombia, see CP Garzón, 'Evaluación de Impacto del problema de vivienda Colombiana' (2010) *Inter-American Development Bank Discussion paper OVE/TDP-10/10.*

[41] The reform of the Colombian health sector in 1993 was founded on the internationally advocated paradigm of privatisation of health care delivery. Taking into account the lack of empirical evidence for the applicability of this concept to developing countries and the documented experience of failures in other countries, Colombia tried to overcome these problems by a theoretically sound, although complicated, model. Some 10 years after the implementation of 'Law 100', a review of the literature shows that the proposed goals of universal coverage and equitable access to high-quality care have not been reached. See T De Groote, P De Paepe, JP Unger, 'Colombia: In Vivo Test of Health Sector Privatization in the Developing World' (2005) 35 *International Journal of Health Services* 125.

the complex array of providers and insurers, the State also had a substantial role to play in regulation. Over time, the contradictions inherent within Law 100 over time produced fault lines which, together with failures of regulation, led to the crisis in the system.

In addition to determining the services provided, Law 100 created a defined benefit package (*Plan Obligatorio de Salud*, POS) which listed the available services. Different packages were created for the affiliation regimes. Consequently, the subsidised regime provided about half of the benefits provided by the contributory regime.

In terms of the role of government participation, the regulation of health has been aimed at efficient public spending coupled with privatisation.

ii. The Right to Health: An Effective Limit on the Market?

Before 1998, there were few conflicts between judges and public authorities protecting the right to health.[42] For a social, economic and cultural right to be protected by the 'writ of protection of constitutional rights' (*acción de tutela*),[43] there had to be an close relationship with a fundamental right. The first cases claimed that the right to health could not be separated from the fundamental rights to life, physical integrity and human dignity. Therefore, the Court in some cases granted the right to health. The right to health adjudication began to give rise to an increase in public spending, notwithstanding the privatisation impulse described above. This increase was described by Uprimny in the following terms: 'While in 1998 about 2 million dollars were required to meet health-related rulings, by 1999 almost 7 million dollars were needed.'[44]

As Colombians demanded their right to health through an ever increasing number of law suits, ruling T-760 of 2008[45] was intended to put an end to the increase in the number of citizens accessing health through Court adjudication. This judgment turned the SER into a fundamental one.

This change has a transcendental consequence. It makes it possible for the demand for the right to health from judges. The Colombian Constitution establishes that the only rights that can be adjudicated by judges are fundamental ones (also called first generation rights). The fact that the Court established the right to health as a fundamental right allows citizens to demand it directly from judges and not, as before, only when the the right to health was linked to the fundamental right to life.

---

[42] 'In spite of the progressive character of the Court's decisions, up until 1998 the judicial protection of social rights did not produce any major conflicts between judges and other public authorities. In fact, before 1998, the number of *tutela* decisions concerning social rights that were upheld was over two per cent, in such a way that judicial activism appeared unacceptable only to the most obstinate of social constitutionalism's opponents', R Uprimny Yepes, 'The Judicial Protection of Social Rights by the Colombian Constitutional Court: Cases and Debates' Research Report (2006), available at www.dejusticia.org/admin/file.php?table=documentos_publicacion &field=archivo&id=69.

[43] 'As reiterated by the Constitutional Court, the 'writ of protection of constitutional rights' (*acción de tutela*) is a procedural institution intended to protect the fundamental rights from injury or threat people by a public authority and, under certain assumptions, by an individual', JC Ortiz Gutiérrez, 'La Acción de Tutela en la Carta Política de 1991: El derecho de amparo y su influencia en el ordenamiento constitucional de Colombia' (2006) 1 (1) *Juris Dictio: La Revista De Asomagister* 8.

[44] 'So, whereas before 1998 only 2,999 actions of this sort were filed against the ISS, in 1998 those actions increased to 10,771', see Uprimny (n 42), 20.

[45] Corte Constitucional (Constitutional Court), Sentencia (Ruling) C-760 of 2008, MP (Judge), Manuel José Cepeda Espinoza, available at www.corteconstitucional.gov.co/relatoria/2008/t-760-08.htm.

Turning again to the T-760 ruling, when this judgment was produced, many Colombians (mostly participants in the contributory regime[46]) were accessing their right to health through demands to the Constitutional Court.[47] In 2008 claims for the right to health had reached a record high.[48] The number of lawsuits related to health was 142,957,[49] representing an enormous burden on the already congested courts nationwide. Ruling T-760 of 2008 was a structural response to the clash between the privatisation of the health system and the understanding of health as a right.[50]

Opinions on the judicial adjudication of the right to health were varied. In favour of the adjudication, some authors argue that SER adjudication is essential to a democratic society.[51] Others believe that the rulings contribute to the human rights fulfillment for socially vulnerable groups.[52]

On the other hand, various neoclassical economists (for example, Rudolf Hommes,[53] Sergio Clavijo[54] and Salomón Kalmanovitz[55]) are extremely critical of the Constitutional Court rulings regarding health. For instance, Kalmanovitz regards the use of claims as an incentive not to participate in the contributory health system, since all the health benefits

---

[46] Defensoría del Pueblo, *La Tutela y el Derecho a la Salud 2010* (writ of protection of constitutional rights and the right to health), (Bogota, Imprenta nacional de Colombia, 2011), 64, available at www.defensoria.org.co/red/anexos/publicaciones/tutelaSalud2010.pdf.

[47] JE Mejía, 'Colombianos consiguen salud a punta de tutelas' (*Revista Semana*, Bogota, 25 September 2009).

[48] Defensoría del Pueblo, *La Tutela y el Derecho a la Salud 2010* (n 23), 27: '[O]f the 344,468 tutelas presented, 142,957 demanded the right to health. An all-time high of 41.5% participation of the tutelas in the country.

[49] O Bernal and C Gutierrez, *La Salud en Colombia. Logros, Retos y Recomendaciones,* (Bogotá, Universidad de los Andes, 2012).

[50] Ibid, 12: 'But it was the Ruling T-760 of 2008, which marked a turning point in the Court's jurisprudence. This ruling involved the rotation of a casuistic approach to the conflicts of 'writ of protection of constitutional rights' (*acción de tutela*), a structural approach that focuses on addressing the underlying systemic failures of individual disputes. To do so, the Court came to the jurisprudential mechanism of complex orders, used by courts in other countries (like the US and India), involving multiple public and private entities and whose compliance is monitored periodically by the Court itself. To do so, the Court accumulated 22 cases that were a sample of the most recurrent conflicts of 'writ of protection of constitutional rights'. In addition to declaring the right to health as fundamental (and therefore capable of being protected an autonomous 'writ of protection of constitutional rights'), the Court issued orders to all relevant actors in the health system to change through deadlines, structural failures of public policy that underline judicialization of health'.

[51] R Arango, *El concepto de derechos sociales fundamentales,* (Bogota, Legis Editores, 2005).

[52] C Rodriguez, 'Beyond the Courtroom: The Impact of Judicial Activism on Socioeconomic Rights in Latin America' (2011) 89 *Texas Law Review* 1669.

[53] The leading economist Rudolf Hommes states his critique in the following terms: 'Moreover, the Court has to be responsible for the economic and political consequences of their actions and must respond to some authority for negligent or catastrophic decisions, or to cause economic damage. Also, it is necessary that the judges exercise self-control and do not let their passions and ideology overwhelm them as has been shown.' See R Hommes, 'Dictadura Constitucional' (*El Tiempo*, Bogota, June 1999).

[54] 'The basic task of economic and social development in Colombia has been seriously threatened by the 'legal instability', aggravated by the activism of the Constitutional Court who served during the years 1991–2000. This Constitutional Court decided to alter the interpretation of laws passed years ago and accommodate various articles of the new Constitution of 1991 to principles based on populist ideas, that were defined as those who order to increase government spending without addressing their negative macroeconomic effects', see S Clavijo, 'Fallos y fallas económicas de las altas cortes: el caso de Colombia 1991–2000' (2001) 12 *Revista de Derecho Público* 27.

[55] 'The decisions taken by the honorable Constitutional Court in relation to the public health system, the electoral administration and other state entities have affected and expanded public spending without justification. In each decision, the Court is generous with resources to these entities, ordering the ISS (Institute of Social Services) to attend sick people that do not contribute to the system or to provide treatments that alter the budget, ordering to the Registraduría to give for free identification papers even if they are repeatedly lost by the citizen, ordering that workers achieve wage levelling undermining the balance of business, and ordering that debtors be fully compensated by the UPAC (Government entity).' See S Kalmanovitz, 'Las consecuencias económicas de los fallos de la Corte Constitucional' (1999) 276 *Economía Colombiana y Coyuntura Política* 124.

can be achieved through adjudication, potentially harming access to health for those who contribute.[56]

The Court rulings have not significantly increased the population's access to health. In fact, many of the claimants were individuals who were part of the private insurance regime, but were occasionally denied the right to health. The right to health adjudication did provide a specific answer to individuals who demanded it from the system. In this sense, it complemented individualistic, market-oriented reforms.

This situation can be described as a paradox created by the Court. On the one hand, when it establishes that the right to health is a fundamental one, it is opening the door for anybody, rich or poor, to demand the immediate protection of this right. On the other hand, people who have no health insurance and belong to the subsidised health regime have less access to the judicial system. In addition, when the Court adjudicates the right to health outside the private insurance regime, the Colombian State created a fund to pay for these rulings. As a consequence, a significant amount of public resources are concentrated on the needs of middle-class individual litigants and not the neediest part of the population.

In addition, this combination of weak State regulation and strong court intervention allowed large pharmaceutical companies to profit enormously. Until the late 1990s, the price of drugs was strictly controlled. By 2004, the regulatory framework was removed and pharmaceutical prices increased rapidly; at the same time, courts adjudicated the right to health and, as a consequence, drugs in Colombia are among the most expensive in the world.[57]

IV. Conclusion

As stated in the introduction, the aim of this chapter has been to present a different perspective on the debate surrounding SER adjudication. It has been demonstrated both in the right to housing and in the right to health, that the rulings by the Constitutional Court have placed limits on liberal reforms (the shift from State intervention to the market in the case of housing and the reduction of public spending in the case of health) but did not have a transformative impact on the general distribution of resources in Colombian society, and in both cases concentrated public resources on the middle class. In this sense, SER adjudication could be understood more as a complement to the market than a counter-hegemonic intervention.

---

[56] Ibid, 125: 'Instead of contributing, each patient can choose to use a tutela. If this action becomes widespread, there will be fewer contributors and that will have a detrimental effect on the existing health system. We turn to ask for justice in this case: the Court is solving the problem for a patient but is endangering the right to health of 12 million citizens who contribute responsibly.'

[57] E Lamprea and T Andia, 'Local maladies, global remedies: rethinking right to health duties' (2010) Presentation at Stanford University Global Justice and Political Theory, available at iis-db.stanford.edu/evnts/6170/Global_Justice_May_21_2010.pdf.

Part VI

The Legal Profession and Globalisation

18

Lost in Translation: On the Failed Encounter Between Bourdieu and Law and Society Scholarship and their Respective Blindnesses

YVES DEZALAY AND BRYANT G GARTH

I. Introduction

The hypothesis formulated by Bourdieu about 'texts which circulate without their contexts' applies to the international circulation of Bourdieu's theories. The reading and reception of texts outside their national spaces is strongly determined by internal battles specific to the field in which the text is received. Those battles determine the possible usages of imported theories, and notably the strategic resources that the potential importers–translators are able to mobilise—shaped in turn by the internal positions that they occupy.

This hypothesis provides an explanation for the striking contrast between the strong interest produced by the publication of Bourdieu's 'The Force of Law' in 1987 and the relatively weak impact of Bourdieu's form of structural sociology on the research methods and agendas in the Law and Society field—despite the fact that Bourdieu is among the most cited scholars internationally in the social sciences.[1]

The argument has two parts. First, the influence of the problematique sketched in 'The Force of Law' was limited by the fact that Bourdieu's sociology of law referred essentially—if not exclusively—to the legal field as structured in Germany, leading to an emphasis on the so-called '*professorenrecht*'. This German structure differs considerably from the US or English legal worlds from which the great majority of Law and Society scholars come. Given this contextual mismatch, any effort to draw on Bourdieu's approach was bound to involve some misunderstanding, reinforced by the inexact English translation of *juristes* as lawyers. The translation obscures the opposition between European jurists of the state, and Anglo-Saxon lawyers who are the product of the autonomisation of legal fields at the margin of the state. More precisely, it obscures the role of the legal field in the construction of the state in Continental Europe and in limiting the bureaucratic construction of state power in the United States.

---

[1] N Truong and N Weill, 'A decade after his death, French sociologist Pierre Bourdieu stands tall: Bourdieu's ideas are making a comeback in education and can be found across the social sciences and the arts' *The Guardian* (21 February 2012) stating that Michel Foucault is one and Bourdieu two as the most cited social scientists.

The recent publication of the lectures given by Bourdieu at the College de France in the period 1989–1992, 'Sur l'Etat', permits some partial correction of this misunderstanding.[2] The lectures suggest lines of reasoning through which Bourdieu had deepened and enriched the hypotheses developed more schematically in 1986 in 'The Force of Law'. While remaining essentially within the historical setting of Continental Europe, Bourdieu sketched a problematique which enlarged both the scope of his analysis and the object of study. He moved beyond jurists in the field of state power towards showing the more general play of oppositions and complementarity between the different fractions which make up the world of law in relationship to the holders of state power. The deepening of this problematique permitted him to open the field of analysis to other national configurations, such as that which developed in Britain with the reforms of the seventeenthth-century civil war. This enlarged and refined perspective allows one to take into account the transformations and breaks that mark the dramatically-changing histories of legal fields, which involve successive geneses, borrowings, breaks, and even revolutions which can be characterised as a succession of golden ages and declines—far from the grand Weberian scheme of a linear progression toward rationality and the autonomy of law.

The first section of this paper will therefore seek to show that, even if still anchored in Continental European history, this more recent problematique developed by Bourdieu can advance Law and Society understanding of the 'Cravath model' of lawyering[3] and the internationalisation of its spaces of practice—whereby this model is at the same time the means and the product.

The second section of the paper focuses more on Law and Society than Bourdieu's approach. It suggests that the analytical power of political and structural sociology contrasts with the mainstream approach of Law and Society scholarship. The mainstream approach draws on the paradigm of Legal Realism—with corresponding objects and silences, even taboos—which is the product of a particular history of the field of state power in the US and the academic, legal and political hierarchies produced by that history. The spread of the Law and Society movement cannot be separated from the complementary and contradictory relationship between law professors and social science researchers. The relationship tends not to favour the kind of reflexive sociology that we believe, drawing on Bourdieu, is indispensable to understanding precisely how hierarchies and links among the academic, legal, bureaucratic and activist components of the legal field determine the problematiques and the objects of the research that characterise Law and Society. More importantly and generally, this reflexive sociology is a prerequisite for the construction of objects of study that do not simply reflect the more or less dominated positions of the producers of research in the field of power.

With a few rare exceptions,[4] this reflexive sociology is almost completely absent in Law and Society research. Yet the scientific relevance of this research and the sustainability of research can be condemned as quickly becoming obsolete by enacting the role of 'handmaidens and sort of technicians that had to supply the technical answers to legal scholars

---

[2] P Bourdieu, *Sur l'État: Cours au Collège de France (1989–1992)* (Paris, Seuil, 2012).

[3] DM Trubek, Y Dezalay, R Buchanan and J Davis, 'Global Restructuring and the Law Studies of the Internationalization of Legal Fields and the Creation of Transnational Arenas' (1994) 44 *Case Western Reserve Law Review* 2.

[4] BG Garth and J Sterling, 'From Legal Realism to Law and Society: Reshaping Law for the Last Stages of the Social Activist State' (1998) 32 *Law & Society Review* 409.

who then had to (1) frame the problem and (2) analyze what the data really meant'.[5] Our second point, therefore, is that it is important to interrogate the sociological contradictions that place obstacles in the way of this more reflexive line of sociological research. We ask why the reflexivity central to Bourdieu's research is almost completely neglected in the borrowings and references to Bourdieu.

II. From the Legal Field to the National Field of State Power

Bourdieu wrote relatively little about law after his long theoretical article, 'The Force of Law', published in 1986. After that effort, he did not return to this theme outside of a few short texts: 'Les robins et l'invention de l'Etat',[6] 'Les juristes, gardiens de l'hypocrisie collective',[7] and 'Esprits d'etat: genese et structure du champ bureaucratique'.[8] In contrast, he made a number of references to the history of law and lawyers on the occasion of his last series of courses on the state offered at the College de France in 1991 and recently published as *Sur l'Etat*.[9]

These recently published articles illustrate how Bourdieu had deepened his analysis beyond the theoretical hypotheses developed in 'The Force of Law'. Bourdieu moved in this later work to treat the legal market more generally and underlined how the demand for legal services was in large part constructed by what the producers offered. His course of lectures examined the genesis and the reproduction of the holders and producers of legal capital in relation to the different powers of the state, a theme that he had treated in a relatively elusive manner in 'The Force of Law'.

This historical focus on the 'clerks' of the law, termed the 'robins', is somewhat more narrow than the topics of 'The Force of Law', but this focus permitted Bourdieu to refine his analysis considerably, notably going beyond the fundamental and over-simplified opposition between theoreticians and practitioners that Bourdieu had borrowed from Weber. Thus, in his course, he took some distance from the very Weberian conception of a '*professorenrecht*' dominated by the theoreticians of 'pure law' by underlining that 'legal capital is not only a capital of theories ... but it is a species of permanent exchange between practical innovations ... and theoretical innovations destined to legitimate small conquests in practice'.[10]

---

[5] Rita Simon quoted in ibid at 459.

[6] P Bourdieu, 'Les robins et l'invention de l'Etat' in *La noblesse d'Etat* (Paris, Seuil, 1989) 539–48.

[7] P Bourdieu, 'Les juristes, gardiens de l'hypocrisie collective' in C Francois and J Commaille (eds), *Normes juridiques et egulation sociale* (Paris, LGDJ, 1991).

[8] P Bourdieu, 'Esprits d'État: Genèse et structure du champ bureaucratique' (1993) 96–97 *Actes de la recherche en sciences sociales* 49.

[9] Bourdieu, *Sur l'État* (n 2).

[10] Ibid, 533.

A. The Internal Fights Between Fractions of Jurists as Fundamental to the Diversification of the Legal Field

Drawing on the works of historians,[11] Bourdieu proposed an 'analysis of the world of the "robins"' in terms of the field, that is to say a differentiated space'.[12] He then opposed various fractions of jurists differentiated by their social origins, their education, and their proximity to royal power.

The first group is consists of jurists of the state who contributed to the creation of the authoritarian state. They represent what can be termed the bureaucratic pole of the legal field or the party of the crown. They are opposed by a different fraction of the '*noblesse de robe*' (the heirs of those who owned the positions of power in the French judiciary and state in the eighteenth century), the '*officiers de justice*', those who inherited the control of the High Courts of Justice. The ideology and objectives of the latter group were inspired in part by the British model. They relied in particular on one key institution, the *Parisian Parlement*, to which the king had delegated the power of applying the law—setting up legal autonomy as a limit on royal power. The third category is that of the 'lower legal clergy ... speaking and being spokespersons for the collective will, popular will, etc, according to the transhistoric alliance between "the intelligentsia proletaroïde" as Max Weber pointed out and the popular classes'.[13] The French Revolution disrupted this hierarchy in favour of the third category, which succeeded in imposing its conception of the nation state as the sole legitimate form of the modern state and then appropriated 'the quasi-monopoly of profits associated with this institution'.[14]

The power of this analysis is that it opens up a fluid conception of the legal field as a 'space of many dimensions [where] things shift in relation to each other'.[15] The positions of the holders of legal capital are quite mobile, since the clerks can operate between many different spaces. They can modify their strategies and the positions they take in relation to the historical and political context that valorises one or other of these spaces.

This metaphor of the legal field as a crossroads[16] is quite rich from a heuristic point of view because it introduces the possibility of using the same general paradigm to examine different national histories of the state and the law.[17] By way of illustration, we can show how this problematique helps to explain the genesis of the British model of the rule of law—constructed against the bureaucratic doctors of Roman law who served as officers of the royal bureaucracy.

---

[11] DR Kelly, *The Beginning of Ideology: Consciousness and Society in the French Reformation* (Cambridge, Cambridge University Press, 1981); K Baker, *Inventing the French Revolution: Essays on French Political Culture in the XVIII Century* (Cambridge, Cambridge University Press, 1990).

[12] Bourdieu, *Sur l'État* (n 2) 516.

[13] Ibid, 515.

[14] Ibid, 544.

[15] Ibid, 518.

[16] This concept was developed by Christopher Charle in 1989 in a short programmatic note where he defined legal professions as 'crossroads professions where social capital is converted easily into diverse other forms of capital: economic, intellectual, political'. See C Charle, 'Pour une histoire sociale des professions juridiques à l'époque contemporaine. Note pour une recherche' (1989) 76–77 *Actes de la recherche en sciences sociales* 117, 119.

[17] Ibid, 556.

B. Common Lawyers versus Officers of the King

The barristers from the time of the fifteenth century were trained at the Inns of Court through a process that could last 10 years and could be compared to a 'finishing school' education.[18] Those who accumulated sufficient social and learned capital were predisposed to serve as agents and intermediaries for the monarchy or for the landed aristocracy—defending independence against royal or religious power. They provided advice and resolved disputes, serving also as Justices of the Peace. The autonomy of the bar was therefore constructed on the basis of capital and activities aimed not only at legitimation, but also at maintaining equilibrium within the field of political power.

Since they were recruited from within the elite of the landed gentry—and to some degree from the new merchant bourgeoisie—the barristers trained and socialised at the Inns of Court were predisposed to become the representatives of the two social groups of which they had become a part. These learned gentlemen became both the champions and the guardians of an equilibrium among various powers against the absolutist claims of the monarchy supported by the bureaucrats and jurists of the state. The parliamentary monarchy that emerged then favoured the emergence of a new elite—the practitioners of the common law—at the expense of the old elite—the doctors of Roman law—which had served the leaders of the royal bureaucracy.

While retaining their privileged relationships with the new ruling classes whose interests were now represented in parliament, these legal practitioners succeeded in legitimating their jurisdictional monopoly and affirming their autonomy with respect to the holders of power. This strategy of autonomisation was facilitated by the fragmentation and decentralisation of the field of power in the context of a civil war and religious battles favouring the emancipation of cities and the growth in power of an alliance between the gentry and the merchant bourgeoisie. The strategy also drew on a mode of familial reproduction through co-opting members and apprentices under the aegis of the Inns of Court, which reinforced the sociological homogeneity of this professional guild dominated by a hierarchy of barristers controlling the judicial power and the learned authority of the law.

This double control of the production of law and the reproduction of lawyers allowed the barristers to thrive in the litigation market. Their monopoly gained credibility because it rested on the affirmation of the need for the law to be independent with respect to the holders of state power—whether central or local. At the same time, however, the guild structure ensured that the bar remained a closed organisation with few members and promoted the decline of the role of the Inns of Court. Intellectual activities diminished at the Inns and they lost their role of educating the inheritors of the elite of the gentry.

C. Internal Fights as a Factor in the Recomposition of Legal Fields: Geneses, Golden Ages, Decline

Even though Bourdieu failed to develop certain lines of comparative analysis himself, he had the insight to see how the fluidity of the world of the state jurists permitted them to serve as go-betweens among different fields of power and successive variations of the field

---

[18] WR Prest, *The Rise of the Barristers: A Social History of the English Bar 1590–1640* (Oxford, Oxford University Press, 1986).

of state power. Drawing on Skinner,[19] he stressed 'the role of the great religious ruptures in the construction of the state'.[20] However, he still did not develop this direction of his research, which without citation has much in common with the theses offered by Berman in his *Law and Revolution*.[21] Consistent with Bourdieu's basic hypothesis, internal fights are crucial to the history of legal fields, including both the period of their geneses and also their crises and recompositions.

Pursuant to this diachronic approach to the legal field, Bourdieu explores the central hypothesis of a parallel genesis for law and the state, a theme that he took up again in his article in 1993. As a counterpoint to this line of research, he also interrogated the effects of contradictions which are the source of tensions, crises, but also of innovations and inventions in the legal field. He remarks also in passing that the internal confrontations between different fractions may degenerate into fratricidal battles so violent that they can sap the fundamentals of the credibility of the field by means of a kind of suicidal collective madness among various fractions of elites, solely intent on disqualifying their opponents, even if it means undermining their own symbolic capital.

D. A Double Game Between the Fields of Power

By comparison with what he wrote in 'The Force of Law', Bourdieu insisted in these courses on the genesis of legal capital through competitive struggles between religious and royal power: 'The jurists, at bottom, served the Church and used resources furnished largely by the Church to construct the State against the Church ... The State was constructed on the model of the Church, but against it.'[22] The strength of these lines of analysis was later clearly shown by Brundage, who reveals in great detail the complexity of the strategies of those with law degrees playing simultaneously in the religious hierarchy and in the royal bureaucracies.[23]

In what Brundage describes as a kind of 'managerial revolution', the very expensive acquisition of legal learning in Medieval and Renaissance Italy appears as the golden path to riches and the accumulation of powers of influence for children of noble lineage.[24] For them, it represented a scholarly reconversion which valorised their relational capital.[25] Their careers then moved quickly because their status as jurists permitted them to serve as counsellors both to kings and princes, and to the Catholic hierarchy. Indeed, grateful for the service of such counsellors, powerful protectors extended the influence of jurists by providing educational stipends and offering ecclesiastical positions to graduates of the University of Bologna and its imitators. Brundage reports that this was the case for a third of the German bishops. This double game was not only very profitable, but also represented a prudential strategy, since it offered a variety of positions to accommodate a historical context where counsellors had to find ways to avoid being the first victims of

---

[19] Q Skinner, *The Foundations of Modern Political Thought* (Cambridge, Cambridge University Press, 1978).
[20] Bourdieu, *Sur l'État* (n 2) 528.
[21] HJ Berman, *Law and Revolution: The Formation of the Western Legal Tradition* (Cambridge MA, Harvard University Press, 1983).
[22] Bourdieu, *Sur l'État* (n 2) 526.
[23] J Brundage, *The Medieval Origins of the Legal Profession* (Chicago, University of Chicago Press, 2008).
[24] Ibid, 274.
[25] Ibid, 267.

antagonisms between competing protective powers.[26] The success of this strategy is evident from the fact that these 'learned' managers and counsellors were able to insinuate themselves into the entourages of both princes and the Church, where they dominated the Curie at the end of the twelfth century[27] and even ultimately at the level of the Papacy, with a succession of popes trained as Doctors of Cannon Law.

E. Legal Capital as Inheritance or Scholarly Merit: Accumulation and Contradiction

Bourdieu also suggests a hypothesis that might be fruitfully developed to better understand the later evolution of legal fields. Apart from these battles of positions in relation to church and state politics, he also notes the structural contradictions inherent in the reproduction of legal capital, since legal capital comes from both inheritance and scholarly achievement. On the one hand, it is a cultural capital that is defined in opposition to aristocratic capital or nobility, giving value to individual merit and scholarly competence rather than inherited title or family lineage—the diploma as against the title of nobility. On the other hand, Bourdieu observes that it is a matter of a false opposition since the doctors of law seek to be recognised as a '*noblesse de robe*'. In the top judicial hierarchy of France, for example, the holders of 'legal offices' purchased from the king, defended the principle of dynastic reproduction against meritocratic promotion.[28]

As mentioned briefly before, this claim to the status of nobility is also sustained by the importance of barriers to entry—as much cultural as financial—that may reserve access to the schools of law only to the most privileged of the 'cadets' of aristocratic lineage—sustained in their studies by their families or as beneficiaries of the support of powerful religious or civil protectors. As mentioned above, grants of an ecclesiastical stipend were critical for these long and costly studies.[29]

Martines further shows that this mobilisation of family capital in legal careers was not limited to scholarly investment.[30] In fact, the first stage in the most successful of these careers involved an early succession of diplomatic tasks that permitted the accumulation of diversified relational capital from the holders of state power, princes of the Church, monarchs or *condotierri* (powerful leaders of mercenary armies in Italy in the period of city states). And there too, the support of great names—one's family or supporters—was necessary in order to be recognised and received. The advantage of family wealth and prominence was also quite direct. Family financial support was usually needed to get through the courses in an ambiance where expected sumptuary demonstrations would likely exceed any stipends.

This phenomenon of the conversion of the social capital of family lineage into learned legal capital, which opened the door to careers in the state, was not limited to the period

---

[26] As an example of these double careers, consider the trajectory of Thomas Arundel (1353–1414), (ibid, 392). This son of an earl was successively Chancellor of England and Archbishop of Canterbury and had numerous protégés who themselves accumulated top bureaucratic positions—Treasurer of England, Chief Justice, Constable of Bordeaux—as well as ecclesiastical ones—Papal Chaplain, Auditor Apostolic Camera, Archbishop of England.

[27] Ibid, 132.

[28] Bourdieu, *Sur l'État* (n 2) 510.

[29] Brundage, *The Medieval Origins of the Legal Profession* (n 23) 121.

[30] L Martines, *Lawyers and Statecraft in Renaissance Florence* (Princeton, Princeton University Press, 1968).

of genesis during the Renaissance. Karady, for example, describes a very similar process in Hungary before the Second World War.[31] This mechanism for the conversion of cultural capital into state capital through investment in legal learning was also exported to colonial societies including, notably, Latin America and Asia.[32] In the case of Brazil, Misceli has shown that the construction by Getulio Vargas of the institutions of a modern state—by opposition to the patrimonial and clientelistic state—was nourished by the reconversion of inheritors of old families from the sugar oligarchy of the North-east, at that time in decline, into the new notables of the state and politics—thanks to the legitimacy of their law degree.[33]

This strong complementarity between family inheritance and a legal diploma—which Bourdieu designated the 'diploma of the bourgeoisie'—did not mean that there were no tensions between these two types of personal resources. More precisely, there is an opposition between different fractions of jurists who seek to valorise one or the other of the forms of capital valued in the field. The inheritors of the '*noblesse de robe*' oppose the new arrivals seeking to make a career of their learned competence, their personal merits, their managerial skills, or their eloquence on behalf of the disadvantaged. Nevertheless, the members of the '*noblesse de robe*'—and their descendants—almost by definition occupy the dominant positions in the hierarchy of the field, drawing on a structural tendency toward the valorisation of family reproduction at the expense of the more intellectual fraction within the legal field,[34] which is also a source of obsolescence or even decline. This kind of process has not been documented by legal historians, since these histories are usually written by and for jurists and therefore serve, as Bourdieu emphasises, 'an internal history, a history without agents'.[35] But one can nevertheless find numerous indicators of this very general tendency toward the relative demise and obsolescence of academic legal capital.

The most flagrant example is doubtless the evolution of the Inns of Court in Great Britain, which lost all intellectual function following the triumph of barristers who then imposed recruitment by co-optation and apprenticeship in conformance with their social origins and political strategy. Elsewhere, one can see this propensity in the histories of faculties of law when they become places for the reproduction of doctrinal exegesis, dominated by the 'guardians of the temple and the texts', seeking to minimise jurisprudential evolutions and refusing to take into account new social realities. As Bourdieu remarked in the conclusion of 'The Force of Law', it is then the dominated of the field or new arrivals who are constrained to invest in the renovation of jurisprudential science. They may, for example, import from social science with the aim of gaining recognition within the law for the new social interests for which they seek to be spokespersons within the legal field.

---

[31] V Karady, 'Une nation de juristes' (1991) 90 *Actes de la Recherche en Sciences Sociales* 106; see also R Dahrendorf, 'Law Faculties and the German Upper Class' in W Aubert (ed), *Sociology of Law* (Harmondsworth, Penguin, 1969) for the faculties of law in Germany after the Second World War.

[32] Y Dezalay and BG Garth, *The Internationalization of Palace Wars* (Chicago, University of Chicago Press, 2002) and Y Dezalay and BG Garth, *Asian Legal Revivals: Lawyers in the Shadow of Empires* (Chicago, University of Chicago Press, 2010).

[33] S Miceli, *Les intellectuals et le pouvior au Bresil* (Paris, AM Metaille, 1983).

[34] *Cf* this famous statement of a senior judge in the French Cour de Cassation, in mid nineteenth century, who was the son of one of the leading writers of the Code Napoleon: 'There is no better guarantee of good justice than a good name.'

[35] Bourdieu, *Sur l'État* (n 2) 536.

The effects of these internal fights are quite often very beneficial to the legal field generally in terms of innovations, but the process can be quite dramatic and conflict-laden. As Bourdieu noted in passing: 'At the core of the field, one kills oneself for things that are imperceptible ... little changes which, often, are not intelligible except to people who operate within the particular universe.'[36] Opposing sides may be completely taken by the logic of symbolic confrontation. They may even fail to see that 'they may be in the process of sawing off the branch on which they are sitting. Very often, the dominant group can contribute to weaken the fundamentals of their domination because, taken by the logic of the game ... they forget that they go a little too far.' The 'passion of internal fights' may therefore become a suicidal enterprise.

Certainly, in European societies, the process of decline that comes in part from resisting any innovation—or more precisely, the loss of credibility in law that results—typically takes place very slowly, especially given the weight of the capital accumulated over a period of centuries and inscribed in institutional, symbolic and linguistic structures endowed with a certain permanence.

In contrast, as we have shown in other articles,[37] in colonised societies where the investment in the law is deeply implicated in colonial and post-colonial politics, this process of losing credibility may be much more brutal and more immediate. Indeed, while the military regimes of the cold war quite often provoked and accelerated this devalorisation of the legal field, the process of losing credibility was already underway because of the political strategies of notable politicians of the law who had abused their double positions in the state and in the law in order to privilege the interests of the oligarchical elites to which they also belonged.[38]

However, as we have shown in other articles,[39] we see the same conjunction of devalorisation of legal capital at the expense of political strategies in European societies between the two world wars, then again in the Welfare States after the Second World War. Even though attenuated in contrast to post-colonial states, lawyers lamented the 'decline of law' according to a formula articulated notably by grand professors such as Georges Ripert and also by young progressive judges such as the members of the 'Syndicat de la Magistrature', who sought to restore the credibility of law—and therefore also their own authority in the field of power—drawing on new ideals combining '*l'Etat de droit*' (from the German notion of '*RechtsStaat*') and social justice.

Rather than serving as an exception to the hypotheses that we have sought to develop, the legal field in the US can be analysed according to the same problematique. In fact, the re-invention of the Cravath model was accomplished through a reinvestment in the production and reproduction of legal learning, parallel with the launching of reformist political strategies at the domestic and international level.[40] These activities addressed an enduring weakness in the social credibility of law according to a process analogous to the

---

[36] Ibid, 502.

[37] Y Dezalay and BG Garth, *Asian Legal Revivals* (n 32).

[38] *Cf* the comment by Nehru that his peers in the law had 'purloined the Constitution'. BPJ Reedy & R Dhavan, 'The Jurisprudence of Human Rights,' in DM Bestty (eds), *Human Rights and Judicial Review: A Comparative Perspective* (Kluwer, 1994) at 182.

[39] Y Dezalay and BG Garth, 'Elite European Lawyers? The Common Market as New Golden Age or Missed Opportunity' in N Kauppi and MR Madsen (eds), *Transnational Power Elites, The European Constellation in the Global Field of Power* (London, Routledge, 2013).

[40] Trubek, Dezalay, Buchanan and Davis, 'Global Restructuring and the Law' (n 3).

situation in other societies constrained to gain a distance with a colonial legal order which left a strong mark on them.

F. Towards a New Genesis: Post-Colonial Reinvention and Hybridisation across the Atlantic

The transplantation of the British common law, and the leadership role of lawyers in the colonies and in the move to independence, paved the way for lawyers and legal legitimacy to become central to the US state. Despite some challenges to their authority, as in the Jacksonian era, lawyers have played a very prominent role in the state and in the economy in the US. By the late nineteenth century the new breed of corporate lawyers was also assuming a position at the top of the legal hierarchy.

Lawyers were not, of course, unchallenged. Their ties to England and the common law occasioned criticism, as did links through business and kinship to local elites. The Jacksonian period is usually presented as the high-water mark of those attacks.[41] The bar began to grow as restrictions on membership were lifted, but by 1860 there were still 'only a few cracks in its façade of social class'.[42] Towards the middle of the nineteenth century stratification within the legal profession began to be more closely identified with clients as corporate wealth began to increase. Railroad attorneys emerged as part of what Konefsky describes as 'a segmented and stratified profession … reinforced by social kinship and family networks'.[43] Lawyers began to concentrate increasingly in cities, to form partnerships, and to specialise in the representation of corporate interests. As the century came to a close and US industry expanded, the emerging law firms that served them began to occupy a unique social position between business and the state.

The main appeal—and success—of the law-firm model rests precisely on the fact that it facilitated this concentration and circulation of resources. Its purpose from inception was to provide the 'robber barons' with an indispensable instrument for realising their projects of industrial restructuring and concentration of financial capital. In the meantime, it also enabled these entrepreneurs to reinvest the substantial profits gained from their business activity into the education sector, notably by setting up and funding law schools, as well as in the state, by supporting reformist policies at home and exporting a combination of 'moral imperialism' and 'dollar diplomacy' abroad.[44]

It is on the basis of this double authority, both moral and political, that the law firms of the Cravath model have been able to impose themselves in business circles, where they have contributed to consolidating industrial dynasties by inciting the robber barons to rebrand themselves as philanthropists and invest in the production of knowledge, in order to encourage and accompany political reform. This mode of production of legal expertise— and of reproduction of the legitimacy of the law—is also at the heart of a strategy of facilitating the exchange of resources and the mobility of elites between the different poles

---

[41] AS Konefsky, 'The Legal Profession: From the Revolution to the Civil War' in M Grossman and C Tomlins (eds), *Cambridge History of Law in America, The Long Nineteenth Century (1789–1920)*, vol 2 (Cambridge, Cambridge University Press, 2008) 77.
[42] Ibid, 86.
[43] Ibid, 89.
[44] Dezalay and Garth, *Asian Legal Revivals* (n 32).

of power. By positioning themselves at the crossroads, lawyers with access to state affairs could combine the leadership of a large firm, and the associated economic gains, with an authority acquired in Washington networks (as 'wise men' or 'elder statesmen'), while maintaining a close connection with the most prestigious campuses (where their generous gifts ensure that they maintain an overview and right of pre-emption in the recruitment of the new generation of elite lawyers).

On the basis of the developments described above, we can summarise the main contributions of Bourdieu's problematique to analyses of the diversity of national legal fields and their respective histories. There are three fundamental axioms. First, research must be undertaken through a sociological problematique—without being constrained by indigenous categories—on the history and composition of the diverse fractions whose oppositions and complementarities are constitutive of national legal fields. Second, it is necessary to relate this history of national legal fields more generally to state power and processes of elite reproduction, particularly in relation to the opposition between the logic of inheritance and the logic of scholarly merit. Third, it is vital to take into account not only the specificity of national legal fields—mixtures of ruptures and path dependencies—but to relate them to a global history in which legal agents have been both the product and the instruments. These connected histories show the national–global role of legal agents as intermediaries and mediators in colonial politics and in hegemonic confrontations among state powers.

In order to undertake this work, one key is to undertake a sociological analysis to question the partial lucidities and the blind spots that derive from positions in academic, legal and political fields and predictably continue to shape Law and Society agendas and research.

III. Towards a Reflexive Sociology of Law and Society

One may apply to different strains of the sociology of law a fundamental axiom of the sociology of science formulated by Bourdieu: the strategies of learned production of the different agents in competition in these fields—and then also the choices of their objects of research as well as their strategies of alliance with professionals, practitioners, bureaucrats or activists—are in great part determined by the positions that they occupy in the hierarchies of fields of learned production.

Further, in the case of legal learning, it is also necessary to take into account the relatively weak autonomy of the sub-field of learned law, which has porous and fluctuating boundaries with the field of legal practice. This internal mobility across boundaries is facilitated by the multiple hats worn by legal elites as learned gentlemen of the law, professor-politicians,[45] or academic entrepreneurs.[46]

This fluidity is evident in the common-law countries modelled on England, where the elite of practitioners, the Queens' Counsels, are considered to be the true scholars in the

---

[45] Dezalay and Garth, *The Internationalization of Palace Wars* (n 32).

[46] Y Dezalay and BG Garth, *Dealing in Virtue: International Commercial Arbitration and the Construction of a Transnational Legal Order* (Chicago, University of Chicago Press, 1996).

law, unwilling to cede legal authority to the new arrivals, the law professors. But this is also true in the legal fields of Continental Europe depicted by Max Weber as a model of '*professorenrecht*'. In fact, the dominant producers—those with the authority 'to speak the law'—are characterised by an ability to combine academic competence with an important mix of political and social capital[47] constructed around networks of alliance within the world of law—the judicial hierarchy and the elite of the bar—but also within the field of state power and parliamentary politics, as well as in the world of business and activism—labour unions, associations, NGOs—and even the media.

As emphasised many times by Bourdieu,[48] this heteronomy of the field of (re)production of legal learning has as a corollary a strong homology of positions—as much between practitioners and learned scholars, as outside the legal field between different fractions of jurists and the social groups whose interests these professional groups translate into the language and forms of the law.

The learned legal capital is then constructed by affinity with the dominant groups in national fields of power. Historians such as Brundage[49] have shown that the reinvention of legal learning in Italy during the early Renaissance—but also later reinventions, notably through the Protestant Reformations[50]—are the product of an alliance between the holders of religious or state power and professors who are often their advisers. These rulers support the academic enterprises and help to finance them—especially by giving their protégés ecclesiastical benefits in order to finance quite costly studies. In exchange, these schools of law select and educate new generations, all predisposed to put their learned competence to work in order to valorise the combined forms of social and relational capital of which they are the product.

Even if these games of alliance are modified with new political configurations,[51] these strategic alliances between the elites of learned law and the dominant groups in the field of state power are found throughout national and colonial histories. The accumulation over time of multiple strata of legal learning helps to produce continuity and stability in the process of social reproduction. This activity has long served to inscribe the interests of dominant social groups within the language of the law. Further, as Berman shows,[52] since it is a matter both of being close to power and seeking to maintain some distance,[53] these clerics and jurists have served as intermediaries in periods of religious and social revolution by facilitating the transition toward new political regimes which are accompanied by recompositions of the legal order that nevertheless preserve a large portion of accumulated

---

[47] A German grand professor stated to Yves Dezalay that it was a matter of the difference between 'true professors' and those who, lacking the power to mobilise multiple forms of social and political capital, were nothing more than simple 'teachers' (*lehrers*), contenting themselves with their contributions to legal knowledge but without the social authority to 'speak the law'.

[48] Notably in 'The Force of Law' where he explained the hierarchy of legal disciplines, such as the civil law versus labour law, by the fact that 'the position of the different specialists in the relationships of power at the core of the field depends on the place in the political field of the groups whose interests are most directly linked to the corresponding forms of law'. See P Bourdieu, 'The Force of Law: Toward a Sociology of the Juridical Field' (1986) 38 *Hastings Law Journal* 805, 818.

[49] Brundage, *The Medieval Origins of the Legal Profession* (n 23).

[50] Berman, *Law and Revolution* (n 21).

[51] Ibid.

[52] Ibid.

[53] EH Kantorowicz, *The King's Two Bodies: A Study in Mediaeval Political Theology* (Princeton, Princeton University Press, 1997).

legal learning. The strength of this symbolic capital, constructed and accumulated in the service of dominant classes, comes in part from the fact that the legal ensemble of principles, categories, and modes of reasoning appears more legitimate because the product of a long history. It appears as a kind of natural, even universal order.

As Bourdieu noted in the conclusion of 'The Force of Law',[54] the social interests of dominant groups are linked to the guardians of the legal order, who are the 'defenders of a (legal) orthodoxy': enshrined in the cult of the text and the primacy of doctrine and exegesis, which is to say the theory that embodies the past, and which typically goes with the refusal to recognise any role for creative values—practically denying economic and social reality and refusing any scientific understanding of this reality.[55] He concludes the analysis by emphasising that it is the dominated of the field, or the new arrivals, who by necessity are forced to invest in the renovation of legal science, even with borrowings from social science aiming to gain recognition in the law for new interests that they seek to speak for within the legal field.

Still, as we are reminded in the 'Noblesse d'Etat', even if opposed to the guardians of the legal order, the new arrivals can only succeed in their strategies of subversion if they play simultaneously on a double register, contradictory as well as complementary, of science and political morality—the promotion of new social rights or access to justice. The double game means that the challenges and oppositions are presented as legal science and legitimate law. At the same time, this approach valorises their positions because success means not only an enlargement of legal markets but also a revival of belief in the law. As Bourdieu states, 'The dominant among the dominated can only succeed in making their interests progress by associating with causes that appear universal, such as through an emancipatory science.'[56] This insight applies nicely to other forms of universals such as human rights or social justice.

The reformers are therefore taken in by the game. In order to contribute effectively to the legal recognition of the social interests that they purport to represent, they must insist on the scientific rigour of their approach, borrowing from social sciences but not putting into question the autonomy of the law—the fundamental basis of the social belief and legitimacy of law. They are captured by a double contradiction. In order to shake up the legal order, they must present innovations as a return to the sources of law. In order to fight to gain recognition of new social groups excluded from the law, they must preserve the fiction of the neutrality of law, since the symbolic power comes precisely from the fact that it does not appear as a simple reflection of social and political relations of power. In other words, the efficacy of the reformist strategies is conditioned on strategies of a double game that permit ruptures as a story of continuity.

This way, the new arrivals oppose their predecessors as dogmatic, conservative and even archaic. But they adopt strategies that serve to inscribe the new state in the forms and the texts of the law and therefore, however precarious, existing social relations. The consolidation of these new legal paradigms is accomplished through a reaffirmation of the autonomy of law that privileges the texts and maintains a distance from their contexts. In short, in seeking to gain recognition for a new orthodoxy, this updating begins the process

---

[54] Bourdieu, 'The Force of Law' (n 48).
[55] Ibid, 18.
[56] Bourdieu, Sur l'État (n 2) 548.

of relaunching the great tradition of exegesis—at least, until these new high priests of the new cycle of doctrinal production are criticised in turn for their own dogmatism.

A. A Tactical Instrumentalisation of Social Science

The social and political alliances that are indispensable to the production of new legal learning impose particular strategies and limits, and the corollary of implied silences and blind spots, taboos and off-limits areas. The various enterprises that have mobilised social science and notably the sociology of law in the service of legal politics—such as the production of new social rights—only succeeds by becoming part of new legal orthodoxies.

In the field of doctrinal production, the new arrivals, anxious to gain recognition for the causes they defend, may profit from collaborators occupying dominated positions—in particular, those from the 'auxiliary' social sciences—by imposing on them a self-limitation on their objects of research. These limitations ensure that the social belief in the law, and ultimately the hierarchy of learning that is fundamental to the legal order, remains unquestioned.[57]

Ronan Shamir's examination of 'The Revolt of the Academics: Legal Realists and the New Deal' in his book on the New Deal[58] clearly demonstrates the relevance of these hypotheses in the relationships between the subfield of learned law and the fields of power—legal and political—in the US. He begins by emphasising the 'dual marginality' of this generation of law professors. They were relegated to the role of 'adjunct' by the elite of legal practitioners. Their competence was mainly in the classification of the law: 'Academics were the librarians, Judges the authors.'[59] Their position was simply as teachers in professional schools using appellate cases as their material. According to Shamir: 'In stark contrast with the vivid intellectual activity in the emerging social sciences,' the law professors were not 'fully integrated—either institutionally or intellectually—into the rest of the academic world'.[60] The revolt of the Legal Realists had therefore to be analysed as a 'collective mobility project' relying on a 'two tiered assault on the established legal order'[61]: 'questioning the field's established hierarchies ... [by] comprehensive challenge of judicial supremacy on the one hand and the privileged position of the bar's elite on the other'[62]—more precisely, 'Challenging the privileged bond between appellate courts and the bar's elite'.[63]

At first, the objective was to question the basis of the authority of the top judicial hierarchy: 'To dethrone the King',[64] they demonstrated the chaotic character, indeterminacy,

---

[57] Cf in this respect, the quite revealing statement by Rita Simon mentioned above that described law and society scholars as 'handmaidens and sort of technicians that had to supply technical answers to legal scholars who then had to (1) frame the problem and (2) decide what the data really meant', see Garth and Sterling (n 4), 459. We find the same perspective from interdisciplinary scholars such as James Willard Hurst that social scientists should be 'on tap' and lawyers 'on top'. See BG Garth 'James Willard Hurst in the Establishment and Definition of the Field of Law and Social Science' (1999) 18 *Law and History Review* 37.

[58] R Shamir, *Managing Legal Uncertainty: Elite Lawyers in the New Deal* (Durham, Duke University Press, 1995).

[59] Ibid, 139.

[60] Ibid, 148.

[61] Ibid, 141.

[62] Ibid, 147.

[63] Ibid, 148.

[64] Ibid, 143.

inconsistency, and above all unpredictability of judicial decisions. In the course of undermining these judicial pronouncements, they also sought to promote 'legitimating alternative sources of law',[65] and also 'different strategies of uncertainty reduction' including a 'social scientific foundation for the study of judicial decisions', as a 'true science'.[66]

Simultaneously, they attacked the monopoly of the case method that stifled reflection on the law through a deductive technique that 'over-emphasized and canonized appellate court decisions'.[67] In order to remedy these defects, they called for the study of 'law in context' and for 'closer relationships with the social sciences', which they intended to attract by opening the doors of the law schools. By bringing them to their own terrain, they not only benefitted from a new image as an 'intellectual vanguard', but they also reaffirmed their own authority, since they were by definition the 'final arbiters of the law'. The position of authority was further facilitated by the fact that they were in position to be 'architects of the new social order' through their privileged relationships with the field of state power in the New Deal.

This alliance with new academic disciplines, which were intellectually prestigious but lacking relational and political power, went hand in hand with a repositioning of alliances in the field of legal and governmental practice. The scientific investment combined with an investment in morality. They denounced a profession which had become 'the obsequious servant of business, tainted with the morals and manners of the market place'.[68] They placed their expertise in the service of the politics of the new bureaucracies of the New Deal by promoting a 'socially informed law' through 'enlightened legislation' able to solve social problems 'too complex, too difficult to be handled by the average judge'.[69]

The incontestable success of this project came from a context that permitted these 'law teachers to escape their dual marginality. … The New Deal opened an entirely new market of legal services, that of the legal expert in the new governmental agencies, and, in the same act, opened the doors of the law schools to the social sciences'.[70]

Nevertheless, this success did not come without its counterpart: 'The alliance with Roosevelt's administration led the realists away from a critical discourse towards an operational one.'[71] In order to appear credible as 'responsible social-legal planners', they had to contribute to reinforce the social belief in the law, constructing the myth of a doubly legitimate law, both from the perspective of the new social science and a political morality conforming to the ideals of the welfare and regulatory state.

B. Law and Society: a Hierarchised Division of Labour of Scientific Rationalisation and the Legal Order

The emergence at the end of the 1960s of the current Law and Society movement signalled the revitalisation of this strategy of mobilisation of the social sciences in the service of legal

---

[65] Ibid, 145.
[66] Ibid, 149.
[67] Ibid, 146.
[68] Ibid, 148.
[69] Ibid, 150.
[70] Ibid, 152.
[71] Ibid, 156.

progress. The themes were a rationalisation of legal regulation and greater social justice[72]—access to justice for the underprivileged and recognition of their rights. This complementarity between the two poles which—employing the terms formulated by Boaventura de Sousa Santos[73]—can be termed 'regulatory' and 'emancipatory', went along with a hierarchised division of labour between lawyers and social science researchers. The professors of law reserved to themselves the key roles, due to the simple fact that they were able to play simultaneously on the double register of scientific competence and the legal authority that goes with greater institutional and relational capital. This hierarchical relationship was built on the opposition and complementary between

> two species of scientific capital: on one side a temporal (or political) power, an institutional and institutionalised power linked to the occupation of eminent positions in scientific institutions ... as well as control over the means of scientific production (contracts, credits, positions, etc.) and the (re)production of legitimate producers of science (power to shape and influence academic careers through nominations, recommendations and appointments...) and on the other side a "pure" scientific capital of personal prestige, which is acquired mainly through contributions recognized by peers.[74]

This division of scientific labour which doubles as a hierarchisation of agents shapes the objects and themes of research. This process is evident with respect to the 'regulatory' pole, which benefits from greater proximity to the institutional resources and market of 'policy sciences'. On the other side, researchers who are more activist and engaged reclaim the 'emancipatory' pole and are able to turn their investment in political legitimacy into a strong scientific visibility. Less subject to bureaucratic necessities, these researchers embody the scientific ideal of the production of knowledge responding to 'social demands'.

Conforming to the adage of making a virtue out of necessity, these investments come at a cost in scientific relevance. These two poles—between which the boundaries are porous and fluctuating—have in common the exclusion from the definition of their objects of research all that touches the structure of the legal field, and therefore that which determines the choice of their objects of study in relation to the positions that they occupy in this hierarchical space. This structural invisibility of hierarchical structures in the field of legal power (and in its relations with the field of state power) is a kind of common denominator of the two topical themes, providing a basis for the alliance between the different fractions that co-exist in the Law and Society movement.

Nevertheless, as a function of their respective positions in the processes of learned production, the two poles of Law and Society invoke perceptively different justifications

---

[72] According to Victor Rosenblum's presidential address to the Law and Society Association in 1970, 'the law itself can in some situations guide the development of cultural values and social institutions, in other situations be utterly ineffective in doing so, and in still other situations have consequences exactly the opposite of those it was intended to produce. The social-scientific investigation of the variables which produce each of these results carried on with the aim of formulating a general theory of the limits of effective legal action seems to me to be essential to the understanding of the relationship between law and social change. Such a theory should be useful to lawmakers as a guide in using law as an instrument of social policy. Another service the social scientist can and should provide the lawmaker is the pragmatic evaluation of the social consequences of specific rules of law to determine how well they achieve their ends and how they might be modified to better achieve those ends'. See VG Rosenblum, 'President's Message' (1970) 5 *Law & Society Review* 3, 4.

[73] B de S Santos, *Toward a New Common Sense: Law, Science, and Politics in the Paradigmatic Transition* (New York, Routledge, 1995).

[74] P Bourdieu, *Usages sociaux de la science: Pour une sociologie clinique du champ* (Paris, INRA Editions, 1997), 29.

to explain their priorities, and thus also their blind spots. The researchers who seek to help policy-makers rely largely on the rigour of their scientific methods. This approach corresponds to the division of labour which allows them to avoid posing questions about the structure of the field in which the process of political decision is inscribed. The social science researchers confine themselves mainly to quantitative analyses with given objectives. The political and professional stakes that weigh on the themes and the categories are, if not hidden, at least bracketed for the purpose of the research. Within the broad Law and Society field in the US, the Society for Empirical Legal Studies well reflects this division.

In contrast, those who work on the themes that are by definition much more political, play less on the scientific register and much more on their engagement in the service of causes for which ideological legitimacy imposes tactical imperatives and self-censure on the researchers. The fact that they are engaging in the service of great causes prevents all forms of reflexive distance, since it might appear as a criticism of the actions of the activist professionals—even a kind of treason. Further, these allies play a determinant role, as much for the definition of the objects and the themes of the research as to validate the results. The support and recognition by the activist practitioners attests to the value of the scholarly analyses.

Even if the modalities and the principles of justification differ, the effects of these blind spots converge to exclude analysis of the structures within the field of legal power. Still, it is not necessary to see this phenomenon as a simple failure of scientific activity. It is above all, the result and the product of the structures of the field—the means by which the structures and hierarchies of legal fields impose their logic on the (re)production of learned representations of the law.

It is therefore significant that one observes very similar phenomena in other national spaces, where the borrowings from the social sciences most often contribute to promote updating and reform strategies, pursued in alliance with state bureaucracies, and also to help the 'lower legal clergy' seeking to gain recognition as legitimate spokespersons for the rights of underprivileged social groups.

C. Social Sciences as Auxiliaries of the 'Legislateur Éclairé' (Enlightened Lawmaker)

As Bourdieu reminds us, 'those who govern today have need of a science capable of rationalizing, in a double sense, domination, capable at the same time of reinforcing mechanisms that assure it and legitimate it'.[75] One can easily transpose these observations about the sociology of religion to legal sociology. The instrumentalisation of social science in the service of policy-makers produces the kind of marketing studies that take as their quasi-exclusive object the behaviour and characteristics of potential clients in order to refine their politics and improve the impact or effectiveness.[76]

---

[75] P Bourdieu, 'Une science qui derange' in *Questions de sociologie* (Paris, Les éditions de Minuit, 1984).

[76] In this manner, the observations of an eminent representative of French legal doctrine, Robert Savatier strangely echo the promotional discourse described above for Law and Society: 'what contemporary jurists desire from sociology, that which can help to guide them, is first in the recognition of social structures that are to be affected by rules of law, next the range of possible reactions that these rules of law will bring according to the play of social factors'. See R Savatier, *Les metamorphoses economiques et sociales du droit prive d'aujourd'hui* (Paris, Dalloz, 1959), 136.

According to the formulas offered by jurists, the social sciences, and more particularly sociology, perform the function of contributing to the modernisation of law. This tactical argument is mobilised—with some prudence!—by reformers, particularly in newer legal disciplines such as social law and labour law. It is a warning addressed to the hierarchy with respect to legal doctrine characterised by the most legally-orthodox positions as well as the most conservative politics.

These modernisers repeat that is not a matter of questioning the legal order, but of avoiding the 'law of jurists' (an expression targeting the guardians of doctrinal orthodoxy and exegetic science) becoming 'antiquarian law', a 'dogmatic law',[77] in order to 'save their discipline from unconditional attachment to the established order'.[78] In short, these reformers remind their peers that in order to be socially credible, the law and the jurists must know how to take into account transformations of the social reality, under penalty of appearing archaic and being disqualified and dispossessed by new sciences of government.

This tactical use of social science, limited to subaltern tasks of reporting on the legal environment and its social context, is in this manner inconsistent with a sociology that would take as its object understanding the functioning of the legal field and interrogating the mechanisms—including the recourse to social science—that contribute to the reproduction of the belief in the law, at the price of a redefinition of positions that consolidate more that threaten the structures and the hierarchies constitutive of the legal order.

The stakes of these false ruptures is only to disturb the hierarchies and internal relations of power sufficiently to permit the promotion of the new arrivals, without in the process weakening the structures and the representations on which rest the belief in the autonomy of these symbolic fields and their legitimacy. As Jean Carbonnier advised: 'Don't shake without discerning the columns of the Temple'. He made this injunction more precise when writing that for this auxiliary science, 'it would be unpardonable to launch by itself, lightly armed as it is, in pursuit of that which the law has most jealously defended, which is its essence, or at least its own image'.[79] This disciplinary imperative addressed to legal sociology made clear that it should stick to its role as an 'ancillary' sub-discipline and thus remain 'respectful' of the legal order that it had to serve. Jean Carbonnier was one of the godfathers of a revival of sociology of law in France in the 1970s, seeking to make the case for the legislative modernisation of family law.

D. A Tactical Interest in the Fable of Pure Science

In a field of scientific production with relatively weak autonomy, scientific ruptures are necessarily linked to ruptures and even political revolutions that favour the emergence of new strategic alliances exterior to the field. As a counterpart, these new alliances, which favour a recomposition of internal hierarchies, also underlie the definition of new objects of research, which appear and give value to a double legitimacy—both in relation to the

---

[77] P Durand, *La connaissance du phenomene juridique et les taches de la doctrine moderne du droit prive* (Paris, Dalloz, 1956).

[78] Citations from Professor Rene David in A Bancaud and Y Dezalay, 'La sociologie juridique comme enjeu social et professionel' (1984) 12 *Revue Interdisciplinaire d'Etudes Juridiques* 1.

[79] J Carbonnier, *Sociologie Juridique* (Paris, Armand Colin, 1972) 272ff.

new political landscape and in regards to the new agendas and paradigms of mainstream academic production.

As was seen in the case of the Legal Realists, the effectiveness of these updating strategies is much greater when the new producers, after having denounced the 'false science' of the guardians of orthodoxy which they oppose, shift gears and reassert the mystification of a scientific approach which permits the law and the jurists to take account of transformations in social demands. For these reformers, it is essential that they protect themselves against the risks of an unveiling which, in publicly revealing their intervention and their interests in the play of alliances, would only weaken the credibility of the new rights by reducing them to arrangements negotiated by learned brokers between law and state politics.

In these plays of alliance, all the participants have an interest in maintaining this fiction, insisting on the scientific objectivity of the relationship between law and society and hiding the role of intermediaries in the process through which new social demands become inscribed in legal categories.[80] This is true for socio-legal scholars—but also for the law professors who are their partners. This boundary is easily maintained by the policy-makers for whom it increases the room to manoeuvre by keeping discreet their specific interests in the world of lobbying. It is even more true for a legal sociology purporting to champion 'causes' and more generally new social demands.

As Bourdieu reminded us,

> this rhetoric of the "social demand" ... is inspired less by a real desire to satisfy the needs or the expectations of such and such category of 'clients' ... or even to gain their support, ... it is part of a scientific strategy whose legitimacy can't be challenged by its opponents, it provides a surplus of symbolic force in the internal competitive struggles over the monopoly of legitimate definition of scientific practice.[81]

The analysis also applies to activist practitioners, such as cause lawyers, who contribute to the promotion of legal practices in favour of dominated social groups. The work of scientific objectification brings them an increase in legitimacy with respect to the process of putting at a distance arrangements and private interests that might otherwise be able to disqualify their efforts. And the strategic importance of this work of universalisation is even greater when it is a matter of marginalised and dominated social groups, since they have little access to the networks and institutionalised forms of rationalisation that are reserved to dominant groups.

---

[80] This 'putting in a direct relationship the text and the context is what I call the 'error of short-circuiting,' an error that consists in putting in relationship a work ... and its (social) manifestations', see Bourdieu, *Usages sociaux de la science* (n 74) 14. He makes this point more precise as follows: 'My hypothesis consists in supposing that between these two poles which are very far apart ... there exists an intermediate universe, which I call the literary, artistic, legal or scientific field, that is to say the universe in which are inserted the agents and the institutions that produce (works or texts). ... In fact, the external constraints, of whatever nature they might be, only operate through the intermediary of the field and are mediated through the logic of the field. One of the most visible manifestations of the autonomy of the field is this capacity to refract, by retranslating constraints and external demands into a specific form.' Ibid, 15.

[81] Ibid, 40.

IV. Conclusion

A blindness not only strongly limits the heuristic relevance of the majority of research on the themes of law and society, but also dooms to failure any effort at comparative sociology, and thus, a fortiori, any interrogation into the international relations between national legal fields, or the emergence of transnational legal fields. In fact, as we have developed in our own works,[82] this international dimension of legal practice is strongly implicated in international hegemonic struggles in which national legal elites are at the same time the missionaries and the mercenaries, the courtiers and the mediators.

Further, the (re)production of legal learning is a key element in the internationalisation of the competition of national legal elites. From the reinvention of legal learning in Bologna for Europe during the early Renaissance, to the recent wave of the restructuring of teaching law according to the model of the American law school, through the exportation of faculties and schools of law as a strategy of co-optation of colonial elites (or as a strategy of the cold war in the case of the Law and Development Movement), the international circulation of students and professors has always been at the centre of the methods for the (re)production of national fields of legal learning.

The international relationships between legal fields is therefore played out in complex games relating at the same time to hegemonic strategies, the competition between different elites and different expertises, but also the interconnection between national histories that have produced different configurations of the field of state power, in which law and jurists have held very specific positions and resources.

In order to begin to understand this international dimension of legal practice, it is then indispensable to analyse the multiple networks of relations that permit these elites of national legal fields to exchange and accumulate different species of symbolic capital—social and economic, political and academic—through which they have constructed their specific model of legal capital, and which determines the respective value of national competences in international markets.

In other words, it is imperative to open the black box that constitutes the unthought and unthinkable of Law and Society scholarship. Failing this, the multiple efforts toward internationalisation, whether seeking to export legal learning (as with the missionaries of law and development), or through comparative sociology, come up against the stumbling block of legal and paradigmatic nationalism—projecting to another national space conceptions of legal practice that are the product of very specific national histories, such as the belief in the virtues of the Socratic method, the notion of 'lawyer' as 'monopolist', and a fortiori that of 'cause lawyer' or the bar as champion of 'political liberalism'.

---

[82] Dezalay and Garth, *Dealing in Virtue* (n 46); Dezalay and Garth, *The Internationalization of Palace Wars* (n 32); Dezalay and Garth, *Asian Legal Revivals* (n 32).

19

BRICS and Politics of Reforming Global Governance: The Case of Investment Arbitration

MIHAELA PAPA[*]

I. Introduction

Are the BRICS countries (Brazil, Russia, India, China and South Africa) the agents of change in global governance or does their rise simply perpetuate established policy trajectories? Do they have the potential to transform highly contested areas of global governance such as investment arbitration? David Trubek's entrepreneurial scholarship at the intersection of global governance, critical legal studies and the sociology of the legal profession sets the foundations for exploring these important questions.[1] This article builds upon and extends David Trubek's efforts to situate emerging powers in the context of complex forces affecting international economic law and policy. It conceptualises emerging powers as agents engaged in the politics of reforming global governance and investigates whether they have the potential to reform investment arbitration governance.

The rise of major emerging powers attracts a lot of attention among theorists and practitioners in the field of international affairs. BRICS countries 'account for nearly 30 percent of the world's land area, 42 percent of the global population, [and] make up 18 percent of the world GDP and 15 percent of the world total trade volume'.[2] Other indicators such as the composite index of national capabilities, natural resource endowments, energy

[*] I would like to thank the Harvard Law School's Program on the Legal Profession for my postdoctoral fellowship, Sarah Weiner for excellent research assistance and the participants in the conference Critical Legal Perspectives on Global Governance: *Liber Amicorum David M Trubek*, held at the European University Institute, 28–30 June 2012, for their insightful comments on the previous version of this article.

[1] See DM Trubek and M Galanter, 'Scholars in Self-Estrangement: Some Reflections on the Crisis in Law and Development Studies in the United States' (1974) 4 *Wisconsin Law Review* 1062; DM Trubek, Y Dezalay, R Buchanan, and JR Davis, 'Global Restructuring and the Law: Studies of the Internationalisation of Legal Fields and the Creation of Transnational Arenas' (1994) 44 *Case Western Reserve Law Review* 407; DM Trubek and A Santos (eds), *The New Law and Economic Development: A Critical Appraisal* (Cambridge, Cambridge University Press, 2006); DM Trubek and L Trubek, 'New Governance and Legal Regulation: Complementarity, Rivalry or Transformation' (2007) 13 *Columbia Journal of European Law* 542; DM Trubek and P Cottrell, 'Robert Hudec and the Theory of International Economic Law: the Law of Global Space' in C Thomas and JP Trachtman (eds), *Developing Countries in the WTO Legal Systems* (Oxford, Oxford University Press, 2009); DM Trubek, 'Developmental States and the Legal Order: Towards a New Political Economy of Development and Law' (2008) *University of Wisconsin Legal Studies Research Paper No 1075*, available at papers.ssrn.com/sol3/papers. cfm?abstract_id=1349163; DM Trubek, 'Reversal of Fortune? International Economic Governance, Alternative Development Strategies, and the Rise of the BRICS' Working paper presented at the conference Critical Legal Perspectives on Global Governance: *Liber Amicorum David M Trubek*.

[2] Y Zhang (Chinese Ambassador to India), 'BRICS Work for Shared Prosperity' *The Hindu* (13 April 2011).

capabilities, and foreign exchange reserves paint a clear picture of these countries' relevance in the global order.[3] Although these countries are spearheading the global economic power shift, their economic credentials do not automatically translate into geo-political influence. Both Japan and the European Union have spent much of their existence as economic powers and political dwarfs, and they have only gradually developed an ability to proactively intervene in world politics.

Some scholars argue that emerging powers are already exerting influence on other stakeholders in the system and envision a major change in policy trajectories.[4] Other scholars doubt that these powers have the capacity to challenge the current world order or emerge as coalitions willing to bear the costs of global public policy leadership.[5] While there seems to be a general consensus that these countries do not view themselves as beneficiaries of the liberal international system, the politics of reform remains less understood. Which emerging powers are the agents of change? What are the actual reform needs in the complex and fragmented system of global governance? What are emerging powers dissatisfied with or what are their incentives for reform? In other words, what are the political determinants of reform that can help us understand the rise of emerging powers in the context of complex forces affecting international economic law and policy? This article seeks to conceptualise the politics of reforming global governance as a prerequisite for thinking about emerging powers' influence in specific subfields. It then draws on this conceptualisation to explore the rise of emerging powers in the field of investment arbitration. The inquiry is focused on the BRICS, a coalition of five emerging powers which are joining efforts to pursue a reformist agenda in global governance and build a multi-polar world order.

Studying the politics of reform in the field of investment arbitration is more than intrinsically important.[6] Investment arbitration is a tool for addressing private foreign actors' claims against a host state, and it may limit the state's policy autonomy in determining issues like water access and gas supply, and environmental and health standards. As such, it has triggered a lot of public anxiety about globalisation and raised concerns that powerful countries and corporations have shaped globalisation to further their own interests and developed rules that work in their favour.[7] The field of investment arbitration now seems to suffer from a phenomenon of self-estrangement.[8] Both scholars and practitioners

---

[3] See LE Armijo, 'The BRICs Countries as Analytical Category: Mirage or Insight?' (2007) 31 *Asian Perspective* 1.

[4] See, eg C Jaffrelot (ed), *Emerging States: The Wellspring of a New World Order* (Cambridge, Cambridge University Press, 2009); AS Alexandroff and AF Cooper (eds), *Rising States, Rising Institutions: Challenges for Global Governance* (Washington, Brookings Institution Press, 2010); K Mahbubani, *The New Asian Hemisphere: The Irresistible Shift of Global Power to the East* (New York, Public Affairs, 2010); A Narlikar, *New Powers: How to Become One and How to Manage Them* (Cambridge, Cambridge University Press, 2010).

[5] See, eg A Cohen, L Curtis, D Scissors and R Walser, 'Busting the Brazil/Russia/India/China (BRIC) Myth of Challenging US Global Leadership' (2010) *Heritage Foundation Web Memo 2869*; C Roberts 'Russia's BRICs Diplomacy: Rising Outsider with Dreams of an Insider' (2009) 42 *Polity* 38; MA Glosny 'China and the BRICs: A Real (but Limited) Partnership in a Unipolar World' (2010) 42 *Polity* 100; AF Hart and BD Jones, 'How Do Rising Powers Rise?' (2010) 52 *Survival: Global Politics and Strategy* 63.

[6] Investment arbitration is a process whereby individuals or enterprises can seek an adjudication of their economic rights against a sovereign state. Investor protections are contained in investment arbitration provisions of international investment agreements and may include, for example, duties to pay market value compensation in case of expropriation or nationalisation, provide fair and equitable treatment to foreign investors and ensure that the host state does not differentiate in treatment of foreign and domestic investments.

[7] For a discussion of concerns with globalisation, see BS Chimni 'International Institutions Today: An Imperial Global State in the Making' (2004) 15 *European Journal of International Law* 1, 1; J Stiglitz, *Making Globalization Work: The Next Steps to Global Justice* (London, Penguin, 2006).

[8] Trubek and Galanter, 'Scholars in Self-Estrangement' (n 1).

have encountered difficulties defining the nature of their work, the utility of the current investment arbitration governance and directions for policymaking. The increasing use of the International Centre for the Settlement of Investment Disputes (ICSID) resulted in extensive criticism of the system, particularly from South American countries. In light of ICSID's handling of $12 billion worth of requests for arbitration over several disputes against Ecuador, Ecuadorian president Raphael Correra publicly denounced ICSID in 2009 and argued that Ecuador's withdrawal was necessary for the country's liberation because ICSID 'signifies colonialism, slavery with respect to transnationals, with respect to Washington, with respect to the World Bank'.[9] Certainly, private actors are dissatisfied with the lack of effective regulation in the investment realm, the uncertainty of the legal frameworks in place and problems with the enforcement of awards. Scholars have been divided on the value of investment arbitration because of its questionable foundation (lack of empirical evidence that investment treaties have a direct influence in attracting foreign direct investment to developing countries); and because of concerns about its bias toward foreign investors and its constraints on domestic policy space.[10] Arguments against using investment arbitration provisions in treaties have become more common, and academics and practitioners are joining efforts to prevent investment arbitration through the use of alternative dispute settlement.[11]

This article first examines the political determinants of reforming global governance: the existence of a reformist coalition, the context of reform, which is defined by the fragmentation and complexity of global governance and institutional dissatisfaction as an incentive to pursue reform. It then investigates the rise of emerging powers and its implications for the field of investment arbitration, which has remained largely unexplored in this format. Do emerging powers display policy convergence in this field? Are they willing and/or able to exert leadership? The analysis of emerging powers' coalitional and country-specific behaviour finds that BRICS countries are unlikely to exert joint leadership as a change-seeking coalition. At the coalitional level, investment has not yet emerged as one of the central themes in BRICS cooperation. At the country level, policies toward investment arbitration vary significantly. Some BRICS countries have already assumed major powers' trajectories in the field of investment arbitration. Other BRICS countries that were reluctant to embrace investment arbitration are rethinking their policies in light of their recent experiences as respondents to claims and increasing interest in protecting domestic investors as they engage abroad.

The concluding section discusses the legal challenges that BRICS countries face in investment arbitration and offers several suggestions for future research.

---

[9] Cited in *Bretton Woods Project* 'ICSID in Crisis: Straight-Jacket or Investment Protection?' (10 July 2009).

[10] See M Sornarajah 'The Retreat of Neo-liberalism in Investment Treaty Arbitration' in CA Rogers and RP Alford (eds), *The Future of Investment Arbitration* (Oxford, Oxford University Press, 2009); G Van Harten, 'Investment Treaties as a Constraining Framework' in SR Khan and J Christiansen (eds), *Towards New Developmentalism: Market as Means Rather than Master* (London, Routledge, 2011); M Waibel, A Kaushal, K-HL Chung and C Balchin (eds), *The Backlash against Investment Arbitration* (Alphen aan den Rijn, Kluwer Law International, 2010).

[11] Debates on treaty disadvantages in Australia and Canada are cases in point. An example of discussions on preventing and managing investment treaty conflict is the Washington and Lee University School of Law and the United Nations Conference on Trade and Development Joint Symposium on International Investment Law and Alternative Dispute Resolution, 29 March 2010.

II. Theoretical Insights: BRICS and the Politics of Reforming Global Governance

The rise of emerging powers is poised to be an economic and potentially political game-changer. As David Trubek pointed out,

> these "emerging powers" are technologically advanced, relatively capital rich, and regionally powerful. [They] can be active competitors in global markets not simply for primary products and for the products of low-wage, low skilled labour but also for advanced and sophisticated products and services. Thus they face the need to maintain global competitiveness[12]

As they are increasingly oriented abroad, their markets are becoming more and more important to other countries and the world economy. In addition, emerging powers 'are increasing their influence in international organisations, they have built up their capacity to deal with international economic law, and they have contributed to the emergence of new approaches to development that challenge the hegemony of neo-liberalism'.[13] As these powers construct their comparative advantages and strategically promote domestic goals, they are transitioning into rule-makers shaping the international system according to their policy preferences. Nonetheless, the impact of emerging powers on governance arrangements and the ways they go about reforming these arrangements are less straightforward. First of all, as this section argues, reform has its own politics. It takes place only if there are entrepreneurial actors willing to move the reform effort forward. The very complexity and fragmentation of global governance raise the question of entry points for reform efforts. Finally, dissatisfaction with the current system is the core incentive for reform and the pursuit of alternative solutions.

A. BRICS as a Reform Coalition

The global policymaking process is complex and involves multiple parties. Changing such a process requires leadership, and it is crucial to create and sustain a sufficiently strong coalition in favour of propositions that move the reform process forward.[14] Such a coalition would need to be able to jointly frame problems, promote particular policy solutions and implement them, deploy power-resources that create incentives, costs, and benefits for others and politically engineer consensus.[15] Are emerging powers such a coalition or are they just an economic acronym?

There is a long tradition of clustering some developing countries into the 'emerging' category to describe those countries undergoing rapid economic growth. The World Bank's use of the 'emerging markets' category or Goldman Sachs' 'emerging economies' cluster

---

[12] Trubek, 'Developmental States' (n 1).

[13] Trubek, 'Reversal of Fortune?' (n 1).

[14] G Sjostedt, 'Leadership in Multilateral Negotiations: Crisis or Transition?' in P Berton, H Kimura and IW Zartman (eds), *International Negotiation: Actors, Structure/Process, Values* (New York, St Martin's Press 1999) 242.

[15] For a discussion of various types of leadership required for transforming complex governance arrangements, see M Papa and NW Gleason, 'Major Emerging Powers in Sustainable Developing Diplomacy: Assessing their Leadership Potential' (2012) 22 *Global Environmental Change* 795.

called BRIC are cases in point.[16] Yet the clustering of emerging countries into a political category has been more controversial. Considering the use of BRIC as an analytical category for political studies from neoclassical economics, realist and liberal institutionalist perspectives, Armijo concluded that the category is 'a mirage' because:

> The four do not share domestic political institutions, international goals, or economic structures and challenges. If the category, nonetheless, provides insight, it must be because this set of countries holds similar implications for the larger *system*—the international political economy—within which it is embedded.[17]

Other scholars have been similarly sceptical, questioning what is the right cluster to examine and suggesting alternative acronyms to describe new blocs of emerging powers.[18]

Russia's initiative to get BRIC countries together as a formal political entity in 2008 facilitated the evolution of cooperation among these countries and cemented BRIC as a political category. Now, together with South Africa, which joined BRIC to form BRICS, BRICS is combining forces to pursue a reformist agenda in global politics and facilitate the creation of a multi-polar world order.[19] BRICS cooperation is deepening through annual summits and the regular cooperation of foreign, trade, finance and other ministers, officials and associations from these countries. Several aspects of BRICS cooperation make it a relevant category for studying the reform of investment governance. The first aspect is BRICS' ambition to engage in reforming global economic governance and create a more equitable and democratic world order. The second aspect is BRICS members' willingness to invest in policymaking. There is a clear commitment to engaging local scholars in producing original research and policy recommendations to enhance problem-solving in global governance, and there is a mechanism to ensure that their output feeds into the political process. Finally, the engagement of BRICS countries in sustained, routine cooperation reinforces their ability to construct common interests and create joint agendas.

B. The Context of Reform: Fragmentation and Complexity of Global Governance

Given that BRICS seeks to become a reform coalition, what needs to be reformed? Global governance structures in place today result from decades of legalisation and judicialisation of the international system.[20] The system's legalisation is reflected in the increasing

---

[16] For example, International Finance Corporation's efforts to promote mutual fund investments in rapidly developing countries in the 1980s were discussed in this context and the very acronym BRIC originates from J O'Neill, 'Building Better Global Economic BRICs' *Global Economics Paper 66*, Goldman Sachs (30 November 2001).

[17] Armijo, 'The BRICs Countries as Analytical Category' (n 3) 38.

[18] See, A Antkiewicz and AF Cooper, *Emerging Powers in Global Governance: Lessons from the Heiligendamm Process* (Waterloo, Ontario, Wilfried Laurier University Press, 2008).

[19] The BRIC countries agreed that their priority was building a more democratic international system founded on the rule of law and multilateral diplomacy and reforming the UN. See, The Joint Communiqué of the Meeting of the Foreign Ministers of the People's Republic of China, the Russian Federation, the Republic of India and the Federative Republic of Brazil (BRIC Meeting Yekaterinburg, Russia, 16 May 2008).

[20] These processes are explained in J Goldstein, M Kahler, RO Keohane and A-M Slaughter, 'Introduction: Legalization and World Politics' (2000) 54 *International Organization* 385; CPR Romano 'A Taxonomy of International Rule of Law Institutions' (2011) 2 *Journal of International Dispute Settlement* 241.

precision of rules and their bindingness, which has brought about the need for greater legal skills and sophistication in institutional engagement. The system's judicialisation or acceleration in the use of third-party institutions for dispute settlement is visible in the rapid growth of international courts and tribunals and other dispute settlement institutions. International relations and international legal scholars have extensively studied international institutions as central analytical units for analysing international cooperation. The former generally analyse three main drivers of institutionalised cooperation: actors' power that shapes the level of cooperation, its rules and payoffs; actors' interests, emerging as actors behave as rational utility maximisers to overcome collective action problems; and knowledge, which drives cooperation through shaping actors' behaviour and identities.[21] The latter examine how law serves several functions, including communication or setting forth standards of behaviour, facilitation or creating arenas where actors seek to set rules for their interactions or find solutions to common problems, and coercion or providing sanctions for non-compliance.[22]

Institutions have traditionally been the focal points of cooperation as well as reform efforts, but the increasing complexity of the international system has led some scholars to question the relevance of institutions. The system's growth created concerns with proliferating jurisdictions and overlapping, parallel and nested agreements, as well as actors' abilities to manipulate the system. Since the late 1990s in particular, legal scholars have talked about fragmentation, and political scholars about the politics of complexity to examine these concerns. Fragmentation scholarship has been prominent in international legal scholarship on the conflict of norms, particularly surrounding the Report of the International Law Commission (ILC) on the Fragmentation of International Law.[23] The ILC report recognised both positive and negative aspects of growth, stating:

> On the one hand, fragmentation does create the danger of conflicting and incompatible rules, principles, rule systems and institutional practices. On the other hand, it reflects the rapid expansion of international legal activity into various new fields and the diversification of its objects and techniques.[24]

The ILC examined the substantive aspects of fragmentation in light of the hierarchy of norms and the Vienna Convention on the Law of Treaties' attempts to bring order to a potentially fragmented landscape of international decisions, but it did not deal with questions relating to the interactions among international judicial institutions or the changes that international courts and tribunals would need to implement to address fragmentation.

---

[21] A Hasenclever, P Mayer and V Rittberger, *Theories of International Regimes* (Cambridge, Cambridge University Press, 1997).

[22] Trubek and Cottrell, 'Robert Hudec and the Theory of International Economic Law' (n 1); A Chayes and AH Chayes, *The New Sovereignty: Compliance with International Regulatory Agreements* (Cambridge, MA, Harvard University Press, 1995).

[23] J Pauwelyn, *Conflict of Norms in Public International Law: How WTO Law Relates to Other Rules of International Law* (Cambridge, Cambridge University Press, 2003); M Koskenniemi and P Leino, 'Fragmentation of International Law? Postmodern Anxieties' (2002) 15 *Leiden Journal of International Law* 553; International Law Commission (ILC) 'Fragmentation of International Law: Difficulties Arising from the Diversification and Expansion of International Law' Report of the ILC Study Group chaired by Martti Koskenniemi, Fifty-eighth session, Geneva 1 May–9 June and 3 July–11 August 2006.

[24] International Law Commission, 'Fragmentation', ibid, 405.

International relations scholars have been concerned with the political aspects of complexity: how do actors in the system move across the webs of governance and how do they affect and are affected by networked politics?[25] Complexity results from both the propensity of actors to create new institutions and the multiplicity of institutions operating within a given social space. It challenges the very idea of institutional stability or institutions acting as focal points for states in the international system, around which states coordinate their bargaining and their expectations.[26] Complexity scholarship has acknowledged positive aspects of growth like the ability to move forward policymaking on an issue by shifting to a more effective institution (for example, landmines negotiations or human rights enforcement), but it has also raised concerns that growth favours powerful countries in the system because they can operate better under complexity, both in terms of shaping the rules of global governance and avoiding them when desired.[27] Having observed how multiple institutions simultaneously influence an issue area, some scholars have shifted their attention from single institutions to new units of analysis such as regime complexes or sets of specialised sectoral and issue-based regimes and other governance arrangements more or less loosely linked together, sometimes mutually reinforcing and sometimes overlapping and conflicting.[28]

Concerns with fragmentation and the politics of complexity have been highly pronounced in investment arbitration. The failure of efforts to negotiate a multilateral agreement on investment resulted in the proliferation of regulatory approaches at multiple cooperation levels and instruments with legal or law-like characteristics.[29] Some of the law was set out in treaties bearing some resemblance to traditional public international law, and some had features of private law. International tribunals and arbitral decision-makers acted as legal entrepreneurs when supplying the actual application of investment provisions or dealing with institutional overlaps (for example, competing norms of the human rights regime or commercial arbitration regime). There are now thousands of Bilateral Investment Treaties (BITs) setting rules for bilateral investment cooperation and dispute settlement, and there is a limited number of multilateral trade agreements with investment arbitration provisions. BITs and trade agreements generally refer investment disputes to the ICSID, a World Bank institution created by a 1965 multilateral convention and whose procedures are specifically tailored for investment arbitration. Other rules commonly used by those outside ICSID are the 1976 Arbitration Rules of the United Nations Commission on International Trade Law (UNCITRAL), which permit ad hoc arbitration in a broad range of disputes, including investment arbitration. The proliferation of international tribunals led to situations where two courts make different judgments and awards when the parties claim and plead the same violations and facts under. This was the case with *CME/Lauder v Czech Republic*

---

[25] See, eg KJ Alter and S Meunier, 'The Politics of International Regime Complexity' (2009) 7 *Perspectives on Politics* 134.

[26] TC Schelling, *The Strategy of Conflict* (Cambridge, MA, Harvard University Press, 1960).

[27] DW Drezner, 'The Power and Peril of International Regime Complexity' (2009) 7 *Perspectives on Politics* 65; E Benvenisti and G Downs 'The Empire's New Clothes: Political Economy and the Fragmentation of International Law' (2007) 60 *Stanford Law Review* 595.

[28] K Raustiala and DG Victor, 'The Regime Complex for Plant Genetic Resources' (2004) 58 *International Organization* 277, 279; S Oberthür and OS Stokke, *Managing Institutional Complexity: Regime Interplay and Global Environmental Change* (Cambridge, MA, The MIT Press, 2011).

[29] The 'messiness' of the system is a common feature of the law of the global space. For an overview of the nature of the investment regime see J Salacuse, 'The Emerging Global Regime for Investment' (2010) 51 *Harvard International Law Journal* 427.

arbitrations, where the tribunal in *Lauder v Czech Republic* found that the Czech government's breach of the US–Czech Republic BIT did not give rise to liability, while Lauder-controlled CME, incorporated in Netherlands, claimed the same violations relying on the Netherlands–Czech Republic BIT and the tribunal came to conclusions diametrically opposing the first award.[30] Similarly, actors can navigate around the system, engaging in 'treaty-shopping' through most favoured nation clauses and by means of corporate group structuring, so there may be extensive activity outside immediate institutional boundaries.

The system's messiness complicates reform efforts. There are many possible reform pathways at various levels of activity, and emerging powers' ability to pick a focal institution to reform, as, for example, they are trying to do with the Security Council or the International Monetary Fund in other issue areas, is constrained.

The density and diversity of international investment agreements resembles what Jagdish Bhagwati would describe as a 'spaghetti bowl' of entangled laws and regulations which is affected by public as well as private actors.[31] This messy prism comprises investment agreements, investment arbitration provisions in these agreements, investment arbitration tribunals and the relationships and flows among them. The prerequisite for strategising about reform is the perception of governance problems and willingness to mobilise to change the status quo.

C. Incentives for Reform: Institutional Dissatisfaction

Policy entrepreneurs willing to reform global governance necessarily define their dissatisfaction with the current system from their subjective point of view—they may perceive institutional decline and need to decide how to address it. The challenge of acting on dissatisfaction has been most clearly conceptualised in the literature through Hirschman's 'Voice, Exit and Loyalty' framework, which assumes that dissatisfied members within an organisation have two key options: to use voice to directly express dissatisfaction within the organisation; or to use exit and leave the organisation.[32] In the choice between voice and exit, voice will lose out because its effectiveness depends on the discovery of new ways of exerting influence and pressure toward organisational recovery, but institutional loyalty may redress this balance and serve as a barrier to exit. This basic Hirschman's dilemma can be applied to global governance institutions, which are unstable and co-exist with multiple overlapping, parallel and nested bodies. I have situated Hirschman's dilemma in the context of institutionally complex global governance, arguing that there are several strategies to respond to dissatisfaction based on actors' decisions to stay in the institution, exit or position themselves in some other way along the disengagement spectrum as shown in Table 1.

'Propensity to disengage' refers to actors' tendency to depart from the current institution. It is low when actors stay engaged in the current institution and increases when they start

---

[30] *Lauder v The Czech Republic*, UNCITRAL, 3 September 2001, 9 *ICSID Reports* 66, (2002) 14 *World Trade and Arbitration Materials*, 35; *CME Czech Republic BV v The Czech Republic*, UNCITRAL, Partial Award of 13 September 2001, 9 *ICSID Reports* 121, 14 *World Trade and Arbitration Materials* 109 (2002).

[31] J Bhagwati, 'U.S. trade policy: The infatuation with free trade agreements,' in J Bhagwati and AO Krueger (eds) *The Dangerous Drift to Preferential Trade Agreements* (Washington DC, AEI Press, 1995).

[32] AO Hirschman, *Exit, Voice and Loyalty: Responses to Decline in Firms, Organizations, and States* (Cambridge, MA, Harvard University Press, 1970).

Table 1. Response to Dissatisfaction along a Spectrum of Disengagement

Propensity to disengage from the current institution	Response to dissatisfaction (Falls along the spectrum of disengagement below—'in' means staying in institution, 'exit' means leaving it)
Low ↓ High	(1) IN – Ignoring Dissatisfaction (2) IN – Voicing Dissatisfaction in the Current Institution (3) IN – Pursuing Other Issue-Related Institutions (4) IN – Setting up a New Institution (5) EXIT – Withdrawing from the Institution (6) EXIT – Pursuing Other Issue-Related Institutions (7) EXIT – Setting up a New Institution

Source: M Papa, State Dissatisfaction in Global Environmental Fora: Explaining the Pursuit of Forum Shopping Doctoral Dissertation (Tufts University, Fletcher School, 2010).

Options (3) and (6) describe institutional shifting whether by leaving the current institution (6) or operating in the current institution and an additional one (3). Options (4) and (7) describe setting up a new institution or forum creation in a related issue area while in or out of the current institution respectively.

expressing dissent, exploring alternatives to current structures and engage in institutional navigation in pursuit of more favourable outcomes. When this conceptualisation is applied to global governance arrangements in the investment realm, emerging powers' dissatisfaction with the system may lead to a number of response strategies. As Narlikar once observed, 'we may expect the new power to show complete socialisation. At the other extreme, however, we may also see the new power using its newfound status to pursue alternative visions of world order.'[33] BRICS already display various institutional choices in the investment arbitration realm.[34] Dissatisfaction with the system may not usurp current institutions, but various options on the disengagement spectrum suggest that there are a number of pathways to challenge their authority. Reform happens as each country shops from among various dissatisfaction options enhancing or undermining its existing choices, and particularly if BRICS decide to jointly pursue costlier and riskier strategies of institutional change and creation.

Dissatisfaction with the current system can also be traced by investing how actors integrate into the existing structures. For example, Johnston examined how state actors socialise into international institutions, by mimicking, which explains pro-group behaviour as a function of borrowing the language, habits and ways of acting as a safe reaction to a novel environment; social-influence or pro-group behaviour as a function of an actor's sensitivity to status markers bestowed by a social group; and persuasion, which explains pro-group behaviour as an effect of the internationalisation of new causal understandings of an actor's environment, such that these new understandings are considered normal, given and normatively correct.[35] Dezalay and Garth demonstrated socialisation of private actors,

---

[33] Narlikar, *New Powers* (n 4).

[34] Discussion draws on M Papa 'Emerging Powers in International Dispute Settlement: from legal Capacity Building fo a Level Playing Field?' (2013) 4 *Journal of International Dispute Settlement* 83.

[35] As conceptualised in AI Johnston, *Social States: China in International Institutions, 1980–2000* (Princeton, Princeton University Press, 2007).

describing how a handful of distinguished European professors and jurists', drew on their legal and social pedigrees to create a legal field of arbitration, which became dominated by social networks initially centred on the International Chamber of Commerce in Paris and then incorporated large Anglo-American law firms and their arbitrators.[36]

Investment arbitration has elements of both international public and private law, so socialisation takes place through government action as well as private actors' choices. The following section examines whether the BRICS countries and the coalition itself adapt to the system or mobilise to change it.

III. BRICS and Investment Arbitration:
Adaptation or Mobilisation?

How does the politics of reform work in the investment arbitration realm? Investment arbitration is a field where state dissatisfaction is latent because states constrain their ability to exercise their power and serve as sovereign guardians of public interest. The extent to which emerging powers can benefit from other states doing the same is only now becoming clearer as these countries' investors need protection abroad and may seek to detour around foreign court systems. The evolution of investment arbitration in BRICS is a reflection of the larger global restructuring of the legal profession and dispute settlement. As David Trubek and his colleagues suggested, the national legal field or the ensemble of institutions and practices through which law is produced, interpreted, and incorporated into social decision-making has become more 'internationalised' through globalisation-influenced shifts in economic activity and changes in the competition among developing countries for foreign investment; the use of legal fields as assets in this competition and their restructuring to create 'modern' laws, 'efficient' courts, and 'business-oriented' legal professions; and international pressures for legal reform.[37] While in each of the BRICS countries there is evidence of internationalisation of dispute settlement, emerging powers have not been equally eager to embrace investment arbitration. This section examines their participation in investment arbitration, first at the country level drawing on data on their bilateral investment treaties and government policies. It then examines the output from BRICS summit meetings to investigate whether there is evidence of joint investment policies at the BRICS level, and whether BRICS countries are potential agents for change.

---

[36] Y Dezalay and B Garth, *Dealing in Virtue: International Commercial Arbitration and the Construction of a Transnational Legal Order* (Chicago, University of Chicago Press, 1996).

[37] Trubek, et al, Global Restructuring and the Law (n 1) 477; see also DB Wilkins, 'Globalization, Lawyers, and the Rule of Law: Private Practice and Public Values in the Global Market for Corporate Legal Services' Paper presented at the *World Justice Forum*, Barcelona (21 June 2011).

A. BRICS Countries' Participation in Investment Arbitration

BRICS countries moved toward opening their economies in the 1990s, facing both an internal push to be more competitive and make their legal systems more attractive to investors, and external pressures from foreign (mostly United States and EU) investors to ensure their investments. Long before emerging powers started using investment arbitration provisions in investment treaties, they embraced the use of international arbitration tribunals for business disputes. BRICS countries (except for Brazil until 2002) ratified the Convention on the Recognition and Enforcement of Foreign Arbitral Awards (New York Convention), which provided for the recognition and enforcement of foreign arbitral awards and for obligatory referral by a national court to arbitration. With respect to using the main international arbitration tribunal for investment disputes—International Centre for Settlement of Investment Disputes (ICSID) BRICS countries have been less forthcoming. The Convention on the Settlement of Investment Disputes between States and Nationals of Other States (ICSID Convention) now has 158 signatories and 147 states have ratified, accepted or approved the Convention.[38] Of these, China is the only one of the BRICS countries that signed and ratified the Convention, and Russia signed but did not ratify it. Both China and Russia's signatures came almost 30 years after the Convention came into force, which indicates that these two countries, as well as Brazil, India and South Africa, have been outsiders to this regime for a large part of its existence. This is an indication of their dissatisfaction with the regime and the institutional benefits it may potentially provide. BRICS countries' policies toward investment arbitration are elaborated in more detail on a country-by-country basis and data on signing BITs is presented in Graph 1.

Brazil has been consistently opposed to investment arbitration and was at the forefront of efforts to reject the ICSID regime in 1964. Its resistance has been based on the belief that foreign investors should not be entitled to more favourable treatment than domestic investors and should be governed by domestic law and only allowed to resort to local courts.[39] A brief period of pro-liberalisation policies in the 1990s resulted in signing 14 BITs, but they were never ratified. While investment arbitration was not a normative fit, Brazil did not have problems attracting inward investment. On the other hand, Brazilian multinationals interested in investing abroad found alternative means of protecting their invesrments such as structuring the investments through other countries' BITs. In 2007, however, the Brazilian government reconsidered its policies toward international agreements and approved guidelines for investment negotiations, including the renegotiation of Mercosur protocols on investments, BIT negotiations with South American countries and investment provision negotiations under free trade agreement with countries outside of South America. The Finance Ministry pushed for investor–state dispute resolution mechanisms to protect Brazilian investors, but there has not yet been any movements on this issue.[40]

Russia has been actively pursuing economic reforms since the collapse of the Soviet Union in 1991, and it has become a party to a large number of BITs—out of 70 BITs, 51

---

[38] ICSID Official website, Member States available aticsid.worldbank.org/ICSID/FrontServlet?requestType=CasesRH&actionVal=ShowHome&pageName=MemberStates_Home.

[39] See J Kalicki and S Medeiros, 'Investment Arbitration in Brazil: Revisiting Brazil's Traditional Reluctance toward ICSID, BITs and Investor—State Arbitration' (2008) 24 *Arbitration International* 423.

[40] US Embassy Brazil, 'Brazil: Investment Agreement Principles: Consolidated GOB, Cable 08Brasilia289' (2008) available at wikileaks.org/cable/2008/03/08BRASILIA289.html.

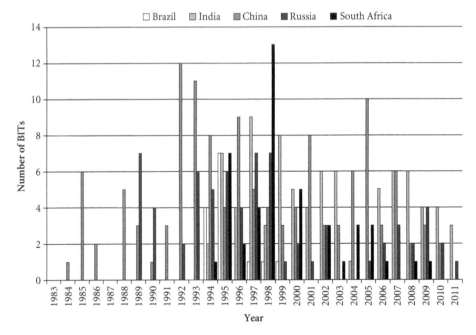

Graph 1. BITs Signed Per Year, 1983–2011(BRICS countries)

Source: UNCTAD Country-Specific Lists of BITs, available at archive.unctad.org/Templates/Page.asp?intItemID=2344&lang=1 and Government of India, Bilateral Investment Promotion and Protection Agreements available ar finmin.nic.in/bipa/bipa_index.asp.

have been ratified. However, Russia has been cautious with respect to investment arbitration provisions, and most of its BITs use a dispute resolution clause limiting the jurisdiction of international arbitral tribunals to hear disputes over the fact of expropriation. In 1994, Russia signed the Energy Charter Treaty because it wanted to encourage foreign investment in the energy sector, but it never ratified it. Part of the reason for non-ratification, as well as for the subsequent treaty withdrawal before the decision in Yukos arbitration, was Russia's concern with investment arbitration provisions. More recently, however, Russian investors' concerns have pushed the government to reconsider investment arbitration. The Indian government's decision to cancel telecom licenses put Russian conglomerate Sistema's $3.1 billion investment in India at risk and reinforced concern about securing investors' rights abroad. A parliamentary working group was set up to address the issue, and the Property Issues Committee of the Lower House recommended reinforcing intra-ministerial cooperation on securing Russian investors' rights abroad, evaluating BITs with other countries and utilising international arbitration.

India had a restrictive approach to foreign investment until the early 1990s, when it progressively opened the economy. It signed over 80 BITs and ratified over 70. India's treaties generally offer strong post-establishment protections including fair and equitable treatment, right to national treatment, non-expropriation without fair compensation as well as direct access to international arbitration. Following the dispute over the Dabhol power plant investment, which resulted in a number of treaty claims by General Electric,

Bechtel, and the foreign banks involved in financing the project, the government sought to limit the reach of investment treaty provisions.[41] India is currently facing a record number of claims against it, and the government remains divided on the value of investment arbitration provisions. When negotiating a trade pact with the EU, India did not yield under EU pressure to include an investment arbitration clause, but the government has not reached consensus on their use more generally. The Commerce Ministry has in principle decided not to include investment arbitration provisions in new agreements and review them in all the existing agreements, while the Finance Ministry believes that this clause should not be reviewed because it can help Indian investors.[42] While Indian investors have only started filing cases against foreign governments (against UK and against Bolivia), the Indian government has become more engaged in protecting investors abroad: its efforts to address continued attacks on investment projects in Nepal and sign a bilateral investment treaty with Nepal are cases in point.

China signed investment agreements with the majority of the world's countries. Its BITs from the 1980s emphasised the right of subrogation in case of expropriation and repatriation of investment and provided for most favoured nation treatment.[43] When China joined ICSID in 1993, it had a reservation for submitting only disputes over compensation resulting from expropriation or nationalisation after the domestic court had established liability. Since the 1998 China–Barbados BIT, China's BITs offer broad access to investor-state arbitration and grant prior consent to ICSID dispute settlement; its free-trade agreements (for example, with Pakistan) also provide for investor–state arbitration if the dispute cannot be settled amicably within a period of six months. China's approach to investment arbitration changed as outbound investments became more significant. Now the trend is for China to give unconditional consent to arbitration before ICSID or an ad hoc tribunal for final determination, and ICSID has become a forum of choice for Chinese investors—the 2007 *Tza Yap Shum v Republic of Peru* case was the first public decision interpreting a BIT with China.[44]

South Africa began to enter into investment treaties in early 1990s, when its post-apartheid government decided to promote foreign investment and provide assurances to investors that their investments would be protected. Yet the government perceived that much of what it signed gave too much power to investors and was not in its favour.[45] Now it has close to 50 BITs and half of them are ratified. The Department of Trade and Industry embarked on a major review of South Africa's BIT policy in 2007 and found that there was

---

[41] Indian official quoted in LE Peterson, 'Bechtel and GE Mount Billion Dollar Investment Treaty Claim against India' *INVEST-SD News Bulletin* (23 September 2003).

[42] Officials quoted in AR Mishra, 'India May Exclude Clause on Lawsuits from Trade Pacts' *LiveMint and Wall Street Journal* (29 January 2012).

[43] This discussion is based on G Wang, 'China's Practice in International Investment Law: From Participation to Leadership in the World Economy' in MH Arsanjani, JK Cogan, RD Sloane and S Wiessner (eds), *Looking to the Future: Essays on International Law in Honor of W Michael Reisman* (Leiden, Martinus Nijhoff Publishers, 2011) and W Shan and N Gallagher, *Chinese Investment Treaties: Policies and Practice* (Oxford, Oxford University Press, 2009).

[44] ICSID, *Tza Yap Shum v Republic of Peru* [2007] ARB/07/6.

[45] Argument put forward by Randall Williams, South Africa's Department of Trade and Industry official at The Third Annual Forum of Developing Country Investment Negotiators; R Williams, 'Nothing Sacred: Developing Countries and the Future of International Investment Treaties' (International Institute for Sustainable Development, November 2009).

no reason why a review of an investor's claim cannot be undertaken in domestic courts provided that these are independent and effective, rather than in international arbitration tribunals.[46] However, South African firms are major regional investors and newer BITs with countries in the region provide for international investment arbitration (for example, the South Africa–Zimbabwe BIT) after a six-month period. Many of the BITs which have been negotiated with African parties have yet to enter into force, but the overall policy for the future is to refrain from entering into BITs except in cases of compelling economic and political circumstances.[47]

This broad overview of BRICS countries' policies toward investment arbitration indicates these countries' different levels of engagement with global investment governance. While all BRICS countries have signed BITs at some point to promote investment (see Graph 1), Brazil is an outsider with a small number of non-ratified treaties but it still participates in the regime through other countries' BITs.

China represents another extreme due to its large number of treaties (more than 100) and its ICSID membership. Accordingly, Brazil has no BITs with other BRICS countries, while China has bilateral investment treaties with all other BRICS countries except for Brazil. South Africa and India have treaties with Russia and China but not with each other. With respect to investment arbitration provisions, China and Russia approached them with caution and in a restrictive way, while India and South Africa had broader provisions and sought to narrow them over time. The question of signing treaties and agreeing to investment arbitration varies across countries due to a number of reasons, such as the negotiating capacity of the government, economic conditions (ease of attracting foreign investors), the existence of treaty sponsors and the nature of the ratification process, but there is also a significant normative component with respect to giving privileged treatment to foreign investors and constraining public autonomy. As these countries began to face claims against their governments at home, and investor protection needs abroad, they have been rethinking their investment arbitration policies.

Assessing the dissatisfaction with the regime is complex as investment arbitration policies are in flux. To be sure, there is no single institution that can serve as a focus of dissatisfaction or reform: there is no central investment arbitration tribunal with interpretative power that BRICS countries accept and neither is there a widely-accepted model investment treaty that would need to be changed. While China has centralised its approach to investment arbitration by integrating into ICSID, other countries do not have such an affiliation and have been experimenting with their investment arbitration policies. On the one hand, Brazil, India, South Africa and Russia have become more assertive in protecting their policy space when negotiating investment arbitration provisions in treaties or trade agreements with major powers. On the other hand, however, they have become concerned about their own investors investing abroad. The result of this tension is a mix of policies in individual BITs and divisions among government departments about the right course of action. At the same time, emerging powers are increasingly thinking regionally about investment cooperation and dispute settlement. India signed the Association of Southeast

---

[46] See South Africa's Department of Trade and Industry Policy Statement 'The South African Government's Approach to Future International Investment Treaties' available at www.jadafa.co.za/LinkClick.aspx?fileticket=9 A6eXZstRl0%3D&tabid=432.

[47] South Africa's Department of Trade and Industry, 'Minister Davies Launched UNCTAD Investment Policy Framework' Media Statement (26 July 2012).

Asian Nations Comprehensive Investment Agreement and established the South Asian Association for Regional Cooperation's Arbitration Council. Brazil engaged in efforts to design an arbitration centre and rules to change the practice of investment arbitration through the Union of South American Nations. South Africa engaged in the Southern African Development Community's efforts to create the framework for broader foreign direct investment in the region. Since problems with protecting emerging powers' outward investments are directly displayed in their regions (for example, cases of Indian investors in Nepal or South African investors in Zimbabwe), regional cooperation channels represent a possible opening for innovation in investment arbitration policies.

B. Coalitional Commitment to Reform Investment Governance

Given that emerging powers have different policies with respect to investment governance, are they displaying any ambition or potential to emerge as a reform coalition in this context? If BRICS countries are committed to acting together in this realm, the main output of BRICS leaders' meetings would need to include statements on investment cooperation. This output represents purposeful joint communication of all BRICS countries through which they offer a direct coalitional account of issues and agendas in coalitional cooperation. Based on the review of BRICS leaders' statements from 2009 to 2012, investment cooperation-related commitments are not explicit and are embedded in larger questions of reforming global economic governance (see Table 2).

Investment is primarily mentioned in the context of increasing investment flows within the BRICS and improving the investment environment more broadly, as well as resisting investment barriers on the grounds of developing a green economy. As Table 2 illustrates, there is a general agreement on the principles for reforming global economic governance, but the preferred institution for global rule-making in this realm remains unclear. G20 was initially considered the 'premier forum' for economic governance reform, but at the 2012 Delhi summit of BRICS leaders, the vision of the G20 mandate became narrower and the UN Conference on Trade and Development (UNCTAD) was outlined as the focal point in the UN system for the treatment of trade and development issues. The two fora, UNCTAD and G20 collaborate, and, per G20 members' request, the UNCTAD Division on Investment and Enterprise reports on G20 investment measures. However, G7/8 (now 20) and UNCTAD have historically pursued different globalisation agendas. G7/8 has often been perceived as the embodiment of the neo-liberal economic project and its support for the rule of the market, deregulation and privatisation. UNCTAD, on the other hand, has been the central promoter of development-friendly integration of developing countries into the world economy and was closely associated with the New International Economic Order earlier in its evolution. Renewed focus on UNCTAD suggests that BRICS countries may seek to emphasise the developmental aspect of investment governance as well as economic governance more broadly and continue their affiliation with developing country-focused institutions and policies.

Although BRICS' response to the financial crisis resulted in a joint multilateral initiative, the fact that BRICS countries are not eager to push for a major reform of global investment policymaking is not surprising. Emerging powers have traditionally resisted multilateral investment cooperation. A Chinese government official once observed that the importance of a multilateral framework for investment should not be overestimated because if the host

Table 2. BRIC(S) Cooperation on Investment

BRIC(S) meetings	Summit-level declarations
2012	*Delhi declaration* (New Delhi, India, 29 March) — believe that the primary role of the G20 as premier forum for international economic cooperation at this juncture is to facilitate enhanced macroeconomic policy coordination, to enable global economic recovery and secure financial stability (para 7); — considering UNCTAD to be the focal point in the UN system for the treatment of trade and development issues, we intend to invest in improving its traditional activities of consensus-building, technical cooperation and research on issues of development and trade (para 17); — intensify trade and investment flows among (our) countries (para 18); — resist trade or investment barriers on the grounds of developing green economy (para 34);
2011	*Sanya declaration* (Sanya, China, 14 April) — support the Group of Twenty (G20) in playing a bigger role in global economic governance as the premier forum for international economic cooperation (para 14); — agreed to continue expanding and deepening economic, trade and investment cooperation among our countries (para. 26);
2010	*BRIC leaders' joint statement* (Brasilia, Brazil, 15 April) — welcome the fact that G20 was confirmed as the premier forum for international economic coordination and cooperation if its member states (para 3); — in order to facilitate trade and investment, we will study feasibilities of monetary cooperation, including local currency trade settlement arrangement between countries (para 12);
2009	*BRIC leaders' joint statement* (Yekaterinburg, Russia, 16 June) — are convinced that a reformed financial and economic architecture should be based, inter alia, on the following principles: democratic and transparent decision-making and implementation process at the international financial organisations; solid legal basis; compatibility of activities of effective national regulatory institutions and international standard-setting bodies; strengthening of risk management and supervisory practices (para 4); — call upon all parties to improve the international trade and investment environment (para 5); — underline our support for a more democratic and just multi-polar order (para 12);

Source: BRICS Information Centre: Official Documents, available at www.brics.utoronto.ca/docs/index.html.

country does not retain sovereign rights to decide when and which sectors are to be opened and under what conditions, foreign investments might be detrimental to economic and social development.[48] She further observed that

> In the framework of General Agreement on Trade in Services (GATS), developing countries have borne the pressure for opening up their domestic service markets to foreign investments, and the Agreement on Trade-Related Investment Measures (TRIMS) has deprived developing countries of some policy instruments useful for effective administration of foreign investments.[49]

Similarly, India has been one of the most powerful voices against discussing multilateral cooperation on investment at the World Trade Organization (WTO) and has argued for dropping the investment issue from the WTO agenda.[50] A possible platform for BRICS engagement in regulating investment cooperation could be through Organisation for Economic Co-operation and Development (OECD) efforts to create a non-binding Model Investment Treaty. While the political dynamics behind the demand for global investment regulation is changing in the BRICS countries, there is not yet a critical mass of interest or an eager constituency to push for policy action and convergence for such regulation at the coalitional level.

C. BRICS' Potential as Agents for Change

Given the initial conceptualisation of the politics of reform and the brief overview of BRICS countries' approaches to investment arbitration, are BRICS countries the likely agents of change in the contested investment arbitration regime? From an evolutionary perspective, investment arbitration governance has been a result of Northern investors' dissatisfaction with the effectiveness of the legal systems, particularly in developing countries, and their unwillingness to rely on these countries' domestic courts in case of disputes. Numerous developing countries accepted the use of investment arbitration provisions and international arbitration tribunals in expectation of investment benefits. Yet BRICS countries' ongoing concerns with signing BITs and trade agreements with investment arbitration provisions with major powers, as well as their reluctance to join ICSID (except for China), indicate that they have not socialised into this field of practice. Furthermore, the full stakes of the investment arbitration provisions that emerging powers agreed to, have become clearer over the past decade as claims against their governments increased. For example, in South Africa, a part of Italian and Luxemburg-based investors' claim focused on the implementation of Black Economic Empowerment measures, which is a crucial policy initiative to rebuild the post-apartheid society.[51] In another case, an international arbitral tribunal found India guilty of violating the India–Australia BIT when White Industries challenged

---

[48] Chinese government expert Li Ling's Presentation at UNCTAD in 1997 cited in 'Bilateral Investment Agreements Play only a Minor Role in Attracting FDI' available at www.twnside.org.sg/title/bil-cn.htm.

[49] Ibid.

[50] KM Chandrasekhar (India's Permanent Representative to the WTO) 'Trade and Investment: Some Issues' presentation at the Permanent Mission of India to the WTO, Geneva (20 March 2003) available at www.twnside.org.sg/title/twninfo16.htm.

[51] ICSID: Piero Foresti, Laura de Carli and others v Republic of South Africa, Case No ARB(AF)/07/1.

the delay in the review of foreign arbitral awards in India, thereby exerting influence over functions of Indian judiciary.[52]

As emerging powers further establish themselves as economic powers, their domestic policies will have greater weight in defining the trajectory of investment governance. Yet in terms of their strategic political engagement at the BRICS level, there is no joint policy commitment to or policy vision for reforming global investment governance. Similarly, BRICS countries are not discussing investment arbitration or prioritising action on strengthening their domestic legal systems during their meetings. Judicial cooperation has been modest and has included BRICS' Supreme Court representatives' meetings in 2010 and exchange programmes for magistrates to share experiences of their countries regarding the organisation and reform of the judiciary rather than international dispute settlement issues. The fact that BRICS countries are having investment disputes among themselves (for example, India–Russia) makes cooperation on reforming the investment regime particularly difficult.

As BRICS countries' investors become increasingly oriented toward investing abroad, they are seeking effective investment regulation. China has adopted investment arbitration and joined ICSID, and other countries have used other methods or are now experimenting with regulation. The private sector in the BRICS countries is often served by top foreign law firms that employ the language, habits and ways of operating often used by major powers' investors. One of the key elements of investment advice is to carefully structure investments, which often takes place through treaty shopping. As the example of Brazil illustrates, it is feasible to use the benefits of the investment arbitration regime without the direct costs of constraining domestic policy space. Private investors in other countries can do the same, so instead of using voice to change the regime through the government, they can bypass the reform effort altogether. The increasing use of international commercial arbitration and BRICS investors' growing engagement in legally challenging environments abroad generate new understandings of the relevance of international dispute settlement, which further undermines the propensity of BRICS governments to reform the investment regime.

IV. Prospects for Reform

The impact of rising powers on global governance outcomes has become one of the central concerns of scholars and policy-makers in the field of international studies. The formation of BRICS as a reformist coalition has opened new political opportunities for changing current governance trajectories. Investment arbitration is a contested regime where emerging powers have traditionally acted as the critics of major powers' policies and as outsiders in dominant institutions like ICSID. As such, emerging powers' behaviour in this field provides a test case for their revisionist potential.

This article first conceptualised the politics of reforming global governance as interplay among three factors: the existence of a reformist coalition, the context of reform, and the

---

[52] UNCITRAL: *White Industries Australia Limited v Republic of India* [2011]

incentive for reform. While BRICS has been established as a reformist coalition, it is not yet displaying commitment to reforming investment arbitration governance. BRICS countries have been guarding their sovereignty in this field, but their outlook on investment arbitration has changed. The central concerns frequently raised by developing countries about the fairness of the regime given the constraints governments assume when signing investment agreements with investment arbitration provisions are now matched by demands for effective protection of BRICS investors. While all BRICS countries have been rethinking their investment arbitration policies following major claims against them or investors' pressure, their current policies vary significantly. Systematic efforts to develop a common BRICS policy (for example comparable to their financial reform efforts) are non-existent, and common interests in cooperating on this issue have not been identified. Yet as BRICS cooperation deepens and spreads, functional cooperation spillovers may be possible provided that countries with two completely opposite policies, China and Brazil, can work together. Future research could examine the convergence of domestic policies in more detail. For example, do the BRICS countries display a similar legal pattern in dealing with developing countries (for example, nature of treaty provisions, regional investment arbitration policies)? Are the sponsors of investment arbitration the same across BRICS? How does the corporate legal elite (domestic and foreign) diffuse treaty shopping practices? How close are the model treaty texts of BRICS countries and could BRICS countries jointly engage in a standard-setting process to design model investment arbitration provisions?

To conclude, building on David Trubek's entrepreneurial research on emerging powers in the context of economic law and policy, this article conceptualised the politics of reforming global governance and BRICS' revisionist potential in investment arbitration. BRICS countries now face several legal dilemmas or challenges, which are, as David Trubek suggests, common to new developmental states.[53] The first legal challenge is creating a flexible yet stable regulatory framework to resolve investment disputes, particularly to ensure returns on BRICS countries' outward investments. While each country can find its own balance, BRICS may also engage in a joint pursuit of alternatives to the current system, thereby mobilising as a reformist coalition. The second challenge is achieving public–private collaboration while avoiding regulatory capture. Criticism of investment arbitration has centred on asymmetries in information, financial resources and technical expertise, which may create conditions conductive to regulatory capture by powerful investors and elite arbitrators. Emerging powers may socialise into the dominant elite and work to address capture at multiple levels of regulation. The final legal challenge is to ensure democratic control and parliamentary sovereignty in this field traditionally characterised by a lack of transparency. Resolving these challenges in the future requires bringing together insights from critical legal studies, the sociology of the legal profession and global governance scholarship, which is an interdisciplinary path David Trubek's visionary scholarship set the foundations for.

---

[53] Trubek, 'Developmental States' (n 1).

20

Corporate Lawyers as an Infant Industry? Legal Market Access and Development Policy

JOHN KM OHNESORGE*

I. Introduction

In an effort to provide an appropriate tribute to his wonderful career, this study develops a set of themes that have been at the centre of Dave Trubek's work for decades, including development economics and the roles of law in developing countries,[1] the structure and regulation of legal professions,[2] debates over industrial policy and 'developmental states', old[3] and new,[4] and global governance.[5] It is enthusiastically Trubekian in frame and aspiration, emphasising, as Dave has done throughout his career, the socio-legal study of the complex interplay between legal institutions, markets and governance.[6] The subject of the essay, that national governments might offer protection and other kinds of support to their domestic legal professions as 'infant industries', may be a new one, but the work that Dave

* For their comments and suggestions I would like to thank the participants of the Conference Critical Legal Perspectives on Global Governance *Liber Amicorum* David M Trubek held at the European University Institute, 28–30 June 2012, the participants in the University of Wisconsin Law School's 2012 Big Ideas Cafe, my colleagues Andrew Coan, Anuj Desai and Jason Yackee, and my outstanding research assistant Andrea Brauer.

[1] DM Trubek, 'Law, Planning, and the Development of the Brazilian Capital Market: A Study of Law in Economic Change' (1971) *Yale Law School Studies in Law and Modernization,* Bulletin Nos 72–73; DM Trubek and M Galanter, 'Scholars in Self-Estrangement: Some Reflections on the Crisis in Law and Development Studies in the United States' (1974) *Wisconsin Law Review* 1062.

[2] RL Nelson and DM Trubek, 'Arenas of Professionalism: The Professional Ideologies of Lawyers in Context' in RL Nelson, DM Trubek, and R Soloman (eds), *Lawyers Ideals/Lawyers' Practices: Transformations in the American Legal Profession* (Ithaca, Cornell University Press, 1992); DM Trubek, Y Dezalay, R Buchanan and JR Davies, 'Global Restructuring and the Law: Studies of Legal Fields and the Creation of Transnational Arenas' (1994) 44 *Case Western Law Review* 407, 408–10.

[3] DM Trubek, 'Law, Planning, and the Development of the Brazilian Capital Market: A Study of Law in Economic Change' (n 1). Although he classifies Brazil as an intermediate rather than a developmental state, Peter Evans provides a helpful summary of Brazil's past developmentalist initiatives. See P Evans, *Embedded Autonomy: States and Industrial Transformation* (Princeton, Princeton University Press, 1995) 60–66.

[4] David Trubek launched the LANDS research project to explore the changing use of law and regulation as a tool for economic and social policy in 2007. See University of Wisconsin Law School, 'Law and the New Developmental State' (LANDS) available at law.wisc.edu/gls/lands.html, providing a list of related research and publications.

[5] See generally, DM Trubek and MP Cottrell, 'Robert Hudec and the Theory of International Law: The Law of Global Space' in C Thomas and JP Trachtman (eds), *Developing Countries in the WTO Legal Systems* (Oxford, Oxford University Press, 2009).

[6] See generally, DM Trubek, 'Max Weber on Law and the Rise of Capitalism' (1972) 72 *Wisconsin Law Review* 720.

has been doing for decades provides an excellent framework through which to construct an initial analysis.

Lawyers have a well-rehearsed repertoire of public-interest arguments for limiting the supply of legal services providers in national contexts, usually focusing on the need for professional licensing standards to maintain quality for the protection of consumers and thus to legitimise the self-regulated legal profession.[7] Sceptics rightly point to the anti-competitive, price-inflating nature of such restrictions, along with the self-serving nature of the lawyers' arguments, and ask whether the benefits of limiting access to the profession really outweigh resulting costs to consumers and society.[8] The basic thrusts and parries of these arguments will be familiar to anyone who has thought about legal market regulation and access to legal services within national borders. If we transpose these arguments onto the international realm, we find counterparts in battles over access to national legal services markets by foreign lawyers or law firms and over the flow of legal services in international trade. Trade in legal services is a relatively recent addition to the universe of trade flows between nations. Yet as wider economic globalisation has transformed the provision of legal services into a global business, countries that are home to major international law firms have pressured others to open their legal services markets to foreign participants. Lawyers have, not surprisingly, sought to resist such pressure using the rhetoric of consumer protection and the maintenance of provider quality familiar from domestic debates over professional licensing.[9] Faced with such arguments, proponents of legal market opening can readily invoke familiar critiques of legal market protectionism developed in domestic debates over professional licensing, and so the debates can proceed.

While legal market access battles will no doubt continue to take place on this familiar rhetorical terrain, they can also take place on a terrain grounded in international trade and development theory, the terrain of 'infant industry' industrial policy. Infant industry arguments also seek to use the public interest to justify protectionism, as well as subsidies, or other types of public support, for local market actors. Rather than invoking consumer protection, however, infant industry arguments focus on an importing society's interest in nurturing local providers of goods, or in this case services, that would otherwise be provided by foreigners absent public support. The costs to society of short-term support, the arguments go, will eventually be outweighed by the benefits society will reap from having national providers. A government's decision to engage in infant industry industrial policy thus presents itself as essentially an investment decision, and by its own logic asks to be judged by whether it results in a positive return.[10]

---

[7] A Blumenthal, 'Attorney Self-Regulation, Consumer Protection, and the Future of the Legal Profession' (1993) 3 *Kansas Journal of Law & Public Policy* 6, 6, 8.

[8] See, eg RL Abel, *American Lawyers* (New York, Oxford University Press, 1989) 151–57, 458–59.

[9] Given the international context, it is not surprising that these arguments are sometimes put in cultural terms. For example, Japan has argued that it needs protection against foreign law firms and lawyers participating in domestic litigation to maintain its traditional reluctance to litigate and to protect its legal culture from becoming overly litigious. ES Lee, 'Trade Barriers in Service/Investment Markets Erected by Korea and Japan' (2007) 32 *North Carolina Journal of International Law and Commercial Regulation* 451, 489.

[10] This would be the case even if global welfare might be increased by the establishment of a new competitor in the global marketplace. Nurturing a permanently uncompetitive national industry solely to increase global competition could not be justified within the traditional infant industry logic, though infant industry policies that fail to produce positive return may in fact have this effect.

Although infant industry arguments may not be entirely new in international legal services debates, they seem to be of growing importance and sophistication. This essay seeks to contribute to that discussion by focusing only on that specific strain of the wider debate over legal market access, and by drawing on the long-standing debates in traditional international trade over the pros and cons, the costs and benefits, of infant industry policies. Following this introduction, Section II provides a basic outline of infant industry arguments in international trade, including the history of the idea, as well as an introduction to the terms of the debate. Section III then evaluates the provision of various types of corporate legal services through the lens of infant industry debates, including the special case of infant industry logic in discussions of 'capacity building' to engage in the provision of legal services related to international governance and international dispute settlement, primarily at the World Trade Organization (WTO). The conclusion, contained in Section IV, is that infant industry arguments probably have limited substantive validity in the legal services context, but the move to invoke the infant industry logic, with its explicit grounding in cost–benefit analysis, encourages a commendable level of rationality when compared to more traditional arguments against market opening. Traditional consumer protection arguments should also be based on a weighing of potential social costs against purported benefits,[11] but this has been rare in the purely domestic context, at least in the US,[12] and there is no apparent reason why the structure of consumer protection arguments would change just because the threatened competition comes from abroad instead of from home. The greatest virtue of infant industry arguments with respect to lawyers, therefore, may be that in their framing, and perhaps ultimate rejection, they encourage more rigorous analysis and debate.

II. Infant Industry Arguments: Pros, Cons and Caveats

Modern infant industry arguments can be traced to the writings of the economist Friedrich List in the early nineteenth century,[13] though the term itself reportedly appears as early as the seventeenth century.[14] Developed by List in response to the arguments for free trade in agricultural and manufactured goods put forth by classical economists, especially David Ricardo, infant industry arguments are an early and enduring example of economic development heterodoxy. Rather than leaving a nation's productive structure to accidents of history and to the exogenous decisions of international market actors, infant industry advocates call on governments to take action restricting imports in, or otherwise supporting, the selected industry. Some infant industry programmes have been tied to inward-focused visions of import substitution industrialisation (ISI), in which the basic objective has been to replace imports with local production. Several possible economic development

---

[11] I thank my colleague Andy Coan for pointing this out.

[12] Abel, *American Lawyers* (n 8) 15–17.

[13] J Viner, *International Trade and Economic Development* (Glencoe, Free Press, 1952) 58. The standard source for List's infant industry arguments is his 1841 work, *Das Nationale System der Politischen Ökonomie*. See generally, F List, *The National System of Political Economy* (SS Lloyd (trans) London, Longmans, Green and Company, 1916).

[14] Viner, *International Trade* ibid, 58.

justifications have been offered for such policies, including preserving hard currency, building domestic industries that provide upstream or downstream 'linkages' with other valued domestic industries,[15] and building domestic industries that improve the country's level of technological sophistication.[16] Inward-focused infant industry arguments can also have more purely political justifications, such as a perceived need to build domestic capacity in steel production for national defence. Infant industry policies can also be tied to outward-oriented developmental policies designed to strategically alter an economy's comparative advantage, and in such cases the goal is that the infant industry eventually grows up to become an exporter of its goods, or in the case of lawyers, its legal services. This latter approach is now generally associated with the export-oriented 'developmental states' of northeast Asia,[17] while the former, more autarchic approach is associated with Latin American ISI.[18]

The above distinction between autarchic and export-oriented infant industry policies is important when evaluating possible justifications for treating legal services as an infant industry, as the plausibility of attaining these alternative goals may be quite different for different countries' legal professions. Whether or not it is a good idea, autarchy in legal services would be a much more attainable goal for most countries than the goal of becoming exporters of legal services, given the current dominance of English and the Anglo-American style of lawyering in the international sphere. The dominance of Anglo-American lawyering can be seen in the overwhelming dominance of US and UK law firms in the global legal services market,[19] and in the fact that Common law, English-speaking India has been the first great provider of internationally out-sourced legal services.[20]

Whether autarchic or export-oriented in aspiration, however, infant industry arguments depend on a belief that short-term costs imposed on local taxpayers, or more typically on local consumers forced to purchase from the protected local industry, will eventually be outweighed by greater benefits to the society once the infant industry has matured. Translated into the world of legal services provision, the costs imposed upon legal services consumers forced to hire protected local firms must be a reasonable price to pay for the greater benefits that society will reap once the local firms have achieved a more competitive status. This highlights the fact that infant industry policies can operate as wealth transfers from one specific group within an economy to another, therefore, one should also ask whether the transferors will ever be made whole, even if society as a whole eventually

---

[15] AO Hirschman, *The Strategy of Economic Development* (New Haven, Yale University Press, 1958) 98–119.

[16] J Cypher and J Dietz, *The Process of Economic Development* (London, Routledge, 2004) 248–308.

[17] See, eg A Kohli, 'Where Do High-Growth Political Economies Come From? The Japanese Lineage of Korea's 'Developmental State' in M Woo-Cumings (ed), *The Developmental State* (New York, Cornell University Press, 1999).

[18] See generally, T Lothian, 'The Democratized Market Economy in Latin America (and Elsewhere): An Exercise in Institutional Thinking Within Law and Political Economy' (1995) 28 *Cornell International Law Journal* 167, 170–75.

[19] For example, in the *American Lawyer* magazine's 2012 Global 100 ranking of law firms only three of the top 100 firms are not based in Anglo-American jurisdictions. The three that are not Anglo-American rank 73rd, 83rd, and 89th. See 'The 2012 Global 100: The Complete Report' *The American Lawyer* (28 September 2012) available at www.americanlawyer.com/PubArticleTAL.jsp?id=1202571230283. The same magazine's new ranking of law firms by market valuation presents an even starker picture, with only one of the most valuable 97 firms, Loyens & Loeff, in 85th place, being from outside the Anglo-American sphere. Ibid.

[20] See generally, T Brennan, 'The Original Outsourcers Head Out' *The Asian Lawyer* (5 December 2012), discussing the founders of Pangea3 LLC, the Mumbai and New York based pioneer in the 'legal process outsourcing' (LPO) industry).

benefits.[21] If, for example, forcing local businesses to hire them is part of an infant industry policy for domestic law firms, one should consider both the overall impact on society and whether the local businesses would ever be compensated by society for their contribution to the local lawyers.

A full accounting of an infant industry policy for corporate lawyers would be beyond the scope of an exploratory essay like this, and in any case would be unique for every economy. The goal of this brief essay, therefore, is to bring some general ideas about infant industry policies into the discussion of legal services, and given the continuing influence of his Brazilian experiences on Dave's career, it is fitting that the essay turns to 1950s Brazil and the Getulio Vargas Foundation (FGV) for inspiration. In a series of lectures offered at FGV in 1951, Jacob Viner, a leading international trade economist of the day, offered a defence of the classical free-trade position with respect to developing countries.[22] In so doing, Viner argued against the newly-emerging heterodox position of Raul Prebisch and others, who had begun to caution developing countries against relying upon agricultural or natural resources exports for development.[23] The work of Prebish and his contemporary, Hans Singer, provided important support for a broader movement in development economics that included infant industry ISI policies, as well as the heterodox intellectual framework known as 'dependency theory'.[24] Although much has been written in the subsequent six decades debating the merits of ISI as compared to more free-market approaches to international trade and development, Viner's 1951 observations are of special interest to this essay because they came early in the modern revival of infant industry thinking. For that reason, they address fundamental issues that should be considered in weighing the extension of infant industry arguments to a field in which the debates have been on quite different terms.[25]

While very sceptical of Prebisch's larger argument,[26] Viner was perhaps surprisingly sympathetic to the infant industry concept *in theory*, proposing that the main objections have been on 'historical and practical grounds'.[27] Expressing this caution over the difficulty of putting infant industry ideas into effective practice, Viner identified the following concerns:

— the arbitrary or irrational selection of industries to favour;
— the spreading of infant industry protection to general protectionism;
— that the protected infant industry tends to languish rather than develop in the absence of competition;
— that although the temporary protection should be removed either when the infant industry no longer needs it, or when it has proved incapable of development even with protection, experience shows that protection tends to become permanent; and

---

[21] Such horizontal, intra-industry wealth transfers are in addition to the more general role of infant industry policies as investments intended to transfer wealth from the present to the future. I am indebted to my colleague Anuj Desai for this insight.

[22] See generally, Viner, *International Trade and Economic Development* (n 13).

[23] Ibid, 60–62; see also J Toye and R Toye, 'The Origins and Interpretation of the Prebisch-Singer Thesis' (2003) 35 *History of Political Economy* 437.

[24] See generally, J Cypher and J Dietz, *The Process of Economic Development*, 2nd edn (London, Routledge, 2004) 158–88.

[25] See generally, n 1 above.

[26] Viner, *International Trade and Economic Development* (n 13) 60–73.

[27] Ibid, 58.

— that even temporary protection to rationally-selected industries tends not to outweigh the costs imposed on the rest of society, which is forced to deal with the protected industry.[28]

Viner also suggested that a society wishing to aid an infant industry would probably be advised to offer the industry a subsidy rather than protection, as the costs of subsidies are more transparent and easier to calculate than the costs of protection, and can also be distributed across society as a whole through taxation and government expenditure, rather than burdening only the domestic consumers forced to trade with the protected infant.[29] Finally, Viner cautioned that by suppressing demand, the artificially high prices that result from protection may stifle the growth of the very industry that is in need of development, whereas subsidies would be more likely to encourage growth in the targeted industry.[30]

III. Legal Services as an Infant Industry

Although Viner expressed his concerns primarily with respect to trade in manufactured goods, the traditional focus of infant industry and other industrial policy advocates,[31] the concerns equally apply in the context of infant industry protection for domestic lawyers. So far, infant industry arguments in the legal services context have focused on the market for legal services related to international business, which has been, and is likely to remain, the contested ground in legal market access debates. Foreign law firms, whether from developed countries or from other developing countries, have so far not sought to penetrate domestic legal markets to provide general legal services. Infant industry arguments in the legal services market context also seem focused on developing countries and their policies toward local law firms, though the boundaries of developed versus developing in legal services may be fluid, and may not track other indicators of development. Given the current global dominance of Anglo-American firms and law practice style, discussed above, it may actually be a small group of countries who are natural exporters of legal services, and a surprisingly large number of countries in which local firms might be expected to seek infant industry support.

Turning then to the first of Viner's concerns, would rational policy analysis lead a country to identify its business lawyers as a promising infant industry, or should one expect to look elsewhere for the actual motives? Few countries are likely to become successful exporters of legal services, so in most cases the benefit side of the cost–benefit calculus would have to be based on benefits derived from autarchic import substitution. From a purely theoretical standpoint, it would surely be possible to construct scenarios in which the benefits of infant industry support for domestic business lawyers would eventually outweigh the costs. Yet the admittedly brief research conducted for this essay produced no evidence that countries

---

[28] Viner, *International Trade and Economic Development* (n 13) 59.
[29] Ibid, 59–60.
[30] Ibid, 60.
[31] Congress of the United States, Congressional Budget Office, *The Industrial Policy Debate* (1983).

have ever, in fact, conducted such analysis.[32] This raises the concern that infant industry rationales are being deployed primarily *ex post facto*, to explain and justify policies taken on other grounds. While *ex post facto* rationales are not necessarily invalid, in a world in which trade in services is growing and is the subject of international negotiation over market access, the costs to countries of protecting specific services markets will only grow.[33] Governments considering protection or other infant industry support for local law firms must therefore consider whether the benefits outweigh the costs. In many societies business lawyers will constitute the kind of focused interest group that historically has been able to obtain trade protection or other government support even at the expense of the wider society.

Turning to Viner's second concern, could infant industry protection offered to business lawyers be limited to them alone, or would it tend to support protectionism with respect to other areas, perhaps in professional services such as accounting, insurance, financial services and so on? Infant industry arguments are certainly made by those industries when faced with foreign competition,[34] though it is unclear if protection for lawyers plays any role in buttressing infant industry arguments by other service providers. In a world where countries negotiate multi- and bi-laterally over access to many professional services markets,[35] a developing country might find a stronger infant industry rationale for supporting a sector other than legal services, in which case it might be rational for it to trade off access to legal services in order to keep the other market closed. Likewise, a government wanting to give up protection of a different services market might find it helpful to have given up protection of legal services, so that the industry resisting liberalisation could not demand the same protection as the lawyers. Such considerations would depend very much on the circumstances faced by individual governments, but it is not unreasonable to accept Viner's underlying point that a decision to provide infant industry support to a sector such as the legal profession could hinder a government's efforts to achieve an optimal trade regime.

With respect to Viner's third objection, that perversely, protection will tend to reduce the impetus to innovate and develop that would be necessary for the infant industry policy to actually work, protection of legal services would seem to raise real dangers. Trubek's research of the European Union's legal market, for example, shows how competition from American law firms in Europe forced European countries to eradicate inefficient legal traditions.[36] Because European countries traditionally limited the practice of law to a small academic and social elite, there were not enough specialised lawyers to deal with the legal

---

[32] Unfortunately, this is hardly surprising. A recent *New York Times* investigation of tax incentives granted to private business by state, county and city governments in the US concluded that an accurate accounting of the effectiveness of the incentives was impossible. Many of the government agencies did not know the value of all their awards, and they rarely kept track of the number of jobs created as a result of the public support. See L Story, 'As Companies Seek Tax Deals, Governments Pay High Price' *New York Times* (1 December 2012).

[33] The primary vehicle for trade in services negotiations is the WTO's General Agreement on Trade in Services (GATS), though bilateral trade agreements can also address services. Countries have chosen both approaches to negotiating access to legal services markets.

[34] TG Berg, 'Trade in Services: Toward a "Development Round" of GATT Negotiations Benefiting Both Developing and Industrialized States' (1987) 28 *Harvard International Law Journal* 1, 17–22.

[35] Twelve major categories of services were identified for coverage within the GATS regime, the so-called W/120 list, one of which is 'other services not included elsewhere'. United Nations Department of Economic and Social Affairs Statistics Division, *Manual on Statistics of International Trade in Services* (Series M No 86, 2010) 14.

[36] Trubek, Dezalay, Buchanan and Davies, 'Global Restructuring and the Law' (n 2) 429–31, 435–36.

complexities resulting from EU integration, and American law firms outperformed them.[37] Europe was forced to loosen its barriers to entry of the legal market to stay competitive,[38] and competition with American firms also pushed the creation of the first large multinational European firms.[39] Similarly, in Japan, the influx of foreign law firms drove the creation of the first large Japanese law firms, even though traditionally most lawyers were sole practitioners.[40]

These dangers relate to Viner's fourth objection, which is that protection intended to be strategic and temporary tends to become permanent even when it should be ended. In the case of legal services, if the infant industry support comes in the form of excluding foreign firms from the market, it is easy to imagine lawyers finding ways to manipulate the levers of state power, specifically the regulation of their profession, so as to perpetuate the protection. As Viner suggested, this should be expected whether the infant industry support has succeeded and the local law firms no longer need the protection, or whether it has failed and they will need support forever. Likely, the rational cost–benefit analysis at the core of infant industry logic—never lawyers' primary argument for limiting access to the profession—will be overwhelmed by more traditional arguments based on consumer protection and the sanctity of the local legal culture. If local firms actually need protection because they are less efficient providers, then confirming the protection may allow them to continue on their course without reforming. Because the industry has been protected from global competition, it will not develop the skills necessary to compete globally.[41] On the other hand, if local firms do use the protection to improve their performance, as envisioned by infant industry supporters, then the result may be that they have simply increased the rents they obtain from their monopoly, which they will work diligently to maintain.[42]

Viner's concern that infant industry protections will become permanent and outlive their usefulness is especially problematic in the legal services context because lawyers argue for barriers to the legal market not only to protect the developing local market but also to uphold the quality of legal services. Barriers to legal services markets exist in developed countries as well requiring attorneys to obtain certain qualifications before practising locally. In the infant industry context, these quality of services arguments will compound with the infant industry competition arguments and there is arguably a heightened risk that the protections will persist after they are no longer needed.[43]

Viner's fifth objection is essentially a simple cost–benefit projection that even if a country manages to avoid the other dangers he raised, the costs incurred in protecting an infant industry are likely to outweigh the benefits. In order to make this analysis more tractable in the context of legal market access, it will be helpful to consider in some detail various

---

[37] Ibid, 429–31.

[38] Ibid.

[39] Ibid, 435–36.

[40] R Hamano, 'The Turn Toward Law: The Emergence of Corporate Law Firms in Japan' in WP Alford (ed), *Raising the Bar: The Emerging Legal Profession in East Asia* (Cambridge, MA, Harvard University Press, 2007) 171–77.

[41] RL Abel, 'Transnational Law Practice' (1994) 44 *Case Western Law Review* 737, 748.

[42] The concern that the industrial policy bureaucracy will be captured by the supported industry, and therefore not administer support programmes in an economically-rational way, has long been at the core of industrial policy and 'developmental state' debates.

[43] See generally, PD Paton, 'Legal Services and the GATS: Norms as Barriers to Trade' (2003) 9 *New England Journal of International Comparative Law* 361 (discussing the interaction between law as a profession and law as a business in the GATS context).

aspects of global legal practice, and different forms that infant industry protection might take. The following breakdown of practice areas and flows may be helpful for this exercise, as different types of practice seem to face different consequences.

Domestic litigation in the protected market. Domestic litigation may be the most commonly-protected market. Even if domestic law allows foreign law firms to establish local offices, the foreign lawyers they bring with them will not be licensed to litigate locally, and it is a common rule that local lawyers working for foreign firms give up the right to appear in court.[44] The protection is thus provided through the limitation placed on the local hirers' practices, but who does that protection benefit, and is that protection likely to help the development of the local infant legal industry? That protection will impose costs on all local litigation clients who might benefit from the organisational strengths of international firms in litigation, because while those clients will be able to hire an international firm for litigation support that falls short of the practice of local law, they will also be forced to hire a local firm to appear in court and to otherwise conduct the litigation. While this will clearly benefit the small group of local lawyers who own the domestic firms, it is less clear that it will benefit the local lawyers who are mere employees of those firms. The employee lawyers capable of engaging in international practice would presumably benefit from a fully-competitive hiring market, in which the presence of fully-functioning foreign firms would exert upward pressure on their wages, and in which they could gain valuable experience by fully practising law with international firms. With the domestically-oriented local lawyers largely unaffected by these hiring rules, the real beneficiaries of the protection would seem to be the owner/employer lawyers, whose numbers in any jurisdiction will depend upon how local practices are organised. The key question will then be whether they are likely to invest the rents gained from this protection in ways that will allow them to eventually compete with the international firms on a level playing field, the infant industry ideal. They may decide to do so but they may instead invest such rents in perpetuating the protective system, as Viner had cautioned.

Domestic regulatory work in the protected market. These markets are somewhat harder to define, and therefore to protect, than domestic litigation markets. However, some jurisdictions do define work obtaining regulatory permissions and approvals as the practice of law, and limit that practice to local lawyers employed by local firms.[45] Local clients might or might not be interested in hiring a foreign firm to assist in such work, but in-bound foreign investors certainly have been. In many jurisdictions foreign investors will, as a matter of course, have retained an international law firm to advise on the local legal and regulatory environment, so requiring those investors to also retain a local law firm to assist with regulatory matters will generally raise the cost of investing. If the local offices of international firms were allowed to hire local lawyers to deliver the regulatory approval and compliance documents, as well as to advise on their terms and perhaps to actually prepare them, then local law firms would feel additional competitive pressure to improve their services and lower their costs, and the regulatory costs to foreign investors would decrease. Leaving the protection in place forces foreign investment projects to be run at least in part through local law firms, and if the infant industry logic holds, at some point the local firms may

---

[44] See, eg MA Cohen, 'International Law Firms in China: Market Access and Ethical Risks' (2012) 80 *Fordham Law Review* 2569, 2570.

[45] This is the case in China, for example.

be able to capture the work entirely. But again, who would benefit from that? The primary beneficiaries might be only the local owner/employer lawyers, as other local lawyers would arguably benefit from an open market in which they would be able to do the same work for either an international or a local firm, whichever offered the most attractive terms. To the extent that countries are in a competition to attract foreign investment, raising the regulatory costs of foreign investments in order to benefit the owners of local law firms would seem to be a questionable choice.

Outgoing work for business clients from the protected market. A third type of practice that should be considered would not involve the practice of law in the protected market, except under a very broad definition, but would involve advice to local clients on legal matters outside the jurisdiction. Countries can try to steer this work to local law firms by preventing international firms from establishing any kind of presence in the jurisdiction, but the more sophisticated local clients will simply deal directly with law firms abroad, if they choose to. They may choose to involve a local firm to help advise on overseas legal matters, but it would be hard to force them to do so as part of an infant industry strategy, especially if they are truly private, rather than state-owned. Perhaps ironically, the best way for the local government to assist domestic law firms to gain expertise in that type of work might be to allow them to affiliate with international firms in ways that would allow them to participate in international transactions engaged in by local clients. Such affiliations seem to attract protectionist criticism, however, as they grant international firms some level of access to local markets at the same time as they allow internationally-oriented local firms access to international markets and international expertise. From an infant industry perspective, however, it might be that encouraging local–international affiliations would be a reasonable strategy, especially with respect to out-bound work for local clients. Local firms would presumably gain access to the technologies of law practice that allow international firms to dominate the global marketplace, while at the same time they would be under some pressure to perform at a high level themselves, as the affiliations would be voluntary, rather than mandatory. On the cost side, local businesses might pay more for legal services obtained from an affiliation, but certainly the costs would be lower than if the government tried to mandate use of local firms only, which, as noted above, might be very difficult to enforce anyway.

Capacity Building for Participation in International Governance. Probably the area of law practice that has received the most sustained attention through the infant industry lens, implicitly if not explicitly, involves the provision of legal services to governments engaged in WTO litigation and other international activities related to trade and investment.[46] Focusing only on WTO litigation, legal capacity to handle such disputes could be built within the government itself, within local private law firms, or both. For example, a government might decide to hire private counsel to handle WTO litigation on its behalf but still feel that it should invest in the training of its own staff in order to better choose and oversee its outside counsel. If the government did not also privilege local firms when hiring outside counsel, then the government's attempts at capacity-building through investment in training its own officials would not fit the classic understanding of an infant industry policy. True infant industry capacity building would involve the government trying to build

---

[46] See generally, GC Shaffer and R Meléndez-Ortiz (eds), *Dispute Settlement at the WTO: The Developing Country Experience* (Cambridge, Cambridge University Press, 2010).

international dispute settlement capacity in local law firms by sending work to them, and while a government trying to grow WTO capacity in local law firms would probably also invest in building its own internal capacity, neither necessarily follows from the other.

Capacity building arguments are sometimes put in terms of building the capacity of local law firms to represent their governments in WTO matters so that those governments can reduce their dependence on foreign firms.[47] The support for local firms would come in the form of the subsidy provided by non-competitive government procurement, rather than through protectionism imposing costs on local private consumers. In keeping with Viner's preference for subsidies over protection, whatever the economic cost to society of nurturing local law firms in this way, it would be relatively widely-spread across society as it would consist of the higher cost, or decreased performance, that the government would incur in order to build the infant industry.[48] Brazil's efforts in this regard have received the most scholarly attention,[49] but efforts by China,[50] and others are receiving attention as well,[51] so we should soon have a better overall picture.

Perhaps the most interesting virtue of viewing such WTO legal-capacity-building efforts through an infant industry lens has to do with determining what is in the national public interest when trade disputes are involved. Taking WTO disputes over anti-dumping measures as an example, there is a well-developed line of argument suggesting that countries as a whole generally lose when their governments impose anti-dumping duties on imports.[52] Indeed, it is probably accurate to say that this is the mainstream position within the economics and the trade law academies, based on a view that the benefit to the importing society's consumers from lower-priced imports will generally outweigh the harm to the local producer.[53] In this view, national anti-dumping measures are generally bad policy which governments undertake because they are overly responsive to motivated and well-organised minorities, the local producers or their employees, and thus subvert the genuine public interest. The same arguments are made against the imposition of countervailing duties on the import of goods produced with the benefit of subsidies from the exporter's government. 'An economist is right to claim that, if foreign governments subsidise their exports, this is simply marvellous for his own country, which then gets cheaper goods and thus should unilaterally maintain a policy of free trade.'[54] In the context of WTO dispute settlement, this means that the country as a whole loses again if its government 'wins' a WTO challenge to such duties, though the government itself will want to win at the WTO level so that it can continue servicing its special interest constituency.

---

[47] See generally, M Papa, 'Emerging Powers in International Dispute Settlement: From Legal Capacity Building to a Level Playing Field?' (2012) 3 *Journal of International Dispute Settlement* 19–20.

[48] Providing infant industry support via subsidising local competitors rather than through limiting imports was suggested by Viner, *International Trade and Economic Development* (n 13).

[49] See generally, GC Shaffer, MR Sanchez and B Rosenberg, 'The Trials of Winning at the WTO: What Lies Behind Brazil's Success' (2008) 41 *Cornell Law Journal* 383.

[50] See generally, Manjiao Chi, 'China's Participation in WTO Dispute Settlement Over the Past Decade: Experiences and Impacts' (2012) 15 *Journal of International Economic Law* 29.

[51] Papa, 'Emerging Powers in International Dispute Settlement' (n 47).

[52] See, eg I Van Bael, 'Lessons for the EEC: More Transparency, Less Discretion, and At Last, a Debate?' in JH Jackson and EA Vermulst (eds), *Antidumping Law and Practice* (Ann Arbor, The University of Michigan Press, 1989) 405–408.

[53] See, eg ML Hurabiell, 'Protectionism Versus Free Trade: Implementing the GATT Antidumping Agreement in the United States' (1995) 16 *University of Pennsylvania Journal of International Business* 567, 600–602.

[54] J Bhagwati, *Protectionism* (Cambridge, MA, MIT Press, 1989) 35.

One does not need to accept this critique in its entirety in order to accept that it will sometimes be valid. How, then, should a country evaluate the public interest when investing in international trade law capacity, and where should resources be put? Fully accepting the criticisms of the preceding paragraph might lead one to conclude that nurturing a local private bar of trade remedy lawyers would be a decidedly mixed prospect. Returning to the case of anti-dumping duties, local exporters subject to anti-dumping measures imposed by other countries would probably benefit if there were local firms with global trade law expertise, and those benefits to the local exporters would not seem to be offset by any harm to other segments of society. However, that same local trade remedy bar would also certainly be interested in representing local producers seeking anti-dumping relief from their government, implicating the critique outlined in the preceding paragraph. Turning back to local exporters, additional qualified trade law firms in the market should lead to competition and lower prices, furthering the public interest. With respect to local producers seeking protection, however, more law firms in the market might well contribute to more questionable cases being brought, as prices drop and competition among the firms increases. Along the same lines, to the extent the local trade remedy bar is used by local producers seeking protection, then the more effective those lawyers are, the more the public interest actually suffers.

Moreover, if the goal of WTO legal-capacity-building is to guarantee that WTO dispute resolution benefits developing nations as much as developed nations, protectionist policies in the legal services market will be insufficient. Shaffer argues that the US and EU's distinct advantage also comes from their use of private–public partnerships in bringing their grievances at the WTO.[55] By collaborating with private actors such as business groups, the US and EU gain access to funds for hiring lawyers, insider market information, and other political resources such as campaign support, lobbying and public information campaigns.[56] In return, however, these private actors pressure their governments to assert their interests instead of necessarily furthering the nation's broader interests.[57] The government of India, for example, has struggled to build a culture of private–public relationships with lawyers and private industry in international dispute settlement.[58] This situation has, however, stifled India's impact at the WTO because private actors such as sophisticated businessmen could compensate where the government lacks capacity.[59] More importantly, US and EU influence over the WTO means they can directly impact the development of WTO law in their favour.[60] Perhaps it follows that if legal capacity building could allow developing nations to become more involved in WTO disputes, those countries could also attempt to impact the development of WTO law. Perhaps any economic loss from protectionist trade policies would be outweighed by the potential for more beneficial top-down

---

[55] GC Shaffer, *Defending Interests: Public-Private Partnerships in WTO Litigation* (Washington DC, Brookings Institution Press, 2003) 5–6.

[56] Ibid, 13–16.

[57] Ibid, 150, 155.

[58] Papa, 'Emerging Powers in International Dispute Settlement' (n 47). See also, M Papa, 'Emerging India in Investment Arbitration: The Role of Lawyers in Regime Participation' (2012), Workshop Discussion Paper, from Globalization, Lawyers, and Emerging Economies, Workshop on India Related Research, Harvard Law School, 13–14 April 2012.

[59] Papa, 'Emerging Powers in International Dispute Settlement' (n 47).

[60] Shaffer, *Defending Interests* (n 55) 156–58.

trade policies. At the same time, countries like India might benefit from a competitive push to change their social norms to become more efficient.

Building trade-law capacity within the government itself raises somewhat different issues, but there is a basic symmetry if one thinks of capacity primarily in terms of raising the odds of winning trade disputes. As was discussed above, a very standard view of trade remedy law would hold that 'winning' at the WTO might not actually further the national interest if it meant that one's own anti-dumping duties would remain in place, while winning at the WTO might further the national interest if it meant that a foreign country would remove the protection that it had imposed. Given the standard picture of government over-responsiveness to private interests seeking protection, perhaps the capacity that governments need most is the capacity to effectively screen potential cases so that wins are likely to actually further the public interest.[61] In developing that capacity it may be helpful to the government to have local lawyers work in private practice to gain expertise in trade remedy law and in WTO dispute settlement, but it might be more efficient to have the local lawyers gain that expertise working for foreign firms rather than supporting the development of a local trade remedies bar, with the potential downsides that could entail.

IV. Conclusion

This paper is based on a very simple premise: people are beginning to talk about domestic legal professions as infant industries that governments should support for economic reasons, and it is therefore important to take a careful look at the costs and the benefits, the winners and the losers, that might follow from such policies. In that exercise, the practical concerns about infant industry protectionism raised by Jacob Viner in his lectures at Brazil's FGV six decades ago provide a useful starting point. Addressing those concerns, it appears far from self-evident that protectionism or other infant industry support for local law firms providing internationally-related legal services will be good public policy. Lawyers are service providers, and if infant industry protection forces the consumers of those services to pay more, and/or receive worse service, than they would if markets were open, then it is important to consider those costs in some detail. This would be true not only with respect to private sector consumption, but also when the consumer is the government. On the other hand, while it may be that infant industry support for law firms would not be good public policy, even attempting the called-for analysis would facilitate a higher level of rigour than is usually seen when restrictive regulation is based on the public interest in consumer protection, the traditional measure. Properly conducting that analysis would not be easy, but would require a powerful intellect and boundless energy. This is clearly a job for Dave Trubek.

---

[61] The aspiration for such state capacity in anti-dumping administration, which would require both expertise and considerable autonomy from local interest groups, is the same aspiration that has been at the core of the 'developmental state' literature for decades. See, J Ohnesorge, 'States, Industrial Policies & Anti-Dumping Enforcement in Japan, South Korea and Taiwan' (1996–97) 3 *Buffalo Journal of International Law* 289.

21

Where the Action is: Globalisation, Law and Development, the Sociology of the Legal Profession, and the 'GLEE-full' Career of Dave Trubek

DAVID B WILKINS

Dave Trubek has always known where the action is. And he has always understood that the most important action is likely to occur in legal spaces far outside of the traditional mainstream. Before even embarking on his academic career, Dave had the good sense to get himself posted to Brazil, where he helped to launch arguably the most innovative experiment in legal education in what we then charmingly called the Third World.[1] Seven years later, Trubek used his Brazil experience to co-author the definitive article demonstrating that where the action is *not* is in creating a field of 'law and development' that consists primarily of exporting the complete American model of law, legal education and legal practice to the developing world.[2] Instead, Dave urged his fellow law and development pioneers to recognise that the real action is in developing an 'eclectic critique' designed to further the normative goal of improving conditions in the Third World, while simultaneously interrogating the very means by which progressive scholars were attempting to achieve this goal.[3] Two years later, this 'eclectic critique' blossomed into the Critical Legal Studies Movement, with Dave Trubek as one of its founding fathers.[4]

For more than two decades, CLS was where the action was in legal education, roiling virtually every corner of the American legal academy, and helping to spark a critical revolution in academic institutions around the world. By the time Dave Trubek arrived as a visitor at Harvard Law School in the autumn of 1986, CLS had become such a potent force that the venerable law school's faculty was literally at war with itself. By the end of his year-long visit, Trubek had become a victim of the bloody internecine conflict at the institution he famously dubbed 'the Beirut of legal education'—but only after miraculously convincing a healthy two-thirds majority of Harvard's equivalent of the Hatfields and the McCoys that his combination of internationalism, empiricism and critical inquiry was where the action

---

[1] DM Trubek, 'Reforming Legal Education in Brazil: From the Ceped Experiment to the Law Schools at the Getulio Vargas Foundation' (2011) *University of Wisconsin Legal Studies Research Paper No 1180*.

[2] DM Trubek and M Galanter, 'Scholars in Self-estrangement: Some Reflections on the Crisis of Law and Development Studies in the United States' (1974) *Wisconsin Law Review* 1062.

[3] Ibid, 1099–100.

[4] See RM Unger, *The Critical Legal Studies Movement* (Cambridge, MA, Harvard University Press, 1983).

was moving in fields ranging from law and development, to the study of the civil litigation system, to the sociology of the legal profession, to legal theory.[5]

I know, because I was there. And whatever else Dave accomplished during his time at Harvard, he managed to transform me from the boring law professor I would have undoubtedly become without his intervention into someone who has been able to build a happy and interesting academic career—mostly by following Dave's lead to where the action is at the intersection of globalisation, law and development, and the sociology of the legal profession.

The rest of this essay is divided into three sections. Section I builds upon Trubek's classic 1984 article entitled 'Where the Action Is: Critical Legal Studies and Empiricism' to make the case for empirically-grounded theory that addresses 'how the world really works', while still retaining an 'eclectic critique' that rejects the kind of 'positive determinism' that too often underlies empirical inquiry.[6] Section II then describes the project on Globalisation, Lawyers, and Emerging Economies—or GLEE as Dave has named our endeavour with characteristic aplomb. GLEE is a multidisciplinary, multinational research collaborative the goal of which is to investigate how globalisation is reshaping the market for legal services in key emerging economies such as Brazil, India and China, and to explore how this process, in turn, is affecting everything from legal practice, to economic development, to sovereignty and democracy in those countries and around the world. As I explain, the core intellectual underpinnings of GLEE—the complex and often contradictory role of law and lawyers in the latest wave of development in the emerging world; the need to de-Americanise the sociology of the legal profession while nevertheless acknowledging the spread of the American Mode of the Production of Law around the world; and the insistence that any meaningful theorising in this area is based on serious empirical inquiry conducted by scholars attuned to the normative, cultural and epistemological constraints on any attempt to understand the facts on the ground—are all grounded in Dave's path-breaking work. Section III concludes by underscoring how the rich insights that Dave has produced by studying people, issues and institutions considered to be at the margins of mainstream American legal thought, are now ironically pointing the way to where the action is for the most mainstream and conservative part of the American legal profession: the corporate bar.

I. Back to the Future: Reclaiming the Critical Tradition in Law and Society—and Claiming the Empirical Promise of Critical Legal Studies

In 1984, Trubek stood at the intersection of two academic movements in which he had played a central role but which now viewed each other with increasing suspicion, and even hostility. The first, as I have indicated, was the Conference on Critical Legal Studies, which

---

[5] JA Kinison, 'Harvard Legal Battle Puts "Critical Legal Studies" on Trial' *The New York Times* (30 August 1987).
[6] DM Trubek, 'Where the Action Is: Critical Legal Studies and Empiricism' (1984) 36 *Stanford Law Review* 575, 619.

Dave helped to establish shortly after returning from Brazil. Dave's roots in the second tradition, Law and Society, were even more central to his intellectual development. Too young to be one of the Law & Society Association's 'founding fathers', Dave imbibed the intoxicating vision of marrying the rigour of social science methodology with law's progressive normative-vision for lawyers to develop 'legal institutions [that] would create order, facilitate social and economic development, and adorn the Republic' as an undergraduate at the University of Wisconsin from such luminaries as Willard Hurst, Lloyd Garrison, Carl Auerbach and Sam Mermin.[7] At firstglance, there would appear to be nothing contradictory about this dual allegiance. After all, both academic movements have always been united in their claim to the legacy of Legal Realism and their opposition to the formalism underlying classical legal thought—and, as a result, the two schools of thought have also been united in their marginality in the mainstream legal academy. But by the mid-1980s, critical legal scholars and traditional law and society scholars were increasingly fighting over what each perceived to be a small but overlapping piece of turf. In 1984, Dave Trubek began a project to try to negotiate a ceasefire to this border war. In typical Trubek fashion, he did so not by denying that there was a legitimate conflict, but by working to get both sides to embrace it.

Trubek's opening salvo was addressed to the Crits. Writing in a journal that had produced some of the most important CLS scholarship, Trubek argued that critical scholars rejected empirical inquiry because of a mistaken belief that those who do such work are inevitably committed to some combination of determinism (believing that their empirical research would reveal the deep truth about the structures that determine social life that exist independent of our will) and positivism (believing that the facts upon which they based these discoveries exist independent of our values).[8] As the article goes on to demonstrate brilliantly, the best empirical work in the law and society tradition relies on neither belief.[9] Instead, citing the ground-breaking work of Stuart McCauley and others, Trubek argues that there is nothing inherently reductionist or essentialist about empirical inquiry. On the contrary, a careful understanding of 'how the world works' is entirely consistent with acknowledging the role that legal consciousness plays in shaping the way that actors like McCauley's consumer-protection lawyers understand and help to create the very conditions that constitute this reality. This stream of 'pragmatic empiricism', as Trubek calls it, is 'interpretivist and empirical at the same time', and capable of shedding important insight on a broad range of legal phenomena.

Trubek is able to proclaim this conclusion with confidence because he and his fellow researchers at the Civil Litigation Research Project (CLRP—one of Dave's less catchy acronyms) had already definitively demonstrated the utility of pragmatic empiricism as a powerful tool for understanding the field of dispute processing. In designing the most comprehensive study of the role of courts ever undertaken—an undertaking whose shear audacity we should pause for a moment to admire—Trubek and his collaborators rejected both doctrinal categories and existing social relationships as the proper unit of analysis. Instead, they framed their inquiry in terms of 'disputes', an admittedly socially-constructed

---

[7] DM Trubek, 'Back to the Future: The Short, Happy Life of the Law and Society Movement' (1990) 18 *Florida State Law Review* 1, 11.

[8] Trubek, 'Where the Action Is' (n 6).

[9] As Dave is quick to concede, there is plenty of empirical work in law and society—and even more outside of that tradition—that is expressly or implicitly premised on one or both of these beliefs.

concept that expressly recognises the role that power and ideology play in the way that individuals 'name' what constitutes a 'dispute', and the interactive process by which those who believe that they have been wronged decide whom to 'blame' for their injury, and what, if anything, they will do to 'claim' redress from the perpetrator.[10] In this paradigm, courts are but one of many institutions where disputes are processed—and whether the primary purpose served by courts is to promote or repress disputes, or to facilitate or frustrate 'access to justice'—remain questions to be investigated and debated, rather than assumed.[11]

In staking out this position, however, Trubek and his CLRP collaborators were implicitly throwing down a challenge to their fellow law and society researchers that was every bit as biting and prescient as the one Trubek would pose to those in the CLS community in 'Where the Action Is' a few years later. In 1990, Trubek formalised this challenge in an equally pro-vocative 'story and a polemic' written on the occasion of the Law & Society Association's twenty-fifth anniversary. That story—told as a first-person critical narrative that paid hom-age to the influence of the Critical Race Movement Trubek helped to nurture[12]—challenged law and society scholars to embrace the indeterminacy, contradiction, and normativity of CLS and its intellectual fellow-travellers.[13] Without this dimension, Trubek argued, even 'critical empiricism' is in danger of foundering on the shoals of a misguided search for objectivity and a defensible distance from politics.

But Trubek resists the siren call of many critical theorists to abandon any and all attempt at empirical inquiry for the theoretical consistency of the ironic shrug or the direct engage-ment of the battlements. In a concluding polemic that only a critic deeply rooted in the law and society tradition could write, Trubek concedes the importance of the very empirical methods that have always given the socio-legal vision its patina of objectivity, even as he insists that these methods be deployed with humility and accountability befitting their status as the creation of men and women, and not of Platonic gods:

> I recognize that many of the techniques and methods that we have developed in our quest for objectivity are useful and important even for those who recognize the socially constructed nature of the knowledge we produce: not making it up; not taking one event as evidence of a trend; demanding intersubjective validation, etc. I want to hold onto much of the tradition of empirical study of law and think the law and society movement is worth preserving for that reason alone. I just want to explicitly acknowledge the responsibility we have for the knowledge we chose to produce and the uses to which it is put.[14]

---

[10] DM Trubek, 'Studying Courts in Context' (1981) 15 *Law & Society Review* 622, WLF Felstiner, A Sarat and RL Abel, 'The Emergence and Transformation of Disputes: Naming, Blaming, and Claiming ...' (1981) 15 *Law & Society Review* 631.

[11] DM Trubek, 'The Construction and Deconstruction of a Disputes Focused Approach: An Afterward' (1981) 15 *Law & Society Review* 727.

[12] See Trubek, 'Back to the Future' (n 7), 5 fn 1 (acknowledging the influence of Trubek's colleague Patricia Williams for showing him how 'personal narrative can be used in a scholarly argument'). As he obliquely hints later in the article, Trubek played a pivotal role in giving a home to the first meeting of the 'Race Crits' and promoting their legitimacy with his often skeptical—and sometimes hostile—CLS elders. Once again at a moment like this, the generosity and bravery of these actions should not be overlooked.

[13] Ibid.

[14] Ibid, 54.

To do this, Trubek urges us to 'Live [*sic*] in the Contradictions'—to learn how to 'live with—and take advantage of—a series of contradictions that exist in our culture'.[15] As Trubek concedes, 'we live in a culture that believes in law and whose legal tradition contains many progressive values'. [16] Yet 'at the same time, ours is a society in which hierarchies of class, race, and gender persist and influence the operations of the law and the production of legal scholarship'. A true pragmatic integration of the core insights of law and society and critical legal studies must acknowledge this essential contradiction, and recognise that while the resulting 'legal studies can foster progressive visions' that any victories—or even understanding—is inevitably 'partial, tentative, and limited'.[17]

And if this balancing act weren't hard enough, a decade later, Trubek challenged us to multiply the contradictions exponentially by 'cracking the red, white, and blue ceiling' and creating a community of scholars committed to an approach to pragmatic socio-legal scholarship that is truly international.[18] The contradictions are multiplied because this internationalisation cannot simply be a cover for a 'new form of US academic hegemony', a danger—given Trubek's own actions in Brazil—that he knows all too well.[19] Instead, the goal must be to create 'a truly effective global socio-legal network' where scholars from many institutions and legal traditions can collaborate as equals.[20] It is only by creating this kind of multinational and multidisciplinary partnership, Trubek insists, that we can ever hope to begin to understand the true 'complexity of the global field'.[21]

It is this complex, contradictory and multidimensional space that the GLEE project aspires to inhabit.

II. Putting the Choir Back Together Again—While Trying not Simply to Preach to it

GLEE grows out of my own quarter-century engagement with the transformation of the legal services market in the United States, and the implications of these changes for lawyers, clients, and society. By the turn of the twenty-first century, it had become clear that this transformation was becoming global, as US lawyers increasingly followed economic opportunity—and their clients—abroad. But as the first decade of the new century drew to a close it was evident that simply to focus on the actions of US (or even US and United Kingdom) lawyers would be to miss an important part—or perhaps *the* important part—of the story, as countries outside the Anglo-American world developed increasingly large and important legal professions and institutions. Yet, aside from a few articles in the popular legal press, there was almost no systematic investigation of these developments, let alone any serious inquiry into *why* the legal profession was changing so rapidly in countries

---

[15]   Ibid, 45–46.
[16]   Ibid, 46.
[17]   Ibid.
[18]   DM Trubek, 'Cracking the 'Red, White, and Blue' Ceiling: Toward a New International Role for the Law and Society Association' (2003) 37 *Law & Society Review* 295.
[19]   Ibid, 299.
[20]   Ibid, 302–303.
[21]   Ibid.

such as Brazil, India and China, or *how* these changes might affect economic development or the rule of law within these countries, or the global legal services market generally.

The GLEE project seeks to begin to answer these questions. It does so by focusing on the most visible marker of how globalisation is transforming the market for legal services in Brazil, India and China (or 'BIC countries'[22]): the creation of a rapidly expanding and sophisticated 'corporate' hemisphere of the bar. To document this transformation and to study its implications, GLEE relies heavily on the intellectual contributions and organisational capabilities of Dave Trubek.

We focus on the corporate legal sector not because we assume that it is the most important part of the bar in the BIC countries, but because it is the segment of the legal profession that is most connected to why these countries have 'emerged' at all. Over the last 20 years, Brazil, India and China have each undertaken numerous economic reforms. Beginning in the 1990s, each country has more or less opened its economy to foreign capital and has become more deeply integrated into the world economy. Since 2000, these countries have also begun to move from a model of globalisation based primarily on in-bound investment, to one in which companies based in these jurisdictions are also significant sources of outward investment.

Predictably, this market opening has fuelled a growing demand for laws, regulations and administrative apparatus to govern this new corporate sector. And with the growth of corporate law has come the need for corporate lawyers capable of operating in this new environment. Today, this new corporate legal elite—by which we mean lawyers who work in law firms of increasing size and scope which serve a clientele composed primarily of foreign and domestic corporations, and lawyers who work in the internal legal departments within corporations based or operating in the BIC countries—has grown significantly in both size and importance in each of these jurisdictions. Although the vast majority of lawyers in the BIC countries remain sole and small-firm practitioners serving individual clients, each of the countries we are studying now has several law firms comprised of hundreds—and in the case of China, more than 1,000—lawyers, as well as in-house legal departments, such as the 500 lawyer general counsel office of India's Tata Group, that are almost as large.

To study the development of this new corporate legal elite, and to understand its implications both in the countries themselves and more generally, it was clear to me that I would need to enlist Dave Trubek's active participation. Since unmasking the pretensions of the original law and development movement in 1974, Trubek, aided by many able collaborators, had been busily creating a 'new law and economic development' movement, albeit one that was always subject to 'critical appraisal'.[23] Not surprisingly, this work had led Trubek to turn his attention back to Brazil and many of the other important emerging economies

---

[22] Astute observers will undoubtedly note, this is BRIC without the 'R' for Russia. Although the project may eventually move to investigate the development of the corporate legal market in Russia (or in Eastern Europe generally), at present we have found it too difficult to figure out how to begin a project in this part of the world. Indeed, to the extent that GLEE moves to other jurisdictions, our acronym is likely to follow its more famous elder relation and go to South Africa (which has now officially added the 'S' to BRICS, at least for some purposes) or another country on what is likely to be the fastest growing region in the world in the coming decades.

[23] DM Trubek and A Santos, *The New Law and Economic Development: A Critical Appraisal* (Cambridge, Cambridge University Press, 2006).

where the globalising corporate sector was developing.[24] This work was an essential foundation for the GLEE project.

But there was more. In addition to his life-long work on law and development, Trubek has also written some of the most important scholarship about why the corporate legal sector has been globalising in the first place—and equally important, how to study the complexity of legal practice and professional ideology in a world that is inherently fragmented, conflictual and multipolar. In 1992, Trubek, in collaboration with Robert Nelson and Rayman Solomon, published an important collection of essays addressing the so-called 'professionalism crisis' thought to be sweeping over the American legal profession.[25] Starting from the premise that '[t]he American legal profession stands at the crossroads of change', the book both chronicles these changes and challenges prevailing orthodoxies about why they are occurring and what their implications are likely to be for professional ideals. Building on the critique of both critical and socio-legal scholarship elaborated above, the book challenges researchers studying changes in the profession to pay attention 'to the ideologies of lawyers themselves; the views they hold about the nature of their work, their relations to clients and each other, and the way they should organize their firms'.[26]

To study this neglected dimension, Nelson and Trubek urge scholars to abandon the idea of 'professionalism' as a unitary and fixed ideology that either, in the traditional account, creates a single and mutually-reinforcing set of institutions and beliefs guaranteeing that lawyers will act as honest fiduciaries for their clients and zealous defenders of the rule of law, or in the critical account, that acts as pure legitimation that blinds both clients and the public to the profession's ruthless and relentless pursuit of its own self interest. Instead, the authors urge scholars to focus on the many 'arenas' where different groups of lawyers construct—and contest—the meaning of professionalism for a range of competing—and often conflicting—purposes, including arenas such as legal education, professional organisations and, most importantly, the workplace.[27] These arenas are neither part of a single unified structure, Trubek and Nelson argue, nor completely autonomous. Instead, they form a complex web of 'semi-autonomous social fields', to borrow Sally Falk Moore's famous insight, where professional ideologies created in one arena, for example legal education, are incorporated, redefined, and resisted in another, for example the workplace—and vice versa.[28] By studying how lawyers create and deploy professional ideology both within and across these various fields, the authors conclude, scholars can 'advance a broader understanding of how the practices of lawyers reflect, reproduce, and alter the social order'.[29]

---

[24] DM Trubek, 'Law and the "New Developmentalism"' in DM Trubek, HA Garcia, D Coutinho and A Santos (eds), *Law and the New Developmental State: The Brazilian Experience in Latin American Context* (Cambridge, Cambridge University Press 2013), DM Trubek, 'Law and Development in the Twenty First Century' in GP McAlinn and C Pejovic (eds), *Law and Development in Asia* (London, Routledge, 2013).

[25] RL Nelson, DM Trubek and RL Solomon, *Lawyers Ideals and Lawyers Practices: Transformations in the American Legal Profession* (Ithaca, Cornell University Press, 1992).

[26] RL Nelson and DM Trubek, 'Introduction: New Problems and New Paradigms in Studies of the Legal Profession' in *Lawyers Ideals and Lawyers Practices*, ibid, 4.

[27] RL Nelson and DM Trubek, 'Arenas of Professionalism: The Professional Ideologies of Lawyers in Context' in *Lawyers Ideals and Lawyers Practices*, ibid.

[28] SF Moore, 'Law and Social Change: The Semi-Autonomous Social Field as an Appropriate Field of Study' (1973) 7 *Law & Society Review* 719.

[29] Nelson and Trubek, 'Arenas of Professionalism' (n 27) 214.

The GLEE project seeks to take up this challenge. Rather than relying solely on either the official pronouncements of bar officials in the countries we study, or on the growing chorus of critical voices decrying the spread of 'corporatisation' around the world, the project identifies 10 interrelated fields of study where the practice and the ideology of the new corporate legal elite within the BIC countries is being simultaneously produced and contested: 'corporate law firms', both those that are being created within the BIC countries and the international firms that are increasingly attempting to serve these markets; 'in-house legal departments', including those in domestic companies and those in foreign multinationals operating in the BIC countries; 'new providers' such as legal process outsourcing organisations or multidisciplinary professional service firms where corporate legal services are being 'unbundled' or 'repackaged' along global supply chains to compete with traditional legal service providers; 'cross-border mergers and acquisitions' and other corporate transactions that form the basis of much of the work done by the corporate legal sector in the emerging world, 'legal education', including law schools in each jurisdiction, foreign law schools seeking to serve these markets, and new for-profit educational companies claiming to fill in the perceived gaps left by these traditional providers; 'professional regulation' by bar organisations and by the state; 'capacity building' in which state and private actors seeks to enlist the newly emerging corporate elite to participate in the institutions of global governance such as the WTO and investment arbitration; 'traditional elites' and other lawyers whose practices and standing are likely to be affected by the emergence of the new corporate elite; 'public interest' lawyers and practices related to the new corporate sector, such as pro-bono, corporate social responsibility, and the development of new organisations or agendas to oppose or constrain the corporate bar or its clients; and 'political economy' which attempts to understand how all of the above changes are likely to affect—and be affected by—the elaboration of the administrative state in each country and the state's overall development strategy.

Needless to say, this is an ambitious agenda. Our goal is to understand the internal dynamics of each of these arenas from the bottom up, and to examine the complex ways that all of these sectors are combining to influence the development of the corporate legal sector within each of the BIC countries. Moreover, as several of the brief descriptions of the topic areas make clear, even this complex task cannot be done without coming to grips with the influence that forces outside of each country are having on the development of the internal legal markets within them. Precisely because the BIC countries have emerged as important economic powers, they have become increasingly attractive markets for corporate lawyers and other legal institutions from the more mature—and increasingly stagnant—legal markets of the North and West, particularly from the US and the UK. As this Anglo-American global corporate legal sector intersects with the new and increasingly globalised corporate legal elite within the BIC countries, the GLEE project will have to determine whether the resulting 'cross-pollination' is likely to produce new transnational arenas in each of the areas we are studying, and if so, how these arenas will relate to the national legal arenas with which they will both coexist and compete.

Once again, Trubek has already anticipated the need for this kind of multilevel inquiry. Long before most American scholars had even begun thinking about the impact of the looming global restructuring on the market for corporate legal services, Trubek, working in collaboration with the brilliant French sociologist Yves Dezalay and two other collaborators, mapped out a way of thinking about this transformation that neither ignores the crucial role played by the rapidly internationalising US and UK legal elite, nor simply assumes that because these firms are currently the dominant players that globalisation will produce a straightforward diffusion of this model around the world.[30] Working from three case studies—merger and acquisition activity in Europe, public interest challenges to NAFTA, and the transformation of the Indonesian legal profession—the authors seek to develop a common framework for studying 'comparative legal development and its relationship to other social processes'.[31]

A central element of this framework is an examination of the clash between the unique norms, practices and institutional structures associated with what the authors aptly label 'The American Mode of the Production of Law'—large law firms organised as 'professional' rather than 'personal' or 'familial' enterprises, an entrepreneurial, instrumental, and business-focused approach to legal practice, and an ideology of law as a 'public' profession committed (at least in theory) to 'access to justice' and the protection of 'individual liberty' against state control—and an older European mode of legal production (and its colonial offshoots) that depends for its legitimacy on an understanding of law as a science practiced by 'great men' who are insulated from clients and the market. As the authors concede, by the early 1990s the American Mode was spreading rapidly to the European continent (after having profoundly reshaped the legal services market in the UK), putting significant pressure on the old European practices in countries such as France. Nevertheless, Trubek and his collaborators find significant evidence that the importance of various aspects of the old European model persist even among the new corporatised elements of the French bar—particularly those aspects that are tied to social class and other deeply embedded aspects of the surrounding economic, political, and social environment in which law is practised. As a result, the authors conclude that we are likely to see the development of a new and hybridised model of legal practice in Europe that differs significantly from the Anglo-American model upon which it is based. This hybridisation, the authors speculate, is likely to be even more pronounced in the developing world, where 'the technical knowledge of business practices that is part of the symbolic capital of the Americanized firms' must compete with the 'connections and the situational knowledge' of traditional legal elites who may be even more entrenched and powerful in countries like Indonesia in the waning years of the twentieth century than they were in Europe during this same period.[32]

As we begin our research on the GLEE project in the second decade of the twenty-first century, it is clear that maintaining this cautionary attitude toward the increasingly held belief that the American Mode of the Production of Law—and indeed the 'Rule of Law' itself—is unproblematicaly diffusing around the world is even more essential than it was when Trubek and his collaborators conducted their case studies in the 1990s. Both the growing global presence of US and UK law firms, and the emergence of an increasing number of large law firms in the BIC countries that expressly mimic the organisational forms and practices of these global players right down to their Anglicised names (China's 1000+ lawyer juggernaut King & Wood—now King & Wood Mallesons as I explain below—being exhibit number one), would seem to confirm the diffusion story. But how much these new-world firms really look like their old-world counterparts—and how much

---

[30] DM Trubek, Y Dezalay, R Buchanan and J Davis, 'Global Restructuring and the Law Studies of the Internationalization of Legal Fields and the Creation of Transnational Arenas' (1994) 44 *Case Western Reserve Law Review* 407.

[31] Ibid, 497.

[32] Ibid, 489.

the new-world branches offices of US and UK firms are really just like the home office back in New York or London, remains to be seen. To return again to China's King & Wood, there is no Mr King or Mr Wood, and there never has been. Nor does the fact that King & Wood and other emerging market law firms have lawyers who are designated as 'partners' necessarily mean that these practitioners have the same kinds of rights to share in the financial rewards or governance of these law firms that we tend to associate with those who hold this title in US and UK.[33] At the same time, as most US and UK law firms in China and other emerging markets have gone from simply trying to replicate their home-base practices (complete with staffing these outposts with ex patriots whose primary claim is their knowledge of US or UK law), to creating increasingly 'Chinese' offices staffed primarily by local lawyers whose claim to expertise is a deep understanding of Chinese culture and institutions and who have deep connections to Chinese business and government elites, it is increasingly apparent that even these signifiers of globalisation are at least as much a sign of what the legal scholar Carol Silver calls the 'glocalisation' (globalisation and localisation pushed together) of transnational legal practice.[34]

Given this reality, it is even more critical that those who wish to take up Trubek's substantive advice about the need for 'a renaissance in comparative legal studies' also heed his advice about how such a research agenda should be carried out.[35] As he and his collaborators conclude, any project of this kind must begin by forging the kind of 'closer linkages among sociolegal scholars around the world necessary for the study of the interaction of law and global processes'.[36] Thus from its inception, the GLEE project has been committed to recruiting top scholars in each of the countries we are studying to work collaboratively in designing both the questions to be studied and the ways that these issues will be addressed. As I write, GLEE has more than 50 scholars from six different countries (including all three BIC countries), representing 12 institutions (once again, including important institutional partners in each of the countries we are currently studying). The participants include legends in their respective fields like Trubek and those new to this kind of research—or indeed, to research at all. Not surprisingly, this kind of multijurisdictional, multidisciplinary (depending upon how you count, we have scholars who are trained in at least six different disciplines), and multigenerational collaboration is labour intensive, expensive and sometimes difficult. But it is essential, quoting Trubek and his collaborators again,

> to develop[ing] a conceptual structure and methodology that will do justice to the complexity of the processes [we seek to understand], while allowing us to see similarities and identify differences caused by variation in national traditions and modes of production of law, regional integration of economies, position in the international division of labor, and local histories.[37]

---

[33] See J Krishnan, 'Peel-off Lawyers, Legal Professionals in India's Corporate Law Firm Sector' (2013) 9 *Sociolegal Review*, forthcoming and S Liu, 'Globalization as Boundary Blurring: International and Local Law Firms in China's Corporate Law Market' (2008) 42 *Law & Society Review* 771. Needless to say, the extent to which even partners in US or UK law firms continue to have these rights is far from certain, DB Wilkins, 'Partner, Schmartner!: EEOC V Sidley Austin Brown & Wood' (2007) 120 *Harvard Law Review* 1264. This complexity complicates any simple diffusion story even further.

[34] C Silver, N De Bruin Phelan and M Rabinowitz, 'Between Diffusion and Distinction in Globalization. US Law Firms Go Glocal' (2009) 22 *The Georgetown Journal of Legal Ethics* 1431.

[35] Trubek, Dezalay, Buchanan and Davis, 'Global Restructuring' (n 30), 497–98.

[36] Ibid, 498.

[37] Ibid, 497.

It also helps us to remember that sometimes to understand the core of a complex practice it is best to study its periphery. I conclude by saying a few words about this uniquely Trubekean insight.

III. Looking Where Others Think the Action is Not

As I've tried to explain, Dave Trubek has always had an uncanny ability to find where the action is, and to develop analytic frameworks that help others to understand and further investigate the trends he discovers. But he has almost always done so by looking in places most others overlook.

A quick look at Trubek's CV makes the point clear. As I've already mentioned, Dave began his career in Brazil, hardly the traditional path for a Yale Law School graduate who had clerked for Charles E Clark, whose work on the Federal Rules of Civil Procedure was the epitome of the legal scholarship of the day. When Trubek entered the legal academy, he continued to devote the majority of his scholarly attention to a country about which most mainstream legal scholars had very little understanding or interest. And just when one might have thought that Trubek would have tried to cash in on his years of investment in the nascent field of law and development, he and Marc Galanter effectively sounded what appeared to be the death knell for this kind of work in their classic article 'Scholars in Self-estrangement'.

Of course, it has not been the death knell and the field of law and development, if not quite mainstream, is now a staple in one form or another in the curriculum of many major law schools around the world—thanks in significant part to Trubek's unwavering commitment. What's more, the country where Trubek has devoted so much of his scholarly energy to building this field has itself moved from the margins of the global regime to the centre (or at least far closer to the centre) of the new world order. Brazil is no longer marginal even in the still far too parochial American legal academy; nor are the insights about the complex relationship among empiricism, critical reflection on existing categories and hierarchies, and the importance of being able to 'live in the contradictions' that Trubek has consistently championed throughout his long and distinguished scholarly career. Indeed, these very themes have become the ordinary religion of the corporate bar in the US, and on the basis of our preliminary research in the GLEE project, around the world. As I have argued elsewhere, in the 'global age of more for less', corporate lawyers face tremendous pressure to justify the value of their work in terms of objective metrics, to 'think outside the box' in designing creative solutions to their client's legal problems, and to live in the contradictions of an indeterminate and globalised world in which these lawyers can no longer shrink from the fact that they are both a 'profession' and a 'business', with all of the complexity and contradiction that this dual status implies.[38]

---

[38] DB Wilkins, 'Is the In-House Counsel Movement Going Global? A Preliminary Assessment of the Role of Internal Counsel in Emerging Economies' (2012) *Wisconsin Law Review* 251; DB Wilkins, 'Team of Rivals? Toward a New Model of the Attorney–Client Relationship' (2009) 78 *Fordham Law Review* 2067; Wilkins, 'Partner, Schmartner!' (n 33).

Given this reality, it is not surprising that Dave Trubek is now studying the transformation of the corporate bar in Brazil and other emerging economies. Nor will it be surprising when his work on the GLEE project produces important insights that shed new light on the overall political economy of these countries—Dave's own part of the project—and the field of law and development that he has stewarded for more than half a century. I am honoured that I will have a front row seat to this exciting process as Dave continues to show us all where the action is for many years to come.

Index